Ancient Christian Texts

Commentary on John

Volume 1

Cyril of Alexandria

TRANSLATED WITH AN INTRODUCTION AND NOTES BY

David R. Maxwell

EDITED BY

Joel C. Elowsky

SERIES EDITORS

Thomas C. Oden and Gerald L. Bray

IVP Academic
An imprint of InterVarsity Press
Downers Grove, Illinois

InterVarsity Press
P.O. Box 1400, Downers Grove, IL 60515-1426
ivpress.com
email@ivpress.com

InterVarsity Press® is the book-publishing division of InterVarsity Christian Fellowship/USA®, a movement of students and faculty active on campus at hundreds of universities, colleges and schools of nursing in the United States of America, and a member movement of the International Fellowship of Evangelical Students. For information about local and regional activities, visit intervarsity.org.

Design: Cindy Kiple
Images: Saints Peter and Paul by Carlo Crivelli at Accademia, Venice/Art Resource, NY
Monogrammatic cross: Early Christian monogrammatic cross from Monastero, at Kunsthistorisches Museum, Vienna, Austria.
Erich Lessing/Art Resource, NY

ISBN 978-0-8308-2911-8

Printed in the United States of America ∞

As a member of Green Press Initiative, InterVarsity Press is committed to protecting the environment and to the responsible use of natural resources. To learn more, visit greenpressinitiative.org.

Library of Congress Cataloging-in-Publication Data

http://lccn.loc.gov/2012041093

Cyril, Saint, Patriarch of Alexandria, approximately 370-444. Commentary on John Commentary on John / Cyril of Alexandria ; translated with an introduction and notes by David R. Maxwell ; edited by Joel C. Elowsky. Downers Grove, Illinois : InterVarsity Press, [2013] — ©2013

xxxi, 375 pages ; 27 cm.
BR65.C953 I413 2013
ISBN: 9780830829118 (hardcover)

2012041093

P 24 23 22 21 20 19 18 17 16 15 14 13 12 11 10 9 8 7 6 5

Y 42 41 40 39 38 37 36 35 34 33 32 31 30 29 28 27 26 25 24

CONTENTS

GENERAL INTRODUCTION

Ancient Christian Texts (hereafter ACT) presents the full text of ancient Christian commentaries on Scripture that have remained so unnoticed that they have not yet been translated into English.

The patristic period (A.D. 95–750) is the time of the fathers of the church, when the exegesis of Scripture texts was in its primitive formation. This period spans from Clement of Rome to John of Damascus, embracing seven centuries of biblical interpretation, from the end of the New Testament to the mid-eighth century, including the Venerable Bede.

This series extends but does not reduplicate texts of the Ancient Christian Commentary on Scripture (ACCS). It presents full-length translations of texts that appear only as brief extracts in the ACCS. The ACCS began years ago authorizing full-length translations of key patristic texts on Scripture in order to provide fresh sources of valuable commentary that previously were not available in English. It is from these translations that the ACT series has emerged.

A multiyear project such as this requires a well-defined objective. The task is straightforward: *to introduce full-length translations of key texts of early Christian teaching, homilies and commentaries on a particular book of Scripture.* These are seminal documents that have decisively shaped the entire subsequent history of biblical exegesis, but in our time have been largely ignored.

To carry out this mission each volume of the Ancient Christian Texts series has four aspirations:

1. To show the approach of one of the early Christian writers in dealing with the problems of understanding, reading and conveying the meaning of a particular book of Scripture.

2. To make more fully available the whole argument of the ancient Christian interpreter of Scripture to all who wish to think with the early church about a particular canonical text.

3. To broaden the base of the biblical studies, Christian teaching and preaching to include classical Christian exegesis.

4. To stimulate Christian historical, biblical, theological and pastoral scholarship toward deeper inquiry into early classic practitioners of scriptural interpretation.

For Whom Is This Series Designed?

We have selected and translated these texts primarily for general and nonprofessional use by an audience of persons who study the Bible regularly.

In varied cultural settings around the world, contemporary readers are asking how they might grasp the meaning of sacred texts under the instruction of the great minds of the ancient church. They often study books of the Bible verse by verse, book by book, in groups and workshops, sometimes with a modern commentary in hand. But many who study the Bible intensively hunger to have available as well the thoughts of a reliable classic Christian commentator on this same text. This series will give the modern commentators a classical text for comparison and amplification. Readers will judge for themselves as to how valuable or complementary are their insights and guidance.

The classic texts we are translating were originally written for anyone (lay or clergy, believers or seekers) who wished to reflect and meditate with the great minds of the early church. They sought to illuminate the plain sense, theological wisdom, and moral and spiritual meaning of an individual book of Scripture. They were not written for an academic audience, but for a community of faith shaped by the sacred text.

Yet in serving this general audience, the editors remain determined not to neglect the rigorous requirements and needs of academic readers who until recently have had few full translations available to them in the history of exegesis. So this series is designed also to serve public libraries, universities, academic classes, homiletic preparation and historical interests worldwide in Christian scholarship and interpretation.

Hence our expected audience is not limited to the highly technical and specialized scholarly field of patristic studies, with its strong bent toward detailed word studies and explorations of cultural contexts. Though all of our editors and translators are patristic and linguistic scholars, they also are scholars who search for the meanings and implications of the texts. The audience is not primarily the university scholar concentrating on the study of the history of the transmission of the text or those with highly focused interests in textual morphology or historical-critical issues. If we succeed in serving our wider readers practically and well, we hope to serve as well college and seminary courses in Bible, church history, historical theology, hermeneutics and homiletics. These texts have not until now been available to these classes.

Readiness for Classic Spiritual Formation

Today global Christians are being steadily drawn toward these biblical and patristic sources for daily meditation and spiritual formation. They are on the outlook for primary classic sources of spiritual formation and biblical interpretation, presented in accessible form and grounded in reliable scholarship.

These crucial texts have had an extended epoch of sustained influence on Scripture interpretation, but virtually no influence in the modern period. They also deserve a hearing among modern readers and scholars. There is a growing awareness of the speculative excesses and spiritual and homiletic limitations of much post-Enlightenment criticism. Meanwhile the motifs, methods and approaches of ancient exegetes have remained unfamiliar not only to historians but to otherwise highly literate biblical scholars, trained exhaustively in the methods of historical and scientific criticism.

It is ironic that our times, which claim to be so fully furnished with historical insight and research methods, have neglected these texts more than scholars in previous centuries who could read them in their original languages.

This series provides indisputable evidence of the modern neglect of classic Christian exegesis: it remains a fact that extensive and once authoritative classic commentaries on Scripture still remain untranslated into any modern language. Even in China such a high level of neglect has not befallen classic Buddhist, Taoist and Confucian commentaries.

Ecumenical Scholarship

This series, like its two companion series, the ACCS and Ancient Christian Doctrine (ACD), is an expression of unceasing ecumenical efforts that have enjoyed the wide cooperation of distinguished scholars of many differing academic communities. Under this classic textual umbrella, it has brought together in common spirit Christians who have long distanced themselves from each other by competing church memories. But all of these traditions have an equal right to appeal to the early history of Christian exegesis. All of these traditions can, without a sacrifice of principle or intellect, come together to study texts common to them all. This is its ecumenical significance.

This series of translations is respectful of a distinctively theological reading of Scripture that cannot be reduced to historical, philosophical, scientific, or sociological insights or methods alone. It takes seriously the venerable tradition of ecumenical reflection concerning the premises of revelation, providence, apostolicity, canon and consensuality. A high respect is here granted, despite modern assumptions, to uniquely Christian theological forms of reasoning, such as classical consensual christological and triune reasoning, as distinguishing premises of classic Christian textual interpretation. These cannot be acquired by empirical methods alone. This approach does not pit theology against critical theory; instead, it incorporates critical historical methods and brings them into coordinate accountability within its larger purpose of listening to Scripture.

The internationally diverse character of our editors and translators corresponds with the global range of our audience, which bridges many major communions of Christianity. We have sought to bring together a distinguished international network of Protestant, Catholic and Orthodox scholars, editors and translators of the highest quality and reputation to accomplish this design.

But why just now at this historical moment is this need for patristic wisdom felt particularly by so many readers of Scripture? Part of the reason is that these readers have been longer deprived of significant contact with many of these vital sources of classic Christian exegesis.

The Ancient Commentary Tradition

This series focuses on texts that comment on Scripture and teach its meaning. We define a commentary in its plain-sense definition as a series of illustrative or explanatory notes on any work of enduring significance. The word *commentary* is an Anglicized form of the Latin *commentarius* (or "annotation" or "memoranda" on a subject, text or series of events). In its theological meaning it is a work that explains, analyzes or expounds a biblical book or portion of Scripture. Tertullian, Origen, John Chrysostom, Jerome, Augustine and Clement of Alexandria all revealed their familiarity with both the secular and religious commentators available to them as they unpacked the meanings of the sacred text at hand.

The commentary in ancient times typically began with a general introduction covering such questions as authorship, date, purpose and audience. It commented as needed on grammatical or lexical problems in the text and provided explanations of difficulties in the text. It typically moved verse by verse through a Scripture text, seeking to make its meaning clear and its import understood.

The general Western literary genre of commentary has been definitively shaped by the history of early Christian commentaries on Scripture. It is from Origen, Hilary, the *Opus imperfectum in Matthaeum*, John Chrysostom and Cyril of Alexandria that we learn what a commentary is—far more so than in the case of classic medical, philosophical or poetic commentaries. It leaves too much unsaid simply to assume that the Christian biblical commentary took a previously extant literary genre and reshaped it for Christian texts. Rather it is more accurate to say that *the Western literary genre of the commentary (and especially the biblical commentary) has patristic commentaries as its decisive pattern and prototype.*

It is only in the last two centuries, since the development of modern historicist methods of criticism, that modern writers have sought more strictly to delimit the definition of a commentary so as to include only certain limited interests focusing largely on historical-critical method, philological and grammatical observations, literary analysis, and socio-political or economic circumstances impinging on the text. While respecting all these approaches, the ACT editors do not hesitate to use the classic word *commentary* to define more broadly the genre of this series. These are commentaries in their classic sense.

The ACT editors freely take the assumption that the Christian canon is to be respected as the church's sacred text. The reading and preaching of Scripture are vital to religious life. The central hope of this endeavor is that it might contribute in some small way to the revitalization of religious faith and community through a renewed discovery of the earliest readings of the church's Scriptures.

An Appeal to Allow the Text to Speak for Itself

This prompts two appeals:

1. For those who begin by assuming as normative for a commentary only the norms considered typical for modern expressions of what a commentary is, we ask: Please allow the ancient commentators to define *commentarius* according to their own lights. Those who assume the preemptive authority and truthfulness of modern critical methods alone will always tend to view the classic Christian exegetes as dated, quaint, premodern, hence inadequate, and in some instances comic or even mean-spirited, prejudiced, unjust and oppressive. So in the interest of hermeneutical fairness, it is recommended that the modern reader not impose upon ancient Christian exegetes modern assumptions about valid readings of Scripture. The ancient Christian writers constantly challenge these unspoken, hidden and indeed often camouflaged assumptions that have become commonplace in our time.

We leave it to others to discuss the merits of ancient versus modern methods of exegesis. But even this cannot be done honestly without a serious examination of the texts of ancient exegesis. Ancient commentaries may be disqualified as commentaries by modern standards. But they remain commentaries by the standards of those who anteceded and formed the basis of the modern commentary.

The attempt to read a Scripture text while ruling out all theological and moral assumptions—as well as ecclesial, sacramental and dogmatic assumptions that have prevailed generally in the community of faith out of which it emerged—is a very thin enterprise indeed. Those who tendentiously may read a single page of patristic exegesis, gasp and toss it away because it does not conform adequately to the canons of modern exegesis and historicist commentary are surely not exhibiting a valid model for critical inquiry today.

2. In ancient Christian exegesis, chains of biblical references were often very important in thinking about the text in relation to the whole testimony of sacred Scripture, by the analogy of faith, comparing text with text, on the premise that *scripturam ex scriptura explicandam esse*. When ancient exegesis weaves many Scripture texts together, it does not limit its focus to a single text as much modern exegesis prefers, but constantly relates them to other texts, by analogy, intensively using typological reasoning, as did the rabbinic tradition.

Since the principle prevails in ancient Christian exegesis that each text is illumined by other texts and by the whole narrative of the history of revelation, we find in patristic comments on a given text many other subtexts interwoven in order to illumine that text. In these ways the models of exegesis often do not correspond with modern commentary assumptions, which tend to resist or rule out chains of scriptural reference. We implore the reader not to force the assumptions of twentieth-century hermeneutics upon the ancient Christian writers, who themselves knew nothing of what we now call hermeneutics.

The Complementarity of Research Methods in This Series

The Ancient Christian Texts series will employ several interrelated methods of research, which the editors and translators seek to bring together in a working integration. Principal among these methods are the following:

1. The editors, translators and annotators will bring to bear the best resources of *textual criticism* in preparation for their volumes. This series is not intended to produce a new critical edition of the original-language text. The best urtext in the original language will be used. Significant variants in the earliest manuscript sources of the text may be commented upon as needed in the annotations. But it will be assumed that the editors and translators will be familiar with the textual ambiguities of a particular text and be able to state their conclusions about significant differences among scholars. Since we are working with ancient texts that have, in some cases, problematic or ambiguous passages, we are obliged to employ all methods of historical, philological and textual inquiry appropriate to the study of ancient texts. To that end, we will appeal to the most reliable text-critical scholarship of both biblical and patristic studies. We will assume that our editors and translators have reviewed the international literature of textual critics regarding their text so as to provide the reader with a translation of the most authoritative and reliable form of the ancient text. We will leave it to the volume editors and translators, under the supervision of the general editors, to make these assessments. This will include the challenge of considering which variants within the biblical text itself might impinge upon the patristic text, and which forms or stemma of the biblical text the patristic writer was employing. The annotator will supply explanatory footnotes where these textual challenges may raise potential confusions for the reader.

2. Our editors and translators will seek to understand the *historical context* (including socioeconomic, political and psychological aspects as needed) of the text. These understandings are often vital to right discernment of the writer's intention. Yet we do not see our primary mission as that of discussing in detail these contexts. They are to be factored into the translation and commented on as needed in the annotations, but are not to become the primary focus of this series. Our central interest is less in the social location of the text or the philological history of particular words than in authorial intent and accurate translation. Assuming a proper social-historical contextualization of the text, the main focus of this series will be upon a dispassionate and fair translation and analysis of the text itself.

3. The main task is to set forth the meaning of the biblical text itself as understood by the patristic writer. The intention of our volume editors and translators is to help the reader see clearly into the meanings which patristic commentators have discovered in the biblical text. *Exegesis* in its classic sense implies an effort to explain, interpret and comment upon a text, its meaning, its sources and its connections with other texts. It implies

a close reading of the text, utilizing whatever linguistic, historical, literary or theological resources are available to explain the text. It is contrasted with *eisegesis*, which implies that interpreters have imposed their own personal opinions or assumptions upon the text. The patristic writers actively practiced intratextual exegesis, which seeks to define and identify the exact wording of the text, its grammatical structure and the interconnectedness of its parts. They also practiced extratextual exegesis, seeking to discern the geographical, historical or cultural context in which the text was written. Our editors and annotators will also be attentive as needed to the ways in which the ancient Christian writer described his own interpreting process or hermeneutic assumptions.

4. The underlying philosophy of translation that we employ in this series is, like the Ancient Christian Commentary on Scripture, termed *dynamic equivalency*. We wish to avoid the pitfalls of either too loose a paraphrase or too rigid a literal translation. We seek language that is literary but not purely literal. Whenever possible we have opted for the metaphors and terms that are normally in use in everyday English-speaking culture. Our purpose is to allow the ancient Christian writers to speak for themselves to ordinary readers in the present generation. We want to make it easier for the Bible reader to gain ready access to the deepest reflection of the ancient Christian community of faith on a particular book of Scripture. We seek a thought-for-thought translation rather than a formal equivalence or word-for-word style. This requires the words to be first translated accurately and then rendered in understandable idiom. We seek to present the same thoughts, feelings, connotations and effects of the original text in everyday English language. We have used vocabulary and language structures commonly used by the average person. We do not leave the quality of translation only to the primary translator, but pass it through several levels of editorial review before confirming it.

The Function of the ACT Introductions, Annotations and Translations

In writing the introduction for a particular volume of the ACT series, the translator or volume editor will discuss, where possible, the opinion of the writer regarding authorship of the text, the importance of the biblical book for other patristic interpreters, the availability or paucity of patristic comment, any salient points of debate between the Fathers, and any special challenges involved in translating and editing the particular volume. The introduction affords the opportunity to frame the entire commentary in a manner that will help the general reader understand the nature and significance of patristic comment on the biblical text under consideration and to help readers find their critical bearings so as to read and use the commentary in an informed way.

The footnotes will assist the reader with obscurities and potential confusions. In the annotations the volume editors have identified Scripture allusions and historical references embedded within the texts. Their purpose is to help the reader move easily from passage to passage without losing a sense of the whole.

The ACT general editors seek to be circumspect and meticulous in commissioning volume editors and translators. We strive for a high level of consistency and literary quality throughout the course of this series. We have sought out as volume editors and translators those patristic and biblical scholars who are thoroughly familiar with their original language sources, who are informed historically, and who are sympathetic to the needs of ordinary nonprofessional readers who may not have professional language skills.

Thomas C. Oden and Gerald L. Bray, Series Editors

TRANSLATOR'S INTRODUCTION

Cyril of Alexandria's *Commentary on John* is an indispensable resource for understanding how Cyril read the Bible. Modern studies of Cyril often pass over this aspect of his thought because he is primarily known for his Christology. The *Commentary on John*, however, provides a window to his thought processes as he grapples with the Scriptures on any number of issues. This commentary, perhaps more than any of Cyril's other exegetical works, puts on full display the chief feature of Cyril's brilliance: a breathtaking mastery of the contents of the Bible.

Biography

Our knowledge of Cyril's early life is sparse and comes to us from writers who lived two centuries or more after Cyril. The church historian Socrates was a contemporary of Cyril, but he describes only Cyril's later career. For his early life, we must turn to John of Nikiu, a seventh-century Coptic bishop and historian, who reports that Cyril was born to Christian parents in northern Egypt, in the town of Mahallê,[1] probably near or identical with the village of Mehallet el-Kobra.[2] The date of Cyril's birth is uncertain, but John McGuckin posits 378 as an approximation.[3]

Cyril became the attendant of his uncle Theophilus, the patriarch of Alexandria, and was ordained lector in the church of Alexandria. Theophilus also took charge of Cyril's education. The *History of the Patriarchs*, composed by Severus, the tenth-century bishop of El-Ashmunien, reports that Theophilus sent Cyril to a monastery on the mount of Nitria in the desert of Saint Macarius for five years.[4] There, Severus relates, he engaged in intense study of the Scriptures, aided by a photographic memory.[5] He is said to have

---

[1]John, bishop of Nikiu, *The Chronicle of John (c. 690 A.D.) Coptic Bishop of Nikiu: Being a History of Egypt Before and During the Arab Conquest*, trans. Robert Henry Charles (London, 1916; reprint ed., Amsterdam: Philo Press, 1981), 76.

[2]Henri Munier, "Le lieu de la naissance de saint Cyrille d'Alexandrie," in *Kyrilliana* (Cairo: Editions du Scribe Egyptien S.A.E., 1947), 200-201.

[3]John McGuckin, *Saint Cyril of Alexandria and the Christological Controversy: Its History, Theology and Texts* (Crestwood, NY: St. Vladimir's Seminary Press, 2004), 2.

[4]B. Evetts, ed. and trans., *History of the Patriarchs of the Coptic Church of Alexandria 2: Peter I to Benjamin I (661)*, in *Patrologia* 1 (Turnhout: Brepols, 1981), 427; cf. Lois M. Farag, *St. Cyril of Alexandria, a New Testament Exegete: His Commentary on the Gospel of John*, Gorgias Dissertations 29 (Piscataway, NJ: Gorgias Press, 2007), 11; this detail is questioned by modern scholars.

[5]Severus comments that "the grace of God was with Cyril, so that when he had read a book once, he knew it by heart" (Evetts, *History of the Patriarchs*, 428).

read through most of the New Testament during most nights of his study.[6] The result of all this is that he memorized the entirety of the Scriptures.[7]

Because these claims about Cyril's abilities are first recorded some five centuries after Cyril's life, one may reasonably suspect that they contain an element of exaggeration.[8] However, the *Commentary on John* displays a facility with the text of Scripture that is consonant with Severus's estimation of Cyril's powers. Cyril is able to matrix together passage after passage throughout Scripture on the basis of the fact that they contain the same word or phrase. For example, in his comment on John 5:35, in which Jesus refers to John the Baptist as "a burning and shining lamp," Cyril calls the reader's attention to other passages throughout the Scriptures that refer to lamps, with special reference to burning and shining.[9] Patristic exegetes often drew connections between passages on the basis of a shared word or phrase,[10] but Cyril's facility at this suggests that he may have had large sections of the Scriptures memorized.

When Theophilus died, Cyril succeeded him as patriarch in 412. Cyril's early episcopal career was stormy, to say the least, characterized by clashes with both the Jewish and pagan communities in Alexandria. These clashes culminated in the infamous murder of Hypatia, a renowned pagan philosopher. She was killed by a Christian mob, with which Cyril's involvement was unclear.[11] His later episcopal career was devoted largely to the Nestorian controversy. Nestorius described Christ in such a way as to give the impression that there were two acting subjects in Christ: a divine subject and a human one. Cyril, by contrast, strongly asserted the unity of Christ and insisted that anything that happens to Christ happens to the Word, not just to his human nature. Thus, for Cyril it was important to confess that Mary is the mother of God (*theotokos*), not just the mother of the man Jesus. Cyril continued his support of this unitive Christology until his death in 444.

Date

Cyril wrote the *Commentary on John* sometime fairly early in his episcopacy, before the

[6]Ibid.

[7]Ibid.

[8]Wickham dismisses the entire *History of the Patriarchs* as "a tissue of legend and misunderstood facts" (Lionel Wickham, *Cyril of Alexandria: Select Letters* [Oxford: Clarendon, 1983], xii-xiii, n. 3). Farag is more sympathetic to Severus (Farag, *St. Cyril of Alexandria*, 15).

[9]Cyril *In Jo.* 5:35 (see p. 165 in this volume). He adduces Ps 132:17 (Ps 131:17 Septuagint [LXX]), Ex 27:20–28:1 and Lk 12:49.

[10]John J. O'Keefe and R. R. Reno, *Sanctified Vision: An Introduction to Early Christian Interpretation of the Bible* (Baltimore: Johns Hopkins University Press, 2005), 45-50.

[11]Popular presentations of the murder of Hypatia, such as that of Charles Kingsley's novel *Hypatia* or more recently that of the movie *Agora*, portray Cyril as the villain responsible for the murder. The difficulty with this interpretation is that it does not take into account the fact that Socrates, the historian contemporary with Cyril who reports the event, has a bias against Cyril. Socrates was a supporter of the Novatians, whose property Cyril had confiscated (Socrates *Ecclesiastical History* 7.7), so he portrays Cyril as a power-hungry tyrant, a characterization that Cyril's modern detractors are only too happy to adopt uncritically. That is not to say that Cyril is innocent in the matter. Indeed, there is plenty of material in the *Commentary on John* to trouble the modern reader, including Cyril's attitude toward the Jews, which I will address below. However, there is no evidence that Cyril was directly involved in Hypatia's murder, and it is equally as possible that the new bishop was simply unable to control the crowds. For a discussion of these matters, see McGuckin, *Saint Cyril of Alexandria*, 1-15.

outbreak of the Nestorian controversy. There is no mention in the commentary of Nestorius or of the particular slogans of the Nestorian controversy, such as *theotokos*. Though Cyril does occasionally attack Antiochene Christology in general, the position he opposes is not unique to Nestorius. Indeed, as J. Mahé has pointed out, Athanasius attacks a similar christological position in his letter to Epictetus.[12] When Cyril does name an opponent, he names Eunomius, not Nestorius. For these reasons, we can establish a *terminus ante quem* for the commentary of 428, the year when the Nestorian controversy broke out.[13]

A *terminus a quo* is somewhat more difficult to establish. The *Commentary on John* is an anti-Arian work, probably written about the same time as Cyril's two other anti-Arian works: the *Thesaurus* and the *Dialogue on the Trinity*. More specifically, the *Commentary on John* was the last of these three works since he refers to both of them in the commentary.[14] Cyril's *Paschal Letters* are helpful in pinpointing when Arianism became a live concern for him. His early paschal letters address issues of the Christian life, and Cyril's main opponents are the pagans and the Jews. In the letter of 424, however, Cyril becomes preoccupied with Arianism.[15] If we assume that the anti-Arian writings were composed about this time, this gives us a *terminus a quo* of about 425 for the *Commentary on John*. The scholarly consensus, on this basis, dates the composition of the *Commentary on John* somewhere between 425 and 428.[16]

Audience

Little attention has been paid to the question of the intended reader of Cyril's *Commentary on John*. Cyril himself says that he is engaging in "doctrinal explanation" (δογματικωτέραν ἐξήγησιν),[17] and he clearly employs the Gospel of John to refute the arguments of the Arians, Jews and pagans. Cyril does not expect, however, that his opponents will read his commentary. Instead, his goal is to equip his readers to respond to the arguments of the opponents.

The main opposing argument is the Arian contention that the Son is not fully God. The Arians claim that the Son is like the Father but not of the same substance as the

[12]J. Mahé, "La date du Commentaire de saint Cyrille d'Alexandrie sur l'évangelie selon saint Jean," *Bulletin de littérature ecclésiastique* 8 (1907): 43-44.

[13]See G. Jouassard, "L'activité littéraire de saint Cyrille d'Alexandrie jusqu'a 428," in *Mélanges E. Podechard* (Lyon: Facultés catholiques, 1945), 159-74.

[14]*In Jo.* 1:4 (p. 36), *In Jo.* 1:10 (p. 58).

[15]Jouassard, "L'activité littéraire de saint Cyrille d'Alexandrie," 168-69.

[16]Lars Koen, *The Saving Passion: Incarnational and Soteriological Thought in Cyril of Alexandria's Commentary on the Gospel According to St. John* (Uppsala: Almqvist & Wiksell, 1991), 24. This consensus was developed in response to an earlier view on the part of German scholars that the *Commentary on John* was written late in Cyril's career (Mahé, "La date du Commentaire de saint Cyrille d'Alexandrie," 41). For views that date the *Commentary on John* earlier than the consensus does, see Noël Charlier, "Le 'Thesaurus de Trinitate' de saint Cyrille d'Alexandrie," *Revue d'histoire ecclesiastique* 45 (1950): 25-81; Farag, *St. Cyril of Alexandria*, 60-67.

[17]*In Jo.* preface (Pusey 3:7.13).

Father. Eunomius, who is the only opponent whom Cyril mentions by name in the commentary, takes that position one step further and claims that the Son is completely unlike the Father. In response to this view, Cyril tirelessly shows the reader from every conceivable angle how to prove that the Son is, in fact, God by nature.

Likewise, Cyril's polemics against the Jews are directed primarily against their refusal to believe that Jesus is God by nature. In fact, Cyril often elides the Arian and the Jewish views of Christ, represented by the Pharisees in John's Gospel, suggesting that they amount to the same thing. This does not mean, however, that the Jews in Cyril's commentary are merely idealized constructs for the sake of argument. There was a real Jewish community in Alexandria[18] with which Cyril often found himself in conflict. Cyril's incessant repetition of the charge that the Jews are unlearned and senseless is one of the most troubling features of the commentary. It seems to stem from Cyril's conviction that the Old Testament witness to the divinity of Christ is so clear that anyone who does not recognize it must be guilty of stupidity or malice.

Cyril does not spend nearly as much time in the commentary opposing the pagans as he does opposing the Arians and the Jews. However, the one pagan error that he consistently feels the need to correct is the idea that human life, including that of Jesus, is controlled by fate. When John states that Jesus' "hour had not yet come" (Jn 7:30), Cyril worries that the reader might infer that Jesus' death on the cross was decreed by fate, so Cyril takes pains to refute that interpretation.[19] He also wants to make sure that his readers do not imagine that fate renders good works meaningless for humans in general. In opposition to such a view, he stresses human free will.[20]

But who, exactly, needs to be able to negotiate the complexities of all these arguments? There is a good deal of evidence in the commentary that Cyril assumes that his readers are charged with teaching the faith, especially to catechumens. Sometimes Cyril rebuts the arguments of his opponents directly, arguments which he considers to arise from the opponents' evil will or madness. At other times, however, Cyril addresses questions that come from those who have a "devotion to learning," questions which are prompted by difficulties in the text of John itself. In those cases, Cyril anticipates that the questions will be posed by the catechumens and that his readers must be able to answer those questions. For example, when Cyril discusses the statement that Jesus' "hour had not yet come," his particular concern is that "some of those being initiated into the mysteries (μυσταγωγουμένων)" might erroneously suppose that Jesus is under the control of fate.[21] Cyril's rebuttal of this view, then, is addressed not to the pagans or to the catechumens but to those charged with teaching the catechumens.

[18] Robert L. Wilken, *Judaism and the Early Christian Mind: A Study of Cyril of Alexandria's Exegesis and Theology* (New Haven: Yale University Press, 1971), 53.

[19] *In Jo.* 7:30 (see p. 296).

[20] Ibid.

[21] Ibid.

Cyril also draws lessons about pedagogy from the text of John, often portraying Jesus as a master catechist. For instance, Cyril presents Jesus' interaction with Nicodemus and the woman at the well as models for how to teach the faith to catechumens.[22] The main pedagogical principles that Cyril wants to impress on his readers are that teachers in the church should be tireless in their attention to detail as well as their efforts in teaching and that they should start at a level appropriate to their students and gradually lead them to the full truth.

One may infer from these concerns that Cyril wishes to raise the level of catechesis in Alexandria. Indeed, in a few places, Cyril makes explicit reference to a lax state of catechesis in his day. He complains that catechumens are being baptized before they understand that Jesus is actually God[23] and that catechumens are too quickly being ordained into the priesthood.[24] Cyril does not say how widespread these deficiencies are, but his constant attention to issues of pedagogy suggests that he envisions his readers to be engaged in the task of catechesis and that his goal in the commentary is to help them accomplish that task more effectively. To that end, he teaches the reader how to respond to the (in his view dishonest) arguments of the Arians, Jews and pagans, as well as how to respond to honest questions posed by devoted students eager to learn the truth.

Structure of the Work

Cyril divides the commentary into twelve books, and the books are further divided into chapters. At the beginning of each book, Cyril provides a list of chapters for that particular book, identified by headings that describe the doctrinal content of each chapter. The modern reader may be tempted to interpret these lists as a table of contents, as if Cyril were trying to superimpose some kind of doctrinal outline on the text of John's Gospel. It would be closer to the mark, however, to understand them as an index of topics.

The chapter headings would serve as a poor table of contents because they do not always provide a comprehensive summary of the material in each chapter. For example, the thesis for book 4, chapter 4 reads, "The holy tabernacle, which led the people through the desert, was a type of Christ, and so was the ark that was in it and the lamp and the altars, both the altar of incense and the altar of burnt offering. These signified Christ himself." Indeed, the bulk of chapter 4 consists of an excursus about the significance of the tabernacle and its furnishings. However, chapter 4 concludes with a discussion of Jesus' statement in John 6:70, "Did I not choose you, the twelve, and one of you is a devil?" This topic, however, is not included in the chapter heading.

Furthermore, Cyril states explicitly how he intends the reader to use these chapter headings. In the preface to the commentary, he informs the readers, "The list of the chap-

[22]*In Jo.* 3:11 (see p. 99); *In Jo.* 4:26 (see pp. 127–128).
[23]*In Jo.* 2:24 (see p. 96).
[24]*In Jo.* 4:26 (see p. 128).

ters below will show the subjects that the discourse covers. I have added numbers to it so that the readers will very quickly be able to find what they are looking for."[25] Thus, Cyril designs the commentary to be used as a reference work. This design makes sense if, in fact, the commentary is intended to aid catechists. When a catechumen has a question about whether souls existed before their embodiment, for example, or how Jesus can be God if he learns something from the Father, the catechist can consult the chapter headings and quickly locate where that topic is discussed in the commentary.

Finally, understanding the chapter headings as an index of doctrinal topics makes sense out of an otherwise odd feature of the commentary: the later books have far fewer chapter divisions than the earlier ones. Book 1, for example, consists of a preface and ten chapters, while Book 9 contains a preface and only one chapter. This is despite the fact that both books are roughly the same length. This can be explained, I believe, by the fact that most of the excurses and doctrinal discussions occur in the first half of the commentary. The second half is a running commentary on the text of John, so it requires far fewer entries in Cyril's index of doctrinal topics. It would seem that by the time he gets to the second half of the commentary, Cyril runs out of new issues to discuss. The second half of the commentary is still a rich resource for displaying Cyril's handling of the biblical text, and it covers such key events as the crucifixion and resurrection, but in general it does not contain as much explicit doctrinal discussion as the first half does.

Style

Cyril's literary style is complex and wordy. His sentences are lengthy, full of interlocking clauses, and his vocabulary can be unusual, even idiosyncratic. I have tried to preserve some of the structure of Cyril's long sentences, but there is no way to replicate the floweriness in English without making the text incomprehensible to the modern reader. For example, Cyril wants to say that the death of Christ overturned the devil's hopes. Instead of using the word *hopes* (ἐλπίδες), however, he uses the more expansive and abstract phrase "the things in the hopes" (τὰ ἐν ἐλπίσι).[26] I have rendered this phrase "hopes," since "the things in the hopes" of the devil would make no sense to the English reader. Another example of stylistic artifice occurs when Cyril says that the person with a pure heart will follow Christ and ascend to the spiritual mountain "at the time of the kingdom of heaven." In this case, the meaning of the words is straightforward, but the triple-nested structure is not: κατὰ <u>τὸν</u> <u>τῆς</u> <u>τῶν</u> οὐρανῶν βασιλείας καιρόν.[27] Cyril has so constructed the sentence that the definite article occurs three times in a row, each in a different case!

Stylistic characteristics such as these are distasteful to the modern reader. What Robert Wilken says of Cyril's *Contra Iulianum* could also be said of the *Commentary on John*:

[25]*In Jo.* preface (see p. 4).
[26]*In Jo.* 6:38-39 (see p. 221).
[27]*In Jo.* 6:15 (see p. 189), emphasis added.

Cyril's style is "prolix and turgid, an unhappy synergy of grandiloquence and affectation."[28] For Cyril, however, the affectation presumably conveyed a sense of erudition and prestige. By the end of the fourth century, Christianity enjoyed secure status as the religion of the empire. Along with this new status came a writing style that no longer reproduced the spoken Greek of the day, as the New Testament did, but one that imitated the glories of the past, drawing heavily on Attic forms.[29]

Before leaving the issue of style, there is one feature of the present translation that deserves some comment: inclusive language. I have tried to use inclusive language where it seemed possible to do so. This is not to suggest that Cyril thought of men and women as equals[30] but to produce a translation that conforms to the standards of English prose.[31]

Manuscript Tradition

The current translation is based on the critical edition of Cyril's *Commentary on John* prepared by P. E. Pusey in 1872, as part of the Oxford Movement's impetus to foster a return to patristic sources. Pusey's critical edition is in turn based on three main manuscripts ranging from the twelfth to the fifteenth centuries which, together, comprise books 1-6 and 9-12.[32]

Books 7 and 8 of the commentary have been lost, except for fragments that have been preserved in various catenas on the Gospel of John. Pusey has compiled these fragments in his critical edition. Twenty-one additional fragments have been discovered since Pusey's time and edited by Joseph Reuss,[33] and those also have been included in this translation with footnotes indicating that they come from Reuss. For the convenience of readers who wish to consult the critical editions, I have placed the page references to those editions in bold roman type within brackets. For appearance's sake, the publisher has often included them at the end of the previous page rather than at the beginning of the new page. Readers should be able to sort out which volume is in mind by the context.

Cyril's Exegesis

Patristic exegesis frequently seems arbitrary or even bizarre to modern readers. One reason for this is that modern readers and exegetes understand the meaning of the text to

[28]Robert Wilken, "Cyril of Alexandria's *Contra Iulianum*," in *The Limits of Ancient Christianity*, ed. William E. Klingshrin and Mark Vessey (Ann Arbor: University of Michigan Press, 1999), 43.

[29]Geoffrey Horrocks, *Greek: A History of the Language and Its Speakers*, 2nd ed. (Chichester: Wiley-Blackwell, 2010), 155-59.

[30]See *In Jo* 4:16 (see p. 122) for evidence to the contrary.

[31]In general I have employed plural pronouns and verbs where the underlying Greek words are singular, as long as the meaning of the sentence does not depend on the subject being singular. In some cases, I have even used "they" as a gender-neutral singular pronoun, retaining the singular verb where that sounded natural.

[32]Codex Barberinus (twelfth century) contains books 1-6; Codex Vaticanus 592 (fifteenth century) contains books 1-4; Codex Vaticanus 593 (fifteenth century) contains books 1-4 and 9-12. Pusey also consulted the codex S. Marci Venetiis 121 (fifteenth century), which agrees with the Vatican codexes and seems to be copied from them (Pusey 3: vii).

[33]Joseph Reuss, *Johannes-Kommentare aus der Griechischen Kirche*, Texte und Untersuchungen zur Geschichte der altchristlichen Literatur 89 (Berlin: Akadamie-Verlag, 1966), xxv-xxvi, 188-95.

correspond to the original intentions of the human author. The exegetical task, from a modern perspective, is to discover this original intent by examining the text in light of the surrounding verses and in light of the historical circumstances of the author.

Patristic exegetes, by contrast, see their ultimate goal as interpreting a given text in light of the overall sweep of God's plan of salvation. Although they do give attention to surrounding verses and sometimes even to the historical circumstances of a text's composition,[34] they see these matters as preliminary steps in the interpretive process. The goal, however, is to explain how a given text fits into the *oikonomia*[35] of salvation. Since patristic authors hold that the Scriptures are inspired by the Holy Spirit, they are confident that the Scriptures convey not only truths contained in the surface meaning of the texts but also truths concerning God's plan of salvation. Exegesis is "spiritual" when its objects are spiritual, that is, not accessible to sense perception, such as forgiveness and salvation.[36]

In this description of patristic exegesis, I have intentionally avoided drawing a contrast between Antioch and Alexandria or between typology and allegory. In the twentieth century, histories of theology commonly intoned that Antiochene exegetes were more concerned with the literal meaning of the text and practiced typology (an exegetical method that is supposedly respectful of the historical context) while Alexandrian exegetes were more interested in spiritualizing the text by practicing allegory (an exegetical method that is supposedly dismissive of the historical context). However, the view that Antioch and Alexandria represent a sharp dichotomy between two exegetical methods that are fundamentally opposed to each other has largely been discredited.[37] When one reads the commentaries produced by both sides (rather than just the polemical literature) one finds that both sides give attention to the literal meaning of the text and that both are ultimately concerned to find the mystery of Christ in the Old Testament.[38]

Cyril's *Commentary on John* is an excellent example of this phenomenon. While Cyril is certainly capable of exegetical moves that strike modern readers as fanciful, most schol-

[34]Cyril, for example, relies on extrabiblical literature to outline the controversies that prompted John to write his Gospel (*In Jo.* preface to book 1 [see pp. 5-6]).

[35]*Oikonomia* is a technical term in patristic literature. In nontheological contexts the word refers to the management of a household. In theological contexts, it refers to God's plan of salvation, his management, if you will, of his household. It can also refer to the inaugurating event of that plan: the incarnation. Where Cyril uses the term in this technical sense, I have rendered it *oikonomia*.

[36]Robert Wilken, "Cyril of Alexandria as Interpreter of the Old Testament," in *The Theology of St. Cyril of Alexandria: A Critical Appreciation*, ed. Thomas G. Weinandy and Daniel A. Keating (London: T&T Clark, 2003), 21.

[37]Henri de Lubac, "'Typologie' et 'Allégorisme,'" *Recherches de science seligieuse* 34 (1947): 180-226; Jacques Guillet, "Les exégèses d'Alexandrie et d'Antioche: conflit ou malentendu?" *Recherches de science religieuse* 34 (1947): 257-302; Frances Young, *Biblical Exegesis and the Formation of Christian Culture* (Peabody, MA: Hendrickson, 1997), 186-213; Frances Young, "Alexandrian and Antiochene Exegesis," in *A History of Biblical Interpretation*, vol. 1: *The Ancient Period*, ed. Alan J. Hauser and Duane F. Watson (Grand Rapids: Eerdmans, 2003), 334-52; Peter W. Martens, "Revisiting the Allegory/Typology Distinction: The Case of Origen," *Journal of Early Christian Studies* 16 (Fall 2008): 283-317.

[38]Guillet, "Les exégèses d'Alexandrie et d'Antioche," 260, 297.

ars have judged Cyril's exegesis to be relatively sober and innocent of the excessive allegory that is supposed to characterize Alexandrian exegesis, so much so that one important study of Cyril's exegesis notes that he has exegetical tendencies "commonly thought to be peculiar to Antioch."[39] One wonders, however, whether the fact that the patriarch of Alexandria practices "Antiochene" exegesis may indicate that the sharp contrast between Antioch and Alexandria is problematic to begin with.

Fundamentally, what is driving Cyril's exegesis is not a particular method but the conviction that the Scriptures are about the economy of salvation carried out by Christ and the commitment to use the Gospel of John to help catechists teach this faith to their catechumens. When Cyril makes connections between passages based on a shared word or phrase, or when he finds a small detail in the Gospel narrative to reveal a larger truth about the economy of salvation, he is acting consistently with this view of the purpose of Scripture.

Cyril's Way of Referencing Scripture

So far I have tried to describe Cyril's approach to exegesis in general terms, but there is one specific feature of the exegetical task that deserves a brief discussion: Cyril's way of referring to texts. Bibles in Cyril's day did not have chapter and verse divisions. They were, however, divided into sections (κεφάλαια) that corresponded to units of sense.[40] English Bibles do something analogous to this when they divide the text into sections and provide headings like "The Wedding at Cana" or "I Am the Bread of Life."

Occasionally, Cyril refers to the section divisions in his Bible, as when he compares the sections dealing with the Samaritan woman at the well, the royal official and the healing at Bethesda on the sabbath. He comments that they all show the Gentiles responding better to Jesus than the Jews do, and he notes that this conclusion flows from "the well-ordered placement of these sections (κεφαλαίων) next to each other."[41] Usually, however, he introduces a quote by identifying the speaker: "Christ says" or "the Evangelist says."

In many cases, he introduces a quote by saying that it says "somewhere" (που) and then goes on to provide the quote.[42] Rarely does Cyril name the book of the Bible from which he is drawing the quotation. The use of the vague term "somewhere" does not, however, indicate that Cyril is unable to remember the source of the quotation. It is merely a citation formula that is equivalent to something like "the Bible says."

This fact becomes clear when one surveys the many occurrences of this formula. First, the quotes that Cyril provides are almost always verbatim; they are not paraphrases. This suggests that he is not treating the quotations casually. Indeed, it would be incredible to

[39]Alexander Kerrigan, *St. Cyril of Alexandria: Interpreter of the Old Testament* (Rome: Pontificio Istituto Biblico, 1952), 443.
[40]Bruce M. Metzger, *Manuscripts of the Greek Bible: An Introduction to Greek Palaeography* (New York: Oxford University Press, 1981), 41.
[41]*In Jo.* 5:1-4 (see p. 137).
[42]See *In Jo.* 1:1 (see p. 17), for example.

suppose that he could recall the verbatim quotes but could almost never remember the source of the quotes. Second, in a discussion of false prophecies, Cyril refers to a pair of passages from Jeremiah. He introduces the first quote by saying, "The Lord of all says most clearly somewhere (που) about them,"[43] and then cites Jeremiah 23:21. Then he adds a quotation from Jeremiah 14:14, introducing it with the words, "And again in Jeremiah."[44] This second introductory phrase reveals that he knows that both quotes are from Jeremiah, even though he introduced the first one with "somewhere." "Somewhere," therefore, should be taken as a formulaic way to cite a text rather than an indication of a lapse of memory. In fact, Cyril may have derived this formula from the New Testament itself.[45]

Advice for Reading

Cyril's *Commentary on John* is not the kind of text one can readily absorb by reading passively. If the reader does not bring questions to the text, reading Cyril will likely be a frustrating experience. Therefore, I offer the following list of suggestions to help the reader who may be new to patristic literature gain entrance into Cyril's world of thought.

- Do not skip Cyril's citation of Scripture in an attempt to "get to the point." Cyril's handling of Scripture *is* the point.
- Ask what connections Cyril is making between different texts and on what basis he is making those connections.
- Notice what passages Cyril finds difficult or challenging and in need of explanation.
- Try to reconstruct or imagine what the Arians might say about a particular text in order to understand why Cyril makes the points he does.
- Pay attention when Cyril launches into a summary of the entire story of salvation.[46] He has multiple ways of telling it.
- Cyril's discussions are often long, but their structure is not overly elaborate. Cyril seems to be writing down (or perhaps dictating) points as they come to his mind on a particular passage or topic. He does not seem to be following a master outline laid out in advance.

Modern readers may not always feel at home with the exegetical moves that Cyril makes, but they will be drawn deeper into the biblical text and be led to consider the story of Christ in fresh and unexpected ways.

[43]*In Jo.* 7:28 (see p. 294).
[44]*In Jo.* 7:28 (see p. 294).
[45]Cf. Heb 2:6, "It has been testified somewhere (πού)."
[46]The classic example of this occurs in his discussion of Jesus' baptism (*In Jo.* 1:31-32 [see pp. 81-85]).

For Further Reading

Fairbairn, Donald. *Grace and Christology in the Early Church*. Oxford Early Christian Studies. Oxford: Oxford University Press, 2003.

Farag, Lois M. *St. Cyril of Alexandria, a New Testament Exegete: His Commentary on the Gospel of John*. Gorgias Dissertations 29. Piscataway, NJ: Gorgias Press, 2007.

Keating, Daniel A. *The Appropriation of Divine Life in Cyril of Alexandria*. Oxford: Oxford University Press, 2004.

Kerrigan, Alexander. *St. Cyril of Alexandria: Interpreter of the Old Testament*. Rome: Pontificio Istituto Biblico, 1952.

Koen, Lars. *The Saving Passion: Incarnational and Soteriological Thought in Cyril of Alexandria's Commentary on the Gospel According to St. John*. Uppsala: Almqvist & Wiksell, 1991.

O'Keefe, John J., and R. R. Reno. *Sanctified Vision: An Introduction to Early Christian Interpretation of the Bible*. Baltimore: Johns Hopkins University Press, 2005.

Weinandy, Thomas G., and Daniel A. Keating, eds. *The Theology of St. Cyril of Alexandria: A Critical Appreciation*. London: T&T Clark, 2003.

Wilken, Robert L. *Judaism and the Early Christian Mind: A Study of Cyril of Alexandria's Exegesis and Theology*. New Haven: Yale University Press, 1971.

CHAPTER HEADINGS

BOOK 1[1]

1. The Only Begotten is eternal and before the ages; on the words "In the beginning was the Word."
2. The Son, who is both God and of the same substance as the Father, exists in his own hypostasis, just as the Father does; on the words "And the Word was with God."
3. The Son is God by nature and is in no way less than or unlike the Father; on the words "And the Word was God."
4. Against those who dare to say that the natural Word in the mind of God the Father is different than the one called "Son" in the Holy Scriptures. Such an evil opinion belongs to the followers of Eunomius; on the words "This one was in the beginning with God."
5. The Son is by nature creator with God the Father since he is from the Father's substance and not taken on as a subordinate; on the words "All things came to be through him."
6. The Son is by nature life. Therefore he did not come into being but is from the substance of God the Father; on the words "That which came into being—in it was life."
7. The Son is by nature light. Therefore, he did not come into being but is from the substance of God the Father as true light from true light; on the words "And the life was the light of all people."
8. The Son of God alone is true light; the creation is not, since it participates in the light as something originate; on the words "He was the true light."
9. The human soul does not exist before the body, nor is embodiment the result of former sins, as some say; on the words "He was the true light which enlightens everyone coming into the world. He was in the world."
10. The Only Begotten alone is by nature the Son of the Father since he is from him and in him; on the words "No one has ever seen God."

[1]These headings are provided by Cyril at the beginning of each book. They are presented here for the convenience of the modern reader.

BOOK 2

1. The Holy Spirit is in the Son not by participation or as something brought in from the outside but essentially and by nature; on the words "And John testified, 'I have seen the Spirit descending like a dove from heaven, and it remained on him.' "
2. The Son is not an originate being, but as God and from God, he is over all things; on the words "The one who comes from above is over all things."
3. The Son is God and from God by nature; on the words "The one who receives his testimony has set his seal that God is true."
4. The properties of God the Father are in the Son not by participation but essentially and by nature; on the words "The Father loves the Son and has given everything into his hand."
5. The Son is not among those who worship, insofar as he is Word and God; rather, he is worshiped with the Father; on the words "You worship what you do not know, but we worship what we know."
6. The Son is not less than the Father either in potentiality or actuality when it comes to any work, but he is of equal might and of the same substance since he is from him by nature; on the words "The Son can do nothing of himself unless he sees the Father doing it. What he does, this the Son does likewise."
7. No God-befitting dignity or superiority is in the Son by participation or addition from the outside; on the words "The Father judges no one but has given all judgment to the Son."
8. Since the Son is God and from God by nature and is the exact image of the one who begat him, he has equal honor and glory with him; on the words "That all may honor the Son just as they honor the Father."
9. The Son is less than God the Father in no respect, but as God from God, he is equal in might in carrying out all his works; on the words "I can do nothing on my own. As I hear, I judge."

BOOK 3

1. A careful investigation of why Christ calls the blessed Baptist not just a lamp but a burning and shining lamp; on the words "He was a burning lamp."
2. The Son is the image of God the Father, which also convicts the Jews of not understanding the words spoken enigmatically by Moses; on the words "You have never heard his voice," etc.
3. Moses indicated the coming of the Savior when he said, "The Lord your God will raise up for you a prophet like me."
4. Often Christ's withdrawals from Jerusalem indicate that grace will be transferred to the Gentiles. The same chapter contains the discussion about the five barley loaves and two small fish; on the words "And after these things, Jesus went to the other side of the Sea of Tiberias."

5. The Only Begotten is the imprint of God the Father's hypostasis, and there is no other imprint besides him that either exists or is conceived of; on the words "Which the Son of Man will give you," etc.
6. Concerning the manna, that it was a type of Christ's presence and the spiritual gifts given through him; on the words "Jesus therefore said to them, 'Truly, truly, I tell you, it was not Moses who gave you bread from heaven,' " etc.

BOOK 4

1. In no way is the Son less than God the Father because he is from him by nature, even though he is said by some to be subject to him; on the words "I have come down from heaven not to do my own will, but the will of the Father who sent me." In this same chapter there is also a most useful discussion of the precious cross of Christ.
2. The holy body of Christ is life-giving; on the words "I am the bread of life," etc., in which he speaks of his own body as bread.
3. The Son is not a participant in the life of someone else, but he is life by nature since he is begotten of God the Father, who is life by nature; on the words "Just as the living Father sent me, and I live because of the Father, so whoever eats me will live because of me."
4. The holy tabernacle, which led the people through the desert, was a type of Christ, and so was the ark that was in it and the lamp and the altars, both the altar of incense and the altar of burnt offering. These signified Christ himself; on the words "Where shall we go? You have the words of eternal life."
5. Concerning the feast of tabernacles, that it shows forth the restoration of the hope due the saints and the resurrection from the dead; on the words "Now the Jewish feast of tabernacles was near."
6. A discussion of rest on the sabbath, showing in various ways what it means; on the words "If a man receives circumcision on the sabbath, are you angry with me because I healed the whole man on the sabbath?"
7. A discussion of circumcision on the eighth day, showing in various ways what it means; on the words "If a man receives circumcision on the sabbath," etc.

BOOK 5

1. Our affairs are not, as the Greeks ignorantly suppose, subject to hours by necessity, but we proceed by our own choice both to the good and to the opposite, and we are directed by the will of God; on the words "They tried to arrest him, but no one laid hands on him, because his hour had not yet come."
2. After the Savior's cross and at his resurrection from the dead, the Holy Spirit made his abode in us permanently; on the words "For as yet there was no Spirit, because Jesus was not yet glorified."

3. The suffering on the cross was not the work of Jewish might, nor did Christ die because of anyone's mistreatment, but he himself endured this willingly for us, in order to save everyone; on the words "These words he spoke in the treasury, as he taught in the temple, but no one arrested him because his hour had not yet come."
4. The Son is God by nature, completely removed from likeness with creation, as far as his substance is concerned; on the words "You are of this world; I am not of this world."
5. The Son is not inferior in power and wisdom to God the Father, but he is his very wisdom and power; on the words "I do nothing on my own, but I speak these things just as the Father taught me."

BOOK 6

1. Physical suffering does not occur to anyone because of sins committed by the soul before birth, nor does God visit the sins of fathers on their children or the sins of anyone on anyone else, punishing those who have committed no sin. Rather, he renders a just judgment for everyone; on the words "Rabbi, who sinned, this man or his parents, that he was born blind?"

BOOK 7 (Fragments)

BOOK 8 (Fragments)

BOOK 9

1. The Son is in the Father by an identity of nature, and the Father, in turn, is in the Son.

BOOK 10

1. The Son is in no way less than God the Father but equal and similar to him in nature; on the words, "If you loved me, you would rejoice that I am going to the Father, because the Father is greater than I."
2. The Son is of the same substance as God the Father, not of a different or foreign nature as some twisted people say; on the words, "I am the vine, you are the branches, and my Father is the vinedresser."

BOOK 11

1. The Holy Spirit is by nature from God, and in the Son, and through him and in his substance.
2. His Spirit (that is, the Holy Spirit) is by nature in the Son and in his substance, just as he is also in the substance of the Father.

3. No one should understand the Son to lack any God-befitting glory, even though he is found to say, "Father, glorify your Son."
4. The fact that he is said to receive something from God the Father will in no way damage the glory of the Son, since there is a godly reason for this fact.
5. The Son will not be excluded from being true God, even though he calls the Father "the only true God."
6. The Son was not stripped of God-befitting glory, even though he is found saying to the Father, "Now glorify me with the glory which I had," etc.
7. The mention of something being given to the Son by the Father will not expel him from God-befitting honor, but he is clearly of the same substance and from him, even if he is said to receive something.
8. Even though something should be said to belong to the Father, it will not be excluded from the kingdom of Christ, for dominion over all things belongs to him as well.
9. The Son has the dignity of divinity by nature, even though he is said to have received this from the Father on account of his humanity and the form of his humiliation.
10. Christ is not holy by participation with another, nor is the sanctification through the Spirit foreign to his substance.
11. The Son is by nature one with God his Father, and he is in the Father, and the Father is in him according to the essential bond and mode of their unity. Likewise we ourselves, when we have received faith in him, are rendered one with each other and with God, bodily and spiritually.
12. The Son is by nature one with God his Father, even though he says that he received unity with the Father as a share of grace.

BOOK 12

1. The Son is by nature God, even though he is found calling the Father his God on account of us; on the words, "I am going to my Father and your Father, to my God and your God."

CYRIL OF ALEXANDRIA
Commentary on John

[1]
OUR FATHER AMONG THE SAINTS CYRIL ARCHBISHOP OF ALEXANDRIA INTERPRETATION OR COMMENTARY ON THE GOSPEL ACCORDING TO JOHN

Preface

"The Lord will give words to those who proclaim the gospel with great power," as the psalmist eloquently puts it.[1] I do not think just anyone should attempt this, however, but only those who are enlightened by grace from above because "all wisdom is from the Lord,"[2] as it is written, and "every good and perfect gift is from above, coming down from the Father of lights."[3] It is dangerous for ordinary people to speak about the essence that transcends all things and about its mysteries, and doing so risks penalty. Silence is the safer course in these matters. Nevertheless, the one who is God over all[4] deprives us of that course even though we think that silence is quite appropriate for us. He says to one of his saints, Paul, "Speak [2] and do not be silent."[5] The statutes of the law stress this even more when they command those who have been called to the divine priesthood to use trumpet blasts to announce to the people what they need to learn.[6] (These statutes are indicating spiritual matters in an earthly type.) When God wanted to give his most excellent law, I do not think he intended the leaders of the people to put their hands over their mouths, according to the text. Just because they were afraid of giving the impression of making a rash attempt at matters high above human understanding, God did not want them to refuse to give instruction so necessary to those whom they were leading to godliness and the knowledge of God, or to choose silence, which would harm those who were progressing toward discipleship.

By contrast, the disciple of Christ strikes fear into our hearts by saying, "Let not many of you become teachers."[7] In addition, the supremely wise preacher of Ecclesiastes figuratively shows the danger of teaching these things. "The one who chops wood," he says, "will be endangered in the process. If the ax head slips, that person grimaces and will need more exertion."[8] He compares the sharp mind with the ax head because it is the sort of thing that pierces through and sinks into the innermost parts even though it is resisted by the thickness and density of the wood. The thoughts in the divinely inspired Scripture are figuratively referred to as "wood." These thoughts turn the books that contain them into a kind of paradise of knowledge; even more, they are in labor, giving birth to the fruit bearing that comes from the Holy Spirit. One tries to split open the wood of knowledge, that is, the divine and mystic thoughts of the divinely inspired Scriptures, when one searches them with painstaking attention and a sharp mind. The great danger, he says, is that the ax head may slip. [3] This happens when the mind is not borne along the lines of the true

Preface [1]Ps 68:11 (Ps 67:12 LXX). [2]Sir 1:1. [3]Jas 1:17. [4]Rom 9:5. [5]Acts 18:9. [6]Lev 23:24. [7]Jas 3:1. [8]Eccles 10:9-10. Cyril is following the LXX here.

understanding of what is written but goes outside right judgment, leaves the straight path, so to speak, and is carried to some other path of interpretation that has turned away from what is right. When this happens to someone, their soul, that is, their heart, will grimace and groan. They will also increase the exertion of those wicked powers that oppose them, which use pointed and perverted words to persuade the mind of the deceived. These powers do not permit the mind to see the beauty of the truth; rather, they have many ways of turning it away and persuading it to go after crazy ideas. For no one says, "Let Jesus be cursed" except by Beelzeboul.[9]

Let no one make the mistake of thinking that this interpretation of the passage is either itself a mistake or that it is based on false reasoning in some way. After all, the Holy Scripture sometimes refers to the thoughts in the divinely inspired Scriptures as "wood," as we said before. For example, God who is over all says something like this to the people at that time through the supremely wise Moses: "If you make war against a city and besiege it for many days to take it, do not destroy its trees by cutting them down with an ax. You may eat from them, so do not remove them. A tree in the woods is not a person, is it, who enters the fort ahead of you? But do destroy and remove the tree that you know does not bear edible fruit."[10] I suppose it is clear to everyone that the God of all would not have deemed it worthy to give such commands to us if he were talking about trees from the ground. Even so, I should demonstrate also from [4] another command that he has no concern at all for such matters, and he places no importance on them. On the contrary, what does he command should be done with their so-called gods? "Demolish their altars," he says, "smash their pillars in pieces, and cut down their groves."[11] And he permits no tree whatsoever to grow next to his own altar. He proclaims clearly, "Do not plant for yourselves any grove next to the altar of the Lord your God."[12] If I need to say anything more about this, I will speak in the manner of the supremely wise Paul, "Is God concerned about trees? Does he not speak entirely for our sake?"[13] Through earthly examples, he leads us to the contemplation of spiritual matters.

Now let us think of the writings of the unholy heretics as cities. They are fortified, perhaps elaborately, with the wisdom of the world and a tangle of deceptive ideas. However, everyone who contends for the holy doctrines of the church arrives to lay siege on them and encircles them, as it were, "taking the shield of faith and the sword of the Spirit, which is the word of God."[14] Such a person is strong in every way and ready for battle against their false speaking, trained to demolish arguments, as Paul says, "and every proud obstacle that rises up against the knowledge of God, and take every thought captive to obey Christ."[15] Such a soldier of Christ, he says, goes around the bitter writings of heresy like an alien land and happens on the most cultivated trees; that is, the soldier finds words that are from the divinely inspired Scriptures, or words spoken by the prophets [5] or even testimonies from the New Testament dragged off for the purposes of the heretics. When this happens, you should not apply your sharp mind like some ax to cut them down and remove them. Just because these words were employed by people who do not know how to interpret them correctly does not mean that you should reject what comes from the mouth of God. Since it bears edible fruit, it will help and nourish you. They sometimes took the words foolishly, but when we turn the words around to the right argument for the faith, not only will we avoid

[9]1 Cor 12:3. [10]Deut 20:19-20. [11]Deut 7:5. [12]Deut 16:21. [13]1 Cor 9:9-10, "Is God concerned about oxen? Does he not speak entirely for our sake?" [14]Eph 6:16-17. [15]2 Cor 10:5.

being caught with an unstrung bow, but also our bowstring will be taut and ready with words against heresy. Immediately, then, he adds an argument to convince the hearers that it is right for those on the side of truth to mount an attack, not to overturn divine sayings but to remove the errors of the opponents. He says, "A tree in the woods is not a person, is it, who enters the fort ahead of you?"[16] Do you really think, he says, that the words of the Holy Scriptures will of themselves arise to attack you like some archheretic? Aren't these words rather defrauded by the folly of the heretics? So do not cut them down, he says. Let them be your food. "But do destroy and remove the tree that you know does not bear edible fruit."[17] The fruit of these people's writing is inedible for the one who wants to know the truth. Let every ax strike them. Let every spiritual lumberjack show strength. Let the strong ax gleam against them by advocating for the truth. The prophet Hosea also masterfully explains to us how useless and profitless the nonsense of the heterodox is: "The sheaf is not robust enough to yield grain, and if it does yield grain, **[6]** strangers will eat it."[18] Those who are eager to alienate themselves from friendship with God will feast on the weak old wives' tales of their own ignorance.

Now as I was saying at the beginning (for I think we must go back to that), the interpretation of the divine mysteries is extremely difficult. But your many words persuade me, my most diligent brother, to offer this work as a kind of fruit of my lips and spiritual sacrifice.[19] Therefore, I do not shrink back from the task because I trust in God who makes wise the blind and does not seek from us what is completely beyond our abilities but accepts equally even the offerings of the poor. The lawgiver commanded, in the beginning of Leviticus,[20] that whoever wants to bring a gift as a whole burnt offering to the Lord is to offer a bull. In this passage he defines the amount of honor due for each type of sacrifice. Nevertheless, he lowers the standard and says that those who might not have enough for this should offer sheep. But he knew full well that sudden grinding poverty would claim some so that perhaps they would be too weak for this. Therefore, he says, "Offer a gift of turtledoves or pigeons."[21] He even honors the one who is too poor for these and who approaches with the most worthless gifts. "Fine flour," he says, "will be their gift,"[22] defining an offering which I suppose is attainable for everyone and does not demand too much even for the deepest poverty. The lawgiver knew very well, I suppose, that it is better to bear fruit even a little than to be bereft of it. People who might otherwise be ashamed that their gifts seem inferior to the gifts of others should not be forced to the conclusion that they should not honor the Lord of all. **[7]**

Since I am understandably persuaded by all these considerations, I have banished all hesitation, that ally of silence, from my thoughts. I think I should honor my Lord with whatever I have, and I will offer, like fine flour wet with oil, a discourse that is nourishing and joyful to those who will read it. I will undertake an immense task and begin the book of John. But because of faith, I am not weak. I must without protest confess that I will speak and think less than is fitting. The great difficulty of the book, or more accurately, the weakness of my understanding, will persuade me rightly to seek pardon for this.

I will muster my discourse for battle, as well as I can, against the false opinions of those who teach wrongly. I will direct the discussion at every point to a doctrinal explanation. I will not extend the length as much as I could. In fact, I will even get rid of the excess. I am anxious to see that what I do

[16]Deut 20:19. [17]Deut 20:20. [18]Hos 8:7. [19]Heb 13:15. [20]Lev 1:3. [21]Lev 1:14. [22]Lev 2:1.

is appropriate. The list of the chapters below will show the subjects that the discourse covers. I have added numbers to it so that the readers will very quickly be able to find what they are looking for. **[9]**

Chapters in Book One

OUR FATHER AMONG THE SAINTS CYRIL ARCHBISHOP OF ALEXANDRIA EXEGETICAL COMMENTARY ON THE GOSPEL OF JOHN

BOOK ONE

God has instructed the thought of the holy Evangelists, and it is truly precise. From a hill or a lookout post, as it were, they scan with an eagle eye in every direction for something to benefit their hearers. With intense zeal, they track down what they think would profit those who thirst for the true exposition of divine teachings and who search with good intentions for the meaning hidden in the Holy Scriptures.

The Spirit does not reveal the truth to those who spend too much effort preparing for battle and who exult in tangled and deceptive arguments rather than rejoice in the truth. That is because the Spirit does not "enter a deceitful soul,"[1] nor does he otherwise allow his precious pearls to be rolled under the feet of swine.[2] Instead, he would rather spend his time with simple minds because they move without guile and **[12]** avoid superfluous sophistry. Such sophistry leads to senselessness and to a departure from the straight royal road because one leans too far to the right. "For the one who walks simply, walks surely," as Solomon says.[3]

The holy Evangelists have a precision in their writing that is quite amazing because they are not the ones who are speaking, as the Savior says, but the Spirit of the Father who is in them.[4] One might with good reason say that the composition of the book of John far surpasses even wonder itself when one looks at the excellence of his thoughts, the sharpness of his reasoning and the unceasing introduction of one idea after another. The Evangelists are like a team of horses in the interpretation of divine teachings that has left the starting gate and is racing towards one goal. The character of the discourse, however, is put together differently for each of them. It seems to me that they are like people who are ordered to assemble in one city but by no means are to travel by one and the same route. One can see that the other Evangelists provide a precise account of our Savior's genealogy according to the flesh. They trace the descendants in order from Abraham down to Joseph,[5] or they go from Joseph back up to Adam.[6] But the blessed John is not overly concerned about these matters. He harnesses the lightning-hot motion of his thoughts to reach for subjects that are beyond human comprehension. He dares to narrate the ineffable and unutterable birth of God the Word,[7] knowing that the "glory of God hides speech"[8] and that the dignity that befits God is greater than all our thought and speech. **[13]** The properties of the divine nature are difficult to utter and even more difficult to explain clearly.

Yet it was necessary in some way to measure heaven with a span[9] and, using the small measurements of human nature, to turn and approach things that are hard for everyone to understand and explain. That way, the road may not be left wide open for false teachers to assail those who are simpler. Since none of the sayings of the saints who have become "eyewitnesses and servants of the word"[10] fetter the evil ideas of such teachers, John gets right to the point, to the chief of all divine doctrines. "In the beginning was the Word," he cries, "and the Word was with God, and the Word was God. He was in the beginning with God."[11]

I think that those who are engaged with the Holy Scriptures need to approach all writings that might be good, noble and free from harm. In this way, by gathering what many people have observed from various points of view about the same thing, and by bringing them all to bear on one point, they will climb to a good measure of knowledge. They will imitate the bee, a wise worker, and build the sweet honeycomb of the Spirit.

Some of those who study these matters most intensely say that after our Savior's crucifixion and ascension into heaven, certain false shepherds and false teachers fell on the Savior's flocks like wild beasts and threw them into great turmoil. They spoke "from their own hearts," as it is written, "and not from the mouth of the Lord,"[12] or rather, not

Book 1 [1]Wis 1:4. [2]See Mt 7:6. [3]Prov 10:9. [4]See Mt 10:20. [5]See Mt 1. [6]See Lk 3. [7]The word ἐξηγέομαι, here translated "narrate," is the same word used in Jn 1:18 to describe what the Son has done in relation to the Father: he has "made him known." [8]Prov 25:2. [9]Is 40:12. [10]Lk 1:2. [11]Jn 1:1-2. [12]Jer 23:16.

only from their own heart but also from the teachings of their father, who is clearly the devil. (For if no one can say, "Jesus be cursed," except by Beelzeboul,[13] how could our claim about their father not be true?) What teachings then did these people **[14]** belch up in opposition to their own head? They ignorantly and impiously insisted that the only begotten Word of God, the eternal light, in whom we all move and have our being,[14] was first called into being when he was born as man of the holy virgin. After taking this ordinary form, he "was seen on the earth," as it is written, "and dwelt with humanity."[15] As for those who were disposed this way and who dared to slander the ineffable and eternal generation of the Son, the word of the prophet commands them, "Come here, you lawless sons, you seed of adulterers and a prostitute. Whom did you ridicule? At whom did you open your mouth and stick out your tongue?"[16] Clearly, your tongue is not bringing out good things from a good heart but is spewing the venom of the bloodstained serpent whom the psalmist references when he says to the one God who is over all, "You have crushed the heads of the serpent on the water."[17]

There was no small disturbance about these matters among the believers, and the consequences of the scandal were consuming the souls of the simple like a plague. Some were dragged away from the true teachings by the nonsense of these teachers and believed that the Word was first called into existence when he became human. Therefore, those of the faithful who were wiser gathered and met together about this. They went to the Savior's disciple (I mean of course John himself) and told him about the disease that was afflicting the brothers, and they disclosed the nonsense of the heterodox teachers. They then urged him to come to their aid with all his might by the illumination of the Spirit and to stretch out a saving hand to those already caught in the nets of the devil. **[15]**

The disciple grieved over the lost, whose minds had been corrupted, and he thought it would be equally catastrophic not to give some forethought to future generations. So he risked writing a book. He left to the other Evangelists the task of explaining the human matters more fully, like the genealogy of the legal and natural birth according to the flesh, while he himself pounced with fire and vigor on the nonsense of those false teachers, saying . . . **[16]**

Chapter One

1:1 In the beginning was the Word.

The Only Begotten is eternal and before the ages.

What do they say to this? I am talking about those who introduce the Son to us as a latecomer in order to deny that he is fully God. "There will be no new god among you," says Holy Scripture.[18] How then is he not new if he was born recently? And how was he not lying when he said to the Jews, "Truly I say to you, before Abraham came to be, I Am"?[19] I presume it is clear to all and everyone agrees that Christ was born through the holy virgin a long time after the blessed Abraham. But how will the phrase "he was in the beginning" at all be maintained and turn out to be true if the Only Begotten came to be at the end of the ages? You will see, I think, from what follows how absurd it is to cut short the eternal existence of the Son and to suppose that he came into existence in recent times. On the contrary, this statement of the blessed Evangelist will serve as a discriminating touchstone for us: **[17]**

[13]1 Cor 12:3. [14]Acts 17:28. [15]Bar 3:37 (Bar 3:38 LXX). [16]Is 57:3-4. [17]Ps 74:13 (Ps 73:13 LXX). [18]Ps 81:9 (Ps 80:10 LXX). [19]Jn 8:58.

In the beginning was the Word.
There is nothing older than the beginning, as long as one does not violate the definition of beginning. For there could never be a beginning of a beginning, or else it would stop being a true beginning because we would have to imagine some other beginning arising before it. Besides, if anything can exist before the real beginning, our discussion will lead us to an infinite regress. Another beginning will always arise before the "beginning" and will show the "beginning" under investigation to be second.

Therefore, there will be no beginning of a beginning according to strict reasoning. Otherwise, any discussion of the beginning would go off into tedium and incomprehensibility. But since the flight ever backwards has no end and extends as far as the regression of the ages, the Son will be found to have come to be not in time but rather to exist eternally with the Father. For "he was in the beginning." And if he was in the beginning, what kind of interpretation, tell me, will have the power to fly over the "was"? When will the "was" stand at the final beginning point if it is always running ahead of the reasoning that is pursuing it and leaping ahead of the thought that is chasing it?[20]

This is the very thing that amazed the prophet Isaiah. He says, "Who can tell of his generation? His life is lifted from the earth."[21] The account of the birth of the Only Begotten really is "lifted from the earth." I mean, it is above every thought of those who are on the earth and over every earthly account so that it remains ineffable. But if it is above the mind and the explanations that are within our power, how could he be originate,[22] since our intellectual capacity is not too weak to describe both the time and the definition of originate beings? **[18]**

Another view of the same thing:
In the beginning was the Word.
No beginning that is the least bit temporal can be applied to the Only Begotten because he is before all time[23] and has his existence before the ages. Furthermore, his divine nature exempts him from having an end because he will always be the same. As the Psalms sing, "You are the same, and your years will never end."[24] From what sort of beginning then, measured in temporal quantity as our beginnings are, will the Son proceed, if he does not have an end (because he is God by nature and for this reason cries out, "I am the life")?[25] A beginning by itself should not be considered a beginning if it has no end. That is because we name a beginning relative to its end, and an end relative to its beginning, at least when we are talking about a beginning measured in temporal quantity, as we are here.

Therefore, since the Son is older than even the ages themselves, he will elude any notion that he came to be in time. Through all time, he "was" in his Father as in a source according to his own statement, "I came from the Father and have arrived."[26] Therefore, since the Father is considered as source, "the Word was in him" because the Word was his wisdom, power, imprint, radiance and image. If there was no time when the Father was without word, wisdom, imprint and radiance, one must confess that the Son, who is these things for the eternal Father, exists eternally. For how is he really the imprint, how is he the precise image, unless he exhibits the beauty of the one whose image he is, since he has been formed in relation to it?

It would not be wrong in the least to think that the Son exists in the Father as in a source.[27] **[19]** For the name "source" in this case indicates only what something is from.

[20]Cyril is envisioning human thought chasing the "was" into the past. [21]Is 53:8 (LXX). [22]"Originate" (γενητός) refers to something that comes into existence from some origin. [23]See 2 Tim 1:9. [24]Ps 102:27 (Ps 101:28 LXX). [25]Jn 14:6. [26]Jn 16:28. [27]The word for "source" (πηγή) denotes a spring of water.

The Son exists in the Father and from the Father. He did not come into existence from outside of the Father or in time but exists in the substance of the Father. He radiates out from that substance like beams from the sun or heat from a fire. These sorts of examples show that one thing can be begotten of another but still always be with it and inseparably attached to it. The one cannot exist in itself apart from the other, yet the integrity of its own nature is truly preserved. How can the sun possibly exist without rays, and how can the sun's rays exist without being in the sun, which emits them? How can fire exist if it has no heat, and where does heat come from if not from fire, or perhaps from something else that is not far removed from the essential quality of fire? Therefore, as these examples show, the fact that something is "in" what it is from does not take away the fact that the two are "with" each other. Instead, the "in" shows that the begotten offspring always coincide with the sources that begat them and that they share in one nature with them, so to speak. The same holds true for the Son. If he is thought and said to be in the Father and with the Father, that does not mean the Son will be alien or foreign or in second place after the Father. Instead, he will always be in him and with him and radiating from him according to the ineffable mode of divine generation.

The saints too refer to God the Father as the "beginning"[28] of the Son only to indicate whom he is "from." Listen to the psalmist predicting through the Holy Spirit the second appearance of our Savior, addressing the Son himself: "With you is the beginning in the day of your power, in the splendor **[20]** of your saints."[29] The day of the Son's power is that day when he judges the whole world and renders to each one according to his works. He will certainly come, and then he will be in the Father and have the Father in him. The Father is the beginningless beginning of the Son's nature, so to speak, but only in the sense of source because the Son's existence is "from" the Father.

In the beginning was the Word.
The discussion of the "beginning" indicated here is speckled with many colors that cross a spectrum of different ideas for us to consider. We are eager to pursue in every direction those things that are profitable and to track down like a hound the true understanding of divine teaching and the precise meaning of the mysteries. "You search the Holy Scriptures," says the Savior, "because in them you think you have eternal life. And these are they that testify about me."[30] Now the blessed Evangelist here seems to call the Father the "beginning,"[31] that is, the authority over all things, so that the divine nature clearly transcends all things. That nature has all originate beings under its feet and is practically borne aloft over those things that are called into being through it.

Therefore, in this "beginning" that is above all and over all "was the Word." He was not "with" everything under the feet of this beginning, but outside all things and by nature "in" the beginning. He is like a coeternal fruit that has the oldest place of all, as it were. That place is the nature of the one who begat him. Therefore, since he springs from the free Father and is himself free, he will possess with the Father the beginning (or dominion) that transcends all things. We should now see how this argument proceeds.

Some, as we said above, foolhardily **[21]** insist that the Word of God was first called into existence when he took the temple from the holy virgin and became human for us. What would be the consequence if the Son turned out to be of this nature? What if he is originate and created and has the same nature as everything else whose origin is from noth-

[28]Ἀρχή. [29]Ps 110:3 (Ps 109:3 LXX). [30]Jn 5:39. [31]The word for "beginning" in Jn 1:1 (ἀρχή) also means "dominion."

ing? What if both the name and the reality of slavery are proven right and true? What created thing can safely gain exemption from servitude to God who rules all things? And what will not bow down before the dominion and authority and lordship over all things, which Solomon himself somewhere indicates when he says, "The throne of dominion[32] is established with righteousness"?[33] The throne of dominion over everything is clearly established for righteousness, and quite rightly so. What is the throne we are talking about now? Listen to God speaking through one of his saints: "Heaven is my throne."[34] Therefore, heaven is established for righteousness, that is, for the holy spirits in heaven.

If the Son was born recently and is one of the creatures created in time, as they contend, then one must confess that he is subject to God the Father along with the other created beings and that he holds the rank of slave and falls under the authority of the dominion like the others. The blessed Evangelist positively pounces on those who teach wrongly, and he removes the Son from all servitude. He shows that the Son is clearly of the substance that is free and rules over all, and he insists that the Son is "in" that substance by nature when he says, "In the beginning was the Word."

He aptly adds "was" to the word *beginning* so we may understand that the Son is not only glorious but also before time. He puts the "was" here to stretch the thinking of the reader to some deep, incomprehensible and ineffable birth outside of time. Since the Evangelist says "was" without qualification, **[22]** at what point will the "was" stand still, since its nature is always to run ahead of the thought that pursues it? Whatever stopping point someone might think it has, it makes that stopping point the beginning of a further pursuit. Therefore, the Word "was" in the "beginning," that is, in the dominion that is over everything. He is from that dominion by nature and possesses the dignity of the Lord. But if this is true, how is he any longer originate or created? How will "was not" intrude where "was" is? In the end, what place can there be for "was not," regarding the Son? **[23]**

Chapter Two

The Son, who is both God and of the same substance as the Father, exists in his own hypostasis,[35] just as the Father does.

And the Word was with God.
The Evangelist has now sufficiently demonstrated that the ignorant views of those who hold such opinions are stale and have strayed from the truth. By saying "in the beginning was the Word," he has closed every loophole for those who claim that the Son is from nothing, and he has utterly stripped them of all their nonsense on this subject. Now he proceeds to the other related and stubborn heresy. He is like a skilled and patient gardener who takes special delight in the work of the pickax. He gets dressed in appropriate work clothes and works hard to present his garden free of annoying thorns. He does not stop piling up the thorns on top of each other but circles around them and uproots the troublesome plants with the hard tooth of his pickax. In the same way, the blessed John carries in his mind the living, active and razor-sharp word of God.[36] With clear sight and a keen mind he inspects the prickly growths of evil that arise from the heterodox, **[24]** and he runs at them full speed, so to speak, and wastes no time cutting them down from every direction. He sees to it that everyone who reads what he has written is kept in the true faith.

[32]Ἀρχή. [33]Prov 16:12. [34]Is 66:1. [35]A hypostasis is a concretely existing individual. To say that the Father and the Son each has his own hypostasis is to say that there is a distinction between them. This statement rejects the position of the modalists, who say that the distinction between Father and Son is a distinction in name only. [36]Heb 4:12.

Notice once again the vigilance of the Spirit bearer. He taught above that the Word was in the beginning, that is, in God the Father, as we said. But since the eyes of his mind were enlightened, he was aware, it seems, that some would arise who would in colossal ignorance say that the Father and the Son are one and the same and would distinguish the persons of the holy Trinity in name only. They would not concede that the Father and Son subsist in their own hypostases so that the Father is really understood to be the Father and not the Son, and that the Son in turn subsists on his own and is not the Father, as the word of truth holds. The Evangelist arms himself against this heresy too as if it were already present and stirred up at that time, or about to be. And for its destruction he immediately adds the phrase "and the Word was with God" to the phrase "in the beginning was the Word." He rightly puts the word *was* in both phrases to indicate that the Son was begotten before the ages; then, by showing that the Word was "with God," he indicates that the Son is one thing and subsists in himself, while God the Father, "with" whom "the Word was," is another. For how could something that is really one in number be thought to be "with" itself or beside itself?

In the considerations that follow, we will show that the heretics hold an ignorant view in this matter. In the process, we will establish an accurate touchstone for the topics of our investigation. **[25]**

Proof by reasoning and scriptural testimonies that the Father subsists in his own hypostasis as does the Son. The Holy Spirit is also counted as God with them, though no evidence about him is marshaled for now.

The Son is of the same substance as the Father, and the Father is of the same substance as the Son. Therefore, they ascend into an exact likeness so that the Father is seen in the Son, and the Son is seen in the Father, and the one shines in the other. As the Savior himself says somewhere, "The one who has seen me has seen my Father," and "I am in the Father, and the Father is in me."[37] He is in the Father, and he has the Father in him. He beautifully corresponds in every detail, as stated above, to the form of the one who begat him; indeed, he genuinely depicts in himself the one who begat him, the one from whom he exists. However, he will not for that reason lose his own subsistence, nor will the Father lose his. Neither will their complete likeness cause any confusion of the hypostases so that we understand the Father who begat to be the same in number as the Son who was begotten of him. We will confess the identity of nature for both, but the proper subsistence of each one surely follows so that we should think of the Father as really the Father and the Son as the Son. In this way, since the Holy Spirit is numbered with them and also counted as God, the holy Trinity will have the proper fullness.

Another: If the Son himself is also the Father, how do we explain the difference in the names? If the Father did not beget at all, why is he called Father? And if the Son was not begotten from the Father, how is he really the Son? **[26]** The names themselves demand such an interpretation. Since the Holy Scriptures proclaim that the Son is begotten, and he truly is, he therefore subsists in himself. And if the relationship of the begotten to the begetter is that of one thing from another, then the Father too exists separately.

Another: The blessed Paul, writing to the Philippians about the Son, says, "who though he was in the form of God did not consider equality with God something to be exploited."[38] Who then is the one who did not

[37]Jn 14:9-10. [38]Phil 2:6.

want to consider equality with God something to be exploited? Do we not have to say that someone who is in the form of God is different from the one whose form it is? This much is clear to all, and everyone admits it. Therefore, the Father and the Son are not one and the same in number, but they are distinct, and they are seen in one another because of the identity of substance, even if the Son is clearly from the Father as one from another.

Another: "I and the Father are one,"[39] says the Savior, because he knows, of course, that he subsists on his own and so does the Father. But if this is not the truth of the matter, why does he obscure the unity by saying "I and the Father" are one? Since he explains the meaning with the plural, it should be clear that he overthrows the conjecture of the heterodox. For it would make no sense to apply the phrase "we are" to the word *one.*

Another: At the formation of humanity, the voice of God is introduced, saying, "Let us make humankind in our image and likeness."[40] If the breadth of the holy Trinity, if I may call it that, is contracted into a singular and they impiously take from the Father and the Son their own subsistences, who is speaking to whom in the statement, **[27]** "Let us make humankind in our image"? If this is so, he ought to say (as they foolishly say), "Let us make humankind in my image and likeness." As it is, however, the author of the book does not say this, but he describes the making with the plural by adding "in our image." He all but cries out with a clear and mighty voice that the enumeration of the holy Trinity is greater than one.

Another: If the Son is the radiance of the Father as light from light, how is he not other than the Father so that he subsists on his own? For it is clear that what is really emitted will be emitted from another and not from itself.

Another: The Son shows that he is from the substance of God the Father when he says at one point, "I came from the Father and have arrived. I am going to the Father again."[41] How then will he not differ from him in hypostasis and number since all reason convinces us to think that something that comes from something else is different from that from which it has come? Therefore, the opponents' argument is not true.

Another: We are justified in believing in God the Father and the only begotten Son and the Holy Spirit. That is why the Savior himself instructs his own disciples, "Go and make disciples of all nations, baptizing them in the name of the Father and of the Son and of the Holy Spirit."[42] If the difference in names is going to make no contribution at all to our understanding, but the one who says "Father" means the Son and the one who names the Son is referring to the Father, **[28]** what was the point of ordering the believers to be baptized not into the Unity but into the Trinity? Since the statement about the divine nature extends to the number three, however, I think it is clear to all that each one of those numbered is in his own hypostasis. But because there is no change in nature, each hypostasis ascends to one divine nature and receives the same worship.

Another: Holy Scripture says that the wrath of God burned up the cities of the Sodomites. It explains how God's anger came on them, and it teaches clearly how the destruction happened. "The Lord," it says, "rained fire and brimstone on Sodom from the Lord,"[43] since this is the portion of the cup that is most fitting for those who make it their practice to commit these sins.[44] What Lord then sent fire from what Lord and consumed the cities of Sodom? It is clear that the Father works everything through the Son, since the Son is his power and his arm. So the Father caused him to rain fire on the Sodomites. When the

[39]Jn 10:30. [40]Gen 1:26. [41]Jn 16:28. [42]Mt 28:19. [43]Gen 19:24. [44]Ps 11:6 (Ps 10:6 LXX).

Lord sends fire on them from the Lord, how are the Father and Son not different from each other, insofar as each subsists on his own? For it says here that the one is from the other.

Another: The prophetic Spirit moved the blessed psalmist and gave him knowledge of the future. Accordingly, the blessed psalmist understood that the human race could be saved only by the appearance of the Son of God, who can easily bring about whatever transformation he wishes. That is why the psalmist asked that the Son be sent to us, since only he is able to save those who have fallen under the oppressive hand **[29]** of the devil. In particular, the psalmist addressed God the Father, saying, "Send out your light and your truth."[45] What kind of light is it and what kind of truth? Listen to the Son, who says, "I am the light" and "I am the truth."[46] But if the light and the truth of the Father, that is, the Son, is sent to us, how can the Son not be different from him, as far as his own subsistence is concerned, even if he is also one with him as far as the identity of substance is concerned? If anyone thinks this is wrong, and the Father and the Son are one and the same, why didn't the Spirit bearer pray differently, crying out, "Come to us, O light and truth"? But since he says "send," the conclusion should be clear that he thinks the sender is different from the one being sent. Of course, we should understand the manner of the sending in a way that is fitting to God.

Another: The Holy Scriptures say that everything was made through the Son, "things visible and invisible, things in heaven and on earth."[47] We worshipers of the truth believe this, and so we employ right reasoning within the bounds of godly doctrine. Therefore, let us examine carefully the words "through the Son" and search out their meaning. Clearly, these words force us to think that the one who does the work is different from the one through whom all the work is done. "Through the Son" necessitates two persons. When it says that the Father creates through the Son, let them explain how "through the Son" can truly and strictly refer to a unitary subject without envisioning another subject alongside and concurring with the first. I think my opponent will be completely at a loss. But since the Holy Scriptures themselves proclaim that the Father has made all things through the Son,[48] **[30]** and we believe it (and I suppose even they do too), how could we not think that the Father subsists on his own by himself, and the Son does as well, without overturning the recognition that the holy Trinity has an identity of substance? **[31]**

Chapter Three

The Son is God by nature and is in no way less than or unlike the Father.

And the Word was God.

The Spirit bearer was not unaware that some would arise in the end times who would speak against the substance of the Only Begotten "and deny the Lord who bought them."[49] They would think that the Word who appeared from God the Father is not God by nature. Instead, they would introduce to us some falsely named bastard, so to speak, who clothes himself in the name of sonship and deity but does not truly have them. Those who do this sort of thing make a home in their mind for the Jewish impiety of Arius. They bring out of their dead heart not the life-giving discourse of pious contemplation but weapons that aim for death. "Their tongue is really a wounding arrow. The words of their mouth are treacherous."[50]

It is as though someone were already straining against the words of truth and all but saying to the holy Evangelist, The Word, my friend, was with God. Fine. We believe your

[45]Ps 43:3 (Ps 42:3 LXX). [46]Jn 8:12; 14:6. [47]Col 1:16. [48]Jn 1:3. [49]2 Pet 2:1. [50]Jer 9:8.

book on this point. Let the Father be and exist on his own, and the Son as well. But what should we think of the Word's nature? **[32]** The fact that he is with God tells us nothing at all about his substance.

When the Holy Scriptures proclaim one God, shall we ascribe this only to the Father, with whom the Word was? Well, what does the herald of truth say to this? Not only was the Word "with God," but also he "was God." Because he was "with God," we recognize him as another besides the Father, and we believe that the Son exists on his own. But because he "was God," we understand him to be of the same substance and to be from him by nature because he is both God and comes forth from God. Everyone agrees that the divine nature is one, so it is inconceivable that the holy Trinity would not completely possess identity of nature and so rise to the "one" that is characteristic of the divine nature. Therefore, he "was God." He did not become God later, but he was God. That is because being eternal is a strict consequence of being God. Something that comes into being in time or is in any way brought into being from what does not exist could not be God by nature.

Since God the Word has eternity on the basis of the word *was*, and he has consubstantiality with the Father because he was "God," what sort of punishment and vengeance must we think they are risking when they imagine that he is somehow less than or even unlike the one who begat him? They do not shudder to go so far in their godlessness that they teach such ideas to others, "not understanding either what they are saying or the things about which they are making assertions."[51]

From the following considerations, however, we will see that the Son who is truly from the Father is not at all less than the Father.

First. The Holy Scriptures call the Son many different names. They say that he is the wisdom and power of the Father, according to the statement in **[33]** Paul, "Christ the power of God and the wisdom of God."[52] Again, he is also called his light and truth, as one of the saints sings in the Psalms, "Send out your light and your truth."[53] He is also called righteousness, according to the passage, "Save me in your righteousness,"[54] for the Father gives life in Christ to those who believe in him. He is also called the counsel of the Father, according to the statement, "You have led me in your counsel,"[55] and again, "The counsel of the Lord remains forever."[56] Because the Son is all these things to God the Father, let those who fawn on the deception of Arius and fill themselves with his madness tell us how the Son is less than the Father. If they are right, if the Son, who is all these things to him, will be shown imperfect because he really has these qualities to a lesser degree, then it is time to say that the Father is not perfectly wise, not perfectly powerful, not perfectly light, not perfectly truth, not perfectly righteous and not even perfect in his counsel. But surely it is impious to think or say this. The Father is perfect because he has everything in himself perfectly. Therefore, it is clear that the Son—the wisdom and power, the light and truth, the righteousness and counsel of the Father—is also perfect. How could he who supplies perfection to his own Father be considered inferior?

Another: If the Son is inferior because he is "with" God the Father, yet he is adored by both us and the holy angels, we will be caught worshiping two gods. For the imperfect will in no way rise to the identity of nature with the perfect. There is a sharp distinction that separates beings of different natures, making them different from each other. The faith, however, is not in a plurality of gods. God the

[51]1 Tim 1:7. [52]1 Cor 1:24. [53]Ps 43:3 (Ps 42:3 lxx). [54]Ps 119:40 (Ps 118:40 lxx). [55]Ps 73:24 (Ps 72:24 lxx). [56]Ps 33:11 (Ps 32:11 lxx).

Father is one, and the Son rises to unity with him, and so does the Holy Spirit, of course. Therefore, no accusation **[34]** against the Son remains. How will an inferior being be admitted any longer into unity with the perfect Father and united with him by nature in an identity of substance?

Another: If the Son is fullness (for "from his fullness we have all received"),[57] how can anything inferior be in him? Opposing attributes cannot be in the same subject at the same time.

Another: If the Son, who is lesser, fills all things, where will the greatness of the Father go? I am speaking in a corporeal way for the sake of example. Lesser and greater have different senses when applied to incorporeal objects.

Another: If God is above every name, yet the Son, who is his heir, is imperfect because he is inferior, then there is no greatness in the one who is over everything, that is, God. But it is absurd either to think or to say this. Therefore, the Son is perfect because God, who is over every name, is also perfect.

Another: If the divine nature is not subject to quantification but whatever is inferior admits of degrees, how could the Son, who is God by nature, be considered inferior? If, as they say, he is inferior to the Father, he will be subject to quantification.

Another: The blessed John says concerning the Son, "He gives the Spirit without measure,"[58] to those who are worthy, of course. Since there is no measure in the Son, he is therefore immeasurable. Since he is God, he surpasses all thinking that operates in terms of quantity. How then can one who is not measured be inferior?

Another: If the Son is inferior and the Father is superior, then they will clearly act differently in our sanctification in proportion to the measure that each one has. The Father will sanctify more and the Son by himself will sanctify less. **[35]** There will also be a twofold Spirit who is inferior in the Son and superior in the Father. Those who are sanctified by the Father will be sanctified perfectly, and those who are sanctified by the Son will be sanctified imperfectly. But this line of reasoning is totally absurd. The Holy Spirit is one, and sanctification is one and perfect, supplied from the Father through the Son by nature. Therefore, the one who has the same activity as the perfect Father is not inferior to him. He has the Spirit of the one who begat him, a good of his own nature, living and hypostatic,[59] just as the Father has.

Another: If the Son was in the form of and equal to the Father, as Paul says,[60] how is he inferior to him? The account of the *oikonomia*[61] with the flesh and the emptying that Paul speaks of[62] on account of it will not, I suppose, strip the Son of the honor he has by nature, because the end of the story is his second coming from heaven. He will surely come, as we have heard, "in the glory of his Father."[63] But how can one who is inferior to the Father really be in the glory of the perfect Father?

Another: One finds God the Father saying somewhere through one of the prophets, "My glory will I not give to another."[64] We must therefore ask those who impiously dishonor the Son—or rather through him dishonor the Father too ("for the one who does not honor the Son does not honor the Father")[65]—whether the Son, whom they suppose to be inferior to God the Father, is nevertheless of the same substance with him. If they say that

[57]Jn 1:16. [58]Jn 3:34. [59]Cyril here uses the word ἐνυπόστατον to describe the Spirit. This does not mean the Spirit is "enhypostatic" in the sense he exists only "in" the hypostasis of another and has no hypostasis of his own. That is how the term later comes to be used to describe Christ's human nature. Here it means that the Spirit exists concretely as his own person. [60]Phil 2:6. [61]*Oikonomia* can mean either God's plan of salvation in general or the incarnation in particular. [62]Phil 2:7. [63]Mk 8:38. [64]Is 48:11. [65]Jn 5:23.

he is of the same substance, why do they senselessly attribute inferiority to him? Things that are of the same substance and nature would not have any superiority among themselves, at least when it comes to the definition of their mode of being. This is, after all, what we are investigating.

Perhaps they will not agree, however, and **[36]** refuse to grant that the Son is of the same substance as the Father since they think he is inferior. In that case, he will be completely different from and alien to the Father. But then how does he have his glory? "For to him was given honor and the kingdom," as the blessed Daniel says.[66] Either God the Father will be lying when he says, "My glory will I not give to another," or if he is telling the truth and has given his glory to the Son, then the Son is not another beside him. He is, rather, the fruit of his substance and a genuine offspring. How could someone whose nature is related to the Father in this way ultimately be inferior to the Father?

Others, simple and unconnected: If the Father is almighty and the Son is also almighty, how is the Son inferior to the Father? That which is imperfect will never rise to the measure of perfection because it always lags behind. If the Father is Lord and the Son is also Lord, how is the Son inferior to the Father? The Son will not be perfectly free if he is inferior in lordship and does not possess full dignity in himself. If the Father is light and the Son is also light, how is the Son inferior to the Father? In that case, he will not perfectly be light, but he will be overcome in part by the darkness. So the Evangelist will be lying when he says, "The darkness has not overcome it."[67] If the Father is life and the Son is also life, how is the Son inferior to the Father? In that case, we will not have perfect life in us even if Christ dwells "in the inner being."[68] Those who believe will be partially dead if the Son, since he is inferior, is not perfectly life. Since we must banish these absurdities as far away as possible, we say that the Son is perfect. He is equal to the perfect Father because of his exact likeness of substance.

Another: If the Son is inferior to the Father and therefore not of the same substance, then he is by nature different from and completely alien to him. **[37]** He is not Son and not even God at all. How could one who is not from the Father be called Son? And how could one who is not from God by nature still be called God? Since our faith is in the Son, we are still, it seems, in error because we do not know the true God. But this is absurd. When we believe in the Son, we of course also believe in the Father and the Holy Spirit. The Son is not alien to God the Father as one who is inferior. He is one with the Father since he is "from him" by nature. Therefore, he is both equal and perfect.

Another: If God the Word, who shines forth from God the Father, is truly Son, our opponents are forced to confess even against their will that he is from the substance of the Father. That is what sonship truly means. How then is one who is the fruit of the Father's substance inferior to the Father, since that substance admits no inferiority into itself? But if he is not from the Father's substance, then he is not Son but some bastard, so to speak, and a son in name only. In that case, the Father would not correctly and truly be called Father either. He is called Father because of the Son, so how could he be thought of as Father if the Son is not Son by nature? But this is absurd. God is the true Father. All the Holy Scriptures indeed cry this out. Therefore, the one who is from him by nature is completely Son. And if so, he is not inferior. Since he is Son, he is of the same substance.

Another: Strictly speaking, God does not

[66]Dan 7:14. [67]Jn 1:5. [68]Eph 3:16-17.

receive the name of family or fatherhood from us, but rather we clearly received it from him. The statement of Paul is trustworthy, who cries out, "From whom every family in heaven and on earth is named."[69] Since [38] God is the oldest of all things, it is clear that we are fathers by imitation. We have been called to his pattern by being made in his image. How then, tell me, are we who are made in his likeness fathers of our own children by nature? How could this be if it does not apply to the archetypal image according to which we are formed? How could anyone grant that the name of family or fatherhood proceeds from God to others if he is not really Father? This obviously turns the whole matter upside down, and we will give him the name "Father" in imitation of us, rather than him giving it to us. This argument will force the heretics to surrender even against their will, since if they are right, the witness to the truth lies when he says that every family in heaven and on earth comes from him. But this is patently absurd. The one who is bold to say, "Do you seek proof of Christ speaking in me?"[70] speaks the truth, and the name "family" flows down from God to us. Therefore, he is by nature the Father of the Word. The one he begat was not at all unlike himself, as though he had less than the Father himself has. For we are made in imitation of him, and the ones we beget are not less than us but altogether equal, at least as far as the definition of their nature is concerned.

Another: Do not let the subtle heretics subject the truth to sophistry with their arguments. Do not let them confess that the Word of God is Son when they grant to him only the honor of mere words, maintaining that he is not of the substance of the Father. How would he be Son at all if he were not Son by nature? Let them tear off the mask of hypocrisy and blaspheme openly, confessing him to be neither God nor Son. Or else, if they are convicted by the entirety of Holy Scripture, [39] if they are shot through by the words of the saints as by stones from a sling, if they feel ashamed in the presence of the truth, if they say that he is both Son and God, let them not think that he is less than the one who begat him. Since the Word is God, how can it be that he receives any inferiority at all just because he is "with" God the Father? A man is called a "son" of a man, and he is, but he cannot be less human than his father. Indeed, no human being can be more or less human than another, nor can an angel, let's say, be more or less of an angel than another angel. Nor can anything else that exists be greater or less than anything that has the same nature and shares the same substance. Therefore, if he is truly Son, we must say that he is from the substance of the Father, bearing all the properties of that substance in himself by nature. If the Father is God by nature, it is clear that the Word who is begotten of him is also God by nature. How then will God be less divine than God?

Another: Where do you people get the audacity to say that the Son is placed in an inferior position from the one who begat him? How could he receive inferiority into himself? Not even a perfect fool would make assumptions about the age of his being, I think, because the Son is before the ages, and he is the creator of the ages.[71] It would be reasonable to suppose that something whose generation is older than all time would not be defined by time at all. Nor is he less than the Father in size because the divine nature is understood to be and is without size, without quantity and without body. In what respect then will inferiority be demonstrated in the one who was begotten? In glory, perhaps someone will say, or in power or in wisdom. Then let them

[69]Eph 3:15. The word for "family" is πατριά, a word which is etymologically related to "Father" (πατήρ). [70]2 Cor 13:3. [71]Heb 1:2.

say how great and how large the Father is in these respects, if one really must speak this way, so that the Son is ultimately thought to be inferior when measured against him. **[40]** Or if the Father's goodness is inconceivable and immeasurable and far surpasses the limit of our understanding, how do the Arians, who are ready to dare anything, say that he is inferior and overthrow the dignity that belongs to him by nature? The lesser is demonstrated by comparison with the greater. But the dignity of the Father is immeasurable, so what proof is there of a shortfall in the Son?

Another: Really, we can respond to the abomination of the unholy heretics by truthfully saying, "Our enemies are without understanding."[72] How could they not be filled up entirely with ignorance, not knowing "either what they are saying or the things about which they are making assertions," as Paul says?[73] The reason we think it is necessary to accuse them is this: if they say and believe that the Son is begotten of God the Father as true God, how is he less than the Father? This will generate a great number of absurd arguments containing blasphemy on every side such that one will refuse even to listen to them. If the Son, who is fully God by nature, will admit inferiority into himself in any respect, then we must think that there is something greater than God. We will not think that the substance of the Father is perfect in absolutely every respect, even though he is God by nature. Instead, he will advance in some direction toward the greater since like the Son, his image, he himself is proven to be of a substance that admits inferiority. He will endure this potentially even if he has not yet endured it. Beings that are capable of admitting something will certainly admit what they are capable of. Therefore, when the time comes for them to undergo this, they will not refuse it. But this is clearly a great blasphemy. The Father will not at all progress toward superiority, nor will he admit inferiority because **[41]** he is God by nature. Therefore, the Son will not admit inferiority into himself since he too is God by nature. Their pet slogan, then, conceived by the ignorance of the heretics, may not be entertained as an accusation against the substance that is higher than all.

Another: [They say that] even though the Word is the Son of God the Father by nature, he is nevertheless inferior to the Father either because of their definition of the dignity that God deserves, or because the Son does not have an unchangeable nature or because he has some sort of deprivation. If so, this accusation will not so much strike him as it will strike the substance from which we believe he exists, since it is caught giving birth to something less than or even worse than itself. Even originate created beings do not undergo this. Everything that is the fruit of generation gives birth to that which is completely similar to itself. But if they are going to say that the Father's divine nature lies above all suffering, then clearly it will lie outside accusation in this matter as well. Since it is the archetype of our good attributes, it will not beget the Son as inferior but as equal and of the same substance, lest God who is so far above us be inferior even to us.

Another by reduction to absurdity: Christ says somewhere to his disciples, "The one who has seen me has seen the Father,"[74] showing that he is equal to God the Father. If he is this way by nature, and if he exists the way that he himself confidently and truthfully affirms, how can he be inferior, as the foolish counsel of some would have it? If he reveals the Father with no intervening variation yet is inferior in himself, the inferiority will reach up to the Father since he appears in his unaltered image, the Son. But **[42]** this is absurd. Therefore, the

[72]Deut 32:31. [73]Tim 1:7. [74]Jn 14:9.

Son, in whom the perfect Father is imaged, is not inferior.

Another: How can the Son admit inferiority to the Father into himself, since he says blamelessly, "All things the Father has are mine,"[75] and again, addressing God the Father, he says, "All that is mine is yours, and all that is yours is mine"?[76] If the Son is inferior, as the foolish counsel of some holds, the inferiority will make its way even to the Father since the Son is telling the truth when he says to the Father, "What is mine is yours, and what is yours is mine."[77] Likewise, the superiority will make its way to the Son since the order makes no difference. The qualities that belong to each one appear in the other. Whatever might belong to the Father belongs also to the Son, and whatever is shown to be proper to the Son is also proper to the Father. Therefore, nothing will prevent us from saying that the Father is less than the Son and the Son is greater than the Father. But it is the height of madness even to think such a thing. Therefore, the one who has the surpassing qualities of substance in common with the Father is equal and not inferior.

Another along the same lines: If all that the Father has belongs completely to the Son and there is perfection in the Father, the Son will also be perfect since he has the attributes and surpassing qualities of the Father. Therefore, he is not inferior, as the impiety of the heretics would have it.

Another by reduction to absurdity in combination with a syllogism: Let them tell us—those who are raining down unquenchable fire on their heads, who reject the uprightness of the divine teachings, who think up the twists and turns of multiple [43] syllogisms to deceive and overthrow the innocent—if the Son is inferior, as they foolishly maintain, is the Father greater than the Son, since he possesses superiority? I think they will surely say that the Father is greater. If not, let them answer: what advantage does the Father have by possessing superiority if he is not superior? If none at all, then every accusation against the Son has just been destroyed. But if he has a significant advantage, he is superior since he possesses superiority. Let them answer, then, and teach us, if they are really wise: why, when the Father begat the Son, did he not beget him equal to himself but inferior? If it seemed better to him to beget the Son equal to himself in every respect, who stopped him from doing so? If something prevented him by force, they will confess even against their will that there is something greater than the Father. The other option is that nothing at all hindered him, and he had the power and knew that it was better to beget the Son as equal, but he decided to beget him as inferior. In that case, the Father clearly had envy and malice toward him because he did not want to give equality to the Son. So if the Son possesses inferiority, as they say, either the Father will be powerless over his own begetting or he will be malicious, according to the conclusions drawn from their syllogisms. But that is absurd. The pure divine nature is above all suffering. The Son is not inferior, so he does not lose equality. The Father is by no means too weak to beget the one from him as equal, and he is certainly not prevented by malice from choosing what is better.

Another: The Savior himself says somewhere that he is in the Father and the Father is likewise in him.[78] It is clear to everyone, I suppose, that it is not fitting to think [44] that the Father can be contained in the Son like one body in another or one vessel in another. Nor is it fitting to think that the Son is somehow loaded into the Father like cargo into a ship. No, the Father appears in the Son and the Son appears in the Father as in an unchangeable identity of substance and a natural unity and likeness. It is just as though someone, looking

[75]Jn 16:15. [76]Jn 17:10. [77]See Jn 17:10. [78]Jn 14:10.

down at his own form in an image, were to marvel at the likeness of his form which is precisely represented and exclaim truthfully, "I am in this picture, and this picture is in me!"

Or to take another example, it is just as though the sweet quality of honey were placed on the tongue and were to say of itself, "I am in the honey, and the honey is in me." Or again, it is just as though the heat which proceeds naturally from fire were to emit a voice and say, "I am in the fire, and the fire is in me." Each of the examples I just mentioned can be distinguished in thought, but they are one in nature. One comes out, so to speak, from what it is in by a kind of indivisible and inseparable procession. Even though the images in these examples depict procession, one item clearly exists in the other, and they are the same in substance. Therefore, if the Father is in the Son by the immutability of substance and the completely unfalsified quality in the image, how will one who is superior enter and be seen in the Son, who according to them is inferior? But since the Father is wholly in him, the Son is completely perfect; he is capable of containing the perfect, and he is the likeness of the great Father. **[45]**

Chapter Four

Against those who dare to say that the natural Word in the mind of God the Father is different from the one called "Son" in the Holy Scriptures. Such an evil opinion belongs to the followers of Eunomius.

1:2 This one was in the beginning with God.

The Evangelist makes a sort of recapitulation of what he has already said on these matters. When he adds the phrase "this one," we see him all but crying out, "The one who was in the beginning, the Word who was with the Father, God who is from God—we present our solemn book about this one and not another." Indeed, he had a good reason for adding the words "this one was in the beginning with God." Since he was enlightened by the divine Spirit with the knowledge of things to come, it seems clear to me—and we can truly say—that he knew that some would appear to serve as workers of destruction, nets of the devil and snares of death. They would bring down to the snare of hell and its chambers[79] any who from ignorance devoted themselves to what they belched up from their wicked hearts. They would resist and fight against their own head, saying that the Word in the mind of God the Father is different from the Son and Word through whom God made everything. This other Word, they say, is very much like, even exceedingly similar, to the Word in the Father's mind **[46]** so that he may be thought of as the Word of the Word, the image of the image and the radiance of the radiance.

The blessed Evangelist rightly reacts to the absurdities in their books, as if he already hears them blaspheming. He has already defined and stated clearly with many words, as was fitting, that the one and only true Word is from God and in God and with God. Now he emphatically adds, "This one was in the beginning with God." Clearly, he was with God as a Son with the Father, as innate, from his substance and only begotten, since he says "this one," and there is no second one.

Although the learned will safely leap over this impiety like a snake lurking in the middle of the road,[80] I think we ought to be zealous and explain the issues related to this godlessness so we can better expose their blasphemy to protect the simple. Therefore, I will present their opinion as best I can in the form of an opposing argument. It will receive its refuta-

[79]See Prov 7:27; 9:18 (LXX). [80]See Gen 49:17.

tion in due course in the ways in which God, who gives wisdom to everyone, will provide.

Eunomius's opinion concerning the Son of God

"The only begotten Son of God," he says, "is not strictly speaking his Word. The Word in the mind of God the Father always moves and exists in the mind of the Father. The Son, however, who is said to be begotten from him, receives that Word that is in the Father's mind. He knows all things because he learned them. It is because of his similarity to that Word that he is called and is the Word."

Then, for the confirmation (so he thinks) of his impiety, he weaves together such arguments from perverted ideas so that, as it is written, "the wretch is bound by the cords of his own sins."[81] **[47]**

"If the Son," he says, "is the very Word who is in God, who is natural and who is in the Father's mind, and if he is of the same substance as the one who begat him, what prevents the Father too from being called and being the Word, since he is of the same substance as the Word?"

And again, "If the Son is the Word of God the Father and there is none other besides him, by what word," he asks, "is the Father found saying to him, 'You are my Son. Today I have begotten you'?[82] After all, the Father clearly did not address him without words, since everything that is said is said solely and entirely in words. And the Savior himself says somewhere, 'I know the Father, and I keep his word.'[83] And again, 'The word which you hear is not mine, but it belongs to the Father who sent me.'[84] The Father converses with him in words. He himself admits at one time that he keeps the Father's word. At another time, he says the Jews were hearing not his word but the Father's. So how could there be any doubt," he says, "that the Son is different from the Word in the Father's mind (in the movement of his intellect) and that the spoken Word who reveals the Father's essence (that is, the Son) is called Word because he participates in and is filled up with that Word?"[85]

These are the evil thoughts that a crazed man strings together for himself. He is not ashamed to disagree with all of Holy Scripture at one fell swoop, thereby showing what is written about him to be true: "When an impious person goes into the depths of evil, he shows contempt."[86] Whoever fights against God has truly dug to the depths of evil by their ignorance. They refuse to be corrected by the truth but are worn out by the rot of their own arguments. We will see from the following that the only begotten Son of God **[48]** the Father is, strictly speaking, his Word.

A sequential refutation of Eunomius's evil opinion

The insane heretic is slow to learn. How could wisdom come into a deceitful soul at all?[87] Or what, tell me, could be more deceitful than those who, as it is written, "turn their ears from the truth" and run more easily to "the myths" of their own imagination?[88] Since what they say does not come from Holy Scripture, they rightly hear this: "Woe to those who prophesy from their own hearts and not from the mouth of the Lord."[89] Who, speaking from the mouth of the Lord, says "Jesus be cursed"?[90] Some of them do this when they criticize pious teachings without restraint, just like one of the holy prophets said, "perverting everything that is right."[91] They say that the

[81]Prov 5:22. [82]Ps 2:7. [83]Jn 8:55. [84]Jn 14:24. [85]Eunomius is employing the Stoic distinction between λόγος ἐνδιάθετος, a "word" or thought which is conceived in the mind, and λόγος προφορικός, a spoken word. Cyril also uses the same distinction, to a different end, to describe his own position in his comments on Jn 8:29 in book 5, chapter 5 (see p. 347 in the present work). [86]Prov 18:3 (LXX). [87]Wis 1:4. [88]2 Tim 4:4. [89]Ezek 13:3; Jer 23:16. [90]1 Cor 12:3. [91]Mic 3:9.

natural Word in the mind of God the Father is different from the one called Son and Word. And for proof of their opinion (as they think of it, but it is really their unbridled impiety), they adduce what our Lord Jesus Christ says in his conversation with the Jews, "I know the Father, and I keep his word."[92] They also adduce what the Father says to him, "I begat you from the womb before the morning star."[93] Then they belch up poison from their own father and say, "The one speaking is different from the one spoken to. The Father speaks to the Son by the Word. Therefore, the innate Word by which the Father carries on the conversation must be different from the Son." And again, "If the Son himself," he says, "insisted that he keeps the Father's Word, how could the one who keeps not ultimately be different from what is kept?"

To this, at least, it is perhaps not difficult **[49]** to respond. "For the Lord will give words to those who proclaim the gospel with great power."[94] Those who are afflicted by such ignorance ought to remember the one who says, "Oh, those who forsake the paths of uprightness to walk in the paths of darkness!"[95] But we ought to cry aloud to our guide in heaven, "Turn my eyes from looking at vanity,"[96] since the babbling of their ignorance is truly nothing but vanity and nonsense.

The Son did not speak of keeping the Father's word because he had some other Word of the Father in himself. Nor did he ever assert that he came to us bringing with him some sort of pedagogue. No, he alone exists by nature in the Father and likewise has the Father in him with no intermediary. "I am in the Father," he says, "and the Father is in me."[97] It is not the innate or any other Word, but the Father, in me.

"How then should we understand what he said to the Jews?" someone may quite reasonably ask us. In answer to this, we will truthfully say what comes into our mind. The Savior was teaching the Jews, a most stubborn people. Little by little he drew his hearers from the worship of the law, and he often cried out, "I am the truth!"[98] all but saying, "Shake off from yourselves, people, the yoke of the law. Receive the worship in the Spirit. The truth has shined, so let the shadow finally depart and the type go far away!" But not everyone thought he acted rightly when he overthrew the teachings of Moses, or rather led them to what is truer, so that some immediately cried out, "If this man were from God, he would not have broken the sabbath!"[99] openly accusing him of sin **[50]** who knew no sin.[100]

In order to defend himself, then, against such foolishness on the part of the Jews, he quietly removes any hint of boasting from his words. He wants to teach them in a subdued tone, not a piercing one, that the Son who knows no sin would do nothing contrary to the will of God the Father. If he were to say more openly, "I know no sin," he would incite them to stone him to death. Their anger would immediately boil over, and they would rush at him, saying, "Only God does not sin. You are a man, so stop saying things which apply to God alone!" They did this at another time, saying that he ought to be stoned because he, a man, made himself God.[101] Since the Savior became a human being and put himself under the law alongside those under the law, he makes the less direct statement that he keeps the Father's will. In so doing, he is practically saying, "I will not transgress the Father's will in any way. Sin comes from departing from the divine law, but I know no sin since I am God by nature. Therefore, I do not grieve the Father with my teaching." So let no one blame the one who is by nature the lawgiver for becoming like us and being a lawkeeper as well. He says that he

[92]Jn 8:55. [93]Ps 110:3 (Ps 109:3 LXX). [94]Ps 68:11 (Ps 67:12 LXX). [95]Prov 2:13. [96]Ps 119:37 (Ps 118:37 LXX). [97]Jn 14:11. [98]Jn 14:6. [99]Jn 9:16. [100]See 2 Cor 5:21. [101]Jn 10:33.

knows the Father not in a simple way as we do (though this would be effortless for him since he is God), but he asserts that he knows the nature of the Father because of what he is. Since he knows that his Father knows no change, he clearly knows that he himself is unchangeable from an unchangeable Father. How could something that knows no change be said to sin? Would it not rather stand unshakably in its own natural virtues? The accusing imagination of the Jews has no basis, then, when they suppose that the Son's thoughts consist of anything other than the will of the Father. For he keeps his word, as he says, and by nature he knows no sin. He knows that the Father [51] cannot experience sinning, since, as true Son, he is of the same substance as the Father.

Since [the Arians] add another passage to their argument, "I begat you from the womb before the morning star,"[102] let us give a pious explanation for this passage as well. We should not think that just because the Father says such things to the Son, there is an innate Word in him and the Son is some other Word besides that one. First, however, let us consider the fact that a prophet, practiced at speaking mysteries in the Spirit, plays for us the role of the Son. In particular, he introduces him as he hears from the Father, "You are my son," and the rest that follows.[103] This human way of speaking will in no way force us to think there are two Words. We will attribute the unavoidable sequencing in these matters to our custom of speech, and we will blame, at least if we do rightly, the weakness of our nature. Our nature has no words or even ways of thinking that could accurately convey the mysteries that are above us or that could faultlessly explain matters that are fitting to God. So we will allow the divine nature superiority over our mind and our reason. When it comes to matters of the divine nature, we will not take the words as they read, but we will take them in a way that is consonant with the dignity and will of that nature. If some of the unholy heretics think that we are using these words incorrectly, and if they will not allow the form of words to transcend ordinary usage, then they will justly hear, "Let the Father be thought to beget as we do, and let him not be denied a womb and the labor of giving birth." After all, "From the womb I begat you," he says to the Son.[104] Perhaps, or rather certainly, they will say that the Father's genuine birth pangs for the Son get their name from their likeness to us. Therefore, [52] let this passage too be understood piously as spoken in human form. Then their bitter and unholy objection stands refuted.

That was, I think, sufficient. However, we think it is necessary to strike down the objections they stubbornly devised, like some swarm of enemies, with the truth of pious teaching. Therefore, come let us bring up each objection on its own. Then let us put forward the refutation of each and, with burning investigation, arm the ever-conquering truth against it. We will state their objection first and then give the arguments that refute it. In this way, we will provoke vigilant thought that leads to careful examination. Like the rush of a flowing river, each objection will propel the noble desire of the readers so that they will always want to learn how to refute it.

Objections or opposing arguments from the heretics

"There has to be another Word," they say, "that exists as a substance in God the Father's mind who is different from his only begotten Son. The Son too is called Word, but only in imitation of that Word. If this were not the case, the result would be absurd. We who think rightly would have to confess that if the Word

[102]Ps 110:3 (Ps 109:3 LXX). [103]Ps 2:7. [104]Ps 110:3 (Ps 109:3 LXX).

is of the same substance as the Father, and the Father is of the same substance as the Word, then there is nothing to prevent the Father both from being and being called the Word, since he is of the same substance as the Word."

The solution to this: No argument, my friend, will force us to think that the Father must be considered and called the Word or even to believe that he could be [the Word] **[53]** just because he is of the same substance as the Word. Objects which are of the same nature certainly do not change into each other, nor do they allow a mixture between the two, so to speak, so that the objects under consideration could contract from a multiplicity to a unity or perhaps even from a dyad into a monad. Just because our ancestor Adam was of the same substance as the child who was begotten of him does not mean that the father will turn into the son or that the son will turn into the father. On the contrary, since he is one with him in a unity characterized by the quality of essence, he will maintain what is his own. Anyone who comes from a father will be considered a son, and anyone who begets another will clearly be a father.

You think that you are constructing a clever argument about this, and that consubstantiality will force objects of the same substance to be one with each other in every respect, allowing no distinction to be in force that would enable each one to exist by itself and in its own condition. But if you are right, what persuaded the judge of all not to punish the father for the son or exact punishment on the son for the father? "For the soul that sins," he says, "will die. The son will not bear the sin of his father, nor will the father bear the sin of his son."[105] The argument of the just judge does not bring the father down to the place of sonship just because the father is of the same substance with the son, nor does it put the son in the position of fatherhood. It recognizes each one on his own. The father does not progress toward the son, and the son does not approach the father. And yet, there is one substance for both. It is undoubtedly clear that no argument will force God the Father to change into the Word just because he is of the same substance as the Word. The Father remains completely in himself even though the one who was begotten of him is considered and is the Word, and therefore the Son. Otherwise, the divine would clearly be in a worse condition than we are. **[54]**

Another solution to the same form of argument, by reduction to absurdity: Since the Son does not change into the Father but is the exact image "and imprint of his hypostasis,"[106] we find him saying to his disciples, "The one who has seen me has seen the Father."[107] But if he is of the same substance with the Father in such a way that each completely pours over into the other, nothing will prevent the Son, it seems, from being considered to be the Father, since he is of the same substance with the Father. He will be able to pass over into that condition with nothing to stop him if the definition of "same substance" is enough to imply this kind of change or movement. So let the Son be considered to be the Father. Let him say to the real Father, since this is now so, "From the womb before the morning star I begat you."[108] In short, let him appropriate to himself every utterance that belongs to the Father. When this has taken place, everything will then be poured together, and that which is eternally in this state (that is, the holy and consubstantial Trinity) will ultimately be contracted into a unity. That is what will happen if the properties that strictly belong to each person disappear due to the definition of "same substance" and the identity of nature overturns the distinction of persons. But this is absurd. Therefore, the Father will not be the Word just because he is of the same substance

[105]Ezek 18:20. [106]Heb 1:3. [107]Jn 14:9. [108]Ps 110:3 (Ps 109:3 LXX).

with the Word, but he will remain unchanged, being what he is, even if he has the same nature or the same substance with his own Word. Thus their objection has been shown to be empty.

Another: If every word is the word of someone—since someone sends it out from the tongue or belches[109] and brings it up from the heart—and if God the Father is the Word just because he is of the same substance with the Word, he will then be his own word, or rather the word of no one, or he will not even exist at all. How will there be a word **[55]** when the one to whom the word belongs does not exist? But this is absurd. The pure divine nature will never be susceptible to nonexistence, nor will the Father ever change into the Word, even though he is of the same substance with the Word. He will remain the Father, and the Son is his Word.

Another: If the divine nature is believed to be unreceptive to all turning and change[110] by definition of its substance, how will the Father leave his own position, so to speak, and be transferred into being the Word? He will be susceptible to turning, since he experienced this turning by necessity. And since he has not preserved what he was from the beginning, he will not be the same. But this is absurd since being changed is completely foreign to the divine nature. The Father will not change into the Word, but he will always be Father, being immutable and unchangeable since he is God.

Another, on the same point, in descriptive form: The only begotten Word and Son of God, showing that he arose as true God from true God the Father, says, "Everything the Father has is mine."[111] Even though the Son is the heir of all attributes that are in the Father by nature, since he is from him by nature, even so he will never have the attribute of being Father. This is one thing that belongs to the Father alone. But the Son will remain without being deprived of anything in the Father even though he is not considered to be the Father. He has all the attributes and special qualities of the Father's nature perfectly in himself. When we apply this same reasoning to the person of the Father, we say that he has all that belongs to the Son naturally, but he can never pass into sonship and be the Word. Since **[56]** he is unchangeable by nature, he remains what he is so that in addition to being God the Father, he may also be unchanged and have in himself the unchangeable Word that appeared from him, that is, the Son.

Another: God the lawgiver accused certain people through his holy prophets, saying, "They did not distinguish between the holy and the common."[112] After all, those who have discernment recognize a great difference, or rather mutual exclusivity, in the character of the holy and the common. But if it is possible to mix together the nature of consubstantial entities so that individuals who exist in their own separate hypostases will run off to become whatever they wish within the same genus or species, what criterion will then distinguish for us the common from the holy? How can we tell the difference if the individual's distinguishing characteristic or defining quality can never be seen, but one thing lies hidden in another on account of the identity of substance? If the distinction between individuals makes no difference, let everything be mixed together with everything else. Let the traitor Judas be Peter or Paul, since he is consubstantial with Peter and Paul. Likewise, let Peter or Paul be Judas, since they are consubstantial with him. But such thoughts are the height of absurdity. Being of the same substance will in no way remove the distinguishing characteristic of individuals who are in the same genus or species with each other. So we in our weakness should not throw such a tantrum at the divine nature so as to force

[109]See Ps 19:2 (Ps 18:3 LXX). [110]Jas 1:17. [111]Jn 16:15. [112]Ezek 22:26.

God the Father to be and be called the Word just because he is of the same substance as the Word. He always remains Father. He can never lose this distinctive characteristic, nor does he yield to the identity of substance so as to possess nothing of his own. That does not mean he will have more than the Son. Rather, he will show the Son to be genuine and to possess the Father's immutability and unchangeability from him by nature. **[57]** This is shown both by the Son possessing his own unique sonship and by the fact that he does not change into the Father, just as the Father does not change into the Son.

Another objection or opposing argument from the heretics: "You are unreasonable," they say, "to denounce as heterodox those who say that the Word innate in God the Father is another Word besides the Son, even though you hear him saying plainly in the Gospel narrative, 'I know the Father and I keep his word.'[113] If, as he himself insists, he keeps the Father's word, then he would have to be completely different from the Word since we must maintain the distinction between the one keeping and what is being kept."

Different solutions in sequence showing clearly that the Son is the Word of God the Father: If the only begotten Son of God the Father is not himself his Word, but there is some other Word besides him in God, which they designate "in the mind,"[114] let those who put forward this contrary opinion tell us whether this Word, conceived by their own ignorance, is hypostatic or not. If they say that he exists by himself and is understood to be in his own existence, they will surely confess two sons. But if they say he is not hypostatic, how will the Son be third from the Father and not rather next to him, as a Son with the Father, since nothing intervenes any longer and cuts the Son off?

Another, along the same line of reasoning: The opponents define a Word in the mind of God the Father who, **[58]** according to their dull imagination, teaches the Son the will of the Father. We must now see how foolish their teaching on this point is.

We should consider the following line of reasoning on this point: The name "Father" entails no intermediary who forces his way between the Father and Son. After all, what would be the intermediary between Father and Son, or between the Son and the Father? But what if, as they ignorantly maintain, an intervening will and a Word in the mind of the Father—which they say interprets his will—cuts off the Son from the Father? Then the Father could no longer be considered completely Father nor the Son Son, at least if we think of the will of God and the Word that interprets it as existing in their own hypostases. But if we grant that they are anhypostatic,[115] then the Son is in God the Father adjacently and without an intermediary. Where then will the Word who is in the Father's mind go? Or what place will the will have if it is understood to be other than the Son?

Another by reduction to absurdity: We believe that the holy Trinity, who is worthy of adoration, is consubstantial, even if the madness of the heretics does not like it. I think that in the case of things that are of the same substance, we should admit a complete resemblance to each other, at least when it comes to natural properties. So if, as some rashly maintain, there is some Word in the mind of the Father besides the Son, then the Son will certainly have a Word in his mind as well since he is the Father's image and the unchangeable imprint of his hypostasis, as it is written.[116] The Holy Spirit too will have a Word just like the Son does on the basis of their equality. Thus the Trinity has doubled on us and **[59]** the divine nature is shown to be compound.

[113]Jn 8:55. [114]ἐνδιάθετος. [115]Not persons. [116]Heb 1:3.

But this is absurd. In simple substances, there is nothing else beyond those substances. Therefore, nothing will prevent the holy and consubstantial Trinity from being connected directly with nothing intervening.

Another in descriptive form: When Holy Scripture puts definite articles in front of nouns, it indicates the one entity that alone is called by that name in the true and strict sense. But when it does not place the article in front, the statement is more general, including everything that is called by that name. Here is a clear example. Many are called gods. But when "the" God is spoken of with the article it refers to him who alone is God in the strict sense.[117] When god is spoken of more simply and without the article, it refers to one of those who happen to be called to this by grace.[118] And again there are many men. But when the Savior says with the article, "the Son of Man," he indicates himself picked out of the multitudes. Since names have this character in Holy Scripture, how should we understand "in the beginning was the Word"? If this means that every word of God is in the beginning, let them show it and we will be the fools. But if the Evangelist put the article in front and refers to the only one who is the Word in the strict sense, crying out, "In the beginning was *the* Word," why do they quarrel in vain and introduce another Word only to expel the Son from the substance of the Father? Considering the absurdity of this, we ought to refuse the foolish counsel of the heterodox.

Another, showing that the Son is formed not after the Word in the Father's mind, as they say, but is the image of the Father himself: They think that the only reason the only begotten Son of God both is and is called the Word **[60]** is that he receives the Word who is in the mind of the Father, and they think he is formed, as it were, with reference to that Word. Well, if that were true, why do we not see him saying to his disciples, "I and the Word of the Father are one. The one who has seen me has seen the Word of the Father"? Since he omits mention of anything else and makes himself alone like the only Father, there is no intermediary who barges in between their likeness, and the Son will be considered to be like his Father, not like someone else besides him.

An opposing argument from the opponents: "We find the Son," they say, "to be different from the Word in God's mind not because we pay attention to our own thoughts on this matter but because we pay attention to the meaning of Holy Scripture. What shall we say when we hear the Son saying to the Father, 'Glorify your Son,' and the Father responding, 'I have glorified him and will glorify him again'?[119] Shall we not certainly grant that the Father responded to the Son with a Word? How then is the one through whom the Father responded not different from the Son?"

Different answers to this in sequence: The unholy heretics deserve our wonder, or rather, our tears. Indeed, one should say to them what was said in the prophets: "Do not weep for one who is dead or mourn for that one, but weep bitterly for the one" who thinks and says such things about the Only Begotten.[120] What could be more wretched than these people if they suppose that this voice, strictly speaking, belonged to the Father, which not only **[61]** the Son heard but also the crowd of Jews standing around, and most of all the choir of holy disciples? For they should envision qualities that are appropriate for God and not try to impose laws that are appropriate for us on matters that are above us. That which strikes the body's ear is a bodily voice, a noise that comes through the lips and through the air, or is contrived by some other mechanism. But the

[117]In English, we often make this point not by adding the article ("the god") but by capitalizing the word ("God"). [118]For example, Moses is "god" to Pharaoh (Ex 7:1). [119]Jn 12:28. [120]Jer 22:10.

will of the Father turns in his mind, as it were, gently with an ineffable voice, and is known only by the Son who is in him by nature since he is his wisdom. To suppose that God uses a voice that operates by sound is utterly unjustifiable if we think that we ought to reserve the qualities that are above creation to the nature that is above all. Besides, our Lord Jesus Christ himself says that the voice did not belong to God the Father. He shows that he does not need an explanation from anyone else to be able to learn the Father's will when he says, "This voice came not for me but for you."[121] He should rather have said, gentlemen, if you are right about these points concerning him, "You have heard with me the voice of the Father." But as it is, he says exactly the opposite, insisting that he needs no voice but that the voice came for their benefit. It was not spoken from the Father, but it came into being for them. And if God the Father made everything through him, then certainly this too was through him, or rather he himself was the voice. The Son did not explain the Father's disposition for his own benefit, since he knew it as the Son. But he explained it for the bystanders to hear so that they might believe.

Another: If they say that the Son needs some innate Word **[62]** so it can teach him the will of God the Father, what will become of Paul, who says, "Christ the power of God and the wisdom of God"?[122] How is the Son the wisdom of the Father if he lacks wisdom and receives perfection from someone else by learning what he clearly did not know? Do we not then have to say that the wisdom in the Father is not perfect? And if the Son is the wisdom of the Father, how could the Father's will be conceived of as something besides him? In that case, it is time to say that the will of God the Father is not perfect in wisdom. But this statement is utterly godless and blasphemous. Therefore, the Son knows what is in his Father not because he has a share in someone else's knowledge but because he himself, as the Word and wisdom and will, "searches also the deep things of God," as it is written somewhere also about the Spirit.[123]

Another: The Holy Scriptures introduce the Son to us as the image and unchangeable imprint of the Father.[124] And the Savior himself says somewhere, "The one who has seen me has seen the Father."[125] But if, even though he has this kind of likeness to him, he does not know on his own what is in the Father, but he needs (so to speak) someone else's explanation to learn it, it is time to think that the Father too is in the same situation. Since he is in the likeness of his Son, he himself will also need someone to explain what lies hidden in his offspring. On top of these absurdities, the divine nature has become susceptible to ignorance as well. But since it is impious to think this, we must move on to more fitting matters. This is clearly what is appropriate and profitable.

Another: "The Spirit searches everything," says the blessed Paul, "even the deep things of God."[126] And he adds, "For what person knows the things of a man except the spirit of the man who is in him? So also no one knows the things of God **[63]** except the Spirit of God who is in him."[127] Since the Holy Spirit, who knows all things accurately, is not only the Spirit of the Father but also of the Son, how then could the Son be ignorant of anything that is in the Father, since he has in himself by nature the Spirit who knows all things? Therefore, it is clearly redundant to think that the Son learns the will of the Father from someone else. There will be absolutely no need for a Word to mediate in vain, as they maintain in their ignorance. The Son knows all things from himself.

Another by reduction to absurdity: They accuse the substance of the Only Begotten by

[121]Jn 12:30. [122]1 Cor 1:24. [123]1 Cor 2:10. [124]Heb 1:3. [125]Jn 14:9. [126]1 Cor 2:10. [127]1 Cor 2:11.

saying that he does not know the will of the Father but uses a teacher, as it were, to learn it. This teacher is another Word conceived by them and which they refer to as "in the mind." So, if they think their opinion on this must prevail, let them tell us whether they will say that the Word "in the mind"—assuming it exists on its own—is by nature equal to the Son or not. If it is not equal, it could be inferior, perhaps, or it could be superior. If they hold it to be inferior, then they will also commit impiety against the Father himself. For there will certainly be something in him inferior to him and other than him, that is, the Word in his mind. But if they say it is not inferior and grant it superiority over the Son, the accusation against the Son will go double for the Father. First, he will be caught begetting something that is in a worse condition than he is. Next, he will also have a Word in his mind that is superior to him, if the Father is of the same substance as the Son, who has been given an inferior position according to them. But I suppose the opponents will likely evade both blasphemies by saying that the Word in the Father's mind is equal in substance to the Son. **[64]** Then the problem is solved. How will one teach the other—the one who knows teaching the one who does not—if they are both equal by nature? Therefore, since their argument is weak on every side, it would be redundant to think that the Son has some intermediary and not rather believe that he is God the Word in God the Father and that he was in the beginning.

Another: The blessed Paul says that the treasures of all wisdom and all knowledge are hidden in the Son.[128] But if he is telling the truth when he says this, how could we still think that the Son needed to be taught by someone else? In whom will we finally seek perfection in knowledge if the one who has all knowledge has been taught by someone else? How can one who is made wise be wisdom? But we ought to pay attention not to their words but to the words that come through the Holy Spirit. The Son has, as Paul says, the treasures of wisdom and all knowledge in himself. Therefore, he will not learn what makes him wise from someone else; rather, since he is in the Father, he has all the Father's knowledge because he is his wisdom. **[65]**

Chapter Five

The Son is by nature creator with God the Father because he is from the Father's substance and not taken on as a subordinate.

1:3 All things came to be through him, and without him, not one thing came to be.

After the blessed Evangelist overturns the intricate objections of the unholy heretics and weaves for us his own subtle and exacting discourse on the Only Begotten, he moves on to another snare of the devil, constructed from an ancient deception. This snare threatens us with the sting of the polytheistic error which has "wounded and cast down many."[129] Widening the road to destruction and flinging open the broad and spacious gate of death, it herded together human souls like cattle bound for hell. It continually served the devil rich food, as it were, and brought to him "choice meats."[130] Because the children of the Greeks were devoted to the wisdom of the world and their minds were saturated with the spirit of the prince of this world, they kept going astray into the error of polytheism and kept perverting the beauty of the truth. Like those who walk in gloom and darkness, they went down to the pit of their own ignorance by worshiping lifeless idols and saying to a tree, **[66]** "'You are my God,' and to a stone, 'You have begotten

[128]Col 2:3. [129]Prov 7:26. [130]Hab 1:16.

me.'"[131] Others, however, struck a discordant note that is related to theirs, but they pursued a more refined error. They thought they should worship "the creation rather than the creator,"[132] and they lavished the glory that is fitting only to the divine nature on the elements that came into being through it.

Therefore, the Theologian has to introduce the Only Begotten to us as the creator and craftsman by nature. He says that everything came to be through him and without him nothing came into being. He did this so that he might close the door on their deceptions forever and show the creator of all things to those who do not know him. By the same words through which he says the creation has been made, he teaches clearly that the one who calls things into being is different from that creation. By his ineffable power, he brought all things into existence from nonexistence. Thus, it is possible from the beauty of the creatures to see proportionately the creator[133] and to recognize the one who is truly God, through whom all things have come to be and are now preserved. I think, then, that he deftly deploys the passage from the Gospel against the false worship of the Greeks, and we believe this is the reason that the Only Begotten was introduced by the voice of the saint as creator and craftsman.

Since it is good to consider the intractable inventions of the heretics, I think it is good also to look at their habits and to say a little about them.

"All things," he says, "came to be through him, and without him, not one thing came to be."

He confers on the Son this God-befitting dignity as well, showing that he is of the same substance with God the Father in every way and saying that everything that belongs to the Father is by nature in the Son. **[67]** As a result, he is understood to be God from God in truth, not god like we are, having recently acquired the name—a name which belongs to us only by grace at that, as it says, "I said, 'You are gods, and all of you are children of the Most High.'"[134] If "all things came to be through him," he would be different from all of them since the term *all things* excludes nothing that belongs to all things. The blessed Paul, of course, understands "all things" the same way. When he was talking about our Savior somewhere in one of his epistles and said that all things were placed under his feet, he quite rightly added, "When it says 'all things,' it left nothing that was not subject to him."[135] Therefore, since we believe that all things have come to be through the Son, we should not understand him to be one of the "all things." On the contrary, we conclude that he lies outside all things, and we exclude him from the nature and species of originate beings. We will finally confess him to be nothing else than God from God by nature. What could anyone place between God and creation? I am not talking about substance, for in that respect there is a great distance between them. I am talking only about his conceptual position in relation to anything else that exists. What other place will the Son have since he is above the nature of creatures, or rather is himself the creator? All things have come to be through him in his role as the power and wisdom of God the Father. These are not qualities that are hidden in the nature of the one who begat him like the innate wisdom and power that happen to be in a human being as well. This wisdom and power exists by itself on its own and proceeds by an altogether ineffable mode of generation from the Father so that the wisdom and power of the Father is understood to be the truly existing Son.

Although the blessed Evangelist says that all things have come into being "through him," I do not think this statement will undermine what we are saying about him. **[68]** Just

[131]Jer 2:27. [132]Rom 1:25. [133]Wis 13:5. [134]Ps 82:6 (Ps 81:6 LXX). [135]Heb 2:8.

because it says that what exists came to be "through him," that does not at all mean that the Son should be introduced to us as an underling or a servant of someone else's will so that he is no longer understood to be the creator by nature. He does not receive the power to create from someone else, but rather he himself alone, since he is the strength of God the Father, works all things as the only begotten Son. Of course, the Father and the Holy Spirit also work with him and accompany him. We understand the Father to be with the Son, not as though the Son were powerless to bring about creation but because the Son is completely in him on account of the immutability of his substance and the utter proximity and unmediated character of the Son's procession from him by nature. It is as though one were to say that the flower itself is with its fragrance by the operation of the sweet smell since the fragrance proceeds from the flower by nature. But the force of this example is weak when it comes to these matters. The nature that is above all surpasses this example too, so these ideas barely scratch the surface.

How should we understand the statement "My Father works until now, and I also work"?[136] The Son denies that God the Father does anything on his own and by himself when it comes to creation. He likewise denies that he works apart from the Father, while his Father's substance is somehow idle. In that case, there would certainly be two creators, not one, if each one works separately and apart, and the Father would receive the ability not to have the Son always in himself, and the Son likewise would be seen not to have the Father always in himself, if it is at all possible that each one does the work of creation by himself and separately, as we said before. **[69]** Furthermore, the Son would by no means be telling the truth when he says, "I am in the Father, and the Father is in me."[137]

Now when we see the Son (as imprint) in the Father and the Father (as archetype) in the Son, we should certainly not understand that to indicate a mere similarity of substance. Rather, we hold that the Son shines forth *begottenly* from the Father's substance and that he is and subsists on his own in and from that substance as God the Word. And we hold that the Father, in turn, is in the Son *connaturally*, as in an offspring of the same substance, and *separately* only because of the difference in what he is and is understood to be. The Father remains what he is even if he is in the Son by having the same nature, just as we say that the sun is in its brightness. And the Son, for his part, will not be understood to be something different from what he is even though he is in the Father by having the same nature, just as the sun's brightness is in the sun. In this way, since the Father is understood to be and is in truth the Father, and the Son is and is understood to be the Son, and the Holy Spirit clearly comes in with them, the number of the holy Trinity arrives at[138] one and the same divine nature.

How would God be understood to be one in any sense if each of those mentioned withdrew into complete individuality and, though separated in every respect from the shared nature of the other and from any essential relationship, they were each called God? Therefore, we should understand the Father, Son and Holy Spirit individually when it comes to their individual existence. We do not mix up the difference of persons or names with the position each one has. But we preserve to each one individually the name and fact of what he is. While believing this, we nevertheless refer them to one divinity when it comes to nature. We refuse to understand them to be completely different because the Son is called the Word, wisdom, brightness, imprint and power of the Father. **[70]** He is Word and

[136]Jn 5:17. [137]Jn 14:10. [138]Literally, "ascends to."

wisdom because of the fact that he is from and in the Father's mind immediately and with no distance and because the Father and Son interpenetrate each other, so to speak. The mind can be seen in the Word and wisdom, and the Word, in turn, in the mind. And there is nothing intervening or separating one from the other. He is also power since power resides, without distance, in those who are naturally capable of it. It cannot be separated from them, the way an accident can, without the destruction of the subject. He is also the imprint since an imprint is always naturally with and cannot be separated from the substance whose imprint it is.

Therefore, since each one is in the other by nature and by necessity, it is clear that when the Father works, the Son will work since he is his natural, essential and hypostatic power. Likewise, when the Son works, the Father works as well, since he is the source of the creating Word, and he is by nature in his own offspring just as the fire also is in the heat that proceeds from it.

It is clear, then, that the opponents repeat their accusation against the Only Begotten in vain. They introduce him to us as one who became a creator by learning, or rather as an underling, because the blessed Evangelist says, "All things came to be through him, and without him, not one thing came to be." I marvel greatly at the unholy heretics. Whatever they think strips away the honor of the Only Begotten in any way and shows him to be second after the one who begat him, at least in their view, this they track down with great zeal and gather from every direction the poison of their own stubbornness. But whatever things are said soundly and correctly and which raise the Son to the glory of the Father, these things they bury in deepest silence, as though they have one sole purpose: to rail in vain at the one who is glorified by all creation. When they hear that "all things came to be through him," **[71]** they vehemently call him an underling, dreaming that the Son is a slave rather than free and a worshiper rather than the Lord. But when they learn that "without him not one thing came to be," they do not rise up to think anything great or admirable about him. The Evangelist says that nothing at all has come into being without him because the Father does not have it in his nature to create in any other way than through his own offspring, who is his wisdom and power. Therefore, the Only Begotten is also the glory of God the Father, since he is glorified as creator through the Son. He works all things, and he brings into being things that are not.[139]

One may understand well the words "without him not one thing came to be" by considering what was said at the creation of humanity: "Let us make humankind," it says, "in our image and likeness."[140] One can see especially clearly in this passage that there is nothing lowly in the Son as in an underling, as they claim. For God the Father does not command the Word, "Make humankind," but he shares his will for humanity in common with the Son, since the Son is with him by nature and in him with no distance, as a coworker, as it were. When he knows something, he does not know it before the Son does since his mind shows itself, without distance or time, in the imprinted Word who is in him.

Now we must allow that divine realities transcend the force of the following example as well. We say that he works with the Son, not conceiving of the two separately lest we think there are two gods, nor conceiving of both as one lest the Son be contracted into the Father or the Father into the Son. But we understand it in this way: as if one were to grant that light exists with the rays that it emits. **[72]** In this case, there seems to be some sort of distinction in thought between the one who begets and the

[139]See Rom 4:17. [140]Gen 1:26.

one who is begotten and comes forth indivisibly. But both are one and the same by nature, and neither is at all apart from the other. Nevertheless, God will be above even this example since he is above being. No created thing is completely like him so that it could be taken, in precise teaching, as an image of the holy Trinity without qualification.

If those insane people think that the words "through whom," when spoken of the Son, are able to bring down his substance from equality and natural likeness with the Father, so that he is an underling rather than creator, let them consider this, come forward and give an answer: What then shall we think about the Father himself, and who shall we assume he is, since the Holy Scripture plainly applies to him the word *through*? "For God is faithful," it says, "through whom you were called into fellowship with his Son."[141] And, "Paul, an apostle of Jesus Christ through the will of God."[142] And again, Paul writes to some, "So that you are no longer a slave but a child. And if a child, then also an heir through God."[143] All of these passages refer to the person of God the Father. Yet no one, I suppose, would rush to the level of madness (unless they happened to think like the aforementioned people) that they would think it reasonable to impugn the very glory of the Father with the name and the status of an underling, just because the word *through* is applied to him also. The Holy Scripture is sometimes indifferent regarding its words without harming the subject matter. When it speaks of topics, it sometimes employs, in a looser sense, both the words and the concepts that it thinks explain them well. But it is better to say of such things, "The glory of the Lord hides speech,"[144] since the total power of words is weak [73] when it comes to a precise explanation of ineffable and God-befitting glory. Therefore, we must not be offended at words that are not very fitting. Rather, we must concede supremacy to the divine and inexpressible nature over the power of language and the sharpness of every mind. In this way, we will be pious in no small degree. [74]

Chapter Six

The Son is by nature life. Therefore he did not come into being but is from the substance of God the Father.

1:4 That which came into being—in it was life.

The blessed Evangelist continues for us his discussion of God the Word. He covers profitably, it seems to me, everything that pertains to the Word by nature in order to put to shame the drunken behavior of the heterodox and to strengthen those who want to excel in the right faith with arguments that lead to that faith. He does not strengthen those who borrow unconvincing arguments from discourses of worldly wisdom but those who marvel at the beauty of the truth by a demonstration of the Spirit.[145] That is what he wants to teach us in this topic.

He just showed us that the Son is the maker and framer by nature when he said, "All things came into being through him, and without him, not one thing was called into being." The Son not only gifts creation by calling it into being, but once it has come into being, he also holds it together through himself. He mixes himself in, so to speak, with those things that do not have eternal being by their own nature, and he becomes life to those things that exist so that once they have come into being, they may remain and be preserved, each one according to the definition of its own nature. Therefore, the Evangelist has to say, "That which came into being—in [75] it was life." Not only does he say that all things came into

[141] 1 Cor 1:9. [142] 2 Cor 1:1. [143] Gal 4:7. [144] Prov 25:2. [145] 1 Cor 2:4.

being through him but also that whatever came into being—in it was life, that is, the only begotten Word of God, the origin and sustainer of all things visible and invisible, in heaven, on earth and under the earth. Since he himself is life by nature, he grants being, life and motion in many ways to all that exists. He does not do this by dividing himself in some way and by changing into each of the creatures that are distinct by nature. Instead, there is one life for all that goes into each creature as befits it and as it is able to participate, even though creation considered by itself is wrought in diversity by the ineffable power and wisdom of the creator.

Since what is brought from nonbeing into being must also decay, whatever has a beginning will also have an end. Only the nature that is divine and above all things is suited to have no beginning or end. The creator deals wisely with this weakness in creatures and devises for them a kind of eternity by his skill. The perpetual succession of each creature into others like it, and the natural progression of one creature into the next generation of the same genus or species, always looking forward step by step in its course, renders the creation ever-shining and always existing with God the creator who sustains it. The strategy is that every creature that exists sows seed in itself according to its kind and likeness, as the ineffable decree of the creator says. Therefore, in everything "there was life," for this is our subject.

Now, most excellent sir, one may say with good reason to the heretic fighting against the truth, how will you respond when you hear the Spirit bearer saying that in all originate things "was the life," that is, the Word who is in the beginning? Will you now dare to say that the Son is not from the **[76]** substance of God the Father so that he is understood to be originate and created? How could one not cry out against your ignorance, and be absolutely right to do so? If the Word was in originate beings as life by nature and has mixed himself together by participation with what exists, he is therefore different from those things in which he is believed to be. How could one who is by nature different from creation not be God who is over creation, in the final analysis? But if you remain shameless and do not stop thinking that the Son is original, even though he is in originate beings as life, than he will be understood to be in himself. Further, if this same one is assumed to be from originate beings just because he is among them, then he will participate in himself, and so will life. But I suppose even the enemy of God will surely see what ignorance it is to think this. Therefore, if the Word who gives life to originate beings is in them in the sense that they participate in him, he himself cannot be included among the beings that participate, but he must clearly be different than they are. If so, then he is not originate, but he is in them as life by nature. We will see this from the following considerations.

Considerations or syllogisms

If the Son is not from the substance of God the Father, but the Father brought him into existence externally, as they claim, then the Son is originate and created. How then is the one who is included among originate beings the one who gives life to everything? What special quality will we then find in the divine nature? Or how does the most wise Paul say, as something admirable about the one who is by nature God, "the one who gives life to all things"?[146] If the Son is originate and gives life to all things, then creation gives life to itself, and it does not need [77] God the creator for this. There is then nothing more in God besides creation since creation does no less than God can do. But this is absurd. There-

[146]1 Tim 6:13.

fore, the Son is not originate but rather God, and so he is also life by nature

Another: The psalmist marvels greatly at the divine nature, and rightly so. In particular, he ascribes to it the most beautiful honor by saying, "With you is the fountain of life."[147] But if the Father subordinates the Son and the Son is not from the Father's substance, and this sort of Son gives life to originate beings and is life by nature since he is the lifegiver, why does the psalmist exert himself in vain, saying that the fountain of life is with God alone? After all, the nature of originate beings is capable of this life-giving power as well, if the Son also gives life even though he is not of the divine substance, as they foolishly maintain. But this is absurd. Therefore, the Son is life by nature as God from God and life from life.

Another: If the Son, even though he is life by nature, is originate and created in that he does not possess his being from the substance of God the Father, as they conjecture, the nature of originate beings will admit of both being and being called life. All things will be life, at least potentially, even if they have not yet actualized the fact. For that which has any natural capacity for something would certainly be that, even if it has not yet become it because it has the potential in its nature. Moreover, if being life is common to the creation and not the special property of anyone alone, why does the Son boast in vain about himself, saying, "I am the life"?[148] I suppose he should have said, "I along with you am the life." That would have been truer if he is life while really being originate. But since he clothes himself alone with being life as a good attribute, it should be clear that he arrays himself not with things originate **[78]** but with the divine substance of the Father to which being life belongs by nature.

Another: A being that participates in life is not, strictly speaking, life, since life is clearly in that being as something other than it. So if originate beings participate in the Son as life, he must be different from the beings that participate in him and lack life. He is not originate, nor does he seek to be made alive by someone else. Therefore, he is God because he is the lifegiver. And if so, he will be confessed to be of the substance of the Father, at least if we worship one God and do not serve some other god besides the one who exists.

Another: When we examine carefully the nature of all that exists, we see God and creation and nothing else in addition to these. Whatever falls short of being God by nature is surely originate, and whatever escapes the condition of being made is surely within the limits of divinity. Since we have well established this, let them tell us—those who exclude the Son from the substance of the Father—how could he give life as life since the divine nature has this as its own property and yields it to no one else? But if one who is originate can also be life, the grace of this excellence will certainly overtake all originate things, and everything will be life by nature. What need will originate beings then have of participating in the Son, and what good would it do them? After all, they too are life by nature. But this claim is not true. They must participate in the Son since they need life. Therefore, only the Only Begotten is life by nature. Because of this, he is not ordered among originate things, but he ascends to the nature of the one who begat him. The Father too is life by nature.

Another: Since the Son is life by nature, he is either different **[79]** from the creation (I mean by nature) or he is of the same nature as creation. If he is of the same nature and the same substance, how is he not lying when he says, "I am the bread of life that comes down from heaven and has given life to the world"?[149]

---

[147]Ps 36:9 (Ps 35:10 LXX). [148]Jn 14:6. [149]Jn 6:48, 33.

After all, creation has the fact of being life from its own resources, and life does not participate in life. That is how it is shown to be life. But if he is not of the same nature, he will also escape being originate and will remove himself from creation along with this good attribute of his. Then creation will not be life by nature. Instead, it needs and participates in life.

Another: If the Son, even while he is life by nature, is of the same nature as created beings since he is not of the substance of God the Father, as they claim, why does the blessed psalmist say that the heavens will perish and wear out like a cloak,[150] while the same psalmist confers on him, so to speak, his own special prerogative, crying out, "You are the same, and your years will never end"?[151] Either he will perish and come to an end with us (since he is of the same nature as we are) and will no longer be thought to be life, or the natural connection with him will pull us up as well so that we will be ever the same, live for endless years and be life. But he will remain always the same, while we will come to an end. Therefore, he is not originate like we are. Since he is from life by nature, he himself gives life, as life, to those things that need life.

Another: Nothing participates in itself. But the creation participates in the Son as life. Therefore, he is not the creation, and neither is the creation life, but the Son is life.

Another: That which gives life is one thing, and that which is given life is another; one is active and the other passive. The Son gives life, and the creation is given life. Therefore, the Son and the creation are not the same, since what acts is not the same as what is acted upon. **[80]**

Chapter Seven

The Son is by nature light. Therefore, he did not come into being but is from the substance of God the Father as true light from true light.

And the life was the light of all people. With these words too, the blessed Evangelist shows us that the Son is God by nature and that in his substance, he is the heir of the good qualities of the one who begat him. Previously, the Evangelist taught that he is life by nature. He is in all things that came into being through him, holding them together, giving them life and granting them by his ineffable power to pass from not being into being. And once they come into being, he preserves them. Now the Evangelist moves to another train of thought, determined to lead us by the hand from every direction to the apprehension of the truth, which is most fitting. Thus, the Word was in all originate beings as life, and humans are among the originate beings on earth. We are rational animals, capable of both mind and knowledge, and we participate in the wisdom from God. Therefore, the Spirit bearer cogently and clearly shows us that the Word is the one who supplies wisdom among people in order that God the Father may be understood to be all in all through the Son[152]—**[81]** life in those who lack life, and light and life in those who lack life and light. That is why he says, "And the life was the light of all people." In other words, God the Word who gives life to everything, who is the life in all things that exist, both enlightens the rational animal and lavishes intelligence on those capable of intelligence. In this way, the following words addressed to the creation are beautifully preserved and have full force: "What do you have that you did not receive?"[153] The originate and created nature has no riches from its own resources. Whatever it does have is certainly from God who bestows both being and how each one ought to be. The Evangelist does well placing the "was" in front of "life" so that he

[150]Ps 102:26 (Ps 101:27 LXX). [151]Ps 102:27 (Ps 101:28 LXX). [152]See 1 Cor 15:28. [153]1 Cor 4:7.

may indicate in multiple places the eternal being of the Word and beat back the nonsense of the ignorant who introduce the Son to us as coming from nothing, a notion that clearly fights against the entirety of Holy Scripture.

Concerning the eternity of the Word with the Father, since we have already treated it sufficiently in the present book and in the book called the *Thesaurus*, we think we should say no more about it. But we will most eagerly examine as carefully as possible the issues raised by the meaning of the words before us. We will hasten to profit both ourselves and those who will read this later, as God opens for us both the door and the mouth for the discussion.[154]

What will the enemy of Christ say to us when he learns that the "life," that is, God the Word who lives forever, is "the light of all people"? What arguments will they sling at us when we come forward saying, If the Son is not God by nature and the fruit of his Father's substance, if the true light does not shine on us from the true light but is subordinate and exterior, as they ignorantly assert, **[82]** then he is of the same nature as created beings, and he will in no way escape being originate? How then, you perfect fools, does he enlighten what is enlightened by him? Is not the enlightener different from what is enlightened? This is plain and clear to everyone. If we were to grant that they are the same in the quality of their substance and their manner of existence, what is it that is greater in the one who has the strength to enlighten and less in the one who lacks light? Whatever quality it is will come to both of them, to each one in turn. That which needs light will be light, and the light will be no different from what is enlightened. Obviously, this line of thought is deeply confused. Reason of necessity separates for us each item that has a name. That which supplies is placed in its own proper nature, and that which receives the supply is placed separately in its own proper nature. Therefore, the Son is not of the same nature as created things, but he will remain in the substance of the Father, being true light from true light.

Earlier, we argued that the Son is life by nature and showed that he is different from what he is in. It is not difficult to transfer this argument and apply this knowledge in the present chapter as well. In order not to leave this labor to others or to seem to be conquered by hesitation, I myself will attempt to transfer the gist of the previous argument, so far as I can. Just as in the former discussion, since he is life by nature he is clearly different from what he was in, so also in this discussion, since he is said to be and truly is "the light of all people," he will be found to be different from the things which lack light and participate in it. We will see this more clearly from the following. **[83]**

Demonstrations by syllogisms that the Son who enlightens is other than the creation that is enlightened.

If the Word was in the creation, as we are discussing, as light by nature, mixing himself through participation with the beings that exist, then he is different from the beings in which he is believed to be. But since he is by nature different from the creation that participates in him and is enlightened by him, how could he not be God over all?

Another: If the enemies of God say that even though the Son is by nature light, he is still among originate beings as one of them, enlightening the things that lack light—first, that means he will be in himself; in addition to this, he will participate in himself, and so will light. This is the consequence of holding that the same person is *in* originate beings and *from* them. But the one who has applied their

[154]See Lk 21:15.

"heart to wisdom,"[155] as it is written, surely sees what great foolishness it is to think this. Therefore, if the Word who enlightens originate beings is in them by participation, then he himself will not be among the beings that participate and are enlightened, but clearly he will be different than they are. If so, he is not originate, but he is light by nature and God in beings that need light.

Another: If the Son is not from the substance of God the Father but the Father brought him into existence externally, as they claim, then the Son is originate and created. How then is he in originate beings enlightening them? What special quality will we then find in the divine nature? How does the supremely wise psalmist say, as an expression of admiration to the one who is God by nature, "In your light we see light"?[156] If the Son is originate and yet enlightens everything, then the creation enlightens itself, and it does not need God the creator for this. There is then nothing more in God than in creation since creation does no less than God can do. **[84]** But this is absurd. Therefore, the Son is not originate but rather God, and so he is light by nature, just as the Father is.

Another of the same: If the Son is originate and is brought into being and yet is the light of God the Father, according to the passage, "In your light we see light,"[157] and, "Send forth your light and your truth,"[158] by the same reasoning, nothing will prevent all originate beings from being called the light of God the Father. If the nature of creatures at all admits of this, it will be potentially common to all and not the property of the Son alone. But this is absurd. It is fitting for the Son alone both to be called and to be the light of God the Father. Therefore, he is not originate, but he is light, as God from God, who enlightens through him all things that need light.

Another: If the Son is light by nature without being from the substance of the Father, but he came into existence externally, as the enemies of God foolishly maintain, he is of the same nature as created things, and he is their brother, seeing that he falls short of the divine substance. How then is he called light, and how is he light? It is said of Saint John the Baptist, "He was not the light."[159] Yet the blessed John the Baptist is light potentially, and not he alone, if one at all concedes that the Son is originate and yet can be light by nature. Once an attribute is situated in a nature, it follows that the attribute is common to all that partake of that nature. But John is not the light. The Son is the light. Therefore, his nature is different, and he is not of the same nature as originate beings.

Another along the same lines: If the Son is light by nature and yet is originate and created—seeing that he does not have his being from the substance of God the Father, as some speculate— the nature of originate beings will be able to be and be called **[85]** light, and originate nature will be light in every respect, because that is how potentiality works. That which has a natural capacity to be something would surely be that fully, even if the actualization has not yet occurred. Since being light is common to the nature of originate things and is not the special property of anyone alone, why does the Son boast in vain about himself, saying, "I am the light"?[160] I suppose he should have said, "I along with you am the light." But since he clothes himself alone with this as his own good quality, not including anyone else, it should be clear that he arrays himself not with originate beings but with the divine substance of the Father, which is light by nature.

Another: That which participates in light is not, strictly speaking, light. Clearly, if one thing is in something else, the two must be

[155]Ps 90:12 (Ps 89:12 LXX). [156]Ps 36:9 (Ps 35:10 LXX). [157]Ps 36:9 (Ps 35:10 LXX). [158]Ps 43:3 (Ps 42:3 LXX). [159]Jn 1:8. [160]Jn 8:12.

different. So if originate beings can participate in the Son as light, he must be different from what participates in him and lacks light. Therefore, he is not originate, nor does he seek to be enlightened from someone else as originate beings do. This means he is God, and he has the power to enlighten. And if this is so, we will recognize that he came from the substance of the Father—at least if we worship one God and do not serve some other god besides the one who actually exists.

Another: When we carefully examine the nature of what exists, we perceive God and creation and nothing else besides these. Whatever falls short of being God by nature is altogether originate. And whatever escapes the condition of being made is completely within the limits of divinity. Now that we have examined these things to the best of our ability, let them tell us—those who drive the Son from the substance of God the Father—how could the Son enlighten as light since the divine nature possesses this property as its own and does not cede it to anything else? If the Son can be light even though he is originate, then the grace of this privilege will immediately extend to all originate beings, and everything will be light by nature. Then why would they need to participate in the Son? Or what more will they gain from such participation **[86]** since they too are light by nature, just as the Son, of course, is also light in them? But creation needs the one who enlightens because it does not have light of its own. Therefore, the Son is by nature God, and consequently he is light since he is able to enlighten whatever lacks light.

Another: Since the Son is by nature light, it is evident that in his mode of being he is either different from the creation or has the same nature it has.[161] If he is of the same origin and substance, there would seem to be no reason for him to say, "I have come as a light into the world."[162] In this view, being light is also the property of creation itself. And light does not participate in light. That is how it is recognized as light. But if he is not of the same nature, and if creation lacks light since it hears the words "What do you have that you did not receive?"[163] the Son, in that case, will have to escape from being originate. He will remove his good attribute, along with himself, from creation. Creation will not be light by nature, but it will lack light and participate in light.

Another: Nothing participates in itself. But creation participates in the Son as light. Therefore, he is not a creature, and creation is not the light. The Son is the light.

Another: It is one thing to enlighten and another to be enlightened. One is active; the other is passive. The Son enlightens, and the creation is enlightened. Therefore, the Son and creation are not the same since that which acts is not the same as that which is acted on.

1:5 And the light shines in the darkness, and the darkness did not comprehend it.

The sage Evangelist races on, cogently expanding the thought of the foregoing material for us with these words as well. I suppose he thought that he had not provided a firm enough grounding for his hearers **[87]** in the knowledge that God the Word really is the light of all people just by saying, "And the life is the light of all people." More than likely, some people would arise who would hear what he said without examining it. They would claim rank and try to teach others that the Word of God really is light but that he does not supply light to all. Instead, he places the light of understanding in whomever he wishes, testing each one to see if they are worthy to receive so bright a gift. The nature of other rational creatures, they claim, gets the power of thought either from its own seeds, as it were,

[161]Cyril uses "mode of being" as an interchangeable term for "nature." [162]Jn 12:46. [163]1 Cor 4:7.

or from God the Father placing mind and understanding in the creatures, since the Son is not strong enough to accomplish this.

The Evangelist cogently says, "And the light shines in the darkness, and the darkness did not comprehend it." He says this to show clearly that God the Word, who was in God the Father, is himself both life and light. He does not exist in some piecemeal fashion, belonging to some and not others; rather, he mixes himself by some ineffable mode of participation with all who exist. In this participation, he is wisdom and understanding (which is what light is called in rational creatures) so that things capable of reason may become rational and things capable of wisdom may have wisdom. This could not happen in any other way.

With great precision, he all but cries out to his hearers something like this: I said, sirs—and I was teaching the honest truth—that the life was the light of all people. I said this, not so that someone may suppose (especially from the present statement) that those who show themselves righteous and good receive light from someone else as a reward for good conduct, but so that you may learn that in the same way the Word is life in all who come into being and gives life to the things that are capable of life, so also he is light in them. **[88]** For those beings who have the capacity for wisdom and understanding, he makes them what they are. In this way, God the Father through the Son in the Spirit is all in all.[164]

He uses the term "darkness" to refer to the nature that lacks enlightenment, that is, the whole originate nature. By calling him "light," he also evokes its opposite, thereby showing that the rational creation which lacks light and lacks participation in light is different. He does this not without purpose, at least in my judgment, but he has in mind, above all, the fact that the nature of originate beings in no way springs from itself. It receives all of its being and its well-being (such as it is) from the creator. That is why it rightly hears the words "What do you have that you have not received?"[165] Along with other things it also possesses light itself as a gift from God. Since it receives light, it clearly does not already have it. Since it does not have light of itself, how could it not be the opposite of light? How could it not be called "darkness"? So "the light shines in the darkness" is a persuasive proof—no, a proof that follows from absolute necessity—that the creation is darkness and the Word of God is light. If the nature of originate beings by participation receives the Word of God, who is light or from light, then it is clear that creation itself, which receives [light], is darkness. The Son "shines" in it as "light shines in the darkness," even if the darkness does not know the light at all. I think this is what "the darkness did not comprehend it" means. After all, the Word of God illuminates everything that is capable of illumination and enlightens everything that has a nature capable of being enlightened. But the darkness does not recognize him. The rational nature that is on the earth, that is, humanity, worshiped the creation rather than the creator. It "did not comprehend the light." It did not recognize the creator, the **[89]** source of wisdom, the beginning of understanding, the root of knowledge. At the same time, because of his love for humanity, originate beings have the light, just as they are supplied with the power of thought which is established when they come into being.

We must indicate once more in these matters that no argument will permit us to think that the Son of God is originate or created; rather, he surpasses our condition in every way, and he transcends the nature of created beings. He is completely other. According to the quality of his nature, he is far

[164]See 1 Cor 15:28. [165]1 Cor 4:7.

different from what they are, just as light is of course not the same thing as darkness, but they are contrary and distinguished into different natures by incomparable differences. Since we have already gone through the argument about this sufficiently in the foregoing, we will move on to what comes next.

1:6-7 There arose a man sent from God. His name was John. He came as a witness to testify concerning the light.

Previously, he explained many things about the Word of God, and with great care he went through the facts that clearly show that the Word is by nature the Son of God the Father. Now, he concerns himself with their faith in what they have already heard him say. Since, as God said through Moses, "Every matter shall be established by the mouth of two or three witnesses,"[166] he wisely introduces the blessed Baptist in addition to himself. Indeed, he brings him in as a most important witness. He did not think that he ought, even if he commanded great respect, to go beyond the law in asking those who read his book about our Savior to believe him. He did not think he should ask them to believe him alone when he explained what transcends our reason and sense. **[90]** Therefore, the blessed Evangelist himself testifies that "the Word was in the beginning, and the Word was God, and he was with God in the beginning"[167] and that "all things came to be through him."[168] He testifies that he was the life in originate beings, "and the life was the light of all people."[169] His purpose through all of these testimonies was to show that the Son is God by nature. The Baptist testifies along with him, crying out with God's voice, "Prepare the way of the Lord! Make straight the paths of our God!"[170] Anyone will surely say that the one who has the dignity of lordship in him by nature is true God. This dignity, truly and strictly speaking, inheres in no one else, since "for us there is one God and Father, and one Lord Jesus Christ," according to the words of Paul.[171] Even though many both in heaven and on earth are called "gods" and "lords" by grace, the Son, with the Father, is the one true God.

Therefore, the pair of holy witnesses offers a lot of weight. What they said deserves a credibility that is finally not subject to anyone's accusation. This credibility is based on the fulfillment of the law and is strengthened by the stature of their persons. So it would have been imbecilic and ignorant for the blessed Evangelist to say anything about himself and to sing his own praises. If he did that, he would deserve to have heard, "You testify about yourself. Your testimony is not valid."[172] Therefore, he lets those who know him form an opinion about him, and he very appropriately goes to his namesake and says that he was "sent from God." He had to show that the holy Baptist did not arrive at his witness about our Savior on his own or with self-chosen zeal but by yielding to what was ordained from above and serving the divine will of the Father. **[91]** Therefore he says, "There arose a man sent from God. His name was John."

We should pay attention to how he targets his discussion and fits it to each character, and how he adapts it to the nature of the subject matter. In the case of the Word of God, he fittingly introduces the word *was*. This word indicates his eternity in every respect. It shows that he is older than every beginning that takes place in time, and it takes away any thought that he might be created. How could anyone think that something that has always existed could also have an origin? In the case of the blessed Baptist, it was appropriate for him to say, "There *arose* a man sent from God," since

[166]Deut 19:15. [167]Jn 1:1-2. [168]Jn 1:3. [169]Jn 1:4. [170]Is 40:3. [171]1 Cor 8:6. [172]Jn 8:13.

he has an originate human nature.[173]

The Evangelist, it seems to me, is very accurate in these matters when he says not simply "there arose," but he adds "a man." By doing so he overturns the thoughtless conjecture of some. Already a story was going around among the people saying that the holy Baptist was not really a man by nature but one of the holy angels in heaven who used a human body and was sent by God to preach. Moreover, they found the pretext for this conjecture of theirs in the fact that God says, "Behold, I send my angel ahead of you who will prepare your way before you."[174] Those who think this are led astray from the truth, not knowing that the word *angel* refers to service, not substance, just as in the story of the blessed Job, of course, one angel[175] after another runs to report Job's various sufferings and to serve him in those incurable calamities of his. Paul himself, who is quite wise, provides this sort of definition for the holy angels when he writes, "Are they not all **[92]** ministering spirits who are sent to serve those who are going to inherit salvation?"[176] Therefore, the blessed John the Baptist is called "angel" by the voice of the Lord not because he is an angel by nature but because he is sent to be a messenger and to cry out, "Prepare the way of the Lord!"

The Evangelist aptly maintains that the angel was "sent by God," showing that his testimony stands completely on solid ground. The one sent by God to preach would not utter anything in his teaching that was not in complete agreement with the will of the one who assigned the mission to him. Therefore, the witness who is taught by God is a true witness. I think this is what "sent by God" means. The wise Paul too, by telling us that he was sent by Jesus Christ,[177] confirmed that he did not learn the power of the mystery from anyone else but learned it "through a revelation" from the one who sent him.[178] And he presented the revelation to us in summary form, so to speak, by saying that he was "sent by Jesus Christ." Therefore, "being sent by God" surely implies being taught by God. No one can dispute the fact that the ministers of the truth zealously seek to tell the truth.

"And the man's name," he says, "was John." The one who was sent has to be recognized by the significance of his name. This name, I think, lends great credibility to his message. When the angel Gabriel, "who stands in the presence of God," as he himself says,[179] announced to Zechariah that Elizabeth would give birth, he added to the announcement, "And his name will be John."[180] It is doubtless clear, and everyone agrees that the angel named him in agreement with the divine will and command. How **[93]** could one who is crowned by God with such honor not be considered to be greater and more distinguished than all praise? Therefore, we must pay attention to the mention of his name, and we do so to our benefit.

The Evangelist has added the phrase "that all may believe through him"[181] as testimony to the fact that the holy Baptist was sent by God. Our opponents resist this, saying, Why doesn't everyone believe the one who was sent from God? How is it that someone who was selected for this by a decree from above was unable to persuade some people? When they say things like this, our reply will be, We should not blame John for laziness in these matters; instead, we should lament the stubbornness of the unbelievers. As far as the intention of the preacher is concerned and the kind of mission he has from above, no one would have been untaught, and no one would have remained an unbeliever. But since the intention of the

[173]The Greek word for "originate" (γενητός) is the adjectival form of the verb "arose" (ἐγένετο). The verb ἐγένετο, to Cyril's ear, implies that John the Baptist came into being. [174]Mt 11:10; Mal 3:1. [175]The Greek word for "angel" also means "messenger." Here it refers to human messengers. [176]Heb 1:14. [177]Gal 1:1. [178]Gal 1:12. [179]Lk 1:19. [180]Lk 1:13; cf. Lk 1:63. [181]Jn 1:7.

hearers is different, and each person has the power over their own choice, some missed out on the benefit because they did not receive faith. Clearly, one must say of them what is found in the prophet, "Let the one who hears hear, and let the one who refuses to hear refuse to hear."[182]

This man came as a witness to testify about the light.

The word *this* is pregnant with meaning about the virtue and fame of the person being presented. The one who was sent by God, it says, is the one who astounded all Judea (and rightly so) by the seriousness of his life and his surpassing discipline. He is also the one who was proclaimed in advance by the voice of the holy prophets. In Isaiah, he is called the "voice of the one calling out in the wilderness."[183] By the blessed David he is called a "lamp prepared for Christ."[184] "This man came as **[94]** a witness to testify about the light." In this statement, John calls God the Word "light." He shows that he is the only one who, strictly speaking, is light itself. There is nothing else alongside him that has by nature the ability to enlighten and that does not lack light. Therefore, the Word of God is alien, so to speak, and of a different nature than creation, since he himself is really, truly and, strictly speaking, the light. Creation, by contrast, participates in the light. Because he is no longer classified with created things and therefore is recognized to be of a different nature, how could he be originate? How could he not be within the limits of the divine nature and full of the good nature of the one who begat him?

1:8 He was not the light, but he came to bear witness to the light.

The Baptist preferred spending time in the desert to living in the cities. He showed unusual endurance in discipline, and he reached the very summit of human righteousness. People quite rightly marveled at him, and some even assumed that he was Christ himself. At least the leaders of the Jews were led to some such notion by the height of his achievement in virtue, and they sent some envoys to him, whom they instructed to ask whether he was the Christ. The blessed Evangelist was not unaware of the opinions circulating among the people about him. This is why he was constrained to write, "He was not the light." He wrote this in order to uproot the error about John and to establish credibility for the one who was sent by God as a witness. Who can surpass his excellent character? How is he not worthy of all wonder? He is clothed with such great virtue and so distinguished in **[95]** righteousness that he imitates Christ himself. The remarkable beauty of his piety causes some to even think that he is the light itself!

Therefore, "he was not the light," says the Evangelist, "but he was sent to bear witness to the light." By saying "the light" with the addition of the article, he shows clearly that this light is in a class by itself, and it truly is. We will not deny that the blessed Baptist, or all the other saints as well, may rightly be called "light" because of what our Savior said about them: "You are the light of the world."[185] And it is said of the holy Baptist, "I have prepared a lamp for my Christ,"[186] and, "He was a burning and shining lamp, and you were willing to rejoice for a while in his light."[187] But even though the saints are "light" and the Baptist is a "lamp," we will not be ignorant of the grace they have and the abundance they receive from the light. The light in the lamp is not its own, nor does the illumination in the saints belong to them, but by the truth shining in them, they were continually shown to be bright and clear. "They are lights in the world,

[182]Ezek 3:27. [183]Is 40:3. [184]Ps 132:17 (Ps 131:17 LXX). [185]Mt 5:14. [186]Ps 132:17 (Ps 131:17 LXX). [187]Jn 5:35.

holding out the word of life."[188] And who is the life whose word they were holding out and so were called light? Surely it is none other than the Only Begotten himself, who says, "I am the life."[189] Therefore, the true light is in a class by himself. He gives light; he does not receive light. By participation in the one light, everything that is called light is understood to be so in imitation of him. **[96]**

Chapter Eight

The Son of God alone is true light; the creation is not, since it participates in the light as something originate.

1:9 He was the true light.

The divine Evangelist profitably repeats what he said before and clearly distinguishes the true light (the Only Begotten) from things that are not the true light (originate things). He makes a clear distinction between that which is something by nature and those that are the same thing by grace; between that which is participated in and those that participate in it; between that which supplies itself to those in need and those that receive the abundance. If the Son is the true light, then nothing else besides him is truly light, nor can anything on the basis of its own power be or be called light. Originate beings will not produce what I just indicated as a fruit of their own nature. Just as they exist from [former] nonexistence, so also they rise up to being light when they were [formerly] not light. They will receive the beams of the true light and be made to shine brightly by participation in the divine nature. By imitation of that nature, they will be called and will be light.

The Word of God is light in his substance. He is not light by participation, that is, by grace, nor does he have this dignity in himself as an accident. Light is not brought in like grace but **[97]** is an immutable and unchangeable good fruit of his uncreated nature that extends from the Father to the heir of his substance. The creation is not light in this way. It receives because it does not have. It is illumined because it is darkness. It has grace that is newly acquired, the dignity that comes from the giver's love for humanity. Therefore, he is the "true light." Creation is not. So when it comes to the identity of nature, because the difference between them is so great and the conceptual wall that separates the Son of God from creation is so high, how could one not assume (for good reason) that they are talking nonsense—or rather that they have lost all good sense—when they say that he is originate, and they class the one who gave a beginning to everything in the same category with created things? It looks to me like they have no idea the level of impiety they are daring to risk since they know "neither what they are saying nor what they are making assertions about."[190]

To those of us who are accustomed to judge the truth more carefully in these matters, the Only Begotten, that is, "the true light," will never be rendered at all originate or created or in any sense the same nature as creation. One may see this from every angle, and quite easily too, especially from the following sequence of ideas collected to help us consider the matter before us.

Considerations or syllogisms through which it is possible to learn that the Son is the only true light, and the creation is not. Therefore, he is not of the same nature as creation.

If the Son is the true light because he is the radiance of God the Father's glory, he will not be of the same nature as creation. Therefore, creation will not be understood to be the radiance of God the Father's glory or to have

[188]Phil 2:15-16. [189]Jn 11:25. [190]1 Tim 1:7.

the potential to be by nature what the Son is.

Another: If all creation is capable of being the "true light," **[98]** why is this title given only to the Son? It would be necessary, I suppose, because of their equality, to hold that created beings too are "true light." But this is not appropriate for originate beings. It is predicated only of the substance of the Son. It applies to him, truly and strictly speaking, but not to creation. How then is he of the same nature as creation? How does he not rather transcend creation, since he is above it with the Father?

Another: Not being true light is not the same as being true light since the terms for each are opposites. The Son is called "true light," and this is by nature. Therefore, creation will not be "true light." Nor will things that are so removed from each other be of the same nature as each other.

Another: If the Only Begotten is not the only true light, but creation is also the true light, what would be the point for him to "enlighten everyone coming into the world"? If originate substance also has this on its own, it would be superfluous for it to be enlightened by the Son. But he does in fact enlighten, and we all participate in him. Therefore the Son and creation are not the same in the quality of their substance, just as what is participated in is not the same as what participates in it.

Another: If being the "true light" does not belong only to the Son by nature, but to creation as well, the psalmist looks superfluous, it seems to me, when he says to some, "Come to him and be enlightened."[191] The light which is completely true would not become light by participation in someone else, nor would it be made bright by illumination from another. Rather, it will be supplied with perfect purity from its own nature. But we see that humanity lacks light since it has a created nature. The psalmist tells the truth when he cries out **[99]** to the Word of God, "You, O Lord, will light my lamp. You, my God, will enlighten my darkness."[192] Therefore, we are not truly light, but we participate in the Word who gives light, and we are by nature different from the true light, which is the Son.

Another along the same lines: If the human mind is called a lamp as the Psalms sing, "You will light my lamp, O Lord,"[193] how will we be true light? After all, the light is brought in and given to the lamp. If only the Only Begotten enlightens the darkness in us, how is he not the true light instead of us? And if this is true, how could he be of the same nature as creation, since he is so far above it?

Another: If creation can be the true light (in the same sense the Son is, of course) then humanity will clearly be "true light," since humanity is part of creation. To whom, then, did God the Father promise through the holy prophets, "The sun of righteousness will arise on you who fear my name"?[194] How would the true light have had any need at all for the sun to shine on it? But in fact, God the Father promised to give it to us since we are in need, and we have been enlightened because we received it. Therefore, the Only Begotten is different from us and from creation, as far as the identity of nature is concerned, since he is the "true light" and by nature enlightens those things that lack light.

Another: If the Son alone is not "true light," but creation is too, this characteristic will clearly also be in us. What kind of consideration, then, led the saints to cry out to God, "Send out your light and your truth"?[195] Tell me, what help did they think we would receive when they sent forth these words so often? If they knew that humanity was in need of light and that we needed something additional from someone else, how will anyone say truthfully

[191]Ps 34:5 (Ps 33:6 LXX). [192]Ps 18:28 (Ps 17:29 LXX). [193]Ps 18:28 (Ps 17:29 LXX). [194]Mal 4:2 (Mal 3:20 LXX). [195]Ps 43:3 (Ps 42:3 LXX).

that humanity is the "true light"? But if **[100]** humanity did not need the Word who enlightens, why did they keep calling in vain on one who could not help them at all? But no one can say that the mind of the saints was led astray from the truth. God the Father himself sends the Son to people because they lack light. Therefore, the Only Begotten is by nature different from creation, just as the one who enlightens is different from the things that lack light.

Another: We see that creation lacks light. The Only Begotten enlightens it; it does not lead itself to the light. Therefore, it is not the "true light" as the Son is.

Another: If that which is truly light by nature has no darkness, and the Only Begotten is "true light," and creation is "true light" in the same way, why does the Scripture say of the Son, "The darkness did not comprehend it"?[196] And why does Paul say of us, "among whom the god of this age blinded the minds of the unbelievers"?[197] And again, the Savior himself says, "While you have the light, walk in the light so that the darkness does not overtake you."[198] I suppose it is clear to everyone that if it were not possible for some of us to be overtaken by darkness, the Savior would not have said this. How then are the Only Begotten and creation the same in their nature? How is the unchangeable the same as the changing? How is one who suffers no harm from evildoers the same as something that is darkened and can be enlightened, since illumination obviously belongs to it as an added feature, not as something rooted in it by nature?

Another: If the Only Begotten is not alone the "true light," but creation is too, since it is of the same nature as him, how shall we lift our voices to God the Father, crying, "In your light we will see light"?[199] If we are the true light, after all, how will we be enlightened in someone else? But if we say these things because we need light from without, **[101]** we are clearly unmasked as those who are not truly light. Therefore, we are not of the same nature as the Word who is so far above us by nature.

Another in descriptive form: We see our Lord Jesus Christ saying in the Gospels, "And this is the judgment, that the light has come into the world, and people loved darkness rather than light because their deeds were evil. For all who do evil hate the light and do not come into the light."[200] But if the Only Begotten is the "true light," and creation can likewise be the "true light," how does he come to enlighten it, and how does it love the darkness? How does it refuse to come into the light at all if it is the "true light"? Attributes that belong to something by nature have their possession firmly rooted, but attributes that are chosen by the will do not have this stability. For example, no one is made a rational human being by their own will. They have this from their nature. People do have it in their will, however, to be good or evil, and similarly they will love righteousness or its opposite by their own power. Therefore, if creation is light by nature, since this is what "true" means, how does it not come into the light? How does it love the darkness, as though it clearly is not true light by nature but rather makes for itself an inclination by choice toward the better or the worse?

Let the opponents dare to say that the qualities that surpass creation are not in the Son by nature that they may be convicted of naked blasphemy and hear from everyone, "The Lord will cut off all lying lips and the tongue that makes great boasts."[201] Or else, if they confess clearly that these good things are in him substantially, let them not join the creation to him in a unity **[102]** of nature since the creation is not like this, as we have just shown.

Another: If the Word of God alone is not

[196]Jn 1:5. [197]2 Cor 4:4. [198]Jn 12:35. [199]Ps 36:9 (Ps 35:10 LXX). [200]Jn 3:19-20. [201]Ps 12:3 (Ps 11:4 LXX).

the "true light" but creation is the "true light" as well in the same way as he is, why does he say, "I am the light of the world"?[202] How can we let him strip our nature of its most excellent quality if it is at all possible that we too are the true light on the grounds that originate substance also has this quality? But if the Only Begotten is telling the truth when he says, "I am the light of the world," it is clearly by relation to him that the creation will be light, and not otherwise. And if this is so, creation is not of the same nature as he is.

Another: If the Son alone is not truly light but this quality resides in originate beings as well, what then will we say when Peter in his infinite wisdom writes to us, "But you are a chosen race, a royal priesthood, a holy nation, God's own people, that you may proclaim the wonderful deeds of him who called you out of darkness into his marvelous light"?[203] What darkness, if any, could there be in us, or what darkness could we have entered into if we too are truly the light? How have we been called into the light if we are not in darkness in the first place? But the herald of the truth was not lying when he boldly said, "Do you seek proof of Christ speaking in me?"[204] Nor was he lying when he said we were called into "his marvelous light," as from darkness, that is, and not in any other way. If this is true, creation is not truly the light, but only the Son is truly and strictly speaking light. Originate beings are light by participation in him, and therefore they are not of the same nature as he is. **[103]**

Other arguments with a list of passages that lead the readers from simpler thoughts to the confession that only the Son of God is the true light and the nature of originate things is enlightened from his abundance; their nature is not light substantially the way he is.

The psalmist says, "The light of your face, O Lord, has been impressed on us."[205] What then is the face of God the Father, whose light has been impressed on us? Surely it is none other than the only begotten Son of God, the exact image, who for this reason says, "Whoever has seen me has seen the Father."[206] It has been pressed on us, shaping us into his form and engraving the illumination through his own Spirit as a divine image on those who believe in him. That is why because of him they too may now be called both gods and the children of God. But if the true light belonged to originate beings, how was it impressed on us? "For the light shines in the darkness," according to the truthful voice of the Spirit bearer. After all, how could light shine in light?

Another: The psalmist says, "Light dawned for the righteous."[207] If it dawned for one who has light and does not lack it, then it is superfluous. But if light dawns for one who does not have it, then only the Only Begotten is light, and creation participates in the light. Therefore, they have different natures.

Another: The psalmist says, "They did not inherit the land with their sword, and their arm did not save them, but your right hand and your arm and the light from your face did."[208] Here he refers to the revelation from the Son through the Spirit and the direction of all that exists as the "light from God the Father's face." It alone saved Israel and **[104]** delivered them from the exploitation of the Egyptians. If the Only Begotten alone is not "the true light," but the same dignity resides also in originate beings, why were those he is speaking about not saved by their own light? Why are they clearly supplied with additions as from an alien and unnecessary light? It is clear, however, that the Only Begotten enlightened those who lack light. Therefore, he alone

[202]Jn 8:12. [203]1 Pet 2:9. [204]2 Cor 13:3. [205]Ps 4:6 (Ps 4:7 lxx). [206]Jn 14:9. [207]Ps 97:11 (Ps 96:11 lxx). [208]Ps 44:3 (Ps 43:4 lxx).

is the "true light," and creation borrows grace from him. If this is so, how could it be of the same nature as he is?

Another: The psalmist says, "Blessed are the people who know a joyful shout. They will walk, O Lord, in the light of your face."[209] Why will they too not walk in their own light? If they too are really the true light just as God the Father's face (i.e., the Son) surely is, then why, tell me, do they barely attain salvation for themselves by gathering illumination from another source? Rather, I think it is evident to everyone from this passage as well that the Word supplies illumination to creation since it lacks it, and creation is saved by receiving what it does not have. How then are the Only Begotten and the creation that came into being through him still the same in substance?

Another: The psalmist says, "He sent forth light in the darkness for the upright."[210] But how was the upright person in darkness at all if that person too is the "true light," if indeed the nature of originate beings has this quality too just as the Only Begotten does? But if the light is sent to the upright because they do not have it, we will not need many words. For the very nature of things will cry out that something that is lacking could not be the same in substance as something that is perfect, nor could that which supplies from its abundance be the same as that which needs the supply.

Another: "Be enlightened, be enlightened, Jerusalem! For your light has come, **[105]** and the glory of the Lord has risen on you!"[211] If the nature of originate beings has the light on its own (and this is strictly speaking what we mean when we say that the Only Begotten is the "true light"), how would Jerusalem have needed anyone to enlighten it? Since it receives enlightenment, which is classified as grace, the Son alone is the true light who enlightens it and who gives it what it does not have. If this is so, how is he not completely different from it by nature?

Another: "Behold, I have given you as a covenant to the people and a light to the Gentiles."[212] How did earthly rational creation lack light at all if the true light is in it by nature? For God gives his only Son to a creation that does not already have light. And by the very fact of receiving, creation proclaims both the poverty of its own nature and the rich dignity of the Word who enlightens.

Another: "And now, O house of Jacob, come let us walk in the light of the Lord."[213] Why do they not walk in their own light instead? Why does the Only Begotten hold the torch for them? Why did he implant in them his own good that belongs to him essentially? But they have no confidence in what belongs to them, so they borrow what belongs to another. Thus, they recognize that they borrow it because they do not have it.

Another: The Savior says, "I am the light of the world. Whoever follows me will never walk in darkness but will have the light of life."[214] Let the creature too dare to utter this statement if it is also truly the light. But if it shrinks back from these words, it will flee from their meaning as well, and it will confess the "true light," that is, the Son.

Another: The Lord says, "While you have the light, believe in the light, so that you may become children of the light."[215] **[106]** Were those who are light by nature—if it is at all possible for originate substance to be the true light—going to lose the light by not believing? How could this ever be? Neglect never deprives people of what belongs to them essentially, but it does deprive them of what they obtain by their will and of what can be added or taken away without destroying the subject. For instance, a person is rational by nature, a shipbuilder by will and suffers bodily

[209]Ps 89:15 (Ps 88:16 LXX). [210]Ps 112:4 (Ps 111:4 LXX). [211]Is 60:1 (LXX). [212]Is 42:6. [213]Is 2:5. [214]Jn 8:12. [215]Jn 12:36.

ailment as an accidental quality. One who is lazy could not possibly lose the faculty of reason, but that person will lose the skill of shipbuilding. And the accidental quality of suffering will be warded off when the person hastens back to the better through medicine. Therefore, that which belongs to people essentially has a rooted stability. So if the nature of originate beings can at all be the "true light," how do those who do not want to believe lose the light, or how will believers become the children of light? If they themselves are "light" by nature, then they are called children innately. So what is the reward for believers? After all, they did not receive faith, but they are children innately. Arriving at the truth from these arguments, we must say that only the Only Begotten is the "true light." Creation lacks light and therefore is of a different nature.

Another: "Jesus said to them, 'The light is with you for a little longer. Walk while you have the light so that the darkness may not overtake you.' "[216] You may skillfully apply the previous argument to these words as well. That which is "light" by nature could never be overtaken by darkness.

Another: John says, "Whoever says he is in the light while hating his brother is still in the darkness."[217] **[107]** Therefore, the light in us attaches to originate beings by choice and will rather than by essence if the one who hates his brother is in the darkness. The Only Begotten is in his essence light because he does not have this dignity as a fruit of his choice. Therefore, the one who is so far above originate beings is not of the same nature as they are.

Another of the same kind: "The one who loves his brother remains in the light."[218] Love grants to originate beings what they do not have, namely, light. But the Only Begotten is light. Therefore, he is different from those in whom he comes to be through love. **[108]**

Chapter Nine

The human soul does not exist before the body, nor is embodiment the result of former sins, as some say.

Which enlightens everyone coming into the world.

The Theologian is trustworthy because he does not think it is enough to say that the Only Begotten is the "true light"; instead, he immediately proves what he had just said, practically shouting it out with a loud voice: I say that he is the true light "which enlightens everyone coming into the world." Someone who is glad to receive divine doctrines, though not without careful investigation, might say, Do not angels enlighten human minds? Tell me, who told Cornelius that he needed to be saved by God by being baptized?[219] And Manoah, the father of Samson—was he not instructed about the future ahead of time by the voice of an angel?[220] And likewise Zechariah the prophet—does he not clearly tells us, "And the angel who talked to me said, 'I will show you what they are'"?[221] And as he goes through the same story, does he not clearly show us that angels used to reveal to him the knowledge of secret things in **[109]** his mind? "For behold," he says, "the angel speaking to me stood there, and the other angel went out to meet with him and said to him, 'Run and tell that young man that Jerusalem will be inhabited abundantly because of the multitude of people and animals in the midst of her.'"[222] What about Daniel, who was extremely wise? When he applies himself to the wonderful visions, does he not get the explanation of what he sees through the voice of the angels? Listen to what he says: "And it happened that when I, Daniel, saw the vision and sought to understand it, behold, something like the appearance of a man stood

[216]Jn 12:35. [217]1 Jn 2:9. [218]1 Jn 2:10. [219]Acts 10:3. [220]Judg 13:11-14. [221]Zech 1:9. [222]Zech 2:3-4 (Zech 2:7-8 LXX).

before me. And I heard the voice of a man in the middle of the Ubal [River], and it called out and said, 'Gabriel, explain the vision to him.'"[223] Therefore, angels can enlighten, and not only angels, but someone can even borrow enlightenment from another person. For instance, when the eunuch who is eager to learn does not understand the prophecies about our Savior, he says to Philip, "I ask you, who is the prophet speaking about: himself or someone else?"[224] Those who run to the teachers of this life do so for no other reason, I think, than this alone. But why do we spend time on these things when we can easily free ourselves by offering as proof the words of our Savior to the holy apostles: "You are the light of the world"?[225]

Someone who is confused will most likely say such things. From us, they will hear the answer, We see that created things are composite, my friend, and there is nothing simple in them. Therefore, the one who can make others wise, if that person is originate, is not wisdom itself but a servant of the wisdom within them. The wise person is wise in wisdom. And the one who by teaching imparts intelligence **[110]** is not intelligence itself but a servant of the intelligence within them. In intelligence they too are intelligent. And again, the one who knows how to enlighten others should not be considered light, strictly speaking, but a lender of the light in them. They loan it out to others by teaching and sharing with others the good that they have received. That is why it is said to the holy apostles, "Freely you have received, freely give."[226] Whatever good was in them is completely given by God. Human nature must not pride itself at all in its own goods, and neither should the nature of the holy angels. For once they are called into existence, all things that exist have their mode of being from God. We will maintain that everything in them essentially is a gift from the creator's generosity and has the grace of the creator as its root.

Therefore, since originate beings are composite, the light in them will not be, strictly speaking, simple and uncompounded. Rather, they have this light, along with everything else they have, by participation and by receiving it from God. Again, we understand the true light (the Only Begotten), which enlightens and is not enlightened by another, to be in a simple and uncompounded nature because the divine withdraws from everything that is double.

That is how it is. But perhaps the opponents will say to us, If the saints were not light by nature, why did the Savior call them light rather than participants in the light? How is creation of a different nature than he if the rational creation is called light just like he is? The disciples heard the words "you are the light of the world."[227] What about that, my good friend?

We will reply, We are called sons of God and gods by the Holy Scriptures in the passage, "I said, You are gods, and you are all sons of the Most High."[228] Shall we then leave what we are by nature and **[111]** climb up to the divine and ineffable substance? Shall we expel the Word of God from his true sonship and take our seat in his place next to the Father? Shall we turn the grace of the one who honors us into a pretext for impiety? May it never be! When the Son is in a position, he is in it unchangeably. But we are placed into sonship, and we are gods by grace. We are not ignorant of what we are. This is the way in which we believe that the saints too are light.

I think that we need to examine and look at this too. The rational part of creation that receives light enlightens others by pouring ideas from one mind into another. Such enlightenment should properly be called teaching rather than revelation. The Word of

[223]Dan 8:15-16. [224]Acts 8:34. [225]Mt 5:14. [226]Mt 10:8. [227]Mt 5:14. [228]Ps 82:6 (Ps 81:6 LXX).

God "enlightens everyone coming into the world" not by teaching the way angels, perhaps, or people do. Instead, by the divine act of creating, he inserts a seed of wisdom, or knowledge of God, and he implants a root of understanding into everything he calls into existence. In this way he makes a living creature rational. He shows that it participates in his own nature, and he sends into the mind luminous vapors, as it were, of his ineffable brightness in a way and a mode that only he himself knows. I should not say too much about these matters, I think. This is why we also see that our ancestor Adam does not become wise in time the way we do, but he obviously has perfect knowledge from the start, from the beginning of his creation. He preserves in himself the illumination, still untroubled and pure, given to his nature by God. He keeps the dignity of his nature uncorrupted.

Therefore, the Son enlightens by creating, since he himself is the true light. But creation is brightened by participation with the light, and this is why it is called and becomes light. It rises up above its own nature because of the grace of the one who glorifies it and who crowns it with various honors **[112]** so that each one who is honored may have a reason to come forward, raise up prayers of thanksgiving and sing out with a loud voice, "Bless the Lord, O my soul, and forget not all his benefits, who forgives all your iniquities, who heals all your diseases, who redeems your life from corruption, who crowns you with love and mercy, who satisfies your desires with good things."[229] The Lord truly "works mercy." Things which are small and insignificant according to their own nature he shows to be great and marvelous through his goodness toward them, just as he, as God, ungrudgingly deemed it necessary to exalt us with his own good attributes. That is why he calls us gods and light. What good titles, after all, does he not give us?

What does he say after that? "He was in the world." The Theologian gives us necessary information with this useful addition because when he says, "He was the true light which enlightens everyone coming into the world," it is not immediately clear to the hearers whether the light enlightens "someone coming into the world" or the true light itself comes into the world as if from some other place and enlightens all people. The Spirit bearer must uncover the truth for us and interpret the meaning of his words by saying immediately of the light, "He was in the world." That way, you may understand the phrase "coming into the world" to refer to a human being and to be predicated of a nature that is enlightened since it is called into existence from what is not. It is as if originate beings are in a certain place seen by the imagination, a place of nonexistence. And when they somehow pass from there into existence, they take up another place, **[113]** a place of existence.[230] Therefore, it is quite proper and fitting for human nature to receive enlightenment from its beginning and to receive understanding which is formed at the same time as it receives its existence from the light who is in the world, that is, the Only Begotten. He fills all things with the unspeakable power of his divinity. He is present with the angels in heaven. He is with those on earth. And he does not even leave hell itself empty of his divinity. Since he dwells everywhere with everyone, he departs from no one. So it is quite reasonable for the psalmist in his wisdom to marvel at this and say, "Where can I go from your Spirit, and where can I flee from your face? If I go up to heaven, you are there. If I go down to hell, you are there. If I take up my wings towards the dawn and dwell at the ends of the sea, even there your hand

[229]Ps 103:2-5 (Ps 102:2-5 LXX). [230]Cyril is here denying that the phrase "everyone coming into the world" implies that human beings existed in some other actual place before they came into the world.

will lead me, and your right hand will uphold me."[231] The divine hand grasps every place and every creature. It keeps creatures in existence. It takes those things that lack life and binds them tightly together with life. It sows the light of intelligence in those capable of understanding. It is not in a place, as we said before, nor does it undergo motion from one place to another since this is proper to bodies; rather, it fills all things as God.

But perhaps someone will respond to this by asking, What do we say, sir, when someone brings up Christ's statement, "I have come as light into the world"?[232] And what about when the psalmist says, "Send out your light and your truth"?[233] Look, he himself clearly says here that he came into the world, so he was obviously not in it. And the psalmist kept asking for one who is not yet present to be sent, **[114]** at least if you take the words the way they appear and consider what it means to be "sent" to us.

To this we say that the Theologian confers on the Only Begotten dignity that is worthy of God. He says that he is always continually in the world as life by nature, as light according to his substance, filling creation as God, not circumscribed by place, not measured by distance, not comprehended by quantity, not surrounded by anything at all, not requiring motion from place to place, but he dwells in everything and forsakes nothing. Yet the Theologian insists that he has come into the world, although he was already in it, by the incarnation.[234] "For he appeared on earth and lived with humankind"[235] with flesh, thereby making his presence in the world more clear. The one who was perceived long ago in the mind is also the one who is now seen by fleshly eyes. He was placing in us a denser perception, so to speak, of the knowledge of God by being recognized through wonders and mighty deeds. The psalmist asks that the Word of God be sent to us to enlighten the world in no other way, it seems to me, than this. Furthermore, I think that the one who loves knowledge should consider this as well: the mind is keener than all speech, and the motion of thought is sharper than the tongue. Therefore, we behold the varied beauty of the divine nature according to the subtlety of the mind and the precise movement in it, but we speak about these things in a more human manner and in speech that is appropriate to us since the tongue cannot stretch out to the measure of the truth. That is why Paul, the steward of the mysteries of the Savior, kept asking for a message from God "to open his mouth."[236] So **[115]** our poverty of speech will in no way bring to ruin the natural dignities of the Only Begotten, but what we say about him should be understood in a way that is fitting to God. Yet one cannot help speaking in a more human way—whether he speaks for our sakes or the saints speak about him in proportion to the limitations of our nature.

I think it would be good to consider what I just said to be enough of an explanation of these matters, but I also think that the pen that serves the divine doctrines should be above sluggishness. So come, let us look at the passage again and examine more carefully how the words "coming into the world" should be understood in a way that is fittingly applied to humanity. "In it was light," as the Evangelist himself testifies to us. We maintain that it is not the light that comes into the world but rather the person who is enlightened. Some people[237] spew forth things "from their own hearts and not from the mouth of the Lord,"[238]

[231]Ps 139:7-10 (Ps 138:7-10 LXX). [232]Jn 12:46. [233]Ps 43:3 (Ps 42:3 LXX). [234]Cyril here uses the word ἐνανθρωπήσις to refer to the incarnation, indicating that the Word became not only flesh but also a full human being. [235]Bar 3:37 (Bar 3:38 LXX). [236]Eph 6:19. [237]Certain Origenist monks had taken the positions Cyril describes in this paragraph. They were opposed by Cyril's uncle Theophilus, his predecessor as Patriarch of Alexandria (Norman Russell, *Theophilus of Alexandria*, The Early Church Fathers [London: Routledge, 2007], 24). [238]Jer 23:16.

as it is written, and say that before the formation of bodies, human souls preexisted in heaven, spending a long time in incorporeal blessedness and enjoying more purely the true good. But when they had enough of the better, they turned downward to the worse and descended into alien thoughts and desires. The creator understandably became angry with them and sent them into the world. He wove them into bodies made from the earth and forced them to bear those bodies as burdens. He shut them up in some cave of strange pleasures, as it were, and decided to teach them by the trial itself how bitter it is to be carried away to the worse and to place no value on the better.

For proof of their ridiculous story they first of all seize on the very passage we are dealing with: "He was **[116]** the true light which enlightens everyone coming into the world." They also seize on other passages from Holy Scripture, "Before I was humbled, I went astray."[239] Specifically, they say (since they are not ashamed to talk nonsense), Aha! The soul says that it went astray before its humbling, that is, before its embodiment. Therefore, it has been justly humbled and bound together with death and decay, just as Paul refers to the body this way when he says, "I am a wretched man. Who will deliver me from this body of death?"[240] If the soul goes astray before it is humbled, they say, and it comes into the world, it is clear that the soul preexisted. How could it sin in the first place if it did not yet exist? It obviously comes into the world by moving from other places.

Because they stitch these things onto the doctrines of the church and heap up the nonsense of their empty explanations in the hearing of the simple, they deserve to hear, "Woe to those who prophesy from their own hearts and see nothing at all."[241] They place visions and auguries and prophecies from their own hearts against the words that come through the Spirit, but they do not realize what madness this enterprise will lead them to. The psalmist says to God, "You are to be feared. Who can stand against your wrath?"[242] It is absolutely absurd to think that the soul preexists and that it is sent down into earthly bodies because of previous sins. We will attempt to prove this as well as we can through the following arguments, knowing that it is written, "Give opportunity to the wise, and they will be wiser. Instruct the just, and they will receive more instruction."[243] **[117]**

Thoughts or arguments of a complex kind and in syllogistic form:

1. Some suppose that the human soul existed before the formation of bodies and turned away toward the inferior and that the descent into the flesh is the penalty for its transgression. But if that is so, how, tell me, does the Evangelist say that it is enlightened when it "comes into the world"? Enlightenment is an honor, I think, and a bestowal of dazzling gifts. No one is punished by being honored, nor is one chastised by being made a participant in divine goods, but by encountering those things that come from the wrath of the punisher. However, since the person "coming into the world" is not in this condition but on the contrary is even enlightened, I think it is clear that the one who is honored with the flesh does not receive the embodiment as a punishment.

2. *Another:* If the soul was a mind that was still pure and living continuously in blessedness before it received a body, but it turned away and descended to what is base and for this reason came to be in flesh, how is it "enlightened" when it "comes into the world"? We would have to say it was bereft of light before it came. But in that case, how could the mind have been pure since it barely attained

[239]Ps 119:67 (Ps 118:67 LXX). [240]Rom 7:24. [241]Ezek 13:3. [242]Ps 76:7 (Ps 75:8 LXX). [243]Prov 9:9.

the beginning of enlightenment when it came "into the world" with the flesh?

3. *Another:* They say that the human soul existed before the body and was therefore a mind that was still pure. It was very appropriately attached to good things by its desire for them. But because it turned aside to the worse, it was sent into earthly bodies, and once it was in the body, it was required to stop being willing to transgress. How is that just? It was not commanded to do this when it was better prepared for virtue, not yet being in bondage to the evils that come from the body. But when it entered the muddy waters of sin—then it is compelled to do this! That is too late. **[118]** However, the divinity would not miss the appropriate time, nor would he ever do wrong, who by nature does no wrong. Therefore, he justly commands us at the proper time with our flesh not to sin since we have only this time of existence in which we "come into the world" with our bodies. We do this by leaving a previous nonexistence as if it were some place and by moving from it into the beginning of existence.

4. *Another:* What was the point, I would like to ask them, of sending into a body the soul that sinned before its embodiment to learn the shamefulness of its own desires through that experience? They do not blush to promote this explanation as well despite the fact that the soul needed to be freed even from imagining evil rather than being thrust down to the very depth of alien pleasures. For the former, not the latter, was a form of healing. Therefore, if embodiment serves to increase the soul's diseases so that it may revel in the pleasures of the body, no one would have praised the chastiser since he injures the sick through the means by which he thought he was helping. If, however, the point of embodiment was for the soul to cease from its passions, how could it emerge after it has fallen into the very depth of desire? Would it not more readily have rejected the beginning of the disease when it was clearly free of what dragged it down into sin?

5. *Another:* If the preexisting soul was entangled in flesh and blood as a form of retribution for a previous transgression, would not those who believe in Christ and thereby receive the forgiveness of sins need to depart immediately from their bodies and to cast away what was wrapped around them as a punishment? How, tell me, does the human soul have complete forgiveness while it still wears **[119]** the instrument of its punishment? But we see that the believers are so far from wanting to be set free from their bodies that together with their confession of Christ, they proclaim the resurrection of the flesh. Therefore, the body, which is honored by the confession of faith, will not be a method of punishment since, by its return to life, it testifies to the divine power of the Savior to do everything effortlessly.

6. *Another:* If the soul sinned during its preexistence, as they claim, and for this reason was entangled in flesh, why does the law prescribe that the more serious crimes are worthy of death, while the one who has committed no sin should live? I suppose it should have commanded those caught in the most shameful deeds to live on in their bodies in order to be punished more severely and those who have committed no sin to be removed from their bodies, if embodiment is really a form of punishment. But on the contrary, the murderer is punished with death, and the righteous person suffers nothing in the body. Therefore, embodiment is not a form of punishment.

7. *Another:* If souls were enfleshed because of previous sins, and if the nature of the body was understood to be a form of punishment for them, how did the Savior help us when he abolished death? Was it not rather decay that showed mercy by removing what punishes us and placing a limit on the wrath against us? One might even say that it is more reasonable to give thanks to decay than to the one who

lays unending punishment on us through the resurrection from the dead. But in fact we do give thanks that we are delivered from death and decay through Christ. Therefore, embodiment is not a form of punishment for the human soul.

8. *Another along the same lines:* If human souls were entangled in earthly bodies to make satisfaction for earlier sins, what thanks, tell me, **[120]** will we give to God who promises us the resurrection? After all, it is clearly a renewal of punishment and a restoration of what hurts us if a long punishment is bitter to everyone, as it obviously is. The resurrection of bodies is therefore a grievous thing since they have the task of punishing wretched souls. But in fact our nature has the resurrection as a gift from Christ, a gift that brings it into a new state of joy. Therefore, embodiment is not a form of punishment.

9. *Another:* The prophetic word somewhere clearly proclaims to us a great and highly anticipated feast. It says, "The dead will rise, and those in the tombs will be raised."[244] But if the embodiment of wretched human souls was really a way of punishing them, why did the prophet not rather grieve when he announced these words as from God? How will the message be good at all when it makes permanent the things that grieve us? If he really wanted to bring joy to those who were embodied because of sin, he should have said, "The dead will not rise, but the nature of the flesh will be destroyed." But on the contrary, he does bring them joy by saying that the resurrection of bodies will take place according to the will of God. So how could the body be a form of punishment, as some foolishly think, since we ourselves rejoice over it, and God is well pleased?

10. *Another:* As God was blessing the blessed Abraham, he promised somewhere that his seed would be like the innumerable multitude of the stars.[245] But if the claim is true that the soul that sinned prior to having a body is sent to earth into the flesh to be punished, then God promised to that righteous man not a seed which has a share in blessing but an ignoble mob of the condemned who run away from the good. In fact, however, God says this to Abraham to bless him. Therefore, the origin of bodies is delivered from every accusation. **[121]**

11. *Another:* The race of the Israelites kept spreading out into a great and innumerable multitude. Furthermore, Moses, the teacher of sacred truths, rightly marvels at this and prays, saying to them, "Behold, today you are like the stars of heaven in number. May the Lord, the God of your ancestors, increase you until you are a thousand times more."[246] But if being with bodies in the world was a punishment for human souls, and if they could not be stripped of bodies, then this statement of Moses turns out to be a curse and not a prayer. It is not so, however. The statement was made as a blessing. Therefore, embodiment is not a kind of punishment.

12. *Another:* God does not say yes to those who attempt to make a request with evil intent. The Savior's truth-telling disciple will become a witness of this for us. "You ask," he says, "and you do not receive because you ask wrongly."[247] If, then, embodiment is a punishment for the soul, how will one not reasonably say that Hannah, the wife of Elkanah, was led very far astray from what is fitting when she raised her prayer to God and asked for a "male child"?[248] She was, after all, asking for the downfall of a soul and its descent into a body. It comes down to this: how could God give her holy Samuel as a son if a soul really had to sin in order to become entangled in a body and fulfill the woman's request? But God did in fact give him, and God by nature gives only good things. By readily granting her request,

[244]Is 26:19. [245]Gen 15:5. [246]Deut 1:10-11. [247]Jas 4:3. [248]1 Sam 1:11.

he frees it from all blame. Therefore, embodiment is not the result of sin, nor is it a form of punishment, as some say.

13. *Another:* If the body has been given to the human soul as a form of punishment, what was it that convinced Hezekiah, the king of Jerusalem, even though he was wise and good, **[122]** to ask with bitter tears to avoid the death of the flesh, to shrink back from taking off the instrument of his punishment and to request to be awarded the addition of years? If he really was good, he should absolutely not have asked to avoid death. Instead, he should have considered being entangled with the body a burden, and he should have given thanks for death rather than for its opposite. How was it gracious for God to promise him, "Behold, I will add fifteen years to your life,"[249] when in fact the promise was an increase in punishment, not a form of kindness—if they are right? But in reality, the promise was a gift from above, and the addition was a grace. Therefore, embodiment is not punishment for souls.

14. *Another:* If the body has been given to the human soul as a form of punishment, what favor did God do for the eunuch who pulled Jeremiah up from the pit[250] when he said, "And I will give your life as a reward, and I will save you from the Chaldeans"?[251] He should rather have let him die in order to honor him by freeing him from prison and punishment. What favor, tell me, did he do the young men of Israel when he saved them from the fire and from the inhumanity of the Babylonians?[252] And why did he rescue the wise Daniel from the fierceness of the lions?[253] But in fact, he does these things out of kindness, and he is glorified because of them. Therefore, dwelling in the flesh is not a form of punishment, or else the same thing would be both an honor and a punishment from God.

15. *Another:* Saint Paul teaches that there will be an examination of each person's life in due course before the divine judgment seat. He says, "For all of us must appear before the judgment seat of Christ, so that each may receive recompense for what has been done in the body, whether good or evil."[254] But if it is only for things done in the body that one is either punished by the judge or considered worthy of a fitting honor, and no mention is made **[123]** of previous sins, and no accusation before birth will be investigated, how then could the soul preexist? Or how could it be humbled because of sin, as some say, when the only time allotted to it is the time in the flesh because only the things done through the flesh are investigated?

16. *Another:* If souls were embodied because of previous sins, how could Paul write to us, "Present your bodies as a living sacrifice, holy and acceptable to God"?[255] If bodies have been given to wretched souls as a form of punishment, how can we present them as a pleasing aroma to God? How can the instrument of our condemnation be pleasing to God? What kind of virtue will it ever be capable of since its nature is to punish and its root is sin?

17. *Another:* Paul shows that corruption extends to the entire human nature because of the transgression in Adam. He says, "Yet death reigned from Adam to Moses, even over those who did not sin in the likeness of the transgression of Adam."[256] How then does he say that death rules over those who did not sin if mortal bodies were given to us because of previous sins? Where in the world are those who did not sin if embodiment is a penalty for stumbling and the fact that we are in this life with the flesh carries with it a preexisting accusation? Therefore, the assertion of the opponents is ignorant.

18. *Another:* The disciples once asked the Savior about someone who was blind from

[249]Is 38:5. [250]Jer 38:7-13 (Jer 45:7-13 LXX). [251]Jer 39:18 (Jer 46:18 LXX). [252]Dan 3. [253]Dan 6. [254]2 Cor 5:10. [255]Rom 12:1. [256]Rom 5:14.

birth. In particular, they said, "Rabbi, who sinned, this man or his parents, that he was born blind?"[257] Since it is written in the prophetic books that God "visits the iniquity of the parents on the children,"[258] the disciples assumed that this was what was happening to the man. **[124]** What then does Christ say to this? "Truly I tell you, neither this man nor his parents sinned; this happened so that God's works might be revealed in him."[259] How does he exempt them from sin, although their lives are not free from blame? Since they were human beings, I suppose they were certainly subject to faults. But it is clear and obvious that these words refer to the time before birth when they were not sinning because they did not yet exist, so that Christ may be telling the truth.

19. *Another:* The blessed prophet Isaiah, explaining the reason why the earth was made, says, "He did not make it in vain, but to be inhabited."[260] The earth surely had to be inhabited and filled not with bare spirits or disembodied and naked souls but with souls that are furnished with bodies appropriate to the earth. Was it therefore the divine will that made the souls sin so that the nature of bodies might come into being to show that the earth was not made in vain? But this is absurd. Therefore, the other alternative is stronger.

20. *Another:* Wisdom, the craftsman of all things, says about herself somewhere in the book of Proverbs, "I was the one in whom he (the creator of all things) rejoiced. Every day I rejoiced continually before him. He rejoiced when he completed the world, and he rejoiced among humanity."[261] Since God exults at the formation of humanity after he completes the world, how would it not be insane to subject the soul to previous sins, saying that it is embodied because of them and thereby punished? In that case, would not God be the creator of a prison rather than a world? Would it not be astonishing for him to rejoice at those who undergo punishment? How could he be good if he takes such delight in things that are so awful? **[125]** But he is in fact good, and so he is surely the creator of good things. Therefore, embodiment will not be a form of punishment.

21. *Another:* If the human soul, by its entanglement in the flesh, is paying a penalty for transgressions that predate its birth in the world, and the body is a form of punishment for it, why was the flood brought on the world of the ungodly,[262] while the righteous Noah was saved?[263] And why did he have this salvation as a reward from God for his faith? Should not those who committed intolerable sins have spent more time in bodies in order to be punished more severely? Should not the good have been freed from the chains which come from the flesh and have been released from the body as an honor for their piety toward God? But I think that the creator of all things is just and that he imposed on each kind of person the judgment they deserved. Since he is just, and he punishes the lawbreaker with the death of the flesh while he gladdens the righteous by life with the body, bodies are therefore not a punishment for human souls. Otherwise, God would seem unjust since he punishes the wicked with grace but honors the righteous with punishment.

22. *Another:* If the soul descended into the flesh and the body to pay a penalty for previous transgressions, how did the Savior "love"[264] Lazarus when he raised him and forced him who was once set free from his chains to return to them? But he did this to help him, and Christ honored the dead man as a friend by bringing him from the dead. The contention of our opponents, therefore, is pointless.

23. *Another:* If the body has been devised and given to the soul as a form of punishment because of its previous sin, as they foolishly say, then it was sin that introduced the nature of human bodies. However, **[126]** "death came

[257]Jn 9:2. [258]Ex 20:5. [259]Jn 9:3. [260]Is 45:18. [261]Prov 8:30-31. [262]2 Pet 2:5. [263]Gen 7:1. [264]Jn 11:36.

through sin."[265] Sin, therefore, is clearly arming itself against itself, destroying the beginning by what follows, and so Satan is divided against himself. "How then will his kingdom stand," according to the words of the Savior?[266] But this way of thinking is not credible. Therefore, the opposite is true.

24. *Another:* God created everything in a state of incorruption. He "did not make death";[267] rather, "death came into the world through the envy of the devil."[268] But if it is true that the body has been given to the human soul as a form of punishment, my friend, why will we blame the envy of the devil which places a limit for us on these grievous things and does away with the body that punishes us? And why on earth will we give thanks to the Savior who binds us again to the flesh through the resurrection? But we do in fact give thanks, and the envy of the devil has brought grief to our nature by inflicting corruption on our bodies. Therefore, the body is not a form of punishment, nor is it a payment for our primeval sin.

1:10 And the world was made through him.

With these words, the Evangelist forcefully shows that the world was made through the true light, that is, the Only Begotten. He called him the Word at the beginning, and he insisted that all things came to be through him, and without him nothing was brought into being. He thereby demonstrated that he was the maker and creator. Nevertheless, he had to take up this particular point and say it again here in order to leave no place for error and destruction to those who are used to perverting the truth of divine teachings. **[127]** After he tells us that the light was in the world, the Evangelist helpfully, forcefully and immediately introduces the Only Begotten as the maker and framer of the whole world, thereby making us secure once again and leading us to a simple and straightforward understanding of the truth. He does this to prevent anyone from twisting what he said into strange interpretations and numbering the light among the parts of the visible world. For example, the sun, moon and stars are certainly in the world, but as parts of the world and as parts of one body. Who would be so stupid and have such folly in their mind that they would suppose that the one through whom the world is said to be made is not completely other than the world? Who would not put the creature in its own place, distinguish the creator from it in thought and exalt his divine nature? After all, what was made has to be by nature different from its maker, or else the maker and what is made are clearly the same thing.

If they were considered the same, having no distinction in their mode of being, then what is made will rise up to the nature of its maker, and the creator will descend to the nature of the creatures. He will no longer be the only one who has the power to create, but this power will be found potentially also in the creatures if there is no way at all to distinguish them from being of the same substance as God. So creation will be its own creator, and the Evangelist will confer an empty honor on the Only Begotten when he says, "He was in the world, and the world was made through him." But he knows that the creator of all things is unique in his nature. Therefore, what is made should not be considered the same as the maker, nor should God be considered the same as the creature, at least among those who know the right way to believe. Instead, the creature will be subject as is fitting for a servant, and it will acknowledge the limits of its nature, **[128]** while the Son will rule over it since he alone has, along with the Father, the ability both to call the things which are not into existence[269] and by his ineffable power to bring that which does not yet exist into being.

[265]Rom 5:12. [266]Lk 11:18. [267]Wis 1:13. [268]Wis 2:24. [269]Rom 4:17.

In the discourse on the holy Trinity, we have already sufficiently gone through the fact that since the Son is by nature God, he is altogether different from creation. Therefore, we will say nothing more about it here. But it will be helpful for us to add the following: by saying that the world was made through him, he raises our mind to consider the Father, and he introduces the words "through whom" along with the words "from whom." That is because all things are from the Father, through the Son, in the Holy Spirit.

And the world did not know him.
Once again, the Spirit bearer is sober and quickly anticipates the sophistry of some, and once again, you will be amazed at his thoughtful reasoning. He called the Son the true light, and he insisted that he enlightens every person coming into the world. In addition to this, he says that "he was in the world and the world was made through him."[270]

But one of our opponents would have immediately objected, If he was the light, my friends, and if he enlightens everyone's heart (to divine knowledge, that is, and to understanding that is appropriate to humanity), and if he was always in the world and he was its maker, how was he unknown and for such a long time? Therefore, he was not enlightening the world. In short, he was not the light.

The Theologian very quickly counters these things by saying, "The world did not know him." He does not say that he was at fault for being unknown. Let the world blame its own weakness. The Son enlightens, but the creature blunts the grace. The creature was loaned the sight to conceive of the one who is God by nature, but it squandered the gift and limited the scope of its contemplation to created things. It shrank **[129]** from going further. It buried the illumination by laziness. It neglected the gift. This is what Paul commands his disciple to be careful of, so that it does not happen to him.[271] Therefore, the indifference of those who are enlightened has nothing to do with the light. The light of the sun rises on everyone but is no help to the blind. Nevertheless, this is no reason for us to blame the sun's rays. Instead, let us blame the defective eye because the sun was giving light, but the eye was not receiving it.

I think we should consider the Only Begotten in the same way. He is the true light, but "the god of this age," as Paul says, "has blinded the minds of the unbelievers to keep them from seeing the light" of the knowledge of God that is in them.[272] We say that people are subject to blindness in this respect: not that they come into a total lack of light (for God-given intelligence is certainly preserved in their nature), but they extinguish it with a foolish way of life. And by turning to the worse, they in a way erode and melt away the measure of grace. That is why it is only right that when the supremely wise psalmist plays the part of such a person for us, he asks to be enlightened, saying to God, "Open my eyes, and I will perceive your wonders out of your law."[273] "For he gave the law as a help"[274] to rekindle the divine light in us and to clear away the darkness imposed by ancient ignorance like a sort of film over the eyes of the heart.

The world, therefore, remains under the charge of thanklessness and dullness in these matters both because it did not know its own maker and because it did not show forth the good fruit of enlightenment. So what the prophetic voice sang about the children of Israel is shown true about the world as well: **[130]** "I expected it to produce grapes, but it produced thorns."[275] The fruit of enlightenment was the true understanding of the Only Begotten. It is like a bunch of grapes hanging on a branch (I mean the branch of human understanding), rather than its opposite, the

[270]Jn 1:10. [271]1 Tim 4:14; 2 Tim 4:5. [272]2 Cor 4:4. [273]Ps 119:18 (Ps 118:18 LXX). [274]Is 8:20 (LXX). [275]Is 5:4 (LXX).

foolishness that leads to polytheistic error, which is like sharp thorns rising up among us that mortally wound the mind with their deception.

1:11 He came to his own, and his own did not receive him.

The Evangelist expands his defense that the world did not know the one who enlightens it, that is, the Only Begotten. From the worse sin of the Israelites, he presses on to strengthen the charge against the Gentiles as well, pointing out the disease of ignorance and unbelief that was imposed on the whole world. Very appropriately he enters into a discussion of the incarnation, and little by little he comes down from sheer theology to an explanation of the *oikonomia* with the flesh which the Son accomplished for us.[276]

It is no wonder, he says, that the world did not know the Only Begotten. It ran away from the understanding that is appropriate for human beings, and it did not know that it was created in honor. It was like the ignorant beasts, as the divine psalmist said,[277] when the very people who above all were supposed to belong to him shook him off when he was present with the flesh. They did not want to receive the one who came for the salvation of all and who gives the kingdom of heaven in return for faith.

Notice how precise his discussion of these matters is. He accuses the world of completely failing to recognize the one who enlightens it, **[131]** as though fashioning a just pardon for it on this account and preparing in advance a reasonable basis for the grace given to it. But in the case of the Israelites, whom he ordained to belong especially to him, he writes, "They did not receive him." It would not be true to say, "They did not know him," because the ancient law proclaimed him, and after that the prophets were the schoolmasters[278] who led them to the understanding of the truth. Therefore, the severe judgment against them was just, and the kindness to the Gentiles was certainly just as well.[279] The world, or the Gentiles, lost their relation to God through the fall into evil, and along with it they lost their knowledge of the one who enlightens them. But those who greatly expanded their knowledge through the law and who were called back to a delightful citizenship with God later fell willingly because they did not receive the Word of God, whom they already knew and who had come to dwell with them as with his own.

The entire world is God's "own" because of the way it was made and because it was brought into being from him and through him. It is even more appropriate that Israel be called his own and gain the glory that goes with it, both because of the election of the holy fathers and because Israel is called the beginning and firstborn of the children of God. God says to Moses somewhere, "Israel is my firstborn son."[280] And again, referring to Israel as one and chosen for himself, he was accustomed to call Israel his own people, saying to Pharaoh, the ruler of Egypt, "Let my people go."[281] A passage from the books of Moses also shows that Israel belongs to God as his own. "When the Most High," he says, "divided the nations, as he scattered the children of Adam, he established the boundaries of the nations according to the number of the angels **[132]** of God. And his people Jacob became the Lord's portion, Israel the allotment of his inheritance."[282] He visited Israel as his own lot and portion, saying, "I was sent only to the lost sheep of the house of Israel."[283] And when he was not received, he transferred

[276]"Theology" here refers not to all articles of doctrine but specifically to discourse about the divine nature. *Oikonomia* is the word Cyril uses to describe the incarnation. [277]Ps 49:12 (Ps 48:13 LXX). [278]Gal 3:24. [279]See Rom 11:22. [280]Ex 4:22. [281]Ex 8:1 (Ex 7:26 LXX). [282]Deut 32:8-9. [283]Mt 15:24.

the grace to the Gentiles. The world, which did not know him in the beginning, was enlightened through repentance and faith, but Israel ran back into the darkness out of which it had come. Therefore, the Savior also said, "I came into this world for judgment so that those who do not see may see, and those who do see may become blind."[284]

1:12 But to all who received him, who believed in his name, he gave power to become children of God.

This judgment is truly just and worthy of God. The firstborn Israel is cast out because it did not want to remain God's own, nor did it receive God's Son when he dwelt among his own. It rejected the bestower of nobility and drove away the giver of grace. But the Gentiles received him by faith. Therefore, it is reasonable that Israel will receive the wages of its senselessness. It will grieve over the loss of good things and receive the bitter fruit of its own foolishness, being stripped of sonship. But the Gentiles will revel in the blessings that come from faith. They will find the bright rewards of obedience, and they will be transplanted into Israel's place. They will be cut off from their natural wild olive tree and be grafted contrary to nature into the good olive tree.[285] Israel will hear, "Woe to you, [133] sinful nation, people full of sin, wicked seed, lawless children. You forsook the Lord and provoked the Holy One of Israel."[286] But one of Christ's disciples will say to the Gentiles, "You are a chosen race, a royal priesthood, a holy nation, God's own people, in order that you may proclaim the mighty acts of him who calls you out of darkness into his marvelous light."[287] When they received the Son through faith, they received the power to be ranked among the children of God.

The Son, by his authority, gives what belongs to him alone by nature and sets it forth as a common possession, making this a sort of image of the love he has for humanity and for the world. We who bore the image of the earthly man could not escape corruption unless the call to sonship placed in us the splendor of the image of the heavenly man.[288] We became participants in him through the Spirit. We were sealed into his likeness, and we ascend to the archetypal form of the image according to which Holy Scripture says we were also made. Once we recover the ancient beauty of our nature in this way and are refashioned in relation to the divine nature, we will be superior to the evils that befell us because of transgression. Therefore, we rise up to an honor above our nature because of Christ.

However, we will not be sons of God unchangeably like he is, but we will be sons of God in relation to him by the grace of imitation. He is the true Son existing from the Father, but we are adopted because of his love for humanity, and we receive as a share in grace the words "I said, 'You are gods, and you are all sons of the Most High.'"[289] The created and servile creation is called to glories above its nature by the mere nod and will of the Father. But the Son and God and [134] Lord will not acquire being God and Son by the will of God the Father or only because the Father wants it that way, but he shines forth from the very substance of the Father, and he possesses the good of that substance by nature. The Son is recognized to be the true Son, and he is proven so by comparison with us. Being something by nature is different from being something by adoption, and being something truly is different from being something by imitation. We are called sons by adoption and by imitation. Therefore, he is Son by nature and in truth. We who are made sons too are compared with him. We enjoy the good that comes by grace rather than the honors that come by nature.

[284]Jn 9:39. [285]Rom 11:24. [286]Is 1:4. [287]1 Pet 2:9. [288]1 Cor 15:49. [289]Ps 82:6 (Ps 81:6 LXX).

1:13 Those who were born not from blood, nor from the will of the flesh, nor from the will of a husband, but born of God.

Those who are called by faith in Christ to God's sonship, he says, have put off the poverty of their own nature. The one who honors them glorifies them by grace, as by a bright robe, and they ascend to an honor beyond their nature. They are no longer called children of the flesh, but rather offspring of God by adoption. Notice what care the blessed Evangelist took in his discussion. Since he was about to say that believers are born of God, he has to devise a safeguard for us. Otherwise, someone might think that believers spring from the nature of God the Father in truth and reach an unchangeable likeness with the Only Begotten. Or they might think that the words "from the womb before the dawn I begat you"[290] apply in a looser sense also to him. That would drag him down to the nature of created beings since he too is said to be begotten of God. **[135]** First he says that the natural Son gave them power to become children of God, thereby introducing the idea of adoption and grace. Then he goes on without danger to say, "They were born of God." This is to show the magnitude of his grace toward them since he gathers, as it were, what is alien to God the Father into a natural kinship and raises what is servile to lordly nobility because of his fervent love toward it.

Perhaps someone might say, "What then do believers in Christ have that is greater or more special compared with Israel since it too is said to be born of God according to the statement, 'I begat and raised sons, but they rejected me'?"[291] I think one must reply to this by saying first that "the law has a shadow of the good things to come, not the image itself of the realities."[292] He did not give this to the Israelites to possess in truth, but it was written for them in the form of a type and a sketch "until the time of restoration,"[293] as it is written. At that time, he will reveal those who call on God the Father with more fitting and truer worship because the Spirit of the Only Begotten dwells in them. The former had the "Spirit of slavery to fear," the latter "the Spirit of sonship" for freedom "in whom we cry, 'Abba, Father.'"[294] Therefore, the people who were going to ascend to sonship through faith in Christ were described ahead of time in Israel in shadows, just as we of course understand circumcision in the Spirit to be typified ahead of time in ancient days in Israel's flesh. In sum, everything that we have, they had in type.

In addition, we say that Israel was called to sonship in type through the mediator Moses. Therefore, **[136]** they were also baptized into him, as Paul says, "in the cloud and in the sea."[295] They were taken from idolatry to the law of slavery when the angel administered the commandment to them in writing.[296] But those who rise to divine sonship through faith in Christ are baptized not into anything originate but into the holy Trinity itself through the Word who is the mediator. He joins what is human to himself through the flesh that was united to him, and he is joined by nature to the Father since he is by nature God. In this way, the slaves ascend to sonship through participation in the true Son since they are called and so to speak raised to the honor that is in the Son by nature. Therefore, we who received the new birth through the Spirit by faith are called born of God, and that is what we are.

Since some recklessly dare to lie about the Holy Spirit just as they lie about the Only Begotten, saying that he is an originate creature and completely removing him from consubstantiality with God the Father, come let us marshal once again the discourse on the

[290]Ps 110:3 (Ps 109:3 LXX). [291]Is 1:2. [292]Heb 10:1. [293]Heb 9:10. [294]Rom 8:15. [295]1 Cor 10:2. [296]Gal 3:19.

right faith against their unbridled tongues and beget the material for aiding ourselves and our readers. My friends, if God's own Spirit—who, because he is God's own, exists essentially in God—is neither God by nature nor from God but is another besides him and is of the same nature as created beings, how are we who are born through him called "born of God"? Either we will say that the Evangelist is certainly lying or, if he is telling the truth and it is so and not otherwise, the Spirit will be God and from God by nature. When we are considered worthy to participate in him through faith in Christ, we are made sharers in the divine nature[297] and are called "born of God." Therefore, we are called gods not only because we **[137]** fly up to glory beyond ourselves by grace but also because we have God now dwelling and abiding in us, according to the statement in the prophet, "I will dwell in them and walk in them."[298]

Let those who are so full of ignorance tell us how we who have the Spirit dwelling in us are the temple of God, as Paul says,[299] if he is not God by nature? If he is an originate creature, why then, when we defile the body in which the Spirit dwells—the Spirit who possesses the entire natural property of God the Father and likewise of the Only Begotten—does God destroy us on the grounds that we are destroying the temple of God? How will the Savior be telling the truth when he says, "Those who love me will keep my word, and my Father will love them, and we will come to them and make our home with them"[300] and dwell in them? Though the Spirit is the one who dwells in us, we believe that through him, we also have the Father and the Son at the same time, just as John himself said again somewhere in his epistles: "By this we know that we abide in him and he in us, because he has given us of his Spirit."[301] How will he be called the Spirit of God at all if he is not from him and in him by nature and is therefore God? After all, if he is originate, as they say, and he is still the Spirit of God, there is nothing to prevent other creatures from being called Spirits of God. This condition could potentially spread to other creatures, if it is at all possible for an originate nature to be the Spirit of God.

It would be quite appropriate to go into a long discourse about these matters and to meditate further on them to overturn the foolishness of the unholy heretics. But since we have already discussed the Holy Spirit sufficiently in the book on the holy Trinity,[302] **[138]** we will refrain from speaking at length here.

1:14 And the Word became flesh.

With these words he has now entered into an explicit discussion of the incarnation. He clearly explains that the Only Begotten has become and is called Son of Man, for this and nothing else is what it means to say that the Word became flesh. It is as if he said more plainly, "The Word became a human being." And when he says this, he is introducing to us nothing strange or unexpected. Holy Scripture often calls the whole creature by the name of the flesh alone, as in the passage in the prophet Joel, "I will pour out my Spirit on all flesh."[303] Surely we will not suppose that the prophet said the divine Spirit would be supplied only to soulless human flesh.[304] That would be ridiculous. But he takes the part for the whole and refers to humanity with the word *flesh*. It must be understood this way and not otherwise. I must, I think, explain why.

A human being is an animal that is both rational and composite, of a soul, that is, and this perishable earthly flesh. When humanity was made and brought into being by God, it did not have incorruptibility or indestructibil-

[297]2 Pet 1:4. [298]2 Cor 6:16; Lev 26:12. [299]1 Cor 3:16. [300]Jn 14:23. [301]1 Jn 4:13. [302]*De trinitate ad Herm.* dial. 7, 63ff. (G. M. Durand, *Cyrille d'Alexandrie Dialogues sur la Trinité*, vol. 3, Sources Chretiennes 246 [Paris: Les Éditions du Cerf, 1978], 140ff.). [303]Joel 2:28 (Joel 3:1 LXX). [304]As Apollinaris taught.

ity from its own nature. These belong essentially to God alone. It was sealed by the Spirit of life, and by its relation to the divine, it gained the good that is above its nature. "He breathed into his face," it says, "the breath of life; and the man became a living soul."[305] **[139]** But when he was punished because of his transgression, he justly heard, "Earth you are, and to earth you will depart,"[306] and in so hearing he was stripped of grace. The breath of life, that is, the Spirit of him who says, "I am the life," departed from the earthly flesh, and the living being fell into death through the flesh alone. The soul was preserved in immortality since the words "earth you are, and to earth you will depart" were addressed only to the flesh. That in us which was in the most danger had to be vigorously restored and called back to incorruption by being intertwined once again with life by nature. That which suffered the evil had to procure the release from evil. The statement, "Earth you are, and to earth you will depart," had to give way since the body that fell was united ineffably with the Word who gives life to all things.

The flesh, when it became his, had to participate in the immortality that comes from him. Fire can put the visible manifestation of its natural activity into wood[307] and practically transform the wood—in which it resides by participation—into itself. It would be downright absurd if fire could do this, but the Word of God, who is over all, is thought not to bestow his own good activity—that is, life—to the flesh. I think this is the reason why the holy Evangelist says that the Word of God became "flesh," indicating the whole creature by the part that is affected. That way, one can see the wound and the medicine at the same time, the patient and the physician, that which fell into death and the one who raised it to life, that which is overcome by corruption and the one who drives corruption away, that which is seized by death and the one who is stronger than death, that which was deprived of life **[140]** and the one who supplies life.

He does not say that the Word came into flesh but that the Word became flesh, so that you do not assume that he came to it temporarily the way he came to the prophets or the other saints, but he truly "became flesh," that is, a human being, as we just said. Therefore, God is both in and with the flesh by nature, on the grounds that he has it as his own. And he is worshiped in and with it, on the grounds that he is considered something else besides it, as the passage in the prophet Isaiah says: "People of stature will come to you, and they will be your slaves. They will follow you bound in fetters. They will worship you and pray to you since God is in you, and there is no God besides you."[308] Notice that they say God is in him, not separating the flesh from the Word. Furthermore, they insist that there is no other God besides him, uniting the Word to that which he carries as his very own, that is, the temple of the virgin. For there is one Christ of both.

And dwelt in us.

The Evangelist gives us a helpful elaboration of what he said, and he brings the meaning of his statement into sharper focus. His statement was that the Word of God became flesh. In order that no one out of great ignorance might suppose that the Word departed from his own nature and was changed into flesh and suffered—which was impossible because the divine, by its mode of being, is far removed from all alteration and from changing into something else—the Evangelist immediately adds the well-crafted phrase "and dwelt in us." That way, when you realize that two things are signified, the dweller and that in which he dwells, you will not think that he turned into flesh, **[141]** but rather that he "dwelt" in flesh, using as his own

[305]Gen 2:7. [306]Gen 3:19. [307]Fire can make wood glow red-hot. [308]Is 45:14.

body the temple that came from the holy virgin. "For in him the whole fullness of the deity dwelt bodily,"[309] as Paul says.

He also reveals another profound mystery to us when he affirms for our benefit that the Word "dwelt in us": We were all in Christ, and the shared properties of our human nature were taken up into his person. That is why he is called the last Adam. He gives all the riches of his tranquility and glory to our common nature, just as the first Adam gave corruption and shame. Therefore, the Word "dwelt in" all people through the one man so that when the one man "was designated Son of God in power according to the Spirit of holiness,"[310] this honor might extend to all humanity. In this way, because of one of us, the words "I said you are gods, and you are all sons of the Most High"[311] might come to us as well. Therefore, the slave is truly freed in Christ and ascends into mystical unity with the one who bore the form of a slave,[312] while at the same time Christ is in us in the sense that we are like him because of our kinship with his flesh. Why, after all, does he "take on not the nature of angels, but the seed of Abraham; therefore, he had to be like his brothers in every way"[313] and truly become human? Is it not therefore perfectly clear to all that he came down into that which was in slavery, not to do anything for himself but to give himself to us "that by his poverty, we might become rich"[314] and that we might ascend by likeness with him to his own exceptional dignity and be shown to be gods and children of God through faith? He who is by nature Son and God "dwelt in us." **[142]** Therefore, in his Spirit "we cry Abba! Father!"[315] The Word dwells in the one temple, taken from us and for us, as he dwells in all people, so that having everyone in himself he might reconcile everyone in one body with the Father,[316] as Paul says.

And we saw his glory, the glory as of the Only Begotten of the Father, full of grace and truth.
He says that the Word became flesh, that is, a human being, and that he came down into kinship with slaves and creatures, but even so he preserves his divine dignity intact and shows once again that he is full of the Father's attributes, which are in him. The divine nature is truly stable in itself. It cannot experience a change into something else, but it is always the same, and it stands firm in its own superiority. Although the Evangelist says that the Word became flesh, he insists that he is not overcome by the weakness of the flesh and that he did not fall away from his primeval power and glory when he clothed himself with our weak and most inglorious body. For we saw "his glory," he says, surpassing that of others. It is the kind of glory that one might confess is appropriate for the only begotten Son of God the Father because "he was full of grace and truth." If one looks at the choir of the saints and measures the incredible achievements of each, one will with good reason marvel and rejoice over the good qualities that are in each one and certainly say that they are filled with the glory from God. **[143]** But the theologians and witnesses say that they have seen the glory and grace of the Only Begotten, not competing with those of others but far surpassing them and ascending to incomparable superiority. His grace has no measure, as if someone else gave it to him, but it is true and perfect in the perfect one, that is, not imported or brought in from the outside as an addition, but it is in him essentially. It is the fruit of the Father's natural quality, which passes over to the Son who is from him.

If any want to put the foregoing to the test with further consideration, let them look for themselves at the incredible deeds done by each one of the saints and those done by Christ our Savior, and they will find the difference to

[309]Col 2:9. [310]Rom 1:4. [311]Ps 82:6 (Ps 81:6 LXX). [312]Phil 2:7. [313]Heb 2:16-17. [314]2 Cor 8:9. [315]Rom 8:15. [316]Eph 2:16, 18.

be as great as we have already said. In addition, there is this as well: they are like the legitimate servants of the house, but he is "like the Son over his house."[317] Also, Holy Scripture says concerning the Only Begotten, "Blessed is he who comes in the name of the Lord."[318] But concerning the saints, it says that God the Father "sent to you all my servants the prophets."[319] They borrowed power from above, but he, as the Lord of powers, says, "If I am not doing the works of my Father, do not believe in me. But if I do them, even though you do not believe in me, believe my works."[320] If the Only Begotten is seen by the works themselves to be as great in power as the Father, he will be extolled proportionately with equal praise since he does equal works. Even though he is in the flesh, he will certainly surpass those who are called to be his brothers the same extent that the one who is God by nature exceeds humanity, and the true Son exceeds those who are sons by adoption.

But since it is written by the blessed Luke, "Jesus advanced in wisdom and grace,"[321] we must note here that **[144]** the Spirit bearer said that the Son has glory "full of grace." To where, then, will that which is full advance? Or what possible addition will he receive since nothing is greater than him? Therefore, he is said to advance not insofar as he is the Word and God but because his works kept showing him to be ever more marvelous and gracious to those who beheld him. It is truer to say that the disposition of those who marveled at him advanced than to say that he who is perfect as God advanced toward grace. Even though this discussion is a digression, these matters are helpful and we should discuss them.

1:15 John testified about him and cried out,

Once again, the supremely wise Evangelist follows the thread of his thoughts and makes the next section balance what came before as it should. When he said concerning the Son of God, "We saw his glory, the glory as of the Only Begotten of the Father,"[322] to make it clear that he is not the only one saying this (since "we saw" is not fitting for one person), he joins with himself the witness of the same name who has one and the same devotion as he does. "I myself bear witness," he says, "for I have seen what I spoke of, and the Baptist likewise bears witness"—an august pair of Spirit bearers and a worthy pair of men nourished together on the truth and not knowing how to lie.

See how very forceful he made his explanation. Not only does he say, "John testified about him," but he usefully adds, "and cried out." He takes his proof for this word from the phrase "a voice of one crying in the wilderness,"[323] and he does this exceedingly well. Some of the opponents could have said, When did the Baptist testify about the Only Begotten? With whom did he communicate about these matters? **[145]** Therefore, he says "he cried out," that is, he does not speak in a corner, nor does he testify quietly in a whisper. You may hear him crying louder than a trumpet. And you are not the only one to hear these things, I say. The message is spread abroad to all. The herald is shining bright. The voice is distinct. The forerunner is not unknown; he is great.

This was he of whom I said, "He who comes after me has come before me, for he was before me."

After he names the witness with the same mind and the same name as he has and shows that this witness used a loud voice in the service of his preaching, he usefully brings up the manner of the witness as well. This statement encompasses the entire question.

[317]Heb 3:6. [318]Ps 118:26 (Ps 117:26 LXX). [319]Jer 7:25. [320]Jn 10:37-38. [321]Lk 2:52. [322]Jn 1:14. [323]Is 40:3.

What then do we find this John crying out about the Only Begotten? "He who comes after me has come before me, for he was before me." The saying is profound, and it demands a great deal of investigation.

The overused interpretation that seems obvious to most people goes something like this. When it comes to the time of his birth with the flesh, the Baptist came before the Savior. Emmanuel clearly followed and came after by six whole months, as the blessed Luke relates. Some think that John says this so that the statement might be understood in this way: "He who comes after me *in age* has come before me." But one with sharper sight can look at the divine words and see, in the first place, how this interpretation leads us to futile thoughts and takes us far away from the matter we must investigate. The holy Baptist was taken as a witness not to show that Christ's time of birth is later and then again earlier **[146]** but to be a fellow witness of "his glory, the glory as of the Only Begotten of the Father, full and grace and truth."[324]

What meaning could one attach to such unsuitable explanations? How could anyone explain this clearly to us if they take the passage under investigation, that is, "He who comes after me has come before me," to refer to a quantity of time? Let us agree and grant that the Lord comes after the Baptist since he was born second when it comes to the time of his flesh. How will he also come "before" him, I mean in time? After all, the due order and progression of the statement bring us to this understanding by analogy with the foregoing. But I think it is clear to everyone that this is not possible. That which comes after something in time would never precede what comes before. Therefore, it is absolutely ignorant and utterly unconvincing to think that the holy Baptist was referring to the time of the flesh when he said, "He who comes after me has come before me." But we will understand this statement in accordance with what preceded it, and we will believe that it means something like the following. The blessed Baptist gracefully raises the discourse from ordinary language to its spiritual meaning. From a kind of image of our affairs, he proceeds to an explanation of subtler thoughts.

Things which always precede by nature are normally considered more glorious than things which are said to follow, and those that follow yield to those that lead. For example, one who is a skilled brass worker, carpenter or weaver leads, so to speak, and has superiority over the one who is considered to follow in training and who is on the way to complete knowledge. But when such a student **[147]** surpasses the skill of the teacher, leaves that skill behind and accomplishes something greater, I assume the one who is overcome will say, not unskillfully, of the student who overcame, "He who comes after me has come before me."

If you transfer the meaning of this example, using the same pattern, to our savior Christ and to the holy Baptist, you will understand it correctly. Take the account of each from the beginning. Everyone kept marveling at the Baptist. He was making many disciples, and a great crowd of people always surrounded him to be baptized. But Christ, though he was greater, was unknown. They did not know that he was true God. Since he was unknown while the Baptist was admired, he seemed in a way to be inferior to the Baptist. He came a little "after" the one who still had greater honor and glory in the eyes of the people. But "he who comes after has come before," since he is shown to be greater and superior to John. The one was now revealed to be God through his works. The other is finally found to come "after" since he does not surpass the measure of human nature.

Therefore, the blessed Baptist said darkly,

[324]Jn 1:14.

"He who comes after me has come before me," instead of, "He who was once inferior to me in honor has been shown more glorious than me, and he surpasses by incomparable superiority the measure that belongs to and is fitting for me." If we understand the statement this way, we will find him to be a witness of the glory of the Only Begotten and not a random expositor of useless subjects. After all, when the Baptist says that Christ is greater than he is, even though he has a great reputation for holiness, what is he doing but witnessing to Christ's exceptional glory?

"Because he was before me." After he said, "He has come before me," he necessarily adds, "because he was before me," ascribing the most ancient glory to Christ and **[148]** maintaining that his superiority over all things did not accrue to him in time but is in him from the beginning since he is God by nature. He says, "He was before me," instead of, "He was always and in every way better and more glorious." By comparing Christ with one originate man, the Baptist casts his vote against all originate beings in favor of the one who is above all things. After all, we will not see the great and glorious honor of the Son only in the fact that he surpasses the glory of John but in the fact that he exceeds all originate substance.

1:16 From his fullness we have all received.

With these words, the Evangelist accepts the true testimony of the Baptist and gives his own clear indication of our Savior's superiority. He shows that, in his essence, he is greater than everything originate both in glory itself, which is what we are specifically addressing now, and in the glorious list of all the other good attributes. The Baptist speaks most excellently and truly, says the Evangelist, when he declares concerning the Only Begotten, "He was before me," that is, far greater and better. For "we all" too who are enrolled in the choir of the saints have enjoyed the great riches of his own good, and human nature is exalted by his superiority rather than its own when it is found to have anything admirable. From "the fullness" of the Son, as from an ever-flowing spring, the gift of divine graces gushes forth to each soul that is shown worthy to receive it. If the Son gives from his natural "fullness," then the creature receives. How could one deny that he has a glory unlike the glory of others but **[149]** his glory is fitting for the Only Begotten whose superiority over everything is a fruit of his own nature and whose supremacy is a dignity that comes from his Father's attribute? I think that the supremely wise Paul too made a distinction in the nature of all things. He was moved by this to a true understanding, and so he addressed the creature, saying, "What do you have that you did not receive?"[325] Not only being but also well-being is given by God to creation. Creation has nothing of its own but is rich only through the generosity of the giver. We must note once again that he says the Son is full, that is, completely perfect in all things. He is so far from any lack that he can supply all things without diminishing himself, while preserving the greatness of his superiority so it is always the same.

1:17 And grace in place of grace, because the law was given through Moses, but grace and truth came through Jesus Christ.

After saying that the glory of the Only Begotten shines brighter than all human glory, and after ascribing to him great holiness which incomparably surpasses the saints, he hastens to prove the point from those who have reached the heights of virtue. So the Savior says of John, "Truly, truly, I say to you, among

[325] 1 Cor 4:7.

those born of women, no one has arisen greater than John the Baptist."[326] But he already set aside this man who is so great and admirable, as John the Baptist himself says, crying out with a loud voice, "He who comes after me has come before me, for he was before me."[327] If John's glory was inferior and yielded to the Only Begotten, how could we come to any other conclusion than that none of the other saints rise to the same **[150]** measure as Christ the Savior when it comes to the glory that is seen in the brightness of their deeds? The saints who lived at the time of the advent were not able to surpass John's virtue, nor did they rise above his stature. Along with him, they will yield the victory to Christ. This is especially so if the blessed Baptist, who possesses the pinnacle of goodness and has left no way for others to surpass him, receives the judgment of inferiority not through the voice of another but has himself sealed the case against him. As a saint, he speaks the truth.

Since Emmanuel had to be shown greater and better than the saints of old as well, the blessed Evangelist must first come to the teacher Moses about whom God said, "I know you above all, and you have found favor with me."[328] We also know from this passage that he is known by God above all: "When a prophet of the Lord arises among you," he says, "I will be known to him in visions, and I will speak to him in sleep. Not so my servant Moses. He is faithful in my entire house. I will speak to him face to face clearly, and not in riddles."[329] Although the supremely wise Moses has such great superiority over the saints of old, the Evangelist shows the Only Begotten to be greater and more glorious in every way so that he may clearly have "first place in all things," as Paul says.[330] Therefore, he says, "And grace in place of grace, because the law was given through Moses, but grace and truth came through Jesus Christ."[331] I, at least, think that the blessed Evangelist wanted to indicate this sort of thing. The great Baptist made a true confession about the Only Begotten, he says, when he announced explicitly, **[151]** "He who comes after me has come before me, for he was before me,"[332] and, "From his fullness we have all received."[333] Let no one think that the Only Begotten surpassed John or the other saints who lived at the time of the advent but was less in glory than the saints of old who were bright with holiness in the time before the advent. One will see him far outstripping the measure of Moses, the Evangelist says, even though Moses possesses greater holiness than those other saints. For the lawgiver clearly maintained that the Lord knew him above all. John, then, was proven by his own words to trail behind the glory of Christ. He comes behind his brightness. Nothing should be sought from him, or that would hinder the search for the truth.

Where then shall we find that the teacher Moses too falls short of the glory of the Lord? Let the one who loves knowledge, he says, examine closely the "grace" of the gospel given to us by the Savior "in place of the grace" of the law that was through Moses. Then one will indeed see that the Son is as much superior to Moses as the way of life the Son decrees is better than the one decreed by the law. For that matter, what he introduces is better than anything introduced by Moses. "For the law," he says, "was given through Moses, but grace and truth came through Jesus Christ."[334]

What then is the difference between the "law" and the "grace" that is through the Savior? Again, the one who is devoted to investigation and is a friend of honest effort will see it. But we will say a few words rather than many since we believe that there is a great number of ideas in these words and it is a bit tedious. The law then condemned the world because through it, God "imprisoned all things under

[326]Mt 11:11. [327]Jn 1:15. [328]Ex 33:12. [329]Num 12:6-8. [330]Col 1:18. [331]Jn 1:17. [332]Jn 1:15. [333]Jn 1:16. [334]Jn 1:17.

sin," as Paul [152] says.[335] It continually showed us to be deserving of punishment. But the Savior frees the world instead. He did not come "to judge the world, but to save the world."[336] The law too used to give "grace" to humanity by drawing the deceived away from the worship of idols and calling them to a knowledge of God. In addition, it pointed out evil and taught good—not perfectly, but profitably nevertheless, the way a schoolmaster does.[337] But the "truth and grace" through the Only Begotten does not introduce the good to us in types, nor does it make shadowy sketches of what is profitable, but with bright and purest pronouncements it leads us by the hand to perfect knowledge of the faith. The law kept giving a "spirit of slavery to fear," but Christ gives a "spirit of adoption" for freedom.[338] Likewise, the law introduces the circumcision of the flesh, which is nothing. "For circumcision is nothing," as Paul writes to certain people.[339] But our Lord Jesus Christ introduces circumcision of the spirit and heart through faith.[340] The law baptizes the defiled in mere water, but the Savior baptizes "in the Holy Spirit and fire."[341] The law introduces the tabernacle as a copy of the true sanctuary, but the Savior raises us up to heaven itself and leads us into the truer tabernacle "which the Lord pitched, and not a human being."[342] It is not difficult to heap up other proofs for what has been said, but we should respect our limits.

Yet we cannot help saying the following for the reader's benefit. The blessed Paul answered the question in a few words. He said, concerning the law and the grace of the Savior, "If there was glory in the ministry of condemnation, much more does the ministry of righteousness abound in glory!"[343] He says that the command through Moses was the ministry of condemnation, but he calls the grace from the Savior the ministry of righteousness. [153] To this grace he grants surpassing glory since, as the Spirit bearer, he most carefully examines the nature of things.

Since the condemning law was given through Moses but the justifying grace came through the Only Begotten, how is the one who issued better decrees, he says, not greater in glory? The psalmist then is telling the truth when he cries out in the Spirit that our Lord Jesus Christ is superior to the whole illustrious multitude of the saints. "Who," he says, "in the clouds will be equal to the Lord, or who among the children of God will be like the Lord?"[344] The spiritual clouds, that is, the holy prophets, will yield the victory to Christ. They know that they must not contend for equal honor with him since the one who is known by God above all, that is, Moses, is relegated to second place. Those who are called children of God at the time of the advent will not be exactly like the one who is Son by nature, but they will acknowledge their limits, especially since the holy Baptist says that he is far behind, and the one who knows hearts says of him, "Among those born of women, no one has arisen greater than John the Baptist."[345] Therefore, the blessed Evangelist is telling the truth when he says that he has seen "his glory, the glory as of the Only Begotten of the Father," that is, the glory which is appropriate to the only begotten Son of the Father, and not to those called to be his brothers and sisters, of whom he is the firstborn. [154]

Chapter Ten

The Only Begotten alone is by nature the Son of the Father because he is from him and in him.

1:18 No one has ever seen God. The only begotten God who is in the bosom of the Father has made him known.

[335]Gal 3:22. [336]Jn 12:47. [337]See Gal 3:24. [338]Rom 8:15. [339]1 Cor 7:19. [340]Rom 2:29. [341]Mt 3:11. [342]Heb 9:24; 8:2. [343]2 Cor 3:9. [344]Ps 89:6 (Ps 88:7 LXX). [345]Mt 11:11.

Note once again the vigilance of the Spirit bearer in these matters. He was not unaware that some would surely question more pointedly what he said about the Only Begotten and say, You said, sir, that you have seen "his glory, the glory as of the Only Begotten of the Father."[346] After that, when you had to clarify for us the explanation of these matters and express an idea that is extraordinary and fitting for God, you proved his superiority over Moses and over the stature of John on the grounds that no one could see his glory in any other way. Yet the blessed prophet Isaiah says, "I saw the Lord of hosts sitting on a throne, high and lifted up, and the house was filled with his glory. And seraphim stood around him, each with six wings. Each one had six wings, and with two they covered their face, with two they covered their feet, and with two they flew. And one cried out to **[155]** the other and said, 'Holy, holy, holy, is the Lord of hosts; the whole earth is full of his glory.'"[347] Again, Ezekiel distinctly cried out to us that he saw cherubim who had a firmament like sapphire hanging over their heads, and he saw the Lord of hosts on his throne. He says the following about this. "And behold, there was a voice from the firmament which was over their heads. And from above the firmament which was over their heads, there was something that looked like sapphire with the likeness of a throne on it. And on the likeness of the throne was a likeness in the form of a man above. And I saw what looked like amber from what appeared to be his waist up. And from what appeared to be his waist down, I saw what looked like fire, and its radiance surrounded him. As the appearance of a rainbow in the clouds on a rainy day, so was the appearance of the radiance around him. This is the appearance of the likeness of the glory of the Lord."[348]

Therefore, since it was not unlikely that some of the more unlearned people would say such things to us, the blessed Evangelist hastens to cut off their attempts, saying forcefully, "No one has ever seen God." For "the Only Begotten, who is in the bosom of God the Father," is himself God. He explained this to us when he said with utmost clarity to the teacher Moses that no one may "see my face and live."[349] And to his own disciples at one point he said, "No one has seen the Father except the one who is from God. He has seen the Father."[350] The Father is visible to the natural Son alone and not to anything else that exists. Therefore, one should conclude that the divine nature sees and is seen in a way that is fitting to God.

Nevertheless, the word of the holy prophets is by no means lying when they cry out that they have seen the Lord **[156]** of hosts[351] because they are not claiming to have seen the nature of God in its very substance. No, they themselves cry out distinctly, "This is the appearance of the likeness of the glory of the Lord."[352] The portrayal of the divine glory was formed obscurely out of material from our experience. More precisely, it was a likeness that conveys God-befitting thoughts like a picture, while the truth of these matters surpasses mind and speech.

Therefore, the supremely wise Evangelist does exceedingly well when he says, "And we saw his glory, the glory as of the Only Begotten of the Father, full of grace and truth."[353] He introduces the proof of this statement from his superiority over all things. Just as the power of the creator of all is seen "proportionately from the beauty of created things,"[354] and "the heavens declare without speech the glory of God, and the firmament proclaims the work of his hands,"[355] so also the Only Begotten will be shown, in turn, to be brighter and greater in glory. As God, he surpasses the perception

[346]Jn 1:14. [347]Is 6:1-3. [348]Ezek 1:25-28. [349]Ex 33:20. [350]Jn 6:46. [351]Is 6:1. [352]Ezek 1:28. [353]Jn 1:14. [354]Wis 13:5. [355]Ps 19:1 (Ps 18:2 LXX).

that belongs to the power of the eye. Where he surpasses creation, there he is understood to be above it and is glorified as such. I think the sense of the passage labors to give birth to this idea and no other. We must note once again that he calls the Son the "only begotten God" and says that he is "in the bosom of the Father" to show once more that the Son is not of the same nature as creation and that he has his own existence from the Father and in the Father. After all, if he is really the "only begotten God," how can he not be different in nature from those who are gods and sons by adoption? The Only Begotten cannot be understood as one among many brothers. He is the only one from the Father. Although, as Paul says, there are many in heaven and on earth who are or **[157]** are called gods, the Son is the "only begotten God," that is, he is excluded from the others, and he is not classified among those who are gods by grace. Rather, he is the true God with the Father. Paul joins them together for us when he says, "For us there is one God, the Father from whom all things are, and one Lord Jesus Christ through whom all things are."[356] Since the Father is one God by nature, the Word who is from him and in him will not remain outside of being God. He is distinguished by the characteristic of the one who begat him, and he ascends in his essence to equal dignity because he is by nature God.

He says that he is in the "bosom of the Father," of course, so you may know that he is in him and of him, as it says in the Psalms, "From the womb before the dawn I begat you."[357] The Son is genuinely from the Father. So he puts "from the womb" here out of a kind of likeness to our situation, since what is born of human beings comes forth from the womb. In the same way, when he says "in the bosom," it is almost as if he wants to show the Son in the Father's womb. This womb begat him, showing him forth in a brilliance that is fitting for God and in a certain ineffable procession into his own hypostasis. However, this womb also has him in it since the divine offspring did not come from the Father by a bodily separation or division. Indeed, the Son says somewhere that he is in the Father, but he also has the Father in himself.[358] The Father's own substance passes over essentially to the Son and reveals the Father in him, yet the Father has the Son in himself. The Son is rooted in him by an unchanging sameness of substance and grows, as it were, from him. This takes place, however, not by division or separation in space but by the Son always being in and with him. In this way, then, we will piously understand the Son to be "in the bosom of the Father," not as some who are accustomed to fight against God have taken it **[158]** "whose condemnation is just."[359] "They pervert all that is right," as the prophet says.[360] They impair the hearing of the simple and "sin heedlessly against members of the family for whom Christ died."[361]

We must also say what it is that they think, say and try to teach others. When the holy Evangelist says that the Son is "in the bosom of the Father," and when the children of the church think in the right way and maintain on this basis that he is from the Father and in the Father, and when they quite reasonably hold that the genuine begetting must be preserved from those who love to fight, then those who are drunk with all ignorance immediately laugh at them and dare to say, Your opinion, sirs, is nonsense. Your thought about God is not well-informed because, when it says that the Son is "in the bosom of the Father," you think he is altogether of his substance, and you ignorantly suppose that he is a fruit of the unoriginate nature. Have you not heard, they say, when Christ himself was talking about the rich man and Lazarus in the parables of

[356]1 Cor 8:6. [357]Ps 110:3 (Ps 109:3 LXX). [358]Jn 14:10. [359]Rom 3:8. [360]Mic 3:9. [361]1 Cor 8:12, 11.

the Gospels, that it came about that Lazarus died, "and he was carried by the angels to Abraham's bosom"?[362] Will you then claim, because Lazarus was "in Abraham's bosom," that he is from Abraham and in him by nature, or will you rightly refuse to say this and agree with us that "in the bosom" refers to love? Therefore, we say that the Son is "in the bosom" of God the Father instead of saying "in his love," as he himself says somewhere, "The Father loves the Son."[363]

When people who love to criticize hit us with these words, though they are fierce only in their railing, **[159]** we will deploy the correct account of the truth, and we will answer, We see, sirs, that "bosom" according to you means love since we just heard you say this. So since "God loved the world,"[364] as the Savior said, and "the Lord loves the gates of Zion,"[365] as the holy psalmist said, shall we without danger say that both the world and the gates of Zion are in the bosom of God the Father? And when he says to the teacher Moses, "Put your hand into your bosom," does he command him, tell me, to love his hand and not rather to keep it hidden? How then will we not provoke great laughter in these matters? Or rather, how will we not sin against the Father himself when we say that all things are in his bosom and make the unique good that belongs only to the Only Begotten common to the rest, so that the Son has no more than the creature?

Therefore, we will say goodbye to their foolishness and walk on the straight road of the consideration of the truth. When the Son is said to be in the bosom of the Father, we will understand him to be from him and in him. When we carefully chew over the meaning of the term, we will find it to be this and nothing else. "The only begotten God," he says, "who is in the bosom of the Father has made him known." When he says "only begotten" and "God," he immediately adds, "who is in the bosom of the Father," so that the Son may be understood to be from him and in him by nature. He says "bosom" instead of "substance" of the Father as from a corporeal example because visible things are in a way types of spiritual things, and things among us lead us by the hand to understand things above us. Corporeal objects are often taken as an image, and they convey to us the understanding of more subtle ideas, even if in their own time they are understood **[160]** the way they seem to be spoken. I am referring to what was said to Moses, "Put you hand into your bosom." And it will in no way hurt our argument to say that Lazarus was placed in Abraham's bosom, but it will support it and concur with our ideas. After all, Holy Scripture practically says this: After Lazarus died and ended his life with the body, "he was carried to Abraham's bosom," which means "he was numbered among the children of Abraham" since God said to him, "I have made you the father of many nations," as it is written about him somewhere: "I have made you the father of many nations."[366]

1:19-20 And this is the testimony of John, when the Jews sent priests and Levites from Jerusalem to ask him, "Who are you?" He confessed, he did not deny but confessed, "I am not the Christ."

The Evangelist recalls his words and hastens to explain to us more fully (which he does very well) what he had already said before in summary form. He had said, "There arose a man sent from God. His name was John. He came as a witness to testify concerning the light."[367] After this, he needs to introduce the manner of the testimony that comes from him. So he says, "When the leaders of the Jewish ranks prescribed by the law sent priests and Levites to him with instructions to ask him what he said about himself, then he confessed

[362]Lk 16:22. [363]Jn 3:35. [364]Jn 3:16. [365]Ps 87:2 (Ps 86:2 LXX). [366]Gen 17:5. [367]Jn 1:6-7.

very clearly, spurning all shame for the sake of the truth. He said, 'I **[161]** am not the Christ.' Therefore, I, the author of the book, did not lie when I said of him, 'He was not the light, but he came to testify about the light.'"

1:21 And they asked him, "What then? Are you Elijah?" He said, "I am not." "Are you the prophet?" He answered, "No."

The Evangelist stated, as an explanation, "He confessed, 'I am not the Christ.'" Now he tries to show how or in what manner the confession took place. And it seems to me that in so doing, he wants to expose the ignorance of the Jews. "Claiming to be wise, they became fools."[368] They are haughty in their knowledge of the law. They urge up and down the commandments given through Moses, and they claim that they study the words of the prophets in exacting detail. But by their foolish questions, they are convicted of being completely ignorant. For the teacher Moses, speaking in the office of prophet to reveal the Lord, proclaimed ahead of time to the children of Israel that "the Lord your God will raise up a prophet like me from your own people, and you will listen to him, just as you requested from the Lord your God at Horeb."[369] And the blessed Isaiah, introducing the forerunner to us, announced ahead of time, "A voice crying in the wilderness, 'Prepare the way of the Lord. Make straight his paths.'"[370] Third, in addition to these, the prophet Joel says concerning the Tishbite (who was Elijah), "Behold, I am sending Elijah the Tishbite to you who will turn the heart of the father to the son and the disobedient to the wisdom of the righteous, lest I come and smite the land utterly."[371]

Now there were three whose coming was announced: Christ, **[162]** John and Elijah. But the Jews expect more to arrive, so it is only appropriate that they hear, "You are wrong because you do not know the Scriptures."[372] After they ask the blessed Baptist and learn that he is not the Christ, they respond, "What then? Are you Elijah?" And when he says, "I am not," they should finally have asked about the forerunner since he was now the only one left. But they ignorantly return to Christ himself, who was revealed as a prophet through the law. See how they are ignorant of Moses when they say, "Are you the prophet?" And he answered, "No," because he was not the Christ as he already made clear.

1:22-23 "What do you say about yourself?" "I am the voice of one crying in the wilderness."

He harshly accuses them of knowing nothing, and he confirms the design or purpose entrusted to him by the prophetic witness. I have come, he says, to make no other announcement than that the expected one is finally at the door. In fact, the Lord is within the doors. Be prepared to go wherever he tells you. You have walked the way that came through Moses. Now take up the way that comes through Christ. This is the way that the choir of holy prophets kept announcing to you ahead of time.

A list of passages about the way of Christ.

Isaiah. "Come, let us go up to the mountain of the Lord and to the house of the God of Jacob. He will teach us his way, and we will walk in it."[373]

The same. "There will be there a completely pure way, and it will be called a holy way. **[163]** No lion will be there, nor will any dangerous wild beasts go up there. But the dispersed people will walk on it."[374]

The same. "I will give a beginning[375] to Zion, and I will exhort Jerusalem onto the way."[376]

[368]Rom 1:22. [369]Deut 18:15-16. [370]Is 40:3; Mt 3:3. [371]Mal 4:5-6 (Mal 3:22-23 LXX). Malachi says this, not Joel. [372]Mt 22:29. [373]Is 2:3. [374]Is 35:8-9. [375]Ἀρχή can mean "beginning" or "dominion." [376]Is 41:27.

The same. "And I will lead the blind on a way which they did not know, and I will make them walk on paths which they did not know."[377]

Jeremiah. "Stand in the ways and ask for the eternal paths of the Lord. See which is the good path, and walk on it. And you will find cleansing for your souls."[378]

What then is the good way that cleanses those who walk on it? Let Christ himself tell you: "I am the way."[379]

1:24 And they were sent from the Pharisees.

Those sent from the Jews were Levites. Some were in the priesthood. They were convicted of asking foolish questions. They thought that Christ was someone else besides the prophet spoken of by the law because after the holy Baptist clarified who he was, saying, "I am not the Christ," they said, "Are you the prophet?"[380] But look, the whole crowd of Pharisees is caught being wise in their own eyes rather than having an accurate knowledge of the divine sayings. "Why then do you baptize at all," they say, "if you are not the Christ or Elijah or the prophet?"[381] Once again it is clear that they bring forth no small madness when it comes to the Baptist. It seems they do not think that he is worthy to be put on the list of those who were expected. They suffer from the pretension that they grew up with, and they consider him to be of no account, even though he was announced ahead of time by the voice of the prophet. **[164]** When they hear, "I am the voice of one calling in the wilderness, 'Prepare the way of the Lord,'"[382] they do not accept the statement. They rebuke him without restraint, as it were, saying, There is nothing in you, sir, that is convincing, marvelous or great. Why do you baptize at all? Why do you who are nothing at all attempt something so great?

This is the custom of the unholy Pharisees. They disparage the one who is already here, and they pretend to honor the one who is coming. They want no one else to seem distinguished so they can gain constant honors from the Jews and obtain sources of revenue for themselves. They even killed the heir, saying, "Come, let us kill him and get his inheritance."[383]

1:26 "I baptize with water."

The blessed Baptist patiently bears with those who rebuke him. He very aptly turns the explanation about himself into the basis for saving proclamation. He is already teaching those sent by the Pharisees, even against their will, that the Christ is indeed within the doors. For I bring an introductory baptism, he says. I use water to free those who are defiled by sin in order to bring them to the beginning of repentance, and I teach people to ascend from the lower to the more perfect. This was to fulfill in deed what I was sent to preach: Prepare the way of the Lord. The giver of greater and most remarkable gifts, the supplier of every perfection in good,[384] "stands among you" as yet unrecognized because of the garment of the flesh. He so surpasses me, the Baptist, that I must consider myself not even in the rank of slave **[165]** in comparison with him. I think it is clear that "I am not worthy to untie the thong of his sandal."[385] By speaking the truth, he does something else that is beneficial. He persuades the proud Pharisee to be humble, and he introduces himself as an example.

"These things," he says, "happened in Bethabara beyond the Jordan,"[386] adding this too as a kind of sign of an accurate and painstaking record. We all by nature and custom, so to speak, when we narrate things that require it, mention also the places in which the events happened. **[167]**

[377]Is 42:16. [378]Jer 6:16. [379]Jn 14:6. [380]Jn 1:20-21. [381]Jn 1:25. [382]Jn 1:23; Mt 3:3. [383]Mt 21:38. [384]See Jas 1:17. [385]Jn 1:27. [386]Jn 1:28.

CHAPTERS IN BOOK 2

1. The Holy Spirit is in the Son not by participation or as something brought in from the outside but essentially and by nature; on the words "And John testified, 'I have seen the Spirit descending like a dove from heaven, and it remained on him.'"
2. The Son is not an originate being, but as God and from God, he is over all things; on the words "The one who comes from above is over all things."
3. The Son is God and from God by nature; on the words "The one who receives his testimony has set his seal that God is true."
4. The properties of God the Father are in the Son not by participation but essentially and by nature; on the words "The Father loves the Son and has given everything into his hand."
5. The Son is not among those who worship, insofar as he is Word and God; rather, he is worshiped with the Father; on the words "You worship what you do not know, but we worship what we know."
6. The Son is not less than the Father either in potentiality or actuality when it comes to any work, but he is of equal might and of the same substance since he is from him by nature; on the words "The Son can do nothing of himself unless he sees the Father doing it. What he does, this the Son does likewise." **[168]**
7. No God-befitting dignity or superiority is in the Son by participation or addition from the outside; on the words "The Father judges no one but has given all judgment to the Son."
8. Since the Son is God and from God by nature and is the exact image of the one who begat him, he has equal honor and glory with him; on the words "That all may honor the Son just as they honor the Father."
9. The Son is less than God the Father in no respect, but as God from God, he is equal in might in carrying out all his works; on the words "I can do nothing on my own. As I hear, I judge." **[169]**

OUR FATHER AMONG THE SAINTS
CYRIL
ARCHBISHOP OF ALEXANDRIA
ON THE GOSPEL ACCORDING TO JOHN

BOOK TWO

INTRODUCTION[1]

1:29 The next day he saw Jesus coming towards him.

In just a short time, the Baptist is revealed to be both a prophet and an apostle since he shows that the one whose coming he kept proclaiming beforehand is now present. Therefore, he leaped over the stature of the prophets, as the Savior himself says somewhere to the Jews when discussing him, "What did you come out into the desert to see? A prophet? Yes, I tell you, and more than a prophet."[2] They prophesied in their day that Christ would be revealed, but when he cried

Book 2 [1]The Greek text has no heading for this introductory section. [2]Mt 11:9.

out that Christ would come, he also pointed him out as present. "The next day," it says, "he saw Jesus coming towards him."

And he said, "Behold the lamb of God who takes away the sin of the world."

The time for "prepare the way" has passed **[170]** because the one for whom the preparation is supposed to be made is at last seen and is before their eyes. The facts of the matter now require other words. He must explain who is present and why the one who has come to us from heaven makes his descent. So he says, "Behold the lamb of God who takes away the sin of the world." The prophet Isaiah also indicated him to us when he said, "He was led like a sheep to the slaughter, and like a lamb before its shearer he was silent."[3] He also says that the ancient law given through Moses typified him, but it saved in part and did not extend mercy to all because it was a type and a shadow. Now, however, the one who was pictured dimly long ago, the true lamb, the spotless sacrifice, is led to the slaughter for all, to drive away the sin of the world, to overturn the destroyer of the world, to abolish death by dying for all, to undo the curse that is against us so that the pronouncement "Earth you are, and to earth you will return"[4] may cease. The lamb is to become the second Adam, not from the earth but from heaven,[5] and to become the source of all good for human nature, the deliverance from imported corruption, the bestower of eternal life, the basis for transformation into God, the source of piety and righteousness and the road to the kingdom of heaven. For one lamb "died for all,"[6] rescuing the entire flock on earth for God the Father—one for all, that he might subject all to God,[7] one for all, that he might gain all[8] so that all might "live no longer for themselves but for the one who died and rose for them."[9] When we were in many sins and therefore deserved death and decay, the Father gave his Son as a ransom for us, one for all, since all are in him, and he is greater than all. One died for all that all may live in him. **[171]** Death swallowed up the lamb for all[10] and vomited forth all in him and with him since we were all in Christ who died and was raised for us and on our behalf.

Since sin is destroyed, how could death, which comes from sin and is its result, not be utterly destroyed as well? Since the root has died, how could the shoot that comes from it still be preserved? Why are we still going to die even though sin is removed? As we celebrate the feast, because of the slaughter of the lamb of God we say, "O death, where is your penalty? O Hades, where is your sting?"[11] "All wickedness," as the composer of the Psalms says somewhere, "will stop its mouth,"[12] no longer able to accuse those who sin out of weakness. "It is God who justifies. Who is it that condemns?"[13] "Christ redeemed us from the curse of the law by becoming a curse for us,"[14] so that we might escape the curse that comes from sin.

1:30 "This is he of whom I said,"

He reminds the hearers of his words and yields to Christ superiority in glory. In so doing, he accomplishes a work, not of love but of truth or even necessity. The creature is subject to the creator even if he does not want to be, the slave to his master, the one who is supplied to the one who supplies. We have already discussed sufficiently above the way in which Christ is "after" John but "came before him because he was before," as he himself confesses. **[172]**

1:31 "I myself did not know him, but for this reason I came baptizing with water: that he might be revealed to Israel."

[3]Is 53:7. [4]Gen 3:19. [5]1 Cor 15:47. [6]2 Cor 5:15. [7]Cor 15:27, 28. [8]See 1 Cor 9:21-22. [9]2 Cor 5:15. [10]Is 25:8 (LXX). [11]Hos 13:14 (LXX); 1 Cor 15:55. [12]Ps 107:42 (Ps 106:42 LXX). [13]Rom 8:33-34. [14]Gal 3:13.

The one who leaped in the depths of his mother's womb at the voice of the holy virgin while she was still bearing the Lord, the prophet before he was born, the fetal disciple, says concerning the Savior, "I did not know him," and he is telling the truth. He is not lying since God knows all things of himself without being taught, but the creature knows by being taught. The Spirit dwells in the saints. He fills what is lacking and graces human nature with his own good, I mean, the knowledge of things to come and the understanding of hidden mysteries. Therefore, when the blessed Baptist says that he does not know the Lord, he is not lying in the least. In accordance with what belongs to humanity and the measure that is proper for creation, he attributes the knowledge of all things to God alone who through the Holy Spirit enlightens a person with the understanding of hidden things. He benefits the hearer greatly by saying that he does not know Christ on his own, but he has come strictly for this reason: that he might "reveal him to Israel." In this way, he makes clear that it was not his idea to rush into bearing witness, so no one thinks he is serving his own will; rather, he is just a worker in the divine plan of salvation and a servant of the will from above which reveals to him the "lamb of God who takes away the sin of the world."

So that the Jews may more easily come to believe in the Savior Christ and have the most worthy conception of him, he says that he came to know the one whom he did not know. That way, they may understand God who revealed him and, struck dumb by the judgment from above, [173] they may receive the message about him. And when they see how great the servant is, they may estimate proportionately the honor of the master. When he says that he has come "to reveal him to Israel," how does that not fully indicate the care that is fitting for a servant? [174]

Chapter One

The Holy Spirit is in the Son not by participation or as something brought in from the outside but essentially and by nature.

1:32-33 And John testified saying, "I saw the Spirit descending from heaven like a dove and it remained on him. I myself did not know him, but the one who sent me to baptize with water said to me, 'The one on whom you see the Spirit descending and remaining is the one who baptizes with the Holy Spirit.'"

After he says above that he does not know him, John the Baptist benefits the hearer by completing his task. He uncovers the divine mystery by showing that God the Father was the one who revealed it to him and by explaining openly how the revelation took place. Through all these things, he assists the mind of the hearers. He says that through these means God taught humanity the mystery concerning Christ. He also shows that those who oppose him are fighting against the decrees from above and recklessly pitting themselves against the mighty will of the Father. This is characteristic of one who has the ability to persuade people to reject their vain counsel and to receive the one who by the Father's good will came for the salvation of all. He testifies that he saw "the Spirit descending [175] from heaven" in the form of a dove and that it remained on him. In addition, he declares that he heard the one who sent him to baptize with water say that the one on whom the Spirit comes and remains is the one who "baptizes with the Holy Spirit." Therefore, the witness is most credible, the sign is supernatural, and the Father who revealed it is above all things.

These things are so. But perhaps the heretic who loves to criticize will leap up and with a loud laugh say, What, sirs, do you say to this?

What argument will you weave to outwit what is written? Look, he says that the Spirit descends on the Son. See here, he is anointed by God the Father, and he clearly receives what he does not have. The psalmist also testifies to this by addressing him with the words "Therefore, God your God anointed you with the oil of gladness above your companions."[15] How then can the Son be of the same substance as the perfect Father since he himself is not perfect and that is why he is anointed?

In response to this, I think we must say to those who overturn the holy doctrines of the church and pervert the truth of what is written, "Awake, you drunkards, from your wine,"[16] that you may be able to gaze at the bright beauty of the truth and cry out with us to the Son, "Truly you are the Son of God!"[17] because, if you really believe he is God by nature, how could he not be perfect? If you say he is not perfect, then it is time for you to profane the Father himself. Where would his perfection have to come from, according to you? How will he not be brought down to the level of his offspring who, according to you, is imperfect since the divine substance in the Son once received the ability to be imperfect, at least according to your foolish and ignorant reasoning? We will not divide that mighty and undefiled nature **[176]** into different Words so that it is imperfect in one and perfect in another. Since the definition of humanity is the same for all and equal in all of us, what human being is less human than another? And no one will be considered more human than someone else either. I think also that one angel will differ in no way from another angel, at least insofar as they are angels, because they are the same species as each other and they are all bound to one nature. How then can the divine nature which surpasses all things and is in its own good state be seen as inferior to originate beings? How can it undergo an experience that the creature cannot experience? How will it in any way be simple and uncompounded if the perfect and the imperfect are clearly in it? It will be composed of both if the imperfect is dissimilar to the perfect—which it is, because if they are similar and there is no difference between them, then everything that is perfect will also be imperfect without distinction. Furthermore, if something imperfect is also perfect, the charge against the Son comes to nothing, even though by your reasoning, he clearly does not have perfection. Not even the Father himself will surpass the Son, even though his perfection is attested, so our problem is solved. But if a great chasm separates the imperfect from the perfect, then the divine nature receives both in the same respect and so it is composite, not simple.

But perhaps someone will say that opposites are incompatible and cannot exist in the same subject at the same time, as white and black skin together on the same body. You, my friend, have presented a very fine and forceful argument for our position. If the divine nature is one thing and is not contrary to itself, how, tell me, could it be receptive of opposites? How will things that are unlike each other come together in one subject? **[177]** Since the Father is by nature God, the Son is by nature God as well. Therefore, he differs in no way from the Father when it comes to being perfect since he springs from his divine and most perfect substance. Must he not be completely perfect who is from a perfect parent, if he is really his unchangeable image and the "imprint of his hypostasis,"[18] as it is written? But I would think everyone would agree with us and consent to this. Or else let someone come forward and say how the Son is the unchangeable imprint of the perfect Father without having perfection in his own nature, as some foolishly maintain. Since he is the imprint and

[15]Ps 45:7 (Ps 44:8 LXX). [16]Joel 1:5. [17]Mt 14:33. [18]Heb 1:3.

image, he too is perfect, just as the one whose image he is.

But, someone says, "John saw the Spirit descending from heaven" onto the Son. He has sanctification from without because he clearly receives it as one who does not have it. So it is time to say explicitly that he is a creature, honored with only a little superiority, but in the same rank as the others since he is perfected and sanctified and has his supply of good things as a recent acquisition. How, then, is the Evangelist not lying when he says "from his fullness we have all received"?[19] How will he be full in his own nature if he himself receives from another? How can God be considered a father at all if the Only Begotten is a creature and not rather a Son? If this is so, the Father is falsely named and the Son is in no way the truth since he has a bastard dignity and a title of mere words. The whole thing, then, will come to nothing since the Father is not truly the Father nor is the Son by nature what he is said to be. But if God is truly Father, then he certainly has from himself the one whose Father he is, namely, the Son.

Furthermore, how will the divinity which is holy by nature give birth to an offspring from itself that is devoid of holiness **[178]** and produce fruit that is its own but which is stripped of the properties that belong to it? If he has sanctification from without, as they foolishly say, then they have to confess even against their will that he was not always holy, but he became so later when "the Spirit descended on him," as John says. How then was the Son holy even before the incarnation? After all, the seraphim kept glorifying him as such by crying "holy" three times in a row. Therefore, if he was holy even before his "enmanment," or rather when he was always existing with the Father, how could he need someone to sanctify him, and this in recent times when he became a man? I am amazed at how this escapes them with all their zeal for investigation. Do we not have to think that the Son could reject sanctification at any time if it is in him not essentially but accidently, just as it is in us and other rational creatures? But is not something that falls from holiness completely in bondage to sin? Does it not squat down toward the worse, no longer preserving the ability to be apart from vice? So the Son will be found to be changeable, and the psalmist lies in the Spirit when he cries out as to him, "You are the same."[20]

In addition to the things said above, let us also examine the following since it introduces a related idea. All reason demands that something that participates is different by nature from that in which it participates. If this is not true, however, and the one is no different than the other, but they are the same, then that which participates in something will participate in itself, which is incredible even to conceive of. How can one be thought to participate in oneself? **[179]** But if the things mentioned are completely distinct from each other by nature, and if the necessity of reason separates them, let those who give the Spirit to the Only Begotten by participation see the depth of impiety to which they sink without realizing it. If the Son participates in the Spirit and the Spirit is holy by nature, then he himself is not holy by nature. He is shown to be barely holy through his connection with another, and he is transformed by grace to a better state than he was in at first.

But let the enemy of God see once again to what ungodliness this view casts them down. First, some change and turning will be detected regarding the Son, as I said before, since he changed according to you and advanced toward the better. Not only is he inferior to the Father, but he will be shown somehow even to have become greater. We will say how by drawing from the divine Scriptures. The divine

[19]Jn 1:16. [20]Ps 102:27 (Ps 101:28 LXX).

Paul says somewhere concerning him, "Each one of you think this among yourselves which is also in Christ Jesus, who, being in the form of God, did not consider equality with God something to be exploited, but he emptied himself, taking on the form of a slave, being born in human likeness. And being found in human form, he humbled himself."[21] Even before becoming human, he was in the form and equality of the Father. But when he became human, he received the Spirit from heaven and was sanctified, according to them. He is shown for this reason to be both better and greater than himself, and he clearly surpasses even the stature of the one who begat him. And if by receiving the Spirit, he ascended to a dignity beyond that of the Father, then the Spirit is greater than even the Father himself since he graces the Son with superiority over him. Who will not shudder at merely hearing this?

It is very difficult even to go through such arguments. **[180]** But there is no other way to fend off the harm that comes from their stubbornness. Therefore, we will say to them again, If the Word of God receives the Holy Spirit and is sanctified when he becomes human, but before becoming human he was in the form and equality of the Father, though not yet sanctified, as they say, then it is time we dare to say that God the Father is not holy—if, indeed, the Word, who completely shares his form and is equal to him in all things, was not holy in the beginning but became barely holy at a later time. Again, if he is strictly speaking the Word of God who receives the Spirit and is sanctified in his own nature, let the opponents tell us: Did he become greater or less than himself, or did he remain the same when he experienced this? If he gains nothing more from the Spirit but remains the same as he was, then stop being scandalized when you learn that "he descended on him." If he was injured and became inferior when he received the Spirit, you will introduce the Word to us as passible, and you will accuse the substance of the Father of injuring rather than sanctifying. But if he is shown to be greater when he receives the Spirit, and he was in both the form and equality of the Father even before he was made better, as you say, then the Father has not ascended to the pinnacle of glory. He will have the same stature the Son had when he shared his form and was equal to him, though the Son advanced to greater glory. I think, then, that this is the right time to say to the ignorant heretics, "Look, O foolish and senseless people, who have eyes and cannot see, ears and cannot hear."[22] "The god of this age" has truly "blinded the minds of the unbelievers, to keep them from seeing the light of the gospel of the glory **[181]** of Christ."[23] We should grieve over them rather than be angry with them because they do not understand what they read.

It will be clear from the following that our reasoning is correct, even if we have not yet demonstrated it plainly in the foregoing introductory material. We bring up once again what Paul says. "Each one of you think this among yourselves," he says, "which is also in Christ Jesus, who, being in the form of God did not consider equality with God something to be exploited, but he emptied himself, taking on the form of a slave, being born in human likeness. And being found in human form, he humbled himself."[24] See how he marvels greatly at the Son, that although he is equal to and shares the form of God the Father, he does not exploit this because of his love for us. Instead, he descends to humiliation through the form of a slave and empties himself by means of his humanity. But if, sirs, he was sanctified by receiving the Spirit when he became human and he was shown to be greater than himself through the sanctification, what

[21]Phil 2:5-8. [22]Jer 5:21. [23]2 Cor 4:4. [24]Phil 2:5-8.

kind of descent into humiliation is that? How was what was exalted humbled? Where did what was sanctified descend? How did it not rather ascend? How was it not rather exalted to a superior condition? What sort of emptying does the filling of the Spirit contain? How could he be thought to have become human for us at all if he was waiting for such a great profit for himself? How did the one who was rich "become poor on account of us"[25] if he was made rich on account of us? How was he rich even before his advent if, according to them, he received in his advent what he did not have, namely, the Spirit? Should he not offer thank offerings to us for the things he gained because of us?

"Heaven is amazed at this," according to the Scripture, "and absolutely horrified, says the Lord." For the people of the heterodox have truly committed "two evils."[26] **[182]** They know "neither what they are saying nor the things about which they are making assertions."[27] They think nothing of so endangering themselves in the most serious matters, or else they would shed bitter tears from their eyes, raise a loud voice to heaven, draw near and say, "Set a watch before my mouth, O Lord, and a strong door about my lips. Do not incline my heart to words of wickedness."[28] For their words, which work extreme harm in their hearers, are indeed words of wickedness. But we expel their nonsense from our heart and walk according to the right word of faith, keeping in mind what is written: "We destroy arguments and every proud obstacle raised up against the knowledge of God, and we take every thought captive to the obedience of Christ."[29] Come then, let us take our mind captive in the subject before us and submit it to the glory of the Only Begotten, bringing all things wisely into his obedience, that is, into the way of his incarnation. "Though he was rich, yet for our sakes he became poor, that we through his poverty might become rich."[30]

Listen for a minute to our words and receive, if you please, our proof in the matter before us. Holy Scripture testifies that humanity was made in the image and likeness of God who is over all. Indeed, the one who drew up the first book for us, Moses, who was known by God "above all,"[31] says, "And God made the man; according to the image of God he made him."[32] He taught us that through the Holy Spirit he was sealed in the divine image, saying, "And he breathed into his face the breath of life."[33] At the same time the Spirit put life into the one who had been formed, he also imprinted his stamp on him, in a manner appropriate to God. Thus **[183]** God, the most excellent craftsman, after he completed the earthly rational creature, gave him the saving command. He was in the garden, as it is written,[34] still keeping the gift, and was illustrious in the divine image of his maker through the Holy Spirit who dwelt in him. But when he was led astray by the deception of the devil, he despised the creator. He trampled on the law that was marked out for him and grieved his benefactor. The benefactor took back the grace that was given to him. When, for the first time, the one who came to life heard, "Earth you are, and to earth you will return,"[35] the likeness to God was then marked with a false stamp through the sin that rushed in, and the engraving was no longer distinct. It became more obscure in him, so to speak, and darkened by the transgression. When the human race reached a great multitude and sin ruled over all of them, it thoroughly plundered the soul of each one, and nature was stripped of the original grace. The Spirit also departed completely, and the rational creature fell into utter irrationality, not even recognizing the creator himself. But the creator of all, after

[25]2 Cor 8:9. [26]Jer 2:12-13. [27]1 Tim 1:7. [28]Ps 141:3-4 (Ps 140:3-4 lxx). [29]2 Cor 10:5. [30]2 Cor 8:9. [31]Ex 33:17. [32]Gen 1:27. [33]Gen 2:7. [34]Gen 2:8. [35]Gen 3:19.

enduring for a long time, finally had mercy on the corrupted world. Since he is good, he hastened to gather together the flock on earth, which ran away, with those above. He also decreed to transform humanity once again to the original image through the Spirit. There was no other way to make the divine imprint shine again in humanity as it did at first.

Therefore, we next discuss how he planned to do this, how he implanted in us the grace that is our refuge, how the Spirit was rooted once again in humanity and how our nature was transformed to its original state. The first man was earthly and from the earth. He had in his power to choose either good or evil, **[184]** since he was the master of the inclination to each. But he was seized by bitter treachery. He inclined toward disobedience, and he fell to the earth, the mother from which he came, and, now overcome by decay and death, he conveyed his penalty to the whole race. Evil increased and multiplied among us, and our thoughts always descended to the worse. Sin reigned, and thus human nature was shown to be stripped of the indwelling Holy Spirit. "For the Holy Spirit of wisdom will flee deceit," as it is written, "and will not dwell in a body enslaved to sin."[36]

Since the first Adam did not preserve the grace given by God, God the Father planned to send us the second Adam from heaven. He sent his own Son, who is by nature without variation or change, into our likeness. He knew no sin at all so that, just as through the disobedience of the first we came under God's wrath, so through the obedience of the second, we might escape the curse, and its evils might come to nothing.[37] When the Word of God became human, he received the Spirit from the Father as one of us. He did not receive anything for himself personally because he himself is the supplier of the Spirit. But the one who knew no sin received the Spirit as man in order to keep the Spirit in our nature and root in us once again the grace that had left us. I think that is the reason that the holy Baptist profitably adds, "I saw the Spirit descending from heaven and remaining on him." The Spirit flew away from us because of sin, but the one who knew no sin became one of us so that the Spirit might become accustomed to remain in us, since the Spirit finds no reason in him for leaving or shrinking back.

Therefore, he receives the Spirit through himself for us, and he restores **[185]** to our nature the original good. Thus he is also said to become poor for our sakes.[38] Though as God he was rich and lacked no good thing, he became a man who lacked everything, to whom it is said somewhere, and exceedingly well, "What do you have that you did not receive?"[39] Although he was life by nature, he died for our sakes according to the flesh in order to conquer death for us and to raise our entire nature with him. (We were all in him because he became human.) In the same way also, he received the Spirit for our sakes in order to sanctify our entire nature. He did not come to help himself but to become for all of us the door, the beginning and the way to heavenly blessings. But if in fact he did not resolve to receive as man or to suffer as one of us, how could anyone have shown that he "humbled himself"[40]? Or how could the "form of a slave"[41] have been appropriately preserved if nothing fitting a slave was written about him? Let not, then, the profound message of the plan of salvation be pulled to pieces—the plan about which the divine Paul himself rightly cries out in admiration, "that through the church, the manifold wisdom of God may now be made known to the rulers and authorities in heavenly places. This was according to the eternal purpose which he realized in Christ Jesus our Lord."[42] The great mystery of the incarnation is truly recognized as wisdom and as fitting to God.

[36]Wis 1:5, 4. [37]Rom 5:19. [38]2 Cor 8:9. [39]1 Cor 4:7. [40]Phil 2:8. [41]Phil 2:7. [42]Eph 3:10-11.

I think that we who choose to be godly and rejoice in orthodox doctrines ought to have such a conception about the Savior. I do not imagine that we too will sink to such irrationality as to think that the Spirit is in the natural Son by participation, and not rather essentially, just as the Spirit is, of course, in the Father himself. Just as the Holy Spirit is of the Father, so in the same way, he is of the Son. **[186]** Thus we read in the Holy Scriptures, "When they had come opposite Mysia," it says, "they attempted to go into Bithynia, but the Spirit of Jesus did not allow them."[43]

If it seems good to someone who loves conflict to resist the arguments about these things and to assert once more that the Spirit is in the Son by participation or that he came to be in him when he was baptized during the time of the incarnation, and he was not in him before, then such a person should be aware of how many great absurdities they will fall into. First, the Savior says that "among those born of women, no one has arisen greater than John the Baptist."[44] And this statement is true. Yet we see the one who has ascended to the summit of human glory and virtue honoring Christ with incomparable superiority. "I am not worthy," he says, "to stoop down and untie the thong of his sandal."[45] How is it not insane—no, ungodly—to believe that John was filled with the Spirit "already from his mother's womb"[46] because this is written about him, but to think that John's master and lord—no, rather the master and lord of all—first received the Spirit when he was baptized, even though the holy Gabriel says to the holy virgin, "The Holy Spirit will come upon you, and the power of the Most High will overshadow you. Therefore, that which is born is holy. He will be called the Son of God"?[47] Let those who are devoted to learning see that this statement is pregnant with great meaning. Concerning John, it says "he will be filled with the Holy Spirit"[48] since the Holy Spirit was in him as a gift and not essentially. But concerning the Savior, it no longer says "he will be filled," and quite rightly so, but "that which is born is holy." It does not even add "will be" since he was always holy by nature as God. **[187]**

I think it is fitting that we hunt down what is profitable from every direction. Now that the voice of the archangel was brought up, come let us do training exercises with it for a little while. "The Holy Spirit," it says, "will come upon you, and the power of the Most High will overshadow you. Therefore, that which is born is holy. He will be called the Son of God." So let the one who from great ignorance resists the right teachings of the church tell us whether the Word of God the Father was Son before the incarnation or whether he had this glory in name only and was a bastard with an alias. If such a person says he was not a Son at all, they will deny the Father. After all, whose Father will he be if there is no Son? Their thought will be contrary to the entire Holy Scriptures. But if they confess that the Son was and was called Son even before the incarnation, how is it that the archangel tells us that the one to be born through the holy virgin will be called the Son of God, even though he was this by nature from of old? Therefore, just as the Son was with the Father eternally since he has the Father as the source of his being, but he was defined as the Son of God[49] at the time of the incarnation because he appeared with a body in the world, in the same way, he has his own Spirit essentially in himself, but he is said to receive it as man. He thereby preserves for humanity a fitting order, and along with humanity, he makes his own the qualities that belong to it for our sakes.

How could the Word in any way ever be thought to be separate from his own Spirit? Would it not be absurd to say that the human spirit—the spirit that is in a human being both

[43]Acts 16:7. [44]Mt 11:11. [45]Mk 1:7. [46]Lk 1:15. [47]Lk 1:35. [48]Lk 1:15. [49]See Rom 1:4.

according to the definition of human nature and for the completion of the living being—was separate from that human being? I think this is perfectly obvious to all. How then shall we separate the Spirit from the Son since the Spirit is in him in this way and united to him essentially? The Spirit comes forth through him **[188]** and is in him by nature so that the Spirit is not understood to be something else besides him, both because of the identity of activity and the unchangeable quality of the nature itself. Listen to what the Savior says to his disciples: "If you love me, keep my commandments. And I will ask the Father, and he will give you another counselor, the Spirit of truth, whom the world cannot receive."[50] See, he explicitly calls the Holy Spirit "the Spirit of truth." But we know that the Savior and no one else is the truth. Listen to what he says: "I am the truth."[51] Therefore, since the natural Son is and is called the truth, see how great the unity is which the Spirit has with him. The disciple John says somewhere concerning our Savior, "This is the one who came by the water and the blood and the Spirit, Jesus Christ. He did not come with the water alone, but with the water and the blood. And the Spirit is the one who testifies because the Spirit is the truth."[52] And because the Holy Spirit dwells in us "in the inner being,"[53] Christ himself is said to dwell there as well.[54] And, in fact, he does. Yes, the blessed Paul teaches this most clearly when he says, "But you are not in the flesh, you are in the Spirit, if in fact the Spirit of God dwells in you. Anyone who does not have the Spirit of Christ does not belong to him. But if Christ is in you, though the body is dead because of sin, the Spirit is life because of righteousness."[55] Give a keen ear, sir, to these words. He named the Spirit of Christ who dwells in us and then immediately added, "But if Christ is in you." In so doing, he ascribes the unchanging likeness of the Son to the Spirit as well, who is his own and who flows forth from him by nature. That is why **[189]** he is called a "Spirit of sonship," and in him we cry, "Abba! Father!"[56] And as the blessed John says somewhere, "By this we know that he is in us, because he has given us of his Spirit."[57]

I think these things are sufficient for the children of the church to be able to ward off the damage that comes from the heterodox. But if anyone is soaked in the unmixed wine of their ignorance and thinks that the Son first received the Spirit when he became human, let them demonstrate that, before the incarnation, the Word of God was not holy, and we will be silent.

One may well marvel, however, that the holy Evangelist always safeguards matters belonging to the divine nature with great care. Since he said above that "no one has ever seen God,"[58] but now he says that the blessed Baptist saw the Spirit "descending on the Son from heaven," he adds of necessity, "I saw the Spirit," but in the form "of a dove." He did not see what the Spirit is nakedly in his own nature, but in the form of the gentlest animal. This was to preserve clearly the natural relationship and likeness with the Son, who says, "Learn from me, for I am gentle and humble in heart."[59] Therefore, the Spirit will not fall away from being God by nature. Indeed, the Spirit has kept himself from ever being seen, except in the form of a dove, and that was because of the need of the disciple. The blessed Baptist says that the descent of the Spirit was given as a sign or token when he adds to his testimony about our Savior that "the one who sent me to baptize with water said to me, 'The one on whom you see the Spirit descending and remaining is the one who baptizes with the Holy Spirit.'" There-

[50]Jn 14:15-17. [51]Jn 14:6. [52]1 Jn 5:6. [53]Eph 3:16. [54]Eph 3:17. [55]Rom 8:9-10. [56]Rom 8:15. [57]1 Jn 4:13. [58]Jn 1:18. [59]Mt 11:29.

fore, [190] I think it is fitting for us to laugh the ignorant heretics to scorn since they take something that was given as a sign to be the truth of the matter, even though it happened economically,[60] as was said before, because of the need of humanity.

1:34 "And I have seen and testify that this is the Son of God."

The witness is reliable. He says what he actually saw. Perhaps he was not unaware of the Scripture, "Declare what your eyes have seen."[61] I have seen the sign, he says, and I understand what it means. I testify that "this is the Son of God," the one who was announced in the law given through Moses and proclaimed by the voice of the holy prophets. Again, the blessed Evangelist says with great reliability, it seems to me, "This is the Son of God," that is, the one and only Son by nature, the heir of the distinctive characteristic of his Father, to whom we who are sons by adoption are conformed, and through whom we are called by grace to the dignity of sonship. Just as from God the Father "all fatherhood in heaven and on earth is named"[62] because he is strictly, primarily and truly the Father, so also all sonship is from the Son because he is strictly, uniquely and truly the Son. He is not a bastard or a son in name only, but he is of the substance of God the Father—not by cutting off or emanation or division or separation, for the divine nature is altogether impassible, but as one from one, always with him, coeternal, rooted in the one who begat him, both in him and proceeding from him indivisibly and without distance. The divine nature is neither corporeal, nor circumscribed by space nor [191] of such a nature as to move from place to place over distance.

It is like heat in fire. The heat proceeds from the fire, and there is a conceptual distinction between the two so that they are not the same as each other. But the heat is from the fire and in it by nature, and it proceeds from it without being damaged by cutting or division or emanation since it remains whole throughout the entire fire. Let us think about the divine begetting in the same way, understanding the meaning of it in a way that is the most fitting to God. We believe that the Son subsists on his own, but we do not place him outside the one ineffable divine nature, nor do we say that he is of a different substance from the Father. In that case, it would not be right to think of him as the Son but something else besides that, and a new God would arise, who would be different than the one who alone exists. How will something that is not of the same substance as the one who is God by nature do anything but completely fall short of being the true God? But since the blessed Baptist, who is both trustworthy and of the highest reputation, testifies that "this is the Son of God," we will confess that the Son is true God in every way and of the substance of the Father. As far as we are concerned, this, and nothing else, is what the name of sonship means.

1:35-36 The next day again John was standing with two of his disciples; and he looked at Jesus as he walked, and said, "Behold the lamb of God who takes away the sin of the world!"

The blessed Baptist already pointed him out earlier, but see, he repeats the same message and shows Jesus to his disciples. He calls him the "lamb of God," and he says that he "takes away the sin of the world," all but leading his hearers to think of the one speaking in the prophets, "I am, I am the one who blots out

[60]"Economically" in this context means "according to the plan (*oikonomia*) of salvation." Cyril is contrasting the way God manifests himself in the plan of salvation with the way he is "nakedly" in his own nature. [61]Prov 25:7 (LXX). [62]Eph 3:15.

your sin, [192] and I will not remember it."[63] The Baptist does not repeat the same explanation about the Savior in vain. It is a mark of excellence in teaching to implant a message that is not yet understood into the souls of the learners without shrinking from repetition but rather enduring it for the benefit of the students. That is why the blessed Paul too says, "To say the same thing to you is not irksome for me, and it is safe for you."[64]

1:37 The two disciples heard him speaking, and they followed Jesus.

Do you see the fruit that goes with the teaching and that the teaching yields? Do you see how much profit is to be found in repetition? So let whoever is entrusted with the task of teaching learn from this to overcome all sluggishness and to consider silence more harmful to himself than to his hearers. Let him not bury his master's talent in idle sloth as in the earth[65] but rather take "his money to the bankers."[66] For the Savior will receive that which is his own with interest, and like a seed, he will give life to the word that was implanted. You have here an excellent example of what has been said. The Baptist, since he did not shrink back from showing the Lord to his disciples or from saying to them a second time, "Behold the lamb of God," obviously helps them so much that they are ultimately persuaded to follow him and now desire to be his disciples. [193]

1:38 When Jesus turned and saw them following, he said to them, "What do you seek?"

The Lord turns to those following him so that they may benefit from his action, and they may learn what is sung in the Psalms, "I sought the Lord, and he heard me."[67] As long as we do not yet seek God through good conduct and a right faith, we remain in a sense behind him, away from his face. But when we thirst for his divine law and follow the holy and excellent way of righteousness, then he will certainly look at us and cry out what is written, "Turn to me, and I will turn to you, says the Lord Almighty."[68] "What do you seek?" he says to them, not because he did not know, but why? He knows everything as God, but he poses the question as the beginning and basis for his discourse.

They said to him, "Rabbi, where are you staying?"
Those whom he asks respond as ones who are well-instructed. They already call him teacher, clearly demonstrating their desire to learn from him. Next, they want to learn where he is staying so they can tell him their need there at the proper time. They did not think it right, it seems to me, to tell him their need when they were on the road. What he says next is a helpful pattern for us.

1:39 He said to them, "Come and see."

He does not show them the house, though they asked him to do this, [194] but he tells them to go straight to it. By this action, which serves as a model, he teaches first of all that it is not good to put off the search for good. Delay is harmful in matters that are profitable. In addition, he teaches that for those who do not yet know the holy house of our Savior Christ, that is, the church, it will not suffice for salvation to learn where it is; instead, one must enter into it by faith and see those things that are done mystically in it.

So they went and saw where he was staying,

[63]Is 43:25. [64]Phil 3:1. [65]Mt 25:18. [66]Mt 25:27. [67]Ps 34:4 (Ps 33:5 LXX). [68]Zech 1:3.

and they stayed with him that day. It was about the tenth hour.
The disciples constantly applied themselves to the knowledge of the divine mysteries. I do not think it is fitting for those who are devoted to learning to have a dainty attitude. They should love to work hard, and they should excel beyond mediocrity in their good efforts with the intention of standing out in displaying single-minded zeal their whole life long. This is what I think the words "they stayed with him that day" reveal in the form of an enigma. But when it says, "It was about the tenth hour," on this very point we make an application that is beneficial and appropriate to everyone. We say that the one who compiles the divine sayings subtly teaches us again that the great mystery of our Savior was not made known at the beginning of the present age but now, as the time draws to a close. As it is written, in the last days, we are all shown to be "taught by God."[69] Take as another image of what I am saying about the tenth hour the disciples who are at the Savior's side. [195] The Evangelist says that once they stayed with him, they clung to him so that those who enter God's house by faith and run to Christ may learn that they must remain with him and not desire to be estranged again either by departing to sin or by rushing back to unbelief.

1:40-42 One of the two who heard John speak and followed him was Andrew, Simon Peter's brother. He first found his brother Simon and said to him, "We have found the Messiah," and brought him to Jesus.

Those who just received their talent immediately make a profit and bring it to their master. Souls who love to listen and learn truly show themselves to be this way. They do not need long discourses in order to profit, nor do they bear the fruit of their teaching months or years later. Rather, as soon as the teaching begins, they attain the goal of understanding. "Give opportunity to the wise," it says, "and they will be wiser. Instruct the just, and they will receive more instruction."[70] So Andrew saves his brother Peter by revealing the entire mystery in a brief summary. "We have found" Jesus, he says, like a treasure hidden in a field or like one pearl of great price, as the parables in the Gospels say.[71]

Jesus looked at him and said, "You are Simon, son of John. You will be called Cephas, which means rock."
The one who sees hearts and inner parts[72] looks intently at him in a divine way. He sees [196] what godliness the disciple will ascend to, what virtue he will attain and what goal he will reach. The one who "knows all things before they come to be"[73] is ignorant of nothing. By this, he teaches the one who is called that, since he is true God, he has knowledge without being taught. He needed no explanation at all, nor did he seek to learn who the man was or from where he came to him. He tells him who his father is and what his name is. And he no longer allows him to be called Simon. He already exercises authority and power over him, operating with the assumption that he has become one of his own. He changes his name to Peter, naming him after *petra*,[74] because he was about to found his church on him.

1:43 The next day, he decided to go to Galilee. He found Philip and said to him, "Follow me."

Philip is of the same mind as the ones before him, very eager to follow Christ. Christ knew that he too would be noble, and that is why he says, "Follow me," using these words as an indication of the grace that is on him. With

[69]Is 54:13. [70]Prov 9:9. [71]Mt 13:44, 46. [72]Jer 20:12. [73]Sus 42. [74]*Petra* means "rock."

them, he instructs Philip to follow him, thereby testifying to his excellent way of life. After all, he would not have chosen him if he were not altogether worthy.

1:45 Philip found Nathanael and said to him, "We have found the one about whom Moses in the law and also the prophets wrote, Jesus, the son of Joseph, from Nazareth."

The disciple is extremely quick to bear fruit so that he might be shown by this to have the same disposition as those before. "He found [197] Nathanael," not by happening on him while Nathanael was walking but by searching diligently for him. For he knew that he was quite willing to work hard and learn. Next he says that he has found the Christ, the one proclaimed by all the Holy Scriptures. Notice that he is not talking to someone he thinks is ignorant but to one he assumes is exceedingly well-versed in the contents of the supremely wise Moses and the prophets. But an untrue conjecture prevailed among the Jews about our Savior Jesus Christ. They thought that he would be from the city or village of Nazareth, even though Holy Scripture says that he is a Bethlehemite according to the following passage. "And you, Bethlehem," it says, "the land of Judah, the house of Ephratha, are very few to be reckoned among the thousands of Judah, for from you will come forth to me the one who will be the ruler in Israel, and his goings are from the beginning, from eternal days."[75] He was brought up in Nazareth, as the Evangelist himself somewhere testifies, "And he went to Nazareth where he was brought up,"[76] but he was not from there. He was from the place we just mentioned, or rather, the voice of the prophet mentioned. So Philip follows the conjecture of the Jews and says, "Jesus from Nazareth."

1:46 "Something good can come from Nazareth."[77]

Nathanael readily agrees that what people expected to be revealed from Nazareth would be great and most fair. It is quite clear, I suppose, that not only did he take Nazareth as an identifier of the one who was expected, but also he collected knowledge from the law and the prophets and quickly attained understanding as one who is very knowledgeable. **[198]**

"Come and see."
Seeing him will be proof enough, he says, and after a mere conversation with him, you will ardently confess and affirm beyond doubt that he is truly the expected one. We must believe that there was a certain divine and ineffable grace flowing out of the Savior's words and enchanting the souls of the hearers because it is written, "They all marveled at the gracious words which were proceeding from his mouth."[78] As the word was effective in power, so also it was sufficient to persuade.

1:47 "Behold a true Israelite in whom there is no deceit."

Since he did not yet make it his practice to show himself through signs, Christ tried in another way to persuade his own disciples (and as many other sensible people who came to him) who could understand that he himself was by nature Son and God, even though he came in human form for the salvation of all. What then was the way leading to faith? Clearly, it was God-befitting knowledge because knowing all things befits God alone. So he affirms Nathanael, not to control his

[75]Mic 5:2 (Mic 5:1 LXX). [76]Lk 4:16. [77]Pusey's Greek text has a question mark so that it conforms to the standard reading, "Can anything good come out of Nazareth?" but Cyril's explanation of the text makes it clear that he takes the verse as a statement, not a question. [78]Lk 4:22.

dispositions by flattery but to prove by the things he knew that as God he knows hearts.

1:48 "Where did you get to know me?"

Nathanael begins to marvel and is called to a faith that is already firm. But he still wants to know where Jesus got this knowledge about him because souls that are devoted to learning and love God are exceedingly diligent. **[199]** And perhaps he suspects that Philip revealed something about him to the Lord.

"I saw you under the fig tree before Philip called to you."
The Savior alleviated his suspicion by saying that he saw him under the fig tree before his meeting and conversation with Philip, even though he was not there in the body. It is quite helpful that he mentions both the fig tree and the occasion because they provide the proof that he saw him. We accept people more readily if they have already learned the details about us.

1:49 "Rabbi, you are the Son of God. You are the king of Israel."

He knows that God alone searches the heart and gives to no other human being the ability to know the mind. He is probably thinking of the passage in the Psalms, "O God, who tests the hearts and inner parts."[79] The psalmist ascribes this special quality too to the divine nature alone, taking the position that it does not belong to anyone else. Therefore, when he realizes that the Lord saw his suspicion while it was still turning around in his mind in voiceless whispers, he immediately calls him "teacher." Already entering eagerly into discipleship under him, he confesses him to be Son of God and king of Israel who has the properties of divinity. As one who is well-instructed, he maintains that this one is certainly also God by nature.

1:50 "Do you believe because I told you that I saw you under the fig tree? You will see greater things than these."

You will be more secure in the faith, he says, when you see **[200]** greater things than these. How would one who believes one sign not certainly be in a better position because of many signs, especially when they are clearly more remarkable than the ones that have already amazed him?

1:51 "Truly, truly, I say to you, you will see heaven opened and the angels of God ascending and descending on the Son of Man."

The statement that seals Nathanael's faith is now common to all. By saying that angels will be seen rushing up and down on the Son of Man, that is, ministering and carrying out his commands for the salvation of those who are going to believe, he says that he will especially then be revealed as the Son of God by nature. For the rational powers surely serve not each other but God. This does not mean there is no subordination among the angels, but this subordination would not rightly be called service.[80] We have heard from the holy Evangelists that "angels came" to Christ the Savior "and ministered to him."[81]

2:1-4 On the third day, there was a wedding in Cana of Galilee, and the mother of Jesus was there. Jesus was invited to the wedding, and so were his disciples. When the wine ran out, the mother of Jesus said to him, "They have no wine." And Jesus said to her . . .

[79]Ps 7:9 (Ps 7:10 LXX). [80]When Cyril says that the rational powers "serve" God and that their subordination to each other is not really "service," he is using forms of the word δουλεία, which refers to the service of slaves to their master. For Cyril, this form of service is appropriately directed only to God. [81]Mt 4:11.

When it is the right time, he finally begins giving signs, even if he seems to be invited to it unintentionally. When a wedding feast is held (and this is clearly done with all reverence), the mother of the Savior is there, and he himself is invited and comes with his disciples, **[201]** though he comes to work miracles rather than to feast with them, and even more to sanctify the very beginning of human birth—I mean so far as it pertains to the flesh. It was fitting for the one who was recapitulating human nature itself and refashioning the whole of it in a better condition not only to impart his blessing to those already called into existence but also to prepare his grace for those not yet born and to make holy their entrance into existence.

Consider a third reason as well. God said to the woman somewhere, "In pain you will bear children."[82] How could we not need to be rescued from this curse as well? How else could we have escaped the condemnation of marriage? The Savior undid this too, since he loves humanity. By his presence, he, the desire and joy of all, has honored marriage in order to drive out the ancient grief of childbearing. "For if anyone is in Christ, there is a new creation. The old has gone," as Paul says, "and has become new."[83] So he comes to the wedding together with his disciples. Those eager to see miracles needed to be present with the miracle worker in order to gather together what he would perform as a kind of food for their faith. And when the wine failed the guests, the mother called the Lord because he was noble in his love for humanity. She said, "They have no wine." She urged him to do the miracle with the conviction that it was in his power to do whatever he wanted.

"Woman, what concern is that to you and me? My hour has not yet come."

The Savior fashioned this excellent response for us as well. It was not right for him to come running to perform the deed or for him to come on his own volition as if to show off as a miracle worker. **[202]** Instead, he needed to come to it reluctantly, because he was invited, and to indulge the need rather than the onlookers. The outcome of people's desire seems more attractive somehow when it is not given at once to those who ask for it, but through a short delay they anticipate it more intensely. Both through this and in other ways, Christ shows that the honor that is due one's parents is most remarkable, since he accepts out of reverence for his mother what he did not yet want to do.

2:5 His mother said to the servants, "Do whatever he tells you."

The woman has great influence over the performance of the miracle, and she prevails by persuading the Lord with an appeal to propriety, since he is her son. She begins the work by preparing the servants of the feast to do whatever they are now instructed to do.

2:7-10 Jesus said to them, "Fill the jars with water." And they filled them up to the brim. He said to them, "Now draw some out, and take it to the steward of the feast." So they took it. When the steward of the feast tasted the water that had become wine, and did not know where it came from (though the servants who had drawn the water knew), the steward of the feast called the bridegroom and said to him, "Everyone serves the good wine first, and then the inferior wine after the guests have become drunk. But you have kept the good wine until now."

The servants carry out their instructions, and the water is transformed into wine by an ineffable power. After all, what could be

[82]Gen 3:16. [83]2 Cor 5:17.

difficult for one who has power over everything? How could the one who calls into being things that are not[84] grow weary from transforming what is already made into **[203]** whatever he wants? They marvel at the matter as something exceptional, since it is not possible for the works done by Christ to appear any other way. The steward of the feast, however, accuses the bridegroom of bringing out the better wine at the end of the feast. And he is not being rude, it seems to me, at least according to the narrative.

2:11 Jesus did this, the first of his signs, in Cana of Galilee, and revealed his glory; and his disciples believed in him.

Many excellent things were accomplished at once through the one first sign. Honorable marriage[85] was sanctified, and the curse against women was taken away. Children will no longer be brought forth in pain[86] since Christ has blessed the very beginning of our coming into being. The glory of our Savior shone like the brightness of the sun, and greater than this, the disciples were made secure in their faith by their marveling.

The discussion of the narrative will stop here. Still, I think we must also consider another way of looking at the words and talk about what is hinted at in the narrative. The Word of God came down from heaven, as he himself says somewhere, to make human nature his own, as a bridegroom does, and to persuade it to be pregnant with the spiritual seed of wisdom. Therefore, the human nature is reasonably called the bride and the Savior the bridegroom, since Holy Scripture raises its language from things that are on our level to an understanding of things that are above us.

The wedding was held on the third day, that is, in the last times of the present age, since the number three gives us a beginning, a middle and an end. This is how **[204]** all time is measured. What was said somewhere by one of the holy prophets clearly fits with this: "He will smite us and bind us up. After two days, on the third day, he will heal us, and we will arise and live before him and know him. We will pursue knowledge of the Lord, and we will find him ready like the morning."[87] He struck us because of the transgression in Adam by saying, "Earth you are, and to earth you will return."[88] That which was smitten by decay and death he bound up once again on the third day, that is, not at the beginning or the middle but at the end times, when he became human for us and made our entire nature healthy by raising it from the dead in himself. That is why he is called "the first fruits of those who have fallen asleep."[89] Therefore, by saying that the marriage was being held on the third day, he signifies the final age.

He also indicates the place since he says it was in Cana of Galilee. Let the one who is eager to learn pay attention once again. The gathering is not in Jerusalem. Instead, the feast is held outside Jerusalem, as if in the country of the Gentiles—"Galilee of the Gentiles,"[90] as the prophet says. I suppose it is perfectly clear that the synagogue of the Jews rejected the bridegroom from heaven, and the church of the Gentiles received him with great joy. The Savior does not go to the wedding of his own accord but because he was invited by the many voices of the saints. But the wine failed the feasters, for the law perfected nothing; the Mosaic letter did not suffice for perfect gladness. Neither did the measure of implanted sobriety reach the point where it could save us. Therefore, it would be true to say also of us, "They have no wine." Our generous God does not overlook our nature, worn out by a lack of blessings. **[205]** He unveiled a wine that is better than the first, "for the letter kills, but the Spirit gives life."[91] The law has no

[84]Rom 4:17. [85]See Heb 13:4. [86]Gen 3:16. [87]Hos 6:1-3. [88]Gen 3:19. [89]1 Cor 15:20. [90]Is 9:1. [91]2 Cor 3:6.

perfect blessings, but the divine instruction in the teaching of the Gospels brings the fullest blessing. The steward of the feast marvels at the new wine because everyone, I think, who is ordained into the divine priesthood and entrusted with the house of our Savior Christ is amazed at his word which is above the law. Christ commands it to be given to him first because, as Paul says, "It is the farmer who does the work who ought to have the first share of the crops."[92] Again, let the hearer think about what I am saying.[93]

2:14 In the temple he found people selling cattle, sheep and doves, and the money changers seated at their tables.

These acts convict the Jews once again of holding the law that was given to them in low esteem and making the writings of Moses of no account since they are looking only for financial gain. Although the law commands those who are going to go up to the divine temple to cleanse themselves first in many ways, those who could have prevented it did not keep out the bankers, the money changers, and others besides, whose business was greed, interest and lust for money (since the entire aim of the merchants is focused on these things). They did not prevent them from defiling the holy court, from entering it with unwashed feet, as it were. In fact, they themselves surely kept ordering them to do it so that God might be shown to speak the truth about them: "Many shepherds have utterly destroyed my vineyard. They have defiled my portion and made my desired portion a trackless desert. It has become a complete ruin."[94] **[206]** The Lord's vineyard was truly destroyed since the vineyard was being taught to trample the divine worship itself, and since it was being turned into a desert of complete ignorance by the sordid greed of its leaders.

2:15 And he made a kind of whip out of cords and drove everyone out of the temple.

The Savior is angry for good reason at the senselessness of the Jews. The holy temple was not supposed to be made into a house of merchandise but a house of prayer, as it is written.[95] He shows his feeling not with mere words but with blows and a lash. He throws them out of the environs of the temple, justly devising a punishment for them that is fit for slaves because they were not going to receive the Son who sets people free through faith. Look at what Paul says, in a beautifully engraved image, as it were: "If anyone destroys the temple of God, God will destroy them."[96]

2:16 "Get these things out of here. Stop making my Father's house a house of merchandise!"

He commands as Lord, he leads by the hand to what is proper as teacher, and he provides the explanation of the offenses along with the punishment, not allowing the one who is rebuked to become enraged from the shame of it. We must note again that he calls God his own unique Father from the conviction both that he is indeed the only one who is from him by nature and that he is truly begotten. After all, if this is not so, and the Word is really a son along with us, as one of us (by adoption, that is, **[207]** and only by the will of the Father), why does he alone seize for himself the boast which is presumably common and available to all by saying, "Stop making my Father's house" rather than "our Father's house"?[97] It would probably have been more consistent to say this if indeed he knew himself to be one of those who are not sons by nature. But since the Word knows that he is from the substance of God the Father and not included among those who are sons by grace, he places himself apart

[92] 2 Tim 2:6. [93] See 2 Tim 2:7. [94] Jer 12:10-11. [95] Mt 21:13. [96] 1 Cor 3:17. [97] Cf. *Thesaurus* 317 (PG 75:539A).

from the others by calling God his own Father. When those who are called to sonship and who have this honor from the outside pray, it is fitting for them to cry, "Our Father in heaven."[98] But since the Only Begotten is the only one from the one Father, he rightly calls God his own Father.

But if, as we give our attention to the passage at hand, we must also spiritually apply it to higher matters, then we must look at the passage differently.

2:14 In the temple he found people selling sheep, cattle, etc.

Look again at the entire shape of God's plan, as far as it concerns us. It is woven throughout with two facts. What I mean is this: Christ joins and feasts with the Canaites (I mean those of Galilee) and eats with those who invited and, thereby, honored him. He aids them with signs and fills up what was lacking in their joy. What good does he not freely bestow? In so doing, he teaches through a type that he will both accept the inhabitants of Galilee, that is, the Gentiles—who invited him, as it were, to be with them by the faith that is in them—and he will lead them to the heavenly bridal chamber, that is, to the church of the firstborn,[99] and make them recline with the saints **[208]** (since the holy disciples reclined at table with the feasters). And they will take part in the divine and spiritual feast, as he says somewhere, "Many will come from the east and the west and will recline at table with Abraham, Isaac and Jacob."[100] Nothing will be lacking in their joy. "For everlasting joy will be on their heads."[101]

The disobedient Jews, however, he will drive out of the holy places and put them outside the holy precinct of the saints. He will not receive those who bring sacrifices. Instead, he will subject them to the punishing whip as they are bound by the cords of their own sins.[102] Listen to him as he says, "Get these things out of here," that you may understand again what he said long ago through the voice of the prophet Isaiah, "[I have had enough of] your burnt offerings of rams. I do not want the fat of lambs and the blood of bulls and goats. Do not come to appear before me. For who has required these from your hands? Tread no more on my courts. If you bring fine flour, it is meaningless. Incense—it is disgusting to me. I cannot bear your new moons and sabbaths and the great day. My soul hates your fasting and rest and feasts. I have had enough of you. I will no longer pardon your sins."[103] He signifies this most excellently in a type by devising a whip of cords for them since whips are a sign of punishment. **[209]**

2:17 His disciples remembered that it is written, "Zeal for your house will consume me."

The disciples obtain full knowledge in a relatively short time, and they already show great progress toward the better by comparing what is written with its fulfillments in deeds.

2:18 "What sign have you to show us for doing this?"

The multitude of the Jews is astonished at this strange authority, while those who serve the temple are very upset because they are being deprived of incalculable profits. But they cannot refute him by saying that he did not speak correctly when he commanded them not to treat the divine temple as a house of merchandise. So they devise delays for the removal of the merchandise, alleging that they should not readily submit to him or indeed accept someone as the Son of God without due consideration when he lacks the testimony of a sign.

[98]Mt 6:9. [99]Heb 12:23. [100]Mt 8:11. [101]Is 35:10. [102]Prov 5:22. [103]Is 1:11-14.

2:19 "Destroy this temple."

To those who seek blessings with good intentions, God most readily grants them. To those who come to tempt him, however, not only does he deny the object that they seek, but also he charges them with wickedness. Thus, the Savior censured the Pharisees who were seeking a sign in other parts of the Gospels by saying, "A wicked and adulterous generation asks for a sign, but no sign will be given to it except the sign of the prophet Jonah. For as **[210]** Jonah was three days and three nights in the belly of the whale, so will the Son of Man be three days and three nights in the heart of the earth."[104] Now what he said to them, he says also to these people with a slight change. For these, just as the former, ask in order to tempt him. This sign would certainly not have been given to people with such an intention except that it was necessary for it to happen for the salvation of us all.

We must note that they made this the pretext of their charge against him, misrepresenting Jesus' words to Pontius Pilate. They say, "This fellow said, 'I am able to destroy the temple of God.'" On this point too, Christ spoke about them in the prophets: "False witnesses rose up against me. They asked me about things I did not know."[105] And again, "False witnesses rose up against me, and injustice lied for its own advantage."[106] He does not drive them to murder when he says, "Destroy this temple." But since he knew they were going to do it without delay, he gives a subtle hint at what is about to happen.

2:20 "It has taken forty-six years to build this temple, and you will raise it up in three days?"

They ridicule the sign, failing to understand the depth of the mystery. They take their own diseased ignorance as a legitimate excuse not to obey him. Since their minds are occupied with disgust at his deed, they understand him to be speaking at random rather than professing something that is possible, so that what is written might clearly be true of them, "Let their eyes be darkened that they may not see, and bend their backs forever."[107] Thus, since they are, in a way, **[211]** always bent downwards and look only at earthly things below, they receive no sight of the highest doctrines of devotion to Christ. God, who is loving toward humanity, is not begrudging them these things, but with fair-minded justice he is punishing those who commit intolerable transgressions.

See how senselessly out of control they are. They show no concern for their own souls. Our Lord Jesus Christ called God his own Father when he said, "Stop making my Father's house a house of merchandise."[108] Therefore, they should now understand that he is Son and God on the grounds that he arose from God the Father. They still believe, however, that he is a mere man and one of us, so they bring up the time spent building the temple, saying, "It has taken forty-six years to build this temple, and you will raise it up in three days?" O you are completely drunk with ignorance, I think one may rightly say to them. If you have a wise mind, if you believe that the temple in your midst is the house of God, how can you come to any other conclusion than that he is God by nature when he dares to say without risk to himself, "Stop making my Father's house a house of merchandise"? I mean how, tell me, would he have needed a long time to build one house? How would he have been too weak for anything whatsoever who in only seven days completed the whole universe with his ineffable power and who has that power merely by willing it? A people who are knowledgeable in the Holy Scriptures ought to have considered these things. **[212]**

[104]Mt 12:39-40. [105]Ps 35:11 (Ps 34:11 LXX). [106]Ps 27:12 (Ps 26:12 LXX). [107]Ps 69:23 (Ps 68:24 LXX). [108]Jn 2:16.

2:21-22 But he was speaking about the temple of his body. When therefore he was raised from the dead, his disciples remembered that he had said this, and they believed the Scripture and the word which Jesus had spoken.

A wise word is readily received by one who is wise, and the knowledge taught by lessons is retained more easily by those who understand. As the pattern of seals is distinctly impressed in wax that is not completely hardened, so also the divine word is readily planted in softer human hearts. That is why the hardhearted person is also called wicked. Therefore, since the disciples have a good disposition, they become wise. They ruminate on the words of Holy Scripture, nourishing themselves to gain more exact knowledge and from there come firmly to faith.

When the body of Christ is called a temple, how could the only begotten Word who dwells in it not be God by nature, since one who is not God cannot be said to dwell in a temple? Or let someone come forward and say what saint's body was ever called a temple. But I do not think anyone can show this. Indeed, I say that what we will find to be true when we carefully search Holy Scripture is that such an honor is attributed to none of the saints. The blessed Baptist, for instance, was beheaded by the insanity of Herod after reaching the pinnacle of all virtue and allowing no one to exceed him in devotion; yet no such thing is attributed to him. On the contrary, the Evangelist came up with a coarser word for his remains, saying this too providentially, it seems to me, to preserve the honor for Christ alone. [213] Thus it is written: when the murderer, namely, Herod, it says, "sent and beheaded John in prison, his disciples came and took his corpse."[109] If the body of John is called a corpse, whose body will be a temple? It is in another sense that we are said to be temples of God because of the Holy Spirit dwelling in us. We are called temples of God, after all, not temples of ourselves.

But perhaps someone will say, How then, tell me, does the Savior himself call his own body a corpse as well? "Wherever the corpse is," he says, "there the vultures will gather."[110] To this we say that Christ did not say these things about his own body, but he is referring in a parable-like way to the future gathering of the saints to him at that time when he appears to us again from heaven with the holy angels "in the glory of his Father."[111] Just as flocks of carnivorous birds, he says, swoop down to fallen bodies with a mighty rush, so also you will be gathered to me. Paul also revealed this to us when he said, "The trumpet will sound, and the dead will be raised incorruptible,"[112] and indeed elsewhere, "we will be caught up in the clouds to meet the Lord in the air, and so we will always be with the Lord."[113] Therefore, that which is taken as an image due to its similarity will in no way damage the force of the truth.

2:23 When he was in Jerusalem at the Passover feast, many believed in his name when they saw the signs which he did.

Christ does not stop saving and helping. He wins over some by his wise words, and he [214] catches others in his net, bringing them to faith by astounding them with divine power. By the things they see him doing, they are persuaded to agree that the one who performs such amazing works must truly be God.

2:24 But Jesus did not entrust himself to them.

The disposition of those who have just believed is not secure, and their understanding is not

[109]Mt 14:10, 12. [110]Mt 24:28. [111]Mt 16:27. [112]1 Cor 15:52. [113]1 Thess 4:17.

established by the new miracles. How could those whose course of catechesis is still green, so to speak, already be rooted in piety? Therefore, Christ does not yet entrust himself to the novices, showing that kinship with God is a great and highly desirable goal. It does not lie ready at hand for those who come to take it, but it is attained by desire for the good, by diligence and with time.

Let those who dispense the mysteries of the Savior learn from these things not to admit a person too soon within the holy veil or to allow neophytes to approach the divine table who are baptized too early and do not at that time believe that Christ is the Lord of all. In order to become a pattern for us in this as well, and to teach us who is appropriately initiated, he receives those who believe, but he clearly does not yet put his trust in them because they do not "believe in him." It is clear from this that newcomers must spend not a little time in catechesis. In this way, they may with difficulty become faithful. **[215]**

2:25 Because he knew all people and needed no one to testify about anyone; for he himself knew what was in everyone.

Along with the other qualities in Christ, this dignity too is fitting for God and is in no created being. The psalmist attributes it only to the one who is truly God when he says, "He alone fashions their hearts. He knows all their deeds."[114] If God alone understands what is in us, and Christ understands it, how is Christ not God by nature "who knows secret things"[115] and knows "deep and hidden things,"[116] as it is written? "For what man knows the things of a man except the spirit of the man that is in him?"[117] Though no one knows, God is not ignorant. He knows, because he is never numbered among the "all people" among whom "no one" is found (since he is outside of everything and everything is under his feet). Paul too testifies to this when he says, "The word of God is living and active, sharper than any two-edged sword, piercing to the division of soul and spirit, of joints and marrow, and discerning the thoughts and intentions of the heart. And before him no creature is hidden, but all are naked and laid bare to his eyes."[118] Since he "planted the ear," he hears all things, and since he "formed the eye, he observes."[119] Indeed, he is portrayed in Job as saying, "Who is this who hides his counsel from me, confines words in his heart and thinks to conceal them from me?"[120] **[216]** The Evangelist has to say, "He needed no one to testify about anyone; for he himself knew what was in everyone," so that we might see that the Son is God by nature.

3:1-2 There was a man of the Pharisees named Nicodemus, a leader of the Jews. He came to Jesus by night and said to him,

Nicodemus is quite ready to believe, but since he is overcome by an unhealthy regard for others and does not ignore other people's opinion, he refuses to be forthright and divides his mind in two. He "cripples" his intention and is weak "in both knees," as it is written,[121] pressed by the argument of his conscience that he should believe because of the surpassing quality of the miracles but estimating that the loss of his leadership over the people is intolerable since he was a "leader of the Jews." Thinking that he can both preserve his reputation with them and secretly be faithful, he makes the darkness of the night a coworker in his scheme, and he comes to Jesus. And by coming in secret, he is convicted of being double-minded.

[114]Ps 33:15 (Ps 32:15 LXX). [115]Sus 42. [116]Dan 2:22. [117]1 Cor 2:11. [118]Heb 4:12-13. [119]Ps 94:9 (Ps 93:9 LXX). [120]Job 38:2. [121]1 Kings 18:21 (LXX).

3:2-3 "Rabbi, we know that you are a teacher come from God, for no one can do these signs that you do unless God is with him." Jesus answered and said to him,

With these words, he thought he could possess the complete faith, and he supposes that it will be sufficient for his salvation [217] merely to marvel at things for which wonder is appropriate. He seeks nothing more than this. When he calls him a "teacher from God" and a coworker with God, he does not yet know that he is God by nature, and he clearly does not understand the message of the *oikonomia* with the flesh.[122] He approaches him thinking he is a mere man and has little understanding of him.

3:3-4 "Truly, truly I tell you, no one can see the kingdom of God without being born from above." Nicodemus said to him,

Faith does not consist in what you think it does, Nicodemus, he says. Talk is not sufficient for righteousness, nor will you establish your godliness with mere words. "For not everyone who says to me, 'Lord, Lord,' will enter the kingdom of heaven, but the one who does the will of my Father in heaven."[123] The will of my Father is that a person be made a participant in the Holy Spirit and that the citizen of earth be reborn into a strange and unaccustomed life and be called a citizen of heaven. And when he says that the rebirth by the Holy Spirit is "from above," he shows clearly that the Spirit is of the substance of God the Father, just as of course he says about himself somewhere, "I am from above."[124] And again, the supremely wise Evangelist says about him, "The one who comes from above is above all."[125]

We will discuss more fully at the proper time the fact that the Spirit is certainly from the substance of God the Father. [218]

3:4-5 "How can a man be born when he is old? Can he enter a second time into his mother's womb to be born?" Jesus answered,

With these words Nicodemus is convicted of still being unspiritual and therefore of not at all receiving "the things of the Spirit of God"[126] since he thinks that so august and illustrious a mystery is foolishness. When he hears of a birth that is from above and spiritual, he still imagines a bodily womb re-experiencing the birth pains of those who are already born, as he tries measuring divine things without transcending the law of our nature. When he finds the height of learning to be unattainable by his own ideas, he falls down and is carried away. Just as objects that are hurled against the dry rocks bounce back again, so also, I think, an ignorant mind, when it strikes ideas that are more vigorous than its own, bounces back down, exhausted. And since such a mind always prefers to dwell within its own limits, it despises the better and higher understanding. Indeed, this is what happens to the ruler of the Jews, and he does not receive the spiritual birth.

"Unless one is born of water and the Spirit, he cannot enter the kingdom of God." Since the man does not adequately understand what having to be born from above means, Jesus instructs him with clearer teaching and sets the knowledge of the mystery more plainly before him. Our Lord Jesus Christ calls the rebirth through the Spirit "from above," [219] showing that the Spirit is of a substance that is higher than all and that through him we become partakers of the divine nature.[127] This is based on Jesus' understanding that as

[122]*Oikonomia* in patristic writings refers to God's plan of salvation in general and, as here, the incarnation in particular.
[123]Mt 7:21. [124]Jn 8:23. [125]Jn 3:31. [126]1 Cor 2:14. [127]2 Pet 1:4.

we enjoy the one who proceeds from the divine nature substantially, we are transformed through him and in him to the archetypal beauty, and in this way, we are reborn into newness of life[128] and refashioned into divine sonship. But Nicodemus, since he did not understand "from above"[129] in this way, surmised that the birth that would happen again is meant in a bodily way. Therefore, he fell into a chain of reasoning which forced him to conclude this was impossible, and he was caught being both foolish and ignorant. So the Savior still has to deal with him more gently, as with one who is weaker in disposition. He removes the veil that seems to be thrown over his words and now says openly, "Unless one is born again by water and the Spirit, he cannot enter the kingdom of God." Since human beings are composite and not simple by nature, mixed from two things—namely, a body with senses and an intellectual soul—they need a twofold healing for the new birth, corresponding to both of the aforementioned. So the human spirit is sanctified by the Spirit, and the body is sanctified by the water, which in turn is also sanctified. Just as water that is poured into a kettle receives an impression of the fire's power by association with the tips of the flame, so also through the activity of the Spirit, perceptible water is transformed into a divine and ineffable power and sanctifies those with whom it comes into contact. **[220]**

3:6 "That which is born of the flesh is flesh, and that which is born of the Spirit is spirit."

By a different reasoning, Jesus moves him to ascend to a higher level of understanding so that when he hears of a spiritual birth, he does not call to mind properties that belong to the body. Just as it is surely necessary, he says, that offspring of flesh are flesh, so also offspring from the Spirit are plainly spirit. When things have different modes of being, their modes of birth certainly will not be the same.

We must note, however, that we say the human spirit is an offspring of the Spirit not as if it were from him by nature—that is impossible—but in the first place, it refers to what did not exist being called into being through him,[130] and in the second place, in the *oikonomia*, it refers to our transformation through him toward God in which he stamps his own impression on us and transforms our mind[131] to his own quality, so to speak. Along these lines, I think you will correctly understand also what Paul said to certain people, "Little children, for whom I am again in the pain of childbirth until Christ is formed in you,"[132] and again, "In Christ I gave birth to you through the gospel."[133]

3:7-8 "Do not marvel that I said to you, 'You must be born from above.' The wind blows where it chooses, and you hear its sound, but you do not know where it comes from or where it is going. So it is with everyone who is born of the Spirit."

An excellent teacher can deal with the mind of the hearers in various ways and go through many ideas, heaping up demonstrations for those things whose explanation seems difficult. So he brings up an example **[221]** as an illustration of the mystery and says, This mundane wind[134] in the air blows through the whole world. It runs wherever it wants and indicates its presence only by its noise. It escapes the notice of everyone's eyes, yet by interacting with bodies by the subtlest breezes it implants some idea of the natural activity

[128]Rom 6:4. [129]Ἄνωθεν, here translated "from above," also means "again." In this passage, Cyril has both meanings in mind simultaneously. [130]See Rom 4:17. [131]See Rom 12:2. [132]Gal 4:19. [133]1 Cor 4:15. [134]The word for "wind" (πνεῦμα) is also the word for "spirit."

that is in it. You should think of the rebirth through the Spirit in this way, he says, led on from small examples to greater ones and understanding what is beyond sense perception by means of the explanation that was put forward as an image.

3:9-10 Nicodemus answered and said to him, "How can these things be?" Jesus answered and said to him,

Long discussion does no good to one who understands nothing. Therefore, what is said in the book of Proverbs is wise: speak "to attentive listeners."[135] The Savior showed this to be true by experience, giving himself to us as a model of it. The teacher will certainly not be open to the charge of being unable to persuade when he says what he knows is right, but it does no good because of the dullness of the hearers. Besides, through this we learn that "a hardening has come on a part of Israel"[136] because "they hear but do not understand."[137]

"You are the teacher of Israel, and you do not know these things?"
Through this one instance, Christ shames all who are adorned with the name "teacher" but are clothed with a mere assumption that they are learned in the law, when in fact they have a mind full of ignorance and are unable to understand not only what they ought to know but also what they ought to be able [222] to teach others. If the teacher is like this, what will the learner be like, since the disciple does not rise above the level of the teacher, as the Savior says? "A disciple," he says, "is not greater than the teacher."[138] Since they were so ignorant, Christ is not lying when he compares them with "whitewashed tombs,"[139] and Paul most eloquently says to the leader of the Jews, "God is going to strike you, you whitewashed wall!"[140]

3:11 "Truly, truly, I say to you, we speak of what we know, and we testify to what we have seen."

He finds the man uninterested in learning, exceedingly uneducated and, because of the extreme dullness of his mind, still unable to be led to the understanding of divine teachings, even after expending a long explanation with various examples on him. Therefore, he reasonably skips careful explanation and finally advises that he should accept with simple faith what he cannot understand. He himself testifies that he knows clearly what he is talking about, showing by the celebrated status of his own person that it would be quite precarious to continue to oppose him. After all, Nicodemus was not likely to forget, since he asserted that he knew that our Savior Jesus Christ came as a teacher from God.[141] But to resist one who is from God, and God—how could this not be fraught with danger? This is a clear case of fighting against God! However, we who have the authority to teach should learn from this that for those who just come to faith, faith in simple arguments is better than a deep discourse and a very complicated explanation. Paul too gave some people milk to drink who were not yet able to partake of more solid food,[142] [223] and the supremely wise Solomon somewhere says to us, "Know well the souls of your flock,"[143] meaning that we should not set instruction indiscriminately before those who come to us, but we should fit it appropriately to the abilities of each.

"And you do not receive our witness."
Knowing that he has the Father and the Spirit naturally in himself, the Savior put "testify" into the plural so that, consistent with the law of Moses, what he said might be confirmed "by the mouth of two or three

[135]Sir 25:9. [136]Rom 11:25. [137]Is 6:9. [138]Mt 10:24. [139]Mt 23:27. [140]Acts 23:3. [141]Jn 3:2. [142]1 Cor 3:2. [143]Prov 27:23 (LXX).

witnesses."[144] He shows that the Jews in no way want to be saved, but by a totally unbridled and heedless stampede, they are carried into the deep pit of destruction. If they cannot understand what is preached because of their great ignorance, and they are not made receptive to faith, what other way of salvation could be devised for them? Therefore, the Savior spoke well and quite rightly when he said that Jerusalem would be without excuse on the grounds that it is bringing down on itself a self-invited ruin. "Jerusalem, Jerusalem," he says, "who will kill the prophets and who stones those sent to it, how often I have wanted to gather your children as a hen gathers her brood under her wings, but you were not willing. Behold, your house is left to you."[145] **[224]**

3:12-13 "If I have told you of earthly things and you do not believe, how can you believe if I tell you of heavenly things? No one has ascended into heaven except the one who descended from heaven, the Son of Man who is in heaven."

Because of your immeasurable foolishness, he says, you rejected a teaching that does not surpass human understanding. So how could I explain to you more divine things? How could those who are most ignorant in their own affairs be wise in matters that are above them? How could those who are weak in lesser matters not find the greater unbearable? If you do not believe me by myself when I speak to you but seek many witnesses for each point, whom shall I bring to you as a witness of the heavenly mysteries? For "no one has ascended into heaven except the one who descended from heaven, the Son of Man."

Even though God the Word has descended from heaven, he says that the Son of Man descended, refusing, after he became human, to be divided into two persons.[146] He does not allow certain people to say that the temple taken from the virgin because of our need is one son and the Word who appeared from the Father is another, except insofar as there is a distinction between what is appropriate to each one by nature. Just as the Word is from God, so also the man is from the woman; but ultimately Christ is one from both, indivisible in sonship and God-befitting glory. How does he confer on the temple from the virgin, as the temple's own properties, those properties that are appropriate to the naked Word alone? Conversely, how does he make his own the properties that are appropriate to the flesh alone? For now he says, "The Son of Man has descended from heaven," but at the time of his suffering he is afraid, terrified and distressed,[147] and he himself is recorded as undergoing the sufferings that are appropriate to the humanity alone. **[225]**

"And as Moses lifted up the serpent in the wilderness, so must the Son of Man be lifted up, that all who believe in him may not perish but have eternal life."

After sufficiently defending himself and explaining the reason why his instruction to Nicodemus does not ascend to the immeasurable and supernatural, he descends again to the acts done in type through Moses from the beginning. He knows that Nicodemus is barely able to come to the knowledge of the truth by being led by the hand through figures, let alone by exacting spiritual reasoning. He must surely "be lifted up," he says, "as the serpent" was lifted up by Moses, showing that searching the historical narrative is absolutely necessary and practically saying to the one who understands nothing, "Search the Scriptures, because it is they that bear witness to me."[148] The serpents

[144]Deut 19:15. [145]Mt 23:37-38. [146]πρόσωπα. Here we may see an early indication of Cyril's later opposition to Antiochene Christology. [147]Mt 26:37. [148]Jn 5:39.

were leaping on those of Israel in the desert. And as they were falling like ears of corn, immeasurably distressed at the danger that visited them unexpectedly, they uttered the most pitiful cries and kept calling for salvation from above and from God. Since as God he is good and compassionate, he commands Moses to raise up a bronze serpent for them,[149] and by this command in particular he orders them to rehearse beforehand salvation by faith. For the medicine for those bitten was to look at the face of the serpent put before them, and faith along with what was seen worked deliverance at the last extremity for those who saw it. That is the historical narrative.

By this deed he, in turn, inscribes the whole mystery of the incarnation typologically. The snake signifies bitter and murderous sin which kept feeding on the entire earthly race, **[226]** biting the human soul in numerous ways and pouring in the multifarious poison of wickedness. There was no other way for us to escape such victorious sin except through help from heaven alone. And so God the Word came to be "in the likeness of sinful flesh in order to condemn sin in the flesh,"[150] as it is written. He came to be made the procurer of indestructible salvation for those who gaze at him by a more intent faith or by searching the divine dogmas. The fact that the serpent was set up on a high base certainly indicates the fact that Christ became known and distinguished so that he was unknown to no one; or it indicates that he was lifted from the earth, as he himself says somewhere, by his suffering on the cross.[151]

3:16 "For God so loved the world, that he gave his only begotten Son that whoever believes in him should not perish but have everlasting life."

With these words, he rushes forward to show openly that he is God by nature, if indeed we must think that one who has appeared from God the Father is certainly also God, not having this dignity as something alien, as we do, but truly being that which he is believed to be. He exhibits a great amount of planning in what he says too. After he ingeniously joins God the Father's love to us, he quite naturally comes to the discussion of it. For he shames the unbelieving Nicodemus, or rather he shows him to be ungodly as well. The failure to come eagerly to believe, even though it is God who is teaching—what else could this be than to cloak the truth with a charge of falsehood? In addition, when he says that he has been given for **[227]** the life of the world, he is urging Nicodemus to consider carefully what kind of penalty would be in store for those who from madness consider such wonderful grace from God the Father to be next to nothing. "For God so loved the world," he says, "that he gave his only begotten Son."

Let the Christ-fighting heretic listen to this again, and let him come forward and tell us what the greatness of God the Father's love is or how we might reasonably marvel at it. He will no doubt say that the wonder of his love is seen in the fact that he gave "his Son" for us and in the fact that he is the "Only Begotten." Therefore, in order that the love of God the Father may remain and be preserved, let him be considered a Son, not a creature—I mean, a Son who is from the substance of the Father, that is, of the same substance as the one who begat him, and who is really and truly God. But if as you say, sir, he is not from the substance of God the Father, he will no longer be by nature Son and God, and the famous wonder of the Father's love will finally come to nothing because he exchanged a creature for creatures and not truly his Son.

Furthermore, the blessed Paul would have no basis for his threat when he says, "Anyone

[149]Num 21:8-9. [150]Rom 8:3. [151]Jn 12:32.

who has violated the law of Moses dies without mercy on the testimony of two or three witnesses. How much worse punishment do you think will be deserved by one who has trampled the Son of God under foot?"[152] Everyone agrees that one who despises tramples under foot. However, such a person tramples not the true Son but a fellow servant with Moses, since a creature is surely akin to a creature by reason of its being made, even if it surpasses the glory of another by its greater or more excellent qualities. Paul's statement, however, is true. The one who tramples the Son will pay a more severe penalty because he is not transgressing against a creature or one of the fellow servants of Moses. Therefore, the Father's love is great and beyond nature **[228]** since he has given his own Son, who is from him, for the life of the world.

3:17 "For God did not send his Son into the world to judge the world, but that the world might be saved through him."

After explicitly calling himself the Son of God the Father, he does not think that he should leave the statement without a witness. Rather, he introduces the proof from the quality of his deeds, so to speak, rendering the hearers more secure in the faith. I was not sent, he says, as the teacher Moses was, to condemn the world with the law or to introduce a command to convict people of sin. Nor do I do the ministry of a servant. Rather, I bring the love for humanity that befits the master. As Son and heir of the Father, I free the slave. I transform the condemning law into justifying grace. I forgive the sins of those who are strangled by the cords of their own transgressions.[153] I came to save the world, not to condemn it. As a servant, Moses had to—had to, he says—become a minister of the law that condemns, but as Son and God, I had to free the whole world from the curse of the law and, by surpassing love for humanity, heal the disease of the world. And if justifying grace is better than the condemning commandment, how does it not then follow that we consider the one who brings such a God-befitting authority and who looses humanity from the bonds of sin to surpass the measure of a slave?

This, therefore, is one message of the passage under consideration, and no ordinary one, I think. A devotion to learning moves me to mention a second message in addition to this, **[229]** which turns through the same revolutions and introduces a sense related to the foregoing. The Savior saw that Nicodemus was stuck in the Mosaic law and clinging to the ancient commandment, that he was shuddering at the rebirth through the Spirit and shrinking back from the new evangelical way of life, thinking, it seems, that this would be more difficult to bear than what was already commanded. As God, Jesus was not ignorant of the fear that sprang on Nicodemus from ignorance. So by using one short statement, he frees him from confusion about this. He shows that the commandment given through Moses is more grievous because it condemns the world. Jesus thus presents himself as a gentle judge by saying, "For God did not send his Son into the world to judge the world, but that the world might be saved through him."

3:18 "The one who believes in the Son is not judged, but the one who does not believe is judged already because he did not believe in the name of the only begotten Son of God."

After he proved by his deeds both that he is the Son of God the Father and that he brings to the world grace which is more marvelous than the ministry of Moses (for how could being justified by grace not be better than

[152]Heb 10:28-29. [153]See Prov 5:22.

being condemned by the law?), he devised for us, as God, another way leading to faith, driving the lost together from every direction to salvation. He holds out before the believer the reward of not being summoned to judgment, but before the unbeliever he holds out punishment. Thereby he brings them in both ways to one and the same road and calls them to come eagerly to faith, some from a desire for grace and others from a fear of suffering. He shows that the charge of unbelief is severe and great, **[230]** since he is the Son and the Only Begotten. The more trustworthy something insulted is, the more one who dishonors it will be condemned for a terrible transgression. He says that the unbeliever "is judged already" in that the unbeliever has already determined that punishment must be decreed against himself by knowingly rejecting the one who bestows freedom from judgment.

3:19 "This is the judgment, that the light has come into the world, and people loved darkness rather than light."

He does not allow the judgment against the unbelievers to remain unexamined; instead, he adds the reason and clearly shows that, according to the passage in Proverbs, "not unjustly are the nets spread for birds."[154] After all, those who prefer to remain in darkness, he says, when it is in their power to be enlightened—how would they not reasonably be the ones who determine that dreadful consequences should happen to them? How would it not be their own choice to suffer sorrows which they could avoid if they would only examine matters correctly, preferring to be enlightened rather than not, and taking care to consider baser matters secondary to more noble matters? Again, he keeps the human mind free from the bonds of necessity. By its own inclinations it tends toward both sides, so that it may justly receive praise for the good and punishment for the opposite, just as he has certainly shown in another place, saying, "If you are willing and obedient to me, you will eat the good of the land. But if you are unwilling and disobedient to me, the sword will devour you."[155] **[231]**

3:20 "For all who do evil hate the light and do not come into the light, so that their deeds may not be exposed."

He profitably goes over what he said and exposes sluggishness in beneficial matters as coming from a love of evil and having as its root the unwillingness to learn those things that would make someone wise and good. Those who do evil flee and refuse, he says, to come into the divine light, not hiding from shame because of evil (since by doing this they would have been saved) but desiring to remain in ignorance of what is right lest they be struck when they transgress and run into the now more pointed accusations of their own conscience. In the end, because they know the good, they will give a more painful account to the judge if they should be unwilling to do what is pleasing to God. But "the one who does the truth," that is, the one who loves and performs the deeds of the truth, "comes into the light so that it may be clearly seen that their deeds have been done in God."[156] They do not reject illumination by the Spirit; indeed, by such illumination they are calmly led to be able to understand whether they have transgressed the divine command and whether everything has been done according to the law of God.

It is therefore a clear proof of an unbridled inclination to evil and of taking pure pleasure in what is worse to be unwilling to learn the things that make one strong enough to run back to the better. But it is clear proof of a

[154]Prov 1:17 (LXX). [155]Is 1:19-20. [156]Jn 3:21.

desire for the best to thirst for illumination and to make God's law a kind of rule and guide for a way of life that is pleasing to him. Knowing this is this case, the divine psalmist sings, "The law of the Lord is blameless, converting souls. The [232] testimony of the Lord is faithful, making wise the simple. The judgments of the Lord are right, gladdening the heart. The command of the Lord is bright, illumining the eyes."[157]

3:22-24 And after these things Jesus went to the land of Judea with his disciples. John was baptizing at Aenon near Salim because there was much water there; and people came and were baptized. For John had not yet been thrown in prison.

After the instruction to Nicodemus has reached its conclusion, the divine Evangelist furnishes us with something else that is most beneficial. Since he was illumined by the divine Spirit to explain the most necessary subjects, he knew that it would be of immense profit to his readers to know clearly how superior the baptism of Christ is and to what degree it surpasses the baptism of John. That is because it was truly not far from his expectation that eventually some would arise who dared from their ignorance to say that there is no difference at all between them and they should be crowned with equal honors—either that, or slipping into even wilder ignorance than this, that the vote of superiority should be taken away from the baptism by Christ and the victory shamelessly wasted on the baptism by water. What rashness is beyond the reach of the uninstructed? Or with what blasphemy do they not rush ahead, those who rise up against the holy doctrines of the church "and pervert everything that is right," as it is written?[158]

The supremely wise Evangelist, then, in order to refute beforehand the reasons for their babbling, introduces to us the holy Baptist himself giving his own disciples the answer to the question. Accordingly, Christ baptizes [233] through his disciples, and likewise John too baptizes (though certainly not through the hands of others), but he was not baptizing in the same springs in which Christ appeared doing this, but "near Salim," as it is written, and in one of the neighboring springs. I mean that by the very act of distinguishing, in a way, the springs of water, he is showing that there is a difference in the baptism and indicating through an enigma that his baptism is not the same as that of our Savior Christ. Yet it was near and close to it, providing a kind of preparation and introduction to the more perfect one. Therefore, just as the law of Moses is said to have a shadow "of the good things to come and not the true form of the realities"[159]—since the Mosaic letter is a kind of preparatory exercise and precatechesis of worship in the Spirit and is in labor with the truth hidden within it—so also you should conceive of the baptism for repentance in the same way.

3:25-26 Now a discussion about purification arose between John's disciples and a Jew. They came to John and said to him,

Although the Jews are powerless to recommend sprinkling according to the law and are not able to advocate cleansing through the ashes of a heifer, they weave a web for John's disciples by which they were planning to distress them in no small measure, even though they are quite easily beaten at their own game. The blessed Baptist's followers were already showing themselves stronger and more intelligent than the Pharisees by marveling at the baptism of their teacher and resisting the purifications of the law. [234] And the Pharisees, who are eager only for invective and are

[157]Ps 19:7-8 (Ps 18:8-9 LXX). [158]Mic 3:9. [159]Heb 10:1.

quite ready for every evil work, are angry at what is going on. They even change their tune and praise Christ's baptism. They do so not because they are rightly disposed or showering true praises on it but because they are stirred up with the sole purpose of distressing their opponents. So they borrow a statement that is contrary to their opinion until their pursuit reaches its goal. They cannot adduce a reasonable proof, nor do they argue for Christ by drawing on the Holy Scriptures. Where could the uninstructed gain such understanding, after all? Merely to confirm their own arguments, they put forward the pretext that very few people come to John, while they come to Christ in droves. Perhaps they thought, in their exceeding foolishness, that they would carry off the prize and speak out in favor of legal purification, thinking it has now prevailed, by placing the baptism that Christ bestows on those who come to him over the baptism at the hand of John. They do indeed distress those with whom they are arguing, but they barely get away with it. And they withdraw from John's disciples far more defeated by their ill-considered battle over words because they are forced to crown the Lord with praise against their will.

3:26-27 "Rabbi, the one who was with you on the other side of the Jordan about whom you testified, look, he is baptizing and everyone is going to him." John answered and said,

The disciples are chewed up by the arguments of the Pharisees. Even though they are concentrating on the very nature of the matter, they cannot prove the Pharisees are lying. They are understandably at a loss, and because they do not know the great honor of our Savior, **[235]** they are astounded at John's shortcomings. Combining words of love with shame and admiration, they demand to learn now why the one he testified about with his own voice surpasses him in fame, exceeds him in grace and, by baptizing, takes into his net not a part of the entire Jewish multitude but already the whole of it. And they were asking this question, it seems, not without divine help since because of their question the Baptist invites them to a painstaking and lengthy explanation about the Savior, and he introduces the clearest difference between the baptisms.

"No one can receive anything except what is given them from heaven."
There is nothing good in human beings, he says, which does not absolutely need to be given by God. It is right for creation to hear, "What do you have that you did not receive?"[160] I think that we must be satisfied with the measure that is apportioned to us and rejoice at the honors given us from heaven, and we should by no means stretch beyond them. We should not dishonor the decree from heaven, treating the honors ungratefully by a continual desire for something better, or fight against the Lord's judgments out of shame because we think it is not right for us to receive something less than what is more perfect. Instead, we should value highly whatever honors God is pleased to grant us. So let not my disciple be ashamed, he says, if I do not leap over the lot given to me, if I do not set my sights on the better but am lowered to the glory that befits a human being. **[236]**

3:28 "You yourselves are my witnesses that I said, 'I am not the Christ,' but I have been sent before him."

He reminds his disciples of the words they have so often heard. He proves them guilty of being paralyzed by forgetting what is beneficial and of nodding off before so solemn a teaching.

[160]1 Cor 4:7.

Ingeniously, at the same time he persuades them to remember the Holy Scripture since they are nourished by a desire to learn the following: Who does the Scripture proclaim Christ will be? And who does it proclaim the Baptist, the forerunner, will be? When they receive the knowledge of each in this way, they will in no way be angry since they see them each in the condition that is fitting for each. Therefore, I need no one else, he says, to witness to this. I have my disciples who themselves have heard. I have confessed my servitude, proclaiming, "I have been sent. I am not the Christ." Let him conquer. Let him prevail. Let him shine brighter, since he is Lord and God.

3:29 "He who has the bride is the bridegroom. The friend of the bridegroom, who stands and hears him, rejoices greatly at the bridegroom's voice. For this reason, my joy has been fulfilled."

Again, the discussion originated from a comparison with our affairs, but it leads to more subtle thoughts. Types of intellectual things can be touched by the hand, yet the coarseness of corporeal examples often introduces a very precise proof of spiritual matters. Accordingly, Christ is, he says, the bridegroom and the ruler of the feast, while I am the one who invites people to the supper and who leads the bride. I consider it my highest joy and most illustrious honor merely to be counted among his friends and [237] to hear the voice of the one who feasts. Therefore, I already have what I long for, and my zealous pursuit has been accomplished. For I not only proclaimed that Christ would come, but also I have already seen him present, and I admit his very voice into my ears. But you, my wise disciples, when you see human nature, which is betrothed to Christ, going to him, and when you observe the nature that is cut off and running away from its love for him ascending to spiritual intimacy through holy baptism, do not be upset that this is not for me, he says. Instead, realize that the bride gladly runs to her spiritual bridegroom, since this is truly right and more fitting. After all, "he who has the bride is the bridegroom," that is, do not seek in me the crown of the bridegroom. The psalmist is not dancing for me when he says, "Listen, daughter. See and incline your ear. Forget your people and your father's house because the king has desired your beauty."[161] The bride is not seeking my bedroom when she says, "Tell me, the one whom my soul loves, where you pasture and where you make your flocks lie down at noon."[162] She has the bridegroom from heaven. Still, I will rejoice in the name and the fact of friendship because I have surpassed the honor befitting a servant.

With that, I think the meaning of the passage before us has been explained very well. And since I have already sufficiently gone through the spiritual marriage,[163] I think it would be wearisome to write any more about it.

3:30 "He must increase, but I must decrease."

He shames his disciples for still being troubled about insignificant matters, for taking offense prematurely at things that should not offend them at all [238] and for not knowing precisely who Emmanuel is and where he comes from. The marvel over his deeds will not be limited, he says, nor will he exceed my honor merely because more people are baptized by him. Instead, he will ascend to a measure of glory that befits God. He must enter into an "increase" of glory and, by the daily addition of signs, bound ever upwards to the greater and shine more brightly to the world. "But I must decrease," meaning that I remain in the condition in which I am found so that I do not

[161]Ps 45:10-11 (Ps 44:11-12 LXX). [162]Song 1:7. [163]See Cyril's comments on Jn 2:11 (p. 91).

sink below the measure once given me. But as he ascends to ever-increasing glory, I decrease to the extent that he rushes past me.

These matters the blessed Baptist explains to us. But our discussion will do well to proceed by way of examples, making clearer the force of what was said. Let a two-cubit stake be placed in the ground. And let a plant be placed next to it, still below the ground but sending green shoots into the air, and by an irresistible force from the roots always pushing toward a greater height. Now if someone were to confer a voice on the stake, and it said concerning itself and the neighboring plant, "This must increase, and I must decrease," one would not reasonably think that it indicated any harm to itself or that its existing length would be shortened. It asserts that it decreases only in this respect: that it is found to be less than the one which always advances toward growth. Or take an example similar to this, that the brightest star cries out, speaking about the sun, "That must increase, but I must decrease." While **[239]** the gloom of night darkens the depths of the atmosphere, one may well admire the morning star shining with its golden light and conspicuous in its full glory. But when the sun has already promised to rise and sprinkles the world with a bit of light, the star is overcome by something greater and yields to it as it advances little by little. It may well speak the words of John since it is experiencing the same thing he says he is undergoing. **[240]**

Chapter Two

The Son is not an originate being, but as God and from God, he is over all things.

3:31 "The one who comes from above is over all."

It is no great achievement, he says, nor is it very admirable if Christ exceeds the glory of humanity since he does not set the bounds of his glory at that point. As God he is above all creation, and he "is over all" that has been made. This does not assume that he is numbered among "all things" but that he is distinct from all things and set above all things in a manner befitting God. He adds the reason, shaming the one who resists him and silencing his opponent. "The one who comes from above," he says, that is, the one who has sprung from the root from above, preserving in himself by nature his Father's natural goodness—everyone agrees that he is "over all." It would be inconceivable not to give the Son exactly the same honor as the one who begat him. After all, how could the Son, who is illustrious because of his identical nature and who is the radiance and imprint of the Father, be less than him in glory? Will not the properties of the Father be dishonored in the Son, and will we not insult the imprint of the begetter if we place the Son in an inferior position? **[241]** I think this will be clear to everyone, and for this reason it is written, "That all may honor the Son just as they honor the Father. The one who does not honor the Son does not honor the Father either."[164] The one who rejoices in honor equal to that of God the Father since he is from him by nature—how could he not be thought to surpass the substance of originate beings? That is what "is over all" means.

I perceive, however, that the mind of the Christ-fighters will never rest, and they will likely come with their incessant babbling and say, When the blessed Baptist says that the Lord came "from above," what argument will force us to suppose that, just because it says "above," he came from the substance of the Father and not rather from heaven or even from his inherent superiority over all things, and that is why he is understood and said to be

[164]Jn 5:23.

over all? When they pelt us with such arguments, they will hear in return, We will not follow your unsound reasoning, sirs, but only the divine Scripture and the sacred writings. We must therefore search in them to see how they define for us the force of "from above." So let them hear one of the Spirit bearers crying out, "Every good and perfect gift is from above, coming down from the Father of lights."[165] See, he says explicitly that "from above" is "from the Father." Knowing that nothing else surpasses originate beings except the ineffable nature of God, he applies "from above" strictly speaking to that nature. Everything else is subject to the yoke of servitude. God alone rises above being ruled and rules. Therefore, he is truly "over all." The Son, since he is God and from God by nature, will not be excluded from this splendor.

But if you think "from above" must be taken to mean "from heaven," **[242]** then let the term be used also of every angel and rational power since those who dwell in the city above come to us from heaven, and they "ascend and descend," as the Savior says somewhere, "on the Son of Man."[166] What then is it that persuaded the blessed Baptist to attribute that which was in the power of many to the Son alone exclusively and to say "the one coming from above" as though he is the only one descending from above? I guess he should have made the honor to be common to the others and said, "Those who come from above are over all." But he knew that the expression belonged to the one Son since he sprang from the highest root.

Therefore, "from above" does not mean "from heaven." Instead, it should be understood, as we already said, in a way that is pious and true. How in the world will he be "above all" if "from above" does not mean "from the Father" but rather "from heaven"? In that case, every one of the holy angels will be "above all" since they come from there. But if each one escapes being numbered among the "all," who then will comprise the "all"? How could the word *all* remain intact and keep its precise meaning if such a multitude of angels desert and destroy the definition of "all"? It is no longer "all" if those who were in the "all" remain outside of it. The Word, however, shines forth ineffably from God the Father, possesses the birth from above as his own and "comes" in the sense that he is from the Father's substance as from a spring. Therefore, he will do no harm to the "all" when he escapes being classified among the "all" as a part. Instead, he will be "over all" as someone besides them by nature and by God-befitting power and by the other attributes that belong to the one who begat him. **[243]**

But perhaps they will be ashamed of the strange results of this line of inquiry, and they will say, "from above" does not mean "from heaven" but "from his inherent superiority over all things." Come then, let us examine more carefully what they are saying and see where their attempt will lead us. First of all, it is completely ignorant and dim-witted to say that the Son comes from his own dignity and that one and the same goes out from his own superiority, as if from a place or a person, to be "over all." In addition, I would very much like to ask them whether they will grant the Son an essential and irrevocable superiority over all things or one that is brought in from the outside as an accident.[167] If they say that he has an acquired superiority and is glorified with imported honors, then they must admit that the Only Begotten can at some point be bereft of glory, stripped of his acquired (as they call it) grace, deprived of being "over all" and shown to be bare of the superiority that they now admire. That is because an accident can be lost since it does not touch the substance of its subject. Therefore, there will be change and alteration when it comes to the Son, and the

[165]Jas 1:17. [166]Jn 1:51. [167]That is, an outer characteristic that is not of the substance of an object or being.

psalmist will be lying and singing vain words to him: "The heavens will perish, but you remain. They will all wear out like a cloak. You will roll them like a garment, and they will be changed. But you are the same, and your years will not come to an end."[168] How is he the same if he undergoes change along with us, and this change happens by alterations for the worse? He even glorifies himself in vain, it seems, when he says, "Behold, behold, I Am, and I do not [244] change, and there is no God except me."[169] How will the passions of the offspring not ascend to the Father himself, since he is his imprint and exact image? God the Father will then be changeable on us, and he will possess his superiority over all things as an attachment. I will not speak of the rest. The archetype must, so to speak, make the qualities of the image his own.

So let's say that they shudder at the troubling absurdities in their argumentation and they now say that his superiority is not acquired but essential and irrevocable. Well then, sirs, how will you not agree with us, even against your will, that the Son is "above all" in that he is God by nature, and therefore he also comes only from the substance of God the Father? If there is nothing originate that is not included in the meaning of "all," and the Son is "over all"—that is, as someone else besides all things, who possesses an essential superiority over all things and is not the same nature as all things—how could he not be thought to be true God? The one who in his essence lies outside the multitude of created things and who by nature escapes being classed among originate beings—what else could he be but God? We see nothing holding a middle position, after all, as far as subsisting substance is concerned. Creation is ruled, and God is understood to be over it. So if the Son is God by nature, and he is begotten ineffably from God the Father, "from above" indicates the nature of the one who begat him. And the Only Begotten is "over all" for this reason, that he too is seen to be of that nature. [245]

"The one who is of the earth belongs to the earth and speaks about earthly matters." The one who is earth-born, he says, will not be able to persuade as effectively as God who is over all. "The one who is of the earth" will speak as a human being and will hold the rank merely of an advisor, entrusting the reins of the desire to believe completely to the students. But "the one who comes from above" as God employs a message with divine and ineffable grace and implants it in the ears of those who come to him. The more superior he is by nature, the more effective he will certainly be. The blessed Baptist says these things to the great benefit of his disciples. When they observed that he was inferior to the glory of the Savior, they were scandalized by this in no small measure. So they went to him saying, "Rabbi, the one who was with you on the other side of the Jordan, to whom you testified—look, he is baptizing, and everyone is coming to him."[170] The Spirit bearer, cutting short their offense and implanting in his disciples a healthy view of the most important matters, explains as well as he can the superiority of the Savior over all things. And he teaches the reason, no less, why everyone was now going to him and why they were leaving behind the baptism by water only and going to the more divine and more perfect baptism, namely, the baptism by the Holy Spirit.

"The one who comes from heaven is over all." This statement testifies, he says, that the difference between those of the earth and God the Word who comes down from above and from heaven is exceedingly great and incomparable. If I am not qualified to teach this, [246] and if my word alone is not enough for you, the

[168]Ps 102:26-27 (Ps 101:27-28 LXX). [169]Is 45:5. [170]Jn 3:26.

Son himself will confirm it by testifying that there is an incomprehensible degree of difference between what is earth-born and the beginning which is over all. When he was arguing with the unholy Jews somewhere, the Savior said, "You are from below; I am from above."[171] The nature of originate beings is below, he says, on the grounds that they are subject to and have to serve God, who calls them into being. But he says that the divine, ineffable and ruling nature is above on the grounds that it has all originate beings under its feet and subjects them to the yoke of its authority. The blessed Baptist did not add these words to his previous statement to no purpose. He did not want his disciples to think he was inventing idle arguments and to think that he was saying that Christ is from above, while he himself is from the earth, just because he was ashamed of being inferior to Christ. Therefore, he has to confirm the force of what he said with what the Savior himself said, and he shows his explanation to be not an empty excuse, as they thought, but rather an exposition of the truth.

Since the other part of the line reads, "For what he has seen and heard, this he testifies,"[172] come and let's discuss this a little. By nature and custom, we gain certainty about every matter especially through two dominant senses: I mean vision and hearing. When we hear and see things for ourselves, we come to speak about them with certainty. While persuading them to run full speed to believe in Christ (since he speaks, he says, of what he knows accurately), he draws again on a sort of comparison with our affairs, so that [247] we may understand what is more divine. And so he says, "What he has seen and heard, this he testifies."

3:32 "And no one receives his testimony."

The blessed Baptist does not say this thinking that no one receives the testimony that Christ is indeed God by nature and that, since he comes from above and from the Father, he is over all. For many have received it and believed it, and Peter even said in front of everyone, "You are the Christ, the Son of the living God."[173] But since he recognizes more clearly than everyone else the great dignity of the one speaking, he marvels at the senselessness of those who do not believe in him, all but shaking his head and slapping his thigh.

CHAPTER THREE

Christ is God and from God by nature.

3:33 "The one who receives his testimony has certified that God is true."

There is no other way to show the ungodliness of those who do not believe except to unveil the glorious uprightness of the believers since what is base is easily recognized by comparison with the good, and knowledge of the better puts the worse to shame. Anyone who assents to the words of the one who has come from above has sealed and confirmed through this understanding that constant truthfulness is characteristic of the divine nature and most agreeable to it. From this it is clear, for those who can see, that the opposite is true as well. The one who fends off the faith will surely bear witness that God is not true.

We must again take note that he removes the Son from consubstantiality with creation and shows through what he says that the Son is God by nature. If the one who believes what he says and receives the testimony that he gives about himself has confirmed and declared that "God is true," how could Christ not be understood to be God by nature, since he is the one who, on the basis of what was just said, is

[171]Jn 8:23. [172]Jn 3:32. [173]Mt 16:16.

testified to be true? **[249]** Or again, let the opponent tell us how the divine nature is honored as being true when our Savior's testimony is received? If he is not completely God by nature, then the one who believes that Christ is telling the truth will not be showing reverence to the divine nature. Instead, according to them, the believer will be showing reverence to one of the fairest creatures. But since the declaration of being true extends to God when Christ is believed, I think it is entirely clear that he is God and not an imposter seizing honor for himself from those who join to praise him.

The enemy of the truth, however, will most likely not agree with these words of ours but will leap up vigorously, not admitting that the Son is God by nature. Again, the opponent will say, You engage in sophistry, sir, and you invent a maze of intricate arguments, always finding some way to reject the simple and right sense. The Word of God has come down from heaven and clearly cries out, "I do not speak on my own, but the Father who sent me has commanded me what to say and speak,"[174] and again, "Everything that I heard from the Father, I report to you,"[175] or also, as the holy Baptist himself testified in what follows, "He whom God has sent speaks the words of God."[176] Therefore, he is referring to the Son when he says "the one who receives his testimony" has certified that God is true. God the Father is actually true, but you are trying to transfer to the Son what belongs to someone else.

What then shall we say to these things? Will the Only Begotten be classified as one of the prophets, carrying out the ministry that belongs to the prophets and doing nothing else? Who does not accept without hesitation **[250]** that the prophets brought us messages from God? What then is exceptional in the Son if this is all he does? How is he over all if he is still classified with the prophets and clothed with the stature that belongs to a slave? How does he make this statement in the Gospels, which assumes that he surpasses the prophets in glory: "If he called them gods to whom the word of God came, and the Scripture cannot be broken, do you say that the one whom the Father sanctified and sent into the world is blaspheming because he said, 'I am God's Son'?"[177] With these words, he clearly separates himself from the company of the prophets and says that they are called gods because the word of God came to them, but he confesses himself to be Son. Grace is partially apportioned among the holy prophets, but in the Savior Christ "all the fullness of the divine nature" has been pleased "to dwell bodily," as Paul says.[178] And for this reason, "from his fullness we have all received," as John maintained.[179] How then is the one who gives at the same level as those who receive? Or how will the fullness of the divine nature be assigned the lot of the servant?

Therefore, let them consider carefully what a great blasphemy their argument risks. We will explain more fully in its own time and place how one should understand the passage, "I do not speak on my own, but the Father who sent me has commanded me what to say and speak."[180] But for the present, I think the objections of the opponents should be turned into a foundation for piety, and we should contend for the dogmas of the church on the basis of what they propose. They insist that the Son has received commands from the Father and does not speak on his own. Whatever he hears, as he himself says somewhere, he hastens to tell us as well. Fine. Let this be so. We will agree, **[251]** since this fact does no harm to the Son, at least as far as his mode of being is concerned. Rather, it introduces quite an elegant way to think through the present subject. So when they hear him saying, "I and

[174]Jn 12:49; cf. Jn 14:10. [175]Jn 15:15. [176]Jn 3:34. [177]Jn 10:35-36. [178]Col 2:9. [179]Jn 1:16. [180]Jn 12:49; cf. Jn 14:10.

the Father are one,"[181] "The one who has seen me has seen the Father,"[182] "I am in the Father and the Father is in me,"[183] let them "receive his testimony," let them "confirm that God (the Father) is true" when he moved the Son to speak what he knew accurately. Let them not disbelieve the words of the Savior, who is explaining to us truths from the Father.

3:34 "For he whom God has sent speaks the words of God."

The Father knows, therefore, that his own Son in him is the same by nature. For this and nothing else is what I think "are one" means. The Father recognizes that he is a Son, not a creature—and I mean a Son from his substance, not one who is honored by the mere name of sonship. The Father knows that the Son is an unchangeable image of his own character. Therefore, the Son is seen perfectly in him, and the Father depicts the Son, who shines forth ineffably from him by nature, in himself; he has the Son in himself, and he, in turn, is in the Son because of the identity of substance.

By considering these things, O heretic, you will release yourself from a bitter disease and us from spending time in argument and investigation. "For he whom God has sent speaks the words of God." If this passage is understood according to its surface meaning,[184] what will there be that is marvelous in the Son? After all, was not each of the holy prophets also sent by God? Did they not also proclaim words from him? Certainly, it was said somewhere to the teacher Moses, "Now come, I am sending you to **[252]** Egypt, and you will say to Pharaoh, 'Thus says the Lord,'"[185] and to the most holy Jeremiah, "Do not say, 'I am too young,' for you will go to everyone to whom I send you, and you will speak everything I command you."[186] What more, then, is in the natural Son who speaks the words of God because he was sent by him? He will be rendered a prophet, it seems, and nothing else when it comes to the way he carries out his ministry.

Therefore, you should understand "has sent" in this passage either to refer to the incarnation and the visitation in this world with the flesh, or you should take it in a more God-befitting and worthy way. For the Father did not hide the Son in himself, but he beamed him forth from his own substance like radiance from a source of light, according to the ineffable and inexplicable mode of divine generation. This too the Only Begotten himself made clear to us when he said, "I came from the Father and have come."[187] The Son came from the Father into his own existence even though he is in him by nature. And what "he came" indicates to us in that passage is the same as what "has sent" communicates in this one. The Word then, he says, who has appeared and flashed out from the Father, will use words that are fitting to God since he is indeed God and from God. Words that are fitting to God are true and are free from the stain of falsehood. Therefore, the one who receives the testimony of the Savior has confirmed that God is true, for he really is God by nature. **[253]**

"For he gives the Spirit without measure." Pay especially close attention now, my good friend, so that you may marvel with us at the sobriety of the saints. Now he says both that the Son has been sent from God and that he speaks the words of God. But he perceives, as it were, that he has clothed the Son with the stature of a prophet, as far as the superficial meaning of the words is concerned, as we just said. So in this passage he raises him above equality with them, and with this one statement he gives us to understand that there is a great, no rather an

[181]Jn 10:30. [182]Jn 14:9. [183]Jn 14:10. [184]Literally, "from what is at hand." [185]Acts 7:34; Ex 4:22. [186]Jer 1:7. [187]Jn 16:28.

incomparable difference. It is impossible, he says, for those who obtained the Spirit by measure to be able to give him to someone else. A saint has never become the supplier of the Holy Spirit to a saint, but the Son supplies to all as from his own fullness. Therefore, "he gives without measure." He does not have, as they do, some small share of the Spirit, and that by participation. Rather, since he has been made the supplier as well, he obviously must have the Spirit wholly essentially in himself. Therefore, the one who has such superiority over the prophets will not speak the words of God on the grounds that he is one of the prophets; but on the grounds that he is God from God, he will pour out words befitting God.

The fact that certain people think the Spirit is given to some by the apostles' hands[188] will in no way oppose what has been said since we should believe them to be invokers of the Spirit rather than suppliers of the Holy Spirit. That is because even the blessed Moses was not commanded to take from the Spirit who was on him, but God reserved this for his own authority alone. He told him that he must put forward the seventy, and he promised to take from the Spirit who was on him and place the Spirit on them.[189] For he knew that only God could accomplish God-befitting deeds. **[254]**

Chapter Four

The properties of God the Father are in the Son not by participation but essentially and by nature.

3:35 "The Father loves the Son and has given all things into his hand."

Since he has said that the Son, who has appeared as God from God, cannot use any other words than those that the one who begat him used, namely, true ones ("for he whom God has sent," he says, "speaks the words of God"),[190] he cogently develops this point with the present passage and says, "The Father loves the Son." We will not grieve God the Father, he says, when we clothe the one begotten from him with equal honor. We will not give offense when we crown the heir of the Father's essential goodness with God-befitting glory. For he "loves," he says, "the Son." Therefore, he will be pleased when the Son is glorified by us, and he will be distressed at the opposite. And let no one think, he says, that his Son is an heir only of this one God-befitting honor, since "he has given all things into his hand," that is, everything which is essentially good in the Father is completely in the power **[255]** of the Son. "Hand" in this passage refers to power, just as when he says through one of the prophets somewhere, "My hand has fixed the sky,"[191] instead of my "power." The Son has all the properties of the Father in himself, not by participation, even though the Father is said to have given them. Otherwise, he would have an acquired divine nature and not a natural one. The Father gives all of his properties to the Son in the same way a man may be thought to have given the properties of human nature to the child that springs from him, or a fire may be said to have given the property of its own nature to the heat that proceeds from it in its activity. In these examples, the act of giving is no loss to those who give (since the things understood to be given do not come forth by way of division or being cut off), and the appearance of receiving is no accusation against those who receive. That is because these words are used only to indicate origin, and the offspring are understood to be a certain natural quality, so to speak, of the ones who beget them. As such, they show what their begetters are according to their substance, and they shine with the natural activity of their own source.

[188]Acts 8:18. [189]Num 11:17. [190]Jn 3:34. [191]Is 48:13.

These cases are adduced as examples, but God is clearly above them. Therefore, we will not blame human speech, which is weak, "for the glory of the Lord hides speech," as it is written.[192] And if we see through a mirror and an enigma, and we know in part,[193] how could we not be far weaker when it comes to words of the tongue? You should then piously understand either that all things have been given by the Father to the Son in this way, or you should take the statement to refer to the *oikonomia* with the flesh, so that it no longer introduces a giving and receiving regarding natural properties but **[256]** places the Son in authority over all originate beings. You may also understand it like this.

"The Father loves the Son and has given everything into his hand."
Let not the slow to hear, he says, be quick to speak when they see that the Lord of all is a man. Nor let them think that the truth is lying and, because of the flesh, reject the necessity to believe in him as God. Let them receive his testimony. Let them eagerly confirm that God is true lest they grieve the Father in heaven. For he "loves his own Son," and the fact that he has given him authority over all things is proof of his love for him. Indeed, the Savior himself said as much: "All things have been handed over to me by my Father,"[194] and again, "All authority in heaven and on earth has been given to me."[195] And just because the Son appears to receive does not of course mean that there is good reason for anyone to accuse him of being lesser. Why? Because he received when he became man, when he humbled himself for our sakes, when the Lord was called a slave, when the free Son became one of the servants. How did he humble himself? How is he said to have descended from equality with God the Father? Do you not see in these words the one who gives in a God-befitting way as well as the one who is said to receive in the way of a human and a servant what he already had as God? It is not strictly speaking a gift from the Father which first put the Son into a position of lordship over all things, but rather it is a return and resumption with the flesh of the authority he had before the flesh. He does not begin to rule creation only when he becomes human.

What kind of humility could anyone say he descended to if he began to rule only when he became human? **[257]** How could he appear in the form of a slave if he is declared Lord only at that time, and then just barely? Away with this absurd line of reasoning! When he became human, he started to rule then in this sense: not that he cast aside God-befitting dignity because of his flesh, but he ascended again even with his flesh to what he was from the beginning. He himself proves that the statements about Christ that they babble about are really a resumption of what he had before when he says, "Father, glorify me with the glory I had in your presence before the existence of the world."[196] Do you see how he asks not for a beginning of glory but for a renewal of the glory he had in the beginning, and that he says this as a man?

Moreover, the one who is eager to learn will wisely heap up proofs from all over the place and be able to understand that "everything" is said to be given to the Son on account of his humanity. But one can especially see this from that awe-inspiring vision of Daniel in which he says that he saw the Ancient of Days sitting on his throne, and he declares that thousands on thousands ministered to him and ten thousand on ten thousand stood before him.[197] And he adds to this, "And behold, one like a son of man was coming with the clouds of heaven, and he came to the Ancient of Days, and he was presented before him. And to him was given dominion, honor

[192]Prov 25:2. [193]1 Cor 13:12. [194]Mt 11:27. [195]Mt 28:18. [196]Jn 17:5. [197]Dan 7:9-10.

and rule; and all people, tribes and languages will serve him."[198] You see how in these words the entire mystery of the incarnation is recorded for us in detail. You see how the Son is said to receive rule from the Father. The bare Word did not appear to the prophet, but one like a son of man.

After all, he humbled himself, as it is written, being found in appearance as a man for our sakes[199] so that when he was first restored to his rule, he might be made a beginning for us and a glorious way into his kingdom. **[258]** Though he is life by nature, he descended for us into death according to the flesh in the place of all so that he might deliver us from both death and decay. He did this by mixing us with himself, so to speak, by his likeness with us, and so rendering us participants in eternal life. In the same way, even though as God he is the Lord of glory, he conforms himself to our dishonor in order to raise up human nature to royal honor. He has become "preeminent in everything," as Paul says,[200] the way, the door, the first fruits of the blessings for human nature from death to life, from decay to incorruption, from weakness to strength, from slavery to sonship, from dishonor and ignominy to honor and royal glory. Therefore, when the Son clearly receives as man what he already had as God, let us not at all be offended, but let us bring to mind the way of the *oikonomia* that is for us and in our place. In this way we will preserve our mind unwounded and unhurt.

3:36 "The one who believes in the Son has eternal life."

The supremely wise Baptist does not testify simplistically or without examination about the fact that life is set forth as a reward to those who believe in Christ; rather, he brings us a proof from the very quality of reality, so to speak. The Only Begotten is life by nature, "for in him we live and move and have our being."[201] He certainly enters us through faith and dwells in us through the Holy Spirit. The blessed Evangelist John testifies to this in his epistles when he says, "By this we know that he is in us, because he has given us of his Spirit."[202] Therefore, Christ will give life to those who believe in him, since he himself is life by nature and dwells in them. **[259]** Paul proves that the Son dwells in us through faith when he says, "For this reason I bow my knees before the Father from whom every family in heaven and on earth receives its name, that he may grant you according to the riches of the glory of his simplicity to be strengthened with power through his Holy Spirit and that Christ may dwell in your hearts by faith."[203] So since life by nature is once again restored to us by faith, how is he not telling the truth who says, "The one who believes in the Son has eternal life"? That is, he has the Son himself and not some other life conceived of besides him.

"But the one who does not believe the Son will not see life."

Perhaps someone will say, Does the Baptist then advocate a different opinion to us and corrupt the teaching of the resurrection, saying that the believer will be given life but maintaining that the unbeliever "will not see life" at all? We will not all rise, it seems, since this implies a distinction. What then will happen to that which was said unconditionally about everyone, "The dead will be raised"?[204] And what is Paul doing when he says, "We must all appear before the judgment seat of Christ that each one may receive recompense for what has been done in the body, whether good or evil"?[205]

Now I suppose that the one who is eager for knowledge should be praised, but all the same,

[198]Dan 7:13-14. [199]Phil 2:7. [200]Col 1:18. [201]Acts 17:28. [202]1 Jn 4:13. [203]Eph 3:14-17. Cyril reflects a variant reading here, or perhaps Cyril adds "of his simplicity" as his own gloss. [204]1 Cor 15:52. [205]2 Cor 5:10.

a painstaking investigation of the Holy Scriptures must be made. See clearly, I beg you, the distinction between the different statements that were made. When it comes to believers, he says that they will have eternal life. When it comes to unbelievers, however, the statement takes a different form. He does not say that they will not "have" life since they will be raised by the common resurrection; rather, **[260]** he says they will not "see" life, that is, they will not arrive at so much as the mere sight of the life of the saints, they will not touch their blessedness, they will remain without a taste of life spent in bliss. That is really life. But to live again in punishment is worse than any death since it holds the soul in the body only for the sensation of suffering.

Paul too introduces such a distinction concerning the word *life*. Listen to what he says to those who have died to evil on account of Christ: "You have died, and your life is hidden with Christ in God. When Christ your life appears, then you too will appear with him in glory."[206] See how he refers to the life of the saints as appearing with him in glory? What about when the psalmist sings to us, saying, "Who is the person who wants life and desires to see good days? Keep your tongue from evil"?[207] Shall we not say that this passage is referring to the life of the saints? I think this is clear to everyone. He certainly does not command some to refrain from evil in order to obtain the future resurrection of the flesh since they will be raised even if they have not stopped doing evil. But he rouses them to that life in which they can surely see good days and spend eternal life in blessedness and glory.

"But the wrath of God remains on him." The blessed Baptist, by adding these words, has shown us more openly what he was getting at before. Let the one who is eager to investigate consider carefully the force of the thought. "The one who does not believe the Son," he says, "will not see life, but the wrath of God remains on him." If it were really possible to **[261]** think that the unbeliever will be bereft of life in the body, he would surely have added immediately, "But death remains on him." Since, however, he calls it the "wrath of God," it should be clear that he is distinguishing between the punishment of the ungodly and the bliss of the saints, calling the true life in glory with Christ "life" and calling the torments of the ungodly the "wrath of God." I will introduce two witnesses of the fact that punishment is often called "wrath" in the Holy Scriptures: Paul and John the Baptist. The one said to those who were converting from the heathen, "And we were by nature children of wrath, like everyone else."[208] The other said to the scribes and Pharisees, "You brood of vipers! Who warned you to flee from the coming wrath?"[209]

4:1-3 Now when the Lord found out that the Pharisees heard that Jesus was making and baptizing more disciples than John (although Jesus himself did not baptize, but only his disciples), he left Judea and departed again to Galilee.

It would seem appropriate to address how the discussion reaches this point, or where the sequence of events started that led to the statement that the Lord found out that the Pharisees had learned what they wanted to know. The fact that the holy Evangelist says "now when the Lord found out" clearly evokes the subject of a previous discussion. He knows all things spontaneously as God, with no one telling him anything. And he knows them first not when they come to be but even "before they come to be," as the prophet testified.[210] However, he waits for the right time for everything, and he yields to the order of

[206]Col 3:3-4. [207]Ps 34:12-13 (Ps 33:13-14 LXX). [208]Eph 2:3. [209]Mt 3:7. [210]Sus 42.

things rather than to his foreknowledge since this is indeed appropriate for the God-befitting *oikonomia*. **[262]**

So when "a discussion about purification arose between John's disciples and a Jew,"[211] there was much argument on both sides. One group, defending their teacher, maintained that the baptism administered by him was now on a higher level than the legal sprinklings and typical purifications of the other group. In fact, it seems they adduced as proof of their position the fact that many were going to him and were very happy to leave the ancient customs given from above. The other group—since their opponents' argument was coming headlong against them and the force of the truth was rushing down like water and washing over the feeble minds of those who stood against it—went contrary to their own opinion and, against their will, said that the baptism bestowed by Christ was far better.

They now began to get the upper hand by using the same reasoning as proof, rising up with the same arguments against those who had defeated them. They asserted that far more are seen going to Christ and that everyone rushes to him rather than to John. That is why I think John's disciples, burning with distress, go to their teacher and say, "Rabbi, the one who was with you on the other side of the Jordan about whom you testified, look, he is baptizing, and everyone is going to him."[212] They are presenting in the form of a question the premises or arguments that come from their quarrel with the Jews. On this basis, then, the Evangelist says that the Lord found out "that the Pharisees heard that Jesus was making more disciples than John," and to avoid their unbridled jealousy and to keep his suffering for its own time, he withdraws from the land of the Jews and goes up again to Galilee. **[263]**

4:4-5 But he had to go through Samaria. So he went to a city of Samaria called Sychar, near the plot of ground which Jacob had given to his son Joseph.

O what great wisdom and pure sobriety! With this explanation he anticipates the questions that he expected would be asked of him. Otherwise, someone would have immediately said, either to someone else or secretly in their mind, Why did our Lord Jesus Christ provide illumination to the Samaritans at an inappropriate time? After all, a Syrophoenician once came to him in tears begging for mercy for her suffering daughter. And what did the compassionate one say to her? "It is not right," he said, "to take the children's bread and throw it to the dogs."[213] He did not think, I believe, that he should lavish the grace allotted to those of Israel on the Gentiles ahead of time. He himself clarifies this when he says, "I was sent only to the lost sheep of the house of Israel."[214] How then, someone might ask, did the one who was sent only to Israel begin to teach the Samaritan race even though Israel had not yet completely rejected grace? In response, he introduces the explanation, persuasive with authority: "He had to go through Samaria." He did not arrange his stay with the Samaritans with the sole purpose of preaching the word to them and transferring to them the entire blessing of all of Israel. But since he "had to go," he teaches them, carrying out the work of wisdom.

Just as fire could never cease from the burning activity that is in it by nature, so also I think that it is impossible for the Wisdom of all not to carry out what is proper to wisdom. Though he says that it is not right **[264]** to take the children's bread and throw it to the dogs, yet he did throw grace to the woman who persisted with many tearful pleas in her request for mercy. No one else legislated the

[211]Jn 3:25. [212]Jn 3:26. [213]Mt 15:26. [214]Mt 15:24.

time of giving. He himself defined the time with the Father as Son and God and Lord. In the same way, he had mercy on the Samaritans as well. He unveiled the ineffable power of his God-befitting authority and gave illumination to the whole land as a by-product of his journey.

Otherwise it would be strange that Israel, already enraged with folly and thirsting for the Lord's blood, is perfectly loved. However, since they do not yet persecute him completely, but still within limits, our Lord Jesus Christ does not yet strip them of grace. He does nevertheless draw out the blessing to others little by little. And the fact that he withdraws from the land of the Jews and hastens to go to the land of a different race because of the inhumanity of his persecutors was a kind of threat, depicted typologically by the nature of his action, that they will presently undergo a complete loss of grace and will send their own good possession, that is, the Christ, to others unless they stop their violence toward him.

4:6 Jacob's well was there, and Jesus, wearied by his journey, was sitting by the well.

Once the Savior crosses the border of Judea and is now with people of an alien race, he rests "at Jacob's well." With this action, he shows us, in another type and enigma, that even though the gospel proclamation departs from Jerusalem and the divine word goes out to the Gentiles, love for the fathers will not be cast out along with Israel. [265] Christ will cling to them again and once again rest and be refreshed as in his saints, preserving to them the unfading grace they had in the beginning. He loves to dwell in the memory of his saints that he may show himself to be a type for us in this also, and become the beginning and the door to the honor given to the fathers.

He rests, "wearied by his journey," as it is written, in order even in this to accuse the ungodliness of those who drive him out. They should have gained his friendship with benevolent honors and cherished him with reverence and fear as a benefactor; instead, they inflict sweat and toil on the Lord so that he is telling the truth when he says of them in the book of Psalms, "And they repaid me evil for good."[215]

The daring of the Jews is seen in these words. How then will the Arians, who are neighbors of their foolishness (or rather, who could rightly be addressed with the words "you have made Sodom appear righteous")[216] answer us on this point? The one group crucifies Christ in the flesh, but the other slanders the Word's ineffable nature itself. See, he was "wearied by his journey." Who is the one who experienced this? Will you then introduce to us the Lord of powers lacking in strength? Will you ascribe the weariness of the journey to the very one who is the Only Begotten of the Father so that the one who cannot suffer is understood to be passible? Or will you do the right thing, avoid such thinking and apply the accusation in these matters only to the nature of the body, or rather say that weariness is proper to the human nature, not to the Word when he is considered (and is) bare and in himself?[217] This is the sense, then, in which the one who possesses all power in his own nature and who himself is the strength of all is said to have grown weary.

Now do not—do not, I say!—divide the one Christ into a pair of sons. He makes the experiences of the human nature his own, even though [266] the one who does not have it in him to grow weary remains impassible when he becomes human. So if he should say something that we think is fitting, or rather necessary, to a human being and therefore not to God, let us not immediately hunt for words, nor let us, when we most need skill for

[215]Ps 35:12 (Ps 34:12 LXX). [216]See Ezek 16:52. [217]I.e., weakness is not proper to the Word apart from incarnation.

godliness, be caught in exceeding ignorance, putting the language of the *oikonomia* with the flesh as far away from us as possible, ascending rashly to the very divinity of the Word and touching from great ignorance matters that are above us. If he did not completely take the name "human," if he did not come to be in the "form of a slave," it would be right to be confused when he says something fit for a slave, or rather to demand that everything be fitting for God. But if we are preserved in a sure faith and are unswervingly confident that, as John says, "the Word became flesh and dwelt among us,"[218] when you see him speaking as flesh, that is, as a human being, receive the discourse that is fitting for humanity in order to keep the proclamation certain. In no other way could we know clearly that, while being God and Word, he became human, unless the impassible is recorded as suffering something and the highest as saying something humble.

It was about the sixth hour.

He shows Jesus appropriately resting at the well. The sun was pouring out its most intense rays on those on earth from the middle of the sky and burning bodies with its unmitigated beams. Going further would not be without harm, but resting a little would be more reasonable, especially when he would have easily refuted the charge of luxury since the fitting time of day is his advocate in the matter.

He does not say that it was precisely the sixth hour, but it was "about the sixth hour," that [267] we may learn not to be indifferent about even the smallest details but to strive for and be concerned for the truth in whatever happens to be before us.

4:7-9 A Samaritan woman came to draw water. Jesus said to her, "Give me a drink." (His disciples had gone into the city to buy food.) The Samaritan woman said to him,

The Savior was not ignorant of the woman's arrival. Since he was true God, he knew quite well that she would soon come to draw cold streams from the well. And when she was there, he began to lure his prey into the snare. Immediately he drew tight the word of his teaching and began to construct his discourse from what was at hand.

The law specified for the Jews that they should in no way be defiled. Therefore, it ordered them to withdraw from every unclean thing and not to mix with foreigners or the uncircumcised. But they carried the force of the commandment much further and followed pointless observances rather than precisely what was said. They did not dare even to touch the flesh of a foreigner, and they thought they would incur total uncleanness if they were found to have anything to do with the Samaritans. Their concern for distinction advanced to such a point that they recoiled from tasting water and food brought to them by the hand of foreigners. In order to get a reaction from the woman so that his unexpected conduct might invite her to investigate who he was, where he came from and why he despised Jewish customs, and so that his conversation may thus [268] reach its goal, he pretends to be thirsty, saying, "Give me a drink." She says,

4:9-10 "How is it that you, a Jew, ask a drink of me, a woman of Samaria?" For Jews have no dealings with Samaritans. Jesus answered and said to her,

Inquiry is the beginning of learning. A question about something is the root of understanding for those who are ignorant of it. The discourse is designed to achieve this beginning.

[218]Jn 1:14.

Therefore, the Savior wisely pretended to place no value on the customs of the Jews.

4:10-11 "If you knew the gift of God and who it is that is saying to you, 'Give me a drink,' you would have asked him, and he would have given you living water." The woman said to him,

Since she did not know the substance of the Only Begotten, which surpasses earth and heaven, and especially since she did not at all know the incarnate Word, the woman called him a Jew. For her benefit he remains silent about this in order to keep to the subject of his discourse with her. He does, however, raise her understanding of him to a higher level by saying that she does not know who it is who asked for a drink or how much grace the gifts bestowed by God have. If she had this knowledge, she would not have allowed herself to lag behind. She would have asked before the Lord did. Through these words, then, he rouses her eagerness to want to learn. Notice how aptly he now carries out his discourse without boasting and says that he is God, even if the woman is slow to be able to understand it. He does this by persuading her to marvel at "the gift of God" and then introducing himself as the bestower of this gift. [269] For "if you knew the gift of God," he says, "and who it is that is speaking to you, you would have asked him." Who would appropriately grant the gifts of God? Would it not be the one who is God by nature?

He calls the life-giving gift of the Spirit "living water." Through this gift alone does human nature—though it is nearly parched to its very roots and already rendered dry and barren of all virtue by the evil work of the devil—run back up to the original beauty of its nature. It drinks in the life-giving grace and blooms with all kinds of good things. It springs up into a virtuous habit and sends forth well-nourished branches of love toward God. God says something of this sort to us also through the prophet Isaiah: "The beasts of the field will bless me, the owls and young ostriches, because I have given water in the desert and streams in the dry land to give drink to my chosen race, my people whom I have preserved for myself to declare my virtues."[219] The soul of the righteous will be "like a fruitful tree," says another of the saints,[220] and "it will spring up like grass between brooks," and it will appear "as a willow beside flowing water."[221]

It is possible for us, in addition to what has been said, to heap up other testimonies from Holy Scripture through which it would also be very easy to show that the divine Spirit is often referred to by the term "water." However, this is not the right time for us to dwell on these matters. Therefore, we will swim on to other matters, pressing on into the great and wide sea of divine meditations.

"Sir, you have no bucket, and the well is deep. Where do you get that living water?" The woman imagines nothing more than she is accustomed to. [270] She does not at all understand the meaning of what he said. She thinks he will raise up the water for her spontaneously from the depths of the well without a rope or any other mechanical device, just like those who are in the business of working wonders through spells and demonic deceit. She means "living water" according to her own definition: that which flows right from the breasts of the spring.

4:12-13 "Are you greater than our father Jacob, who gave us this well, and who drank from it along with his sons and flocks?" Jesus answered and said to her,

The woman stops herself as quickly as pos-

[219]Is 43:20-21. [220]Jer 38:12 (LXX). [221]Is 44:4.

sible. She sees that she did not understand his meaning in a way that is holy and altogether right. It was impossible that she who was, on the whole, enjoying the divine discourse should receive no benefit at all toward sobriety. So she thought it was possible that the one speaking was not a magician but a prophet (and one of those who is distinguished by his holiness), and that for this reason he promises to offer her living water even without the usual buckets. Or, she thought he may have found much better water for her use from another spring. Therefore, she immediately changes her conversation for the wiser and compares a saint with a saint, so to speak, saying, "Are you greater than our father Jacob, who gave us this well?" You may perceive her quick intelligence from the fact that she no longer wonders whether he is promising water without a rope, but she thinks he is speaking only of the quality of its taste.

The Samaritans then are foreigners since they are colonists of the Babylonians, but they count Jacob as their father in two ways. Since they live in a land that borders and is a neighbor to the Jews' land, a little of the Jewish worship rubbed off on them, and they were accustomed to boast of the fathers of the Jews. Besides, [271] it was really true that the majority of the inhabitants of Samaria sprang from the root of Jacob. For Jeroboam son of Nebat, after he gathered the ten tribes of Israel and the half-tribe of Ephraim, departed from Jerusalem during the reign of Rehoboam son of Solomon. He took Samaria and built houses and cities in it.

4:14-15 "Everyone who drinks of this water will thirst again, but whoever drinks of the water that I will give them will never thirst. The water that I will give them will become in them a spring of water gushing up to eternal life." The woman said to him,

"Are you greater than our father Jacob?" The Samaritan woman poses this question as if it were a great problem that is difficult to overcome. Again, the Savior with the greatest skill avoids boastful words by not saying explicitly that he is greater; instead, he persuades her to consider him superior by the quality of his deeds. To do this, he shows the incomparable difference that there is between spiritual water and earthly perceptible water by saying, "Everyone who drinks of this water will thirst again." But those who have their fill of my water, he says, not only will be raised beyond ever thirsting again but also will have in themselves a spring that is able to nourish them to eternal life. The one who gives greater gifts is greater, he says, than the one who has less, and the one who is inferior will not come away with the same glory as the one who conquers.

Next we must realize that the Savior here calls the grace of the Holy Spirit "water." If anyone should become a participant of it, they will then have a supply of divine knowledge springing up in them so that they no longer need admonition from others. Instead, they will be sufficient and capable [272] to exhort with ease those who thirst for the divine and heavenly word. These were the saints, prophets and apostles during their lives while they were still living on earth, and the heirs of their service, concerning whom it is written, "Draw water with joy from the springs of salvation."[222]

4:15-16 "Give me this water so that I may not thirst or come here to draw." Jesus said to her,

Again, she speaks about and imagines only ordinary things, and she does not understand what he says at all. She thinks that the goal of our Savior consists entirely in freeing her from

[222]Is 12:3.

petty chores, and she limits the grace of God to the fact that she would no longer thirst. Not even in mere thought does she receive the things above.

"Go, call your husband, and come here." It would be correct and not untrue to say that the minds of women are effeminate, and a soft mind dwells in women which has no ability to understand quickly. The nature of men is more apt for learning and far more ready for reasoning since it has a mind that is awakened for sobriety and, so to speak, burning and virile. For this reason, I think, he told the woman to call her "husband," subtly convicting her of having a heart that is exceedingly slow to learn and unpracticed in discourse leading to wisdom but at the same time planning something else most beautiful. [273]

4:17-19 The woman said to him, "I have no husband." Jesus said to her, "You are right in saying, 'I have no husband,' for you have had five husbands, and the one you have now is not your husband. You have spoken the truth." The woman said to him,

Who cannot see that the Savior asked the question about the nonexistent husband not out of ignorance that she was bereft of a lawful husband but as a pretext for revealing what was hidden? For he was able—able with difficulty—to help her marvel at him no longer as one of us but now as above humanity because of his incredible knowledge of her situation. He also helped her by approving her statement that she has no husband, even though she wasted away with so many men, because it is not the coming together from love of pleasure but the lawful consent and common bond of pure love that makes a marriage that is above reproach.

"Sir, I see that you are a prophet." With difficulty, she brightens toward sober-mindedness, although not yet perfect, since she still calls the Lord of the prophets a "prophet." Nevertheless, little by little she shows herself to be better than before. She is in no way disturbed by the accusations; instead, she seizes the meaning of the sign for her benefit and thus departs from her effeminate heart. She ascends in some measure to a vigorous mind and stretches the eye of her heart to an unaccustomed understanding of things. Therefore, it follows that we should marvel at the patience together with the power of our Savior who easily refashions our uninstructed understandings to a remarkable disposition of mind. [274]

4:20-21 "Our fathers worshiped on this mountain, but you say that the place where one should worship is in Jerusalem." Jesus said to her,

Thinking that the Lord is truly a prophet and a Jew, she boasts greatly in the customs of her country and contends that the counsel of the Samaritans is greater than the assumptions of the Jews. After all, the Jews, since they still accepted a coarser understanding about the divine and incorporeal nature, maintained that the God over all should be worshiped "only in Jerusalem" or its neighbor Zion, assuming that the entire ineffable and incomprehensible divine nature had once and for all made its dwelling there and was enclosed in temples made with hands. Therefore, they are convicted of being totally without understanding by the voice of the prophets of God, which says, "Heaven is my throne, and earth is my footstool. What house will you build for me, says the Lord, or what is the place of my rest?"[223] The Samaritans, moreover, are no farther along than the

[223]Acts 7:48; Is 66:1.

ignorance of the Jews. Their land as well as their ignorance borders that of the Jews. They do not escape just ridicule since they similarly think that both prayer and worship must take place on a mountain called Gerizim. The pretext for their ignorance was the fact that the blessing was given on Mount Gerizim, as we find written in Deuteronomy.[224] The woman puts this question to the Savior as some great and unsolvable problem, saying, "Our fathers worshiped on this mountain," and so forth. [275]

"Believe me, woman, the hour is coming when you will worship the Father neither in Jerusalem nor on this mountain."
He condemns alike the ignorance of all, saying that the form of worship will be transformed so that it is truer. A place will no longer be sought, he says, in which they think that God dwells strictly speaking, but "each one in their own place will worship the Lord,"[225] as one of the holy prophets says, as one who fills all things and is able to contain them. He says that his sojourn with the flesh in the world is the hour and the time for the change of such customs.

Observe how he uses the most elegant leading in his conversation to guide the mind of the woman to an understanding of the Son by calling God "Father." How could a Father be thought of at all, after all, if there is no Son? [276]

Chapter Five

The Son is not among those who worship, insofar as he is Word and God; rather, he is worshiped with the Father.

4:22 "You worship what you do not know. We worship what we know, for salvation is from the Jews."

He speaks once again as a Jew and a human being, since the handling of the situation demands this way of speaking. (After all, Christ would not have missed an opportune moment.) Still, he attributes more understanding to the worship of the Jews. The Samaritans worship God in a simple and unexamined way, but the Jews do so as they receive through the law and the prophets the knowledge of the One Who Is, as far as they are able. Therefore, he says that the Samaritans do not know, but he maintains that the Jews in some ways know well and that from them salvation, namely, himself, will be revealed. Christ is from the seed of David according to the flesh, and David came from the tribe of Judah. As a human being, he classifies himself among those who worship, even though he is worshiped with God the Father both by us and the holy angels. Since he put on the form of a servant, he carries out the worship that is fitting for a servant without ceasing to be God and Lord and the object of worship. He remains the same even though he also [277] became human and even though he preserves in every way the character of the *oikonomia* with the flesh.

If you see a great and supernatural humility, approach as a wonderer—not an accuser or a blamer but an imitator.

Paul wants us to be shown as such when he says, "Each one of you have the same mind in yourselves which is also in Christ Jesus, who, though he was in the form of God, did not consider equality with God something to be exploited, but emptied himself, taking on the form of a slave, being born in human likeness. And being found in human form, he humbled himself."[226] Do you see how the Son became an example of humility for us when, though he was equal to and in the form of the Father, as it is written, he came down for our sakes into willing obedience and humility? How then

[224]Deut 27:12. [225]Zeph 2:11. [226]Phil 2:5-8.

could the form of obedience and the form of humility appear except through deeds and words which are beneath his God-befitting dignity and which are far less than the bare Word had when he was with the Father and not intertwined with the form of a slave? How can we say he descended at all if we do not allow him to endure anything unworthy of him? How did he come to be in human likeness, as Paul says, if he did not imitate what is fitting for human beings? Worship is an act that is most fitting for human beings. It is placed in the category of a debt, and it is offered by us to God. Therefore, he worships as a man since he became human, but he is always worshiped with the Father since he was, is and will be true God by nature.

Our opponent, however, will not endure this but will rise up against us saying, Do not be surprised when we say that the Son worships. **[278]** We do not think that he must worship the Father in the same way as, for example, we or the angels do. But the worship of the Son is exceptional and is far superior to our own.

What then shall we say to these things? You think you are going to mislead us, sir, by clothing the Only Begotten with the most noble servitude possible and gilding this servile honor with words of deceit. Stop praising the Son with dishonor that you may continue to honor the Father. "For the one who does not honor the Son does not honor the Father either," as it is written.[227] What good, tell me, will it do for the freedom of the Only Begotten if his worship of the Father is made separate from ours? As long as he is found to be among the worshipers, he will certainly be a slave, even if he were to be considered an exceptional worshiper. He will be no different from the creatures when it comes to being originate. He will differ only with respect to the other superiorities, as Michael is superior to human beings or the other rational powers are superior to the saints. These powers are seen to have essential superiority over those on earth, either because of their holiness or by a superabundance of glory, to the glory of God, the artificer of all things. Nevertheless, the fact that they are classified as originate because they are created is in common with the rest. Therefore, the Word who is in and from the Father by nature will in no way escape being originate even if his worship is said to be exceptional. In that case, how will what is created still be Son, and how will a slave and a worshiper be by nature Lord?

I, at least, think that royal and lordly honor manifests itself in being worshiped, while the status of a servant and a slave is defined by worshiping. By falling down before someone, **[279]** we confess that we must think of his nature as superior and above all. So then all of creation was addressed by the all-wise Moses, "You shall worship the Lord your God, and him only shall you serve,"[228] so that to whomever servitude belongs by nature, and whoever falls under the yoke of the divine nature, this one must surely worship and submit to the garb of adoration. By saying "Lord," he distinguishes him from the slave, and by saying "God," he distinguishes him from the creature. They are conceived of together and contrasted, the slave with the Lord by nature, and that which is brought into being with the unoriginate divine nature.

Since the Son is eternally in the Father and, as God, is Lord, I am at a loss to show how he clearly owes worship. But let them proceed with their nonsense. The Only Begotten, they say, will worship the Father not as a slave or a creature but as a Son worships the one who begat him. We must then import worship into the definition of sonship and say that the Son must certainly worship the Father on the grounds that his being consists in this, just as

[227]Jn 5:23. [228]Mt 4:10; Deut 6:13.

ours consists in being reasoning mortal creatures, receptive of intellect and knowledge. The other option would be to refer his worship to external motions of his mind or mere inclinations of his will. If the total and necessary obligation to worship has been implanted in the Only Begotten by nature, as they think and say, how will they not be caught nakedly blaspheming the Father himself? After all, it is completely necessary to conceive of him too in this way, since the Son is his image and imprint, and whatever things are in exact likeness will surely differ in no way from each other. But if they say that **[280]** the Son offers worship to the Father only in his will, they are guessers rather than knowers of the truth. What then would prevent others from saying, as they fabricate a dangerous piety, that the Father wills to worship the Son, even though he is not a worshiper by nature? But, says the opponent, fitness itself has excepted the person of the Father from this and will subject the Son to it, who worships the Father not unwillingly.

What are you saying, sir? Do you offer us divinations from shrines or Greek tripods, or do you come like Shemaiah of Nehelam, belching things from your own heart and not from the mouth of the Lord?[229] Do you not blush as you trot out "what is fitting" against us, as if this were invincible in these matters? Do you not think it is fitting for the one who is by nature God to have his begotten Word be God whom all creation worships? Do you not think it is fitting for him to be called and to be by nature the Father of a Son who is worshiped rather than who worships? I think I am saying nothing that the truly wise would find disagreeable. How shall we specify that it is fitting for the Father to be worshiped by his own offspring when this idea inflicts such damage on both of them?

First, one who does not worship will not have the same honor or be the unchangeable natural image of one who does. That is because one who worships does so as an inferior. Moreover, this inferiority is not quantitatively measurable, the way one would measure a natural property, since one who is God or Lord cannot be inferior. Instead, the difference lies in the definition of their modes of being.

Next, how will he be shown to tell the truth when he says, "Whoever has seen me has seen the Father"?[230] And how does he say that he must be honored in no less degree than the Father[231] if he does not have equal glory because he is a worshiper? In addition, we will find the Father himself **[281]** in disarray—and not just any disarray. It is his glory to beget one who is as he is by nature. By contrast, it is no small disgrace to have an offspring who is of a different kind and alien to oneself and to suffer something which even the nature of originate beings shrinks from. By the decree and will of the creator of all, those creatures that receive the power to bear do not bear offspring that are worse than themselves. "For," he says, "let the earth bring forth grass and the fruit tree bearing seed according to its kind and likeness."[232] So the divine nature will be in second place after the originate beings since they have this quality, but it does not. He alone will be found to lack what has been decreed to be fitting and well-suited for the succession of creatures.

Who then, sirs, could endure you saying that it is fitting for the Son to worship the Father? But when you add to this argument of yours that the matter is not unwilled by the Only Begotten, and you fortify this unproven starting point merely by drawing on what is fitting—come, let us examine this from the Holy Scriptures from which I think it is most fitting to track down with zeal the proof of every disputed question. The law commanded that "the half-shekel" be paid by each of the

[229]Jer 29:24 (Jer 36:24 LXX); Jer 23:16. [230]Jn 14:9. [231]See Jn 5:23. [232]Gen 1:11.

Jews to God who is over all,[233] not to devise a way to gain wealth or a contribution of money to no purpose but to give instruction that shines forth in the clearest types. First, it teaches that no one is lord of their own head, but we all have one Lord, and we are enrolled for service by the payment of the tribute. In addition, it depicts mental and spiritual fruit in coarser words and deeds. **[282]** "Honor the Lord," it says, "with your righteous labors, and give him the first fruits of your righteousness."[234] This came to pass through the teaching of the gospel when the worship according to the law was now brought to a close. We think we must no longer worship the Lord of all by bringing outward gifts, hastening to pay the half-shekel, which is made of corruptible matter. Since we are true worshipers, we worship God the Father in spirit and in truth.[235] We must suppose that this understanding is hidden in the letter of the law.

When the Lord was in Jerusalem, the collectors of the half-shekel asked Peter, "Does not your teacher pay the half-shekel?"[236] "And when he came home," as it is written, "Jesus spoke to him first, saying, 'From whom do kings of the earth take toll or tribute? From their sons or from others?' And when he said, 'From others,' Jesus said, 'Then the sons are free. However, not to give offense to them, go to the sea and cast a hook, and take the first fish that comes up, and when you open its mouth, you will find a shekel. Take that and give it to them for me and for yourself.'"[237] Do you see that the Son did not endure being under the tax, nor did he undergo, as one who is under the yoke of slavery, an act that is fit for a slave? Knowing the free dignity of his own nature, he maintains that he owes nothing servile to God the Father. "Then the sons are free," he says. How then is slave-befitting worship something that is not against his will? How could one who shrank from the mere type of a thing **[283]** still accept the truth of it? Shall we not consider worship to be a kind of tribute and spiritual fruit bearing and say that it is a form of service? For why did the law bind service to worship by saying, "You shall worship the Lord your God and him only shall you serve"?[238] Worship is a sort of gate and road for service by works since it is the beginning of servitude toward God. Therefore, the psalmist says somewhere to certain people, "Come, let us worship and fall down before him. Let us weep before the Lord our maker."[239] Do you see how the duty of falling down follows from and is joined to worshiping? I cannot say what could be more fitting for a slave than that, at least in the eyes of those who estimate the quality of things rightly.

But if our opponents persist, still swaggering in unchecked shamelessness, and do not cease from their ignorant reasoning in these matters, let them look through all of Holy Scripture and show us that the Son worshiped God the Father when he was still the bare Word before the time of the incarnation and the garb of servitude. Now he worships blamelessly as a man, but then not yet. But they will not be able to show this from the divine and Holy Scriptures. Instead, gathering together guesses and ideas that come from unsound thinking, they will rightly hear, "You are wrong, because you know neither the Scriptures nor" the glory of the Only Begotten.[240]

We will not seek a proof from without, but we shall know from his own words that he does not worship as Word and God. Since he came to be as we are, however, he accepted this experience too, in a way that befits a human being, because of the *oikonomia* with the flesh. Why, after all, does he say to the **[284]** Samaritan woman, "You worship what you do not know, but we worship what we

[233]Ex 30:13. [234]Prov 3:9 (LXX). [235]Jn 4:23. [236]Mt 17:24. [237]Mt 17:25-27. [238]Mt 4:10; Deut 6:13. [239]Ps 95:6 (Ps 94:6 LXX). [240]Mt 22:29.

know"? Is it not clear to everyone from this statement that, since he uses the plural number and numbers himself among those who worship from necessity and servitude, he says these things on the grounds that he came to be in human nature, which is a slave? What, tell me, would have prevented him from applying worship to his own person in the singular if he wanted us to consider him a worshiper? He should have said, "I worship what I know," so that he would not be combined with others and would appropriate the force of the statement to himself alone. But as it is, he says "we" most excellently and with all security as one who is already classified among the slaves because of his humanity, as one numbered among the worshipers and as a Jew by nationality.

4:23 "But the hour is coming and is now here when the true worshipers will worship the Father in spirit and in truth, for the Father seeks such as these to worship him. God is spirit, and those who worship him must worship in spirit and in truth." The woman said to him,

He indicates the present time of his arrival, and he says that the types will be transformed into truth and the shadow of the law into spiritual worship. He says that through the instruction of the gospel, the true worshiper, that is, the spiritual person, will be led by the hand to a way of life that is pleasing to the Father and will more readily rush to friendship with God. For "God is spirit" in contrast to embodied nature. Therefore, he rightly receives the spiritual worshiper who does not carry the form of their godliness in a Jewish way in form and types but who shines forth in an evangelical way through achievements of virtue **[285]** and carries out true worship by the rightness of divine doctrines.

"We know that the Messiah is coming who is called Christ. When he comes, he will explain everything to us."

When Christ teaches that the time and the hour is coming, or rather is already here, in which the true worshipers will offer spiritual service to God the Father, the woman immediately takes flight with thoughts that are higher than usual to the hope that is spoken of by the Jews. She confesses that she knows that the Messiah will come in his own time, but to whom he will come she does not precisely say. It seems she accepts what everyone was saying about him without careful investigation since she is a laughter-loving and carnal woman. She is not altogether ignorant, however, that he will be revealed to Israel as a bearer of more refined teachings. This too she found out, no doubt, from the stories about him.

4:26 Jesus said to her, "I am he, the one who is speaking to you."

Christ reveals himself not to untaught or completely unlearned souls, but he shines forth and appears to those souls who are already more prepared to want to learn and who, giving birth to the beginning of faith in simple words, hasten on toward the knowledge of the more perfect. The Samaritan woman was shown to us to be such a woman. She applied her mind to truly divine ideas more coarsely than she ought, but she was not completely removed from the desire to know something. First, she does not immediately give Christ a drink when he asks for it. When she sees him breaking (to speak in a human way) the national customs of the Jews, she first asks him to tell her about the transgression. **[286]** By her mention of it, she all but invites the Lord to give an explanation. "How is it that you, a Jew," she says, "ask a drink of me, a woman of Samaria?"[241] But when, as the

[241]Jn 4:9.

catechetical discourse proceeds, she receives his accusation as medicine for salvation and finally confesses him to be a prophet, she puts another question to him, saying from a desire to learn, "Our fathers worshiped on this mountain, but you say that the place where one should worship is in Jerusalem."[242] Then he began to teach that the time is coming, or rather is already here, in which the true worshipers will reject the worship on earthly mountains and will offer to God the Father higher service in the spirit. But she considers the best of all to be fitting for the Christ alone and reserves the more perfect knowledge for his times, so she says, "We know that the Messiah is coming, who is called Christ. When he comes, he will explain everything to us."[243] Do you see how ready for faith the woman was already getting, and how she was advancing from insignificant questions to a higher disposition? And so, he needs to uncover for her with clearer words what she desires and to take what was reserved in good hope and place it right in front of her by saying, "I am he, who is speaking to you."

Therefore, let those who have the teaching task in the church entrust to the newcomers the message of catechesis for rumination, and thus let them finally show the newcomers Jesus as they lead them up from a little instruction to a more perfect knowledge of the faith. But those who take a foreigner and a convert and place him within the inner veil, entrust him with sacrificing the lamb with hands that are still unwashed and crown him with the honor of the priesthood [287] when he is not yet catechized—they had better prepare a mighty account for the day of judgment. It is enough for me just to mention this.

4:27 Just then his disciples came.

The arrival of the disciples is the end of his conversation with the woman. Christ is silent, it says. After implanting the glowing spark of faith into the Samaritans, he relies on the passage of time for it to be kindled into a mighty flame. This is how you should understand his statement, "I have come to cast fire on the earth, and how I wish it were already kindled!"[244]

And they were astonished that he was speaking to a woman.

Again, the disciples are astonished at the gentleness of the Savior, and they marvel at his meek way. He does not, like those who are fierce in their excessive caution, think it right to shrink back from talking to a woman, but he extends his loving kindness to all. By this act, he shows that since the creator is certainly one, he does not assign life through faith only to men, but he takes the female race as well into his net to the same life.

Let the one who teaches in the church profit from this as a model, and let him not refuse to help women. After all, one must certainly be directed not by one's own will but by the need for preaching.

But no one said, "Why are you speaking?" or, "What do you want with her?"

It was the work of wise disciples who knew how to preserve the honor that befits their teacher not to appear to go off into strange conjectures with superfluous questions because he was speaking with a woman. Instead, with modesty and fear they shut up their tongue within their teeth and waited for the Lord to speak of his own accord [288] and to offer them a voluntary explanation. We must therefore marvel in this passage at Christ for his gentleness and at the disciples for their wisdom, understanding and knowledge of what is fitting.

[242]Jn 4:20. [243]Jn 4:25. [244]Lk 12:49.

4:28 So the woman left her water jar and went away into the city.

The woman who, two or three days ago, had many men now shows herself to be stronger and superior to the cares of the flesh. And she who was often easily caught by illusory pleasures reaches beyond the so-called necessities of the flesh, disregarding both thirst and drink, and is forged anew into another disposition through faith. Immediately, she exercises love, the fairest virtue of all and the way of affection for others. She runs into the city, quickly announcing to the others the blessing that she had found. The Savior was echoing within her, at least so it seems, and whispering secretly in her mind, saying, "Freely you have received, freely give."[245] Let us learn from this not to imitate that timid servant who accordingly buried his talent in the earth,[246] but let us be eager to put it to work. This famous woman does this well. She shares with others the good that fell to her. The water she has come to draw is no longer taken from the breasts of the fountain, nor does she carry her earthen water jar home again, but with divine and heavenly grace and with the all-wise teaching of the Savior, she fills the storehouses of her understanding.

We should learn from this type and sketch that by utterly despising things that are insignificant and corporeal, **[289]** we will receive better things, and many times more of them, from God. What is water from the earth, after all, compared with wisdom from above?

4:29 And she said to the people, "Come see a man who told me everything I have done. He cannot be the Christ, can he?"

O marvelous change! O truly great and God-befitting strength, resplendent with unspeakable wonder! The woman who understood none of what was said at first and who therefore rightly heard, "Go, call your husband, and come here,"[247] is already a worker skilled in speaking who initiates others into the mysteries. You see how skillfully she conversed with the Samaritans. She does not immediately say that she has found the Christ, nor does she introduce Jesus to them at first in her account. That is because, finding her hearers not unaware of her ways, she would rightly have been rejected on the grounds that she far exceeded the level of discourse that is appropriate for her. Therefore, she prepares them ahead of time with wonder, and by first amazing them with the marvel, she makes the road to faith smoother, so to speak. "Come and see," she says ingeniously, all but crying out with more fervent words. Merely seeing will suffice for faith and will fully convince those present with remarkable miracles. For the one who knows hidden facts and has this great God-befitting dignity—how will he not run successfully to the fulfillment of whatever he wishes?

4:30 They left the city and were on their way to him.

The ready obedience of the Samaritans is an indictment of the hard heart of the Jews, and the inhumanity of the latter is revealed by the gentleness of the former. Let the one who loves learning see the difference of disposition between the two in order **[290]** to marvel, quite rightly, that Jesus leaves the synagogue of the Jews and gives himself to foreigners. The law of Moses announced to the Jews both that Christ would come and to whom he would appear. Moreover, the august chorus of prophets proclaimed him and practically pointed to him present at the door, saying, "Behold our God! Behold the Lord!"[248] And last of all John, who is great "among those born of women,"[249] openly established that he has

[245]Mt 10:8. [246]Mt 25:18. [247]Jn 4:16. [248]Is 40:9-10. [249]Mt 11:11.

already appeared and is dwelling with us, saying, "Behold the lamb of God, who takes away the sin of the world!"[250] And, more marvelous than all these things, the Savior revealed himself through many deeds of power and God-befitting authority. What are they doing who rush heedlessly into strange counsels? They unjustly thirst for blood. They hatch ungodly plots. They are stubborn in their envy. They drive from their own land and city the life, the light, the salvation of all, the way to the kingdom, the forgiveness of sins and the bestower of sonship. Therefore, the Savior was right when he said, "Jerusalem, Jerusalem, the city that will kill the prophets and that stones those sent to it! How often I have wanted to gather your children together as a hen gathers her brood under her wings, and you were not willing! See, your house is left to you, desolate."[251] But the Samaritans show themselves superior to the madness of the Jews. They overcome their own ignorance by their ready obedience, and after they hear about just one miracle, they go running to Jesus. They were not persuaded by the voices of the holy prophets, **[291]** or the preaching of Moses or the pointing of John. Instead, one woman tells them about him—and she was a sinner at that! Therefore, let us too with good reason admire the Savior's judgment against them and exclaim, "You are righteous, Lord, and your judgment is right."[252]

4:31-32 Meanwhile, his disciples were urging him, "Rabbi, eat something." But he said to them,

The divine Evangelist arranges the composition of his book with the highest degree of excellence. He leaves out nothing which he believes will be at all useful to the readers. Hear then how he introduces Jesus again to us as an example of the most remarkable behavior. I do not think anything has been placed in the writings of the saints in vain, but even that which someone thinks is insignificant is sometimes found to be pregnant with a profit that is not to be despised. So when the conversion of the Samaritans had begun and they were not yet to the point of expecting him (for as God, he knew they would come), he is wholly and entirely intent on the salvation of those who are called. He disregards bodily food, although he is wearied "by his journey," as it is written,[253] so that he might thereby help the teachers in the churches and persuade them to disregard all weariness and to consider zeal for those who are being saved to be more important than care for the body. "Woe," says the prophet, "to those who do the work of the Lord carelessly."[254] In order that we may learn that the Lord was accustomed to go without food especially at such times, he introduces the disciples all but on their knees, begging him to take a little of their provisions as food since it is necessary and he cannot do without it. **[292]** "For they had gone into the city to buy food,"[255] which they had obtained and now had.

"I have food to eat that you do not know about."

The Savior gracefully weaves his answer from the subject at hand. He all but hints that if they knew that the conversion of the Samaritans was at the door, they would have persuaded him to cling to that as his food rather than to nourish his body. From this one can learn how much love the divine nature has for humanity because it considers the return of the lost to salvation to be its food and delicacy.

4:33-34 So the disciples said to one another, "Surely no one has brought him something to eat?" Jesus said to them,

Since they did not yet understand his dark

[250]Jn 1:29. [251]Mt 23:37-38. [252]Ps 119:137 (Ps 118:137 LXX). [253]Jn 4:6. [254]Jer 48:10 (Jer 31:10 LXX). [255]Jn 4:8.

saying, the disciples were thinking of the things that often happened in their own experience. They descended to everyday ideas, suspecting that someone had brought him food and that it was perhaps costlier or sweeter than what they came up with.

"My food is to do the will of him who sent me and to complete his work."
He completely tears away the veil from his speech, and he makes the truth absolutely explicit. He now introduces himself as a type for future teachers of the world. He has a steadfast and noble zeal for teaching what is necessary, **[293]** which leads him rightly to consider the care for the necessities of the body to be secondary. When he says that "doing the will of the one who sent him" and "completing his work" is the finest food for him, he delineates the task of the apostolic ministry and indicates clearly what sort of disposition they ought to have. They must, it seems, be resolutely focused on the concern for teaching, and they must be so far removed from the pleasures of the flesh that sometimes they do not even accept the service which seems necessary merely for the avoidance of death.

Let this be enough to say for the present since it directs us to the type and pattern of the apostolic way of life. But if we must add something more doctrinal to what we have already said, he says that he was sent, namely, from God the Father. This could refer to the incarnation, in which he shone on the world with the flesh by the good will and approval of the Father. Or it could refer to the fact that, as Word, he proceeds in a way from the mind who begat him. He is sent and fulfills his decree, not because he was taken on as a minister of another's will but because he himself is at the same time the living Word and clearest will of the Father as he readily saves the lost. Therefore, by saying that it is the work of the one who sent him, he himself is shown to be its fulfiller because all things are from the Father, through the Son and in the Spirit.

I think it is perfectly clear to everyone that the Son is the Word, counsel, will and power of the Father. But it is no trouble to prove it from Holy Scripture as well. One may see that he is the Word in the passage, "In the beginning was the Word, and the Word was with God, and the Word was God."[256] One may see that he is the counsel in the psalmist's statement addressed to God the Father, "In your counsel **[294]** you guided me, and with glory you received me."[257] And one may see that he is the will in the statement, "Lord, in your will give strength to my beauty."[258] The living and hypostatic will of the Father (that is, the Son) strengthens the beauty of the saints (that is, their vigor for every virtue). You may understand that he is also the power from this: "Command, O God," he says, "your power, and strengthen, O God, that which you have furnished for us."[259] You see in this passage in precise detail that by the good pleasure of God the Father, his power (that is, his Son) was made flesh in order to strengthen this body which he furnished for us. If he had not tabernacled among us, the nature of our flesh would not at all have put off the weakness that comes from decay. Therefore, since the Son is the good will of the Father, he "completes his work" by being revealed as salvation for those who believe in him.

But perhaps someone will respond, If the Son himself is the will of the Father, what "will" was he sent to fulfill? That which is fulfilled must be different from the one who fulfills it. What then do we say to this? The assigning of names does indeed demand a difference in the things signified. When it comes to God, however, there is often no difference, and a discussion of the highest nature is exempt from accuracy in these

[256]Jn 1:1. [257]Ps 73:24 (Ps 72:24 LXX). [258]Ps 30:7 (Ps 29:8 LXX). [259]Ps 68:28 (Ps 67:29 LXX).

matters. Its properties are spoken of not altogether as they are in truth, but so that the tongue can explain them and the human ear can hear them. The one who sees in an enigma,[260] after all, also speaks in an enigma. What will you do when the one who is simple by nature enters the story as double by saying concerning the Israelites, And they made their children pass through the fire, "a thing which I did not command them, nor did it enter my heart."[261] Must not [295] the heart be different from the one in whom it is? How can we still understand God to be simple? Therefore, the things of God are spoken of in a human way. They are understood in such a way that they are fitting to God, and the limits of our tongue will not harm the nature that is above all. So even if the Son is found speaking of the will of the Father as something other than himself, you should make no distinction but attribute to the weakness of words in the *oikonomia* the fact that they cannot say anything greater or signify their meaning in any other way.

Let these words serve as proof for understanding the Son also to be the will of the Father. In the passage before us, however, there is no reason to understand the Son as the will of the Father. Rather, we will take it to refer to the good intention to save the lost, without differentiating between Father and Son.

4:35 "Do you not say, 'Four more months and then comes the harvest'?"

Again he takes the occasion for his discourse from what is going on at the moment, and from the realm of coarser sense perception he fashions an explanation of spiritual ideas. At that time it was still winter, and the tender sprouting and fresh stalk of the seed was barely bristling from the ground. But when four months had passed, it was ready to fall into the hand of the reaper. That is why he says, "Do you people not say, 'Four more months and then the harvest comes'?"

"I tell you, lift up your eyes, and see how the fields are already white for harvest."
That is, lift up the eye of your understanding a little from earthly affairs and behold that the spiritual [296] sowing has whitened, as if already progressing to the threshing floor, and calls the reaper's sickle to itself. By the likeness to the events in the narrative, you will see the meaning. You should understand the spiritual sowing and the multitude of spiritual ears to be those who were tilled beforehand by the voice of the prophets and brought into the coming faith by Christ. They are white in the sense that they have already become ripe and ready for faith, and they have been confirmed in their piety. The sickle of the reaper is the shining, sharp word of the apostles which cuts off its hearers from the worship prescribed by the law and transfers them to the threshing floor, that is, the church of God. There they are pounded and pressed by noble toil, and they are made into pure wheat, worthy of the storehouse of the one who gathers them.

4:36-37 "The reaper is already receiving wages and is gathering fruit for eternal life, so that sower and reaper may rejoice together. For here the saying holds true, 'One sows and another reaps.'"

It is the time of the Word, he says, who calls to faith and shows the hearers that the proclamation of the law and the prophets has reached its completion. The law, by its worship in types, foreshadowed the one who was coming, that is, Christ. After that the prophets, interpreting the Spirit's phrase "yet a little while,"[262] referred to him beforehand as

[260]1 Cor 13:12. [261]Jer 19:5; 32:35 (Jer 39:35 LXX). [262]Heb 10:37; Is 26:20.

coming and already here. Since he has already come within the doors, the word of the apostles will not relegate to a distant hope what is expected but will point it out as already present. That word will "reap" from their legal worship **[297]** those who are still slaves to the law and who devote themselves only to the letter, and it will transfer them like sheaves into the evangelical way of life and disposition. It will also cut off the worshipers of idols from their polytheistic error and bring them to the knowledge of the God who truly exists. To summarize everything briefly, it will transform those who still are concerned with earthly matters to the life of the angels through faith in Christ.

The word of the reapers will bring this about, he says. Their word, however, will not go without wages, since it will certainly gather for them "fruit" that nourishes "to eternal life." Nor will those who receive rejoice for themselves alone, but as ones who have labored at the work of the prophets and harvested the seed sown by the prophets before them, they will form one company with the prophets. I think that the supremely wise Paul, who has gained clear knowledge of the types of things to come, uses this idea as the basis for his statement concerning the holy fathers and prophets: "All of these, though they were perfected through faith, did not receive the promise, since God had provided something better for us so that they would not be perfected apart from us."[263] After all, the Savior thought that the reaper should "rejoice" with the one who had earlier sown the seed.

4:38 "I sent you to reap that for which you did not labor. Others have labored, and you have entered into their labors."

Now he reveals the whole mystery to them. He removes the cloak of enigma from his words, and he makes the sense of what he means perfectly clear. Since the Savior loves the prophets and the apostles, he does not take the labor of the former out of the hands of the apostles, nor does he give the apostles complete credit for those who are going to **[298]** be saved through faith in him. Instead, he mixes, as it were, the labor of each with the mutual effort of the other, and he says (for good reason) that the honor of both will be one. He maintains that the apostles have entered into the work of the holy prophets, not allowing them to horn in on the glory of those who preceded them but persuading them to honor them as those who led the way in both labor and time. Who will refuse to admit that this is certainly a most beautiful lesson for us as well?

4:39 Many Samaritans from that city believed in him because of the word of the woman who testified, "He told me everything I have done."

Again, Israel is condemned by these words and is shown to be harsh and uninterested in learning by the ready faith of the Samaritans. The Evangelist marvels greatly, saying that "many believed" in Christ "because of the word of the woman," even though those who are led by the law to this knowledge neither received the words of Moses nor recognized that they ought to believe the message of the prophets. With these words he prepares, or rather wisely fashions, a defense ahead of time for the fact that Israel will with good reason be thrust out of the grace and hope that is in Christ, and the multitude of Gentiles and foreigners who are more ready to believe will come in instead.

4:40-41 So when the Samaritans came to him, they asked him to stay with them; and he stayed there two days. And many more believed because of his word.

[263]Heb 11:39-40.

He explains in simple words what took place, but he prepares, as it were, another proof [299] that Israel must rightly be expelled from hope and that foreigners must be transplanted into it. The Jews, with their bitter and intolerable conjectures, commit outrages against Jesus even as he is working various miracles and shining in God-befitting glory. They are caught behaving like shameless drunkards to the point where they exile him by rushing to drive out of their city the one who showers them with joy. The Samaritans, however, are persuaded by the words of one woman and come to the conclusion that they should go running to him. And when they did, they earnestly begged him to come into their city and bestow on them his saving message. Christ readily agrees to both requests, knowing that grace will not be without fruit. After all, many "believed because of his word." Let the one who loves God and is pious know then from these words that Christ gets up and leaves those who grieve him, but he dwells with those who gladden him with obedience and good faith.

4:42 They said to the woman, "It is no longer because of what you said that we believe, for we have heard for ourselves, and we know that this is truly the Savior of the world."

Faith comes to the Samaritans from a greater source, no longer from what they learn from others but from what they marvel at now that they have heard for themselves. They say that they know he is clearly "the Savior of the world," and in so doing, they make the confession of their hope in him a pledge of their faith.

4:43-44 After two days he went from there to Galilee. For Jesus himself testified that a prophet has no honor in his own country.

He leaves Samaria once he has sown the [300] saving word. Like a farmer, he hid the faith in those who dwell there, not that it might be bound by the silence of those who received it, quiet, as it were, and buried, but that it might be planted in the souls of all, that it might continue to spread and advance and hasten toward more evident power. But since he passes by Nazareth, which lies in the middle (in which he grew up, according to the narrative, so that he now comes from there and is a citizen of that place) and goes down to Galilee, he has to explain why he passed it by. So it says that "Jesus himself testified that a prophet has no honor in his own country." We naturally look down on the familiar even if it should be great and valuable. Furthermore, the Savior certainly did not think that he should seek honor from them like a vainglorious braggart, but he knew clearly that for those who have no thought that they should honor their teacher, the word of faith would no longer be sweet and acceptable. So he passes them by with good reason. He does not think it worthwhile to expend useless labors on those who do not profit from it or to cast grace in this way before those who despise it. It is not right, after all, that those who sin so greatly do so without being punished since it is certainly agreed and indisputable that those who knowingly despise him and spurn such a remarkable gift will suffer the most extreme punishment.

4:45 So when he came to Galilee, the Galileans welcomed him since they had seen all that he had done in Jerusalem at the festival; for they too had gone to the festival.

The Galileans do not welcome Jesus in an unexamined way. [301] Instead, they are rightly astonished at the miracles that they had already seen him do. By their reverence toward him they condemn the madness of the Jews, and they are found to be far superior in disposition to those instructed by the law.

4:46 So he came again to Cana in Galilee where he changed the water into wine.

Christ loves to dwell in those who are well disposed, and on those who more readily perceive and acknowledge the benefits they received, he lavishes a rich supply of even greater blessings. He comes then to work miracles in Cana, thinking that it is fitting to provide further help to the people there, considering that he has previously sown, as it were, the impression that he can do all things by the signs which he had already accomplished there.

4:46-48 Now there was a royal official whose son lay ill in Capernaum. When he heard that Jesus had come from Judea to Galilee, he went and begged him to come down and heal his son, for he was at the point of death. Then Jesus said to him,

The official approaches him with the conviction that he can heal, but he does not yet understand that he is God by nature. He calls him "Lord," but he does not at all give him the true dignity of lordship. He should have immediately fallen down, not indeed that he may come to his house and go down with him to the sick boy, but rather that he may with authority and God-befitting command drive away the disease that fell on the boy. Why did the Lord need to be present with the sick person, since he can easily heal even one who is absent? How is it not utterly ignorant to suppose that he is [302] superior to death but to think that the one who is filled with God-befitting power is in no way God?

4:49 "Unless you see signs and wonders, you will not believe." The official said to him,

A mind that is still hard dwells in those who are deceived, but the wonder-working power of the word that calls them to faith will be all the greater. That is why the Savior said that they need "wonders" in order to be easily reinstructed in what is profitable and to acknowledge the one who is God by nature.

"Lord, come down before my child dies." The official is quite immature in his understanding. He is a child in his request for grace, and he talks baby talk without realizing it. He would have formed a more worthy conception of him if he did not believe that Jesus would have power only when present, but instead believed that he would certainly act even when absent. As it is, however, the official thinks and acts most foolishly. He asks for a power that befits God, but he does not think that Jesus fills all things as God or that he will be more powerful than death, even though he urges Jesus to gain the advantage over the one who had almost overcome, since the child "was at the point of death."[264]

4:50 Jesus said to him, "Go; your son will live."

This is how he should have approached in faith, but Christ clearly does not make an issue of our ignorance. What is more, since he is God, he does good even to those who stumble. He teaches the man what he should have been admired for doing, even though he did not do it, showing himself to be at the same time the one who provides the most beautiful gifts and the one who supplies blessings in prayer. For implicit in the word *go* is faith, [303] and in "your son will live" is the fulfillment of what he longed for, carried out with a great and God-befitting authority.

4:50-51 The man believed the word that Jesus spoke to him and started on his way.

[264]Jn 4:47.

As he was going down, his slaves met him and told him that his son was alive.

The single command of the Savior immediately heals two souls. For the official, it works unaccustomed faith, and it rescues the boy from bodily death. Which is healed first, it is hard to say. Both happened at the same time, I suppose, since the disease made its departure at the command of our Savior. The servants meet him and announce the healing of the child, demonstrating the swiftness of the divine command. (Christ clearly arranges this too.) And by the fulfillment of his hope, they quickly strengthen their master who is weak in faith.

4:52-54 So he asked them the hour when he began to recover, and they told him, "Yesterday at the seventh hour the fever left him." The father knew that this was the hour when Jesus had said to him, "Your son will live," and he and his whole house believed. This was now the second sign that Jesus did after coming from Judea to Galilee.

He asks them the hour that the sick child turned for the better to see if it coincides with the time of grace. And when he learns that it does and the time was no different, he is saved with his entire household. He attributes the power of the miracle to the Savior Christ and brings to Christ a firmer faith as a fruit of his thanksgiving for what had happened. **[304]**

5:1-4 After this, there was a festival of the Jews, and Jesus went up to Jerusalem. Now in Jerusalem there is a pool which in Hebrew is called Bethesda, which has five porticoes. In these lay a great multitude of the sick, the blind, the lame and the paralyzed, waiting for the movement of the water. For an angel of the Lord used to go down into the pool at a certain time and stir up the water. The first one to go into the pool after the stirring of the water was made healthy from whatever disease they had.

There is a reason the blessed Evangelist immediately connects the Savior's return from there to Jerusalem with what he said earlier. His goal was probably to show how superior the foreigners were to the Jews in ready obedience and what a great difference is obvious between the two in both disposition and way of life. In this way and no other can we learn that by the just decree of God, who rules everything and who shows no partiality,[265] there is a good reason why Israel falls away from hope and the fullness of the Gentiles is brought in instead.

It is not difficult to test what has been said by comparing the sections of the text.[266] He showed that with one sign he saved the city of the Samaritans, and with another he likewise saved the royal official in Galilee, and through him he certainly helped the people there a great deal. After testifying in these accounts to the great readiness of the foreigners to obey, he brings the miracle worker back to Jerusalem and shows him accomplishing a deed that is fitting for God. He miraculously frees the paralytic, after all, from an old illness, just as he did for the royal official's son who was certainly dying. But the one believed together with his whole household and confessed Jesus to be God, while the others, who ought to have been amazed, immediately want to kill him and persecute **[305]** their benefactor as a

[265]Rom 2:11. [266]Cyril's term for "sections" (κεφάλαια) refers to numbered divisions of the biblical text of his day. The stories of the Samaritan woman at the well, the royal official in Galilee and the healing at Bethesda on the sabbath each comprise a "section" of the biblical text. These divisions are not the same as modern chapter divisions but originate from Eusebius. See Kurt Aland and Barbara Aland, *The Text of the New Testament*, 2nd ed. (Grand Rapids: Eerdmans, 1989), 252.

blasphemous transgressor. In so doing, they pronounce an even more shameful judgment against themselves in that they are caught falling behind the understanding and the reverence for Christ that the foreigners have. So this too was said of them in the Psalms as to the Lord Jesus, "You will place them in back."[267] For those who have been ranked first because of the election of the fathers will come last after the calling of the Gentiles. When "the fullness of the Gentiles comes in, then all Israel will be saved."[268]

The well-ordered placement of these sections next to each other gives birth to this line of thought. Now we will make a painstaking investigation, piece by piece, of the meaning in the verses.

5:5-6 One man was there who had been ill for thirty-eight years. When Jesus saw him lying there and knew that he had been there a long time,

After the Jews celebrate their festival of unleavened bread, in which it is their custom to slaughter the sheep (at the time of the Passover, that is), Christ leaves Jerusalem and mingles with the Samaritans and foreigners and teaches among them since he is grieved by the intractability of the Pharisees. And as soon as he returns at the time of the holy Pentecost (since this was the next festival in Jerusalem), he heals the paralytic at the waters of the pool. The paralytic had spent a long time in his illness since it was his thirty-eighth year, but he had not yet attained the full number of the law, I mean four times ten or forty.

Our explanation of the history will end with this. **[306]** We must transform, however, the type of the letter into a spiritual understanding.[269] Jesus is grieved and leaves Jerusalem after the slaughter of the sheep, and he visits the Samaritans and Galileans and proclaims his saving word among them. What else could this refer to but his departure from the Jews, which took place after his slaughter and death in Jerusalem on the precious cross? That is when he gave himself to the Gentiles and foreigners by commanding that his disciples be shown, after his resurrection from the dead, that he goes ahead of all of them to Galilee.[270] But the fact that he returns to Jerusalem at the end of the weeks of holy Pentecost shows, in types and enigmas, that our Savior will once again return to the Jews, because of his loving kindness, in the last times of the present age. At that time we who have been saved by faith in him will celebrate the most holy feasts of his saving passion. The fact that the paralytic is healed before the fullness of time according to the law indicates, through the type of what happened, that after Israel irreverently rages against Christ, it will be sick and paralyzed and spend a long time in idleness; however, it will not go off into complete punishment but will be visited by the Savior and healed at the pool by obedience and faith. The fact that forty is the number of completion according to the divine law would not be at all difficult for any to learn who read the Holy Scriptures just once.

5:6-7 Jesus said to him, "Do you want to be made well?" The sick man answered him,

It is a clear proof of Christ's utmost goodness **[307]** that he does not waste a moment waiting for requests from the sick but anticipates their request with his loving kindness. He runs, you see, to the one who is lying down, and he has compassion on the one who is sick and helpless. But the question about whether he wanted to be freed from his illness was not an

[267]Ps 21:12 (Ps 20:13 LXX). [268]Rom 11:25-26. [269]The explanation of the "history" is an elucidation of the bare facts of the narrative. The "spiritual understanding" provides the higher meaning of those facts in the context of the cosmic story of salvation. [270]Mt 28:7.

inquiry made from ignorance about something that was clear and evident to all, but an act to stir up more fervent desire and to urge him to ask with the greatest zeal. The question of whether he wanted to receive what he longed for contains the suggestion and implication that Jesus can supply it and is already prepared to do it. He is only waiting for the request of the one who receives grace.

5:7-8 "Sir, I have no one to put me in the pool when the water is stirred up; and while I am making my way, someone else steps down ahead of me." Jesus said to him, "Stand up."

At the day of holy Pentecost, angels used to come down from heaven and stir up the water in the pool. They would make the splash from this the herald of their presence. The water would be sanctified by the holy spirits, and whoever of the multitude of the sick went down first would emerge relieved of the suffering that afflicted them. The power of healing, however, was meted out only to the first one to seize it. But this too was a sign of the benefit of the law by the hand of angels which extends only to one race, that of the Jews, and heals no one else besides them. For from Dan, so-called, to Beersheba, the commandments of Moses were spoken, ministered by angels on Mount Sinai in the days of holy Pentecost, as it was later defined. For this reason, **[308]** the water of the pool was not stirred up at any other time, thereby signifying the descent of the holy angels into it. Since the paralytic had no one to throw him into the water, bound as he was by the disease, he lamented the lack of healers, saying, "I have no one," that is, no one to bring him down into the water, because he certainly expected Jesus to tell him and advise him to have someone do this.

5:8-9 "Stand up, take your mat, and walk." At once the man was made well, and he took up his mat and began to walk. Now that day was a sabbath.

The command is God-befitting and contains the clearest proof of superhuman power and authority. He does not pray for the man lying down to be released from his disease lest he too seem to be one of the holy prophets. Rather, as the Lord of powers, he commands it to happen by his own authority. He tells him to go home rejoicing and to put his mat on his shoulders so that it will be a reminder to those who see it of the healer's power. Immediately the sick man does what he was told, and by obedience and faith, he brings about the grace he so eagerly desired. But since in the foregoing we introduced him as an image and type of the multitude of the Jews who will be healed in the end times, come let us take up considerations that are consonant with this idea just as we did above.

Christ heals the man on the sabbath, and immediately when he is healed, he commands him to break the custom of the law by inducing him to walk on the sabbath, burdened with his mat on top of that. This despite the fact that God distinctly cries out through one of the holy prophets somewhere, "And you shall not carry a burden **[309]** out of your houses on the sabbath day."[271] I do not suppose that anyone who is sober-minded would say that the man is rendered a despiser and a trampler of the divine commands, but Christ was revealing to the Jews in a type that they will be healed through obedience and faith in the last times of the age. This is what I think "sabbath" indicates since it is the last day of the week. Once they receive healing through faith and are transformed into newness of life, they must consider the oldness of the letter of the law to be of no account, and they must reject the

[271]Jer 17:22.

worship characterized by enigma in shadows as well as the vain observance of Jewish custom. I think the blessed Paul too takes this as an occasion for discussion and writes to those who, after believing, are returning to the law, "I tell you that if you are circumcised, Christ will be of no benefit to you."[272] Again, "You who are justified by the law are cut off from Christ. You have fallen away from grace."[273]

5:10 The Jews said to the man who had been healed, "It is the sabbath. It is not lawful for you to carry your mat."

I think it could not be a better time to cry out to them, "Behold, a foolish and senseless people, who have eyes and do not see!"[274] What could be more ignorant than this, or what could involve a greater lack of perception? They do not even admit into their mind that they ought to wonder at the power of the healer. They are bitter critics, and this is the only thing they know how to do well. So they lay on the man who just barely recovered from a long disease the charge of breaking the law, and they ignorantly command him to lie down again, thinking that honor for the sabbath is shown by having to be sick. **[310]**

5:11-12 But he answered them, "The man who made me well said to me, 'Take your mat and walk.'" They asked him,

This statement is pregnant with the wisest meaning and rebuffs the stubbornness of the Jews. Since it is not lawful, they say, to take your mat and go home on the sabbath, and since they contrive a charge of breaking the law against the man who was healed, he must marshal a more spirited defense against them. He says that the man who was revealed as the giver of health commanded him to walk. This amounts to saying something like, I say that he is most worthy of honor, sirs, even if he commands me to violate the honor of the sabbath. He has such strength and grace that he drove away my disease. If excellence in these matters belongs not just to anyone but corresponds to God-befitting activity and power, he says, how could the one who does these things sin? Or how could the one who has God-befitting power advise actions that are not at all pleasing to God? These words have a pointed meaning.

5:12-14 "Who is the man who said to you, 'Take up your mat and walk'?" Now the man who had been healed did not know who it was, for Jesus had disappeared in the crowd that was there. Later, Jesus found him in the temple and said to him,

The mind of the Jews is thirsty for blood. They search out the one who commanded this, planning to implicate him with the man who was miraculously made well. He alone, it seems, dared to distress them over the sabbath—he who had just passed through snares and inescapable traps and was even snatched from the very gates of death. However, the man cannot tell them who the physician is, even though they really want to know. This is because Christ had concealed himself well in accordance with his plan **[311]** in order to escape the momentary heat of their wrath. He does not flee as though he could suffer something that he does not will to suffer—by necessity, as it were—but he gives himself to us as an example even in this act.

"See, you have been made well. Do not sin anymore, so that nothing worse happens to you."

He was hidden at first in accordance with his plan, and he appears again in accordance with

[272]Gal 5:2. [273]Gal 5:4. [274]Jer 5:21.

his plan, observing the fitting time for each. It was not possible that he who knew no sin[275] should do anything without a fitting reason for it. So he made soul-benefitting instruction the occasion for his conversation with him, saying that he must no longer transgress so that he is not afflicted by worse evils than before. With these words he teaches not only that God stores up people's transgression for the coming judgment[276] but also that he scourges people in various ways while they are still living in the body, before the great and manifest day of the one who will judge all.[277] The supremely wise Paul will testify that we are often smitten when we stumble and grieve God, crying out, "For this reason many of you are weak and ill, and some have fallen asleep. If we judged ourselves, we would not be judged. But when we are judged by the Lord, we are disciplined so that we may not be condemned along with the world."[278]

5:15 The man went away and told the Jews that it was Jesus who had made him well.

He points out Jesus to the Jews not so that they might dare to do something terrible to him and be caught in blasphemy but so that if they too wanted to be healed, they might know the wondrous physician. Observe how this was his intention. He does not come like one of the accusers **[312]** and announce that Jesus is the one who told him to walk on the sabbath. He says Jesus is the one who made him well. This is the behavior of one who is doing nothing but identifying his physician.

5:16-17 Therefore, the Jews started persecuting Jesus and trying to kill him, because he did this on the sabbath. But Jesus answered them,

This statement does not contain a simplistic explanation of the madness of the Jews. The Evangelist indicates quite clearly not only that they persecute him but also why they are not ashamed to do it, when he says "because he did this on the sabbath." They persecute him ignorantly and blasphemously as though the law prevented one from doing good on the sabbath, as though it were not permissible to have mercy and show pity to the sick, as though one should strip off the law of love, the praise of brotherly kindness, the grace of gentleness. What virtues could one show that the Jews did not spurn at every turn, since they did not know the purpose of the lawgiver regarding the sabbath, and they rendered its observance useless? As Christ himself says somewhere, each of them leads their own ox or sheep to drink,[279] and "a man receives circumcision on the sabbath in order that the law of Moses may not be broken," and yet they are angry "because he healed the whole man on the sabbath."[280] Because of their great stubbornness and ignorance, they do not prefer the one made in the divine image even to irrational animals. They think that they are allowed to and ought to have mercy on a sheep on the sabbath and free it from hunger and thirst without incurring blame, but **[313]** any who are gentle and good toward their neighbor on the sabbath are subject to the charge of transgressing the law to the ultimate degree.

Moreover, so that we may see that their foolishness knows no bounds and that they rightly ought to hear, "You are wrong because you do not know the Scriptures,"[281] let us draw on the Holy Scriptures and show that Jesus was long ago depicted clearly, in a type, being indifferent about the sabbath. When the supremely wise Moses in old age, as it is written, took leave of human affairs and was transferred to the mansions above by the judgment and decree of God who rules over all, Joshua the son of Nun obtained and

[275]See 2 Cor 5:21. [276]See Rom 2:5. [277]Acts 2:20. [278]1 Cor 11:30-32. [279]Lk 13:15. [280]Jn 7:23. [281]Mt 22:29.

inherited the rule over Israel. When he placed ten thousand armed soldiers around Jericho as he was planning to capture and overthrow it, he arranged for the Levites to carry the ark around the city for six whole days, but on the seventh day, that is, on the sabbath, he commanded the innumerable multitude of soldiers to shout along with the trumpets.[282] In this way the wall was thrown down, and they rushed in and conquered the city. They did not honor the untimely rest of the sabbath, nor did they refuse the victory on the sabbath because the law prevented it. Neither did they oppose the command of Joshua, but they followed the leadership of the man completely free from blame.

There is a type in these passages. The truth came, that is, Christ, who destroyed and conquered the fortification of corruption set up against human nature by the devil. And when Christ is seen doing this on the sabbath, as he introduces and initiates that victory in the case of the paralytic, they foolishly get angry and **[314]** condemn the obedience of their fathers. They do not allow nature to overcome the abuse it endures from illnesses on the sabbath, even to the point where they must zealously persecute Jesus when he does good on the sabbath.

"My Father works until now, and I am also working."

Christ is speaking on the sabbath day, as it were. That is what "until now" has to mean so that the statement may have a fitting interpretation. The Jews are ignorant and do not know who the Only Begotten is by nature. They attribute to God the Father alone the giving of the law through Moses, and they maintain that they must believe him alone. Clearly he is attempting to persuade them that he does all things with the Father and that since he has the nature of the one who begat him in himself (because of the fact that he is not something other than the Father is, as far as the identity of substance is concerned), he will never think anything other than what seems good to the one who begat him. Since he is of the same substance, he will also will the same things, or rather since he himself is the living will and power of the Father, he works all in all with the Father.

In order then that he might fend off the vain murmuring of the Jews and put to shame those who are persecuting him in those matters where they thought it good to be angry, as though the honor of the sabbath were being despised, he says, "The Father works until now, and I am also working." It is as though he wants to say something like, If you believe, my friend, that God, who by his will and counsel crafted everything and set it in place, also rules creation even on the sabbath day, so that the sun rises, rain-bearing fountains are likewise let loose, fruit springs up from the ground, not refusing to grow on account of the sabbath, **[315]** and fire performs its own work, ministering to human needs without being prevented, then know and admit with certainty that the Father does what is God-befitting even on the sabbath. Why then, he says, do you ignorantly blame the one through whom he works all things? For God the Father will work in no other way than through his power and wisdom, the Son. That is why he says, "I am also working." He puts to shame, therefore, the unbridled anger of his persecutors by reducing their arguments to absurdity, showing that they are not so much opposing him as speaking against the Father, to whom alone they were zealous to ascribe the honor of the law, not yet knowing the Son who is from him and through him by nature. This is why he says that God is uniquely his Father, ingeniously leading them to this most beautiful and precious lesson.

[282] Josh 6.

5:18 For this reason the Jews sought all the more to kill him, because he not only was breaking the sabbath but also was calling God his own Father, thereby making himself equal to God.

The mind of the Jews is devoted to inhumanity. By what should have healed them, they are made all the more sick so that they rightly hear, "How will you say, 'We are wise'?"[283] When they should be softened in their thinking and transformed by suitable reasoning to godliness, they are already plotting murder against the one who proves by his deeds that he has in no way sinned against the divine law by healing a man on the sabbath. Along with their anger on account of the sabbath, they weave in the truth as a charge of blasphemy, binding themselves tightly in the snares of their own transgressions to the point of unquenchable wrath. They seemed to be godly in their distress that he, being a man, said that God was "his own Father." **[316]** But that was because they did not yet know God the Word, who came to be in the form of a slave for us, who is the life gushing from God the Father, that is, the Only Begotten. Truly and strictly speaking, God is called and is a Father for him alone, not for us. We are adopted. We ascend to the dignity that is above our nature by the will of the one who honors us, and we gain the titles "gods" and "sons" on account of Christ who dwells in us through the Holy Spirit. They concentrate only on the flesh without recognizing God who dwells in the flesh, so they cannot endure him springing up to a level that is beyond human nature by calling God his own Father. (After all, by saying "my Father," he would reasonably give this impression.) And they think that the one who has God as his own Father must be equal to him by nature. Indeed, they are right on this one point, for so it is and not otherwise. Since they understand then that these words bring this meaning along with them, they are all the more angry when they pervert the correct word of truth. **[317]**

Chapter Six

The Son is not less than the Father either in potentiality or actuality when it comes to any work, but he is of equal might and of the same substance since he is from him by nature.

5:19 Jesus answered and said to them, "Truly, truly, I tell you, the Son cannot do anything on his own, but only what he sees the Father doing; for whatever the Father does, the Son does likewise."

What we said in the foregoing, he explains again in another way, catching his hearers in a net from every side to lead them to the discovery of the truth. The message was not received at first because of the weakness of those who could not understand, so he puts it in another form. In a variety of ways, he introduces a message that goes through the same ideas. This too is an act of an excellent teacher, namely, not to make the message rush past and fly by the understanding of the students but to make it exquisite and diversely fashioned so that by frequent changes of expression, it strips away the difficulty in the things under consideration. By mixing then what is human with what is fitting for God and by combining both into one intermediate statement, he gently crouches, as it were, beneath the dignity that is fitting for the Only Begotten, while at the same time he surpasses human nature. As Lord, and at the same time as one who is classed among the slaves, he says, **[318]** "The Son cannot do anything on his own, but only what he sees the Father doing; for whatever the Father does, the Son does

[283] Jer 8:8.

likewise." By being able to do exactly the same works as God the Father and by doing them in the same way as the one who begat him, he testifies to the identity of substance with him. For things that have the same nature as each other will act in the same way. But those whose mode of being is different would not have the same way of doing everything. Therefore, as true God from true God the Father, he says that he can do these things equally with him; however, in order to make it clear that he is not only equal to the Father in power but also thinks the same in all things and has one will with him in all things, he says that he "cannot do anything on his own, but only what he sees the Father doing."

It is as though he were to say more explicitly to those who tried to persecute him for healing a man on the sabbath, You think that the honor of the sabbath has been violated, but I would never have done this if I did not see the Father doing something similar. He acts to sustain the world even on the sabbath, though he does it through me. Therefore, it is impossible, he says, for me, the Son who is from him by nature, not wholly to will and to do the Father's works in all things—not as one who receives the example of what to do from without by being taught or as one who is called to bring his will into line with the Father's will by deliberation. Rather, by the laws of uncreated nature I ascend to the same will and action as God the Father. His inability to do anything of himself is exceptionally well defined in these words. I think we should understand the matter reverently in this way and take captive "every thought to obey Christ," as it is written.[284] **[319]**

But perhaps the enemy of the truth will not believe this and will make the statement a kind of food for their own ill counsel, saying, If the Son were equal to the Father and were under no necessity to attribute superiority to him on account of the inferiority of his own nature, what induced him to say so openly that he cannot do anything on his own, but only what he sees the Father doing? Clearly in these words, they say, he admits that he cannot at all do these things on his own. He admits this, that is, as one who knows the one who is greater and superior. Now overcome our argument with your sophistry.

What then shall we say to this? Once again the enemy of Christ puts on a tough front to the point of blasphemy, but since he is drunk from his ignorance, he does not even realize what he is doing. We must test carefully, sir, the meaning of what has been said and not readily spring on reasoning that comes from ignorance. To what kind of equality with the Father do you think we must bring the Son down because of the statement that he "cannot do anything on his own, but only what he sees the Father doing"? Does he then say these things as one who does not have equal power, even though from the very words under consideration one can see that the Son is equal in strength to the Father rather than lacking in God-befitting power? Clearly, he does not say, "The Son cannot do anything on his own unless he receives the ability from the Father." This is what someone who is really weak would say. No, he says "but only what he sees the Father doing." I think no one could dispute the fact that the sense of sight does not make us powerful but enables us to look at things. Therefore, when the Son says that he looks at the works of the one who begat him, he is not showing himself to be weak but a zealous imitator and beholder. We will say more carefully how this is in what follows. And he will teach clearly in what follows that through his **[320]** identical and comparable work, I mean in all things, he is shown to have equal power. He will teach this when he himself says concerning his Father, "For whatever the

[284]2 Cor 10:5.

Father does, the Son does likewise." How then is he inferior who is preeminent with activity that is equal to that of God the Father? Could the offspring of fire have a different activity than fire without changing its activity? How could this ever be so? How then will the Son do "likewise" the works of the Father if on account of his inferiority he falls short of equal power with him?

We have applied these thoughts to the current question from the passage before us. Let us go through other considerations as well and see if the nature of the Son anywhere admits of being second to that of the Father. Let us treat power along the same lines. They either confess that the Son is true God from God by nature and actually from the substance of the Father, or they say he is God but blasphemously add that he lies outside the substance of the Father. If they say he is not from the substance of the Father, he will neither be God by nature nor a true Son. For that which is not from God by nature could not at all be considered God by nature, nor could he be a Son unless he were begotten from the substance of the Father. So they are bringing in a new and bastard god.

But if they will not say this because they blush at the absurdity in their teaching, they will grant that the Only Begotten is truly from the Father and is truly God by nature. How will he be inferior to the Father or weak in anything without **[321]** this fact also accusing the substance of his Father? If it is possible for one who is God by nature to be at all weak, what is to prevent the Father from being in this condition, since the divine and ineffable nature now has the ability to suffer and has already been shown to suffer in the Son, according to them? Therefore, the divine will not be impassible, nor will it repose in sameness and wholly unchangeable blessedness. Who then, tell me, will endure those who hold such opinions? Who, when the Holy Scriptures cry out that the Son is the Lord of powers,[285] will not be reluctant to say that he needs to be strengthened and that he is imperfect in that which strictly speaking belongs only to him (and to the Father and the Holy Spirit as well)?

Our opponent will reply, We say that the Father surpasses the Son in the following respect. The one is the originator of the works since he has perfection both in power and in knowledge of all things. The other first becomes a spectator; then he acts in a like manner, receiving into himself the imitation of the Father's activity, so that by the likeness of the works he too is considered God. He teaches us this when he says that he "can do nothing of himself, but only what he sees the Father doing."

What are you saying, you reckless person? The Son receives impressions of the Father's activity in himself so that for this reason he is considered God? Then he will be God by instruction, not by nature! Just as knowledge or skill, for example, is in us, so also dignity is in him, and he is an artificer of the works of the divine nature rather than true God. He is, of course, certainly different from the skill that is in him, even though that skill is fitting for God. How then do angels in heaven worship one who is outside the boundaries of the divine nature and whose glory is in his skill alone? How do we worship him without blame since the Holy Scriptures command us not to worship anyone besides the **[322]** one who is really God? "You shall worship the Lord your God," it says, "and him alone shall you serve."[286] But the holy multitude of angels, of all things, could not have erred in what is fitting. Yet they worship the Son, and along with us they serve him, recognizing him to be God by nature, not by instruction, as those people foolishly say. They do not perceive, it

[285]Ps 24:10 (Ps 23:10 LXX). [286]Mt 4:10; Deut 6:13.

seems, what great absurdities they will fall into from this position.

First, the Son will admit change and turning from the lesser to the greater, even though he himself says through the prophet, "Behold, behold! I am, and I do not change."[287] And the psalmist will certainly lie in the Spirit when he cries out to the Son, "You are the same!"[288] That is because he waits, as they say, for the Father to do something, as a guide and teacher, that he may see it and imitate it. How could such a one not seem to ascend from ignorance of certain matters to knowledge and to turn from the worse to the better, at least if we consider knowing something good to be better than not knowing it?

Next, what other absurdity do we see? Let those who introduce God as a teacher rather than a Father tell us, Does the Son wait to see the works of the Father in ignorance, or does he have the most precise knowledge of them? If they say that he knows as he waits, they will clearly show him doing something completely superfluous, and they will show the Father carrying out a most idle task. The one, as though ignorant, watches what he knows in detail, and the other tries to teach one who already knows. Who cannot clearly see that such ideas are absolutely ridiculous?

But perhaps they will not say this but will opt for the opposite alternative. **[323]** They will maintain that of necessity he waits for the Father to work in order to learn by seeing. How then did he know "all things before they came to be"?[289] Or how will he not be lying when he says about himself, "I am a God nearby, says the Lord, and not a God far away. Will anything be hidden from me?"[290] How is it not absurd and ignorant to believe that the Spirit searches and knows the deep things of God[291] but to think that the supplier of the Spirit stands in ignorance of the works of the Father and of his own Spirit inasmuch as he is lacking in knowledge? Will they not also reject the fact that the Son is wisdom since he is completely ignorant and learns by being taught? He will be a recipient of wisdom rather than wisdom itself by nature. Wisdom, after all, is that which makes wise, not that which is made wise, just as light of course is that which illuminates, not that which is illuminated. Therefore, he will be something other than the wisdom in him.

This means first of all that he is not simple but ultimately composed of two things. On top of that, he will cease to be God, I mean God by nature and according to substance. The divine nature will not endure learning from anyone at all or endure being doubled by synthesis since simplicity is its own good and perfect property. Furthermore, if the Son is not God by nature, how does he perform and carry out works that are fitting for God alone? Will they then say that merely seeing the Father working is enough to give him God-befitting power and that through mere sight he attains to being God by nature and is able to do whatever things the one who shows him does? In that case, there is nothing to prevent many others from being made gods since the Father wills to show them too the way of his works, **[324]** and the distinguishing characteristic of the Father's substance will consist in learning something above and beyond. The one who is taught, as they claim, is found to rush up to the dignity that belongs to the divinity by nature and say, "I and the Father are one. Whoever has seen me has seen the Father."[292]

Let them weigh then how great a pile of blasphemies they heap up by choosing to think this way, and let them think truly of the Son as it is written. The Son is not a doer or miracle worker (and therefore God) because he sees the Father's works or because the Father is the

[287]Mal 3:6. [288]Ps 102:27 (Ps 101:28 LXX). [289]Sus 1:42. [290]Jer 23:23; 32:27 (Jer 39:27 LXX). [291]1 Cor 2:10. [292]Jn 10:30; 14:9.

originator of his works but because a certain law of nature, as it were, carries him to the unchangeable sameness with the one who begat him, even though he shines forth and is revealed through the exact likeness of the works. Let us set down once again, if you please, the section of text and examine it with more careful scrutiny to see precisely what the meaning of the words is, and let us now see how we should understand them in a godly way: "Truly, truly, I tell you, the Son cannot do anything on his own," he says, "but only what he sees the Father doing; for whatever the Father does, the Son does likewise."

Do you see how through the exact identity of their works, he shows himself to be like the Father in all things so that he might be revealed through this to be the heir of his substance as well? The Savior says these things with the understanding that the one who has the same works must incontrovertibly be understood to be God by nature. Let no one be scandalized when he plainly says regarding the *oikonomia* that he "cannot do anything on his own, but only what he sees the Father doing." Since he was now clothed in the form of a slave **[325]** and had become human by being united to the flesh, he did not speak freely, nor did he fully let his language loose to the point of God-befitting boldness. But he sometimes used speech which, because of the *oikonomia*, was fitting both for God and for man. He was, after all, really both in the same.

That is one explanation, and it is true. But I think we should explain the matter before us in another way as well and pay sharper attention to the precision of our understanding. "The Son cannot do anything on his own," he says, "but only what he sees the Father doing." The word *cannot* or the quality of being "unable" is predicated of certain people or attributed to certain objects that exist. This predication, we say, is not at all indicative of necessity or weakness. It often denotes the steadiness of natures and implacable stability of substances with reference to what each thing mentioned either is or has become, and it denotes what each can do by nature and without change.

Let our argument be made, if you please, also by way of examples. For instance, when a man says he cannot carry a piece of wood somewhere, probably because it is unwieldy or heavy, he is referring to his innate weakness. But when another man says, "Since I am rational by nature and begotten by nature of a rational father, I cannot do anything, as it were, on my own and of myself which I do not see belonging to the nature of the one who begat me," then the "cannot" shows the stability of his substance and his inability to change into something other than what he is. I cannot, he says, of myself overcome the excellent qualities that belong to my nature so that I stop being a rational animal. I do not see the ability to undergo such a thing in the nature of my father. In this way then you should understand Christ when he says, "The Son cannot do anything on his own, but only **[326]** what he sees the Father doing." Do not blame the works of the Son, he says, since in his own thoughts and in the natural motions of his mind, he is beholding the substance of his Father. And whatever he sees that nature fittingly perform, he does these works and no other, since he is not able to undergo anything which is contrary to that nature because he is from it. For example, the nature of the Father has the will to show mercy. The Son sees this inherent in that nature and is merciful since he is from him by nature, and he cannot become anything other than what that nature is. Just as he has his substance from the Father, so he also has the good properties of his substance, simply, that is, and without composition as God. For this reason, he wisely adds the words, "for whatever the Father does, the Son does likewise," to the previous statement and gathers together in these words the whole meaning, so to speak, of, "He cannot do anything on his own, but only what he sees the Father doing." You should consider the reason why the Son says these things and apply yourself with great diligence to what we have said.

So when he had mercy on the paralytic on the sabbath day, the Jews tried to persecute him. But Christ shames them by showing that God the Father is merciful on the sabbath day. He did not think he should ever prevent anything that is connected with our salvation. Indeed, he started off by saying, "My Father works until now, and I am also working."[293] But when they are clearly upset at these things because of their tremendously bad counsel, he adds, "The Son cannot do anything on his own, but only what he sees the Father doing; for whatever the Father does, the Son does likewise." Since, he says, the Father does not refuse to have mercy on the sabbath, and since I see him full of compassion all the time, I too in the same way have mercy all the time. I cannot somehow cut out the Father's **[327]** substance from myself by not appearing and being as he is by nature. I carry out his works in every way since I am from him.

But to say that the Father is the originator of the works partakes in the ultimate ignorance. How could he ever originate anything alone by his own power, since he has the Son as his operative power for everything—his Son who is with him eternally and who reveals his will and activity in any matter? But if they ignorantly maintain that he awaits the separate activity of the Father for each work in order to imitate it faithfully, let them show us what the Father ever did on his own power by himself, or what paralytic he healed and then gave that action to his Son as a type.

5:20 "The Father loves the Son."

Christ convicts those who were heedlessly blaspheming against him on account of the sabbath of going stark raving mad in their vain anger. He gives them a crystal-clear proof of the matter by saying that he is loved by his Father. If in fact "the Father loves the Son," it is clear that he loves not one who grieves him but one who pleases him in what he does and accomplishes. In vain then do they persecute the one who does not refuse to show mercy on the sabbath, and they are caught resisting the decrees of God the Father by doing this. They think they should hate, after all, the one the Father loves. But of course it is certainly clear that the Father would never have loved him if he transgressed the will of his Father and were accustomed to do whatever he wanted by himself on his own. Since the Father justly loves him, the Father clearly agrees and consents to the breaking of the sabbath, **[328]** and he demonstrates that there is nothing in that act over which God, the Lord of the law, might reasonably become angry.

"And shows him all that he himself is doing."

He adds this to the preceding words for rather weighty reasons, and I will say why. Human fathers are sometimes overcome by natural affection and put up with sons who grieve them. Even when they see them attempting to disobey their will, they often endure it because an intense love for their children dwells within them which convinces them to overcome all meanness of spirit toward them. But this is not the way God the Father loves the Son, he says. The Son cannot do anything which the Father himself does not do by nature. Since he has one substance with the Father, he is called by certain physical laws, so to speak, to an identical will and power. Therefore, the Son does nothing, he says, contrary to what is pleasing and fitting to the Father, nor does he boast in the Father's love like an unbridled lover of novelty. But what-

[293]Jn 5:17.

ever he sees the Father do (in his thoughts, as it were), he certainly carries out, kept by the identity of substance from falling away in any respect from what is fitting to God. He has no share in change or alteration, but he remains unceasingly "the same," as the psalmist says somewhere.[294] Again, the Father shows the Son "all that he himself is doing," not as though setting before him lessons written on a tablet or as though teaching one who is ignorant (for he knows all things as God), but he depicts his entire self in the nature of his offspring. He shows his own natural properties in him so that from those things which **[329]** the Son is and is shown to be, the Son may know what sort of Father he has and who the Father is by nature. That is why Christ says, "No one knows who the Son is except the Father, and no one knows who the Father is except the Son,"[295] since the exact knowledge of each lies in both, not by being taught but by nature. Furthermore, God the Father sees the Son in himself, and the Son, in turn, sees the Father in himself. That is why he says, "I am in the Father, and the Father is in me."[296] Let the expressions "seeing" and "being seen" in this discussion be understood in a God-befitting way.

"And he will show him greater works than these, so that you will be astonished."

In the foregoing, the Evangelist says that "the Jews sought to kill Jesus, because he was not only breaking the sabbath but also was calling God his own Father, thereby making himself equal to God."[297] So he disposed of the accusation about the sabbath by showing the Father himself working on the sabbath, spending many words on this point. He is trying to teach them that he is in equality with the Father even though he became human for our sake. This is what the argument still lacked. Therefore, he says, "And he will show him greater works than these, so that you will be astonished." And what does he want to show us with this statement?

The paralytic, he says, has been healed "who had been ill for thirty-eight years."[298] The power of the healer is truly marvelous, and his authority is entirely fitting for God. No sensible person would blame such a miracle worker, I think, for saying he is God, especially since he is the Son, equal in all things to the one who begat him. But since you imagine the most evil and unreasonable things, he says, **[330]** and you are scandalized by this mortal body, you must learn that my authority and power will not stop at this point. You will be witnesses, even against your will, of greater miracles, namely, the resurrection of the dead. And then you will be even more astonished when you see the God-befitting strength and glory that resides in me, whom you now charge with blasphemy and are not ashamed to persecute just because I said, "I am the Son of God."[299]

We have already discussed at great length how God the Father shows his works to the Son.

5:21 "For as the Father raises the dead and gives them life, so also the Son gives life to whomever he wishes."

See again in these words the clear proof of his equality. How can the one who equally effects the resurrection of the dead be inferior in any respect? Or how could the one who is bright with the same properties be of a different nature or alien to the Father? The ability to give life is a property of the divine nature which is in the Father and the Son alike. But the Father does not give life to some on his own and by himself, while the Son gives life to others on his own and separately. The Son does everything since he has the Father

[294]Ps 102:27 (Ps 101:28 LXX). [295]Mt 11:27. [296]Jn 14:11. [297]Jn 5:18. [298]Jn 5:5. [299]Jn 10:36.

naturally in himself, and the Father does everything through the Son. But since the Father has the power to give life in his own nature, just as the Son does, Christ refers to the power to resurrect the dead as belonging to each one on his own. **[331]**

Chapter Seven

No God-befitting dignity or superiority is in the Son by participation or addition from the outside.

5:22 "The Father judges no one but has given all judgment to the Son."

He introduces another God-befitting and extraordinary action in order to persuade them through many proofs that he is truly God by nature. Who else would be fit to judge the world except only the one who is God over all? The Holy Scriptures address him regarding this judgment, saying at one point, "Arise, O God, and judge the earth,"[300] and at another point, "God is judge, putting down one and lifting up another."[301] He says, however, that "judgment" has been given to him by the Father not on the grounds that he lies outside this authority but on the grounds that he is a man according to the *oikonomia*, thereby teaching that "all things" are more fittingly ascribed to the divine nature, which he has as he enters the world. In that he is Word and God, he inherently has authority over all things, but in that he has become human, to whom it says somewhere, "What do you have that you did not receive?"[302] he confesses that it was fitting for him to receive that authority.

Perhaps one of the opponents will say to this, See! The Son explicitly says that he has received "judgment" from the Father. Clearly, one who receives does not have. How then could the one who gives with authority not be greater and of a superior nature than the one who must receive? **[332]**

What then do we say to these things? Our preceding argument has been not unskillfully constructed, I think, in that it introduces a consideration that is especially appropriate for the present time, namely, that of the incarnation. It perfectly fits the *oikonomia* with the flesh when he was called a slave and when he humbled himself, being made in our likeness. Since it seems good to you to despise the simpler doctrines and undertake an elaborate investigation, let us go through your objections. First let us say, The one who is said to give something does not necessarily or in every case grant it to someone who receives because they do not have, nor is the giver always greater than the receiver. Otherwise, what will you do when you see the holy psalmist saying in the Spirit, "Give glory to God"?[303] Shall we think then that God stands in need of glory or that we who are commanded to offer it to him are greater than the creator because of this? But not even you, who do not shrink from blasphemy, will dare to say this, since the divine nature is full of glory even though it does not receive it from us. That which has something inherently and receives it as an honor could never be considered inferior to those who offer glory to it as a gift. One may then see that very often the one who has received something is not inferior to the giver, and the Father is not of a superior nature to his own offspring just because "he has given all judgment" to him.

Next, we must consider this as well. To judge or to render judgment are activities or acts related to substances rather than truly substances themselves. When we give a judgment, we are acting; we are being what we are according to our own characteristics. But if we were to grant that judging or rendering judgment belonged to substances, how could we not, **[333]** even against our will, confess

[300]Ps 82:8 (Ps 81:8 LXX). [301]Ps 75:7 (Ps 74:8 LXX). [302]1 Cor 4:7. [303]Ps 68:34 (Ps 67:35 LXX).

that some could not exist at all, except as judges, and that their substance would cease to exist when the judging ends? But to think this is absurd. Judging then is an activity and nothing else. What then has the Father given the Son? He does not give something additional as from his own nature when he entrusts all judgment to him, but rather he gives him an activity over against those who are judged. How then will he be greater because of this or be of a superior nature because he added something that was not in the Son, since the Son says, "Everything that the Father has is mine"?[304]

So listen to how giving must then be understood. Just as God the Father has the ability to create and creates all things through the Son as through his own power and strength, so also he has the power to judge, and he will exercise that power through the Son as through his own righteousness.[305] Just as though fire were said to supply a certain "burning" to the activity that is from it by nature, so also if we reverently interpret "he has given" along the same lines, we will escape the snare of the devil. But if they shamelessly persist in asserting that glory is added to him from the Father because of his appearing as judge of the earth, let them teach us how he could still be considered the "Lord of glory,"[306] if he is crowned with this glory in the end times? **[334]**

Chapter Eight

Since the Son is God and from God by nature and is the exact image of the one who begat him, he has equal honor and glory with him.

5:23 "That all may honor the Son just as they honor the Father. Anyone who does not honor the Son does not honor the Father who sent him."

The cause and reason for the things enumerated above now comes to light, namely, that the Son should be honored equally with and like the Father. If you recall briefly and remember the previous passages, you can consider the meaning of the statement with precision. This is why he said that God was his own Father, "making himself equal to God,"[307] and why he showed that he had equal strength and skill by saying, "Whatever the Father does, the Son does likewise."[308] And he made it quite clear that he is both life and the giver of life by nature, just like the one who begat him, by adding, "For as the Father raises the dead and gives them life, so also the Son gives life to whomever he wishes."[309] He explained that he would also be the judge of all, with his Father's consent and approval in everything, when he said, "The Father judges no one but has given all judgment to the Son."[310] What then is the reason for these statements? What induced the Only Begotten to say all this? "That all may honor the Son," he says, "just as they honor the Father." If he has everything the Father has, as far as **[335]** God-befitting dignity is concerned, how would it not be right to crown him with equal honors who lacks nothing pertaining to identity of substance?

What then do those who "pervert all that is right," as the prophet Isaiah says,[311] say to this? If, they say, because of the statement "that all may honor the Son just as they honor the Father," you think that the Son should be revered with honors equal to those of the Father, you do not realize that you are wandering far from the truth. The words "just as" do not introduce a strict equality of actions among the things where they are placed, but they often designate a kind of similarity, as for example when the Savior counsels, "Be merciful just as your heavenly Father is merciful."[312] Are we then to be merciful in the same way as the Father because of the "just as"? Again,

[304]Jn 16:15. [305]See 1 Cor 1:30. [306]1 Cor 2:8. [307]Jn 5:18. [308]Jn 5:19. [309]Jn 5:21. [310]Jn 5:22. [311]Mic 3:9. [312]Lk 6:36.

Christ says to his Father concerning the disciples, "You loved them just as you loved me."[313] We will not grant, however, that because of the "just as," the disciples were loved in the same way as the Son. Why then do you invent ingenious explanations and twist the words into blasphemy, though they lay no necessity on the hearers that they must honor the Son to the same degree as the Father?

What then shall we say to these things? The enemies of God bark at us with bitter words, but "outside are the dogs," as Paul says, "outside are the evildoers, outside" of the right faith "are the mutilators of the flesh."[314] We, however, are sons of the truth and children of the light. Therefore, we will glorify the Only Begotten along with God the Father not in a different way but in equality of honor and glory as God from God, light from light and life from life. Too much inquiry about what is to be received by faith is not without danger; nevertheless, we must test the meaning of "just as" so that the opponents do not think too much of themselves. When the words "just as" are applied to things that are dissimilar **[336]** in nature, they certainly do not introduce exact equality, as far as we are concerned, but a similarity and likeness, as you yourselves acknowledged before. But if they are applied to things that are like each other in every respect, they indicate equality in all things and likeness and whatever other synonyms you can think of. For example, the sun in the sky is bright, and silver from the earth is likewise bright, but the nature of the things mentioned is different. Now suppose that any rich person on earth says to the household servants, "Make the silver shine just as the sun." In this case we quite rightly say that matter from the earth does not ascend to equal brightness with the sun but to a certain similarity and likeness, even though the words "just as" might be used of it. Or, take Peter and John, let's say, from the holy disciples, who are not wanting in exact likeness with each other in their nature and in their reverence toward God. Now let the words "just as" be applied when someone says about them, as in the text under consideration, "Let John be honored by all just as Peter is." Will the words "just as" then be powerless so that equal honor need not be paid to both? I do not think anyone will say this because anyone will see that there is nothing to prevent equal honor.

According to this analogy, when the words "just as" are applied to the Son and the Father, why should we shrink from crowning both with equal honors? Since he examined the future ahead of time as God and considered your ignorant and slanderous opposition, he has inserted the words "just as" not by themselves or bereft of appropriate support for them, but he has fortified them beforehand by fitting proofs and shown previously that he is God by nature. **[337]** He made God his own Father, after all. After he established beforehand that he is both God the creator and the true life, and after he introduced himself altogether glorying, so to speak, in the attributes of God the Father, he adds at just the right time, "that all may honor the Son just as they honor the Father." Now what objection will come up? What is to prevent the one in whom the properties and excellent qualities of his begetter reside essentially from ascending to an equal degree of honor? For we will already be found honoring the very nature of the Father as it shines forth beautifully in the Son. That is why he says next, "Anyone who does not honor the Son does not honor the Father who sent him." The charge of dishonoring the Son and the implication of blasphemy will reach all the way up to none other than the very Father himself, just as the Father sends forth the Son from the fount of his own nature even though he is seen to be eternally

[313]Jn 17:23. [314]Phil 3:2.

with him throughout all of Holy Scripture.

Yes, says the opponent, let the charge of dishonoring the Son reach whatever you please, or rather let it reach God the Father himself. He will be angry, and with good reason, though not entirely angry, that his nature was insulted in the Son, according to our carefully worked out argument. Since he is his image and imprint, formed most excellently after his divine and ineffable nature, he has a good reason to be angry, and he will transfer the wrong entirely to himself. It would indeed be most absurd if one who insults the divine imprint does not pay the full penalty of sinning against the archetype, just as one who insults the images of earthly kings is punished as having indeed transgressed against the ruler himself. We will find that something like this has been decreed by **[338]** God for us as well. "Whoever sheds human blood," it says, "instead of that blood shall their own be shed, for in the image of God I made humanity."[315] Do you see then, he says, very clearly in this passage, that if the image is wronged, and not the full divine nature, God the Father deems it right to get angry? Therefore, let Christ's statement, "Anyone who does not honor the Son does not honor the Father," be understood and taken in this way.

Will the Only Begotten then be classed with us as external to the substance of the Father? How is he still God by nature if he has slipped completely out of the limits of the divine nature and is placed in some nature that is his own and other than that of the Father? We do wrong, it seems, when we raise the order of the holy Trinity to one principle of divinity. We must—we must—worship the Father as God and attribute to the Son and the Spirit some glory of their own, splitting them into different natures, as it were, and defining for each one his own mode of being.

The Holy Scriptures, however, declare to us one God and class the Son and the Spirit with the Father since the holy Trinity is brought up into one principle of divinity through the exact identity of substance. Therefore, the Only Begotten is not alien to the nature of the one who begat him. He would not be considered truly a Son at all if he did not shine forth from the substance of his Father, since that is the definition and mode of true sonship for everyone, and there is no other. But if there is no Son, the fact that God is Father will surely be taken from him as well. How then will Paul speak the truth when he says about him, "from whom all fatherhood in heaven and on earth is named"?[316] If he has not begotten the Son from himself in a God-befitting way, how is there an origin of fatherhood in him which reaches by imitation to those who are in heaven and on earth? **[339]** But God is truly Father. The Only Begotten, therefore, is Son by nature and is certainly within the bounds of the divine nature. God will be born of God, just as a human being, for example, is born of a human being, and the nature of God the Father, which is above all, will not err by bearing fruit that is not appropriate to it.

But since they blasphemously and foolishly say that it is not the nature of God the Father that is insulted in the Son when the Son does not receive appropriate glory from some, but rather the Father does well and has good reason to get angry that his image is dishonored in him—we must ask them in what sense they would have the Son be and be called the image of the Father? Or rather let us anticipate their argument and with apt reasoning spell out beforehand the kinds of images there are. In this way, the results of our investigation will be clear and crisp. The first kind of image is characterized by identity of nature in identical properties, like Abel from Adam or Isaac from Abraham. The second consists only in the likeness of imprint and the precise representation

[315]Gen 9:6 (LXX). [316]Eph 3:15.

of the form, like the picture of a king on wood, or made in some other way, representing him as excellently and skillfully as possible. Another kind of image is taken to refer to habits, manners, way of life and inclination toward things that are good or bad, as for example when one says that someone who does good is like Paul and someone who does not is like Cain. The fact that they are equally good or bad brings about and reasonably confers a likeness with each one. Another kind of image is that of dignity, honor, glory and excellence, as for example if someone were to succeed another in command and do with authority everything **[340]** that is proper and fitting for the predecessor. In another sense, an image concerns some other quality or quantity of a thing, its shape and proportion (for we must keep it short).

So let those most painstaking investigators of the divine image teach us whether they think we must ascribe to the Only Begotten the essential and natural likeness, and whether they say that the only begotten Word proceeding from the Father is the image of the Father in this sense, like Abel from Adam, who preserves the entire nature of his parent in himself and bears the complete principle of human nature. Or will they be unable to endure this, though they are compelled to confess the Son as truly God from God by nature, and turn aside like they usually do to fight against the truth and advance to the second kind of image which is understood to pertain only to form and imprint and shape? I think, however, that they will shrink back from saying this. No one will suppose, even if they were a complete babbler, that the divine nature can be quantified or circumscribed by a shape or measured by an imprint or that the incorporeal can at all be subject to corporeal things. Do they then say that he has been shaped in his habits, manners and will, so they are not ashamed to dress him in this image? How is he still understood as God by nature if he has his likeness with him only in will but exists by himself in his own way as something else? They will surely acknowledge that he subsists, after all. What more then will be in him beyond creation? Shall we not believe that angels too hasten to carry out the divine will, while they exist as something besides God by nature? And what about when this is understood of us as well? **[341]** In that case, does the Only Begotten himself teach us foolishly to overstep our nature and aim for the impossible when he says, "Be merciful just as your heavenly Father is merciful"?[317] After all, this undoubtedly says that we should gain the image of the Father by identity of will. Paul too became an imitator of Christ, the image of the Father by mere will, as they foolishly say.

But they will probably abandon these miserable ideas too, and, as though thinking something better and greater, they will surely say this: The Only Begotten is the image of God the Father with respect to identity of wills; with respect to dignity, glory and God-befitting power; with respect to the activity of creating and performing miracles; with respect to reigning and ruling over everything; with respect to judging and being worshiped by angels, humans and all creation in general. Through all these things, as he shows us the Father in himself, he says not that he is of his hypostasis but is the "imprint of his hypostasis."[318]

In that case, as we just said, the Son is none of these things by nature but lies outside them all, at least according to your most senseless reasoning. He is neither true God, nor Son, nor king, nor Lord, nor creator, nor powerful, nor even good in his own will by nature, but he is found merely to boast about what is God-befitting. Just as the application of colors to a drawing on a tablet beautifies merely by

[317]Lk 6:36. [318]Heb 1:3.

its variety to the eye but brings nothing real, so also the beauty of God the Father's honors in the Son is decorated merely with bare names, and it is smeared on him on the outside like paint. **[342]** Or rather, the divine nature is sketched in him, and it appears in mere type.

How then will they not be found fighting against the Holy Scriptures outright, so that they deserve to hear, "You stiff-necked people, uncircumcised in heart and ears, you always resist the Holy Spirit. As your ancestors did, so do you."[319] When do the Scriptures not call the Son true God, or when do they take him outside the substance of his parent? Who has dared to say that he is neither the creator by nature, nor king, nor almighty, nor to be worshiped? The divine psalmist says somewhere as to the Only Begotten himself, "Your throne, O God, is forever."[320] And Thomas, the disciple with the greatest understanding, likewise calls him God and Lord.[321] He is also called almighty and creator by the voice of every saint, not on the grounds that he has this dignity as something imported, as you say, but on the grounds that he is by nature what he is said to be. And for this reason he is worshiped both by the holy angels and by us, even though the Holy Scriptures say that we must worship no one else except the Lord God alone.

So if they believe that his God-befitting dignity is imported and given to him, and they think that we should worship such a person, let them know that they are worshiping a creature rather than the creator,[322] painting for themselves a fresh and new god rather than acknowledging the one who is really God by nature. But if, while they say that the Son is outside the substance of God the Father, they confess that the Son himself is true God, king, Lord and creator, and that he has the Father's properties and characteristics in himself essentially, let them see to what end this kind of thinking risks leading them. **[343]** Nothing at all in the divine nature will be found worthy of confidence since the nature of originate beings too can now be in truth what the divine nature is understood to be. For the Only Begotten has been shown, at least by the opponents' feeble argument, not to be of the divine nature but nevertheless truly to have in himself its characteristics. Who will not shudder merely to hear the blasphemy of these teachings? Everything is turned upside down. The nature that is above all things descends to be classed with originate beings, while creation itself contrary to reason leaps up to a level that is above and not designed for it.

Therefore, let us swim away from these absurd teachings as from a ship sinking in the sea, and let us hasten to the truth as to a safe and calm shore. Let us confess the Son to be the image of God the Father, not plastered over, so to speak, with perishable honors or glorified only with names that are fitting for God but corresponding exactly in his essence with the likeness of his parent and being by nature the exact same as what the one who begat him is understood to be, that is, true God from God in truth, almighty, creator, glorified, good, to be worshiped, and whatever else may be added to these things that is fitting for God. Then, by showing him to be like God the Father in all things, we will also show him to tell the truth that if any should not want to honor the Son, neither do they honor the Father who sent him. That is what our inquiry is about, and that is the origin of the investigation of the things just discussed. **[344]**

5:24 "Truly, truly, I tell you, anyone who hears my word and believes him who sent me has eternal life, and does not come under judgment, but has passed from death to life."

[319]Acts 7:51. [320]Ps 45:6 (Ps 44:7 LXX). [321]Jn 20:28. [322]See Rom 1:25.

He sufficiently demonstrated in the foregoing that the wretched Jews sin not only against the Son when they find fault with whatever he teaches or does among them, but they ignorantly sin against the Father himself. The effect of his words is to wrap their impudence in fear and to persuade them to live more moderately in the hope of things to come. Then at last he catches them in his net and brings them to obedience. He constructed his message concerning these things not unskillfully. Since he knew that the Jews were still sick and were still scandalized by him, he directs their faith back to the person of God the Father, not excluding himself, but as one who is honored as well in the Father on account of the identity of substance. And he affirms that those who believe not only will be participants in "eternal life" but also will escape the danger of judgment, that is, they will be justified.[323] Thus, he holds out fear mixed with hope. In this way, he is able to make his message more effective and powerful to the hearers.

5:25 "Truly, truly, I say to you, the hour is coming and is now here when the dead will hear the voice of the Son of God, and those who hear will live."

After saying that believers will pass from death to life, he introduces himself as the one who fulfills the promise and accomplishes the whole [345] thing. At the same time, he hints to the Jews that the power shown in the case of the paralytic is truly marvelous, but the Son will be revealed doing even more remarkable things, driving away from human bodies not only sickness and the infirmities of disease but overthrowing even death itself and the corruption that presses on us. This is what it says a little earlier, "The Father loves the Son and shows him all that he is doing. And he will show him greater works than these, so that you will be astonished."[324] For the greater wonder is shown in the resurrection of the dead. At the same time, he is preparing something that will probably frighten the hearers in no small degree. He clearly states that he will raise the dead and bring the creature to judgment so that by the expectation of one day standing before him and giving an account of everything, they might be found more hesitant in their audacious attempt to persecute him and might more readily receive the word of his teaching and guidance.

This then is the main point of the section.[325] We must now explain it according to the letter. The common explanation (it seems) is that the time will come when the dead will hear the voice of the one who raises them. And they suppose that it is no less present even "now," either because Lazarus, for example, is going to hear the voice of the Savior or because they say that "the dead" are those not yet called by faith to eternal life but who will surely rise to life once they have received the teaching of the Savior. This way of looking at it does indeed preserve a plausible appearance, but it is not at all accurate. Therefore, we will ruminate once again on the meaning of the words and **[346]** attach to them a more suitable sense. In this way we will define the passage precisely.

"Truly, truly, I say to you, the hour is coming and is now here when the dead will hear the voice of the Son of God"—the hour, namely, when "those who hear will live." With the first words, he signifies the time of our resurrection at which, he teaches, those who sleep will be raised by the voice of the judge to answer for their life in the world. That way, as I said before, he intends the fear that arises from this to be a kind of bridle for them and persuades them to live a very good and wise life. With the next words, he shows that the

[323]Justification is not Cyril's primary way of describing salvation, though he does employ it. He understands it to refer to God's declaration of innocence, which takes place when the sinner comes to faith or, as here, on the last day. [324]Jn 5:20.
[325]See p. 136, n. 266 on the division of the biblical text into "sections."

time has come when people must believe in him, but he also says that eternal life will be the reward for their obedience, all but saying something like, All will come to judgment, sirs, namely, at the time of the resurrection. But if it seems bitter to you to be punished and endure infinite penalties at the hands of an offended judge, do not let the time of obedience pass by, but lay hold of it while it is still here and hurry to rise to eternal life.

5:26-27 "For just as the Father has life in himself, so also he has granted the Son to have life in himself; and he has given him authority to execute judgment, because he is the Son of Man."

Note once again the diplomacy of these words that you may marvel at the shape of the statement and not fall into offense from ignorance and call down destruction on yourself. The Only Begotten—who is human as far as the nature of his body is concerned, and who appears as one of us on the earth while he is still in the [347] flesh and who teaches the Jews many lessons in matters pertaining to salvation—he has clothed himself with the brightness of two God-befitting deeds. He distinctly maintains that he will both raise the dead and summon them to be judged at his own judgment seat. But it was extremely likely that his hearers would be upset by this, suspecting and accusing him with good reason because he "was also calling God his own Father, thereby making himself equal to God."[326] By mixing the message fitted for human nature with God-befitting authority and majesty, he steals away the weight of their wrath, saying more mildly and mutedly than he had to, "For just as the Father has life in himself, so also he has granted the Son to have life in himself." Do not marvel, he says, if I, though I am now like you and I appear as a human being, promise to raise the dead and threaten to bring them to judgment. The Father has given me the power to give life. The Father has given me the authority to judge. But when he had healed the fickle ear of the Jews with these words, he also gives zealous attention to the benefit of what follows and immediately explains the reason he says he has received life and authority. By adding the phrase "because he is the Son of Man," he explains that the human nature has nothing of itself.

I think it is now superfluous to say that the Only Begotten is life by nature and not a participant of life from someone else, and in this way he gives life just as the Father does. We have expended no short discussion on this at the beginning of the book, under the words "that which came into being—it was life."[327]

5:28-29 "Do not be astonished at this; for the hour is coming when all who are in their graves will hear his voice and will come out—those who have done good to the resurrection of life, and those who have done evil to the resurrection of judgment."

He is referring in these words to the time of the resurrection of all [348] when, as the divine Paul wrote to us, "The Lord himself will descend from heaven with a cry of command, with the voice of an archangel, with the trumpet of God"[328] to judge "the world with righteousness"[329] and to repay each one according to their works. By a repetition of the same things, therefore, he leads the most uninformed mind of the Jews to the ability for a clear understanding that he will work even greater wonders than in the case of the paralytic, and he will be revealed as the judge of the world. After profitably contrasting the healing of one sick person with the resurrection of the dead, he shows that the action that destroys death and removes corruption from everyone is

[326]Jn 5:18. [327]Book 1, chapter 6, pp. 32-35 above. [328]1 Thess 4:16. [329]Ps 98:9 (Ps 97:9 LXX).

greater and more remarkable, and he reasonably and necessarily says of the lesser miracle, "Do not be astonished at this." Of course we will certainly not suppose that with these words he is speaking against the glory of his own works or commanding his hearers to derogate those things people would normally marvel at. Rather, he wants those who are astounded at this to know and believe that what they are wondering at so far is a small matter. For he will raise by a God-befitting word and action not only those who are sick with small illnesses but also those who are already submerged by death and overcome by invincible decay. That is why he introduces what is greater and says, "The hour is coming when all who are in their graves will hear his voice." He who by his word brought things that once did not exist into being—how could he not be strong enough to bring what has already been created back into being? Each must be the effect of the same activity and the admirable accomplishment of one authority. **[349]** For our benefit he adds that they will come forth from their graves—those who were caught in shameful deeds and who lived in wickedness to endure endless punishment, and those who are illustrious in virtue to receive a reward for their virtue, eternal life. He introduces himself with these words, as we said before, as the dispenser of what is appropriate for each one. And at the same time he persuades them so that they either are driven to choose a more self-controlled life by fear of terrible punishment or hurry to strive more intently for the good as they are spurred on in some way by the desire for eternal life. **[350]**

Chapter Nine

The Son is less than God the Father in no respect, but as God from God, he is equal in might in carrying out all his works.

5:30 "I can do nothing on my own. As I hear, I judge; and my judgment is just, because I seek not my own will but the will of the Father who sent me."

Pay close attention to the words, and understand the force of their meaning in an intelligent way. Because the Jews did not know the deep mystery of the *oikonomia* with the flesh, nor did they recognize God the Word dwelling in the temple from the virgin, they were often kindled by a misplaced zeal to savage behavior and fierce anger "not according to knowledge," as Paul says.[330] In particular, they kept trying to stone him because "being a man, he was making himself God,"[331] and because "he was calling God his own Father, thereby making himself equal to God."[332] Since they were so ignorant and did not at all put up with God-befitting words but kept thinking and saying petty things about him, the Savior according to the divine *oikonomia* acts like a child with them; yet he still offered them a mixed explanation, neither completely avoiding statements that are appropriate to God nor altogether rejecting human language. After saying something worthy of divine **[351]** authority, he immediately keeps the ignorant anger of his hearers in check by adding something human as well. But when he says something human on account of the *oikonomia*, he does not allow what belongs to him to be viewed only in a lowly way, since he often shows through superhuman power and words that he is God by nature.

You will find this type of astuteness in the passage that is now before us. What did he say before? "For as the Father raises the dead and gives them life, so also the Son gives life to whomever he wishes."[333] Again, "For the hour is coming when all who are in their graves will hear his voice."[334] In addition to this, they will come out to be judged and to receive recom-

[330]Rom 10:2. [331]Jn 10:33. [332]Jn 5:18. [333]Jn 5:21. [334]Jn 5:28.

pense in proportion to whatever works they did. Now someone who says that he can give life to whomever he wishes, just as the Father does—how could he not be understood to have clothed himself in God-befitting power? And someone who explicitly says that he will be the judge of all—how could he not with good reason terrify those who think that he is only a man? It was likely, after all, that since they were Hebrews and instructed in the sacred Scriptures, they were not completely ignorant that God will be the judge of the world since it is often sung even among them, "Arise, O God, judge the earth."[335] And again, "God is judge."[336]

Since he knew that the ignorant people of the Jews were upset by these things, he rids them of their usual anger by saying in a more human fashion, "I can do nothing on my own. As I hear, I judge." As far as one can say from the surface meaning, then, he mocks the understanding of the Jews since the form of expression gives the impression of a certain weakness and an authority that is not altogether free. But it is not so in truth, since the Son is equal to the Father in all things, **[352]** and so he has the same activity and authority in all things by nature. He says that he cannot do anything on his own, but he judges as he hears, showing himself in yet another way to have the same knowledge and the same power as God the Father.

For the Father should not be understood to act in any matter by himself alone without the Son since the Son is his strength and power. Therefore, "all things were made through him, and without him nothing came into being."[337] The Son, in turn, will not do anything by himself without the Father being with him. That is why he says, "I do nothing on my own, but the Father himself who remains in me does the works."[338] Of course, we will not suppose that the Son is strengthened by the Father out of weakness or that his authority over all things is supplied to him. In that case, he would no longer be God by nature since he would have the beauty of his divinity as an import, as it were. Even the Father himself would no longer exist in the invincible superiority of the good if the Word, the imprint of his own nature, needs power and authority from someone else. That is because we would have to seek a supplier of these things for the archetype in the same way as for the image, and thus our argument will go into an infinite regress and run into a deep sea of blasphemies. Since the Son, however, is from the substance of the Father, he takes to himself by nature all the properties of his begetter, and he ascends essentially to one divine nature with him on account of the identity of nature. He is in the Father, and he has the Father in himself. That is why he often ascribes the power of his works, truly and without blame, to the Father. In so doing, he is not placing himself outside of that power, but he is assigning all things to the activity of one divine nature. There is one divine nature in the Father and in the Son and in the Holy Spirit. **[353]**

We have already demonstrated elsewhere that the Son is not inferior to the Father either in power or activity in anything, but he is like him in every respect and has equal power. We demonstrated this under the passage, "The Son cannot do anything on his own, but only what he sees the Father doing; for whatever the Father does, the Son does likewise."[339] But since I think it is fitting and right to overcome all laziness and to show the most devoted zeal in divine doctrines, come, let us imitate the sailors on the sea and wind back up, like a rope, the entire argument of the section.[340] In this way one can see that the Son is not accusing his own nature by saying

[335]Ps 82:8 (Ps 81:8 LXX). [336]Ps 75:7 (Ps 74:8 LXX). [337]Jn 1:3. [338]Jn 8:28; 14:10. [339]Jn 5:19. See Book 2, chapter 6, pp. 142-47 above. [340]See p. 136, n. 266 on the "sections" of the biblical text.

that he can do nothing on his own, but rather he is exposing the folly of the Jews and explicitly demonstrating that they have trampled on the law of Moses itself. The fact that he immediately adds the words "as I hear, I judge" to the words "I can do nothing on my own" frees the Son from all accusation that he cannot act on his own power, and it clearly shows that he loves his Father and agrees in all things with the one who begat him. If he borrowed power from the Father as if he were weak, let's say, and did not have sufficient power on his own, should he not rather have said, "I can do nothing on my own, but I receive the ability from the Father"? But in fact this is not what he says. Instead, he adds to his statement about not being able to do anything on his own the statement about judging just as he hears. Thus it is clear that he inserts the words "I can do nothing" not because of the weakness of his activity in anything but because it is not possible for him to transgress the will of the Father in any matter whatsoever. Since **[354]** we understand the Father and the Son to have one divine nature, their will will certainly be the same also. Neither in the Father, nor in the Son nor in the Holy Spirit will the divine nature ever be understood to be at odds with itself; rather, whatever seems good to the Father, let's say, is the will of the entire divine nature.

Therefore, the Son necessarily introduces himself as one who consents and agrees with the Father in whatever decree seems right to him, explaining that he cannot do anything that is not completely in agreement with the mind of the Father. This is what the words "on my own" indicate to us. If he were to say that he cannot sin, no one would rightly think that he is submitting to a charge of weakness but rather that he is expounding an admirable and God-befitting property of his nature, since he is giving us to understand that he is immoveable and unchangeable. In the same way, when he confesses that he can do nothing on his own, we will rather be awestruck, seeing his immutability as a fruit of his immutable nature, than inappropriately considering the inability to be indicative of weakness.

So let these things be said in proportion to our level, but let the one who is devoted to learning search out something better. Indeed, we will not shrink back from explaining the passage in another way as well, lowering our speech a little below the bounds of the divine nature and the superiority of the Only Begotten. Since the Son truly became and was called a human being, we will transfer the force of the ideas to the *oikonomia* with the flesh and show that what follows is akin and connected to what preceded. He testified clearly that "all who are in their graves will hear his voice" and that they will come forth to be judged. Once he has proceeded to the discussion of him judging the world, **[355]** he promises to be a just judge not only when he says the resurrection of the dead will take place, but he also declares that even now he fairly and justly judges the matters of this life.

Hear now what the issue was and what the discourse was about. For our sakes he was born of a woman. As Paul says, "He does not take hold of angels, but the seed of Abraham. Therefore, he had to become like his brothers in every respect."[341] Since he became man and came to be in the form of a slave, he who as God and Lord is the lawgiver also came to be under the law. He speaks, therefore, sometimes as one under the law and sometimes as one over the law, and he has undisputed authority to do both. He speaks now with the Jews as a human being and one who keeps the law, as one who does not know how to transgress the commands issued from above or to do anything from his own will which does not agree with the divine law. This is why he says, "I can

[341]Heb 2:16-17.

do nothing on my own. As I hear, I judge." By testifying that he can do nothing on his own that is not completely in agreement with the law and that he judges and renders a verdict in matters just as he hears—that is, because the law tells him—he exposes the disobedience of the Jews and lays bare the heedlessness of their behavior. The words "I can do nothing on my own" beautifully hint at this, placed in contrast with, You heedlessly transgress the commandments that have been given to you, and you fearlessly dare to do everything on your own. In every matter you are zealous to render judgments that do not follow the commands from God. You teach "human precepts as doctrines,"[342] and make your own will a law. **[356]**

Next we will discuss the way the material is arranged and how he introduces himself as a just judge but them as judges who are in no way just. He healed the paralytic on the sabbath. He had mercy on a man who spent a long time in sickness, demonstrating right and good judgment in his case. It was right to have compassion on the sick man, even on the sabbath, and not to shut off his mercy out of respect for the sabbath, showing the vainest reverence. Just as the Father too is active even on the sabbath to govern his creatures, through the Son of course, so the Son is as well. He did not think that one who needed mercy on the sabbath should be deprived of it because of the sabbath, since he knew that the Son of Man is Lord even of the sabbath.[343] Nor was humanity made for the sabbath, but the sabbath for humanity.[344] Therefore, the Savior's judgment in these matters was right and good when he did not restrain his mercy for the sick man on account of the sabbath, but even on the sabbath he did what as God he knows how to do. (For the divine nature is the source of his goodness.) The Jews are upset because of the sabbath and therefore want to kill him who did no harm. But how is their judgment concerning him not completely dissonant with the divine laws (since it is written, "You shall not kill the innocent and the righteous"),[345] and how is their judgment not devised from their own cruelty rather than from the Holy Scriptures?

Understand Jesus then to be speaking in this passage with a certain emphatic significance to those who are angry at the good works he is doing, who denounce his holy judgments, who follow only their own ideas and who define as law, so to speak, that which seems right to them even though it is contrary to the law. **[357]** He says, "I can do nothing on my own," that is, I do everything according to the law given through Moses. I cannot stand to do anything on my own. "As I hear, I judge." What does the law intend? "You shall not show partiality in judgment because the judgment belongs to God."[346] Why then "are you angry with me," he says, "because I healed the whole man on the sabbath,"[347] when you do not condemn Moses for commanding that infants must be circumcised even on the sabbath? "Do not judge by appearances, but judge with a right judgment. If a man receives circumcision on the sabbath in order that the law of Moses may not be broken,"[348] then you are upset for no reason when you see a whole man healed on the sabbath. Therefore, I judged rightly, but you did not, since you do everything on your own. "I can do nothing on my own. As I hear, I judge; and my judgment is just, because I seek not my own will," like you do, "but the will of the Father who sent me."

Since we have already discussed at length the manner of sending and the way he was sent, we will refrain from speaking about these things now.[349] But we must make the profitable observation that he says that the law is God the Father's "will."

[342]Mt 15:9; Is 29:13. [343]Mk 2:28. [344]Mk 2:27. [345]Ex 23:7. [346]Deut 1:17. [347]Jn 7:23. [348]Jn 7:24, 23. [349]Cyril discusses this in his comments on Jn 3:34 in book 2, chapter 3, p. 112 above.

5:31-32 "If I testify about myself, my testimony is not true. There is another who testifies on my behalf, and I know that his testimony about me is true."

The supremely wise Solomon gathers together the qualities in which one could most reasonably pride oneself and which make his lifestyle enviable, and he says, "A righteous man accuses himself at the beginning [358] of his speech,"[350] and again, "Let your neighbor praise you and not your own mouth, a stranger and not your own lips."[351] It is truly burdensome and intolerable to the hearers that some people do not want to be praised by the voice of others but incessantly testify to their own excellent and outstanding deeds. But such language is distrusted, and for good reason. For we are called by a certain natural and unavoidable attraction of self-love to be eager not to ascribe anything bad to ourselves but always to clothe ourselves, not altogether truthfully, with claims we think make us seem decent and good.

When our Lord Jesus Christ declared that he judges justly, explicitly saying that he cannot do anything on his own and that he makes the will of the Father the measuring stick, so to speak, for all his actions, he came forward as a witness for himself by saying this. And even though he was a true witness, he had to consider the sophistry of the Pharisees and what they were going to say in their ignorance (since they did not know that he was God by nature). So he brings it up before they do and says, You will surely say, following the custom of the many and not advancing beyond the simplicity that is fitting for the Jews, "You testify about yourself. Your testimony is not true."[352] But you will hear this in reply, he says. I am still putting up with your blasphemies, and I am by no means very angry with you for belching up words from the ignorance that is most dear to you. I grant you for the sake of discussion that you are right in saying even this. Let it be that you reject my voice. "There is another who testifies on my behalf." He is referring in these words to [359] God the Father who is in heaven, who has already testified in many ways to the genuineness of the substance of his own offspring and whose testimony, he says, he knows is true, showing that his own judgment is in fact trustworthy and true. He does not want to make room for malice and provide a loophole for those who are accustomed to hold false opinions about him by admitting that he is telling lies, so to speak, about himself. Therefore, after he makes a necessary concession to what is appropriate and customary, granting that one who praises and approves himself should not be considered completely honest, he returns to his rightful standing as God. He says that he knows the Father's testimony "is true," all but teaching this: Since I am true God, he says, I know myself. And the Father will say nothing about me that shows favoritism. I am by nature exactly what he himself may declare me to be. In the former part, then, there was a consent of condescension, so to speak, and a hypothetical rather than a true statement. But when he says he knows the Father's testimony is true, there is a demonstration of God-befitting credibility.

We should further note that the Father is different from the Son by virtue of his own hypostasis. He is not introduced as a Son-Father, like some uneducated heretics think.

5:33 "You sent messengers to John, and he has testified to the truth."

We have just maintained that it is shameful and not without a share in the utmost foolishness that anyone be seen as an admirer of their own good qualities, even if they could avoid

[350]Prov 18:17 (LXX). [351]Prov 27:2. [352]Jn 8:13.

lying because of their great virtue. Similarly, it is also a neighboring and sister absurdity, so to speak, to say that any who are not called to testify about something should go and appear of their own accord before the judges or before those who wish to investigate. Such a person would seem **[360]** (and this would not be far from the mark) not at all eager to tell the truth but to want very badly to give their testimony, not to make known what the nature of the matter is but rather what seems right to them. Most skillfully then, or rather as God, does our Lord Jesus Christ overturn in advance the accusation of the Pharisees in these matters and say, "You sent messengers to John." Not on his own accord, he says, did the Baptist give free testimony concerning his judgment about me. He is clear of that charge. "You sent messengers to John" to ask him, "and he has testified to the truth." When he is asked by those who were sent to him whether he was the Christ, "he confessed and did not deny. He confessed, 'I am not the Christ, but I have been sent before him.'"[353] "He has testified," therefore, "to the truth," because Christ is the truth.

5:34 "Not that I accept human testimony, but I say this so that you may be saved."

He does not dismiss John's words as useless, nor does he declare the witness to the truth to be of no effect. Otherwise he would rightly have seemed to inflict absurdity on himself, unreasonably dismissing from credence the one whom he himself sent to cry out, "Prepare the way of the Lord! Make straight the paths of our God!"[354] But since he is fighting the immeasurable disobedience of the Jews, he proceeds to greater and more remarkable things. He says that testimony about himself must not be received from human words, but rather that a more glorious proof should be made from the authority that befits the one who is God by nature and from the superior quality of the divine miracles. Sometimes someone will reject a human voice even if that person **[361]** were perhaps numbered among the saints. Some did not shrink from doing this but kept opposing the words of the prophets, crying out, "But speak and report to us another error."[355] In addition to this, some who had fled to Egypt from Jerusalem or from the land of Judea, namely, Azariah son of Hoshaiah, John son of Kareah, and all the arrogant men, as it is written, openly disbelieving the prophecies of Jeremiah, said, "You are telling a lie. The Lord did not send you to us to say, 'Do not go to Egypt.'"[356] But what kind of opposition could the proof from miracles receive? What manner of stubbornness will the testimony from God the Father's surpassing qualities still allow the faultfinders? Indeed, Nicodemus, who was one of their leaders and ranked among those in authority, gave incontrovertible testimony from his miracles, saying, "Rabbi, we know that you are a teacher who has come from God; for no one can do these signs that you do, unless God is with them."[357]

Since then it is not beyond the malice of the Jews to disbelieve even the holy Baptist himself, who offers testimony in words at least, he says again ironically, The blessed Baptist "has testified to the truth,"[358] even though he is questioned by you. But since nothing is unchallenged by you, and you are accustomed to launch recklessly into all kinds of abuse, you have likely rejected his voice. Since this too seems right to you, so be it. Let's say I am persuaded. I agree with you. For you I will put aside the voice of John as well, and along with you I will object to the admissibility of his testimony. **[362]** I have the Father as a witness from above. Then to teach

[353]Jn 1:20; 3:28. [354]Is 40:3. [355]Is 30:10. [356]Jer 43:2 (Jer 50:2 LXX). [357]Jn 3:2. [358]Jn 5:33.

that the statement contains a concession for the sake of argument, he profitably adds, "I say this so that you may be saved," that is, "I made this statement to you not because it is true but for the sake of argument, so that by every means you may be saved."

And here our second book will end.

The Second Book of Cyril Patriarch of Alexandria on John is Finished. [363]

Chapters Treated More Fully in the Third Book

1. A careful investigation of why Christ calls the blessed Baptist not just a lamp but a burning and shining lamp; on the words "He was a burning lamp."
2. The Son is the image of God the Father, which also convicts the Jews of not understanding the words spoken enigmatically by Moses; on the words "You have never heard his voice," etc.
3. Moses indicated the coming of the Savior when he said, "The Lord your God will raise up for you a prophet like me."
4. Often Christ's withdrawals from Jerusalem indicate that grace will be transferred to the Gentiles. The same chapter contains the discussion about the five barley loaves and two small fish; on the words "And after these things, Jesus went to the other side of the Sea of Tiberias."
5. The Only Begotten is the imprint of God the Father's hypostasis, and there is no other imprint besides him that either exists or is conceived of; on the words "Which the Son of Man will give you," etc.
6. Concerning the manna, that it was a type of Christ's presence and the spiritual gifts given through him; on the words "Jesus therefore said to them, 'Truly, truly, I tell you, it was not Moses who gave you bread from heaven,'" etc. **[365]**

OUR FATHER AMONG THE SAINTS CYRIL ARCHBISHOP OF ALEXANDRIA ON THE GOSPEL ACCORDING TO JOHN

BOOK THREE

Chapter One

A careful investigation of why Christ calls the blessed Baptist not just a lamp but a burning and shining lamp.

We have just barely stayed our pen on the second book and swum through the wide and deep sea of divine contemplations, thinking by doing so that we would reach the end like a ship coming into port. But just as we are about to dock our ship on the mainland, we see the beginning of another ocean, that is, our course on the sequel. The subject matter itself shames us into putting all our effort into the task, and we are no less persuaded by the statement made by someone, "The fruit of good labors is glorious."[1] Come then, let us rise up to a courageous purpose of mind and entrust our helm to our good and loving God. **[366]** Let us unfurl

Book 3 [1]Wis 3:15.

the expanse of our understanding like a sail, be filled with the grace of the Spirit like the sound of a fair wind from the stern and embark on a deep investigation. After all, Christ is the one who "makes a road in the sea and a path in the water."[2] Our second book ended with the words "not that I accept human testimony, but I say this so that you may be saved."[3] Let us begin the third book, picking it up with the next line where Christ is discussing John the Baptist.

5:35 "He was a burning and shining lamp, and you were willing to rejoice for a while in his light."

He compares the holy Baptist with a "lamp" inasmuch as, in human measure, he provided illumination before his arrival. But he did not use his own light since the light in a lamp is not its own, but it is brought in and added from the outside. In this way you will see in the saints also the illumination from Christ in the Spirit. Therefore, thinking and acting with the greatest wisdom, they confess with their own voice, "From his fullness we have all received."[4] The Only Begotten is light by nature inasmuch as he beamed forth from the light, I mean the substance of the Father. The creation, by contrast, participates in him. Whatever is endowed with the power to reason and think is like a vessel most excellently fashioned by God, the master craftsman of all things, with the capacity to be filled with divine light.

The blessed Baptist, therefore, is a "lamp" in the aforementioned sense. With this carefully planned statement, the Savior **[367]** reminds the ignorant Pharisees of the voice of God the Father who says somewhere of him, "I have prepared a lamp for my Christ."[5] Christ now most beneficially and necessarily adds these things to what he said before. When he was closing off every opportunity for unbelief for the Jews and drawing them together from all sides to believe in him, he certainly seemed to agree that John's testimony should not be accepted, saying, "Not that I accept human testimony."[6] So that they may not think that the Lord is really and truly so disposed toward his forerunner as the form of the words suggests, he himself, in order to further his present purpose, does not say anything about John, but he introduces him as proclaimed by the voice of the Father. He thought that he should, out of reverence for God the Father, put to shame the one who resists, or rather that he should now openly unmask the one who fights against God as recklessly opposing the very words of God the Father.

So he says, "He was a lamp, and you were willing to rejoice for a while in his light." He needed not only to show that the Pharisees were easily going astray from what is right and by their unholy behavior rejecting the will to believe but also to convict them of being fickle. He needed to show that they were totally unaccustomed to persevering in a desire for good things. After barely getting acquainted with and praising, at least in mere words, those who seemed holy to them, they were not ashamed to change quickly to the opposite disposition. This is what I think is meant by the words "you were willing to rejoice for a while in his light." After all, at first they marveled at the holy Baptist as an ascetic, as a lover of God, as an example of all piety. But those who honor the marvel then turn around **[368]** and insult it because they cannot put up with him saying, "Prepare the way of the Lord! Make straight the paths of our God!"[7] This they are caught clearly doing by their unbelief.

And now, having kept the well-worn way of explaining the passage that common people are used to, we have set forth its meaning to the

[2]Is 43:16. [3]Jn 5:34. [4]Jn 1:16. [5]Ps 132:17 (Ps 131:17 LXX). [6]Jn 5:34. [7]Is 40:3.

best of our ability. But since the word of the Savior draws us to deep meanings and clearly all but demands that we grasp more precise explanations, by indicating not simply that John was a "lamp" but also "burning and shining," we thought it necessary to pay closer attention to the force of the words and to track down the beauty of the truth. So we will put forward the statement itself once again for our consideration. "He was a lamp," it says. This by itself was sufficient to indicate the holy Baptist so that the hearers would remember the statement in prophecy about him, "I have prepared a lamp for my Christ."[8] But since he adds to the word *lamp* the words *burning* and *shining*, it is doubtless clear that he is bringing the hearer not only back to the voice of the prophet but also to a certain regulation in the law that prefigures in appearance and shadow the torch bearing of John, which he accomplished beautifully by testifying to the Lord Christ. He also convicts the Pharisees, who think they are wise because they continually deal with the words of Moses, of being unlearned and of seeming wise rather than being truly instructed in the law. This then is the entire point of the passage. But I think that we should bring forward the divine oracle itself and now demonstrate incontrovertibly that the blessed Baptist is not simply a "lamp" but also "burning and shining." **[369]**

When God was ordaining the arrangements of the holy tabernacle, after the completion of the ten curtains, he said to the teacher Moses, "And you shall command the children of Israel, and let them bring to you refined pure beaten olive oil to burn for light, so that the lamp may always burn in the tabernacle of the testimony outside the veil that is before the covenant. Aaron and his sons will burn it from evening until morning before the Lord. This is a perpetual statute throughout your generations for the children of Israel. And you take to yourself both Aaron your brother and his sons from the children of Israel to serve me as priests."[9] So far the divine oracle.

We must now proceed to the interpretation of it, as far as possible. The refined and pure oil seems to suggest the purest serene nature of the Holy Spirit which penetrates us incomprehensibly like oil and nourishes, preserves and increases illumination in the soul as in a lamp. Thus we believe that the divine Baptist radiated the light of his testimony concerning our Savior, receiving the power of enlightening from no other source than from the spiritual oil that has the ability mightily and effectively to kindle the divine light within us. The Savior himself indicated this in an enigma when he said, "I have come to cast fire on the earth, and how I wish it were already kindled."[10] The blessed Baptist then was, in type, the "lamp" that was always "burning and shining" in the tabernacle of the testimony. And its shining in the tabernacle of the testimony indicates full well that the illumination from him is received in the churches, and he will not lie outside the **[370]** holy and divine court of the Savior.

But the fact that the lamp is seen outside the veil seems to suggest that he will bring a simpler introductory illumination, saying, "Repent! For the kingdom of heaven is at hand!"[11] He reveals nothing at all, however, of what is hidden within the veil, that is, the mysteries of our Savior. John did not baptize into participation in the Holy Spirit, nor did his illumination bring people within the veil. He was in the outer tabernacle "while it was still standing," as Paul says.[12] And when it says, "Aaron and his sons will burn it from evening until morning before the Lord; this is a perpetual statute throughout your generations," I think that the statement should be understood as follows. "Aaron and his sons" intimate those who carry out the work of priests in the churches of their time, that is,

[8]Ps 132:17 (Ps 131:17 LXX). [9]Ex 27:20–28:1. [10]Lk 12:49. [11]Mt 3:2. [12]Heb 9:8.

teachers in the churches and ministers of the divine altars. These are commanded to keep the spiritual lamp, that is, John, always burning. This is the meaning of the words "they will burn it from evening until morning." The entire time that the light of the lamp is supposed to shine is the space of a night. This signifies the length of the present age since we understand the coming age to be light. The lamp burns, however, or is kept bright when it makes its torch bearing always perceptible to those who believe in Christ and when the voice of the priests of that time testifies that it is telling the truth when it says these things about Christ.

So that God may teach you that by this statement he was prefiguring the forerunner of the Savior, he immediately adds the **[371]** election of the priests. You will reach this understanding by ruminating on the overall structure of the section[13]—and it is not without sophistication, it seems to me. At the completion of the tabernacle, the command about the lamp is introduced, and immediately after that the appointment and function of the priests. This corresponds to the fact that at the completion of the law and the prophets, the voice of the forerunner shone forth, the "voice of one crying in the desert," as it is written, "Prepare the way of the Lord! Make straight the paths of our God!"[14] And immediately after him is the selection and appointment of the holy apostles by Christ since the Lord chose "twelve whom he also named apostles."[15]

With that our contemplation of the lamp is complete, so let us look once again at the voice of the Savior. "He was a burning and shining lamp," he says, "and you were willing to rejoice for a while in his light." He charges the Pharisees with having an unlearned disposition and being difficult to lead to obedience. He accuses them further of being sick with incomparable ignorance and not being able to understand what they profess to know. He accuses them of being very far removed indeed from an accurate knowledge of the law and entirely ignorant of what the lawgiver was prefiguring in outline through Moses. By saying, "He was a burning and shining lamp," he puts them to shame most likely for not yet understanding what was sketched in the enigmas of the law long ago.

Now by saying, "You were willing to rejoice for a while in his light," he portrays them always putting their own will before the decree from above and habitually following only those whom they wish. Although the lawgiver, he says, has ordained that the lamp shine and burn always, you did not want it to shine always **[372]** but only "for a while," that is, for the very briefest moment. Though you marveled at first, you quenched, as far as you are concerned, the light of the lamp by most senselessly denouncing the one sent from God. You not only refused to be baptized but you also prevented him from baptizing others. After all, you sent messengers to him to ask, "Why are you baptizing?" That is, Why are you enlightening people to repentance and a knowledge of the Christ? Therefore, the Savior brought a charge of folly and transgression alike against the senseless scribes and Pharisees, fighting on behalf of the words of John. I think the blessed Luke understands this when he states it well and cries out against their madness, saying, "And all the people who heard this," namely, the Savior's words, "justified God, having been baptized with the baptism of John. But the Pharisees and lawyers rejected God's purpose for themselves, not having been baptized by him."[16]

5:36-37 "But I have testimony greater than that of John. The works that the Father has

[13]Cyril is referring to the regulations in Ex 27–28. See p. 136, n. 266 on the division of the biblical text into "sections."
[14]Is 40:3. [15]Lk 6:13. [16]Lk 7:29-30.

given me to complete, the very works that I am doing testify about me that the Father sent me. And the Father who sent me has himself testified about me."

Even though he was the lamp, he says, portrayed in the ordinances of the law and announced ahead of time by the voice of the holy prophets as one who would some day appear and shine before the true light, announcing to you that you should make ready the way of the Lord God, he did not perhaps seem credible to you. This despite the fact that he is so great in virtue. That is because of your own absurd and unbridled folly. Therefore, I now proceed to a greater matter. You will probably say nothing against it because you are ashamed by the very beauty of the truth, even against your will. I am no longer [373] exalted by words and human judgments, nor do I think that I must collect testimonies of mere words about myself, but I will commit my case to witnesses more important and far greater than words. From the very greatness of my deeds, I am already making clear that I am God by nature and from God the Father. I do no harm to my own laws when I reshape whatever I want and transform what was said enigmatically to the ancients from the coarseness of the letter to a spiritual understanding.

Let the one who is devoted to learning consider that when Christ says that his works testify full well that he is God by nature, he is explicitly teaching that it would not be possible for anyone to have God-befitting activity and power immutably unless he were also God by nature. His works testify nothing else about him, I think, than this. If he is viewed as a completer[17] of the works of the one who begat him and carries out on his own power whatever is quite clearly fitting for the Father alone, how could it not be clear to everyone that he has the same nature as the Father and that he shines forth with the same properties as his parent and has the same power and activity as him because he is from him?

Yet he says that the works are received from the Father either because he was speaking with the *oikonomia* in mind, putting it more humbly than necessary on account of the garb of the human nature and the form of a slave, or because he was using the idea of "giving" to extol the good pleasure and approval of God the Father regarding all his miracles. In the same way also he maintains that he was sent in that he emptied himself, as it is written,[18] of the honor that is absolutely God-befitting on account of his love for us. He humbled himself, and we will find the lowliness of this humbling in no [374] other way than in the way he sometimes speaks as a human being. The psalmist agrees with this when he says in a human fashion for our sakes, speaking for him, "I have been established by him as king on Zion his holy mountain, declaring the decree of the Lord."[19] He who was always king with the Father, who as God shared a throne and a seat with the one who begat him, says that he was appointed king and Lord. He says that what he had as God, he received when he appeared as man. A man does not reign by nature, but both the name and the fact of lordship are completely from without. [375]

Chapter Two

The Son is the image of God the Father, which also convicts the Jews of not understanding the words spoken enigmatically by Moses.

5:37-38 "You have never heard his voice or seen his form, and you do not have his word remaining in you because you do not believe in the one whom he sent."

One can see that the arrangement of the ideas

[17]This term recalls Jesus' reference to the "works that the Father has given me to complete" above. [18]Phil 2:7. [19]Ps 2:6-7.

poured out in the passage before us is not simple but contains a swarm of hidden meanings that very easily escapes the mind of the uninquisitive hearers and can perhaps only be understood by those who investigate more keenly. What induced Jesus, perhaps someone will say, when he was saying that his God-befitting activities testify to him, to come to a topic so unrelated as though it belonged to the subject? I am referring here to the statement that the Pharisees have never heard the voice of God the Father or seen his form, nor do they have his word dwelling in them. And I will agree, and so will everyone else, I suppose, that their difficulty would not be improper. Therefore, by the activity and grace of the Spirit, I will try to say what meaning we will attach to the passage before us and what explanation we will prepare for it, as we hold to the truth on all sides. **[376]**

It is the custom of Christ the Savior, when he engages in beneficial conversations with the especially ignorant Pharisees, as he often does, to gaze into the depths of their heart and to examine in a God-befitting way the unspoken lines of thought that are turning and stirring in their minds at that moment. To these thoughts in particular he gives answers, discourses and sometimes even accusations regarding the Pharisees. He does not at all keep to the sequence of his own words, but he shrewdly responds to whatever they are planning and thinking to themselves. And he shows by this that he is by nature God, since he knows what lies in the depths and searches hearts and the inward parts.[20]

Receive the clearest proof for this, if you will, from the other Evangelists, I mean Luke and his companions. It is written in the Gospels that Pharisees and teachers of the law had gathered together from all the surrounding area of Judea. "And behold," it says, "men were carrying a paralyzed man on a bed, and they were trying to bring him in and place him before Jesus. But finding no way to bring him in because of the crowd, they went up on the roof and let him down with his bed through the tiles into the middle of the crowd in front of Jesus. And when he saw their faith, he said to the paralytic, 'Man, your sins are forgiven you.' And the scribes and Pharisees began to reason, saying, 'Who is this who is speaking blasphemies? Who can forgive sins but God alone?' But Jesus, knowing their thoughts," it says, "answered them, 'Why do you think this in your hearts? Which is easier, to say, "Your sins are forgiven you," or **[377]** to say, "Rise up and walk"?'"[21] Do you see how he does not wait for an answer in spoken words or murmuring, but as God he answers their inner thoughts?

You will find another image of the matter, fashioned in the same way. The blessed Luke says, "On another sabbath, he entered the synagogue and taught. And there was a man there whose right hand was withered. The scribes and Pharisees were watching him closely to see if he would heal on the sabbath so that they might find an accusation against him. But he knew their thoughts," it says, "and he said to the man who had the withered hand, 'Come and stand here.' And he got up and stood there. Then Jesus said to them, 'I ask you, Is it lawful to do good on the sabbath, or to do evil?'"[22] Do you see that here too his answer unveiled them, since he sees the very heart of those who were foolishly trying to accuse him? We will suppose that this sort of thing was seen by the Savior in the thoughts of the Pharisees also in the passage before us. And if you do not shrink back from reviewing everything that was just said, you will see that his discourse does not depart from the straightforward arrangement of topics.

This great and long discussion with them first came about because of the paralyzed man

[20]See Ps 7:9 (Ps 7:10 LXX); Ps 26:2 (Ps 25:2 LXX). [21]Lk 5:18-23. [22]Lk 6:6-9.

who was healed on the sabbath. With various devices and arguments, Christ tried to persuade those who were stubbornly upset at the healing on the sabbath that it was right both to have mercy on the sabbath and to do good to all. In addition, he tried to persuade them that the law made the sabbath rest a shadow of the more remarkable reality. Above all, **[378]** since as far as they were concerned he violated the honor of the sabbath and thereby transgressed the law, he quite vigorously asserted that he was sent from God the Father, and he kept saying clearly that the Father bears witness to him and will approve of all that he does.

In response to this, the Pharisees consider the matter in their minds, at least in a way that is persuasive to reason. Inasmuch as they sit at the feet of the letter of the law and always allege that they know the commandments of Moses, they think, What is he saying? How will God the Father approve of him since he breaks the law? When has he testified, or what decree did he make about him? We know from the Mosaic writings that God descended on Mount Sinai, his form was seen by the fathers and his voice (it says) was heard. He spoke to the whole assembly[23] and commanded them to keep the sabbath day by giving them this clear order: "Remember the sabbath day, to keep it holy. Six days you shall labor and do all your work, but the seventh day is a holy sabbath to the Lord your God. You shall do no work on it."[24] And we heard none other than God saying these things, it says. The multitude of fathers heard the voice from God, and after them the word of God was in us. But who is this fellow?

When he sees that they are thinking these things, he accuses them of being completely ignorant, saying, "You have never heard his voice or seen his form, and you do not have his word remaining in you because you do not believe in the one whom he sent." The typological events of that time, which pictured for them the descent of God on Mount Sinai—these events they do not understand, nor do they take them as images of spiritual realities, but they think that the divine nature can be seen with bodily eyes, **[379]** and they believe that it uses a corporeal voice. I think we must clearly show that the Savior's statement about them is true and that they have never heard the voice of God the Father, nor has anyone seen with bodily eyes his form, that is, the Word who is like him in all things. We must demonstrate this fact by subjecting what is written in Exodus to a spiritual investigation and test. The passage reads, "And Moses led the people out of the camp to meet God, and they stood at the foot of Mount Sinai. The entire Mount Sinai was smoking because God had descended on it in fire, and the smoke was going up like the smoke of a kiln, and all the people were completely amazed. The sound of the trumpet grew very loud. Moses was speaking, and God answered him with a voice."[25] Thus far, then, the oracle of the supremely wise Moses. I think that we must even now charge the Jews with sinking into absurdity concerning the glory of God because they both thought they saw his very form and heard a voice that was inherent in the divine nature.

Come then, let us take courage from the abundance and grace of the Savior and refine the coarseness of the letter of the law into spiritual insight. In this way the statement about God to the Pharisees will most clearly be shown true, "You have never heard his voice or seen his form." The fact then that Moses led the people to meet with God, as it is written, will be a clear sign and a statement in an enigma that no one can go to God unled and without understanding, but rather they are led by the law to understand those things they seek to learn. We should understand Moses, **[380]** after all, to be the law, as in the state-

[23]Deut 5:22. [24]Ex 20:8-10; Deut 5:12-14. [25]Ex 19:17-19.

ment by somebody, "They have Moses and the prophets."[26]

Standing at the foot of the mountain, by contrast, when God has already descended and is on it, suggests the readiness of mind and the eagerness of those who are called to serve him, not refusing in any way to apply themselves even to things that are above their power or higher than their nature, since God is with them. The partakers of the Savior are certainly like this. That is why they show even superhuman courage and say, "Who will separate us from the love of Christ? Will hardship, or distress, or persecution, or famine, or nakedness, or peril or sword?"[27] For all terrible things are tolerable to the godly because of their love for Christ. Though hardship rise up like a mountain, they will prevail over every danger, and they will not withdraw their mind from love toward God.

God is said to come down, not to some low ground, but he appears above somewhere and on a mountain so that you may understand for yourself something like this: that although the divine nature comes down to our understanding and makes itself intelligible to us, it still exists in both words and thoughts that are very far above us. The height and intensity of the dogmas concerning the divine nature are signified by the mountain which, he tells us, is completely blackened by smoke. Words about the divine nature, after all, are truly pungent and not very clear to us, stinging the eye of the understanding like smoke. That is why the supremely wise Paul testified that we see in a mirror and an enigma.[28] Moreover, the psalmist says somewhere that he, namely, God, has made "darkness his hiding place,"[29] suggesting by "darkness" his incomprehensibility of which the smoke surrounding the fire on the mountain may well be taken as a type. **[381]**

The divine nature itself descends in the form of fire at that particular time, which is appropriate and necessary due to the nature of the matter. It was fitting—it was fitting, I say—that he who called Israel to service and understanding through the law that was about to be given should appear as an enlightener and an avenger. Both these things are accomplished through fire.

And the "sound of the trumpet," it says, "grew very loud," so that some meaning like the following may be woven together for us. You see, the law was announced by God, but not full blast at first because of the weakness of the students. It was announced in a stutter, so to speak, without the full force of the trumpeter. That is also why Moses called himself "slow of speech."[30] When the right time came, which raised the believers in Christ from the shadow of the letter to spiritual worship, the sound of the divine trumpet came out much stronger, and the saving gospel proclamation resounded, so to speak, throughout the whole world. It was not heard only in the country of the Jews, like the law with its feeble voice and petty proclamation, nor was it being announced from Dan to Beersheba, but rather, "their voice went out to all the earth," as it is written.[31]

And what else does it say? "Moses was speaking," it says, "and God answered him with a voice."[32] Let the mind of the well-informed be sharp. Let them preserve carefully the certainty that is inherent in the divine oracles. Moses is speaking, and God answers him with a voice—certainly not his own voice, it does not say that—but simply and without qualification "with a voice." This voice is miraculously produced in a human way through the sound of words. After all, what **[382]** works are too hard for God? What is there that God could not do with the greatest ease if he wanted to? So Moses was speaking, and God answered him with a voice. That is the type; let us see the truth. In the holy Gospels, the Lord says, "Father, glorify your

[26]Lk 16:29. [27]Rom 8:35. [28]1 Cor 13:12. [29]Ps 18:11 (Ps 17:12 LXX). [30]Ex 4:10. [31]Ps 19:4 (Ps 18:5 LXX). [32]Ex 19:19.

Son," and the Father answers with a voice, "I have glorified him and will glorify him again."[33] But the Savior showed that the voice did not truly belong to God the Father by saying to those who were then present, "This voice has come into being for your sake, not for mine."[34] See how he clearly insisted that the voice was created since it is not fitting to suppose that the divine nature uses a voice with sound even though it conforms itself to our needs and speaks by virtue of the *oikonomia* for our sakes.

We had to introduce these considerations into the present discussion. Indeed, we considered it altogether necessary for the readers that Jesus be shown truthful when he says to the Jews concerning the one who begat him, "You have never heard his voice or seen his form, and you do not have his word remaining in you because you do not believe in the one whom he sent." The Spirit himself also testifies that the Pharisees were puffed up to the point of extraordinary boasting. They kept pretending that the divine word was with them and in them, and they kept asserting foolishly that they had advanced to remarkable wisdom. The Spirit testifies against them when Christ says to them through the prophet Jeremiah, "How will you say, 'We are wise, and the word of the Lord is with us'? In vain have the scribes used a lying pen. The wise have been put to shame. They have been terrified and taken. What wisdom is in them? They have rejected the word of the Lord."[35] How could they not be condemned, since they have rejected the living and hypostatic Word of God, [383] since they have not received faith in him but have dishonored the imprint of God the Father and refused to look at his truest "form," so to speak, through his God-befitting power and authority?

The divine and ineffable nature is grasped by us (as far as possible) in no other way than through what it accomplishes and works. That is why Paul tells us to go from "the greatness and beauty of created things" to a corresponding contemplation of the creator.[36] The Savior too leads us to this understanding about himself when he says, "If I am not doing the works of my Father, do not believe me. But if I do them, even if you do not believe me, believe my works."[37] And somewhere he quite rightly censured his own disciple, Philip, for thoughtlessly supposing that he could arrive at insight into God the Father in some other way, even though he had it in his power to look at his uncreated image, which shows with precision the begetter in itself. "Have I been with you so long, and you did not know me, Philip? The one who has seen me has seen the Father."[38]

5:39-40 "You search the Scriptures because in them you think you have eternal life; and it is they that bear witness to me. And you refuse to come to me that you may have life."

The easy and well-worn understanding of the passage, taken by many, persuades us to suppose that the Savior told the Pharisees in the imperative mood that they ought to search the Scriptures to gather testimonies about him unto life. But when he places the conjunction (I mean "and") in the middle and joins it with "you refuse to come to me," he is clearly indicating something else that is related to what he just said, [384] but a little different. If we are supposed to understand it in the imperative, how could we not say, given this structure, that the whole passage ought to say, "Search the Scriptures because in them you think you have eternal life; and it is they that bear witness to me. And when you have searched them, come to me"? But he is blaming them for not wanting to come even though led to it by the search when he says, "And you refuse to come to me."

We will therefore look for something more

[33]Jn 12:28. [34]Jn 12:30. [35]Jer 8:8-9. [36]Wis 13:5; cf. Rom 1:20. [37]Jn 10:37-38. [38]Jn 14:9.

apt that follows from what preceded it, and we will certainly read it not as an imperative but conjunctively, as it were, and with a comma. The understanding of the passage then will be something like this. He sees them always running to the books of Moses and ignorantly gathering from them material for opposing him, neither seeking nor accepting anything else that would bring about in them the faith they should have. So he shows them, as the situation demands, that their labor in searching for these things is useless and vain, and he explicitly accuses them of having engaged in a great and most profitable task in a way that is not appropriate for its use. What good is it, tell me, that you search the Holy Scriptures, he says, thinking through them to ascend to eternal life, but when you find that they bear witness to me and call me eternal life, you refuse to come to me that you may have life? As a result, he says, you do not realize that you are doing the greatest damage to your own souls from the very source that ought to save you, since you are sharpened by the words of Moses only to oppose me, but the truths by which you could gain eternal life never so much as enter your mind. **[385]**

There is much said both in the law and in the holy prophets concerning life by nature, that is, the Only Begotten. I think this is clear to all who are devoted to learning.

5:41-42 "I do not accept glory from human beings, but I know that you do not have the love of God in you."

Again he perceives, or rather he sees in a God-befitting way, that the stubborn and unruly band of the Pharisees is cut to the heart, certainly not because he was blaming them for not searching the Scriptures as they ought but rather because he said, "You refuse to come to me." They believed that the diseases that they were prone to could also prevail over the Savior. They were apparently thinking, and this too from their great ignorance, that the Lord was now being ambitious toward them and that he wanted to obtain honor for himself from everyone by calling them to be his disciples. When they had gotten this sort of assumption in their mind, they expected soon to be deprived of their authority over the nation, and they were cut to the heart in no small way when they saw the heir wanting to demand the fruit of the vineyard. And so, as far as their wrath and envy at his statement is concerned, they practically say the same thing as in the Gospel parables, "Come, let us kill him and get his inheritance."[39] Therefore, he takes away the assumption that was sown in them by their thoughtlessness and uproots beforehand the shoots of envy and malice by saying in plain words, "I do not accept glory from human beings." I do not call hearers, he says, to be my disciples, hunting for honors either from you or from others the way you do, nor would I receive this as a reward for my teaching since I have the fullest glory from **[386]** myself, and it is not inferior to glory from you. But I have said that you refuse to come to me because I know clearly that "you do not have the love of God in you." Since you are bereft of love for God, he says, how could you come to me, the only begotten God who has appeared from God?

5:43 "I have come in the name of my Father, and you do not receive me. If someone else comes in their own name, you will receive them."

So that the Pharisees may not think that the Lord is railing at them in vain by saying, "You do not have the love of God in you," he immediately adds this to the foregoing to show that what he said was true. I will prove to you by

[39]Mt 21:38.

one fact that I am not lying when I say that you are bereft of love for the divine, he says. I came in the name of my Father in that I persuade you to be eager to do all things to the glory of God the Father. But by your unbelief, you shook off the one who has come from above and comes forth from God. But you will surely receive (for as God I know the things to come) the imposter who does not give glory to God the Father and who demands credence from you yet acts in his own name. I think the blessed Paul understands this as well when he says something true both about the Jews and the son of lawlessness, "Because they refused to love the truth and so be saved, for this reason God sends them a strong delusion so that they believe what is false, that all may be judged who did not believe the truth but took pleasure in unrighteousness."[40] This statement then is a proof that the Pharisees were not slandered with empty words [387] by our Savior Christ since it introduces a prophecy of an event that will happen in its own time.

5:44 "How can you believe when you accept glory from human beings and do not seek glory from the only God?"

He now accuses the Pharisees of being ambitious and of prizing honors from human beings, covertly suggesting that they commit a great wrong when they foolishly put the diseases of their own soul on God who knows no disease at all. Next he says that they are held fast by love of glory and thereby lose the fairest prize, faith in him. Paul clearly says this to us as well. "If I were still pleasing people," he says, "I would not be a servant of Christ."[41] It happens naturally then by necessity, as it were, that those who hunt for honors from human beings fall from the glory that comes from above and from the only God, as the Savior says. Now he says "only" to distinguish God from the gods of the Gentiles. He does not put himself outside the honor of the "only." After all, the fullness of the holy and consubstantial Trinity ascends, as we have already often said, to the one nature and glory of the divinity.

5:45 "Do not think that I will accuse you before the Father. Your accuser is Moses in whom you have placed your hope."

After saying that the Pharisees were eager to live in love of glory rather than in piety and teaching that for this reason they turned aside into immeasurable unbelief, he also says that they will be accused by Moses himself in whom they were accustomed to boast quite vehemently. For example, when the man born blind at one point says [388] to them of Christ, "Do you also want to become his disciples?" they immediately cry out and say explicitly, "You are his disciple, but we are disciples of Moses."[42] So your Moses himself will accuse you, he says, on whom you have placed all your hope. And he, despised along with the others, will cry out before God against the ignorance that is in you.

But we will certainly not suppose that his statement to the Jews, "Do not think that I will accuse you," means that those who do not believe in him will be free from Christ's accusation. Otherwise, what will we say when we hear him say, "Everyone therefore who acknowledges me before others, I will acknowledge before my Father in heaven; but whoever denies me before others I will also deny before my Father in heaven"?[43] Is it not reasonable for us to suppose that whoever meets with a denial by Christ will at that time be accused before God the Father by that denial? I think this is obvious to all. Therefore, the Jews are certainly not free from accusation since they have denied Christ through their long unbelief; rather, this statement applied to them has a different and

[40]2 Thess 2:10-12. [41]Gal 1:10. [42]Jn 9:27-28. [43]Mt 10:32-33.

most natural meaning. They shake off his admonition, and they hold his divine and heavenly teaching to be of no account, but they live by the necessity of always keeping the law of Moses so that they cry out, exposing themselves, "We know that God has spoken to Moses, but as for this man, we do not know where he comes from."[44] Therefore, he quite fittingly accuses them of transgressing the very law of Moses in which they boast, and he says they will need no other accuser, but the law of Moses alone will suffice for them because by it they will fall under an appropriate and reasonable accusation since they do not believe in him, **[389]** even though the voice of the judge, that is, Christ, is silent.

5:46 "If you believed Moses, you would have believed me, since he wrote about me."

After he says that the Jews will be accused by the all-wise Moses and that they have received an indictment for their lack of faith in him, he beneficially brings this charge as well. He teaches that he did not denounce them in vain, and he repudiates their baseless suspicion that he just loves to rail at people, since it is evident that what he says is not untrue. So be it then, he says. You reject my words; I will put up with not being believed. Receive your own Moses. Give credence to the one whom you admire, and you will surely come to know the one whom, not knowing, you dishonor. Break through the types which labor to give birth to the truth. I am the one sketched in his books. Therefore, Moses himself will accuse you, he says, when he sees you disbelieving his writings about me.

Now that we have explained the meaning of the passage before us, we should perhaps proceed to the next passage, leaving it to those who truly love learning to investigate the images of Christ given by Moses. That is because his books are full of passages, and he says a great deal, yet it is difficult to understand and full of very subtle and hidden meanings. However, lest we seem to let sluggishness get the better of us and shrink back for no reason from such an admirable labor by cloaking the books of Moses in difficulty, we will set ourselves to this too, knowing that it is written, "The Lord **[390]** will give words to those who proclaim the gospel with great power."[45] But since the discussion about these things is very lengthy, as we have said, and since Moses prefigured the mystery of Christ with many types, we will not deem it necessary to heap up an immeasurable multitude before the readers, but we will select one from all of them and endeavor to provide clear proof that the statement of our Savior was true that he made to the Jews, "If you believed Moses, you would have believed me, since he wrote about me." **[391]**

CHAPTER THREE

Moses indicated the coming of the Savior. From Deuteronomy, concerning Christ.

"The Lord your God will raise up for you a prophet like me from your brothers. You will listen to him. You requested from the Lord your God at Horeb on the day of the assembly, 'Let us not hear again the voice of the Lord our God or see this great fire any more so that we will not die.' And the Lord said to me, 'Everything they said is right. I will raise up for them a prophet like you from their brothers, and I will put my word in his mouth, and he will speak to them just as I command him. Whoever does not listen to whatever the prophet says in my name, I myself will punish them for it.'"[46]

Deuteronomy contains a kind of repetition and summary of the books of Moses. Therefore, we cannot take from it a type or image of

[44]Jn 9:29. [45]Ps 67:12 (LXX). [46]Deut 18:15-19.

the legal priesthood. However, since we who think rightly about all things on account of Christ are not accustomed to being without understanding, we will say to the readers, prying open the meaning of this passage, See how it speaks to us plainly about the mystery concerning Christ, skillfully molded after the likeness of Moses by the most subtle insight. **[392]** "The Lord your God will raise up for you a prophet like me," he says, "from your brothers." He himself explains—and that quite passionately—what insight this statement brings to us by this likeness to him when he adds explicitly, "You requested from the Lord your God at Mount Sinai on the day of the assembly, 'Let us not hear again the voice of the Lord our God or see this great fire any more so that we will not die.'" He asserts that he was at that time spoken of as the mediator, while the assembly of the Jews was still powerless to deal with things above nature and therefore prudently declined what was beyond their strength, that is, the sight of God, which astonishes the vision with unaccustomed images, and the supernatural echo of trumpets, which is intolerable to the hearers.

Therefore, the mediation of Moses was instituted as a medicine for the weakness of the people at that time so he could give to the assembly the decrees of God. You should, however, transfer the type to the truth and by this passage understand Christ as the mediator between God and human beings who, when he was born of a woman for us, made known through a human voice the ineffable will of God the Father. This will is made known to him and him alone insofar as he is understood to be both his Son and his wisdom who knows all things, "even the deep things of God."[47] It is not possible for the eyes of the body to deal with the pure and naked divine and ineffable glory of the substance that surpasses everything, since "no one will see my face and live," he says.[48] Therefore, the only begotten Word of God had to conform himself to our weakness, clothing himself with this human body according to the ineffable mode of the *oikonomia*, and he had to make clear to us the will from above, that is, from God the Father, saying, "Everything that I heard from **[393]** the Father I will report to you,"[49] and again, "I have not spoken on my own, but the Father who sent me has himself given me a command about what to say and speak."[50] Therefore, as an image of mediation Moses of old should be understood as a type of Christ who most excellently provides the Israelites with the decrees from God. The mediation of Moses, however, is ministerial, while the mediation of Christ is free and more mystical since he touches the parties that are being mediated and reaches both, I mean the mediated human nature and God the Father.

As the Only Begotten of God, he is God by nature, not as though he were separated from the substance of his begetter but clinging to it, as he is also understood to be of it. He is also a human being, since he made himself like us and became flesh, in order that through him what was far separated by nature might be joined to God. So when Moses says, "The Lord will raise up for you a prophet like me," you should understand this in no other way than as we have just said, since God himself puts his seal on this statement by saying, "Everything they said is right. I will raise up for them a prophet like you, and I will place my word on him, and he will speak to them whatever I command him."[51] For the Son "upholds all things by his powerful word," as Paul says,[52] and he makes known to us the voice of the Father, inasmuch as he is ordained by him as a mediator, as is sung in the Psalms as by Christ himself: "I have been appointed king by him on Zion his holy mountain, announcing the decree of the Lord."[53]

[47]1 Cor 2:10. [48]Ex 33:20. [49]Jn 15:15. [50]Jn 12:49. [51]Deut 18:17-18. [52]Heb 1:3. [53]Ps 2:6-7.

If it seems good to anyone to adduce other passages for proof of what kind of likeness is meant, they may take the lawgiver's "like me" and compare it with the passage, "It was said to those **[394]** of old, Do not commit adultery, but I say to you,"[54] do not lust. They may also take "like me" to indicate a kind of leader and guide so people can understand the will of the Father that makes the royal road to heaven passable. In the same way, the blessed Moses certainly arose as a teacher to the ancients of the instruction that comes through the law, everywhere adding to his words the statement, "that you may live long and the Lord your God may lead you into the land he swore to your fathers."[55] And when he adds to his statement, "Whoever does not listen to whatever that prophet says in my name, I myself will punish them for it,"[56] let the ignorant Jews, who harden their mind to the point of utter deafness, now see that they are pouring out self-chosen destruction on their own heads. They will be under the wrath of God, receiving a total loss of blessings as wages for their drunken violence against Christ. After all, if they believed Moses, they would have believed Christ since he wrote about him.

5:47 "But if you do not believe his writings, how will you believe my words?"

There are very good reasons why some may find this statement quite unclear. They will not miss the point of the statement and wander into untrue conjectures if they suppose that the writings of Moses are superior to the words of the Savior. After all, the statement appears to say something like this, and insofar as one can take it without a precise examination, it gives a more favorable estimation to the writings of Moses than to the words of the Savior. By saying, "But if you do not believe his writings, **[395]** how will you believe my words?" he gives us to understand that the writings of Moses are superior to his own words. But the very nature of the matter will show that such an incredible idea is ludicrous. How could the writings of Moses be considered superior to the words of the Savior when types and shadows came through Moses but the truth comes through Christ?[57] It would not perhaps be difficult to expend many words on this topic, but I think it would be superfluous to discuss the pros and cons of matters that are clear—matters that need no external proof but have their proof within themselves. Why should anyone waste time going into detail in such arguments and chopping up what is by no means difficult into uncalled for loquacity?

The Savior's statement then means something like this. If you—though you have the law written by Moses, he says, and though you study his writings up and down—think nothing of transgressing them, submerging what you often read into a strange forgetfulness, how could you be better disposed to my words? Or how could you show yourselves more ready for and obedient to my voice since you do not often—or even ever—attend to it? Instead, you hear it on the side, as it were, and there is scarcely even one time when you admit it into your bodily ears.

You may either take these words in this way or consider them in another way. Labor and investigation in these matters provide very useful learning. The writings of Moses then introduce a certain instruction and figure by type of the mysteries of Christ, and the details sketched out in Moses are elements, in a way, of the knowledge of Christ, which we have demonstrated more fully in what we have already examined. But Christ is the goal of the law's instruction. As it **[396]** is written, "Christ is the fulfillment of the law and the prophets."[58] So how could they now reach more perfect knowledge who have not received

[54]Mt 5:27-28. [55]See Deut 4:40; 5:16; 11:9, 21; 22:7. [56]Deut 18:19. [57]See Jn 1:17. [58]See Rom 10:4.

"the basic elements of God's word,"[59] he says, and who by their folly thrust away the law that leads them by its rather clear letter? Or how could the greater now be acceptable to them when they make no room at all for the small and inferior? **[397]**

Chapter Four

Often Christ's withdrawals from Jerusalem indicate that grace will be transferred to the Gentiles. The same chapter contains the discussion about the five barley loaves and two small fish.

6:1 And after these things, Jesus went to the other side of the Sea of Tiberias.

First I suppose it is necessary to tell the readers that the Lord clearly did not make his withdrawals from Jerusalem without a good reason. He arranges events on almost every occasion, and he inscribes mysteries in the nature of the events as on a tablet. What the point of the withdrawal is and what it indicates we will make clear in due time when the sections before us have reached their termination. After dividing everything into small portions and explaining what is profitable from the Scriptures, and so placing it before the readers for their understanding, we will offer the final consideration of the whole, epitomizing in summary fashion what was said in many parts. But I think we must first address the passage that is now at hand.

"After these things," it says, "Jesus went to the other side of the Sea of Tiberias." After what things? We must investigate this without negligence. Now Christ was revealed in Jerusalem as a wondrous physician. **[398]** He healed a man "who had been ill for thirty-eight years"[60] not by giving him medicine, not by devising a disease-repelling remedy but rather by his word, as God, and by his almighty authority and by a God-befitting nod. "Arise," he said, "take your bed and go to your home."[61] Since it is the sabbath, the Jews are ignorantly upset, who suffer under the coarseness of the letter, who are bound more than he by the foolishness they had grown up with, who are sick because they take an idle rest from all that is good, who are paralyzed in their mind and feeble in their disposition. To them one might reasonably say, "Be strong, you weak hands and palsied knees."[62] But they are angry, saying that the honor due the sabbath ought to be paid even by the lawgiver himself. They condemn Christ as a transgressor without letting what is written enter their mind: "Ungodly is the one who says to the king, You are a transgressor."[63] They received a sharp rebuke from the Savior for these things. He prepared a great and lengthy discourse to show that the rest on the sabbath had been decreed typologically to the ancients and that "the Son of Man is lord of the sabbath."[64] But they are fit for no good thing. Instead they are quite ready to be completely stubborn. They oppose the one who teaches them what they need to learn, and they want to kill the one who would make them wise, repaying him "evil for good," as it is written.[65]

"After these" deeds and words, then, the Lord departs from Jerusalem by necessity, as it were. And since the Passover of the Jews was near, as we will find in what follows shortly, he sailed across the Sea of Tiberias, **[399]** or the lake by that name in the land of the Jews. What drove him away in particular and induced him to go to other places so far removed from Jerusalem was that, as we have just said, the Passover of the Jews was near. Therefore, I think we should demonstrate that Jesus did very well to avoid being found in Jerusalem at that time.

The law of Moses commanded that the Jews hurry from all the surrounding countryside to

[59]Heb 5:12. [60]Jn 5:5. [61]Mt 9:6. [62]Is 35:3. [63]Job 34:18. [64]Mt 12:8. [65]Ps 35:12 (Ps 34:12 lxx).

Jerusalem to celebrate in type the feast of tabernacles there. The spiritual person will perceive here the gathering of all the saints into Christ when they will be brought together from the whole world after the resurrection of the dead into the city that is above, the heavenly Jerusalem. There they will offer the thank offerings of the true tabernacle, that is, of the solidification and permanence of their bodies, since corruption has been destroyed and death has fallen into death.

As far as one may speak of what happened according to the narrative, the crowd of those going up to Jerusalem knew no number, and it is likely that the Pharisees at that time had great influence as they pretended to support the law, crying out in the midst of such a multitude against the transgressor, or one who they thought was a transgressor. It is not at all difficult to fire up the immeasurable swarm of common people when one says they have been wronged and tries to stir them up even against those who do no harm to them. Like water or fire, they are blown about in every direction by impulses that are unexamined and without forethought, and they plow ahead toward everything **[400]** that brings suffering. The Lord was not unaware of these facts, so he stole away with his disciples from Jerusalem and went "to the other side of the Sea of Tiberias." By these words too, we see that he does exceedingly well to avoid the Jews who want to kill him since the blessed Evangelist himself says, "After these things, Jesus went about in Galilee. He did not want to go about in Judea because the Jews were trying to kill him."[66]

Perhaps someone might say, I grant that he avoids going around in Judea so that he might not undergo death before his time, but whether he avoids the feast I do not yet know. Well then, those who were called his brothers approach Christ in Galilee and say, "Get up from here and go to Judea so that your disciples too may see the signs that you perform."[67] The Lord replies to them, "You go up to the feast. I am not going to this feast because my time has not yet fully come."[68]

It is clear and evident then that the Savior withdrew from Jerusalem not only being sent into voluntary banishment from there but also loathing the cruelty of the unbelievers. He eluded the fierceness of his persecutors' shots and by his skill deflected the arrow of envy. So he secretly withdraws, though he could suffer nothing even if he were present, to engrave for us a beautiful type not of cowardice but of godliness and love for the neighbor. We will be led by the hand from the type to a knowledge of something beneficial, and we will learn that when our enemies persecute us, even if absolutely no harm could be found in our remaining, yet by retiring and evading the brunt of their assaults and escaping from the heat of the moment, we will find that the wrath of those who wrong us is past its prime, **[401]** and we will undercut the rashness of their arrogance. By doing so we are helping those who are unjustly unkind to us rather than being helped ourselves. Clearly this means we are seeking not just our own good but also the good of others. It is a work of love then to offer no opposition to those who wish us ill. So let us not be satisfied with the ability to suffer no harm even when present. That causes sharper anger among them, as it were, because they do not have more power than the one they hate. Love, as Paul says, "does not seek its own."[69] Christ was pure in this regard.

When you have fixed the keen eye of understanding on what is written, you will marvel to find the finest arrangement in the withdrawals of our Savior, from Jerusalem, I mean. He often is driven away by the madness of the Jews and stays with foreigners. He seems to be both kept safe by them and to enjoy the honor he deserves. By this he gives a

[66]Jn 7:1. [67]Jn 7:3. [68]Jn 7:8. [69]1 Cor 13:5.

decree of superiority to the church of the Gentiles, and through the godliness of others he convicts the Israelites of hating God. He manifests the savagery of the one through the gentleness of the other so that they might appear in every respect to be rightly and deservedly expelled from the promise given to their fathers.

But when the Lord departs from Jerusalem, he does not stay in one of the surrounding cities, nor does he spend the night in the neighboring villages, but he goes "to the other side of the Sea of Tiberias." By this clear act he all but threatens those who blasphemously decide that they should persecute him that he will depart so far from them and will separate himself from their entire nation so as to render the road of conversion back to him impassable for them. The sea, after all, is impassable for human feet. He will be found to say something like this to them somewhere in what follows: **[402]** "You will seek me, but you will not find me. Where I am going you cannot come."[70] The way of righteousness is extremely smooth and easy to travel, containing nothing rough for those who go to him by faith. But it is rugged and steep, or rather impassable, for those who provoke him to anger. As one of the holy prophets says, "Therefore the ways of the Lord are straight and the righteous will walk on them, but the ungodly will stumble on them."[71] Therefore, the distance across the sea signifies the difficulty, or rather impassability, for the Jews of the way to him since God declares that he hedges up the way of ungodly souls, saying in the prophets, "Therefore, behold, I hedge in her way with thorns, and she will not find her path."[72] What the thorns indicate in that passage, the sea indicates in the present passage since it separates the insulted one from those who choose recklessly to insult him, and it separates the holy from the unholy.

But the type seems to us to be pregnant, as it were, with another hidden meaning. When Israel was sent forth from the land of the Egyptians, the pharaoh was greatly stirred up and followed them, angered by the unexpected success of the nation. He was eager boldly to implement his envious and grievous designs in battle. He followed them thinking he could force back into slavery those who after a long time had just barely escaped from his service. But God carried the people through the midst of the sea. The pharaoh was in hot pursuit and did not allow his anger to abate in any way. He was foolishly seduced by his fierce anger to fight against God, and he was swallowed up in the midst of the sea with his whole army. Only Israel was saved. **[403]** But let Moses now come forward, who grieved beforehand over the madness of the Jews, and let him say to them in his anger over their irreverence toward Christ, "You wicked and adulterous generation, is this how you repay the Lord?"[73] He brought you through the midst of the sea and through mighty waves, and you drive him across the sea and do not blush to persecute him? Therefore, this is what will happen to you, O Jew. The sea will at last swallow you up since death belongs to the persecutors, not to those persecuted, both for them at that time and now in the case of Christ and the unholy Jews. The divine David sings to us somewhere: "Do not let the flood drown me," he says, "or the deep swallow me up."[74] He is hinting at the disastrous shipwreck of the Jewish synagogue and begging not to be swallowed up with them by the depth of their ignorance. For the Egyptians, however, and for their ruler, the danger at that time was to their earthly bodies. But the Jews are punished more severely in that they are affected with respect to what is more honorable. They undergo a punishment of the soul, receiving wages proportionate to their evil deeds. The pharaoh was rightly

[70]Jn 7:34; 8:21. [71]Hos 14:9 (Hos 14:10 LXX). [72]Hos 2:6. [73]Deut 32:5-6. [74]Ps 69:15 (Ps 68:16 LXX).

punished since he was greedily trying to bring what was free into slavery. Correspondingly, Israel is justly punished for not entering into slavery under the Lord of all. What the former was in the power of his greed, as it were, the latter is also found to be because of their great arrogance toward God.

We must note that he calls the Lake of Tiberias a "sea" in accordance with the words of the Holy Scriptures: "The gathering of waters" the creator called "seas."[75] Among the secular writers too there is often no distinction so that some of them sometimes do not hesitate to call a sea a lake. **[404]**

6:2-4 A great crowd followed him because they saw the signs which he was doing for the sick. Jesus went up to the mountain, and there he sat down with his disciples. Now the Passover, the feast of the Jews, was near.

When Christ left Jerusalem according to the words of the prophets, "I have forsaken my house and abandoned my inheritance,"[76] when he spurned the unbelieving and stubborn people of the Jews, he gave himself to foreigners. Then "a great crowd" followed him, but he went up "to a mountain" surely in accordance with what he predicted: "And I, when I am lifted up from the earth, will draw everyone to myself."[77] He was lifted up from the earth when he ascended to the cross for us, but he was lifted up in another way when he ascended to God-befitting honor and glory as "to a mountain."

We do not dishonor him as a man like Israel does, but we worship him as God and Savior and Lord. Among them he was considered to be some humble man, nothing at all. So they did not shrink from calling him a Samaritan. And, dishonoring him even more severely, they used to call him the son of a carpenter. But among those who believe in him, he is admired as a mighty worker and God, a performer of miracles. And you may hear how godly the intention of his followers is. "Because they saw the signs he was doing for the sick," they thought they ought to follow him zealously. They were led in due progression from the works performed to the knowledge of the one who performed them, and from his God-befitting authority they understood that the one clothed with that authority is by nature Son. And this is the way by which the Savior commanded us to reach faith in him. **[405]** "For the very works that I am doing," he says, "testify about me."[78] And again, "If I am not doing the works of my Father, do not believe me. But if I do them, even though you do not believe me, believe my works."[79] Therefore, just as "from the great beauty of creation" God "the maker of all is seen,"[80] so also by the same line of reasoning, from the divine signs the performer of the signs is seen, and the faith of his followers should rightly be admired.

But I think that a more elaborate and complex meaning is hidden in these words. We see that the Evangelist says not only that the followers of Christ were glad to see his signs but also what signs they justly admired. He adds "which he was doing for the sick" in order to demonstrate that the attitude of his followers was the opposite of that of the Jews. The one group irreverently gets angry that he healed a sick paralytic, but the other group not only marvels at these this while he is present but also goes with him at his departure, as a wonder worker and God. So let us, who have registered Christ as our ruler, flee the ignorance that is characteristic of the Jews. Let us stay with him with endurance, which is what the wisest disciples patiently did. They did not allow themselves in any way to be separated from him or be deserters, but by their very deeds they cried out what Paul says with vigor, "Who will separate us from

[75]Gen 1:10. [76]Jer 12:7. [77]Jn 12:32. [78]Jn 5:36. [79]Jn 10:37-38. [80]Wis 13:5.

the love of Christ?"[81] Let us follow him then, as he is persecuted and flees the stubbornness of those who fight against him, so that we may go up "to the mountain" and sit there with him, that is, that we may spring up into glorious and excellent grace by ruling with him, just as **[406]** he himself said: "You who have followed me in my trials, at the renewal when the Son of Man sits on the throne of his glory, will also sit on twelve thrones, judging the twelve tribes of Israel."[82] I think that the statement that the disciples stay with the Savior and go up on a mountain to sit with him suggests these ideas.

6:5-7 When Jesus raised his eyes and saw that a great crowd was coming to him, he said to Philip, "Where will we buy bread for them to eat?" He said this to test him, for he already knew what he was going to do. Philip answered him,

Christ devised an excellent lesson for his disciples, fit for the holiest men, persuading them even in the most difficult circumstances to overcome their cowardice when it comes to hospitality and to cast hesitation in this regard far away and instead to attain to this virtue with zealous activity. What could be greater than this for those who know and will the things by which they might fittingly purchase for themselves friendship from above? After all, when a crowd of no small size was coming to him and an unnumbered multitude was pouring like water into the place where he was staying, he immediately ordered that preparations be made to feed them. It is not unlikely that the zeal even of someone very rich would wane because of the number of those they see, startled into fear of not being able to be hospitable. But Christ shows that it is no great thing when our love is extended to a few, but he wants us to prevail with youthful vigor over things even beyond our hope, grounded by confidence in him for courage in all good things. **[407]**

The meaning of what we have said does not depart from the main point of the narrative. After transferring these matters to a spiritual understanding and stripping away the coarse appearance of the type, we now put it more plainly: God foresees those who seek him through noble zeal and faith as from a mountain, that is, from exalted and God-befitting foreknowledge. As Paul says, "Those whom he foreknew and predestined to be conformed to the likeness of his Son, these he also called."[83] So Christ "raises his eyes" as if to show that those who love him are worthy of the divine gaze, just as it was certainly said to Israel in the form of a blessing, "The Lord lift up his countenance on you and give you peace."[84]

Not only the grace of the divine gaze, however, is in store for those who honor him, but the blessed Evangelist adds something else as well and shows the Lord not without forethought for the crowds but already preparing food for a banquet. Through this you may understand what is delivered to us in Proverbs, "The Lord will not starve the righteous soul."[85] For he sets himself before them as bread from heaven, and he will nourish the souls of those who fear him. He prepares for them everything necessary for life, just as it says in the Psalms, "You have prepared their food, for thus is your provision."[86] And Christ himself says somewhere, "Truly, truly, I say to you, whoever comes to me will never hunger."[87] That is because, as we said before, he will grant food from heaven, and he will bestow the manifold grace of the Spirit. Moreover, he prepares to give food to those who come to him without even waiting to be asked. "For we do not know how to pray as we ought,"[88] **[408]** but he

[81]Rom 8:35. [82]Mt 19:28; Lk 22:28. [83]Rom 8:29-30. [84]Num 6:26. [85]Prov 10:3. [86]Ps 65:9 (Ps 64:10 LXX). [87]Jn 6:35. [88]Rom 8:26.

anticipates us in reaching out for those things that preserve us to eternal life.

So he says to Philip, "Where will we buy bread?" We must look into why he says this to Philip even though the other disciples were standing by and adhering to him. Philip was a questioner and eager to learn, but he was not overly sharp when it comes to his ability for quick apprehension of more divine matters. You may learn this by considering for yourself that after following the Savior for a long time, gathering various lessons about his divinity and acquiring the richest understanding about him through both deeds and words, he says to Jesus at the end of his *oikonomia*, as if he had not yet learned anything, "Lord, show us the Father, and we will be satisfied."[89] But he was quite rightly reeducated as one who spoke out of simplicity. "I have been with you all this time and you do not know me, Philip," says Christ.[90] Therefore, Christ exercises his disciple in the faith and poses a question aimed at one who is dull in his understanding and advancing slower than he should to the apprehension of more divine matters. This is what "test" means in this passage, even though, as the blessed Evangelist maintains, "he already knew what he was going to do."

The words "where shall we buy" demonstrate the lack of concern for money on the part of those who were with him and their voluntary poverty for the sake of God, since they did not even have enough to buy the necessary food. At the same time, he accomplishes something else with his skillful composition of the statement. He says "where" not in vain, as to people who have taken no trouble to prepare anything at all, but to those who are accustomed to be completely unconcerned about money. He thereby most cleverly excludes and cuts off hope in money and all but **[409]** persuades them to come to the point where they ask the Lord to create food by his unspeakable power and God-befitting authority if he wants those who have nothing to feed those who are coming to him. This was all that remained, and he was calling them to find their only hope there, "the iron wound of necessity," as the Greek poets say.

6:7 "Two hundred denarii worth of bread is not enough for each of them to get a little."

Philip advances feebly, though not to the point of recognizing Jesus' power to do all things (and that with ease). Instead, when he hears the words "Where will we buy?" that were spoken to test him, he is immediately seized by those words, and he looks only at the monetary way of doing things, assuming that the matter will be accomplished in no other way than the common law that everyone is accustomed to, that is, generous spending. Therefore, as far as the disciples' lack of desire for money and their lack of possessions are concerned, and as far as Philip's own understanding is concerned, which does not perfectly perceive the extraordinary honor of our Savior, generosity toward the crowds is somehow turned into an impossibility. But it does not turn out this way. The will of the Savior brings the matter to completion. "What is impossible for human beings is possible for God,"[91] and the divine power proves superior in every way to the course of nature in our affairs. It can accomplish all things miraculously, even things which exceed our understanding. **[410]**

6:8-10 One of his disciples, Andrew the brother of Simon Peter, said to him, "There is a boy here who has five barley loaves and two small fish. But what are they among so many?" Jesus said,

He thinks and reasons like Philip, and he himself is convicted of having the same kind of

[89]Jn 14:8. [90]Jn 14:9. [91]Lk 18:27.

understanding of the Savior. He does not recognize his power, nor is he led by the preceding miracles to recognize Jesus' power to do all things most easily. He points out what the boy has, but he is clearly weak in faith. "What are they," he says, "among so many?" However (for we must say it), he should advance not haltingly but quickly to the recollection of the miracles Jesus already performed. He should consider that it is a work in no way foreign or alien to the one who changed the nature of water into wine, who healed the paralytic and drove away so great a sickness with one word, that he should also create food from nothing and divinely multiply the very little that was found at hand. The authority that did the former—how could it not also do the latter? Therefore, the pair of disciples answered more feebly than they should have.

However, we must consider this again. Those lapses that appear to be small failings in the saints often are not without a share of profit. There is something wrapped up in them that is beneficial in the very failing that exposes their weakness. In this case, the above-mentioned holy disciples thought and explicitly said first that "two hundred denarii worth of bread is not enough for each one to get a little." And then, concerning the five loaves and two fish, they asked, "What are they among so many?" **[411]** They raise wonder to the skies and render the Savior's power more glorious when they indicate with their own words a multitude that has not yet been satisfied, and the power of their unbelief is turned into a good witness for Christ. With these words they admit that such a large amount of money will not be enough for the crowds to have even a little enjoyment. And with the same words they crown the ineffable power of the host when he, though there was nothing (for as Andrew says, "what" are the boy's supplies "among so many?"), very richly outdid his work of love toward the crowds.

We find the same sort of little faith in the desert in the all-wise Moses as well. The Israelites were weeping, and, incited to a foul lust for the tables of Egypt, they kept imagining the unclean fleshpots, turning aside to the strangest craving for onions, garlic and vulgar things of that kind.[92] They also disregarded the good things of God and kept assailing Moses their mediator and leader. But God was not unaware of the things for which the multitude was eagerly groaning. Indeed, he promised to give them meat. But since the promise of generosity was made in the desert and that feat seemed difficult as far as the human mind is concerned, Moses approaches him and cries out, "The people I am with number six hundred thousand on foot, and you said, 'I will give them meat, and they will eat for a month.' Are there enough flocks and herds to slaughter for them?"[93] And what does God say to this? "Will not the hand of the Lord suffice?"[94] What could be impossible for God?

Therefore, one may rightly respond also to the words of Philip **[412]** and Andrew, "Will not the hand of the Lord suffice?" Let us too take this event as an example and consider littleness of faith to be the most extreme sickness, surpassing all evil. If God does something or promises to do something, let it be received in utterly simple faith, and let God not be accused because of our weakness in some matter, just because we cannot understand how things that are above us can happen. It would be fitting for a good and sober person who has sound reasoning to consider as well how even the eye of the body will surely see not as far as it might wish, but as far as it is able and the limit of our nature permits. It cannot distinguish things that are situated at too great a height, even if it imagines them in general. It barely gets the slightest glimpse of them. This,

[92]Num 11:4-5. [93]Num 11:21-22. [94]Num 11:23.

I think, is how the human mind operates as well. It stretches and reaches to the limits given to it by its creator, even if it is wholly purified. It sees nothing above itself, but it yields, even against its will, to those things above its nature since it has no way to grasp them. By faith then and not by investigation are the things above us received. And as the one who so believes is admired, so the one who has fallen into the opposite is in no way free from blame. The Savior himself testifies to this for us when he says, "The one who believes in the Son is not judged, but the one who does not believe has already been judged."[95]

Now that we have taken up a discussion about the duty not to disbelieve God, let us take up again, for the edification of those who will read this, a passage from the Holy Scriptures and put it forward to illuminate the punishment for unbelief. Now Moses (since I am returning to the teacher Moses) was once commanded in the desert, when the people were oppressed by an unbearable thirst, **[413]** to take Aaron and smite the rock with his rod that it might gush with springs of water. But he, not wholly persuaded by the words of the one who commanded him but faint-hearted because of his human nature, said, "'Listen to me, you rebels. Must we bring water out of this rock for you?' And Moses raised his hand and struck the rock twice with his staff, and much water came out. And the Lord said to Moses and Aaron, 'Because you did not believe me, and so did not treat me as holy before the Israelites, for this reason you will not lead this assembly into the land which I have given them.'"[96] Should it not be clear to everyone from this how bitter the wages of unbelief are? If Moses, great as he was, was rebuked, whom will God spare? On whom will the one who is no respecter of persons not inflict his wrath for their unbelief? After all, God was not willing to spare even Moses, to whom he said, "I know you above all, and you have found favor with me."[97]

6:10 "Make the people sit down." Now there was much grass in the place; so the men sat down, about five thousand in all.

The Savior observed his accustomed gentleness and took away the sharpness of his reproaches. He does not bitingly rebuke his disciples, even though they were quite asleep in their faint-heartedness and little faith toward him. Instead, he leads them through his very actions to an understanding of the things that they do not yet believe. The words "make the people sit down" have no small force. They practically show Jesus saying something like, **[414]** You who are slow to understand my power and realize who it is who is speaking to you, make the men sit down so that you may marvel when you see them filled from the nothing that is set before you. Make the men sit down. This is the only option left for them since two hundred denarii could not have obtained the necessities of life for the crowds. But that which human money lacks in its ability to save, my power will procure, which calls everything into existence and creates from what does not exist. It was not Elijah the prophet who rendered the widow's flask of oil unfailing or her jar the source of unspent nourishment.[98] And the one who gave this power to him—would he not be able to multiply nothing and to make what was simply on hand a source of his ineffable bounty and the beginning and root of unexpected grace?

It is not unbelievable that Christ intended these things in what he said. The blessed Evangelist, for his part, indicates for our edification that "there was much grass in the place," showing that the place was fit for men who needed to sit down. Notice how although the multitude that was fed was mixed, that is,

[95]Jn 3:18. [96]Num 20:10-12. [97]Ex 33:12. [98]1 Kings 17:14.

there were women present with their children, he counted only the men, following, it seems to me, the custom of the law. God commanded the teacher Moses and said, "Count up the whole assembly of the Israelites by family, by their fathers' houses, by the number of their names, by their head, every male twenty years old and above."[99] The prophet did what he was commanded, and he put together a long list of names. **[415]** And it is clear that he disregarded women and children but enrolled the multitude that had reached young manhood. All that is manly and vigorous is honorable in the book of God, and not what is infantile in its intention toward good things. Thus by this he honors the custom of the law, and he forms a spiritual understanding of it.

Shall we not say with good reason, when we look at the entire meaning of the passage, that Christ rightly turns away from and leaves the violent and boastful people of the Jews, but he very gladly receives those who come to him, and he fattens them up with heavenly food, providing them with spiritual bread that strengthens the human heart?[100] He feeds them not grudgingly but joyfully and without care, taking great delight in this godly act. This is what the fact that the crowds sat on the grass means for us so that what the Psalms say is fitting for each one of those considered worthy of such a grace: "The Lord is my shepherd, I shall not want. In a place of grass, there he has made me rest."[101] In great delight and luxury is the mind of the saints fed by the abundance of the Spirit, according to the statement in the Song of Songs, "Eat, drink, and be drunk, you neighbors."[102]

Although many were there and the crowd was mixed, as we have already said, he mentioned only the men sitting, passing over the women and children to make an edifying point. He is teaching us through an enigma that food will be supplied from the Savior more fittingly and properly to those who act like men (toward the good, that is) and not to those who are effeminate, resulting in a disposition that is not good, or to those who are infantile in their understanding so that they cannot understand what they need to know. **[416]**

6:11 Then Jesus took the loaves, and when he had given thanks, he distributed them to those who were seated; so also the fish, as much as they wanted.

He gives thanks as a type for us and a model of the reverence that we ought to have. As man, he ascribes to the divine nature the power of the miracle. This was his custom. He helped, by his example of reverence, those to whom he was revealed as a teacher of excellent truths, and according to the *oikonomia*, he hid his divine dignity for the time being until the time of his passion was at hand. That is because it was a pressing concern for him that this be hidden from the prince of this world. Therefore, in other cases too he uses words that are fitting for human beings as man, but he heals the mind of the hearers, sometimes enticing them with great wisdom, as in the words, "Father, I thank you that you have heard me."[103] Do you see how human his speech is, and how it can trouble the understanding of the more simple? But when he says this as man, he immediately explains the way of the *oikonomia* and the reason for hiding his will, arranging his words with great skill to rebuild the mind of the simple, which had received a shock. "For I knew," he says, "that you always hear me."[104] For whom then does he say these things? "I have said this for the sake of the crowd standing here," he says, "that they may believe that you sent me."[105] Should it not then

[99]Num 1:2-3. [100]Ps 104:15 (Ps 103:15 LXX). [101]Ps 23:1-2 (Ps 22:1-2 LXX). [102]Song 5:1. [103]Jn 11:41. [104]Jn 11:42. [105]Jn 11:42.

be clear from these words that in order to help us in various ways and to accomplish the hidden purpose of his *oikonomia* with the flesh, as befits him, that he sometimes speaks in a more lowly way than the condition he is actually in? Just as "I thank you" is taken according to the *oikonomia* in those words, **[417]** so also here. [The word *blessed* is taken of the loaves.][106]

We must note that instead of "gave thanks," Matthew says "blessed,"[107] but the versions of the saints differ in no way. Paul shows that both are the same when he says, "All food from God is good, and nothing is to be rejected since it is sanctified by the word of God and prayer."[108] So that which is sanctified by the prayer of supplication, which we are accustomed always to make over the table, is surely blessed.

It is fitting that nothing profitable should be left unexamined. Come then and let us say a little about the five loaves that the boy had and the two small fish. The very kind of things they found and especially the number are pregnant with mystical meaning. Why, someone who loves knowledge might say, were there not rather four loaves and three fish? And why not five loaves and four fish? Why was it necessary at all to recount the number of what they found? Why did he not say more simply and absolutely that the immeasurable multitude of followers was fed with the very little that they found? But the fact that the blessed Evangelist was quite eager to recount these details too certainly gives us something to interpret that we must investigate.

So he says that there are five loaves (and these are made of barley) and two small fish, and with these Christ feeds those who love him. I myself think (and let the one who loves knowledge watch for something better) that the five barley loaves signify the fivefold book of the all-wise Moses, that is, the whole law, since it introduces, as it were, the coarser food through the letter and the narrative. **[418]** The fact that they are made of barley hints at this. The two small fish signify the food that comes from the fishermen, that is, the most delicate writings of the Savior's disciples. And these two, he says, the apostolic and evangelical preaching, shine forth among us. Both of these come from fishermen and are spiritual writings. The Savior then mixes the new with the old, and, with the law and the teaching of the new covenant, he feeds the souls of those who believe in him unto life, that is, eternal life. That the disciples were fishermen is, I presume, evident and clear. Even though not all of them happened to be fishermen, there were nevertheless fishermen among them. So our statement will not depart from the truth on this point.

6:12-13 When they were satisfied, he said to his disciples, "Gather up the fragments left over so that nothing may be lost." So they gathered them up and filled twelve baskets with the fragments from the five barley loaves, left by those who had eaten.

One might think that it was to save the leftovers that Christ commanded his disciples to gather them up. But I think everyone will rightly imagine that he would not allow himself to stoop to such pettiness. And why do I say Christ? None of us would either. After all, what leftovers could be expected from five barley loaves? But there is an important purpose behind the statement; it makes the miracle perfectly obvious to the hearers. There is such an exercise of God-befitting authority in this act that not only was so great a multitude satisfied from five barley loaves and two small fish, but in addition, twelve baskets of fragments were gathered. Most importantly, it

[106]I have followed Pusey in bracketing these words even though they stand as part of the previous sentence in Greek. They seem to be a marginal notation summarizing the next point Cyril makes. [107]Mt 14:19. [108]1 Tim 4:4-5.

seems that the miracle refuted another suspicion. By the discovery of the fragments, **[419]** it confirms the belief that there was certainly and truly an abundance of food, and not rather an appearance of a vision that deceived the eyes of both those who feasted and those who served them.

But what is greater and more remarkable and especially edifying to us is this: Notice how by this miracle he makes us quite eager in our desire to show hospitality with great joy. He all but cries out to us by his deeds that the things of God will not fail the one who shares and rejoices in the way of love for others and wants to fulfill what is written: "Break your bread with the one who hungers."[109] We find that the disciples at the beginning were seized by hesitation about this. But since they had such a disposition, the Savior gave them an abundant harvest of fragments. By this he teaches us as well that when we spend a little bit for the glory of God, we will receive more abundant grace in return according to Christ's statement, "A good measure, pressed down, shaken together, and overflowing will be put into your lap."[110] Therefore, we must not hesitate to share out of love for our brothers, but we must progress to a noble boldness and put hesitation and fear, which persuade us to be inhospitable, as far away from us as possible. Being confirmed in hope by faith in the power of God to multiply even small amounts, let us open our hearts to those in need according to the command of the law. "You will surely open your heart," it says, "to the needy brother among you."[111] After all, when will you be found merciful if you remain hard in this life? When will you fulfill the command if you allow the time in which you can do it to slip by in idleness? **[420]** Remember the psalmist, who says, "In death no one remembers you. In Hades who will acknowledge you?"[112] What fruit do the dead have? Or how will one who has gone down to Hades now remember God by fulfilling his command? "God has hedged them in," as it is written.[113] This is what the supremely wise Paul was teaching us when he wrote to certain people, "While we still have time, let us do good."[114]

Let these things be said to us for our edification from the narrative. When we took what was said spiritually (since we must do nothing other than this), we said that the five barley loaves suggested the books of Moses and the two small fish suggested the wise writings of the holy apostles. Now I suppose we must consider a mystical and spiritual meaning for the gathering of the fragments as well, which follows the sequence of the account. Now the Savior commanded the crowds to sit down. He blessed the loaves and the fish and distributed them, through the ministry of the disciples, that is. And when those who had eaten were miraculously satisfied, he commanded them to gather up the fragments, and twelve baskets were filled, one for each disciple, it seems, since that is how many disciples there were. What shall we conclude from this except that Christ is surely and truly the master of the banquet for those who believe in him and that he nourishes those who come to him with divine and heavenly food, namely, the teaching of the law and the prophets as well as the Evangelists and the apostles. He himself, however, is certainly not the one who does these things, but the disciples serve us the grace from above. They are not "the ones speaking," as it says, "but the Spirit of the Father **[421]** is speaking" in them.[115] The holy apostles, however, will not go unrewarded in their labor in this. When they have distributed to us the spiritual food and have served us the good things that come from our Savior, they will receive the richest reward and find the fullest grace of honor from God. I think this, and nothing else, is what it means that a full basket was gathered for each

[109]Is 58:7. [110]Lk 6:38. [111]Deut 15:11. [112]Ps 6:5 (Ps 6:6 LXX). [113]Job 3:23. [114]Gal 6:10. [115]Mt 10:20.

one at the command of Christ after their labors and the service lavished on the guests. And there is no doubt that, after them, the realities signified by the type will pass also to the rulers of the holy churches.

6:14 When the people saw the sign which Jesus had done, they said, "This is the prophet who is to come into the world."

Those who know how to evaluate God-befitting actions marvel at the sign. They are regulated by human reasoning rather than being sick with a beast-like lack of reason, as the ungodly Jews were who, when they ought to have benefited from the manifestation of what was accomplished, lost even the power of right reasoning. They thought that Jesus must now be stoned because he was often seen doing miracles. Those who marvel, then, are better in no small degree than the foolishness of those people, since by this one great sign they are persuaded that he is surely the one foretold to come into the world as a prophet. Notice what a great difference comes to light, I mean, between the race of Israel and those who are located outside Judea. The one, although they were spectators of many things not unworthy of wonder, are not only hard of heart and inhuman, [422] but also they want to kill him unjustly who was eager to save them. And by their wild folly they drive him from their city and their country. The others, who live outside Jerusalem and who thereby signify the race of foreigners, glorify him because of just one sign, and they nobly determine that the judgments about him must be received by faith without doubt. By all these things, Israel is justly shown to be self-condemned and self-invited to a final just rejection, while the Gentiles now rightly deserve to obtain their share of pardon from above and the love of Christ.

6:15 Now Jesus, knowing that they were about to come and seize him to make him king, withdrew again to a mountain by himself alone.

One may quite rightly judge them absolutely praiseworthy. They were easily persuaded by the great miracle that the most outstanding of all qualities fittingly belong to Christ and that it is right to ascribe to him the height of honor as his portion. After all, what else could it mean that they wanted to choose him as their king? Among other things, one may reasonably admire this too: Christ is shown to be an example for us of contempt for glory. He flees those who want to give him due honor, and he declines the highest kingdom there is among us. Now it was not truly something he wanted, because he rules all things with the Father. Yet to those who look away to the hope to come, he gives the understanding that what is great to the world is small to them and that it is good for them not to seek the honors in this life, or rather this world, even if those honors offer themselves, [423] so that they may ascend to the honor from God. It is truly unseemly that those who are pressing on toward divine grace and thirsting for eternal glory should want to shine in these matters.

We must therefore avoid love of glory, the sister and neighbor of arrogance, which is not far distant from its borders. Let us flee the illustrious honor of the present life as something unjust, and instead let us seek the holiness found in humility, yielding to each other as the blessed Paul admonished us: "Each one of you think this among yourselves which is also in Christ Jesus, who being in the form of God, did not consider equality with God something to be exploited, but emptied himself, taking on the form of a slave, coming to be in human likeness. And being found in human form, he humbled himself and became obedient to the point of death, even death on a cross. Therefore, God also highly exalted him and gave him the name that is above every name."[116] Do you see how the voluntary humility has a glorious end, and a measured attitude is shown to be the root of many good things for us? The Only Begotten, who was in the form of God the Father, humbled himself by becoming human for us. But even though he appeared in this life with the flesh, he did not remain humbled. He returned to his original honor and God-befitting glory even though he became human.

One may think that this is how it is in our case as well. When we bring ourselves down from the vain glories of the present life and seek what is humble, then we will surely receive the glory from above in return, and we will ascend to being gods by grace and will be called children of God by our likeness to the true and natural Son. **[424]** And, to say something similar to the passage before us, let us refuse the highest earthly excellence, the mother of all honor, if it comes to us, since we keep our mind on heavenly things, and we live for things above rather than things on earth.

But this passage is not without a share of spiritual meaning for us. Therefore, we will repeat it, summing up, as it were, the entire import of the things that happened and going through the passage before us from the beginning. In this way, what is about to be said will be clear to us, especially when the blessed Evangelist adds, as if hinting at something necessary and not to be rejected, "He withdrew to a mountain by himself alone." Christ left Jerusalem to avoid the inhumanity of the Jews, which clearly is the same as when it was said, "I have forsaken my house and abandoned my inheritance."[117] After he crossed the Sea of Tiberias and was very far removed from their folly, he went to the mountain with his disciples. We said that this indicates the impassable and trackless nature, so to speak, of the road to him, for the Jews. It also indicates Christ's withdrawal in anger at his suffering until the time, that is, the proper time, and that Christ will be manifest together with his disciples when he departs Judea and goes to the Gentiles, transferring his grace to them. From the mountain, he looked down on his followers and, what is more, gave thought to their nourishment. This, we said, signifies in a type, as it were, the watching over from above that is due the saints according to the passage, "The eyes of the Lord are on the righteous,"[118] and the fact that Christ is not without concern for those who fear him. Next, the great crowd was miraculously fed from the **[425]** five loaves and two small fish. We determined that these should be understood to be the juxtaposition by the apostles of the writing of the saints, both old and new, for those who love Christ. In addition, the chorus of the disciples will receive from God rich fruit from their ministry to us, and after them, those who preside over the holy churches of God, since the initial type was for all in those positions. Then the spectators marvel at the sign and want to seize Jesus to make him king. But he realizes this, and he "withdraws to a mountain alone," as it is written. When the Gentiles marveled at Christ as a wonder worker and as God, when everyone registered him as king and Lord, then he was taken up alone into heaven and absolutely no one followed him. He, the first fruits from the dead,[119] has gone up alone into the great and truer mountain in accordance with what the psalmist said: "Who will ascend the mountain of the Lord, or who will stand in his holy place? The one who has innocent hands and a pure heart."[120] Such a person will follow Christ and ascend to the spiritual mountain at the time of the kingdom of heaven. He "withdrew to the mountain," that is, he ascended into heaven, not to avoid being king over those who believe in him but to defer the time of his more manifest reign until his return to us from above. Then he will descend in the glory of the

[116]Phil 2:5-9. [117]Jer 12:7. [118]Ps 34:15 (Ps 33:16 LXX). [119]1 Cor 15:20. [120]Ps 24:3-4 (Ps 23:3-4 LXX).

Father. He will no longer be recognized through signs, as before, to be Lord truly and by nature, but because of his God-befitting glory he will be confessed without a doubt to be king.

Therefore (for I will bring together the breadth of what has been said and say it again briefly), when through signs he was believed and recognized as God after he departed from the Jewish people, everyone was eager to make him king. But he ascended alone into **[426]** heaven, keeping the more open manifestation of his kingdom for the proper time.

6:16-17 When it was evening, his disciples went down to the sea. They got into a boat, and they started across the sea to Capernaum.

After he miraculously accomplished the first sign, his flight and withdrawal are, according to the *oikonomia,* found to be the root and occasion of another sign. And the wonder worker goes "from strength to strength," as it is written.[121] Since he was being sought as king by those who were astonished at his first great miracle, and he was refusing worldly honors in accordance with the preceding discussion, he surely had to leave that place, or rather their whole country. So in order that he might seem to have sailed away, and in order to dissipate the intensity of those who were seeking him, he instructs his disciples to depart before him. But he himself remains, taking advantage of the opportunity to go on to the next sign. It was his most earnest endeavor to strengthen through every occasion and deed the mind of the apostles so that they might believe in him. Since they were going to be teachers of the world, and they were going to "shine like stars in the world," as Paul says,[122] he led them, as was necessary, to all things beneficial. This was not to show kindness to them alone but also to those who would be led by them into an unerring conception of him.

But, perhaps someone will say, why, after that great miracle, is Jesus' power to walk on the sea itself immediately introduced? Such a person will hear a credible reason in reply. When he willed to feed the crowds, **[427]** Philip and Andrew supposed that he would be powerless to do it. The one said that the greatest amount of money would barely suffice for them to get just a little, while the other indicated that five loaves and two small fish were found with one of the children, but that is nothing to such a great crowd. From all their own words, so to speak, they thought that he could do nothing outside the due course of our affairs. Crucially, then, in order to exempt himself from such a petty conception and to bring the still feeble mind of the apostles to understand that he miraculously does everything he wants, without being prevented by the nature of things and without being hindered in the least by necessary consequences, he placed the wet nature of water under his feet, even though it was not used to being under human bodies.[123] As God, all things were possible for him. When it was evening then and time was exhausting the diligence of those seeking him, the chorus of holy disciples went down to the sea, and immediately they begin to sail off, obeying their God and teacher in all matters without delay.

6:17-18 It was now dark, and Jesus had not yet come to them. The sea became rough because a strong wind was blowing.

Many events are profitably arranged for the same purpose, and the circumstances drive the disciples to a more zealous search for the Savior. The darkness of the night troubles them because it is deep, hovering like smoke over the raging waters and taking from them

[121]Ps 84:7 (Ps 83:8 LXX). [122]Phil 2:15. [123]Following the variant οὐ μελετήσασαν instead of the text, μελετήσασαν.

all knowledge of where they should ultimately steer. The ferocity of the wind causes them no little turmoil [428] as it treads on the waves with a howl and raises them to an unaccustomed height. And though these things had already taken place, "Jesus had not yet come to them," it says. The danger was especially in this fact, and the absence of Christ was causing the sailors' fear to increase.

Those who are not with him are therefore hit by a storm. They are cut off or seem to be absent from him due to the fact that they have left the divine laws and are separated by sin from the one who is strong enough to save them. So if being in spiritual darkness is heavy and drowning in the bitter sea of pleasures is hard to bear, let us receive Jesus. This will free us from danger and from the sin that leads to death. The type of what we just said will be seen in what happens. He will surely come to his disciples.

6:19-20 When they had rowed about twenty-five or thirty stadia,[124] they saw Jesus walking on the sea and coming near the boat, and they were terrified. But he said to them, "It is I; do not be afraid."

When they are separated from the land by a great distance, and it is likely that in their trouble there is no way to be saved (since they are now in the middle of the sea), then the much longed-for Christ appears to them. Thus he is able to provide a most welcome salvation to those who are in danger, when fear had already cut off all hope of life for them. He appears miraculously to them, since this was arranged especially for their edification. They are astonished when they see Jesus going through the midst of the sea and on the very waters, and the miracle increases their fear. But Christ immediately frees [429] them from these things by saying, "It is I; do not be afraid." All tumult surely must go far away, and those for whom Christ is now present must clearly be far above all danger! This makes us aware of how to have a bold and youthful mind in the midst of temptations and how to have intense endurance which comes from hope in Christ, strengthened in the courage that we will surely be saved even though many fears from temptations pour in around us.

Notice how Christ does not immediately appear to those in the boat when they set sail, or even at the beginning of the danger. He appears only when they are many stadia from the land. That is because the grace of the Savior does not visit us at the beginning of the circumstances that trouble us but when fear is at its height, and the danger already shows itself to be strong, and we find ourselves in the midst of waves of trouble, so to speak. Then Christ appears unexpectedly. He attends to our fears and will free us from all danger when, by his ineffable power, he changes what we dread into a sea of tranquility.

6:21 They wanted to take him into the boat, and immediately the boat reached the land toward which they were going.

The Lord frees the sailors not only from danger by miraculously shining on them, but he frees them from toil and sweat as well when by his God-befitting power he thrusts the boat to the opposite shore. They were expecting that they could barely make it if they kept rowing, but he delivers them even from this labor, showing himself to be a worker of many wonders in just a little time in order to give them full assurance. [430] So when Christ appears and shines on us, we will succeed without struggle even beyond our hope, and we who are in danger through not having him will then need no labor to be able to succeed at

[124]A stadium is about 200 yards, so they rowed about three to three and a half miles.

what is profitable when he is present. Christ then is the deliverance from all danger and the accomplishment of achievements beyond hope for those who receive him.

Now since we have discussed each element of the passage individually, let us join the interpretation of the elements with the sequence of what came before and work out the spiritual interpretation. We said, then, that Jesus ascended into heaven as to a mountain (when he was taken up, that is) after his resurrection from the dead. When this has taken place, however, his disciples alone and by themselves swim through the waves of the present life as through a sea, giving us a type of successive teachers of the church for all time. They encounter many great temptations, and they endure no little danger from their teaching, namely, from those who oppose the faith and fight against the gospel proclamation. But they will be rescued from both fear and all danger, and they will even rest from the hardship of their labor when Christ appears to them hereafter in God-befitting power and has the whole world under his feet. This is what I think walking on the sea indicates, since the sea in the Holy Scriptures is often taken as a type of the world, in accordance with the statement in the Psalms, "The sea is great and wide. There are creeping things without number, small animals and great alike."[125] So when Christ comes in the glory of his Father, as it is written, **[431]** then the boat of the holy apostles (that is, the church) and those who sail in it (that is, those who by faith and love toward God are above the affairs of the world) will immediately and without effort reach "the land toward which they were going." Their goal was to reach a beautiful shore, so to speak, that is, the kingdom of heaven. And the Savior confirms this understanding of all that has been said when he says to his disciples at one point, "A little while and you will no longer see me, and then a little while and you will see me,"[126] and at another point, "You will have trouble in the world; but take heart, I have overcome the world."[127]

But the Lord comes down from the mountain in the night and visits his disciples, who are watchful. In fact, it is not without fear that they see him coming. They tremble so that something we need to understand might be shown to us through these events. For he will come down from heaven as in the night, while the world is asleep in a way, and snoring in much sin. Therefore, he says somewhere also to us, "Keep watch, because you do not know at what hour your Lord is coming."[128] And the parable of the virgins will no less teach us this. It says that five are wise, but five are foolish. When the bridegroom was delayed, "they all became drowsy and slept. And in the middle of the night, there was a cry, Behold the bridegroom! Come out to meet him!"[129] Do you see how the bridegroom is announced to us in the middle of the night? What the shout is and how the meeting takes place, the divine Paul will make clear when he says at one point, "The Lord himself will come down from heaven with a command, with the voice of an archangel and with the trumpet of God,"[130] and at another point concerning the saints who are raised up, "We who are living, who are left, will be caught up together with them in the clouds **[432]** to meet the Lord in the air, and thus we will be always with the Lord."[131] The fact that the disciples are smitten with fear even though they see him coming, and they are overtaken even while they are toiling and awake, shows that the judge will be fearful to everyone when he arrives. Even the righteous will surely cower before him, as though tested by fire, despite the fact that they are always looking ahead for the coming one and do not shrink from toil in virtue, nourished as they are by sobriety together with diligent watch-

[125]Ps 104:25 (Ps 103:25 LXX). [126]Jn 16:16. [127]Jn 16:33. [128]Mt 24:42. [129]Mt 25:5-6. [130]1 Thess 4:16. [131]1 Thess 4:17.

fulness. But the Lord does not board the boat with his disciples like a fellow sailor. Instead, he anchors the boat at the shore. Christ will not appear in order to keep working with those who worship him for the accomplishment of virtue but in order to give to those who are already achieving it the end that they are looking forward to.

6:22-23 The next day the crowd that had stayed on the other side of the sea saw that there was no other boat there except the one his disciples boarded, and that Jesus had not gotten into the boat with his disciples, but his disciples had gone away. However, boats came from Tiberias near the place where they had eaten the bread after the Lord had given thanks.

The miracle does not escape their notice, I mean, Jesus walking on the very sea, even though it happened during the night and in the darkness, and it was arranged secretly. The crowd of those who usually followed him notice—due, it seems, to their great watchfulness—that he neither sailed with his disciples nor crossed in another boat. Only the apostles' boat was there, which they took and went ahead of him. Nothing then of what is good escapes notice, even if perhaps it is done secretly by someone. And from this we will see the truth of the saying, [433] "There is nothing hidden that will not be revealed, nothing secret that will not be made known and come to light."[132] I maintain then that the one who wants to follow the footsteps of Christ, as far as it is possible for someone to be molded into his pattern, must not be eager to live a life of boasting or be dragged off into pursuit of praise when practicing virtue, or, if one should enter an incredible and exceedingly ascetic life, want to be praised immoderately because of it. But one must desire to be seen only by the eyes of the divinity, who reveals what is hidden and brings what is done in secret into the clearest understanding.

6:24 Now when the crowd saw that neither Jesus nor his disciples were there, they themselves got into the boats and went to Capernaum looking for Jesus.

These people follow him perhaps because they marvel at the signs, but they surely do not receive the benefit from the signs which leads to the appropriate faith. Instead, they give a kind of payback to the wonder worker by merely praising him, though this is not undesired. This is a coldhearted disease of the mind and of a soul that is in no way accustomed to being led to choose what is profitable. The cause of this is that they only delight in the pleasures of the flesh, and they eagerly jump at the paltriest temporary food rather than running to spiritual goods and trying to gain what would nourish them to eternal life. You may learn this with diligence also from what follows. [434]

6:25 And when they found him on the other side of the sea, they said to him, "Rabbi, when did you get here?"

Their speech takes a form that comes from those who love him. It feigns sweetness, but it is convicted of being totally senseless and childish. At meeting such a great teacher, they should not have said anything without a purpose, nor should they have hurried to learn nothing. Why did they need to be eager to ask him when he arrived? What good would it likely have done them to learn this? Wisdom must then be sought from the wise; let a prudent silence be preferred to uneducated words. The disciple of Christ commands that our words must be "seasoned with salt."[133]

[132]Lk 8:17. [133]Col 4:6.

Another of the wise exhorts us to this, saying, "If you have something intelligent to say, then answer; if not, put your hand over your mouth."[134] How bad it is to be condemned for an undisciplined tongue we will learn from another. "If any among you," he says, "think they are religious and do not bridle their tongues but deceive their hearts, their religion is worthless."[135]

6:26 Jesus answered them and said, "Truly I say to you, you seek me not because you saw the sign, but because you ate the bread and had your fill."

We will say something that is indeed commonplace, but it is not worn out by too much familiarity. Great teachers often become not a little angry when they are questioned about vain and useless matters. And we will find that they experience this certainly not out of arrogance but because they are distressed at the ignorance of the questioners. Now I suppose that such a point is well-made when it comes to us and those like us. **[435]** The Savior too brings a heated rebuke against those who asked those things, charging that they spoke without learning and inquired without understanding. They asked not because it was their duty to seek the things by which they might become honest and good but because they were seeking a bodily reward, and a worthless one at that. After all, what could be less than daily food, and that not lavish? We must practice both reverence and love for Christ, then, not to find anything corporeal but to gain salvation from him. Let us not say good words to him, as they say "Rabbi," while devising smooth talk as a pretext for gain and for a limitless harvest of riches. Let those who attempt this not be unaware that they will run up against Christ, who brings a sharp rebuke and reveals the evil that is hidden in them.

It is fitting to admire once again the thoughtful composition of this passage. When he saw that they were seized by the aforementioned disease, like a skilled physician and master of his craft he devised a double medicine for them, weaving the edifying rebuke together with the most remarkable sign. We will find the sign then in his knowing their thoughts, and you will see the rebuke in the fact that the wonder worker authoritatively tells them that it is not out of reverence that they hasten to seek him.

The benefit is twofold. By clearly understanding their plans and revealing them with precision, he shows that they are ignorant because they think they will escape the notice of the divine eye as they heap up wickedness in their heart while practicing sweetness with their tongue. This rebuke is characteristic of one who persuades them to depart from their disease in these matters and to cease from a sin that is not small. After all, the one who has this conception of God is truly arrogant and lawless.

By rebuking them as sinners for their own good, he restrains in some way the future course of evil. For **[436]** that which has no hindrance creeps on and extends itself, but when it is discovered, it is almost ashamed in a way, and it coils up into itself like a rope. So the Lord helps them even when he is rebuking them, and with the very remarks which might be taken as a blow to them, he is shown to do good to them.

We must understand from this that even if some people praise or flatter the rulers of the churches with kind words but do not walk uprightly in the faith, it is not right for the rulers to be carried away by the flattery or to lend silence in return for faults, as a kind of reward for praise, to those who need correction. Instead, they should rebuke them boldly and persuade them to progress toward the better, or at least they might help others through the

[134]Sir 5:12. [135]Jas 1:26.

rebuke, as Paul says: "Rebuke the sinners before all so that the rest may have fear."[136]

So far we have looked at the passage piece by piece. But now I think we must show that the subsequent parts of the narrative are necessarily connected to what we have already seen before. We said then previously that our Savior's descent from the mountain is a type of his second coming to us from heaven that will take place in the future, and we added in summary of the entire meaning that he appeared to his disciples when they were watchful and still laboring, and he freed them from fear and immediately put their boat at the shore. What is depicted to us in these passages through types, we there made clear.

But observe now that after Jesus comes down from the mountain, some are late in following him and come to him last of all. They come "on the next day." **[437]** This too the Evangelist added not without care. Then when they meet him, they try to flatter him with kind words, but Christ strikes them with a sharp and boiling critique. He does this so that we, in turn, may consider the fact that after the Lord comes to us from heaven, the pursuit of good things is vain and useless for people, and the desire to follow him then is at the wrong time. But if any approach him, thinking to appease him with the kindest words, they will no longer meet a kind and gentle judge but an accusing and harsh one.

You will see the flattery of those accused and the accusation itself in the words of the Savior when he says, "Many will say to me in that day," that is, the day of judgment, "Lord, Lord, did we not cast out demons in your name?" But he says, "Then I will declare to them, Truly I say to you, I never knew you."[137] You did not seek me, he says, with pure motives, nor did you have a desire to excel in holiness. These are the things by which I would have known you. But since you practiced a mere imaginary piety in order to seek gain, I justly declared that I did not know you.

"Lord, Lord" in this passage is equivalent to "Rabbi" in that one.[138] So whoever thinks punishment is a bitter thing, let them not fall into cowardice or succumb to various transgressions while looking to the goodness of God; instead, let them prepare "their works for their departure," as it is written, "and make everything ready in the field,"[139] that is, while they are in this world. The Savior, after all, interpreted the world as a field.[140] So let them prepare for the exhibition of their holiness and righteousness before the divine judgment seat. For they will not see a judge who is merciful after it is too late, or one who yields to pleas for **[438]** mercy. They should have believed in him without delay when he was calling them to salvation, when the time of mercy was allowing them both to seek forgiveness for past transgressions and to seek kindness from God who saves them.

6:27 "Do not work for food that spoils, but for food that remains to eternal life,"

Paul too teaches us something of this sort when he broadens the discussion to a more universal and general level, saying, "The one who sows to the flesh, from the flesh will reap corruption; but the one who sows to the Spirit, from the Spirit will reap eternal life."[141] He says that they sow to the flesh who hand over the reins, as it were, to the pleasures of the flesh and set out at a run to whatever they want. They make no distinction between what is beneficial to them and what injures and harms them. They are completely unaccustomed to considering what is right in the eyes of the lawgiver. They are heedlessly dragged away to the mere pleasure of the moment, and

[136]1 Tim 5:20. [137]Mt 7:22-23. [138]Cyril is referring to Jn 6:25, where the crowds ask, "Rabbi, when did you get here?" [139]Prov 24:27 (LXX). [140]Mt 13:38. [141]Gal 6:8.

they prefer nothing to what is seen.

By contrast, he maintains that they sow to the Spirit who expend the entire energy of their mind on whatever the Holy Spirit wills us to excel in, employing so great a concentration on the cultivation of good things that, if a natural and unavoidable principle had not planted in them care for the necessary nourishment of the flesh, they would never have endured to descend even to this. So I think it befits us to make no provision at all "for the pleasures of the flesh"[142] but to be devoted to those things that are most necessary and to be eager to practice whatever raises us to the eternal and divine **[439]** life. After all, to marvel at the luxuries of the body and consider nothing superior to a full belly is truly brutish and shares in the most extreme lack of reason. But to be devoted to good things, to be extremely eager to excel in virtues, to submit to the laws of the Spirit, to seek readily the things of God which are able to supply us on the road to salvation—I will grant that these are truly fitting for those who know their own nature and are not ignorant that they have been created as rational animals in the image of the creator. Therefore, as the Savior himself says somewhere, "Let us not worry about what we will eat or what we will drink or what we will wear"[143] because we know that "the soul is greater than food, and the body is greater than clothing."[144] Let us think about how the more honorable part of us may do well.

Though the body does well and is fattened by the luxuries that belong to it, there is no profit to the wretched soul. On the contrary, much harm will come to it. It will go into the eternal fire because those who have done nothing good must be punished for it. But when the body is bridled by reason that is fitting and has been yoked under the laws of the Spirit, both must surely be saved together. It is most absurd then for us to make such provision for the flesh, which is temporary and even now will perish, that we think it must lack absolutely nothing that is dear to it; while we treat the soul as an afterthought and place no value on concern for it. This despite the fact that we ought, I think, to be eager to incline toward care for the soul to the same extent that the soul is better than the flesh. In this way, **[440]** by preferring what is superior in comparison with what is inferior and by casting the right vote in this matter, we will become holy and wise jurors and will not cede right reason to others but will crown our own heads with it. So "let us not work," as the Savior says, "for food that spoils." After it goes into the stomach and for the briefest time mocks the mind with the paltriest pleasure, it goes into the sewer and is conveyed again out of the stomach. But spiritual bread strengthens the heart[145] and preserves a person to eternal life. Christ himself promises he will supply us with this bread when he says "which the Son of Man will give you," knitting what is human together with what is God-befitting and yoking together the entire mystery of the *oikonomia* with the flesh in the world. He is also hinting in a way at the mystical and more spiritual food by which we live in him, sanctified in body and soul. We will see him say this more plainly in what follows, so let that discussion be kept to its due time and place. **[441]**

Chapter Five

The Only Begotten is the imprint of God the Father's hypostasis, and there is no other imprint besides him that either exists or is conceived of.

6:27 "which the Son of Man will give you. For on him God the Father has set his seal."

He was not unaware, as God, of the charges

[142]Rom 13:14. [143]Mt 6:31. [144]Mt 6:25. [145]Ps 104:15 (Ps 103:15 LXX).

that would arise from Jewish ignorance or of the reasons why they often became angry without understanding. He knew that, looking only at the flesh and failing to recognize God the Word in it, they would think to themselves, Who is this who usurps statements that are fitting for God? After all, who could provide people with food that sustains them to eternal life? This sort of thing is alien to human nature; it befits God alone, who is over all.

So the Savior defends himself in advance, and by inserting a well-timed statement he puts to shame their expected babbling. He says that the "Son of Man" will grant them food that nourishes them to eternal life, but he immediately stresses that he has been "sealed" by the Father. "Sealed" either stands for being anointed (since one who is anointed is sealed), or it shows that he has been patterned after the Father by nature. It is as though he said, I will not be unable to give you food that **[442]** remains and raises you to eternal life and luxury. Even if I look like one of you, that is, as a human being with flesh, I have nevertheless been anointed and sealed by God the Father to an exact likeness with him. You will see him in me, he says, and me in him by nature, even though I was born as a man from woman for you according to the ineffable plan of salvation. I have the power to do all things with God-befitting authority, and I will in no way fall short of the strength inherent in my Father. If God the Father gives you spiritual food that preserves you to eternal life, clearly the Son will give it as well since he is his exact image, even though he has come to be in the flesh. This image, of course, is understood to be a likeness in all things, not in the manner of a fleshly resemblance or in the manner of things that are understood to be at all in bodily form, but in God-befitting glory and equal power and royal authority.

Next we must note that when he says that the "Son of Man" will supply God-befitting blessings and that he has been sealed to the image of God the Father, he permits no division that cuts off the temple of the virgin from the true sonship; instead, he defines himself and wants to be understood as one. Christ is in fact truly one for our sake, wearing a royal purple robe, as it were, as his own clothing (I mean the human body) or a temple that is of course composed of body and soul since Christ is one from both.

But, most excellent sir, the enemy of Christ will reply, give the truth the power to conquer; stop outwitting us with sophistries, ignobly twisting the words however you wish. Look at it **[443]** with clarity: even with these words the Son is not proven to us to be of the substance of the Father but rather a representation of his substance. Let us take an example, they say, of what we are talking about. A seal or signet ring is pressed into wax, perhaps, or some other matter that is capable of receiving it. And after it has impressed only a likeness of itself, it is taken away again by the one who pressed it in, without losing anything of itself. In the same way, the Father, once he has wholly imposed and impressed himself onto the Son in some way with a most precise likeness, surely does not have a Son who is part of himself, as from his essence or considered to be from his essence, but he has him as an image only and a precise likeness.

Let the one who is devoted to learning then see that even now the opponent leaps on us like a serpent, rearing a head filled with venom. But the one who crushes the heads of the serpent[146] will crush this one too and give us the power to escape their manifold stubbornness. So let the one who has just made our ears ring with fearful words tell us, Does not the seal or the signet, which is made of wood, perhaps, or iron or gold, surely seal with some imprint whatever it impresses? Can a seal

[146]Ps 74:14 (Ps 73:14 LXX).

either exist or be conceived of apart from its imprint? I think that anyone, even on their side, would be drawn by what is right to the truth itself and agree, even against their will, that it will by all means seal with an imprint; but, at least according to right reasoning, it will never seal apart from an imprint.

Since then, as the Holy Scriptures testify to us, the Son is the "imprint of the hypostasis" of God the Father,[147] that is, he is both in and from that hypostasis by nature, with what does he mark his seal? Through whom else will the Father seal his own imprint? No one will deny that the **[444]** Father is altogether in a God-befitting form, that is, the Son who is the form of the one who begat him,[148] whom if one were to see spiritually, they would clearly see the Father. For this reason, he says that he is in him by nature, even though he is understood to be from him as far as his distinct existence is concerned, just as radiance, say, is both in and from what is shining. Radiance is something different from what is shining, at least according to a mental distinction, but at the same time it is not different when viewed in relation to what is shining because it is said to be from it, and it is also in it. These things are not understood in the manner of something whose substance is divided and cut off from the whole since they are planted by identity of substance in those things from which they exist, and they are believed to be from them. They proceed by a kind of shining in thought, as it were, to something else distinct, but not by division.

So the Word from the substance of the Father is sealed by the Father not as bare Word or without flesh. Rather, through him those things are sealed that are brought up to likeness with God, as far as possible. That is how we understand in the statement of certain people, "The light of your face has been marked on us, O Lord."[149] After all, it says that the Son is the face of God the Father, and that face is also his imprint. But the light from him is the grace that extends to creation through the Spirit. Through that grace, we are remolded to God, as it were, through faith. We receive through him, as through a seal, our being conformed to the Son, who is the image of the Father, so that our being made in the image and likeness of the creator may be beautifully preserved in us. Since everyone agrees that the Son is the face of God the Father, he would certainly also be the imprint with which God seals.

Yes, says the opponent, we believe that God seals the saints through the Spirit, but **[445]** your point does not relate at all to the question at hand. Therefore, we will take it up again and say, The seal that is imagined to be made of iron, say, or gold imprints its image in the matter on which it is pressed without losing anything of itself, but it marks what receives it only by the action of being pressed on it. In the same way we understand the Son to have been sealed by the Father: he has nothing of his substance, but he possesses only an accurate likeness of it, and he is different from him just as an image is different from an archetype.

Oh, boundless insanity and reckless arrogance! How easily you have forgotten the things we just went through! We have said that the Son is the imprint of the Father and that through him something else, not himself, is sealed so that he is not understood to be the imprint of himself. But you incorrectly reject our argument on this point and do not blush to ascribe to him only a likeness in activity. Therefore, the Son will be God by imprint only, according to you—not at all by nature, but only by being formed and well-shaped in the likeness of the one who begat him. Perhaps the likeness is no longer of the one who begat him at all since it is time for you by these arguments to take away the begetting as well,

[147]Heb 1:3. [148]Phil 2:6. [149]Ps 4:6 (Ps 4:7 LXX).

or rather you must take it away, even if you do not want to.

Now concerning the necessity to believe that the Son has been begotten of the Father, we have already expended many words, or we will do so in its own time. It is more fitting for us to proceed to the issue at hand and put to those who are accustomed to heedless babbling the question, Will they not surely say that what is given can also be taken away and confess that what is in any way added can also be lost? Does it not happen at some point that everything is rejected that is not rooted in something by nature? [**446**] This is obvious even if none of them should admit it.

The Son, then, will at some point possibly be stripped of his likeness since he is sealed, you say, only by the activity of the Father on him, without having the security that comes from natural endowments. Instead, he is understood to be, and is, completely other than the one who begat him and completely cut off from his substance. You did exceedingly well and foresaw matters with the most cunning reasoning. You insured the Father's safety by saying that he thought it right to give nothing of himself to the Son except his likeness only, so that no suffering may be understood to apply to him. This is unspeakable silliness on your part. After all, you were unaware, it seems, that since God the Father does all things without suffering, he will also beget without suffering and is superior to fire (since the argument forces us to come down to this level), which begets burning without undergoing suffering or division understood corporeally.

Let those who are eager only for conjecture and who heedlessly view blasphemy not as an unholy thing but a virtue, hear this: if they say that the Son is classified with the Father only by the property of likeness, he will have no security when it comes to his good properties, but he will surely risk the fact that he is God by nature, and there is a possibility that he will also admit of a change for the worse. After all, the statement, "You are the seal of likeness,"[150] was made to the governor of Tyre, and reason demands that we attribute these words to the person of the devil. The one to whom this statement is addressed, however, is found to have fallen from the likeness.

So now you see quite clearly from these instances how merely being in the likeness of God is no guarantee of unmoved stability in spiritual things, and how [**447**] being rightly sealed in the nature of the creator does not mean that they will endure unalterably in whatever good properties these beings may be in. For they too fall and are brought down, often changing into a worse mind than they had at the beginning. It is possible, then, according to this principle, that since the Son ascends to likeness with the Father by identical action alone, without resting on any natural support but maintaining his stability by the inclination of his will alone, he could undergo change. Or, even if he were not to suffer change, he would find that his not suffering was the fruit of an admirable choice rather than the steadfastness of his natural stability as God.

What then, most excellent sirs? Has the Son stopped being true God on us? And if this turns out to be so, according to you, why do we worship him? Why is he glorified along with God the Father? And why is he borne aloft on the highest powers as God? Were the holy seraphim themselves ignorant, along with us, that they were led far astray from what is right, glorifying one who is not God by nature? They err, it seems, when they call one whose honor equals theirs the Lord of Sabaoth.[151] Or shall we not say that the highest powers (the rulers, thrones, authorities and dominions)[152] are eager to show themselves conformed to God,

[150]Ezek 28:12 (LXX). [151]Is 6:3. [152]Col 1:16.

as far as they are able? After all, if an animal of the earth (I mean a human being), which is so insignificant compared with those creatures, has been honored with the glory of being conformed to God, why would we not think that far better honors are allotted to those who are far better than we? How then do they call him Lord of Sabaoth and encircle him like bodyguards, ministering to him as to the king of all?[153] Why does he sit with the Father himself—at his right hand at that—the slave with the master, the creature with the creator? **[448]** As for an absence of suffering and alteration that comes from attention and watchfulness, would it not be more fitting to ascribe this to originate beings rather than to one who is God in his essence, who has impassibility by nature? This is obvious even if they will not say so. Who then will endure these babblers, or how will they not rightly hear, "Woe to them who are drunk without wine"?[154]

But perhaps they will be ashamed of the absurdities that result from such arguments and progress to the point where they will say that the Son was sealed by the Father into his exact likeness. And so they will say, he is in an unchangeable nature, even though he is not from the Father.

How then, tell me, will what is not from God by nature bear his properties? And how will what does not proceed from the divine nature according to the true mode of generation be found to have an essential share in the qualities of the divine nature? It is, I think, clear and agreed on by all that the properties of the divine nature are completely inaccessible to the creation and that the qualities that belong to it by nature would never arise, in an equal and identical way, in anything else that exists. For example, immutability exists in God by nature, and so it does not exist in us at all. A kind of stability, however, makes us like that immutability, through attention and watchfulness, which do not allow us readily to go after what we should not.

But if it is at all possible, as they claim, that one of the divine properties exists in something that is not from the divine by nature, and it will exist in the same way as it exists in the divine nature, what, tell me, is ultimately to prevent all the divine properties from descending and existing in those who are not God by nature? After all, if nothing at all prevents one property (I mean immutability) from finding a place, the rest will find a place as well. And what follows from this? Utter confusion. Will not the superior descend below and the inferior ascend above to the place on high? What **[449]** is now to prevent the most high God from being dragged down to our level and us, in turn, from becoming Gods, just like the Father, when there no longer is or is perceived to be any difference between us, since the qualities that belong to God alone will come to us and exist in us by nature? But since God the Father, it seems, contains in himself alone the properties by which we would be like him, we remain human beings, and the angels, along with us, remain what they are, not ascending to the level above all things. If God should want to show himself superior to jealousy, as it were, by placing his own attributes in the power of all, there would surely be many Gods by nature, capable of creating the earth, heaven, and all other creation. Once the qualities that are in the creator by nature reside in them, how could they not become like him? What prevents that which shines with equal good properties from appearing in equal glory?

But surely the enemies of God see what a great multitude of bizarre ideas this line of thinking heaps on us, and that multitude cries out against the dullness that is in them. As it is, the divine will remain in its own nature, and the created will participate in it through a spiri-

[153]Is 6:3. [154]Is 28:1 (LXX).

tual relationship but will in no way ascend to the dignity that unchangeably belongs to the divine. Equipped with this argument, we will find that immutability is in the Son essentially. Therefore, he is God by nature, and in the end he is necessarily from the Father so that nothing that is not from the Father by nature may reach equal divine dignity.

But since they put forward their argument to us as incontestable, saying that the Son is other than the Father as an image in relation to its archetype—and through this sophistical ingenuity they think they are severing him from the substance of the one who begat him—they will be caught in no small ignorance **[450]** having practiced making all their assertions to no effect, as if those assertions were truly able to bring about the purpose they have in mind. Why in the world are they straining at this in vain? On what basis do they cut the Son off from the Father merely because of the difference there is in his own existence? The fact that he exists in his own person does not, of course, show that he is alien to the substance of the one who begat him. He is, as everyone agrees, from the Father on the grounds that he is from his substance, and he is also in the Father because he exists in him by nature. You will hear him say in one place, "I came from the Father and am come,"[155] and at another, "I am in the Father, and the Father is in me."[156] He will not withdraw to a personhood that is completely and in every way separate, seeing that the holy Trinity is understood to be in one divine nature. Since, however, he is in the Father in a way or position that is inseparable, because of his consubstantiality, he will also be understood to be from him in a procession that is manifested ineffably, as in the case of rays of light. After all, he is light from light. Therefore, he is in the Father and from the Father, inseparably and at the same time divisibly, since he is understood to be an imprint as well as an image with its own existence over against its archetype. However, we will not simply assert this point, but we will confirm it with examples from the law, fortifying on all sides the power of the truth against the heterodox.

Now the law instructed the Israelites to bring a ransom for every person, "half of a double drachma."[157] And one stater contains a double drachma. Even in this, Christ himself was once again sketched for us. He offered himself for all and by all, as it were, a ransom to God the Father. And he is considered to be in one drachma, as it were, but not separable from the other because there are two drachmas in one coin, as we already said. This is how **[451]** the Son may be understood in relation to the Father and the Father in relation to the Son. Both are in one and the same nature, but each one is distinguishable in turn since each exists in his own person, yet without being completely cut off or one being divided from the other. Just as there are two drachmas in one coin, and each has an equal share in the mass and neither has a lesser amount, so also you may understand the absolutely unaltered quality of the Son's substance over against God the Father, and, conversely, of the latter's substance over against him. Then you will have a sound principle for understanding everything that is said about him.

6:28-29 They said to him, "What must we do, to be doing the work of God?" Jesus answered and said to them,

The inquiry does not come from a good intention, nor, as one might suspect, does the question proceed from a desire to learn on their part. It comes from sheer false pretense. As if deigning to learn nothing beyond what they already knew, they all but say something like, The writings of Moses are sufficient for us, sir.

[155]Jn 8:42. [156]Jn 14:10. [157]Ex 30:12-13.

We know all we need to know about what one should strive for who is acquainted with the divine works. What new thing will you bring in addition to what was appointed at that time? What strange thing will you teach that was not announced to us before through the divine words? The question then comes out of folly rather than out of a true desire to learn.

You have this sort of situation also in blessed Matthew. A certain young man, overflowing with a wealth of possessions that is not at all easy to acquire, was intimating that he would enter into the due service of God. When he came to Jesus, he eagerly asked what he must do to be found an heir of eternal life.[158] **[452]** The Lord said to him, "Surely you know the commandments: you shall not murder, you shall not commit adultery, you shall not swear falsely," and whatever else goes with these.[159] But he, speaking as one who lacked none of these things, or even as one rejecting an explanation that fell far short of his own behavior, said, "All these things I have kept from my youth. What do I still lack?"[160] So he joined arrogance to ignorance in the words "what do I still lack?" And they did the same thing when, from sheer pretense and an inflated view of their own wisdom, they said, "What must we do, to be doing the work of God?"

A more moderate view of oneself, then, is a good thing, and it is the work of a noble soul to rely on teachers for a thorough knowledge of what is profitable and so to yield to whatever lessons they are pleased to offer, since they have greater knowledge. After all, how could they be at all accepted among the rank of teacher if they have no more understanding than the mind of their students would have, when the students' progress toward the greater will barely make it to their level, according to the Savior's statement, "A student is not above the teacher,"[161] and, "It is enough for the student to be like the teacher"?[162]

6:29 "This is the work of God, that you believe in the one whom he has sent."

Next, the Lord most vehemently attacks the senselessness of the questioners, though still secretly and obscurely. Now someone might suppose, as far as the simplest sense of the statement is concerned, that Jesus is giving them no other command than that they should believe in him. When one examines the sense of the words, however, one will see that they refer to something else since he was fashioning his discussion of these matters exceedingly well, fitting it to the senselessness of the questioners. **[453]** Since they thought that they had sufficient learning from the law for how to do works that are pleasing to God, they irreverently reject the teaching of our Savior. "What must we do," they say, "to be doing the work of God?"

He, however, needed to show them that they were still very far removed from worship that is dear to God and that they knew nothing at all of what was truly good—they, that is, who devote themselves to the letter of the law and fill their mind with mere types and figures. And so—and this is with great significance—he contrasts the fruit of faith with the worship of the law and says, "This is the work of God, that you believe in the one whom he has sent." In other words, it is not what you thought, he says, looking only at the types. Rather, know this, even if you do not want to learn it, that the lawgiver was never pleased with your sacrifices of oxen, and you did not need to sacrifice sheep to God, as though he willed or demanded it. What good is frankincense, though it swirl in the air with its fragrant smoke? What will a goat profit, he says, or costly offerings of cinnamon? God does not eat the flesh of bulls or drink the blood of goats.[163] He knows "all the birds of heaven, and the bloom of the fields is with"

[158]Lk 18:18. [159]Lk 18:20. [160]Mt 19:20. [161]Mt 10:24. [162]Mt 10:25. [163]Ps 50:13 (Ps 49:13 LXX).

him.[164] He hates and rejects your festivals, and he does not smell the offerings in your assemblies, as he himself says somewhere.[165] Nor did he speak "to your fathers concerning whole burnt offerings and sacrifices."[166] Therefore, this is not "the work of God." The work of God is "that you believe in the one whom he" himself "has sent." And indeed, salvation through faith is truly superior to worship that is of the law and in types, and grace that justifies is superior to the commandment that condemns. **[454]**

The work then of a soul who loves God is faith in Christ. It is far better to strive to become wise through the words about him than to attend to typological shadows. In addition to this, you should next marvel at the following. Although Christ is not in the habit of answering those who question him to test him, he does answer the present question as part of his *oikonomia,* even though he knew they would not profit from it and that it would be for their condemnation, just as he says in the case of others, "If I had not come and spoken to them, they would not have sin, but now they have no excuse for their sin."[167]

6:30-31 Then they said to him, "What sign do you do that we may see and believe you? What work do you perform? Our fathers ate manna in the desert, as it is written: 'He gave them bread from heaven to eat.'"

The disposition of the Jews reveals itself little by little, though it is somewhat hidden and still buried in less than clear reasoning. They said from their ignorance, "What must we do, to be doing the work of God?"[168] As we said before, they thought the command of Moses was enough to enable them to be guided into all wisdom. They thought this wisdom would enable them to know how to do what is pleasing to God. But although their intention was unknown, it is now being laid bare and, little by little, comes to the fore more plainly. "For nothing is hidden," according to the voice of the Savior, "that will not be revealed."[169]

Why then do they say, "What sign do you do?" They are saying that the blessed Moses is held in honor, and quite rightly—he was appointed as a mediator between God and humanity—and even he gave a sufficient sign. **[455]** All who were with him "ate manna in the desert." But you, since you come to us in a greater position than his and do not shrink from adding to the decrees of old, with what signs will you convince us? What wonders will you show us to introduce yourself as an author of new teachings to us? By these words, our Savior's statement is shown to be true when he said that they thought they should seek him not in order to marvel at him for the things he did in a way befitting God but because they ate the loaves and were satisfied.[170] They are convicted by what they now say because they demand a sign from him—and not just any sign, but the sign that Moses (so they thought) performed when he fed the people who came out of Egypt—not for one day but for the entire forty years in the desert by the supply of manna. It seems they have absolutely no understanding of the mysteries in the Holy Scriptures. They do not think it right to attribute the performance of the miracle to the divine power of the one who worked it; instead, with utter ignorance they crown the head of Moses for it. Therefore, they demand from Christ a sign equal to that one, granting nothing marvelous at all to the sign that was shown them for a day, even if it should perhaps be found great; instead, they insist that the provision of food should extend indefinitely. Even with that, he would have barely shamed them into assenting and considering the power of the Savior to be most glorious and to think of his teaching as something they ought to

[164]Ps 50:11 (Ps 49:11 LXX). [165]Amos 5:21. [166]Jer 7:22. [167]Jn 15:22. [168]Jn 6:28. [169]Lk 8:17. [170]Jn 6:26.

listen to. And so it is clear that, even if they do not say it altogether clearly, they pay no attention to signs whatsoever, but under the pretext of wanting to marvel at them, they are zealous to serve the impure pleasures of the belly. **[456]**

CHAPTER SIX

Concerning the manna, that it was a type of Christ's presence and the spiritual gifts given through him.

6:32 Then Jesus said to them, "Truly, truly I say to you, it was not Moses who gave you bread from heaven."

Here too the Savior accuses them head-on of a lack of understanding and of the deepest ignorance of the writings of Moses. They certainly should have clearly known that Moses was administering gifts from God to the people and, conversely, from the Israelites to God. He himself was not the worker of any of the miracles, but he was a servant and underling of whatever the supplier of all good things might will to do for the benefit of those he called out of slavery. So what they were impiously imagining, Christ quite vehemently intercepts. How then could it not be replete with foolishness and blasphemy to take qualities that are fitting and due to the divine nature alone and ascribe them to human honor rather than to the divine nature? Since he deprived the teacher Moses of the miracle and removed the wondrous deed from his hand, it should certainly be clear that he ascribes the glory to himself instead, along with the Father, even if he should avoid stating it more clearly because his hearers were not instructed. After all, it was **[457]** truly not beyond the realm of expectation that they would be enraged and inflamed to a fever pitch of anger, as though Moses were being insulted by these words, without inquiring in any way into the truth of the matter or recognizing the honor of the one speaking. They heedlessly pursue only the necessity of honoring Moses. And there is no good reason for this when he is compared with what is superior to him.

Let us learn then to practice reverence toward our holy fathers with more discernment and reason and to render, as it is written, "fear to whom fear is due and honor to whom honor is due."[171] We will do no wrong at all if we attribute to each one what is fitting in proper proportion since "the spirits of the prophets are subject to the prophets."[172] But when a statement is introduced about Christ our Savior, then we must say, "Who among the clouds will be equal to the Lord, or who will be like the Lord among the sons of God?"[173]

6:32-33 "But my Father gives you the true bread from heaven. For the bread of God is the one who comes down from heaven and gives life to the world."

It was necessary not only to deprive Moses of God-befitting authority, as they understood it, and to show that he was a servant of the miracle working rather than the bestower of it, but also to show that the miracle itself, even though wondrously wrought, was a small thing and that in comparison with the greater, it was nothing at all. Think of Christ crying out something like, You, sirs, consider great deeds to be small and paltry, and you confine the lavish generosity of the Lord of all to the narrowest limits. With no small ignorance do you consider the manna to be "the bread from heaven," even though it fed only the race of the Jews in the desert, **[458]** while the other peoples throughout the world are countless. You thought that God wanted to show such constrained love for humanity that he provided

[171]Rom 13:7. [172]1 Cor 14:32. [173]Ps 89:6 (Ps 88:7 LXX).

food for one people alone. But in fact, those gifts of food were types of more universal blessings, and they were a partial demonstration of his generosity in general, as a pledge to those who first received it. However, now that the time of truth is at our door, "my Father gives you bread from heaven." This bread was sketched in shadows by the provision of manna to the ancients. Let no one think, he says, that this is the true bread from heaven, but let them rather acknowledge him who clearly has the power to feed the whole earth and, in short, to give "life to the world."

He accuses the Jew then of clinging to events that occurred in type and refusing to investigate the beauty of the truth. That was not the manna in the strict sense, but rather the only begotten Word of God himself was the manna, who comes from the substance of the Father, since he is life by nature and the one who gives life to all. Since he sprang from the living Father, he too is life by nature; and since giving life is the work that belongs to one who is life by nature, Christ gives life to all things. As our bread, which is taken from the earth, does not allow the weak nature of the flesh to decay, so also he, through the operation of the Spirit, gives life to the spirit, and not only that, but he preserves the body itself in incorruption.

Now that our meditations have come to the subject of manna, it would not hurt, I think, to consider and say a little bit about it, bringing forward piece by piece a passage about it from the books of Moses. In this way, once we have explained the passage with clarity, **[459]** we will see correctly everything the passage intends concerning it. We will demonstrate at every step that Christ himself is the true manna who is understood to be supplied to the ancients in type from God the Father. This is the beginning of the passage: "On the fifteenth day of the second month after they had gone out of Egypt, the whole assembly of the Israelites began to grumble against Moses and Aaron. And the Israelites said to them, Would that we had died, struck by the Lord in the land of Egypt, when we sat by the fleshpots and we were eating bread to the full! For you have led us into this desert to kill this whole assembly with hunger."[174]

Now the subject of the historical narrative is clear and quite easy to see, and I think it requires no discussion to probe the obvious meaning. So we will look only at what is spiritual as we discuss it. The Israelites, then, while still in the land of Egypt, were typologically keeping the feast to Christ, as God commanded them. By taking part in the banquet of lamb, they barely escaped the violence of the tyrant Pharaoh and shook off the intolerable yoke of slavery. Then, after they miraculously crossed the Red Sea, they were in the desert. They were starving there, so they began to crave flesh to eat, and they were dragged down to their accustomed desire for bread. So they began to grumble against Moses, and they stooped so far as to repent of the gift of God for which they ought to have given thanks without measure.

Egypt then would be darkness, and it should be understood as the condition of the present age and the worldly state of affairs. We were enrolled in it, as in some country, and we endure a bitter servitude there, **[460]** working in no way for God but accomplishing only what delights the devil. We hurl ourselves down to the pleasures of the impure flesh like mud or stinking mire, enduring toil that is profitless and without pay and pursuing a love of pleasure that is not without its own demands, if I may put it that way.

However, when the law of God addresses us in a spiritual way, and we then see the bitter slavery in these passages, then, oh then do we thirst for a departure from all evil and come to

[174]Ex 16:1-3.

Christ himself as to the source and door of freedom! When we are furnished with security and grace through his precious blood, when we have left the carnal condition of this life, like some turbulent and stormy sea, and we end up outside all worldly uproar, we then come to a more spiritual and purer state, living in the desert as it were.

But the one who is instructed by the law in virtue does not escape the testing of that virtue. Therefore, when we now find ourselves in this condition, we fall into temptations that test us, and we are sometimes devoured by a reminder of carnal desires. Then the desire sets us on fire with overwhelming intensity, and we often cry out from weariness, even though the divine law has called us to freedom, as we hunger, so to speak, for our former accustomed pleasures. And since we place little value on the labors we have already undertaken for self-control, we no longer view worldly slavery as evil. The will of the flesh is in fact sufficient to drag the mind into faintheartedness regarding blessings.

"And the Lord said to Moses, Behold, I will rain bread from heaven for you."[175] Now you can see quite clearly in this passage **[461]** what is sung in the Psalms, "He gave them the bread of heaven; mortals ate the bread of angels."[176] But it is clear to everyone, I think, that of the rational powers in heaven, none could be thought to be both bread and food besides the Only Begotten of God the Father. Therefore, he is the true manna, the bread from heaven, who is supplied to every rational creature by God the Father. And going into the order of the passage before us, we say this: Observe how the divine grace from above draws human nature to itself and saves it in manifold ways, even though that nature is sometimes sick because of what it is accustomed to. The desire of the flesh falls on the mind, pushes it down like a stone and forces it tyrannically to its own will. But Christ leads us back again, as with a bridle, to a desire for better things, and he brings back those who were ill to a God-loving disposition. Behold! Behold! To those who are slipping down into bodily pleasures, he promises to supply food from heaven, namely, the comfort of the Spirit, the spiritual manna. That is because through this we are strengthened for all endurance and courage, and we gain the benefit of not falling due to weakness into what is not right. The spiritual manna, therefore, that is, Christ, was strengthening us for godliness in ancient times as well.

Now that we have gone into a digression out of necessity, I do not think it is right to allow the subject to remain unexamined since it has much that brings us profit. Someone then may reasonably say, Why does God, who loves both humanity and virtue so much, lag behind in his promise when he should have acted before their request? He in no way punishes those who were so perverse in their disposition, although he punishes them **[462]** later when they are sick with the same desire and are imagining abundant bread and fleshpots and indulging in a yearning for the foulest onions. We will find in Numbers that certain people are punished, and the place where they were then encamping was called "the graves of lust, for there they buried the people who lusted."[177]

Now as to the first point, we will say that it is altogether fitting for him to wait for their desires to arise and so to demonstrate his provision at the right time. After all, for those who are well off, the gift is most welcome when certain desires appear before it and precede it, creating a thirst for what is not yet present. But the human soul would have no sense of gratitude without striving and laboring for the pleasures of being well off.

But perhaps you will say that there was no petition at all on their side, but rather grumbling, apostasy and outcry, since this would be

[175]Ex 16:4. [176]Ps 78:24 (Ps 77:24 LXX). [177]Num 11:34. The Hebrew name is Kibroth-hattaavah.

closer to the truth. In response to this, we say that a petition through prayer would be fitting for those who are perfect in disposition, but grumbling, however it happens, on the part of those who are weaker from weariness will in some way participate in this, and the Savior, who loves everyone, is not altogether angry at this. Just as for those who are still babies, crying sometimes suffices as a request for their needs, and by it the mother is often summoned to find out what will please the infant, so also for those who are still babies and have not yet progressed to understanding, their crying, so to speak, from weariness has the force of a petition to God. He does not punish them at first, even though he sees them weakened by earthly desires, but he punishes them after a time for the following reason, it seems to me. Those who had just departed from the Egyptians had not yet received the manna, nor do they have the bread from **[463]** heaven that strengthens the human heart. So they understandably fall into fleshly desires, and for this reason they are forgiven. But once they have been fed by the Lord, as it is written, and they prefer corporeal goods to spiritual ones, they now undergo a most just punishment, and over and above their suffering they will be assigned a memorial of their suffering. The name "graves of lust" is given to the place of their punishment.

"And the people will go out and will gather the daily portion each day."[178] We will consider the perceptible manna a type of the spiritual manna. And the spiritual manna signifies Christ himself, while the perceptible manna alludes to the coarser teaching of the law. Now the gathering is daily for good reason, and the lawgiver prevents them from keeping any for the next day. By this he subtly indicates through an enigma to the ancients that when the time of salvation comes to light in which the Only Begotten appears in the world with flesh, the types of the law will be made void, and gathering food from them will be vain since the truth itself now lies before us for our pleasure and enjoyment.

"On the sixth day, they will prepare what they have brought in, and it will be double what they have gathered."[179] Observe again, that you may understand, that he does not allow them to gather perceptible manna on the seventh day, but he commands what was already provided and gathered to be prepared as food beforehand. That is because the seventh day signifies the time of our Savior's advent, during which we keep the sabbath in holiness by ceasing from the works of sin as we receive for food both the fulfillment of our faith and the knowledge that already adorns **[464]** us through the law. We certainly do not still gather it from necessity, as it were, since a more glorious food lies before us, and we have the bread from heaven. Twice as much manna is gathered before the holy seventh day. And you may understand from this, it seems to me, that when the law comes to a close, reaching the fulfillment of its time, and the holy seventh day is now beginning, that is, the advent of Christ, the procurement of heavenly goods will be in a sense twice as much, and the grace will be double since it introduces the gospel teaching in addition to the benefits from the law. This is what the Lord himself may be understood to teach when he says somewhere in the form of a parable, "Therefore every scribe who has been trained in the kingdom of heaven is like a rich man who brings out of his treasure what is new and what is old."[180] What is old is from the law, but what is new comes through Christ.

"And Moses and Aaron said to the whole company of the Israelites, 'In the evening you will know that the Lord brought you out of Egypt. In the morning you will see the glory of the Lord when the Lord gives you meat to eat

[178]Ex 16:4. [179]Ex 16:5. [180]Mt 13:52.

in the evening and bread to the full in the morning.'"[181] Moses is promising the Israelites that quail will be supplied to them by God in the evening, and he insists that by this they will know clearly that the Lord led them up out of Egypt. But in the morning, he says, you will distinctly see the glory of the Lord when you receive bread to the full. Again, consider the difference between each of the statements. The quail signifies the law since this bird always flies low to the ground. You may also view in the same way those who are led by the law to a piety that is low to the ground through types, **[465]** concerning sacrifices, I mean, and purifications and Jewish washings. These are a little above the earth and seem to rise above it, but they are in fact in the earth and about it since that which is perfectly good and exalted in understanding is not in the law. Furthermore, it is supplied in the evening. This statement signifies to us either the obscurity of the letter or the dark condition of the world that does not yet have the true light, that is, Christ, who after becoming human says, "I have come as a light into the world."[182] He says that the Israelites will know that the Lord brought them up out of Egypt. Only a general knowledge of the salvation through Christ is seen in the books of Moses because grace is not yet present personally. He was suggesting this very thing when he added, "In the morning you will see the glory of the Lord when he gives you bread to the full." When the mist of the law is dispersed like night and the spiritual sun rises on us all, we will see the glory of the now present Lord in a mirror,[183] obtaining the bread of heaven to the full, I mean, Christ himself.

"In the evening, quails came up and covered the camp. And in the morning, when the dew lifted around the camp, behold, on the face of the desert was a small white thing like coriander seed."[184] Notice once again the arrangement of the ideas. Concerning the quail, he says that they covered the camp. But concerning the manna, he says that in the morning, when the dew lifted, it came down around the camp on the face of the desert. The **[466]** teaching of the law, I mean the teaching in types and figures that we have compared with the appearance of quails, covers the synagogue of the Jews. "There is," as Paul says, "a veil over their heart" and "a hardening in part."[185] When morning comes, that is, when Christ is now risen and flashes forth to the whole world, and when the dew lifts, that is, the coarse and mist-like introduction of the law's commands (since Christ is the end of the law[186] and the prophets), then indeed the true manna from heaven will surely come down to us, I mean the gospel teaching. It will come not on the synagogue of the Israelites but "around the camp," that is, to all the Gentiles, and "on the face of the desert," that is, the church of the Gentiles. Concerning this church it is said somewhere that "more are the children of the desolate than of her who has a husband."[187] That is because the grace of the spiritual manna is scattered over the whole world. This grace is also compared with coriander and called a "small thing" because the power of the divine word is truly subtle and cools the seething passions. It lulls to sleep the fire of carnal motions within us and enters into the depths of the heart. They say that the activity inherent in the natural property of this herb, that is, coriander, provides a most cooling effect.

"When the Israelites saw it, they said to one another, 'What is it?' For they did not know what it was."[188] Since they are not accustomed to something miraculously coming into being and they cannot say from their experience exactly what it might be, they say to one another, "What is it?" And what they said as a

[181]Ex 16:6-8. [182]Jn 12:46. [183]2 Cor 3:18. [184]Ex 16:13-14. [185]2 Cor 3:15; Rom 11:25. [186]Rom 10:4. [187]Is 54:1. The Greek word for "desolate" is the adjectival form of the word for "desert." [188]Ex 16:15.

question they make the name for the thing, and they call it in the Syrian language "manna," **[467]** that is, "What is it?" And you may understand from this how Christ was going to be unknown among the Jews. Experience showed that what prevailed in the type also had force in the truth.

"And Moses said to them, Let no one leave any of it until morning. They did not listen to Moses, however, but they left some of it until morning, and it bred worms and stank. And Moses was angry at them."[189] Now the morning in this passage signifies the bright and shining time of the advent of our Savior, when the darkness of the law was scattered, as it were, along with the diabolical mist among the Gentiles, and the Only Begotten arose on us like light, and the spiritual daybreak was revealed. So the blessed Moses commands that the typical manna not be left until morning. When the aforementioned time rises on us, the shadows of the law are now superfluous and completely out of season because of the truth that is now present. Paul has shown that the righteousness based on the law is useless now that Christ has appeared. He says concerning Christ, "For his sake I have suffered the loss of all things," that is, glorying in the law, "and I consider them rubbish that I may gain Christ and be found in him, not having a righteousness of my own based on the law, but one that is by faith in Jesus Christ."[190] So do you see how as a wise man he took care that none was left till morning? But those who kept it till morning are a type of the Jewish multitudes who were not going to believe in him. Their eager desire to keep the law according to the letter would be the cause of rottenness and worms. **[468]** Do you hear how the lawgiver is furious with them?

"And Moses said to Aaron, 'Take one golden pot, put a full omer of manna in it, and place it before God to be kept.'"[191] This is truly the right time for us to be filled with wonder at this and say, "O the depth of the riches and wisdom and knowledge of God!"[192] Truly incomprehensible is the knowledge hidden in the God-inspired Scriptures. "A great depth," as it is written, "who can find it out?"[193] You see then how our last comment fits this passage. Since Christ himself has been revealed to us as the true manna, and he was shown to the ancients in the form of an image through a type, he needs to teach in the present passage what sort of virtue, and whose virtue, will fill those who treasure up the spiritual manna in themselves and bring Jesus into the inmost recesses of their hearts through right faith in him and perfect love. You hear how a full omer of manna was placed in a golden vessel by the hand of Aaron to be kept before God. The holy and truly pious soul, as it perfectly labors to give birth in itself to the message about Christ and as it receives the entire heavenly treasure, will be a precious vessel, as of gold. It will be offered to God the Father by the high priest of all, and it will be brought into the presence of the one who holds all things together and preserves them so that it too may be protected, since he does not allow even what is perishable in its own nature to perish utterly. The righteous one then is described as having the spiritual manna (that is, Christ) in a golden vessel, as it were, and ascending **[469]** to incorruption (which is like being in the sight of God) and remaining to be kept (that is, to a long and endless life).

Christ rightly then convicts the Jews of being senseless beyond measure and of thinking that the manna was supplied to the ancients by the all-wise Moses. He shows that their reasoning stops at this point, and they do not even consider any of the things foretold through Moses. He says, "Truly I say to you, it was not Moses who gave you" the manna.[194] They should have thought about it and

[189]Ex 16:19-20. [190]Phil 3:8-9. [191]Ex 16:33. [192]Rom 11:33. [193]Eccles 7:24. [194]Jn 6:32.

realized that Moses contributed the mere service of mediation. The gift was not an invention of human hands but a work of grace from above. This grace sketches what is spiritual with items that are coarser, and it signifies for us the bread from heaven. This bread gives life to the whole world; it does not show partiality, as it were, by feeding one race, that of Israel.

6:34-35 They said to him, "Lord, give us this bread always." Jesus said to them,

The intent of the Jews is clearly laid bare by these words, even though they very much desire to hide it. See how no one can claim that the truth is lying when it says that they were not quick to follow him because they saw the signs but because they ate of the bread and had their fill.[195] They could reasonably be accused of great dullness, and I suppose it is truly necessary to say to them, "Behold, O foolish and senseless people, who have eyes and do not see, ears and do not hear."[196] After all, with many words, as one can see, Christ our Savior is drawing them away from carnal ideas and with his all-wise teaching making them fly **[470]** to spiritual insight. Nevertheless, they do not ascend above what is profitable to the flesh. When they hear about bread that gives life to the world, they still imagine bread from the earth since their belly is their god, as it is written,[197] and they are overcome by the evils of the stomach so that with good reason they hear that their "glory is in their shame."[198]

You will find this discussion quite similar to that with the Samaritan woman. Christ our Savior spends a long time in discussion with her and teaches her about the spiritual water, unambiguously saying, "Everyone who drinks of this water will thirst again, but whoever drinks of the water that I will give them will never thirst. The water that I will give them will become in them a spring of water gushing up to eternal life."[199] She is carried away, however, because of her dullness. She forsakes the spiritual fountain and, giving no consideration to it at all, sinks down to the gift of perceptible wells and says, "Sir, give me this water so that I may not thirst or come here to draw."[200] The statement of the Jews, therefore, is related to her statement. Just as she was effeminate because of her nature, in the same way, I think, these too have nothing manly, so to speak, or vigorous in their understanding, but they are feminized, resulting in unmanly desires of the belly. [201] They show what is written about them to be true: "For the fool will speak foolishness, and the fool's heart will think vain thoughts."[202]

6:35 "I am the bread of life."

It is the custom of Christ the Savior, when he explains the divine mysteries that are already foretold, to weave explanations of them that are enigmatic and not very clear. **[471]** He does not allow his word, which is so august, to lie unveiled before those who have only profane and unholy desires so that his words are trampled by them. When he has hidden it in layers of enigmas, however, he does not make it invisible to those with understanding. When he sees some of his hearers who have no learning and who understand nothing at all of what he is saying, he makes clear whatever he wants to show. Removing, as it were, all mist from what he is saying, he sets the knowledge of the mystery before them, stripped bare and easy to see, thereby rendering their unbelief without excuse.

He himself teaches that it was his custom, as we said, to use obscure and rather hidden language when he says in the book of Psalms,

[195]Jn 6:26. [196]Jer 5:21. [197]Phil 3:19. [198]Phil 3:19. [199]Jn 4:13-14. [200]Jn 4:15. [201]Cyril again uses here the conventions of his day in speaking of the feminine as the weaker of the sexes. [202]Is 32:6.

"I will open my mouth in parables."[203] And the blessed prophet Isaiah will no less confirm our explanation of this and show that we have made no mistake when he cries out, "Behold, the righteous king will reign, and the rulers will rule with judgment, and he will be a man who hides his words."[204] He says that the one who utters the following has ruled over us as a righteous king: "I have been appointed king by him on Zion, his holy mountain, declaring the decree of the Lord."[205] And he calls the holy disciples princes who live together in judgment, that is, rightness in all things. They came to Christ the Savior, who often hides his words, and said, "Explain to us the parable."[206] And once when he hears the question, "Why do you speak to the crowds in parables?"[207] he is found to explain the reason with the greatest clarity: "that seeing," he says, "they do not see, and hearing they do not hear, nor do they understand."[208] They were completely unworthy, it seems, since God who judges justly decreed this sentence on them.

[472] The Savior then devised ten thousand turns in his discourse. But when he began to see that his hearers understood nothing, he then says more plainly, "I am the bread of life." He all but pounces on their immeasurable lack of reason, saying, You have superiority over all only in incomparable ignorance. When God announces that he will supply you with bread from heaven and makes you so great a promise in feeding you with manna, you limit the divine generosity. You are not ashamed to stop the grace from above at this point, not realizing that it is a small thing both for you to receive such material blessings from God and for God to give them. So do not believe, he says, that that is the bread from heaven. For "I am the bread of life," who was foretold to you in ancient times in promise and shown to you in type, and I am now present fulfilling the promise I made. "I am the bread of life," not bodily bread, which puts an end only to suffering from hunger and frees the flesh from perishing of it; rather, I remold the whole living being completely unto eternal life and render humanity, which was created to exist forever, superior to death. By this he also hints at the life and grace that comes from his holy flesh, by which the property of the Only Begotten, that is, life, is introduced into us.

We must recognize (since I think we must be devoted to knowledge and zealously track down what brings us profit) that for the entire forty years, God supplied the Israelites with typological manna while Moses was still with them. But when he met the common end of life, and Jesus[209] was now appointed as the commander and general of the Jewish ranks, **[473]** he brought them across the Jordan, as it is written,[210] circumcising them with knives of stone.[211] And when he had brought them into the promised land, he arranged for them to be fed with bread since the all-wise God had now stopped the supply of manna. The type, therefore, will now be transformed into something truer. When Moses was taken away, that is, when the types of the worship of the law became useless, Christ became for us the true Jesus since he saved "his people from their sins."[212] Then we crossed the Jordan. Then we received the circumcision in spirit through the teaching of the twelve stones, that is, the holy disciples. The prophets wrote concerning them, "Holy stones are rolled on the land."[213] The holy stones that go around and run through the whole world are surely those through whom we have been circumcised with a circumcision in the spirit, not done by hands, namely, a circumcision by faith.[214] So when we are called into the kingdom of heaven by Christ (since this, I think, is precisely what it means that some entered the promised land),

[203]Ps 78:2 (Ps 77:2 LXX). [204]Is 32:1-2. [205]Ps 2:6-7. [206]Mt 15:15. [207]Mt 13:10. [208]Mt 13:13. [209]Jesus is the Greek spelling of Joshua. [210]Josh 3. [211]Josh 5:3. [212]Mt 1:21. [213]Zech 9:16. [214]Col 2:11.

then there is no more typological manna for us, since we are no longer nourished by the letter of Moses. But finally the bread from heaven, that is, Christ, nourishes us to eternal life both by supplying us with the Holy Spirit and by participation in his own flesh, placing into us participation with God and destroying death that comes from the ancient curse.

"Whoever comes to me will never hunger, and whoever believes in me will never thirst."

Something is concealed in this passage that we must discuss. It is the custom of Christ the Savior not to argue heatedly about the praises due the saints, but on the contrary to crown them with glorious [474] honors. However, when some of the more unlearned, who do not recognize how superior he is to the saints, give greater glory to them, he changes their mind to their great benefit so that they have a more appropriate understanding, as they consider who the Only Begotten is, knowing that he will surely surpass the saints with an incomparable superiority. He does not, however, make his discussion of this matter crystal clear, but somewhat obscure and free of all boasting. Yet by the observation or comparison of his deeds, his words win the vote of superiority.

For example, he was once talking to the woman from Samaria to whom he promised to give living water. But the woman understood none of what he was saying, and she replied, "Are you greater than our father Jacob, who gave us this well?"[215] When the Savior wanted to convince her that he was both greater than Jacob and in no small measure more worthy of belief, he proceeded to the difference between the waters, saying, "Everyone who drinks of this water will thirst again, but whoever drinks of the water that I will give them, it will become in them a spring of water gushing up to eternal life."[216] And what does this persuade us to think but surely this, that the giver of better gifts is certainly superior to the one with whom he is compared?

Here too he is practicing this sort of explanation and teaching. The Jews were looking down on him and daring to be arrogant, insisting up and down on Moses the lawgiver and repeatedly maintaining that they must follow his words rather than Christ's. They considered the supply of manna and the water gushing from the rock to be the most outstanding proof of superiority over all, even over our Savior Jesus Christ himself. [475] When they did this, as a matter of course, he followed his usual method and did not say plainly that he was greater than Moses, due to the unbridled audacity of his hearers and their great propensity toward anger. But he proceeded again to the miraculous deed itself, and by comparison with the greater, he proves it to be small. "Whoever comes to me will never hunger," he says, "and whoever believes in me will never thirst." Yes, he says, I will agree with you that the manna was given through Moses, but those who ate it were hungry again. And I will grant that water was given to you from the womb of the rocks, but those who drank it thirsted again, and the aforementioned gift gave them only a little temporary enjoyment. But whoever comes to me "will never hunger, and whoever believes in me will never thirst."

What then is Christ promising? Nothing corruptible; rather, he is promising that blessing[217] in the participation of his holy body and blood, which raise a person completely to incorruptibility so that they need none of the provisions that drive away the death of the flesh. I am referring here to food and drink. Next it seems that in this passage he calls either the sanctification by the Spirit or the divine and Holy Spirit himself "water." This designation is often used in the Holy Scrip-

[215]Jn 4:12. [216]Jn 4:13-14. [217]"Blessing" (εὐλογία) is a name for the Eucharist.

tures. The holy body of Christ then gives life to those whom it enters and preserves them to incorruptibility when it is mixed with our bodies. After all, it is understood to be the body of none other than him who is life by nature. It has in itself the full power of the Word, who is united to it. It is endowed with the Word's qualities, as it were, or rather it is filled with his activity by which all things receive life and are kept in existence.

Since these things are so, **[476]** let those who are baptized and have tasted grace know that if they go to church sluggishly and barely at all, if they stay away for a long time from the blessing of Christ, if they feign a reverence deserving of punishment, they will, by refusing to participate in him mystically, decline to be made alive and exclude themselves from eternal life. This refusal, although it may seem to be the fruit of reverence on their part, turns into a snare and a stumbling block. They should instead hurry to obtain strength and zeal so that they show themselves intent on being cleansed from sin. They should also try to practice the most beautiful way of life and so to run with all boldness to participation in life.

But since Satan is multifarious in his deception, he never allows them to think they ought to be sober-minded. Once he has defiled them with evils, he then persuades them to shrink from that grace. That grace would likely bring them back to sobriety from the pleasure that leads to evil, as from wine and drunkenness,[218] to see and consider what is profitable to them. Let us break his chains[219] then and shake off the yoke imposed on us by his oppression and serve the Lord in fear, as it is written.[220] Showing ourselves superior to carnal pleasures through self-control, let us approach the divine and heavenly grace and ascend to holy participation in Christ. This—this is how we will overcome the deception of the devil, and, by becoming participants of the divine and heavenly nature,[221] we will ascend to life and incorruptibility!

6:36 "But I said to you that you have seen me and do not believe."

He struggles with them, using many words, and in every way he urges them to salvation by faith. **[477]** But as God he was not unaware that they would run off to their companion unbelief like some familiar sister and place no value on him who calls them to life. So in order that they may know that Jesus was not unaware of what sort of people they would turn out to be, or to put it more aptly, that they might learn that they are under divine wrath, he brings another charge against them: "But I said to you that you have seen me and do not believe." I foreknew, he says, and clearly foretold that you would surely remain obstinate and, holding fast to your cherished unbelief, be left without a share in my gifts.

And when did Christ say this to them? Remember that he said to the blessed prophet Isaiah, "Go and tell this people, You will indeed hear, but you will not understand; you will indeed see, but you will not perceive. For the heart of this people has become dull."[222] Will not this statement be proven true also by the events before us? They saw—they saw—that the Lord was God by nature when he fed the innumerable multitude that came to him with five barley loaves and two small fish, which he broke up! But although they saw it, "they do not believe" because of the hardening that came like mist on their understanding from the divine wrath. They certainly and without a doubt deserved to suffer this since, when they were entangled in stumbling beyond measure and bound by the unbreakable ropes of their transgressions,[223] they did not receive him who had the power to free them when he

[218]See Joel 1:5. [219]See Ps 2:3. [220]Ps 2:11. [221]2 Pet 1:4. [222]Is 6:9-10. [223]See Prov 5:22.

arrived. This is the reason why "the heart of this people has become dull."

But the following incident will show you even more clearly that because of the greatness of the sign, the Jews realized that Jesus was God by nature. Because they were amazed at what had happened, just as the Evangelist says above, **[478]** they tried to "seize him to make him king."[224] Therefore, the Jews have no more excuse for their lack of understanding. Although they are astonished for good reason at the divine signs, and they have just witnessed works that are proportional to the power of the miracle worker,[225] they practically shrink back from faith in horror, and they leap off the right road, willingly doing a somersault, as it were, into the very depth of destruction.

6:37 "All that the Father gives me will come to me."

It was not fitting for the Lord simply to say, "You have seen me and do not believe." He needed to introduce into the discussion also the reason for their hardening so that they might learn that they have fallen under the divine wrath. Like a skilled physician, then, he both shows them their sickness and uncovers the cause of the sickness, not so that they may remain silent once they have learned about it but so that in every way they may appease the creator of all, who is grieved at them, and for good reason. After all, he would never have been grieved unjustly. The one who knows how to give just judgments would not have rendered such a judgment against them if reason had not summoned him to it, leading inexorably to the necessity of accusing them.

Of course, when the Savior maintains in this passage that all that God the Father should give him will come to him, he is not implying that he himself is unable to bring the believers to himself, since if he willed to do this he would have accomplished it quite easily "by the activity that enables him to subject all things to himself," as Paul says.[226] But since it seems somehow necessary and more fitting to say that those in ignorance were illumined by the divine nature, **[479]** as man he again ascribes the working of the more God-befitting activities to the Father. It was his custom, after all, to do this, as of course we have often said.

Furthermore, it is likely that when he says that "all that he gives him" will be brought to him by God the Father, he is hinting at the people from the Gentiles who are about to be with him but as of yet do not believe. This is a statement of one who is skillfully threatening both that they will fall away from grace and that in their place all who are brought from the Gentiles by the kindness of God the Father will ascend to the Son as the one who is Savior and lifegiver by nature. This is so that as they partake in the blessing[227] that is from him, they may now be made participants of the divine nature and thus be raised to incorruptibility and life and be remolded into the original form of our nature. Therefore, just as someone might bring a sick person to a doctor to drive away the oppressive sickness, in the same way we will say that God the Father brings to the Son those who show themselves worthy of salvation from him. Hardness of heart, therefore, is bitter and absolutely fatal to those who have it. And this is why the prophetic word falls on the Jews, as it distinctly cries out, "Circumcise yourselves to God, and circumcise your hardness of heart, men of Judah and inhabitants of Jerusalem."[228] Not for them, however, but for us has God the Father kept the circumcision of the heart, that is, the circumcision by the Holy Spirit that is performed in the manner of one who is a Jew inwardly.[229] It is right then to flee from their unbelief and zealously to avoid hardness of

[224]Jn 6:15. [225]See Wis 13:5. [226]Phil 3:21. [227]The Eucharist. [228]Jer 4:4. [229]Rom 2:29.

heart, and instead to be refashioned into a more responsive disposition, if we are to avoid the wrath that is on them as we would avoid destruction. **[480]**

"And the one who comes to me I will never cast out."

He says that conversion through faith will not be without profit for those who come to him. He needed to show that being brought by God the Father is truly desirable and is the cause of a myriad of blessings. Those who are called to me by grace from above and come, he says, will have the most excellent blessings. "I will never cast out the one who comes to me," that is, I will not send them away like a useless pot as is said by one of the prophets, "Jechonias was despised like a pot that has no use. He was thrown away and cast out into a land that he did not know. Earth, earth, hear the word of the Lord! Record this man as banished."[230] Therefore, they will not be banished, he says, nor will they be cast out as worthless or remain without a share in my generosity, but they will be brought into my storehouse and dwell in heavenly mansions, and within them they will see themselves possessed of all hope beyond human understanding. "For eye has not seen and ear has not heard nor has it entered into the human heart what God has prepared for those who love him."[231]

Most likely, the words "I will never cast out the one who comes to me" indicate that the believer who comes by divine grace will not be handed over to judgment. You will find that this is what "out" means, as in that parable in blessed Matthew. "The kingdom of heaven," he says, "is like a net that was thrown into the sea and caught fish of every kind. When they pulled it up and brought it ashore, they gathered the good into baskets but threw out the bad."[232] We understand that the good are brought together into the divine and heavenly courts because of his statement that the good are gathered into baskets. But by his **[481]** statement that the useless are cast out, we will see that the ungodly will fall away from all good and go into judgment. Therefore, when Christ says, "The one who comes to me I will never cast out," let us understand it to mean that the people who come to him by faith will never fall under punishment.

With these words, he also seems to imply quite a clever threat against those unusually senseless people. The threat is that if they do not will to be converted expeditiously to the right faith, they will be excluded from all blessings and be separated from friendship with him, even against their will. The same words by which he promises not to cast out the one who comes to him also indicate that he will surely cast out the one who does not come.

Cyril Of Alexandria, on the Gospel According to John, Book 3. [483]

Chapters in the Fourth Book

1. In no way is the Son less than God the Father because he is from him by nature, even though he is said by some to be subject to him; on the words "I have come down from heaven not to do my own will, but the will of the Father who sent me." In this same chapter there is also a most useful discussion of the precious cross of Christ.
2. The holy body of Christ is life-giving; on the words "I am the bread of life," etc., in which he speaks of his own body as bread.
3. The Son is not a participant in the life of someone else, but he is life by nature since he is begotten of God the Father, who is

---

[230] Jer 22:28-30. [231] 1 Cor 2:9. [232] Mt 13:47-48.

life by nature; on the words "Just as the living Father sent me, and I live because of the Father, so whoever eats me will live because of me."

4. The holy tabernacle, which led the people through the desert, was a type of Christ, and so was the ark that was in it and the lamp and the altars, both the altar of incense and the altar of burnt offering. These signified Christ himself; on the words "Where shall we go? You have the words of eternal life."
5. Concerning the feast of tabernacles, that it shows forth the restoration of the hope due the saints and the resurrection from the dead; on the words "Now the Jewish feast of tabernacles was near." **[484]**
6. A discussion of rest on the sabbath, showing in various ways what it means; on the words "If a man receives circumcision on the sabbath, are you angry with me because I healed the whole man on the sabbath?"
7. A discussion of circumcision on the eighth day, showing in various ways what it means; on the words "If a man receives circumcision on the sabbath," etc. **[485]**

OUR FATHER AMONG THE SAINTS CYRIL ARCHBISHOP OF ALEXANDRIA ON THE GOSPEL ACCORDING TO JOHN

BOOK FOUR

Chapter One

In no way is the Son less than God the Father because he is from him by nature, even though he is said by some to be subject to him.

6:38-39 "I have come down from heaven not to do my own will, but the will of the Father who sent me. And this is the will of the one who sent me, that I will lose nothing of all that he has given me, but I will raise it up on the last day."

On the surface, this statement may seem difficult. It may even seem to come very close to causing offense regarding the faith. One might expect us to fall into insuperable difficulties from our opponents because of this statement. But there is nothing at all difficult in it. "For all things are clear to those who understand," as it is written, "and right **[486]** for those who find knowledge,"[1] that is, to those who reverently study to interpret and understand the mysteries contained in the divine Scriptures.

With these words, then, Christ gives us a kind of proof and a clear assurance that the one who comes to him will not be cast out. You know it was for this reason, he says, that I came down from heaven, that is, I became human according to the good pleasure of God the Father, and I did not refuse to undertake even works I did not want to do, until I should nullify the power of death and gain eternal life and resurrection from the dead for those who believe in me. What then was this that Christ both willed and did not will? It was his dishonor from the Jews, the abuse and violence and assaults and scourgings and spitting, and in addition to these things, false

Book 4 [1]Prov 8:9.

accusations, and finally on top of it all, the death of the body. Christ endured these things willingly for us, but if it had been possible for him to accomplish his earnest purpose for us without suffering, he would not have willed to suffer. However, since the Jews were certainly and unavoidably going to inflict these things on him, he accepts suffering, and he makes what he does not want into his will. He does this because of the benefit that comes from his suffering, and God the Father agrees with him and concurs that he must bear all things willingly for the salvation of all. In this we will see most of all the immeasurable kindness of the divine nature since for our sakes it does not refuse to choose rejection.

From the following, you will understand that the suffering on the cross is both unwilled in a sense by Christ our Savior and willed because of us and the good pleasure of God the Father. **[487]** When he was about to ascend to him, he began a dialogue with God in the form of a prayer, saying, "Father, if it is possible, let this cup pass from me; yet not as I will, but as you will."[2] Since the Word was God, immortal and incorruptible, and he was life itself by nature, he could not cringe before death. I think this is perfectly clear to all. Since he has come to be in the flesh, however, he yields to enduring what is proper to the flesh, and he allows himself to cringe before death when it is at the door so that he may show himself truly human. That is why he says, "If it is possible, let this cup pass from me." If it is possible, Father, he says, without undergoing death to obtain life for those who have fallen into death, if death may die without me dying (according to the flesh, that is), let this cup pass, he says. But if this may happen in no other way, he says, not as I will, but as you will. You see how weak human nature is found to be, even in Christ himself, as far as that nature is concerned. But the Word, who is united to it, raises up in it courage worthy of God and re-educates it to a vigorous determination so that it does not entrust itself to what seems right to its own will but follows the divine purpose running full speed to whatever the law of its creator calls us.

You may learn that we are telling the truth about these matters also from the following: "For the spirit is willing," he says, "but the flesh is weak."[3] Christ was not unaware, after all, that it is far beneath God-befitting dignity to seem inferior to death and **[488]** to feel fear because of it. Therefore, he included a fervent defense in what he said. On the one hand, he said that the flesh was weak because of what is proper to it and what belongs to its nature. On the other hand, however, he said the spirit was willing, since it knows that it suffers nothing harmful. Do you see how death was not willed by Christ both because of the flesh and because of the ignominy of the suffering, but at the same time it was willed until he brings the whole world to its fitting consummation intended by the good pleasure of the Father, that is, salvation and life for all? Is he not found surely and truly indicating the same idea to us when he says, "This is the will of the Father," that of those who are brought to me, "I should lose nothing, but I will raise it up on the last day"?[4] As we taught before, God the Father, in his love for humanity, brings the one who lacks life and salvation to Christ, since he is life and Savior.[5]

But I perceive that what I am saying grates on the enemies of the truth. There is no way they will agree with what we have just said. Instead, they will come screaming with a piercing cry, Where are you wandering with our subject, sir, and to what end are you devising these intricate back roads of thought and dragging the discussion away from the

[2]Mt 26:39. [3]Mt 26:41. [4]Jn 6:39. [5]See Cyril's comments on Jn 6:37 (Book 3, chapter 6, pp. 214-15 above).

truth? It seems you are embarrassed, they say, to admit the involuntary subjection of the Son. Is it not obvious to us from his statement that he will in no way lead and rule over the plan of what is to be done, but he is instead subject to the will of the Father? After all, he knows himself to be so far below equality with him that he is somehow forced to take what he does not want and make it his will, and he must do not what seems good to him, but rather what seems good to the Father. Do not tell **[489]** me, they say, that he is subject as man, twisting his statement to refer to the incarnation. Behold, as you see, while he was still God and bare Word and unentangled with the flesh, "he came down from heaven," and even before he put on the form of a slave, he was subject to the Father who was his superior and ruler.

With terrible and lightning-fast words you overtake us, sir, or so you no doubt think! But in fact, these words of yours do not take the straight path but strut right off the well-traveled royal road. You have forsaken the highway, as the saying of the Greeks has it, and you press ahead to cliffs and rocks. Vainly do you contend, in opposition to us, for the Son's obedience to the Father, mentioning it everywhere—as though anyone who is thinking in the right way about this imagines that one ought to hold the opposite of what we've been saying and instead resolve to agree with you on this point. After all, we will refuse to think that the holy and consubstantial Trinity ever has a disagreement among himself, nor is he divided into different opinions, nor does he somehow parcel out what seems good to each, whether it be the Father, the Son or the Holy Spirit. They agree about everything because they are clearly from one divine nature. There is certainly always one and the same will in the entire holy Trinity. Let's move on from this prolonged argument about this! Let the love for arguing, which argues when it is least necessary, be silent. Since no one is upset by this point, it is superfluous for you to go on contending for it.

But since you—accustomed as you are to being absolutely intractable in your thinking and reasoning—call the Son's agreement with the Father's will a subjection of necessity, we will now discuss with you what seems fitting on this point. If this statement were brought forward by you in simplicity, we would have good reason to **[490]** be silent, and we would certainly not probe the lack of distinctions in the statement. But since we see that it has been put forward in bad faith, we must oppose it, trusting in the power of the Holy Spirit and not in our own words.

The Son maintained that he kept himself from his own will not in every respect, or absolutely, or for every intention whatsoever or for every action, but he says that he kept the will of the Father in a specified action, giving forethought as God for our defense against your arguments—at least it seems that way to me. He endures what he did not want and makes it his will for our sakes. I am referring to his suffering on the cross, which is pleasing also to his Father, as we said before. In fact, one can see the proof given right away, and one can see clearly the intention he has that led the Son, as he himself says, to leave his own will and fulfill that of the Father. "This," he says, "is the will of the Father, that I will lose nothing of all that he has given me, but I will raise it up on the last day." The suffering on the cross is seen to be truly unwilled and at the same time willed by the Only Begotten, as we said before. But we will zero in on it in what follows with a more careful investigation that will simplify the truth for the readers.

I will proceed first, however, to an investigation of the subjection you mention, namely, that it is already established and unhesitatingly confessed by you that the wills of the holy Trinity always coincide into one will and purpose. Tell us then, you clever sophists, whether the essence of the Son consists in the name and fact of subjection. [491] Tell us whether this is his nature as, say, human nature is for a human being, or whether he is already existing in his own mode when he subjects himself to the Father, as for example one might imagine in the case of an angel or some other rational power. These beings, since they are and subsist, are capable of turning to subjection.

If you say that the essence of the Son consists in subjection to the Father, he will be a subject rather than a Son. How then, tell me, will you not be shown to be utterly foolish? How could subjection itself be thought to subsist by itself without being in something else that exists? Ordinarily, such qualities are nothing but accidents[6] of necessarily preexisting subjects in which they arise. They are seen to concern substances or are considered to be accidents in substances rather than subsisting by themselves. Take lust, for example, which calls us and carries us to something that exists. It could not exist in itself, but it is conceived in one who is by nature receptive to it. In the same way, subjection to another's will, since it indicates a certain turning toward the necessity of being subject to others, will not be understood to exist in its own nature, but it will be (as a passion or will or desire, perhaps) in something that exists. Besides, the name and the fact of subjection could not, strictly speaking, be understood to be said of anyone absolutely. No one will recognize whether it is good or bad if you do not specify whom the person is subject to. After all, one may be subject to God, but also to the devil. And just as "wise" is a neutral term (for some are "wise to do evil,"[7] but "the wise will inherit glory,"[8] where it is clear that the wisdom is to the good), so also "subjection" has a certain neutrality about it and does not convey the truth definitively. That is because it is not at all clear to whom the subjection will be. Therefore, the nature of the Son is also unclear to us, if it should be understood by you as subjection. [492] Without knowing whom he is subject to, one would not be able to say what the truth is.

We shall see that subjection can never exist of itself in its own mode of being, as we now bring forward a more down-to-earth and obvious argument concerning these matters. Take an argument along these lines. If we grant that for human beings, let's say, existence consists in being subject, we must conclude that when people are not subject, they do not exist at all. How then was it said by the psalmist to someone who already is and exists but is not yet subject, "Be subject to the Lord and beseech him"?[9] Do you see then how utterly foolish it is to think that subjection subsists of itself? Therefore, we must agree that the Son is and exists in his own nature before, and only then say that he is subject to the Father. What then, tell me, is there to force the one who is of the substance of the one who begat him, who is the exact imprint of his nature, to fall from equality with him because of obedience? We think and speak rightly, so we know that he is of the same substance as the one who has begotten him. We confer on him equality in all things, and we will consider him in no way inferior in God-befitting honor. You, however—go ahead and see how you will expel from equal honor with the Father, because of his aforementioned submission, the one who glories in equal possessions because of his identity of substance.

But this very fact, says the opponent, will support our argument: the fact that the Son is subject to the Father and gives no thought to his own will but rather yields to the will of the Father, that is, to one who is above him and greater than he.

But this very fact, sir, which according to your own statement you think will help your argument, will turn out to be nothing other

[6]Outward characteristics. [7]Jer 4:22. [8]Prov 3:35. [9]Ps 37:7 (Ps 36:7 LXX).

than the fruit of your own ignorance. If [493] we were deciding who is superior in dignity and who is greater in glory, your babbling in that case would have seemed to have a point (though just barely). But since we are examining the mode of consubstantiality, how will you not be caught being quite ignorant when you attribute to God the Father superiority over his offspring in this matter? We will not grant that superiority or inferiority or such qualities belong to substance strictly speaking, just as we were saying before about subjection; rather, they are from the outside, and they merely pertain to substances. A subject that already subsists and exists beforehand will perhaps receive superiority or inferiority in comparison with something else. But if there is nothing that underlies and subsists beforehand pertaining to which these qualities arise, how could they exist of themselves when they are understood and defined under the classification of accident?

Therefore, in telling us of greater or lesser, you will not touch the substance of the Only Begotten or even of the Father. Instead, with mere external superiorities or inferiorities you will exalt the Father, so you think, and you will rail against the Son, even though you hear him crying out distinctly, "Anyone who does not honor the Son does not honor the Father," and that everyone ought to "honor the Son just as they honor the Father." [10] Subjects that cannot be separated into alien otherness but have one and the same substance ought to receive equal glory; at least that is what Christ was most excellently teaching when he would not receive "human testimony" about himself,[11] as he himself put it, but came forward himself as his own witness, who is credible and more worthy than all who exist. And he who is truth by nature will surely speak the truth, as we can prove from the very [494] nature of things.

You will probably grant that superiority and inferiority do not belong to the actual substance of anything, but rather they pertain to substances. For example, a man, let's say, will not be greater or less than another man with respect to his being conceived of and called a man. A man will neither be less than another man insofar as he is man, nor will he be greater insofar as he is man. That is because the principle of nature is seen to be equal in the case of all people. The same reasoning would hold in the case of angels and every creature that is counted among creation. Such qualities are therefore found to be utterly out of place regarding the substances themselves; rather, they are accidents of the substances or they pertain to substances, as we have stated above. How then will the Father be greater than the Son; how is God by nature greater than God by nature? The fact that the Son was begotten of him will surely force you, even against your will, to grant that he is of the same substance as him.

Now that it has been established and indisputably admitted that the Son is God by nature, let us investigate, if you please, whether when we ascribe honor to him equal to that of the one from whom he exists, we will in fact be conferring glory on the begetter. Or, more to the point, let us investigate whether we will be doing the opposite when we insult the begotten with lower and lesser honors. After all, it is the Father's glory to beget one who is the same by nature. But the opposite will surely happen if the Son were to lose the natural condition befitting him (although it is not even appropriate to say this!); he would either be inferior in his glory or inferior in anything else that certainly should have belonged to him. In this way, he may clearly be seen to be perfect and true God in all things. If his nature is thus and he honors [495] the Father, do not mock, sir, or be found guilty of ignorantly reproaching what least deserves it.

[10]Jn 5:23. [11]Jn 5:34.

It is certainly appropriate to be amazed also at how he honors and loves the one who begat him, since every species of virtue has as its source and root, as it were, the substance that is above all things. The good qualities appear first in that substance, and then they flow down to us who are made in the image of that substance. For this reason, the lawgiver proclaimed to us that we should honor our father and mother, and he added a most excellent reward to this. He knew, I suppose, that the greatest act of all—an act so great that it is immune to criticism—was to show himself the bestower of a long life. Now in this way, by subjection and obedience to our parents, we are not rendered foreign to them by nature. But being what they are, human beings from human beings, and having and preserving the definition of humanity perfectly, we practice obedience as something in the category of an excellent virtue. This is how you should think of the Father and the Son as well. Being what he is, namely, God from God, perfect from perfect, exact imprint of the substance of his begetter, he will think nothing other than whatever the Father may think, whose counsel and Word he is. He will have the identical will as the Father, compelled by the law of consubstantiality, so to speak, to will all the same good things together with him.

So do not be offended, sir, when you hear him saying, "I have come down from heaven not to do my own will, but the will of the one who sent me." What we were saying at the beginning, we will say again. Christ made this statement about a definite and distinct matter. **[496]** He says these words to teach that he considers dying for all to be willed on the one hand because the divine nature has willed it but unwilled on the other because of the suffering on the cross—and this insofar as the flesh is concerned, which seeks to avoid death. We have already expended many words, but it is fitting for us to see from the very nature of things that suffering on the cross is clearly unwilled, in a sense, by Christ our Savior in that he is a human being. We say then that it was the work of Jewish madness that Christ was going to be crucified no matter what, and this was going to happen without delay at their hands. They were not without practice in the audacity to do such a thing because of what they had already done both to the holy prophets and to whichever saints would have been alive at that time. Since there was no other way to raise what had fallen into death back to life except for the only begotten Word of God to become human (and once he became human he certainly had to suffer), he made what was unwilled into something willed, and the divine nature accepted this because of its love for us.

Wisdom, the craftsman of all, that is, the Son, turned the fabrication of diabolical perversity (I mean his death according to the flesh) into the way of salvation for us and the door of life. The devil's hopes were overturned, and the devil learned the hard way by experience that it is difficult for him to fight against God. The divine psalmist too seems to me to agree with what I have said about this and suggests something like it when he says concerning Christ and the devil, "In his snare will he humble him."[12] The devil laid death as a snare for Christ, **[497]** but he has been humbled in his own snare. Death has been destroyed in the death of Christ, and the tyrant who did not expect to fall was rendered powerless.

It is not difficult to include a long discussion about this, but we will address what is at hand. If the death of Christ was not truly and strictly speaking the work of the will of the Jews and the fruit of their unholy audacity but it was only divine judgment that led him to this suffering, as some think, then would it not be fitting and even necessary that the decree be carried out through human hands, and not

[12]Ps 10:9-10 (Ps 9:30-31 LXX).

otherwise? And how, tell me, would those who are servants of the inexorable decree of God now be justly punished? And how would it have been better for the wretch by whom Christ was betrayed "if that man had never been born"?[13] After all, if the passion were considered to be willed by Christ and in no sense unwilled by him, what penalty could reasonably be exacted from one who is made a servant of the Lord's will and of the things that are inevitably going to happen? Will it not be clear to all that whatever is decreed by the ineffable divine nature must surely happen, and that it must surely happen through agents of some kind? It is possible to see by these arguments and many others that, even though the Son "came down from heaven" to undergo death for all, willingly and at the same time unwillingly, in order to raise everyone "on the last day" because this was decreed by the Father himself for the benefit of all, he does not intend on that account to be considered any different in nature or inferior in any way to the one who begat him.

In fact, I suppose that our opponent is already embarrassed and will not oppose us on this point. **[498]** But to the one who resists and has resolved that further strife is a fitting course, I say the following: if the Son "has come down from heaven" not to do his own will, as he himself says, but that of the Father, and if perhaps the explanation we just gave about the meaning of this passage does not please you, is it not then necessary to say that their wills are somehow opposed to each other and their counsel is divided into contraries? Of course it is. If nothing separates them, there is certainly one will in both, but if he overcomes his own will, which is different from that of the Father, and carries out the Father's will instead, how can we intelligibly say that there is one will, and not rather one will against another?

Let us see then what the Father's will is, since in this way we will also get to know the other will and learn where it may aim. The Father's counsel then, as the Savior himself has said, is that of "all that he has given" him, the Savior should lose nothing, "but he will raise it up on the last day." No one will deny that the Father's will is good and loving. But when we turn to consider the contrary will of the Son, we will find it neither loving nor at all good, since it intends the complete opposite of the Father, not wanting to save us and certainly not wanting to raise us from the dead. How then is he still the good shepherd? How was it that he gave us a sign of his loving kindness by giving his life for us? After all, if he "came down from heaven" of his own accord, how is it that he does not carry out his own will, since he does not destroy what is brought to him but even raises it up on the last day? But if this is not his will, and he is instead serving the will of the Father (namely, when he both raises and saves those who are lost and overcome by death), how will it not be true for us to say that the Son is neither good nor in fact **[499]** loving in any other way? Let the enemies of Christ then cease, since their argument is convicted of blasphemy from every side, and let them stop barking at us with their bitter words about these matters.

6:40 "For this is the will of my Father, that all who look at the Son and believe in him may have eternal life; and I will raise them up on the last day."

Now that he has defined the good will of the Father, he clarifies it and sets it forth more expansively to the hearers for their investigation by taking it up again. He explains clearly what the way of approach would be and what profit people will obtain by being led to it. The Father, then, gives to the Son, who has

[13]Mt 26:24.

the ability to give life, the things that lack life. He gives in this way: through knowledge he inserts something into each one, that is, he inserts the true conception concerning the Son and the ability to have a pure understanding that he is God from true God the Father, so that being so disposed and being adorned by these insights concerning him, each one may be brought to the reward of faith, that is, a long and endless life in blessedness. The Father, then, brings to the Son, through knowledge and God-befitting insights, those to whom he has decreed the divine grace. The Son receives them and gives them life. By placing his own good attribute into those who by their own nature are corruptible, and by pouring the life-giving power of the Spirit into them like a spark of fire, he refashions them completely, making them immortal.

But when you hear that the Father brings and that the Son grants the ability to live again to those who run to him, do not run off into strange ideas so that **[500]** you think each one acts separately on his own with respect to whatever is suitable for his nature. Understand, rather, that the Father is a coworker with the Son, and the Son in turn is a coworker with the Father, and our salvation and rising again from death to life is a work of the entire (so to speak) holy Trinity. Know too that the Father is sufficient for every strength and need, and so is the Son and the Holy Spirit as well. Blessings come to us through the entire holy Trinity, and God the Father is found to be entirely all in all,[14] through the Son in the Spirit.

We must also note, however, that the importance of believing in the Son is found to be very great. After all, it has the reward of life. And if God the Father is known in his natural Son, who could endure any longer those who remove him from the substance of the Father and who have a mouth with no gate to stop blasphemy against him? By the same words with which he promises that he can raise to life that which has fallen into death, he ascends to a natural identity with the one who begat him, since no change now separates them. After all, giving life is a work that is proper to life, and if the Father is life by nature, then the one who is from him by nature, that is, the Only Begotten, will surely also be understood to be life.

6:41 Then the Jews began to grumble about him because he said, "I am the bread that came down from heaven."

Those who understand none of what Christ said are angry again. Their uninstructed mind is especially unmasked by these words. Since they are not able to grasp **[501]** the thoughts which would likely transform them to the better, their mind ends up in uncalled-for pettiness. Will we not find that Christ's statement to the Jews about these matters is true? Why then are they angry? What line of reasoning has brought them to this point? Why are they grumbling? Instead, they should have given closer attention to what he said and from it now examine the truth of the matter. And by the great works that he did they should have arrived at a well-substantiated understanding of whether Christ may be lying when he calls himself the "bread" (that "came down from heaven" no less) or whether he is telling the truth and it is really so. After all, that is how good judges are rightly led to the discovery of what is profitable to them. But because they are not looking for this at all, they are angry, even though Christ showed himself really to be the true bread of life by what had already happened, contrasting himself with the manna that was supplied in type and shadow in the desert to their fathers.

[14] 1 Cor 15:28.

"Whoever comes to me," he says, "will never hunger."[15] He says this on the grounds that those who ate that manna had a short and quite perishable refreshment for the flesh, but those who go to him by faith will ascend not to a benefit like the one they had back then, but they will reap the continuous grace of the blessing.[16]

The mind of the Jews then is led astray because it looks only at earthly matters. This, therefore, is what is sung about them: "Let their eyes be darkened that they may not see, and bend their back always,"[17] so that, never looking up to the knowledge of the divine mysteries, the evil may come to an evil end because of their own senselessness and their utter powerlessness in unbelief. And when we recall the **[502]** writings of Moses, we will find that grumbling at the finest gifts belongs to the Jews as a kind of inheritance. But this fact leads to a bitter end, as the experience of the ancients shows, and the experience of our contemporaries shows no less. The former were grumbling in the desert and making a thankless outcry against God, but "they were destroyed by snakes," as the wise Paul also testified somewhere.[18] The latter are grumbling against Christ and insulting both the lawgiver and the redeemer by such sustained unbelief. But he will command "the serpent, and it will bite them," as it is written,[19] and they will be set before the all-consuming beast as a feast, since unbelief by necessity always meets a catastrophic end.

6:42 And they said, "Is this not Jesus the son of Joseph, whose father and mother we know? How then does he say, 'I have come down from heaven'?"

How ignorant can they be when their understanding is darkened by such unmitigated inebriation! "The heart of this people has become fat," as it is written.[20] It sees absolutely none of what it ought to understand clearly, and it thinks and utters utterly ridiculous ideas. Since they study the writings of the supremely wise Moses and revel in the preaching of the holy prophets, they certainly should have understood that Christ was expected to come to us not apart from the flesh or bodily dress; rather, it was foretold that he would appear in human form and be found in this common garb of all.[21] That is why the prophetic voice proclaims to us that the holy virgin "will conceive and bear a son."[22] And the Lord is found to have sworn to the blessed David the truth, **[503]** which he promised that he would never deny: that he would place someone from the fruit of his loins on his throne, as it is written.[23] He announced ahead of time that a "rod will come out from the root of Jesse."[24]

But they do not perceive it, rushing as they are into such great absurdity. They think that if they know the mother (according to the flesh) of the one foretold to arrive with flesh, they must for this reason certainly deny that he has come down from heaven. Even though we will find that this descent did not happen as far as his body is concerned, nevertheless the divine Word was in the body from the virgin, as in his own temple.[25] He arrived to us from the Father above, and for the salvation of all he took on "the seed of Abraham" so that he may be made "like his brothers in every way"[26] and call human nature to adoption by God. He is thereby shown to be at once both God and a human being. But the Jews do not understand our Savior's *oikonomia* with the flesh, and because they know his mother and father (though he is not his father), they have no qualms about getting angry when Christ says he came down from heaven.

[15]Jn 6:35. [16]"Blessing" refers to the Eucharist. [17]Ps 69:23 (Ps 68:24 LXX). [18]1 Cor 10:9. [19]Amos 9:3. [20]Is 6:10. [21]See Phil 2:7. [22]Is 7:14. [23]Ps 132:11 (Ps 131:11 LXX). [24]Is 11:1. [25]Jn 2:21. [26]Heb 2:16-17.

Even here there is some benefit to be found. These thoughts lead us in our own situation to contemplate the great loss we will suffer if we do not examine the virtue of the saints with the spiritual eyes of our heart and if we do not focus on their hidden glory but despise what God considers great and honorable due to the frequent insignificance of their bodily appearance. God says the following concerning the saints somewhere in the prophets, addressing the many as one person: "Blessed is the man who has believed in the Lord. The Lord will be his hope. He will be like a tree flourishing next to water, and he will put down his roots in a moist place. In the year of the drought he will not fear, and he will not stop **[504]** bearing fruit. The heart is deep beyond all things, and it is the man, and who will know him? I the Lord search hearts and test the inner parts."[27] Now when we in our arrogance disparage one who is known by God and who is admirable in the virtues just mentioned, looking only at the outward and perishable flesh and making the lowliness of the flesh a pretext for a mean spirit toward them, how will we not be caught opposing the king of all and so endure limitless punishment, since we sometimes call the high low and put light for darkness and define sweetness as bitter?[28]

Therefore, we must preserve for the saints the honor that is appropriate for them, and we must look at them through their inner hidden glory rather than the fleshly condition in which they might be found. Yet most of us cannot bear to think that what is lowly in the world is worthy of any honor or glory at all, even if it should be distinguished in virtue, since we focus only on gaining riches and we do not look with righteous eyes on glory that is easily destroyed and even now about to perish. So we place no value on right judgment. The disciple of the Savior ridicules such people, and with very good reason, saying, "Hypocrites, if a person with gold rings and fine clothes comes into your assembly, and if a poor person in dirty clothes also comes in," and you tell the rich person to take the seat at your right hand, but you tell the poor person, " 'Stand there,' or 'Sit at my feet,' have you not made distinctions among yourselves?"[29] It is, however, fitting to observe from this how great an accusation they would in fairness incur who admire external clothing and not internal **[505]** good qualities. Riches and the glory of riches would most likely bring some alien and illegitimate glory to those who possess them, but glory in the heart and distinction in good deeds are genuine and native riches to those who have them, not remaining with the flesh and rotting away with it but dwelling with the soul while it lives within throughout this life, and then when it departs, flying away with it to wherever the ruler of all may will. The Father's mansions are many, as we have heard.[30]

Therefore, we should by no means be forced to honor the one who is famous for riches and who lavishes money on the petty glories of the earth, which are like a picture. Instead, we should honor those for whom the glory of their works gives birth to undying fame from God and whose inner beauty flashes, making them shine with all kinds of good qualities.

6:43-44 Jesus answered and said to them, "Do not grumble among yourselves. No one can come to me unless the Father who sent me draws them, and I will raise them on the last day."

The Jews look down on Jesus because they are ignorant of his Father in heaven, and they do not recognize in the slightest that he is by nature the Son of the ruler of all; they look only at his earthly mother and Joseph. For this reason he answers them rather heatedly, and he

[27]Jer 17:7-10. [28]Is 5:20. [29]Jas 2:2-4. [30]Jn 14:2.

immediately displays a divine characteristic for their benefit. As God, he knows both their secret whisperings and the thoughts that enter their minds. By this very fact, he gives them to understand that they are falling from the truth and have made their conception of him far too small. [**506**] The one who knows hearts completely and who searches the movements in the mind—how is it not necessary now to crown him with God-befitting glory and to raise him up as far above human pettiness as God is above the earth? So he uncovers the thoughts still buried in unuttered accusations and makes known the secret whispered grumblings among them and says, for the reason we just mentioned, "Do not grumble among yourselves."

Then, showing that the mystery concerning him is a good taught by God among human beings and the knowledge concerning him is a work of grace from above, he says that no one is able to come to him who is not drawn by the admonition of the Father. This is the plan of one whose only aim is to persuade them that they should weep and mourn over the harm they have already done him, and seek to be freed and to be drawn also to salvation by faith in him through the will of the Father and through the aid from above. This aid makes the road easy for them in this matter and smoothes, as it were, the road that was made quite rough when they sinned.

For their benefit he maintained that he would raise the believer from the dead, thereby presenting himself to the ignorant as true God by nature. After all, the ability to give life and to compel one who has been overcome by death to return to life would rightly pertain only to the nature of God and would be ascribed to nothing originate. Giving life is characteristic of one who lives, and not of one who borrows that grace from another. [**507**]

6:45 "It is written in the prophets, 'And they will all be taught by God.'"

Since he, as God, recognizes the ignorance in his hearers, he does not leave this statement without a witness. He shows that it was already proclaimed and announced before from above through the holy prophets. In so doing, he both removes the pretext from those who imagine that they should speak against him, and he lays bare no less their ignorance by which they are unable to see this, even though they are led by the law to the understanding of things to come. He persuades them therefore to consent even against their will, since it was not likely that they would oppose even the voices of the holy prophets that God would teach the mystery concerning him to the worthy, and he would reveal his own Son by ineffably speaking to each one, implanting in them the understanding of these things in a God-befitting way.

But after he says above, "No one can come to me unless the Father who sent me draws them," he shows that the drawing is not by necessity or force by adding,

"Everyone who has heard and learned from my Father comes to me."

Where there is hearing and learning and benefit of instruction, there is faith, by persuasion, that is, and not by force. The knowledge of Christ is given by the Father to the worthy as an aid out of love rather than by force. That is because the word of doctrine requires that free will and free choice be preserved to the human soul, that [**508**] it may ask for the just rewards of its good deeds, or if it falls from what is right and heedlessly transgresses the decree of the lawgiver, that it may receive the most reasonable punishment.

We must also know that even if the Father should be said to instruct some people in the mystery of Christ, he will not do this by himself, but he will accomplish it through the Son as through his own wisdom. It is consistent, after all, to think that the revelation of knowledge that is in them from the Father will not be without wisdom. And the Son is the wisdom of the Father. Therefore, the Father will accomplish this revelation through wisdom, his own offspring, in those who are worthy.

Furthermore, to speak simply and altogether truly and not otherwise, one would not miss the mark by saying that all actions or intentions that belong to God the Father regarding anyone belong to the entire holy Trinity, and they are likewise the actions or intentions of both the Son himself and of the Holy Spirit. For this reason, I think, when God the Father is said to reveal his own Son and to call to him those who are more ready to believe, the Son himself is also found to do this and the Holy Spirit no less. The Savior says to the blessed Peter, after he has most courageously confessed his faith in him, "Blessed are you, Simon son of Jonah! For flesh and blood have not revealed this to you, but my Father in heaven."[31] But in other cases, he himself is seen doing this. Paul, for example, boasts quite appropriately about himself, crying out concerning the mystery of Christ, "For I did not receive it from a man, nor was I taught it, but it came through a revelation of Jesus Christ."[32] And you may see that the Holy Spirit himself no less reveals Christ to us. The most wise John, for example, writes, **[509]** "As for you, the anointing that you received from him abides in you, and so you do not need anyone to teach you, but his anointing teaches you about all things."[33] And the Savior himself says somewhere concerning the Paraclete, that is, the Spirit, "I still have many things to say to you, but you are not able to bear them now. But when he comes, the Spirit of truth, he will lead you in all truth. He will not speak on his own, but whatever he hears he will speak, and he will declare to you the things to come. He will glorify me because he will take what is mine and declare it to you."[34] Since he is the Spirit of truth, he will enlighten whomever he enters and will lead them to an understanding of the truth.

And when we say these things, we do not sever into diversity or completely divide the Father from the Son, or the Son from the Father, or the Holy Spirit from the Father and the Son. Rather, we define those characteristics that attach to each one, which seem to be attributed to each individually, to be the will and actions of the entire divine nature. That is because one divine nature really exists and is so proclaimed, seen in the holy and consubstantial Trinity. The divine and indivisible nature will act through itself in an undivided way as far as the unity of the divine nature is concerned, even though it upholds each of the aforementioned in his own subsistence. For the Father is what he is, and the same goes for the Son and the Holy Spirit.

In addition to what we have said, we must also consider the following. Relative terms entail both sides of the relation, and one may see the indication of one in the other. Therefore, it is altogether necessary that the Son be revealed through the Father and the Father, in turn, be revealed through the Son. Each is certainly included in the other, and if anyone should know the one who is God by nature to be the Father, they will certainly know **[510]** the Son who is begotten of him, and of course vice versa, since whoever confesses the Son will not be ignorant of the one who begat him.

Therefore, insofar as God is Father and is understood and proclaimed to be so, he implants knowledge of his own offspring in the hearers. And insofar as the one from him is called and truly is Son by nature, he proclaims the Father. Therefore, the Son says the following, addressed to him, "I have made your name known to human beings."[35] Since the Son was known by those who believed, he says that the Father's name had been made known. But God

[31]Mt 16:17. [32]Gal 1:12. [33]1 Jn 2:27. [34]Jn 16:12-14. [35]Jn 17:6.

the Father may be understood to implant the knowledge of his own offspring in us not with a voice booming from above and resounding through the earth like thunder but with divine illumination shining in us for the understanding of the God-breathed Scripture. And you will find even in this case the work of the Son in us. It is written somewhere concerning the holy disciples, "Then he opened their eyes," namely, to understand the Holy Scriptures.[36]

6:46 "Not that anyone has seen the Father except the one who is from God; he has seen the Father."

Again he foresaw as God that they would in no way receive the revelation through the Spirit, nor would they understand the knowledge from above by illumination, but because of their great ill will, they would reject the very duty of seeing the Father and, if we may put it this way, of being taught by the sight of his very face which, they supposed, was once the case with their fathers, when the glory of God descended on Mount Sinai. He leads them back **[511]** and turns them as with a bridle to the imperative of not having a coarse conception of God or imagining that the invisible nature will ever be visible. No one has ever seen the Father, he says.

He is probably hinting at the teacher Moses because the Jews, reasoning quite foolishly in this matter as well, thought that because he entered the "darkness,"[37] he saw the ineffable nature of God and beheld with bodily eyes that which is by nature the undefiled beauty. So that he does not seem, however, to egg them on to their usual rashness by saying something more explicit against the supremely wise Moses, he says indefinitely of all alike what he might also say about Moses: "Not that anyone has seen the Father." Stop demanding what is above nature, he says, and stop being carried by irrational impulses to what is inaccessible to everything originate. The divine and incomprehensible nature, after all, has withdrawn and eluded not only our eyes but also the eyes of every creature, since all things are included in "no one."

But by defining himself alone as the one who is from God and has seen the Father, he places himself outside the "all things" of which "no one" may be understood to refer. Since he is outside all things, and since no one sees the Father, but he alone is not deprived of seeing him, how could he not be understood to be—not among the "all things" as one of them—but outside the "all things" as superior to all? Moreover, if all things are said to be from God and no one sees the Father (since "all things are from God" according to the statement of Paul),[38] and if he alone sees the Father because he is "from God," then, in order to understand "from God" correctly, we will take it in his case alone to mean "from the substance of the Father." Otherwise, as we just said, **[512]** how does being "from God" let him rise to see the Father, since all things are said to be "from God"? Therefore, "from God" will be employed in a looser sense of creatures since all things are "from God" in the sense of being created because they are brought into being by him. But in the case of the Son, "from God" will be understood in a different and truer sense to mean from him *by nature*. Therefore, since he is not numbered with all things but is outside and above all things with the Father, he will not share the weakness of all things, because he is exempt from being the same nature as they are. And since he rises up to the nature of the one who begat him, he will surely see the one from whom he is.

How or in what way he will either see the Father or be seen by the Father is not something that our tongue can say, but this must likewise be understood in a God-befitting way.

[36]Lk 24:45. [37]Ex 20:21. [38]1 Cor 11:12.

6:47 "Truly, truly, I say to you, whoever believes in me has eternal life."

Faith then is the door and way to life, and the ascent from decay to incorruption. But there will be no less wonder for the hearers in the arrangement of these words. When he perceives that they understand nothing at all, and he sees that they do not even think that they should believe the words of the holy prophets, he cuts off as far as possible their feebleness in believing human arguments by an oath to the truth. He sets before believers highly desirable rewards, he all but forces them against their will through attraction, namely, their desire for these things, and he persuades them to come to what is being proclaimed to them. After all, what could be more valuable than eternal life, at least to those for whom death is bitter and the suffering of decay springs on them? **[513]** This too is the mark of a wise teacher, I mean to re-educate for the better, by every means that invites them to life, those who have chosen to think foolishly. And since he himself is eternal life, he is promising to grant himself to those who believe, which is the meaning of the passage, "that Christ may dwell in our hearts through faith."[39] **[514]**

Chapter Two

That the holy body of Christ is life-giving, in which he speaks of his own body as bread.

6:49-50 "I am the bread of life. Your fathers ate manna in the desert and died. This is the bread that comes down from heaven, so that one may eat of it and not die."

What was announced beforehand by the prophet Isaiah can be seen quite clearly in this passage, "I was revealed to those who did not seek me. I was found by those who did not look for me. I said 'here I am' to the nation that did not call on my name. All day long I held out my hands to an unbelieving and argumentative people."[40] He takes the shell completely off of his words and removes the entire wrapping, so to speak, and he now shows himself unveiled to the Israelites by saying, "I am the bread of life," that they may learn that if they have the desire to be stronger than decay and to strip off death itself, which fell on us because of transgression, they will have to come to participation in the one who can give life, who both destroys decay and nullifies death. This work is truly most fitting and proper to life by nature.

Since, however, they keep insisting that the manna was given to their fathers in the desert, they did not receive the bread that truly came down from heaven, that is, the Son. And so he makes a necessary comparison **[515]** between the type and the truth so that they may recognize not the former [the type] as the bread of heaven but him who proves to be the bread of heaven by nature. Your fathers and ancestors, he says, gave the nature of the body its due by eating the manna, thereby gaining temporary life. And yet, even when they gave the flesh its daily food from the manna they still only barely managed to stave off imminent death. The clearest proof of the manna not being the true bread from heaven, he says, is that those who participated in it received no help toward incorruption by it. And it is likewise a sign that the Son is truly and strictly speaking the bread of life that those who have once participated in him are made stronger than the very bonds of death and have been mixed together with him in some way through fellowship with him. We have already stated in many places that the manna is understood as an image or shadow of Christ and foreshadowed the bread of life but was not itself the bread of life.

[39]Eph 3:17. [40]Is 65:1-2.

Furthermore, the psalmist supports us when he cries out in the Spirit, "He gave them bread from heaven; mortals ate the bread of angels."[41] In a way, this statement seems to be made by the Spirit bearer about the Israelites, but this is not so. Rather, the intent of the statement is focused on us. Is it not silly and completely senseless to suppose that the holy angels in heaven, even though they have an incorporeal nature, partake in coarser food, the sort which this earthly body desires, and that they need this help to be preserved in life? I don't think that it is that difficult to understand, however, that since they are spirits, they would also require that sort of food, namely, spiritual and intellectual food. How then is the bread of angels said to have been supplied to the ancestors of the Jews if the prophet speaks the truth when he cries these things? **[516]** But it is clear that since the typological manna was an image of Christ, who holds all things together and preserves them in being, who nourishes the angels and gives life to earthly things, the prophet was calling that which was presented in shadows by the name of the truth—because the holy angels cannot partake in earthly food. In doing so, he drew his hearers, even against their will, away from their coarse conception, so to speak (I mean concerning the manna), and raised them to a spiritual word, namely, that concerning Christ himself, who is the bread even of the holy angels themselves.

Therefore, those who ate the manna, he says, have died since they received no participation in life from it. It was not really life-giving, but it was taken as an aid against fleshly hunger and as a type of the truer manna. Those who take the bread of life into themselves, however, will have immortality as a reward. They will give no thought at all to decay and the evils that come from it, and they will ascend to a boundless and never-ending long life in Christ. It will in no way undo our argument on this point that those who participate in Christ still must taste bodily death because of what is proper to their nature. Even though they undergo what is human, slipping away into this common end, nevertheless, as Paul says, those who live to God will live in the future.[42]

6:51 "I am the living bread that came down from heaven. If anyone eats of this bread, they will live forever."

"To say the same things to you is not troublesome to me, and for you it is a safeguard," writes the divine Paul to certain people,[43] instructed also in this, I think, by the very words of the Savior. **[517]** Those afflicted by wounds do not need just one dose of medicine. They need all kinds of treatment, and the dispensation of the medicine forces the suffering to surrender not by just one administration but by continual application. In the same way, I think that the roughest souls and most withered minds should have all kinds of remedies prepared by their teachers, and these remedies should come one after another. The result would be that this aid would be able to soften the soul not with just one lesson but with that lesson being presented later as well—even if it came in the same words. Therefore, the Savior often sets the same statement before the Jews, turning it around in various ways. Sometimes it is enigmatic and clothed in great obscurity. At other times it is set free, delivered and loosed from all ambiguity, so that the unbelievers may now lack nothing for their condemnation but the evil may die an evil death, they themselves thrusting the sword of destruction into their own soul.

Christ, therefore, no longer concealing anything, says, "I am the living bread that came down from heaven." The former bread,

[41]Ps 78:24-25 (Ps 77:24-25 LXX). [42]See Rom 14:8. [43]Phil 3:1.

he says, was a type and shadow and image. Hear him now speaking explicitly and no longer veiled, "I am the living bread. If anyone eats of this bread, they will live forever." Those who ate the former bread died because it was not life-giving. But the one who eats this bread, that is, me or my flesh, "will live forever." We must therefore at the same time guard against and avoid becoming hardened to the words that lead to godliness, since Christ persuades us not once but many times. There should be no dispute, after all, that they will surely be guilty of the most serious charges who have fallen headlong into extreme madness and who, through their boundless unbelief, rage like drunks against the teacher of the most beautiful lessons. For this reason, he says concerning **[518]** the Jews, "If I had not come and spoken to them, they would not have sin; but now they have no excuse for their sin."[44] Those who did not through hearing receive the word of salvation into their hearts will perhaps meet with a more lenient judge, pleading that they did not hear at all, even though they will certainly give account for not having sought to learn. But those who are often instructed by the same admonitions and discourses for the pursuit of what is beneficial, yet foolishly think that they should deprive themselves of these incomparably beautiful lessons, will suffer the most bitter punishment and encounter a (so to speak) offended judge and will not be able to find an excuse for their madness that will convince him.

"And the bread that I will give for the life of the world is my flesh."

I die, he says, for all that I may give life to all through myself, and I made my flesh a ransom for the flesh of all. Death will die in my death, and fallen human nature will rise with me, he says. For this reason I have become like you, a human being, that is, and of the seed of Abraham, that I may be made like all my brothers.[45] Understanding well what Christ just said to us, the blessed Paul himself says, "Since therefore the children share in flesh and blood, he himself likewise partook of the same, so that through death he might destroy the one who has the power of death, that is, the devil."[46] In no other way could the one who has the power of death ever be destroyed (and death itself), if Christ had not given himself for us, one **[519]** in place of all, as a ransom. For he was in the stead of all. That is why he says in the Psalms somewhere too, offering himself to God the Father as a spotless sacrifice for all, "Sacrifice and offering you did not desire, but a body you prepared for me. In whole burnt offerings and sin offerings you took no pleasure. Then I said, 'Behold, I have come. It is written about me in the roll of the book. To do your will is my desire.'"[47] Since "the blood of bulls and goats and the ashes of a heifer" were not sufficient to purge sin,[48] nor would the slaughter of irrational animals ever have destroyed the power of death, Christ himself comes to undergo in some way punishment for all. "By his stripes we were healed," as the prophet says,[49] and "he himself bore our sins in his body on the tree."[50] He was crucified in the place of all and for all, so that since one has died for all, we all may live in him.[51] It was "not possible for him to be held" by death,[52] nor could decay have overpowered one who is life by nature.

That Christ offered his own flesh "for the life of the world" we will learn also from his words, "Holy Father, protect them," and, "For them I sanctify myself."[53] He says in this passage that he sanctifies himself not in the sense of advancing himself toward sanctification by purifying his soul or spirit, as it is understood of us, nor in the sense of participa-

[44]Jn 15:22. [45]Heb 2:17. [46]Heb 2:14. [47]Ps 40:6-8 (Ps 39:7-9 LXX). [48]Heb 9:13. [49]Is 53:5. [50]1 Pet 2:24. [51]2 Cor 5:15. [52]Acts 2:24. [53]Jn 17:11, 19.

tion in the Holy Spirit. After all, the Spirit is in him by nature, and he was and is always holy, and will be so forever. But he says "I sanctify" in this passage to mean, "I offer and present myself as a spotless sacrifice for a pleasing aroma." For that which is brought to the divine altar was sanctified, or called holy, according to the law. **[520]**

Therefore, Christ has given his own body for the life of all, and through it he makes life dwell in us again. How he does this I will explain as I am able. Since the life-giving Word of God has taken up residence in the flesh, he has transformed it so that it has his own good attribute, that is, life. And since, in an ineffable mode of union, he has completely come together with it, he has rendered it life-giving, just as he himself is by nature. For this reason, the body of Christ gives life to those who participate in it. His body drives out death when that body enters those who are dying, and it removes decay since it is fully pregnant with the Word who destroys decay.

But perhaps someone will say, fixing the eye of the mind on the resurrection of those who have fallen asleep: Those who have not received faith in Christ or become participants in him will not come to life again at the time of the resurrection. What? Will not every creature who has fallen into death return again to life?

We say yes to this; all flesh will live again. The prophetic word foretells that the dead will be raised. We consider that the mystery of Christ's resurrection extends to the whole of humanity, and we believe that first in him our entire nature has been freed from decay. All will rise in the likeness of him who was raised for our sakes and has all people in himself, in that he is a human being. And just as in the first-formed we fell into death, so also in the first-born for us, all will rise again from the dead, but "those who have done good to a resurrection of life," as it is written, "and those who have done evil to a resurrection of judgment."[54]

Now I, at least, would grant that **[521]** to rise again for punishment and to receive resurrection only for torment is immeasurably more bitter than death. In a stricter sense, therefore, true life must be understood to be life in Christ, in sanctification and blessedness and unfailing delight, since the wise John too has this true life in mind when he says, "Whoever believes in the Son has eternal life, but whoever does not believe in the Son will not see life, but the wrath of God will remain on them."[55] You must see, he says, that the one caught in unbelief will not see life, even though the expectation is that every creature will return to life and rise again. It is clear then that the Savior rightfully called life that which was prepared for the saints—the life in glory, I mean, and sanctification. And no right-minded person will doubt that one ought to pursue it by coming to participation in the life-giving flesh.

Since the Savior called himself bread in many of the passages already before us, let us next see whether he wants to bring to our mind also through the present statement any of the things foretold and whether he is reminding us of the passages found in the Holy Scriptures in which he was signified long ago in the form of bread. It is written then in Numbers, "And the Lord spoke to Moses and said, 'Speak to the Israelites and say to them, "When you enter into the land into which I am leading you, when you eat of the bread of the land, set apart a wave offering, a special offering to the Lord; set apart bread, the first fruits of your dough, as a wave offering, as a wave offering from your threshing floor. Thus you will set it apart, the first fruits of your dough, and give it to the Lord as a wave offering throughout your generations."'"[56]

The **[522]** law typified these things enig-

[54]Jn 5:29. [55]Jn 3:36. [56]Num 15:17-21.

matically then, and with a coarse wrapping, as it were, of the letter; yet it foretold the actual true bread which comes down from heaven, that is, Christ, and which gives life to the world.[57] Observe how, after Christ was made human like us according to our likeness, there was offered to God the Father a certain first fruits of our dough (as it were) and a special offering (as it is written) when he was shown forth as the firstborn from the dead[58] and ascended to heaven itself as the first fruits[59] of the resurrection of all. He was taken from us. He took on the seed of Abraham, as Paul says,[60] and he was offered up from all and for all in order that he might give life to all and be offered to God the Father as the first handful from the threshing floor.

Furthermore, since he was the true light, just as he gave to his disciples the grace of this fact (since he says, "You are the light of the world"), in the same way, since he is the living bread that gives life to all and holds everything in existence, by a similar comparison which was also foreshadowed through the law, he typified the holy choir of the apostles in the twelve loaves. He says in Leviticus, "And the Lord spoke to Moses and said, 'Command the Israelites that they bring you olive oil, pure and beaten, for light to keep the lamp always burning outside the veil in the tabernacle of testimony.'"[61] Then he continues, "And you will take fine flour and make twelve loaves from it, and each loaf will be of two tenth parts. And you will put them in two rows, six loaves in each row, upon the pure table before the Lord. And you will put pure frankincense on each row, and salt, and it will be on the loaves as a memorial set before the Lord."[62]

Now the lamp that gives light in the holy tabernacle outside the veil we said in the foregoing is the blessed John, **[523]** nourished with the purest oil, that is, with illumination from the Holy Spirit. But he is outside the veil because his message is catechetical. "Prepare the way of the Lord," he says, "and make straight the paths for our God."[63] Of what is within the veil, that is, the hidden mystery concerning Christ, he reveals very little. "I," he says, "baptize you with water for repentance, but the one coming after me is mightier than I. I am not worthy to carry his sandals. He will baptize you with the Holy Spirit and with fire."[64] Do you see then how he shines with a simpler message calling to repentance, while he entrusts the revelation of what is within the veil to the one who baptizes with fire and the Spirit? We have taken up this matter at more length at the beginning of the book on the words "he was a burning and shining light,"[65] but we have just now touched on it in a cursory fashion because it was necessary to show that after John's arrival, the preaching of the holy apostles was near and immediately at hand.

For this reason, I think, once the passage has foretold him through the lamp, it presents us with the contemplation of the twelve loaves. "You will make," it says, "twelve loaves, and each loaf will be of two tenth parts."[66] It is the custom of Holy Scripture always to take the number ten as perfect and to recognize it as the fullest number since the sequence and arrangement of the subsequent numbers proceeds and extends as far as you want by receiving a kind of revolution and multiplication of the numbers into the same numbers. It commands then that each loaf be of two tenth parts that you may see the perfection in the disciples in the equal pair, I mean both active virtue and that of contemplation. **[524]** It profitably commands two rows to be made, all but indicating the position that was likely their custom to take, always receiving the Lord in the middle of them and always accustomed to

[57]Jn 6:33. [58]Col 1:18; Rev 1:5. [59]1 Cor 15:23. [60]Heb 2:16. [61]Lev 24:1-3. [62]Lev 24:5-7. [63]Is 40:3. [64]Mt 3:11. [65]Jn 5:35. See book 3, chapter 1, pp. 164-66. [66]Lev 24:5.

surrounding him as their leader. In order that we may learn that, as Paul says, they are the aroma of Christ to God the Father,[67] it commands that frankincense be placed on the loaves and that they be sprinkled with salt. For it was said somewhere to them, "You are the salt of the earth."[68] It also profitably commands that the loaves be offered on the sabbath days since the disciples appeared in the last times of the age, and the sabbath is the last day of the week—and not only that, but because at the time of our Savior's coming, we kept the sabbath spiritually since we rested from sin. And it happened that the holy apostles were shown forth to us at that time, and we, nourished by their divine writings, ascend to a life of holiness. That is why it commands that on the sabbath days the loaves be placed specifically on the holy table, that is, in the church, since the whole is often indicated by the part. What could be holier than the holy table of Christ? Therefore, the Savior was typified ahead of time in the law as bread, and the disciples, by their likeness to him, were typified as loaves, since all things have their true reality in Christ, but when it comes to us these things only exist by likeness to him, through his grace.

6:52-53 Then the Jews began to fight among themselves, saying, "How can this man give us his flesh to eat?" So Jesus said to them,

"All things are plain to those who understand and right for those who find knowledge," as it is written,[69] but even that which is very easy to learn is dark to the ignorant. [525] The hearers who are truly intelligent store away the more obvious teaching in the treasure chest of their understanding. They admit no delay in this, but they search and study with unceasing devotion to learning those subjects whose meaning seems difficult. With great profit they rush, it seems to me, to do what the swiftest hunting dogs are said to do, who have from nature a very keen sense of smell and who always run around the hiding places of their prey. And does not the wise and prophetic oracle call us to such a habit, saying, "Seeking, seek; and dwell with me"?[70] The seeker must seek, that is, they need to bring a focused enthusiasm to the task and not be distracted by fleeting thoughts. The more difficult something is, the sharper the mind that is needed for them to apply themselves, and they must storm the gates of what is hidden with a more spirited mental approach. But whenever anything surpasses the unpracticed and uninstructed mind, that is most assuredly what it rages against with its unbelief. It shuns anything that prevails over it as though it were something fraudulent, ascending from uneducated brashness to ultimate arrogance. That which is unwilling to give way to anyone, after all, or to think that anything is greater than itself—how would it not in the end fit the description we have just given?

We will find, as we focus on the nature of the matter, that the Jews too fell into this disorder. They should have had no problem accepting the words of the Savior, since they had already marveled many times before at his God-befitting power and incontestable authority over all things. And, they should have devoted themselves to the matters that were hard to understand and should have sought instruction [526] in those matters that upset them. But instead they ignorantly ask "How?" concerning God, as though they did not know that this word is full of all blasphemy. After all, God has the ability to accomplish all things without effort. But since they are unspiritual, as the blessed Paul says, they do not receive "the things of the Spirit of God,"[71] but so august a mystery is found to be foolishness to them.

[67]2 Cor 2:15. [68]Mt 5:13. [69]Prov 8:9. [70]Is 21:12. [71]1 Cor 2:14.

We then should derive some benefit from this and set our own life right by the things that make others fall. In the reception of the divine mysteries we should maintain an unquestioning faith and not apply the word *how* to anything that is said, since it is a Jewish word and therefore worthy of extreme punishment. After the leader of the Jewish synagogue (Nicodemus) said, on hearing the divine words, "How can these things be?"[72] he was justly ridiculed and heard, "You are the teacher of Israel, and you do not know these things?"[73] Let us then be found more skillful in the hunt for what is beneficial, even if it comes through the wickedness of others, and let us avoid saying "How?" to what God does. Instead, let us rather take care to attribute to him the knowledge of the way he does his own works.

Just as no one will know what God is by nature, but the one is justified who believes "that he exists and that he rewards those who seek him,"[74] so also no one will know the manner of everything he accomplishes. However, by referring the issue to faith and ascribing to God over all the ability to do everything, one will receive the reward of such a good understanding, which is not to be despised. The Lord of all himself wants us to have such a disposition. He says through the prophet Isaiah, "'My counsels are not like your counsels, nor are my ways like your ways,' says the Lord. 'But as **[527]** heaven is far from the earth, so my ways are far from your ways and your thoughts from my mind.'"[75] How will one who is so far above us in wisdom and power not also perform miraculous works and surpass our understanding?

I would now like to introduce another argument, and not a bad one it seems to me. Those in this life who take up the science called engineering often promise to do something great, and their method escapes the mind of the hearers before they see it done. But when we see their skill, we take it on faith even before the attempt itself, not venturing to contradict them. How then, one might say, would they not be liable to terrible accusations, and for good reason, who dare to dishonor God (the most skillful of all) with their unbelief, who do not refuse to say "How?" to whatever he does, even though they know he is the supplier of all wisdom, and even though they are taught by the entirety of Holy Scripture that he can do everything?

If you persist, O Jew, in saying "How?" I too will imitate your ignorance for your sake and say to you, How did you come out of Egypt? And how, tell me, did Moses' rod turn into a snake? How did his hand become leprous, and how was it restored again, as it is written? How did the water change into the nature of blood? How did you cross through the middle of the sea "on dry ground"?[76] How, through a tree, did the bitter water of Mara become sweet? How was water supplied to you from the breasts of the rocks? How was the manna brought down to you? How did the Jordan stand in its place? Or how was the impregnable wall of Jericho knocked down by a mere shout? Will you never stop saying "How"? **[528]** You will be caught already marveling at a great many deeds, and if you apply your "How?" to them, you will completely disbelieve the entire Holy Scripture and overthrow all the words of the holy prophets, and above all the holy writings of your Moses himself. Therefore, you should rather have believed Christ, assented to his words without hesitation and rushed to learn the manner of the blessing, instead of thoughtlessly raging at him like a drunk, saying, "How can this man give us his flesh to eat?" They also say "this man" in arrogance, since their immoderate speech hints at some such meaning.

[72]Jn 3:9. [73]Jn 3:10. [74]Heb 11:6. [75]Is 55:8-9. [76]Heb 11:29.

"Truly, truly, I say to you, unless you eat the flesh of the Son of Man and drink his blood you have no life in you."
Christ is truly longsuffering and full of mercy, as one can see from the present passage. He has no desire to prevail over the pettiness of the unbelievers; instead, he once again lavishes on them the life-giving knowledge of the mystery. As God he overcomes the arrogance of those who grieve him, and he speaks the words that will raise them to an endless life. He does not yet teach in what way he will give them his flesh to eat because he knew that they were in darkness and could not at all understand the ineffable. Instead, he shows them for their benefit what great good will come to them from eating, in order that perhaps by persuading them to desire a life of unending pleasure, **[529]** he may teach them more readily to believe. For those who have already believed, the ability to learn appropriately follows. This is what the prophet Isaiah says: "If you do not believe, neither will you understand."[77] Therefore, after faith is first rooted in them, the understanding of what they do not know should be brought in next, but inquiry should not precede faith.

That is why, I think, the Lord has good reason for not telling them in what manner he will give his flesh to eat, and he calls them to the duty of believing before investigating. For those who had already believed, he broke the bread and gave it to them saying, "Take, eat, this is my body."[78] Likewise, passing the cup to everyone, he said, "Take, drink of it all of you; this is my blood of the covenant, which is poured out for many for the forgiveness of sins."[79] Do you see how to those who are still ignorant and who refuse to believe without investigation, he does not explain the manner of the mystery, but to those who have already believed he is found to declare it most clearly? So let those who out of ignorance have not yet received faith in Christ hear, "Unless you eat the flesh of the Son of Man and drink his blood, you do not have eternal life in you." They remain completely without a share or a taste of life in holiness and blessedness who have not received Jesus through the mystical blessing.

He is, after all, life by nature, inasmuch as he was begotten of the living Father. And his holy body too is no less life-giving, since it is in some way brought together and ineffably united with the Word who gives life to all. Therefore, it is counted as his, and it is considered to be one with him. He is indivisible after the incarnation except for the knowledge that the Word, who comes from God the Father, **[530]** and the temple, which comes from the virgin, are not the same in nature. That is because the body is not of the same substance as the Word of God. But they are one by that coming together and ineffable concurrence.[80] And since the flesh of the Savior has become life-giving (in that it has been united to that which is by nature life, namely, the Word from God), when we taste of it, then we have life in ourselves, since we too are united to that flesh just as it is united to the Word who indwells it.

That is why, when he raises the dead, the Savior is found to act not by a word alone or by God-befitting commands, but he rushes to employ his holy flesh in particular as a kind of coworker as well, thus showing that it has the power to give life since it has now become one with him. His body, after all, really belonged to him and not to another. So when he raised the synagogue leader's daughter by saying, "Child, arise," he took her by the hand, as it is written.[81] By giving life as God through his all-powerful command and by giving life through the touch of his holy flesh, he displays one joint activity through both. Moreover, when he went

[77]Is 7:9 (LXX). [78]Mt 26:26. [79]Mt 26:27-28. [80]The Council of Chalcedon (451) will also account for the unity of Christ by saying that the two natures "concur" (συντρέχω). [81]Lk 8:54.

into a city called Nain, and "a dead man was being carried out, the only begotten son of his mother," again he "touched the bier and said, 'Young man, I say to you, arise.'"[82] He does not give the activity of raising the dead only to his word, but that he may show that his own body is life-giving, as we have already said before, he touches the dead and through his body places life into those who have already succumbed to decay. And if through the mere touch of his holy flesh he gives life to that which has decayed, how will we not gain the life-giving blessing more richly when **[531]** we also taste the blessing?[83] After all, he will surely transform those who participate in the blessing so that they will have his own good attribute, that is, immortality.

And don't be amazed at this or say to yourselves in a Jewish fashion, "How?" Instead, recognize that water is cold by nature, but when it is poured into a kettle and joined with fire, it then all but forgets its own nature and departs into the activity of that which has overcome it. In the same way then, we, even though we are corruptible because of the nature of our flesh, leave our own weakness by being mixed with life and are transformed into the property of that life. It was necessary—necessary—not only that the soul be recreated in newness of life by the Holy Spirit[84] but also that this coarse earthly body be sanctified and called to incorruption by a coarser participation that is of the same kind as the body.

Let not the Jew, however, who is slow to understand, think that we have discovered some new form of mystery. They will see it in the ancient writings, I mean those of Moses, already prefigured, and bearing the force of the truth because it was also accomplished with mere outward forms. What, tell me, put the destroyer to shame? What made it so that their ancestors did not perish along with the Egyptians when all-conquering death was arming against the firstborn? Should it not be clear to all that it was because they were persuaded by the divine law and sacrificed the lamb, and because they tasted of its flesh and anointed the doorposts with its blood,[85] that death was forced to pass them by since they were sanctified? The destroyer, that is, the death of the flesh, was poised for battle against the entirety of human nature on account of the transgression of the first-formed man. **[532]** At that time we first heard, "Earth you are and to earth you will return."[86] Since Christ, however, was going to overthrow such a terrible tyrant by entering into us through his holy flesh as life, the mystery was typified ahead of time to the ancients. They tasted the flesh of the sheep and were sanctified and saved by its blood, while the one who was appointed to destroy passed by those who were participants in the lamb, according to the will of God.

Why then are you upset, O Jew, now that you are called from types to the truth when Christ says, "Unless you eat the flesh of the Son of Man and drink his blood, you have no life in you"? You should have come with more confidence to the understanding of the mysteries because you were instructed ahead of time by the books of Moses and led by the ancient figures to the duty of believing without doubt.

6:54 "Whoever eats my flesh and drinks my blood has eternal life, and I will raise them up on the last day."

Here too we should especially admire the holy Evangelist for crying out explicitly, "And the Word became flesh."[87] He did not hesitate to say, not that he became "in flesh" but that he became "flesh," in order to show the unity. Moreover, we certainly do not say either that God the Word from the Father has been transformed into the nature of the flesh or that the flesh passed into the Word. Each

[82]Lk 7:12, 14. [83]"Blessing" is a name for the Eucharist. [84]See Rom 6:4. [85]Ex 12:7. [86]Gen 3:19. [87]Jn 1:14.

remains what it is by nature, and Christ is one from both. But in a way that is ineffable and beyond human understanding, the Word has been united to his own flesh and has transformed all of it into himself, so to speak, by the activity that can give life to what lacks life, and he has driven decay from our nature and dislodged death, **[533]** which prevailed long ago through sin.

Therefore, whoever eats the holy flesh of Christ has eternal life because the flesh has in itself the Word, who is life by nature. For this reason he says, "I will raise them up on the last day." Instead of saying that "my body" will raise them (namely, those who eat), he has put "I" on the grounds that he is not different from his own flesh. He is certainly not different in nature,[88] since he refuses to be at all divided into a pair of sons after the union.[89] I, therefore, he says, who came to be in them, that is, through my flesh, will raise on the last day those who eat. It was indeed impossible that the one who is life by nature not completely conquer decay and overcome death. Therefore, even though death, which sprang on us through transgression, forces the human body to the necessity of decay, nevertheless, since Christ comes to be in us through his own flesh, we will surely be raised. It is incredible, or rather impossible, that life not give life to whomever it should enter. Just as if one were to take a spark and bury it in a great heap of chaff so that the seed of fire may be preserved, so also our Lord Jesus Christ hides life in us through his own flesh, and like a seed he places immortality in us, abolishing all the decay that is in us.

6:55 "For my flesh is true food, and my blood is true drink."

Again he contrasts the mystical blessing with the provision of manna and the taste from the cup with the streams from the rocky hollows. What he has already said before in other words **[534]** he says again here, weaving the same discourse in many ways. He does not order them to marvel too much at the manna but rather to receive him as the bread of heaven and the supplier of eternal life. "Your fathers," he says, "ate manna in the desert and died. This is the bread that comes down from heaven, so that one may eat of it and not die."[90] The nourishment of the manna lasted for a little while, he says. Only for a moment did it elude the needs of the body and put away the harm that comes from want, but then it was powerless again since it did not impart eternal life to those who ate it. It was not then "true food," that is, the bread from heaven. The holy body of Christ, however, which nourishes to immortality and eternal life, is the "true food."

Moreover, they also drank water from the rock. And what did they get from that, he says, and what benefit was there for those who drank? They have died, after all. This too then is not "true drink." But the precious blood of Christ is found to be truly "true drink," uprooting all decay from the foundations and dislodging death, which had taken up residence in human flesh. That is because it is the blood of not just anyone but of the one who is by nature life itself. Therefore, we are called both the body and members of Christ[91] since we receive the Son himself into ourselves through the blessing.

6:56 "Whoever eats my flesh and drinks my blood remains in me, and I in them."

With these words he leads us into the myster-

[88]Cyril is flexible in his use of the term "nature" (φύσις). Here he implies that the Word and his flesh are no different in nature, but in the previous paragraph he states that "each remains what it is by nature." This flexibility reflects the ambiguity of the term before it was defined by the Council of Chalcedon in 451. [89]We see here a reference to that which is characteristic of Antiochene Christology. [90]Jn 6:49-50. [91]1 Cor 12:27.

ies in many ways. Since this statement is hard for the more uneducated to understand, demanding the understanding of faith rather than investigation, he spells it out with various approaches by going around and around the same material. **[535]** He sheds light on what is useful about this matter from every angle, planting the most excellent desire for it as a kind of foundation and groundwork for faith. "Whoever eats my flesh," he says, "and drinks my blood remains in me, and I in them." If someone were to join wax with other wax, they will surely see that one has come to be in the other. In the same way, I think, the one who receives the flesh of our Savior Christ and drinks his precious blood, as he himself says, is found to be one with him, mixed together, as it were, and mingled with him through participation so that they are found in Christ, and Christ in them.

Christ was in a way teaching us this also in the Gospel of Matthew when he said, "The kingdom of heaven is like yeast that a woman took and mixed into three satons of flour until all of it was leavened."[92] Who then the woman is, and what the three so-called satons are, and even what a saton is, will be discussed in its own place; for the present, we will speak only of the yeast. Just as Paul says, "A little yeast leavens the whole lump,"[93] so also the least portion of the blessing mixes our whole body into itself and fills us with its own activity. In this way Christ comes to be in us, and we also in him, since it would indeed be true to say that the yeast is in the whole lump, and the lump, by the same reasoning, comes to be in all the yeast. There you have the understanding of the statement in brief.

If we love eternal life, however, if we pray to have the supplier of immortality in ourselves, let us not, like some of the more negligent, refuse to be blessed, nor let the devil deep in wickedness fashion a harmful piety as a trap and a snare for us. Indeed, it is written, the devil reminds me, "Whoever eats of the bread and **[536]** drinks of the cup in an unworthy manner eats and drinks judgment on themselves."[94] And I have examined myself, and I see that I am not worthy.

When then will you be worthy? we will reply to whoever says this. When will you present yourself to Christ? If you are always going to be frightened by your stumbling—and you will never stop stumbling (since "who can understand their errors?" as the holy psalmist says)[95]—you will be found completely without participation in the saving sanctification. Therefore, you should decide to live a more reverent life in accordance with the law and so participate in the blessing, believing it to drive away not only death but also our diseases. When Christ has come to be in us, he puts to sleep the law that rages in the members of our flesh.[96] He kindles reverence toward God and deadens our passions, not counting against us the transgressions we are in but rather healing us as people who are ill. He binds up what has been crushed,[97] he raises what has fallen, and he does this as the good shepherd who has laid down his life for the sheep.[98] **[537]**

CHAPTER THREE

The Son is not a participant in the life of someone else, but he is life by nature since he is begotten of God the Father, who is life by nature.

6:57 "As the living Father sent me, and I live because of the Father, so whoever eats me will live because of me."

The meaning of this passage is unclear and wrapped in no small difficulty. It will not, however, skip off into impenetrability. Indeed, it will be understood and comprehensible for those who choose to think rightly. Now when

[92]Mt 13:33. [93]1 Cor 5:6. [94]1 Cor 11:29. [95]Ps 19:12 (Ps 18:13 LXX). [96]See Rom 7:23. [97]Ezek 34:16. [98]Jn 10:11.

the Son says that he has been sent, he is referring to nothing else but becoming flesh. When we say "becoming flesh," however, we mean that he became a complete human being. The Father then has made me human, he says. And because I, God the Word, was begotten as life from that which is life by nature, I have filled my temple (that is, my body) with my own nature now that I have become human. In the same way, whoever eats my flesh "will live because of me." I have taken on mortal flesh, but since I have dwelt in this flesh—I, who am life by nature because I am from the living Father—I have transformed all of my flesh into my own life. I have not been overcome by the decay of the flesh, but rather I have overcome it as God. Just as, therefore—I will say it again, shrinking from nothing that is profitable—just as **[538]** I have become flesh, he says (since this is what being sent refers to), and I live because of the living Father (that is, I preserve in myself the natural qualities of my Father), whoever receives me into themselves through participation in my flesh will live, being wholly transformed into me, the one who can give life because I am from a life-giving root, that is, God the Father.

He maintains that he has become flesh from the Father even though Solomon says, "Wisdom has built herself a house,"[99] and the blessed Gabriel attributes the creation of the divine body to the operation of the Spirit when he says to the holy virgin, "The Holy Spirit will come upon you, and the power of the Most High will overshadow you."[100] The Son maintains this in order that you may understand that since the divinity is one in nature and is in the Father and the Son as well as in the Holy Spirit, none will act separately in any instance, but whatever may be said to happen through one, this is completely the work of the entire divine nature. After all, since the holy Trinity is one by the principle of consubstantiality, the power over everything will surely also be completely one. All things are from the Father, through the Son, in the Spirit.

What we have often said, we will say again: to say the same things, even if it is burdensome, is nevertheless a safeguard.[101] It is the custom of Christ the Savior for our benefit to attribute those things that exceed human power to the activity of the Father because Christ humbled himself when he became human. And since he received the form of a slave, he does not spurn the limitations befitting a slave, except that he will not be excluded from doing all things with the Father. The one who begat him accomplishes everything through him, as the Savior himself says: "The Father himself who dwells in me does the works."[102] **[539]** He grants then to the *oikonomia* with the flesh what is appropriate, while he attributes to God the Father the acts that exceed human power. Building a temple in the virgin, after all, surpasses human power.

The opponent, however, will respond, How else could the Son have revealed what he is by nature or how else could he have shown clearly that the Father is greater than he, if not by saying, "I live because of the Father"? If the Father supplies life to the Son, who will reach such a level of stupidity that they completely fail to recognize that what participates in life cannot be the same as that which is life by nature or that which can give life?

Against this we too will adduce the word of truth and say fittingly, "Fools will speak foolishness, and their heart will think vain thoughts to commit lawless deeds and to speak error against the Lord."[103] What could be more lawless, after all, than this notion of the heretics? How do they not speak the ultimate error against Christ who gives life to all when those utterly insane people do not blush to say that he lives by participation in the life of

[99]Prov 9:1. [100]Lk 1:35. [101]See Phil 3:1. [102]Jn 14:10. [103]Is 32:6.

another just as his creatures do? Will the Son not then be a creature, seeing that a creature too is a participant in life but is not itself life by nature? A creature must surely be distinct from the life that is in it. If they think the two can be the same, however, let them say that every creature is life. But I do not think that anyone in their right mind would do that. Therefore, the Only Begotten is not a creature either; rather, he should be understood to be life by nature.

Indeed, how else could he be telling the truth when he says, "I am the resurrection and the life"?[104] Life is that which gives life, not that which needs life from another, just as wisdom too of course is understood to be that which **[540]** can make wise, not that which receives wisdom. Therefore, according to you, the truth will lie, and Christ will not be telling the truth when he says, "I am the life." The brilliant choir of saints too will speak falsely as they utter words through the Holy Spirit and call the Only Begotten life. Our divine psalmist is found saying to God the Father, "With you is the fountain of life."[105] And the wondrous Evangelist John says in his epistles, "That which was from the beginning, which we have heard, which we have seen with our eyes, which we have beheld and our hands have touched, concerning the word of life—and the life appeared, and we have seen it, and we testify to it and announce to you eternal life, which was with the Father and has appeared to us."[106] Do you see also from John's statement that the psalmist is telling the truth when he says to God, the Father of all, "With you is the fountain of life"? For the Son was and is with him as the fountain of life. The Spirit bearer will assure us with his own words that he says these things of the Son, since he writes, "And we know that the Son of God has come, and he gave us understanding so that we may know him who is true; and we are in him who is true, in his Son Jesus Christ. He is the true God and eternal life."[107]

Now who, tell me, will endure the hair splitting of the heretics any longer? Who will not rightly cry out against the irreverence of those who dare to say that the Son is a participant in the life of another, despite the fact that the holy and God-breathed Scripture says no such thing about him but rather cries out explicitly that he is God by nature, the one who is true, the fountain of life and eternal life? How could he be understood to be true God who needs life from another **[541]** and is not himself life by nature? Or how could he still be said to be the fountain of life who is aided by the supply of another to be able to live?

All right, says the opponent, we will grant that the Son is life in this sense: he is life insofar as he can give life on the basis of having the living Father in himself.

But this will not be enough, sirs, to defend you from blasphemy against the Only Begotten. In this too your argument will be exposed as being ignorant and crumbling to pieces. After all, to have to say that the Son is called life because he can give life to things that are receptive to life, and to say this on the basis of him having the Father in himself—how is this not full of immeasurable ignorance? You certainly do not seem to know what "by nature" and "from someone by nature" mean as compared with "by adoption."

For example, fire is hot by nature, and other things are hot by participating in its activity, like iron or wood. But they would not be called fire just because they are heated, since they have an alien, not a natural activity in themselves. The rationale of this example will apply to us as well. Grammar, let's say, or geometry are held to be species of rational knowledge. When someone becomes skilled at grammar, however, or the other one, they are not themselves considered to be grammar or geometry,

[104]Jn 11:25. [105]Ps 36:9 (Ps 35:10 LXX). [106]1 Jn 1:1-2. [107]1 Jn 5:20.

but from the grammar that is in them they are called grammarians, and it's the same with the other case.

In the same way, life by nature is completely different from those things in which it comes to be, transforming what is not life by nature into itself. You say that the Father is in the Son, as he might be in matter, for instance, so that since the Father is life by nature, [542] the Son too may give life. Now when you say this, you are incoherently claiming that the Son is life (rather than a participant in life from another) even though he is called to the dignity of being the supplier by relation and not by substance. Just as no one would reasonably call heated iron fire, even though it contains the activity of fire from having been heated by the fire; and just as no one with a brain would call a grammarian grammar because they can lead others to that science, so also I think no reasonable person would call the Son life because he can give life to others (since he is not life by nature, according to them, but he is life because he is implanted with the activity of the Father) or because the Father dwells in him.

What then, tell me, would finally prevent us from thinking that the Son is one of us, namely, of a corruptible nature, if the phrase "he lives because of the Father" means that he is supplied with life from the Father, as they think it does? He would have perished, after all, according to the logic of their position, if he did not have the living Father in himself. If we agree that he is telling the truth when he says, "I am in the Father, and the Father is in me,"[108] then he has the Father, who is life by nature, in himself; but he himself, though he is not life by nature, is also in the Father. And so—I do not utter the blasphemy, even though it is necessary to speak to refute the irreverence of God's enemies—the Father will be caught having in himself that which is devoid of life, that is, decay and a decaying nature.

Because the nature of the matter forces us to think thus concerning the Son, we must look further and go through various considerations, since our goal is to refine our investigation with due precision. You say that God the Father is life by nature. Good, since he is. But he is also in the Son. This too your argument grants. I would now ask you [543] a reasonable question. I would like to know this: What will he do regarding his Son when he is in him? Will he grant a share of his own life to his offspring as to one who lacks it and does not have life of himself? How then is it not completely necessary to think that the Son is devoid of life? And that which is devoid of life—how could it be anything other than subject to decay? But in fact, the Father will not grant a share of his own life to his offspring. The Son is life even if the Son should not receive it from the Father.

How then do some babble on with no restraint and slander the Son and say that he lives on account of the fact that he has the Father, who is life by nature, in himself? If he lives even apart from the Father, since the Son is essentially life itself, then he no longer lives "because of the Father," that is, because of participation in the Father. But if he has the Father as the supplier of his life, he will be shown not to have his own life. He borrows life from another and, as we said at the beginning, is a creature rather than life, and his nature is subject to decay. How then could he call himself life? Either he will be able to say without danger, "I am the life," or, if that statement is perilous because a creature will not be able to rise to God-befitting honors, then the Son must know himself to be life by nature. How will he be the "imprint of the hypostasis"[109] of the one who begat him, and how will he be his image and precise likeness? Or how was Philip wrong when he said, "Show

[108]Jn 14:11. [109]Heb 1:3.

us the Father, and we will be satisfied"?[110] After all, it really is fitting to think that one who has seen the Son has not yet seen the Father, if indeed the Father is life by nature but the Son participates in the Father's life. One would never see that which gives life in one who receives life, or one who lacks nothing in one who is in need. Therefore, according to this other [544] way of thinking, he will be lying when he says, "The one who has seen me has seen the Father."[111]

Those who love the godly teachings of the church, however, see what great absurdities will follow from their nonsense. Therefore, let them "turn from them and pass by," as it is written, and "make their paths straight and set right their ways."[112] Let them gaze at the simple beauty of the truth, believing that God the Father is life by nature, and the Son begotten of him is life in the same way. Just as he is said to be light from light, so also he is life from life. And just as God the Father enlightens those things that lack light through his own light (the Son), and he makes wise those things that are receptive of wisdom through his own wisdom and he strengthens those things that lack strength through his own strength, so also he gives life to as many things as need life from him through his own life which flows from him, that is, his Son.

So when he says, "I live because of the Father," do not think that he is admitting that he lives because he receives life from the Father, but rather he maintains that he lives because of the fact that he was begotten of the living Father. It was not possible for him who is from the living Father not to live. Just as if someone were to say concerning our own situation, I am a rational man because of my father because I was born as a child of a rational man, so also you should understand it in the case of the Only Begotten himself as well. "I live," he says, "because of the Father." Since the Father who begat me is life by nature, and I am his natural and genuine offspring, I gain by nature what is his, that is, being life, since this is what the Father is. And since he is understood to be and is one from one (since the Son is from the Father, even though he was with him eternally), he quite reasonably glories in the natural attributes of the one who begat him, as his own. [545]

6:58 "This is the bread that came down from heaven. It is not like the manna that your fathers ate and died. Whoever eats this bread of mine will live forever."

The result of great blessings, he says, must be great, and the blessings supplied by grace from above must appear fitting for God and worthy of divine generosity. If you have completely accepted in faith that the bread came down from heaven, let it produce unending life in those who long for it, and let it have the unceasing activity of immortality. This would, after all, be clear proof that the bread is from heaven, that is, from God, since we say that it is fitting for the eternal to give what is eternal, not the enjoyment of a fleeting delicacy which can barely last for an instant. No one who is wise will consider that bread to be the bread from God and from above any longer, especially when the ancestors were overcome by death after they had eaten it, and it failed to ward off the damage of decay. And no wonder! That bread could not make one immortal. Therefore, no one could correctly consider it to be from heaven or say that it is from heaven. The work fitting for what has come from there is to render those who participate in it superior to both death and decay.

Next we will establish by an indisputable proof that this is the bread from heaven: the bread that comes through Christ, that is, his body. It makes the one who has tasted it live

[110]Jn 14:8. [111]Jn 14:9. [112]Prov 4:15, 26.

forever. In this fact, we see that we should above all believe that the divine nature does not deign to give only a little. It gives every gift superabundantly, even if the gift surpasses our understanding so that the more simple disbelieve it because of the magnitude of the grace. **[546]** With such a wealthy hand, how could the desire to give richly not be present? Therefore, Paul too marvels and says, "Eye has not seen and ear has not heard and it has not entered the human heart what God has prepared for those who love him."[113] And the law typified great gifts in small examples, "having a shadow of the good things to come but not the image itself of the realities," as it is written,[114] so that the blessing[115] of Christ is seen in the food of the manna. Those shadows of the things to come were prefigured to the ancients.

6:59 These things he said in the synagogue, teaching in Capernaum.

Now that the supremely wise Evangelist has introduced the explanation of the marvelous mysteries to us, he naturally attributes to Christ the Savior the origin of these teachings, shaming the opponent by the notoriety of Christ's person and frightening away ahead of time those who were going to come to speak against him. Sometimes the illustriousness of the teachers makes the hearer more ready to believe and demands a more spirited assent from the learners.

He does exceedingly well to add "in the synagogue." This expression almost explicitly indicates that not one or two people heard Christ saying these things, but he is seen openly teaching everyone "in the synagogue," just as he himself says through the prophet Isaiah, "Not in secret have I spoken, nor in a dark place of the land."[116] He was speaking freely about these things, making the judgment against the Jews irrefutable and rendering the accusation of not believing in him all the more grievous for the unbelievers. If they had not yet been instructed in so great **[547]** a mystery, they might reasonably have avoided punishment by pleading utter ignorance, and they would have received a more moderate sentence from the judge. But since they know and are often instructed in the mystery, yet they insult him with their unbelief, how would they not for good reason be punished, finally deprived of all mercy and pay the most bitter penalty to the one they dishonored? The Savior himself has said this sort of thing about them. "If I had not come," he says, "and spoken to them, they would not have sin. But now they have no excuse for their sin."[117]

We must therefore guard against, or rather renounce, disobedience as the bringer of death and consider faith in what Christ teaches to be the giver of life. In this way we will escape being punished with them. And he adds that Christ said these things "in Capernaum" to show that he remembered accurately. How could one who knows both the place and the town make a mistake about the explanation of the teaching?

6:60-61 Many of his disciples, when they heard it, said, "This is a hard saying; who can accept it?" But Jesus, knowing in himself that his disciples were grumbling about this, said to them,

This is the custom of those without understanding. They always find fault with more subtle teachings, and they ignorantly ridicule any insight that surpasses them, because they do not understand it. They should have hastened to learn and to be refined by what was said. They should not, however, have risen up against such wise words and called "hard" what deserves their wonder. They are undergo-

[113]1 Cor 2:9. [114]Heb 10:1. [115]"Blessing" refers to the Eucharist. [116]Is 45:19. [117]Jn 15:22.

ing the same sort of experience that [548] one may see endured by those who have lost their teeth. These hurry to more delicate food and often spurn the more wholesome food; they sometimes disparage what is superior, all the while refusing to admit the disease that forces them to reject the better food. Foster brothers of ignorance and bereft of sound mind, they shrink back from knowledge that they ought to hunt down with the greatest exertion and attain with intense determination.

The spiritual man then will delight in the words of our Savior and will rightly cry out, "How sweet are your words to my throat, sweeter than honeycomb to my mouth!"[118] But the unspiritual Jew ignorantly considers the spiritual mystery to be foolishness, and when admonished by the words of the Savior to rise up to an understanding that is fitting for humanity, they always fall down to foolishness, which is their foster brother, calling evil good and good evil, as the prophet says.[119] They take after their fathers and will be caught imitating the ignorance of their ancestors also in these words. The one group, when they were supplied with manna from God and participated in the blessing from above, were brought down to their usual coarseness and sought after the foul smells in Egypt, longing to see onions and leeks and fleshpots.[120] The other group, when they are admonished to receive the life-giving grace of the Spirit and taught to feed on the true bread that has come from God the Father, turn aside to their own error, "being lovers of pleasure rather than lovers of God."[121] And just as their ancestors found fault with the nourishment of the manna, daring to say, "Our soul is dried up" by this manna,[122] so [549] also they reject the true bread, not blushing to say, "This is a hard saying."

Therefore, the hearers of the divine mysteries must be wise. They must be approved moneychangers so that they know the genuine and the counterfeit coin, and they neither bring undue incessant questioning to matters that are to be received by faith nor waste faith (which is sometimes harmful) on matters that need investigation. But they grant to everything that is said what is fitting, and they go on a straight path, as it were, refusing to turn to either side. After all, it is right for the one pursuing a right faith in Christ to travel on the royal road.

6:61-62 "Does this offend you? Then what if you were to see the Son of Man ascending to where he was before?"

From an exceedingly great ignorance, some of those taught by Christ the Savior were offended by this statement of his. When they heard him saying, "Truly, truly, I say to you, unless you eat the flesh of the Son of Man and drink his blood, you have no life in you,"[123] they understood themselves to be invited to some savage cruelty, as though they were being told inhumanly to eat flesh and gulp blood and were being compelled to commit acts that are horrible even to hear. They did not know the beauty of the mystery or the most beautiful *oikonomia* that is found in it.

In addition, they must have reasoned this way: How could the human body implant in us eternal life? What help will it be for immortality, since it is of our nature? Christ then, knowing their thoughts (since "all things are naked and laid bare to his eyes"),[124] heals them again, [550] leading them in many ways to understand what they still do not know. It is quite senseless for you, sirs, he says, to be offended at my words. If you cannot yet believe, even though you are often taught the mystery that our[125] body will put life into you, how will you maintain your position, he says,

[118]Ps 119:103 (Ps 118:103 LXX). [119]Is 5:20. [120]Num 11:5; Ex 16:3. [121]2 Tim 3:4. [122]Num 11:6. [123]Jn 6:53. [124]Heb 4:13. [125]Gk ἡμέτερον.

when you see it fly up to heaven? I do not merely promise that I will ascend into heaven itself, lest you again say "How?" But the sight of it will stand before your eyes, shaming every opponent. So if you see, he says, "the Son of Man ascending" into heaven, what will you say then? You will be convicted of no small degree of senselessness. After all, if you do not think that my flesh can implant life into you, how will it ascend into heaven like a bird? If it cannot give life because it does not have the nature of giving life, how will it walk on the air? How will it ascend into the heavens? This too is equally impossible for the flesh. If, however, it ascends contrary to nature, what is now to prevent it also from giving life, even though it does not have the nature of giving life as far as its own nature is concerned? He who made the earthly into the heavenly will also render it life-giving, even if its nature is corruptible considered on its own.

We must observe, however, that he does not allow himself to be divided into two christs,[126] as the foolish counsel of some has it. He keeps himself completely indivisible after becoming man. "The Son of Man ascends," he says, "to where he was before," even though the body from the earth was not above prior to this time, but only the Word was above when he was still by himself before coming together with the flesh. Paul has done well then to include in his epistles the phrase "one Lord Jesus Christ."[127] For there is one Son both before the incarnation **[551]** and after the incarnation, and we will not consider his body to belong to someone other than the Word. For this reason he says that the Word, who came down from heaven above, is also the Son of Man. He became flesh, after all, according to the blessed Evangelist; he did not come into the flesh by a change (since he is unchangeable and immutable as God), but he dwelt in his temple (I mean the one from the virgin) and truly became human. By saying that he will "ascend to where he was before," he gives his hearers to understand that he has come down from heaven. Thus it was likely that they would understand the force of his statement and heed him not merely as a man, but they would know that he is also God the Word in the flesh and believe that his body will be life-giving as well.

6:63 "It is the Spirit that gives life; the flesh is of no benefit."

It was not completely without reason, he says, that you have attributed to the flesh no ability to give life. When the nature of the flesh is considered alone and in itself, it will clearly not be life-giving. It will in no way give life to anything that exists, but it itself needs the one who can give life. However, when the mystery of becoming human is diligently investigated and you learn who dwells in that flesh, you will be altogether confident, he says—unless you accuse even the divine Spirit himself—that it can give life, even though the flesh of itself is of absolutely no benefit. Since it has been united to the life-giving Word, it has risen to the power of the better nature and has become life-giving in its entirety; it did not drag down to its own nature him who is in no way inferior. So even though the nature of the flesh is in itself too weak to be able to give life, nevertheless it will do so because it has the life-giving Word, and it is full of his entire activity. **[552]** The body belongs, after all, to him who is life by nature, not to anyone earthly. The statement "the flesh is of no benefit" would rightly hold true for those who are earthly. Neither the flesh of Paul, for example, or that of Peter or anyone else will work this in us, but only the exceptional flesh of Christ our Savior, in whom dwelt "all the

[126]Here again we see a reference to Antioch. [127]1 Cor 8:6.

fullness of the deity bodily."[128] Indeed, it would be quite strange to think that while honey imparts its own quality to those things that are not sweet by nature and can transform whatever it is mixed with into itself, the life-giving nature of God the Word does not raise up to its own good quality the body in which it dwells. Therefore, the statement "the flesh is of no benefit" will be true of all others, but in the case of Christ alone it will not hold, because in his flesh dwells life, that is, the Only Begotten. He says that he is Spirit, "for God is Spirit,"[129] and according to the blessed Paul, "The Lord is Spirit."[130] And when we say these things, we do not take away from the Holy Spirit his own subsistence, but just as Christ calls himself the Son of Man because he has become man, so also he names himself from his own Spirit. His Spirit, after all, does not belong to someone other than him.

"The words that I have spoken to you are spirit and life."

He now fills his whole body with the life-giving activity of the Spirit since he calls his flesh "spirit" without overturning the fact that it is flesh. Because his whole flesh is utterly united to him and clothed with life-giving power, it now ought to be called "spirit" as well. And this is no wonder, **[553]** nor should you be offended at it. After all, if "the one who is united to the Lord is one spirit with him,"[131] how could his own body not even more be called one with him? Therefore, he is indicating in the passage before us something like this: I perceive from the reasoning within you, he says, that you foolishly conclude that I told you that my earthly body is by nature life-giving, but that is not the intent of my statement. The entire explanation to you was about the divine Spirit and eternal life. The nature of the flesh does not render the Spirit life-giving, but the power of the Spirit makes the flesh life-giving. "The words," therefore, "that I have spoken to you are spirit" (that is, spiritual and concerning the Spirit) "and life" (that is, life-giving and concerning him who is life by nature). He does not set aside his flesh when he says this, but he teaches us what is true.

We will repeat what we have just said, taking it up because it is profitable: the nature of the flesh itself by itself would not be able to give life, since what would be left for the one who is God by nature? It should not be considered alone and by itself in Christ, however, because it has the Word, who is life by nature, united to it. So when Christ calls it life-giving, he is testifying that the power to give life belongs not so much to it as to himself or to his Spirit. Because of him, his body is life-giving since he transformed it so that it has his own power. But how this is so cannot be grasped by the mind or spoken by the tongue but must be honored by silence and faith that is above the mind.

That the Son is often called by the name "Spirit" in the **[554]** Holy Scriptures, we will learn in what follows. The blessed John writes concerning him, "This is the one who came through water and Spirit, Jesus Christ, not with water only but with the water and the Spirit. And the Spirit is the one who testifies because the Spirit is the truth."[132] See, he calls the truth "Spirit," even though Christ cries out distinctly, "I am the truth."[133] Furthermore, Paul writes to us and says, "Those who are in the flesh cannot please God. But you are not in the flesh; you are in the Spirit, if in fact the Spirit of God dwells in you. Anyone who does not have the Spirit of Christ does not belong to him. But if Christ is in you, the body is dead because of sin, but the Spirit is life because of righteousness."[134] See, in this passage, after he has shown that the Spirit of God dwells in us, he says that Christ himself is in us. The Spirit of the Son is indistinguishable from the Son,

[128]Col 2:9. [129]Jn 4:24. [130]2 Cor 3:17. [131]1 Cor 6:17. [132]1 Jn 5:6. [133]Jn 14:6. [134]Rom 8:8-10.

at least by reason of their identical nature, even though the Spirit would be understood to have individual existence. Therefore, he often makes no differentiation, sometimes naming the Spirit and sometimes naming himself.

6:64-65 "But there are some of you who do not believe." For Jesus knew from the beginning who were the ones who did not believe and who was the one who would betray him. And he said, "For this reason I said to you that no one can come to me unless it is granted to them by my Father."

In this very statement one may see explicitly fulfilled what was announced beforehand through one of the holy prophets, "You will surely hear and not understand; you will surely see and not perceive. For the heart of this people has become fat, [555] and they have stopped their ears and shut their eyes, lest they should at all see with their eyes and understand with their heart and turn, and I will heal them."[135] They became earwitnesses, after all, of the Savior's teachings, learning not from some other saint but being instructed in the mysteries by the voice of the Lord of all. Nevertheless, though they saw him with their bodily eyes, they grew fat from their own lack of understanding and, closing the eye of their mind, turned away from the sun of righteousness by not receiving the illumination of evangelical instruction. They were wicked and guilty of many past offenses already. That is why the wise Paul testified to us, "A hardening has come on part of Israel."[136]

Furthermore, since it was not the work of just any wisdom to recognize God hidden in human form, he says that no one can come to him who has not yet received understanding from God the Father. And this is quite reasonable. After all, if "every good and perfect gift is from above, coming down from the Father of lights,"[137] how could recognizing Christ not also be a gift from the right hand of God? And how could the understanding of the truth not be understood to outstrip all grace? The more this knowledge shows itself to bestow the highest gifts, the more fitting it would be that it depends on divine generosity.

The Father, however, does not give knowledge of Christ to the impure, nor does he impart the most beneficial grace of the Spirit to those who are practiced at going off into strange unbelief, since it would not be right to pour costly perfume on mud. Therefore, the blessed prophet Jeremiah commands that those who want to draw near to Christ by faith must first be purified by the [556] desire for every good work. Jeremiah cries out, "Seek God, and when you find him, call on him. And when he draws near to you, let the wicked forsake their way and the lawless man his plan, and let them return to the Lord, and they will find mercy, for he will abundantly pardon your sins."[138] You see how he says that we must first depart from our original way and forsake our lawless plans that we may obtain forgiveness of sins, through faith in Christ, that is. For we have been justified "not by works of the law"[139] but by his grace and the forgiveness granted to us from above.

But perhaps someone will say, In that case what prevented him from forgiving the Jews and lavishing remission on Israel along with us? After all, that would be fitting for the perfect good. How will he be telling the truth, one might say, when he says to us, "I have not come to call the righteous, but sinners to repentance"?[140]

What then shall we say to this? The grace of the Savior was first devised only for those of Israel. He was sent, as he himself maintained, only to the lost sheep of the house of Israel.[141] And it was possible, at least for those who wanted to believe, also to ascend to eternal life.

[135]Is 6:9-10. [136]Rom 11:25. [137]Jas 1:17. [138]Is 55:6-7. [139]Gal 2:16. [140]Mt 9:13. [141]Mt 15:24.

Some, who lived more nobly and were searchers of the truth, received the grace of God the Father as an aid to salvation and were saved through faith. The swaggering Pharisee, however, and the hard-hearted high priests and elders of the people along with them, did not want to believe, even though they had been instructed beforehand by Moses and the prophets. Since, on account of their bad counsel, they finally showed themselves unworthy of eternal life,[142] they did not attain the illumination from God the Father.

[557] You also have a type of this in the ancient writings. Just as those who did not trust God in the desert were not allowed to enter the promised land, so also those dishonoring the Lord through unbelief are not allowed to enter the kingdom of heaven, of which the promised land was a type. And God is not "unjust to inflict wrath on us."[143] Since he is righteous by nature, he will surely decide correctly and direct his judgment in accordance with his own nature, even though we ourselves may not understand the path of his *oikonomia* that is above us.

The blessed Evangelist truly profits us when he says that Jesus knew all things and that he was not unaware of who would disbelieve him and who would be a servant of impiety against him. In this way he may be recognized as God, as the one who "knows all things before they come to be."[144]

6:66 After this many of his disciples turned back and no longer went about with him.

Wisdom is always hard for the unwise, and what may be thought to bring no small profit, they often view as harmful. Just as for those whose bodily sight is diseased, the light of the sun is an enemy but it is a relief to sit in dark places, so also for those whose minds are sick, the more difficult teachings are hateful and those that are obscured by challenging concepts are nauseating, even if they should hold great benefit. Insignificant matters, by contrast, are agreeable and more pleasing, even though sometimes they produce nothing profitable.

Will we not find this statement to be true in the passage before us? Although Christ is placing before them the great divine mystery [558] and through various considerations opening the understanding of it and now all but drawing back the veil of the temple to reveal the inner tabernacle—they still loathe such a wise and heavenly statement, and they turn away once again to ignorance befitting animals. "They turned back," as the Evangelist says, and refused to "go about with him" any more. This is truly falling backward. For this reason he says also through the prophet Jeremiah to senseless and contentious Jerusalem, which nourishes unbelievers, "You have turned from me, says the Lord; may you go backward."[145] Indeed, according to true reasoning, falling backward is a consequence of turning from the good, and God is all good. Therefore, the wretched people "turned back" and fell backwards, no longer walking with the Savior but turning as it were to other paths and being dragged down to their usual passions.

Next let us see if we do not find a type of this too in the words of Moses. When they had ridden through long roads and traveled over that wild desert and were finally at the promised land, Joshua the son of Nun and some others with him were sent by divine command to spy out the land. When they had viewed the whole land, they returned to Moses, and some of them began to give a bitter report to the assembly. The land, they said, that we have spied out has fierce inhabitants, and we have seen sons of giants there.[146] And they went on adding whatever things would strike fear into the hearers. But after them,

[142]Acts 13:46. [143]Rom 3:5. [144]Sus 42. [145]Jer 15:6. [146]Num 13:32-33.

Joshua tried to crown the land with many praises, and he exhorted them, saying, "The land that we have spied out [559] is exceedingly good. If the Lord chooses us, he will lead us into it."[147] But the ancestors of the Jews contended that it would be fitting to stone Joshua.[148] Condemning God, who is strong enough to do anything, for having no power, "they sat down and wept,"[149] as it is written. And with this they understandably provoked the Lord of all. Since they were so unbelieving and arrogant, they fell away from the promise. "As I swore in my wrath," he says, "they will not enter my rest."[150]

Then what? God commands them to return and go back again. He says to Moses, "Tomorrow, depart and turn back by way of the Red Sea."[151] Because they did not want to enter the land to which they were called, they are driven to turn around and are forced to retrace the same road again. They would not follow the words of Joshua, nor when they heard that the land was good did they honor the advisor with assent. So what they suffered then, these suffer now. Although they are taught the way of eternal life and exhorted to hurry into the kingdom of heaven, they commit outrage with their unbelief. Therefore, with justice they "turned back," forfeiting by their own stubbornness the further accompaniment of their guide to salvation.

6:67 So Jesus said to the twelve, "You do not want to go away too, do you?"

Our Lord Jesus Christ is not urging the holy apostles to leave him, nor is he exhibiting to them full and free amnesty for their action, nor is he allowing them readily to turn away as though they would suffer no harm from doing so. Rather, he is cleverly threatening them that unless [560] they show themselves superior to the ignorance of the Jews, they too will be sent back and no longer go about with him but will depart to destruction. It is certainly not the worshipers who are great in number who will be precious in the sight of God, but those who stand out in right faith, even though their number be few. That is why the divine Scripture says those who are called are many, but only the chosen and tested will be received, and they are very few.[152]

In fact, this is what the divine Word himself has been testifying to us. It is as though the Savior said to his disciples, If you completely believe my words without hesitation, if you put away doubt and accusation and with simple faith receive the mystery, if it seems bitter to you and full of intentional brutishness to accuse my words of being hard, if you refuse to say in a Jewish manner, "How can this man give us his flesh to eat?"[153] then I will gladly see you with me and rejoice to live with you and love you as genuine. But if you choose to think like those who have fallen back, then I let you run away with them and indeed justly drive you away with them. I will not run out of worshipers because the gospel proclamation will be spoken not only to Judea but is already going to the whole world and calling them into one company, as it were, and gathering them with no difficulty to the knowledge of the truth.

"Note then the kindness and severity of God," as Paul says:[154] severity for the unbelievers, but kindness for those who are going to acknowledge him, if they continue in his kindness, as Paul also maintained somewhere,[155] or else they too will be cut off. The one who did not spare the natural branches, after all, will not spare those who were grafted in either.[156] [561] Let the one who limps from ignorance of the faith know and learn, then, through these words that unless they should

[147]Num 14:7-8. [148]Num 14:10. [149]Num 11:4; 14:1. [150]Ps 95:11 (Ps 94:11 LXX). [151]Num 14:25. [152]Mt 22:14. [153]Jn 6:52. [154]Rom 11:22. [155]Rom 11:22. [156]Rom 11:21.

choose to put an end to this disease, they will turn back. Furthermore, since they will no longer have their guide to eternal life, they will descend into the gloom of hell and wail over their bad judgment. "In that place," he says, "there will be weeping and gnashing of teeth."[157]

Jesus is probably also suggesting something else profitable to us by saying to his disciples, "You do not want to go away too, do you?" He did not want us to think that the disciples themselves were carried away by Jewish ignorance and had sunk down with the unbelievers or otherwise cried out with them against him, alleging that his teachings were hard and that he was trying to instruct his hearers with impossibilities. So he profitably inquired whether they had the desire to depart with them so that through this he might call them to a confession of the right and pure faith, which is what happened. **[562]**

Chapter Four

The holy tabernacle, which led the people through the desert, was a type of Christ, and so was the ark that was in it and the lamp and the altars, both the altar of incense and the altar of burnt offering. These signified Christ himself.

6:68 Simon Peter answered him, "Lord, to whom shall we go? You have the words of eternal life."

Through one chief they all speak, preserving the discipline that is truly fitting for the saints, that they may be found to be a type of sober and admirable reasoning for those who come after them in this instance as well. It was not fitting for them to speak in the hearing of their teacher with everyone leaping up en masse, trying to get ahead of everyone else and usurping the role of speaker in an unbecoming way. It was fitting, rather, for them wisely and eagerly to yield to those who were first in both counsel and rank. For this reason, Paul too says, "Let two or three prophets speak, each in turn."[158] Just because they were honored by the grace of prophecy, that does not mean it was decreed that they should make speeches in disorder. On the contrary, precisely because they were saints, they were commanded to speak in an orderly fashion to their hearers. It was therefore an act of discipline befitting the saints to allow only him who had the greater rank to answer for all. **[563]**

"To whom shall we go," he says, which means, Who will lead us into mysteries like this? To whom will we go to find something better? "You have the words of eternal life." These words are not hard, as they claim, but they raise us up to the most exceptional thing of all, an unending eternal life that is free from all decay. By these words it will certainly be clear to us that we must sit at the feet of only one teacher, Christ, and learn from him unceasingly and without distraction. We must make him our leader. He knows well how to guide us into eternal life. This—this is how we will ascend to the divine heavenly courts and, as we enter the church of the firstborn, how we will revel in blessings that surpass the human mind. The very nature of the matter will without doubt prove that it is good and salutary to want to follow Christ alone and be with him always. But we will see this no less also from the ancient Scriptures.

When the Israelites had stripped themselves of the oppression of the Egyptians and were pressing on to the promised land, God did not command them to make a disorderly march, nor did the lawgiver permit them to go wherever they wanted, since there was no doubt that without a leader, they would surely go astray. That is why it is written as a pattern for us in the book called Numbers, "On the

[157]Mt 8:12. [158]1 Cor 14:29, 27.

day the tabernacle was set up, the cloud hid the tabernacle, the house of the testimony. And in the evening there was on the tabernacle an appearance of fire until morning. So it was continually; the cloud covered it by day and the appearance of fire by night. When the cloud went up from the tabernacle, **[564]** only then did the Israelites set out. And in the place where the cloud stopped, there the Israelites camped. At the command of the Lord the Israelites will set out, and they will also keep the command of God by not setting out. At the voice of the Lord they will camp, and at the command of the Lord they will set out."[159] Do you see how they are commanded to follow and to set out with the cloud when it sets out, and to stop and rest with it? At that time for the Israelites, being with their leader meant salvation; and now for us, not departing from Christ means salvation. For he himself was with the ancients in the form of the tabernacle and cloud, and also the fire.

Next, we will transfer the content of the narrative, as we are able, to the spiritual. When "wisdom," as it is written, "built herself a house"[160] and set up the truer tabernacle (that is, the temple from the virgin), God the Word, who was in the bosom of God the Father,[161] came down into it in an incomprehensible and God-befitting manner. He did this so that for those who have already been enlightened and who walk "as in the day," as Paul says,[162] he might become a cloud that gives shade and relieves the burning heat of the passions that come from their weakness. For those who are still ignorant and going astray, however, and living as in the night and darkness, he becomes a fire that illuminates and transforms them into the fervor that comes from the Spirit. We believe that all who are good are on fire by the Spirit. I think that the cloud appears over the tabernacle by day and the fire by night for no other reason than the interpretation we have just given.

Those who were commanded to follow did not receive orders to journey at will but to set out with the tabernacle and to stop with it so that you may learn through this type **[565]** the same point Christ makes: "Whoever serves me must follow me, and where I am there my servant will be also."[163] Steadfastness in following and zeal for sitting at his feet is what it means to accompany him without interruption. Now accompanying Christ the Savior and following him is by no means understood in a bodily way; rather, it is accomplished through virtue in deeds. The wisest disciples fixed their mind on that virtue. Refusing (as deadly) to turn back with the unbelievers, they cry out for good reason, "Where can we go?" meaning, We will always be with you and cling to your commands and receive your words. We will not accuse them in any way or, with the uninstructed, think that what you say is hard as you lead us into the mysteries. Instead, we will think, "How sweet are your words to my throat, sweeter than honey and honeycomb to my mouth."[164]

Such then is the meaning of this passage. Next we will learn that the tabernacle was a type of Christ for the ancients by applying discriminating attention to what was said to the holy Moses concerning it. Now perhaps the discussion of these matters may seem to be a digression to some, but it will bring no little profit. I think we must carefully examine these matters with great intensity, disregarding the finger pointing of those who accuse us for no reason. God's statement then goes this way (since we will set forth the shadow of the letter piece by piece like this and refine it as we are able): "And the Lord spoke to Moses, saying, 'In one day at the new moon of the first month, you shall set up the tabernacle.'"[165]

[159]Num 9:15-20. Cyril's citation omits some phrases that are in the LXX. [160]Prov 9:1. [161]See Jn 1:18. [162]Rom 13:13. [163]Jn 12:26. [164]Ps 119:103 (Ps 118:103 LXX). [165]Ex 40:1-2.

Someone devoted to learning might reasonably ask, What induced the Lord of all to order that the tabernacle be set up in one day [566] rather than two or three, and at the new moon not of just any month but of the first? These matters should occasion for us a great deal of investigation, and quite reasonably so, since nothing is said by the Holy Scriptures in vain. So we will pursue these issues in order. Now the tabernacle that was set up signifies the holy body of Christ and, so to speak, the pitching of his precious tabernacle, in which all the fullness of the deity was pleased to dwell bodily.[166] Moreover, he commands it to be set up in one day, and this most wisely and according to plan, so that by the one day you may understand the present age in which alone he became human. And it is fitting for us to understand the new moon to be nothing other than the advent of the Savior that renews us, by which "the old things have passed away, and everything has become new."[167] After all, a new season has been revealed to us in Christ, expelling the oldness of the law's worship and re-creating us into a new and fresh life through the teachings of the gospel. Indeed, it renews those who have grown old from sin and have come near to vanishing[168] so that they have the beginning of righteousness. It destroys the oldness of the imported decay, and by the newness of incorruption, it cleanses those who have sped on their way to eternal life by faith. "If anyone is in Christ, there is a new creation," as it is written.[169]

Now he commands the divine tabernacle to be raised in the first month when the beauty of springtime shines forth, washing away, as it were, the sorrow of winter, when the earth is warmed softly by suns that are now brighter and purer, [567] when "the vines bloom"[170] and the farmer revels in the sweet smell of flowers, when the plains bear grass and all the fields bristle with rows of corn, as certain of the Greek poets say, when "the winter is past," as it is written, "and the rain is gone and the time for pruning has come."[171]

You should understand all these things spiritually. The winter at its end and the rain that is past are the temptations that fall on us from the tyranny of the devil and his violence against all creation, since the power of the demons has been destroyed in the days of Christ. Moreover, the bright sun has risen on us, namely, he of whom God the Father says, "And the sun of righteousness will arise on you."[172] By the heat of the Spirit, this sun warms to righteousness those who have fainted in sin. And you should understand the spiritual vines and flowers and ears of corn too to be the saints who stand out in multifaceted reverence toward God and abound with many kinds of virtuous fruit (since we must speak concisely).

The spring brings forth flowers, prepares the whole earth to grow grass, crowns the meadows with new blooms, renews the youth of tree trunks long dry due to the intolerable violence of winter, improves their appearance, surrounds them with their usual leaves and prepares the farmer who tends them to glory in their natural fruits. We will find that something similar happens in our case as well. We who were long dry because of sin reigning over us and destitute of fruit that leads to virtue have sprung up again to righteousness through Christ, and we bring to the farmer of our spirits fresh and new fruit that now comes through faith. This is how we understand, [568] with good reason, what was said by one of the holy prophets in the person of Christ, "I am he that speaks; I am present as the season on the mountains."[173] What the season on the mountains (that is, the springtime) does, we have already stated clearly.

[166]Col 2:9; cf. Col 1:19. [167]2 Cor 5:17. [168]Heb 8:13. [169]2 Cor 5:17. [170]Song 2:13. [171]Song 2:11-12. [172]Mal 4:2 (Mal 3:20 LXX). [173]Is 52:6-7.

Profitably then he commands that the tabernacle be erected in one day, which offers a type of Christ so that by it you may understand that he died once in this one present time. He will certainly not be born or die in the future since he has already been born and has died and has risen from the dead. Resurrection, which is a kind of pitching of the holy tabernacle, must follow death. And it is in the new moon because we have a new age in Christ, since whatever is in him is a new creation. And the first month is taken to indicate a renewal of human nature from death and decay to life and incorruptibility, its present change from barrenness to fruitfulness and its escape from the tyranny of the devil, like that winter that is now over and past.

Next he shows us Emmanuel in another way in type and outline, saying, "And you will place the ark of the testimony in it, and you will cover it with a veil."[174] In the foregoing, the Word was indicated to us by the whole tabernacle (since it was the house of God, and God dwelt in it, that is, the holy body of Christ), but no less is the same one signified to us by the ark in particular. It was constructed of incorruptible wood that you may think of his incorruptible body.[175] And the whole thing was covered with pure gold, as it is written, inside and outside.[176] That is because all facets of him are honorable and royal, both the divinity and the humanity, **[569]** and he has preeminence in all things, as Paul says.[177] Gold is taken to be a type of honor and excellence above all things. The ark then, built of incorruptible wood overlaid with gold, also had the divine law placed in it as a type of God the Word dwelling in and united with the holy flesh. The law, after all, is also the word of God, though not hypostatic like the Son is.

Moreover, it is covered by the veil. And indeed God the Word made human was in a certain way unseen by the many, having his own body as a cloak and hiding in his own flesh as behind a veil, so that because of this some people did not recognize his God-befitting dignity. One time they tried to stone him, charging that he, being a human, said that he was God.[178] Another time they said without blushing at all, "Is this not Jesus, the son of Joseph, whose father and mother we know? How does he now say, 'I have come down from heaven?'"[179] The placing of the veil over the ark then indicates that Jesus will not be recognized by the many. Therefore, the ark too was a type of him.

For this reason it also went before the Israelites in the desert, standing in for God at that time. He was, after all, the leader of the people. The psalmist too is a witness, saying, "O God, when you went out before your people, when you marched through the desert, the earth shook and the heavens dropped rain."[180] Even though the ark always marches before and goes ahead, God is explicitly said to go before.

You may have even clearer proof in addition to this when you consider the following. At one point God commanded the Israelites through Moses to go up boldly to Mount Seir and besiege the Amorites.[181] But **[570]** those commanded fell into intractable cowardice, and because they looked to their own strength for success rather than trusting in help from above, they sat down and wept by the mountain, as it is written.[182] The lawgiver was justly provoked by this and threatened that he would not lead them into the promised land. Scarcely were they cut to the heart by this threat and driven to a hasty change of mind when, by a second disobedience, they tried to go up and take up arms against the Amorites. But God announced beforehand through Moses what was going to happen. "Do not go up to them,"

[174]Ex 40:3. [175]Ex 25:10. [176]Ex 38:2. [177]Col 1:18. [178]Jn 10:33. [179]Jn 6:42. [180]Ps 68:7-8 (Ps 67:8-9 LXX). [181]Deut 1:7, 19. [182]Deut 1:45.

he said, "and do not fall in front of your enemies, for I am not with you."[183] But they were overcome by the disease of disobedience, and they forced their way up the mountain, as it is written.[184] But the ark of God, it says, did not go up with them. It remained in the camp.[185] Do you see that when God says, "I am not with you," the ark does not go up with the disobedient, showing clearly to those with more understanding that it stands in the place of God their leader?

Or again, it was carried around Jericho by the priests, and Jericho's high wall fell, not by setting up siege engines and battering rams but by trumpets and shouting. And we will find this to be true in Christ. He is the one who is carried by the holy priests and who overturns all the might of the devil, not with weapons but with a shout and a trumpet, that is, the apostolic and evangelical proclamation, and with the united praise of all the people, confessing their Lord with the right faith.

We see this fulfilled also in the mystical doxologies in which the priestly trumpet, that is, the voice of the liturgist, leads the people, and in this way the power of the adversaries falls and is crushed. **[571]** "For our weapons are not fleshly," according to Paul, "but they have divine power."[186] The prophet Habakkuk makes clear that Christ is carried in a way by the saints and rests on them when he says, "You will mount your horses, and your chariot will be your salvation."[187] And the Savior himself will teach this no less when he says to Ananias concerning Paul, "Go, for he is my chosen vessel to carry my name before all the Gentiles."[188]

Yes, "and you shall bring in the table," it also says, "and arrange its setting, and you shall bring in the lampstand and set up its lamps."[189] And you may recognize Christ through both of these. He is figured in a way by the table that has loaves set on it because in him all are nourished to eternal life, namely, by participating in his holy flesh, according to his statement: "I am the bread that came down from heaven and that gives life to the world. If anyone eats of this bread, they will live forever. And the bread that I will give for the life of the world is my flesh."[190] Therefore, what is set on the table, that is, the loaves, indicate the holy body of Christ, which nourishes everyone to eternal life.

When the blessed David and his companions were hungry, as it is written, they ate the showbread.[191] Let us see whether this incident too sketches some mystery. According to the law's command, no one was permitted to taste the showbread except for the priests alone. Nevertheless, even though David and his companions were not from a priestly tribe, they partook of the most holy food so that through this again the faith of the Gentiles and **[572]** of part of Israel might be signified. Now Christ was designated for the Israelites since they were holier "because of their fathers" and the law,[192] but the multitude of other races ran to him, so to speak, and even though they were unholy because of their straying, they ate the bread of life. And David was with them, serving as a type, as it were, of the saved of Israel, which the blessed Isaiah calls a remnant.[193] For many of them believed in Christ.

This then is how Christ may be understood through the holy table. Next, he is the lampstand since he shines throughout the whole house, that is, the world. "For I am the light of the world," he says.[194] And it holds seven lamps, not just one.[195] That is because he shines in many ways and enlightens the souls of the believers with different gifts. And the lampstand is made of pure gold[196] because it is superior to all and precious. It also has a solid stem, as it is written,[197] because there is

[183]Deut 1:42. [184]Deut 1:43. [185]Num 14:44. [186]2 Cor 10:4. [187]Hab 3:8. [188]Acts 9:15. [189]Ex 40:4. [190]Jn 6:51, 33. [191]Mt 12:3-4. [192]Rom 11:28. [193]Is 10:22. [194]Jn 8:12. [195]Num 8:2. [196]Num 8:4. [197]Num 8:4 (LXX).

nothing hollow or lightweight in Christ. It has lilies[198] because of the sweet smell of sanctification, according to the statement, "I am a flower of the plain, a lily of the valleys."[199] Moreover, the seven oil funnels[200] signify the supply of divine graces. The prophet Zechariah, however, testified that two olive branches were around the lampstand[201] so that you may understand that two peoples received mercy, whom he called "sons of fatness." He says they "stand by the Lord of the whole earth,"[202] even though Zechariah sees the branches around the lampstand. This gives the clearest proof that the lampstand is Christ, who has set next to himself both the people of the Gentiles and the people of the Jews through obedience and faith in him.

Next, he continues to point him out to us in many ways. **[573]** "And you shall set up the golden altar to burn incense before the ark. And you shall place a covering, a veil, over the door to the tabernacle of testimony. And the altar of burnt offerings you shall place next to the door of the tabernacle of testimony. And you shall cover the tabernacle and sanctify everything in it all around."[203]

We must pay attention to how Christ is described to us through both altars. After he has ordered that the golden altar, on which incense is offered before the ark, be put aside, and after he has said that a covering is to be stretched across the middle of the doors of the tabernacle so that no one can see inside, he commands that the altar of burnt offerings be placed next to the doors of the tabernacle of testimony. It is not invisible or hidden since it is outside the veil. See him then through the altar of incense as a sweet aroma ascending to God the Father (for this is what incense signifies) and through the altar of burnt offering as an offering and a sacrifice offered for us. The golden altar was hidden by the veil since the glory of Christ was hidden, but the other one, the altar of burnt offering where the sacrifices were, was visible since the death of Christ was evident and known to all.

Now their position makes a difference. The one was in front of the ark; the other was by the doors of the tabernacle. The position of the one, the golden altar, in front of the ark in the sight of God the Father, as it were, suggests through an enigma that the glory of the Son is wondrous, according to the statement, "No one knows who the Son is except the Father."[204] The position of the other, the altar of burnt offering, at the very doors of the tabernacle contains a type of his death and his sacrifice for all and signifies that we can approach God the Father in no other way **[574]** than through the sacrifice of Christ, according to his statement, "I am the door,"[205] and, "No one comes to the Father except through me."[206]

Further, he commands that the tabernacle be covered all around, encompassing everything in it, so that it is seen as one and not many. That is because Christ among us is one, even though he is perceived in various ways: as a tabernacle because of the veil of his flesh, as the ark that has the divine law (since he is the Word of God the Father), as the table since he is food and life, as the lampstand since he is intellectual and spiritual life, as both the altar of incense since he is the pleasing aroma of sanctification and the altar of burnt offering since he is the sacrifice for the life of the world. And everything in it is sanctified because Christ is completely holy, however he is perceived.

Since then the holy tabernacle was their leader, those of Israel were ordered both to set out and to rest with it. God was profitably teaching and instructing us that God the Word made flesh for us is our leader and guide on the road to salvation and that by assenting

[198]Num 8:4. [199]Song 2:1. [200]Zech 4:2 (LXX). [201]Zech 4:3. [202]Zech 4:14. "Sons of fatness" appears in the LXX of this verse. [203]Ex 40:5-6. [204]Lk 10:22. [205]Jn 10:9. [206]Jn 14:6.

to his commands without hesitation we ascend to eternal life. Those who had been instructed in the mysteries with many words did not want to do this, and they "turned back and no longer went about with him."[207] The blessed Peter, however, is most wise. He says to the Savior, "Where can we go?"[208] It is truly most fitting for the saints not to depart from God in any way but to hurry to be with him spiritually.

6:69 "And we have come to believe and know that you are the Christ, the holy one of God."

Wondrous is the faith of the holy apostles, fervent [575] their manner of confession and most desirable and excellent their understanding. For they did not just turn back and fall away, like certain of the more ignorant or like those who called the Savior's word hard. Nor were they called to faith in such a way that they were easily carried away by levity. Rather, they were already certain and convinced ahead of time that their instructor of the mysteries was full of life-giving words and that he was the bringer of heavenly teachings. This faith is exceedingly sure. A faith that is otherwise would easily and rightly be rejected. Since it does not have certainty as its root, it is quite readily eroded from the human mind.

Indeed, the Savior himself, when he is speaking in parables about the sower, says that what fell on the rock dried up because it had no root. He is saying enigmatically that any mind that is dried up and cannot receive the word that is cast onto it is rock. The wretched Jews also experienced this because of their exceedingly great ignorance and were being taught by the voice of the prophet, "Rend your hearts and not your garments."[209] Just as the precepts of farming advise that the earth be cut open by a plough before the casting of the seeds, so also I think that those who go to receive the divine words ought to open up their heart in some way by the desire for them. By receiving them in this way, they make their soul pregnant like a plot of land bearing fruit.

In the certainty of faith, then, the most wise disciples say that they have "come to know" and are sure that he is the "Christ, the Son of the living God." And again on this point you will find their words put together with great wisdom. They mention both terms: "believe" and "come to know," bringing both together [576] as the same thing. After all, it is necessary both to believe and to know. And just because the more divine truths are attained by faith, that does not at all mean we should abandon investigation into these matters; rather, we should try to ascend at least to a measure of knowledge that is "in a mirror and an enigma," as Paul says.[210] And he does well not to say "come to know" first and then "believe," but he puts faith first and brings in knowledge second. That is because knowledge is after faith and not before it, as it is written, "Unless you believe, you will not understand."[211] First a simple faith is laid in us like a foundation. Then knowledge is built on top of it little by little, raising us to "the measure of the stature" in Christ and to "mature" and spiritual "manhood."[212] That is also why God says somewhere, "Behold, I will lay a foundation for Zion, a chosen precious cornerstone."[213] Christ is for us a beginning and a foundation for sanctification and righteousness, through faith, that is, and in no other way. For that is how he dwells in us.

Observe how they say throughout in the singular number with the article prefixed, "You are the Christ, the Son of the living God," separating the true Son, by whose likeness we too are sons, from those who are called to adoption by grace, on the grounds that he is one and exceptional. They also call him "the Christ" in the singular. But know that

[207]Jn 6:66. [208]Jn 6:68. [209]Joel 2:13. [210]1 Cor 13:12. [211]Is 7:9 (LXX). [212]Eph 4:13. [213]Is 28:16.

at this point he is not called Christ on his own account or because he is this in his essence (like he is the Son in his essence), but he is called truly and uniquely one because none of the anointed ones[214] are like him, except insofar as he is called Christ by his likeness to us. Son is a name and a true reality that is proper to him and set apart as his own, while Christ is common to us. Since he was anointed in that he was made human, he is Christ. If, therefore, **[577]** we attribute the anointing to the need of the human nature, he would be understood as Christ by likeness to us, and not in the same way as he is the Son. However, he is still one and unique—both by nature and by excellence, both before the flesh and with the flesh. He is not two as some think, who do not seem to understand the depth of the mystery.

The Word of God the Father, after all, did not come down into a man as the grace of the Spirit comes down on one of the holy prophets, but he himself truly became flesh, as it is written,[215] that is, he became man. He is indivisible, then, after the union, and he is not divided into two persons,[216] even though we recognize that the Word of God is one thing and the flesh in which he has come to dwell is another. Since the whole chorus of holy apostles confirms for us the faith concerning these matters, in that they say that they have "come to know" that he is "the Christ, the Son of God" in the singular, we will not accept, if we think rightly, those who ignorantly dare to institute something new beyond this.

6:70-71 Jesus answered them, "Did I not choose you, the twelve, and one of you is a devil?" He was speaking of Judas Iscariot, the son of Simon. He, though one of the twelve, was going to betray him.

He intensifies his reproach, and he ties them down with sharper words, cutting off what is flabby and lazy in their will to be made wise. He almost seems to say something like, O my disciples, now is the time for watchfulness and purpose and a mind intent on the desire for salvation. The road to destruction is extremely slippery. It drags down not only the feeble mind but also the one that thinks it already stands securely. **[578]** Sin is a fearful thing and has many forms. It bewitches the human mind with many different pleasures, and with the smoothest desires, as it were, it drags the mind to things that are not fitting. Your situation, he says, will be the example of what I am saying. I will tell you to begin with, I did not choose any of those who have fallen back out of frivolity as I chose you who are good (since as God I knew what was in you), but Satan seized one of you through greed, and my judgment certainly was not deceived. In humanity there is free will and choice to go to both, either to the right or to the left, that is, to virtue or vice.

By his severe accusation, then, he rouses them to a fitting watchfulness and at the same time makes each one more steadfast regarding himself. He does not yet say clearly who will betray him, but by placing the burden of impiety simply and indefinitely on one, he was putting them all in the contest and summoning them to more careful watchfulness as each one was dreading the loss of his own soul. At the same time, with these words he was accomplishing something else profitable for the faith of the disciples. When they have confessed that they know and have firmly believed that he is the "Son of God,"[217] he shows that he knows the future, thus demonstrating that their confession of him was sure, as it were. After all, knowing the future does not belong to anyone who exists except to the one who alone is by nature God, concerning whom it is written, "Who knows all things before they come to be."[218] He also called the servant of

[214]The word he uses here is "christs," which means "anointed ones." [215]Jn 1:14. [216]πρόσωπα. [217]Jn 6:69. [218]Sus 42.

the diabolical will the "devil," and he was not deceived. Just as "the one who is united to the Lord is one spirit with him,"[219] so also the reverse is true. **[579]**

Chapter Five

Concerning the feast of tabernacles, that it shows forth the restoration of the hope due the saints and the resurrection from the dead; on the words "Now the Jewish feast of tabernacles was near."

7:1 And after these things, Jesus was going about in Galilee. He did not want to go about in Judea because the Jews were trying to kill him.

After these things, he says (referring to both words and deeds), Christ gladly spent time in Galilee. This is what I think "go about" shows. By adding the reason, he shows that being with them was not by his choice but rather happened by necessity. The Jews, he says, wanted "to kill him." For this reason, he granted himself to another race for a long time, refusing to "go about in Judea." Now I think these words do nothing less than accuse Israel for its exceeding stubbornness, at least if being with the Gentiles is found to be far better than living with Israel. This then is what was spoken by the prophet Jeremiah: "I have forsaken my house; I have abandoned my inheritance; I gave my beloved soul into the hands of her enemies."[220] The fact that Christ became an outcast because of the **[580]** unholiness of his persecutors and went away to the Galileans—how is that not plainly giving his own soul into the hands of her enemies? The Gentiles are, after all, enemies of Christ because they serve another and worship the creature rather than the creator,[221] since they have not yet received faith in him. He himself teaches this clearly when he says, "Whoever is not with me is against me."[222] And I think everyone will admit that before they had the true knowledge of God and faith, the Gentiles were not with Christ; therefore, they were against him and classified as enemies by this statement.

Now if this is so (and it clearly is), so great an abomination was practiced among those of Israel that he was better off going to live with his enemies (with whom it was least fitting for him to want to spend time) than to live with his relatives according to the flesh (which would have been appropriate and more fitting). Since they were related to him, they ought to have loved him. It was most reasonable then for Christ to go to the Gentiles. By this very act he was saying in a way that if they did not stop persecuting him and sending away their benefactor by their madness, Christ would give himself completely to those outside and go over to the Gentiles. Just as we say that he hints at this by this act, so also we will find that through an ancient figure as well he threatened to depart from Jerusalem.

When he was decreeing the laws about sacrifices, as it is written in the book of Leviticus, he appointed beforehand, as an image of Christ, that a calf be brought forward as a gift and whole burnt offering to the Lord.[223] He then sketches him in another way, saying, "If his gift to the Lord is from the flocks, from the lambs or the kids as a whole burnt offering, **[581]** he shall bring forward a spotless male and lay his hand on its head, and they shall slaughter it by the side of the altar to the north before the Lord."[224] We must then investigate how the mystery of Christ is expressed to us in this passage as well.

I think that first we should speak about the placement of both the temple itself in Jerusalem and the divine altar so that in this way we may understand what it means that the sheep does not look straight ahead but is turned to

[219]1 Cor 6:17. [220]Jer 12:7. [221]Rom 1:25. [222]Lk 11:23. [223]Lev 1:2-17. [224]Lev 1:10-11.

the north. Now the territory of the Jews lies in the southern part of the earth, and the temple looks east and opens its doors toward the first rays of the sun. But the divine altar itself, right next to the holy of holies in the sight of God, as it were, shows its front to those who come from the east, its two sides looking one south, the other north.

You may have proof that these things are just as we have said from the passage in the prophet Ezekiel. When he was learning of the death of Phaltias,[225] that is, in a spiritual vision, he says, "And I looked, and behold, there were twenty-five men with their backs toward the temple of the Lord and their faces away from it. And they were worshiping the sun in the east."[226] Now if a man worshiping the rising sun has the temple behind him, is it not necessary to suppose that the front of the temple is turned toward the east? And the divine altar itself followed this pattern, as we have said. Therefore, the front access both of the temple itself and of the divine altar was to the east. And there were two sides, one to the south and the other to the north. The remaining side, which is conceived of as the back, faced west. **[582]**

Since what we have said is so, we will find to the north the neighbor of the Jews, Galilee, that is, the land of the Gentiles, "Galilee of the Gentiles," as it is written.[227] Since our Lord Jesus Christ was about to depart from the land of the Jews after his saving passion and go to Galilee, that is, to the church of the Gentiles, the sheep that was taken for the sacrifice as a type was slaughtered at the side of the altar so that it might look north, according to that statement by the psalmist about Christ, "His eyes look toward the Gentiles."[228]

And since the blessed Evangelist says that he refused to be with the Jews since they were plotting to kill him, we will add the following to what has been said: we will not consider Christ's withdrawal to occasion a charge of cowardice, nor on this account will we accuse him who has all power of weakness, but we will accept the manner of the *oikonomia*. It was necessary that he endure the cross for all not ahead of time but in his own time.

7:3-5 So his brothers said to him, "Leave here and go to Judea so that your disciples also may see the works you are doing. For no one acts in secret who seeks to be known openly. If you do these things, manifest yourself to the world." For not even his brothers believed in him.

The reputed brothers of the Savior, not yet knowing that God the Word dwelt in his holy flesh, nor knowing when they say this that **[583]** he became human, still have a small conception of him and far too limited a picture of the grace and excellence that is in him. They see no more than others see, and they are deluded by the common opinion of him, thinking that he too was actually begotten of their father, Joseph, not seeing the hidden constitution of the mystery. It seems that while many miracles are being done secretly by Christ in Galilee, they try to persuade him to seek empty glory, and they advise him to receive the admiration of the spectators as some great thing. They assume that this is the only reason he himself wants to do each of the miracles he performs, only to be admired by the spectators and to revel in human praise like those who habitually seek glory. See how they advise him to go up "to Judea" to perform miracles there instead, not so that "his disciples" may believe in him but so that "they may see the works he is doing." After all, if you want to be known, they say (since this is what it means to be "manifest"), do not be a wonder

[225]Phaltias is the name the LXX gives for Pelatiah, whose death is recorded in Ezek 11:13. [226]Ezek 8:16. [227]Is 9:1 (Is 8:23 LXX). [228]Ps 66:7 (Ps 65:7 LXX).

worker in secret and do not flee being "known openly," since you are preeminent in your power to do all things. In this way you will be known "to the world" and more famous among the spectators. This, then, is what they are saying in this passage.

The most wise Evangelist, however, profitably indicates that "his brothers did not yet believe in him." Indeed, it would have been quite strange if those who through faith had already received full knowledge of him as God were guilty of such cold words. What they say is prudent at the time, however, since they do not yet believe. But after they understand the great mystery concerning him and believe, they ascend to such a point of reverence and virtue that they are both called apostles **[584]** and attain illustrious piety.

You have this as well sung ahead of time by the voice of the prophets. Indeed, the blessed Jeremiah says, addressing our Lord Jesus Christ, "For even your brothers and the house of your father, even they have rejected you; they have cried out, they are gathered together behind you. Do not believe them, for they will speak fair words to you."[229] His brothers, who rejected him before they had faith and who from what we just said practically tried to shout him down, were gathered together through faith and have spoken fair words about him, both helping others and contending for the message of the faith. After the prophet mentions the brothers, he very carefully and profitably adds "the house of your father," lest they be thought to have come somehow from the holy virgin rather than from their father, Joseph, alone.

7:6 Jesus said to them, "My time has not yet come, but your time is always here."

The Savior's words are always concealed by shadow. That is why it is written of him, "And he will be a man who hides his words."[230] And who among those who think rightly will not say that he fashioned this statement profitably as well? Therefore it is "not yet" the time for absolute openness, he says, or for an unveiled revealing to all, since the mind of the Jews is not yet ripe for understanding so that they might be able to receive my words without anger and wrath. Nor does the present time allow me to be made known fully to the world, since the Jews are not yet completely departing from grace, and they have not yet raged against me to the point where I must finally go to others. That is why he says that his time "has not yet **[585]** come," and he says that their time has come and is always "here." After all, we say that those in the world may do what they want without any necessity hindering them or summoning them to a time-sensitive plan that tells them what they should or should not do, as was of course the case with Christ. On the contrary, the way of life for those who have chosen life in this world is relaxed and free from more laborious care, always ready and open to a period of pleasure that may unfold, as it were, and readily permitting those who practice it to go wherever they wish.

When, therefore, actions must be subject to plans, not every time is appropriate to do what needs to be done; instead, there is an appropriate time for each act, just as the nature of the matter may demand. But for the one who has chosen to live unhindered, no such limitation will be imposed; rather, the way lies quite ready and open to wherever one wishes to go.

7:7 "The world cannot hate you, but it hates me because I testify about it that its deeds are evil."

Quite cleverly does the Savior now reprove his brothers, who are still too worldly-minded and disposed. He introduces a second skillful

[229]Jer 12:6. [230]Is 32:2 (LXX).

defense, as it were, whereby he shows not only that they do not know who he is by nature but also that they are still so far removed from love toward him that they choose to live in harmony with those who admire the life of the world rather than the life of virtue. It would have been most absurd indeed to teach all the others [586] what is useful, with all the wrapping around the instruction removed, yet not to bestow on his reputed brothers in far greater measure the things which they were going to learn with great profit, now that they have the supplier of wisdom.

This is the custom of Christ the Savior. Sometimes he seizes a well-timed opportunity and constructs long catecheses for his hearers. All people love what is related to them, he says, and an identical way of life miraculously leads to the same disposition. "The world does not hate you" since you still think like it, "but it hates me" since it does not take kindly to being accused by me for its disgraceful behavior. Therefore, you will go to the festival without risk, but not me. I will surely dispute with them and tell them while I am there what is good for them. But correction is bitter for those who love pleasure, and it has the power to provoke to wrath the one who does not have appropriate self-control.

Next, the Lord helps us through these words as well. Indeed, it is not good to rebuke thoughtlessly or to offer guidance to everyone through reproof but to keep in mind what is written: "Do not rebuke the evil, lest they hate you"[231] (since hatred is not harmless for us), but rather be eager to speak "into the ears of those who listen," as it is written.[232] The world loves sin, but the Lord is a corrector of those who do not act rightly, and it is fitting that the correction is often given through rebuke. To enumerate sin at all is to rebuke those who love it, and to condemn iniquity is to chastise those who have it. When, therefore, necessity summons the teacher to rebuke and the manner of healing requires him to go down this road, [587] the one who is instructed unwillingly by the rebukes gets extremely angry. At that point, evil deeds must surely arise from hatred. That is why the Savior says that he is hated by the world; he recognizes that it cannot yet bear exhortation accompanied by rebuke, even though it should do so for its own profit. The mind that is under the tyranny of iniquitous pleasure surely gets angry at the advice that tries to persuade it that it ought to be sober. The Savior says these things not completely refusing a stay in Jerusalem or refusing to give correction that would clearly be profitable to the sinners but intending to do this too, along with everything else, in due time.

And note that he says something similar to his disciples as well. As he is encouraging them and teaching them not to be too distressed over what will happen to them when they proclaim him to the world and encounter a myriad of trials because of it, he says, "If you were of the world, the world would love you as its own. But since you are not of the world, for this reason the world hates you."[233] Here he is not calling the visible creation "world," but those who set their mind on the things of the world.[234] Indeed, for these people, anyone who does not love the same things—and intensely—is considered hard and hostile and is classified as an enemy. But the one who consents with them and is bound with them to the same shameful behavior by an identical lifestyle is considered a close and dear friend.

7:8 "You go up to this feast. I am not going to this feast became my time has not yet fully come."

The Lord now clearly refuses to feast with the Jews or to go along to partake [588] in shad-

[231]Prov 9:8. [232]Sir 25:9. [233]Jn 15:19. [234]See Rom 8:5.

owy festivities with them. What was once said to a few, albeit to those reputed to be his brothers, will potentially be extended to the whole race of Israel. No one can say, at least in the strict sense, that Jesus avoided being with his brothers because of their behavior, since he is obviously with them in Galilee. We should rather surmise that his purpose in staying with them was related to his supposed relationship with them according to the flesh which was generally assumed. It is clear then that since the whole multitude of the Jews is being introduced as a type by means of his brothers, Christ refuses to feast with them according to the statement by one of the holy prophets: "I hate, I reject your feasts, and I will not smell the aroma in your festal gatherings. Therefore, even if you bring me whole burnt offerings and sacrifices, I will not accept them, and I will not look at the sight of your peace offerings. Remove from me the noise of your songs; I will not listen to the hymn of your instruments."[235]

"For God is Spirit, and those who worship him must worship in spirit and truth,"[236] according to the voice of the Savior himself. Since he is Spirit, he would naturally take pleasure in spiritual honors and offerings, of which the sacrifices of oxen and sheep and offerings of frankincense, fine flour, wine and olive oil were appointed by the command of the law as a type, indicating through more visible outlines the many hues of virtue of those who worship in spirit. You then, he says, who still love the shadow and are coarsely and Jewishly disposed concerning these matters, you go up to the assembly that is in shadows and types. But I take no pleasure in that kind of feasting. I do not go up to this feast, namely, the one in type and outline, since I have no delight in it. **[589]** Instead, I await the time of the true assembly, which has not yet fully come. Then—then, he says—I will be with my company, rejoicing in the brightness of the saints and the glory of the Father, shining forth with ultimate brilliance.

But he says it belongs to him and calls the time his own since the feast is his and he is the master of the feast. The blessed Jeremiah ascribed it to him, saying to those who have neglected reverence toward God and have placed no value on the desire to excel in goodness, "What will you do on the day of the assembly and in the days of the feast of the Lord?"[237] You, he says, who reject toil for the Lord and do not have the bright robe of love for God, what will you do in the day of the assembly? How will you enter the divine and heavenly feast? How would the master of the banquet not rightly throw you out of the most illustrious chorus of the invited guests, saying, "Friend, how did you get in here without a wedding garment?"[238]

Related to this and conveying the same thought to us would be the passage from the prophet Zechariah. "And it will come to pass," he says, "that whoever is left from all the nations that came against Jerusalem will go up every year to worship the king, the Lord Almighty, and to celebrate the feast of the tabernacles."[239] He says that those who are left will go up to worship the great king and observe the feast of the tabernacles. That is because although many have been invited by grace, those who go up to the city are not many. For "few are chosen,"[240] says the Savior, that is, few are left from every nation. And when he says they will go up to worship, **[590]** he shows that they no longer observe the worship of the law but the worship in spirit, and that they observe the feast of the tabernacles in truth, all but sending up with a clear voice that song in the Psalms, "Blessed be the Lord, for he has heard the voice of my supplication. My heart hoped in him, and I was

[235]Amos 5:21-23. [236]Jn 4:24. [237]Hos 9:5. [238]Mt 22:12. [239]Zech 14:16. [240]Mt 20:16. Not all manuscripts of Matthew have this statement.

helped, and my flesh revived."[241]

The flesh has revived and will live again, and not without Christ. For he himself has become for us the source of resurrection and the door of the truer tabernacle. And this was what was said through one of the holy prophets, "I will raise up the fallen tabernacle of David."[242] After all, the fallen tabernacle of Christ, who is of the seed of David according to the flesh, was the first raised to incorruption by the power of God the Father, as one of the apostles said to the Jews about him, "This man, handed over to you by the definite plan and foreknowledge of God, you killed by taking and crucifying him by the hand of lawless men. But God raised him up, having loosed the pangs of death, because it was not possible for him to be held by it."[243] And again, "God raised this Jesus, and of that we are all witnesses."[244] It is not difficult to see that it is the custom of Holy Scripture to call Christ, who is from David according to the flesh, David.

7:9-10 After saying this, he remained in Galilee. But after his brothers had gone to the feast, then he also went up, not publicly but in secret.

He is glad to stay in Galilee, and when he is banished from the land of the Jews, he dwells there happily and safely so that the multitude of the Gentiles might be shown nobler than those who are reputed to be learned in the law, **[591]** even though the Gentiles are completely uninstructed because of the error that still grips them. By this he shows his just love toward them and his most reasonable hostility toward those of Israel. How could the one who "knows all things before they come to be"[245] not be so disposed that he deems the church of the Gentiles already worthy of divine love since it is so easily called to faith in him, but he shakes off and justly loathes Jerusalem as senseless?

Even before the time of his coming, he is said to desire her beauty, according to the cry of the psalmist,[246] but he called stiff-necked Jerusalem a prostitute and adulteress, and what names of this sort did he not call her? For example, he says to her most clearly through the prophet Ezekiel, "Therefore, O prostitute, hear the word of the Lord."[247] And by the voice of Jeremiah she is charged as an adulteress when he cries, "As a woman leaves her husband, so the house of Israel has left me," says the Lord.[248] Since, according to the foreknowledge of God-befitting counsel he has observed the beauty of the church of the Gentiles and the shamefulness of the synagogue of the Jews in its wicked ways, he loves the one in advance and comes to her as to a bride in the bridal chamber, but he is roused in advance to hatred toward the other, reserving for the proper time the fullness of what they each deserve. He neither wholly brings punishment on those of Israel ahead of time nor wholly gives himself to Galilee before the saving cross. That is when he could justly and for good reason withdraw from his love toward them.

Now after he said that he would not go up to this feast but let his brothers go if they wanted to, he goes up after them alone, since he insisted that his time had not yet come. **[592]** He is not saying one thing but doing the opposite of what he says. That would be lying, though it says that deceit, that is, lying, is not to be found in his mouth at all.[249] No, he is in fact zealously doing what he promised. He does not go up to feast with them but to admonish them, and, since he came to save, he goes up to the feast to say and teach things that lead to eternal life. That this was his intention will clearly be shown by the fact that

[241]Ps 28:6-7 (Ps 27:6-7 LXX). [242]Amos 9:11. [243]Acts 2:23-24. [244]Acts 2:32. [245]Sus 42. [246]Ps 45:11 (Ps 44:12 LXX). [247]Ezek 16:35. [248]Jer 3:20. [249]Is 53:9.

he did not want to accompany those who were going up but barely went up at all and went secretly, not with the openness and joy of those going to a feast.

Indeed, when he was finally going up to his saving passion, he went up not secretly but was carried on a colt, as a type of the new people. He had an innumerable company of children preceding him, bringing to realization the sketch of the people who would be born, about whom it is written, "A people that is created will praise the Lord."[250] And the children preceding him were crying out, "Blessed is he who comes in the name of the Lord! Hosanna in the highest!"[251] Therefore, by going up secretly he shows that the Christ came to Jerusalem not to feast with them but to dispute against them. As we said before, he does not completely depart from Israel until he obviously has a good reason for doing so, when he has been handed over to death.

As for him saying that he will not go up but afterward not refusing to go up, you will find an ancient type of this fulfilled in the book called Exodus. The divine and most holy Moses was spending a long time with God on the mountain, waiting for the law that he was going to give. But Israel was making a calf in the desert, paying no attention to reverence toward God. **[593]** But the lawgiver rightly gets angry at these things. He cries out against the levity of those who so readily turned aside to what is not right, threatens to destroy them once and for all and finally says to the holy Moses, "Depart and go up from here, you and your people whom you brought out of Egypt, to the land which I swore to Abraham, Isaac and Jacob, saying, 'I will give it to your seed,' and I will send my angel before you.'"[252] Then Moses says to him, "If you yourself do not go with me, do not lead me up from here. How will it be truly known that I have found favor with you, I and your people, unless you go with us?"[253] And the Lord said to Moses, "What you have said I will do, for you have found favor with me."[254] You see how as he grieved over the apostasy of Israel, he maintained that he would not go up with them to the promised land but said that he was sending an angel with them, yet out of respect for Moses and the memory of the fathers, he granted them pardon and promised again to go with them.

After he denied, then, that he would feast with the Jews—since they dishonor God by their arrogance and violence and by their denial of him (just as those did by making the calf)—he does not get excessively angry at the offenses of those grieving him. Instead, he keeps the promise to the holy fathers, and he goes up to teach and set before them the doctrines for their salvation. He does not entrust this ministry to an angel (just as he did not then either), but he himself accomplishes even the salvation of the ungrateful. **[594]**

7:11 Now the Jews were looking for him at the feast and saying, "Where is that man?"

The Jews are searching for Jesus not so that they may believe in him once they have found him—in that case, he would have preempted their search and offered himself according to his statement, "I was found by those who did not seek me; I was made manifest to those who did not ask for me"[255]—but they do it falling (because of their exceedingly great transgression) into the vain toil of the Greeks. They are more zealous for Greek customs than for those things that would likely enlighten them by grace from above.

Now the Greeks, who seem to be wise, are filled with worldly and demonic wisdom. They expend long and keen discourses, spin cycles of vain ideas and weave a spider web, as it is written,[256] as they pretend to investigate the

[250]Ps 102:18 (Ps 101:19 LXX). [251]Mt 21:9. [252]Ex 33:1-2. [253]Ex 33:15-16. [254]Ex 33:17. [255]Is 65:1. [256]Is 59:5.

nature of truth or goodness or justice. Fashioning for themselves something like a mere shadow of true knowledge, they remain without any taste whatsoever of virtue in deeds. And remaining barren of the real wisdom from above,[257] they practice their repeated word exercises to no useful purpose. The Jews, who are neighbors and relatives to their ignorance, seek Jesus not so they may believe in him once they have found him, as the nature of their actions made clear, but so that by heaping much abuse on him, they may bring unquenchable fire onto their own heads.

And there is another sense in which we shall consider their search to be completely idle: they only pretend to search for him, because he is not there. "The wonder worker must be present at the feast," they say, since they are hunting for the pleasure and enjoyment of being amazed and not at all for the benefit that comes from it. But having wrapped themselves in the glory of their knowledge of the law [595] and thinking that they have been instructed beyond measure in the Holy Scriptures, they forget the voice of the prophet which says, "Seek God, and when you find him, call on him. When he draws near to you, let the wicked forsake his way and the lawless man his plan, and let him turn to the Lord, and he will find mercy."[258] Do you see how it will not be enough for salvation only to seek, but those who find must also turn to him, namely, through obedience and faith? This is how the ignorant and straying people of the Jews could have been saved.

But since in this too they are found to be exceedingly foolish, they will in the end hear with good reason, "How can you say, 'We are wise, and the word of the Lord is with us'? In vain have the scribes used a false pen. The wise were ashamed, alarmed and taken. What wisdom is in them? They rejected the word of the Lord."[259] How did those who refused to receive the word not reject it? Or how do those who ignorantly say, "Where is that man?" not dishonor the word? The expression "that man," after all, belongs to the senseless and to those who do not think it is in any way right to marvel at him, even though because of his exceedingly great miracles, they ought to have the most preeminent conception of him.

7:12 And there was muttering about him among the crowds. Some were saying that he was a good man, but others were saying, "No, he is deceiving the crowd."

The good is always hard to hunt down and difficult to find, and to be able to track the beauty of the truth is difficult for the many to accomplish. This is especially true for the more unlearned and for those who do not have an acute understanding, who by the most foolish turns of vacuous reasoning incline toward whatever seems easier to them. Since they cannot bear to test the nature of whatever comes on them, [596] they will never arrive at the true quality of things, even though Paul says, "be approved bankers," and urges us to "test everything"[260] so that by careful investigation we come to the prize of what is profitable.

Let them hear then, who from their stupendous senselessness do not marvel at Jesus but think it right to condemn him indiscriminately, "Taste and see that the Lord is good."[261] Just as those who identify choice honey by the quality of its taste perceive what they are seeking by just a little sample, so also those who try even a little of the Savior's words will recognize that he is good and, once they learn this, will marvel. Therefore, the wiser of the Jews advocate for Christ and offer a right judgment about him. Together they praise him as good, no doubt having in mind the most likely conclusion: that the power to accomplish feats clearly worked by God would not belong

[257]Jas 3:17. [258]Is 55:6-7. [259]Jer 8:8-9. [260]1 Thess 5:21. [261]Ps 34:8 (Ps 33:9 LXX).

to anyone unless he were God by nature or a partaker in God, and for this reason good. He would deserve both the approval of all and the empowering by grace from above, even though this was not the case for Christ because Christ himself is the Lord of powers.

But those who did not hesitate to call him a deceiver, though he guides us on the unerring path of righteousness, are swimming in the most absurd opinions and have left the truth far behind. Let the deranged Jew then hear, "Woe to those who call evil good and good evil, who put darkness for light and light for darkness."[262] For bringing an accusation against the good is ranked on the same level as advocating evil, and removing the most just condemnation from what is shameful is ranked on the same level as casting undeserved blame on those who are on the side of good. The accusation against their abuse was also foretold. **[597]** "Woe to them," it says, "for they turned from me. Wretched are they, for they sinned against me. I redeemed them, but they spoke lies against me."[263]

7:13 Yet no one spoke openly about him for fear of the Jews.

There is muttering among the Jews, and "for fear of the Jews" it says that no one can "speak openly." The divine Evangelist then calls the leaders of the Jews simply "Jews" because he does not think it right, it seems to me, to call them elders or priests or anything else of the sort. He is pierced with grief in his godly zeal over those whom God quite rightly accuses of destroying his spiritual vineyard, saying in the prophets, "Many shepherds destroyed my vineyard. They defiled my portion. They made my desirable portion a trackless desert. It has become a complete ruin."[264] How can we not think, after all, that the Lord's vineyard has truly been destroyed by their brutality when they showed that even to praise the good or merely to be amazed at what deserves amazement was dangerous? Who among the wise will doubt that this inflicts a more burdensome punishment on the leaders of the Jews along with the others?

Look at this! The whole people fear and tremble before them. They are not instructed in the law or taught to live in an appropriate way, even though they are quite determined to submit to whatever their leaders decree. Fear, after all, is proof of the ultimate submission. They were being compelled to transgress **[598]** rather than to examine wisely the decree of the lawgiver, and they were being compelled (in that they did not even dare to praise the good) to render a judgment of evil that was by no means free, but coerced, against whomever the others chose, so that they condemned as shameful the one who is worthy of praise and wonder.

If a highly skilled seafarer who is stationed at the rudder of the ship and has the ship entrusted to him should steer it into the rocks, he himself would be held responsible for the wreck. Or if an experienced horseman were driving the swiftest ponies and by a flick of the reins could point their easily-directed flight wherever he wanted, but he dashed the wheels against a rock, it would not be reasonable to attribute the cause of the accident to the ponies but to the driver himself. In the same way, I think, the leaders of the Jews, who have the people not only honoring them but being subject to them in fear as well, would themselves justly pay the penalty for the destruction of all since they managed the people contrary to the divine decrees. The prophet Jeremiah testifies that they themselves have become the occasion for the destruction of the people when he says, "The shepherds became foolish and did not seek the Lord. Therefore, the whole flock had no understanding and was scattered."[265]

[262]Is 5:20. [263]Hos 7:13. [264]Jer 12:10-11. [265]Jer 10:21.

7:14 When it was about the middle of the feast, Jesus went up into the temple and began to teach.

It is fitting for our Savior to teach in the temple. Where else should we hear the divine voice than in the place where the divinity is believed to dwell? Now God exercises care for everything, and he must not be considered to be circumscribed by place; **[599]** rather, as far as his own nature is concerned, he is completely uncontained by the things that exist. Yet it is somehow more fitting that we suppose that he dwells in holy places, and it is quite reasonable to think that we should hear the decree of the divine nature especially in sacred places.

Again, what was pictured to the people of old in type and shadow, Christ now transforms into truth. God says to the holy teacher Moses, "And you shall place the mercy seat on top of the ark, and into the ark you shall place the testimonies that I shall give you. And I shall make myself known to you from there, and I shall speak to you from above the mercy seat, between the two cherubim that are on the ark of the testimony, concerning all the commands I give you for the Israelites."[266] And our Lord Jesus Christ, "when it was about the middle of the feast," as it is written, enters as God into the holy places dedicated to God and there addresses the crowds, although he went up in secret. Just as, then, the descent of God to the mercy seat in the tabernacle was secret and even then was scarcely perceived when the time for his speaking had come, and just as God spoke at that time with one person, the blessed Moses, and no one else, so also Christ now instructed one race, that of the Jews, and he converses with one people, since he had not yet unfolded his general grace to the Gentiles.

The blessed Evangelist very carefully says not simply that he "entered" but that he "went up" into the temple because it is a high matter, far exceeding base lowliness, to enter the divine school and stay in the holy places. And the type of this act is true for us. Christ was, after all, the one who sanctifies the temple, and Moses of old was a type **[600]** of this when he poured sanctified oil on the tabernacle and sanctified it, as it is written,[267] even though the man needed to be sanctified by the holy places rather than him sanctifying them. But the actions done in type on account of the truth have no importance. Indeed, it is rather for the sake of the truth that those things were formed in shadows, as one may see also in the case of the holy prophets. One was commanded to live with a prostitute against his will.[268] Another was commanded to go around naked.[269] Yet another was commanded to lie on his right side for many days.[270] These actions were commanded for the sake of what came out of them, not at all for their own sakes. In the same way, then, the blessed Moses too was commanded to sanctify the tabernacle, even though he needed to be sanctified by it, in order that Christ might be understood in him to sanctify his own temple, although he lived with flesh among the Jews and in that flesh he addressed the crowds, just as God did from the mercy seat long ago.

7:15 The Jews marveled saying, "How does this man have such learning, when he has never studied?"

The marvel of the Jews strikes no sour note, but there is something quibbling about their statement on this point. It was quite likely, after all, that they would be astonished when they saw him strangely excelling in both speech and knowledge—especially one who had not benefitted from anyone instructing him. The human mind is capable of wisdom, and if someone is not yet wise, their nature is

[266]Ex 25:21-22. [267]Lev 8:11. [268]Hos 3:1-3. [269]Is 20:2. [270]Ezek 4:6.

still highly adapted to the attainment of knowledge and understanding of some subjects. But among those who do not have much practice in words, the natural ability is stopped up in a way and dulled. Among those, however, who are accustomed to go through such **[601]** labors and to revel in word exercises, that ability is quite bright and prepared for a noble sobriety, and that person is found to have no small store of speech and intellectual abilities. The Jews then are astonished since they do not yet view Christ the Savior as God by nature but still as a mere man. They marvel that he is rich in wisdom even without having its provider, training in reading, because he knows letters without being taught. This too, therefore, along with the rest, is an accusation of the Jews' lack of understanding. It should not have seemed strange to them that Wisdom, the artificer of all (that is, the only begotten Word of God) who was hidden among them in human form, should not need education.

Next we must look at their statement to receive further benefit. Above, when they are looking for Jesus, they say, "Where is that man?"[271] on the grounds that they know him only by his miracles and that they do not yet clearly know who exactly he is or from whom or where he comes. In this passage, however, they say, "he has such learning, when he has never studied," on the grounds that they are not ignorant of anything about him, but they know everything clearly. Thus the general search for him was undertaken by the common people, and the words "Who is that man?" were uttered contemptuously by those who did not know exactly who he was. Those who knew him made the other statement. Therefore, those who were not ignorant will suffer a more severe penalty than those who were. For the one group, their ignorance is an excuse, but for the other, their knowledge condemns them. For this reason it is also said to be better for some not to have known the way of truth.[272] Knowledge brings greater punishment because "they are lovers of pleasure rather than lovers of God."[273]

Now Jesus, as the Jews said in amazement, knew letters **[602]** without studying. Moses, by contrast, was instructed "in all the wisdom of the Egyptians," as it is written,[274] yet it was as though he knew nothing at all, even though he was exceedingly wise among them, because he was being instructed in better knowledge by words from above. The wisdom of the world is proven feeble by the more divine and more powerful wisdom by which or through which we are instructed on matters concerning Christ and receive the knowledge that is truly from above and from God.

Christ, then, is the perfect good in all things. He is the one wisdom and knowledge of all. Concerning this wisdom, we understand him to have his brilliance innately, not by being taught. Indeed, the prophet Isaiah says of him somewhere, "Before the child knows good or evil, he will refuse evil to choose the good."[275] Certainly we will not foolishly suppose that the divine and heavenly offspring turns away from evil and applies himself to the good by a discernment of reasoning or by choosing the better. No, it is as though one should say of fire that it refuses cold. The fact that its essence is not receptive of cold indicates not a choice of wills in it but rather the most steadfast adherence to the property of its own nature. So it is also with Christ since all good things are in God by nature and are not introduced from the outside. In this way wisdom too was in him, or rather, he himself was strictly and properly the full solid Wisdom through which the creatures in heaven and on earth, the ones that have partial wisdom by participation, receive their rationality.

[271]Jn 7:11. [272]2 Pet 2:21. [273]2 Tim 3:4. [274]Acts 7:22. [275]Is 7:16 (LXX).

7:16 Jesus answered and said, "My teaching is not my own, but his who sent me."

We will find what was written by one of the wise men to be most true: "The Spirit of the Lord has filled **[603]** the world, and the ear of hearing hears all things."[276] But to those who in utter foolishness, or rather blasphemy, think that anything uttered will escape God's attention, the divine psalmist says somewhere, "Understand, you senseless ones among the people. You fools, be wise at last. The one who planted the ear, does he not hear?"[277] How could it possibly happen that the one who implanted the sense of hearing in those who were made by him does not hear absolutely everything?

Note then that in this statement too, the Lord is God by nature. For he is not ignorant of the secret whisperings of the Jews in the crowd. He receives them in his ears, as it were, in a God-befitting way, even though they say nothing openly about him out of fear of the rulers. And when on one occasion some of those who had gathered at the temple marveled at him and were probably thinking or saying quietly to each other, "How does this man have such learning, when he has never studied?"[278] he once again shows them, as the situation demands, that he is equal to God the Father, who studied nothing at all but has knowledge of everything by nature without being taught because he surpasses all understanding and soars above all wisdom that is in creation. It was possible then also from other actions to demonstrate this and to assure his hearers that whatever is in his Father also clearly belongs to him because of the identity of nature. He used to do this in other situations as well from his ability to do the same things and to have an identical activity in all things, understandably attaining the same honor. "For whatever the Father does," he says, "the Son too does likewise."[279] And again, "Just as the Father raises the dead and gives them life, so also the Son gives life to whom he wills."[280]

But here it was most timely and fitting, I suppose, **[604]** to give proof of what was most relevant to the discussion. The discussion among those considering these matters was about the fact that he had knowledge and he was devoted to learning even though he had not studied. So he needed to show that this understanding was in him just as it is of course in the Father. How then did he prove it? He proved it by the fact that he has wisdom equal to the Father's, even though according to true and sober reasoning, he himself is Wisdom and from God the Father. Since he is like him in all things, he says that he teaches the same things as the Father without any change. Either he says that this teaching is the Father's because of the utter similarity between his teaching and that of the Father, or he says that his teaching is the Father's because he himself is the Wisdom of the Father, through which the Father speaks and decrees all things.

Along with this, he orchestrates something else that brings no small profit for the salvation of his students. When they saw a man, they did not receive his word as from God because of his earthly flesh. Because of this, they seemed to suffer from a plausible unbelief, so he profitably attributes his teaching to God the Father while at the same time speaking the truth. He persuades them to accept what he says because they feared that if they resisted the decrees from above any longer, they would appear to be enemies of God.

Next, we must recognize that by saying again that he was sent, he does not show himself to be second in honor to the Father. That is because being sent must not be understood in a manner fitting a slave, even though since he has clothed himself in the form of a slave, he could without blame say even this

[276]Wis 1:7, 10. [277]Ps 94:8-9 (Ps 93:8-9 LXX). [278]Jn 7:15. [279]Jn 5:19. [280]Jn 5:21.

about himself. He has been sent, rather, in the same way as a word from the mind, as the sun's rays from the sun itself. For these examples are emergent, so to speak, from the items in which they exist since they seem to come out, but they exist naturally and inseparably in the items from which they come. When a word has come forth from the mind **[605]** and a ray from the sun, let's say, we should not at all suppose that for this reason what begat them is deserted by what has gone out. Instead, we will see the former existing in the latter and the latter existing in the former. A mind, after all, will never be without words, and a word will never fail to be shaped by the mind in it.[281] We should understand the other statement [about being sent] on analogy with this.

7:17 "If anyone does his will, they will know whether my teaching is from God, or whether I speak on my own."

We ought to accept the word of truth without any doubt or examination and believe that what was said just once cannot be other than it was declared to be. Because of the unbelievers, however, he does not allow his words to go without proof, but he brings forward a most evident and utterly clear refutation, fine-tuning the form of his words with great skill. What that skill is, and what the logic of his plan is, we shall say next.

They were trying to kill him because of the paralytic, I mean the one who was healed on the sabbath day. He gently undercuts, then, those who are already plotting something terrible against him, and along with that, he clearly exposes those who are giving birth to bloodlust against him, showing that they choose to fulfill their own desires rather than the will of the lawgiver. Then you will know with certainty, he says, that my teaching is from God the Father, if you should choose to follow his will rather than your own. But the will of God the lawgiver is to abstain from murder. Then—then, he says—when you are not preoccupied with unjust hatred and you are not driven like a wild animal into random rage, you will know clearly "whether my teaching is from God, or whether I am speaking on my own." He weaves together, then, reproof with profit, **[606]** and he justly accuses them of mocking for no good reason whatever he teaches, even though God the Father agrees with him and has the same will as him, or that which is also true teaches with him and interprets with him.

He puts "on my own" instead of "privately and completely cut off from agreement and the identical will of the Father." Now I suppose that no one who thinks rightly will imagine that he is accusing his own words of being spurious, but he says this on the grounds that his words could never diverge from the will of God the Father. The Father speaks, after all, through his own Word and wisdom, his own offspring. But this offspring speaks without at all dissenting from him. How could he?

7:18 "The one who speaks on his own seeks his own glory."

He gives this clear indication that he is not at all working for his own glory by his teaching and that he does not use any strange words foreign to the law, since that would be speaking "on his own." Instead, he is advising them to follow what has already been prophesied. He is merely removing the useless and coarse shadow of the letter and persuasively transforming what already lies hidden in types into the spiritual sense. That is what he says also in the Gospel according to Matthew: "I have not come to abolish the law, but to fulfill it."[282] Here he hints at this obliquely. The gospel way of life entails merely a transformation of the

[281]In Greek, "mind" (νοῦς) can also refer to the meaning of a word. [282]Mt 5:17.

letter into truth. And since it has transformed the Mosaic type into something more fitting, it has the knowledge of worship in the Spirit. Christ then is not speaking "on his own," that is, he is saying nothing foreign to what has already been foretold. He does not send Moses away, after all, nor does he teach people to reject the instruction in the law; **[607]** instead, he teaches them to take what is sketched in type and fill it in with the truth, as with a brighter color.

With exquisite mastery he ascribes honor and glory to God the Father, thus gaining the good will of the Jews. Since the Jews did not know the Word who had appeared from God the Father, but they thought that the law had been given by God the Father alone, he understandably maintains that he himself is also glorified when the law is kept, and he suffers the contrary if it should not be kept as it ought. But even though the Son shares in the glory of the Father, and God the Father spoke to Moses through him, nevertheless he agrees with their suppositions according to the *oikonomia*.[283] By saying nothing "on his own" that is not decreed by the law, he confesses that he is not at all striving to build up his own glory but that which is due the law.

In addition to this, we must also observe the following. He strikes an indirect and obscure blow at the Jews, who are ignorantly falling into the very vices they blame on him and who habitually seize glory for themselves rather than for God, the Lord of all. And I will explain how. They fell away from the commandments of the law and were carried away to whatever pleased them, "teaching human commandments," as it is written, "as doctrines."[284] For this Christ appropriately convicts them as transgressors and offenders against the lawgiver himself in that they persuaded their hearers not to live by his decrees but to be devoted to their doctrines. Therefore, although Christ now says absolutely and without qualification, "The one who speaks on his own seeks his own glory," he is rebuking the disease of the Pharisees' madness because by choosing to speak their own words, they are stealing the glory of the lawgiver and applying to themselves what belongs to God, **[608]** and that is why they inevitably plot to kill him.

That is the particular reason he rebukes them for transgressing, and that is the occasion in the plan of his discourse for the language about striving to keep the law and thereby honoring God the Father. "The one who seeks the glory of the one who sent him," he says, "this one is true, and there is no unrighteousness in him."[285] As a result, it is characteristic of those who seek not God's will but their own, that they are not true but utterly unrighteous. For they are not "true" in that they slander the law and replace it with their own will. And they are most unrighteous in that they reject the righteous judgment of the lawgiver and put their own ideas above the Lord's. Christ therefore is righteous and true, falling under none of the accusations just mentioned.

7:19 "Did not Moses give you the law? Yet none of you keeps the law. Why are you trying to kill me?"

Through many inventions,[286] the Savior's discourse arrives at its one purpose. He indirectly rebuked the Pharisees in the foregoing, as was fitting, for thinking that the commands from above did not have to be obeyed but that they should introduce their own ideas and eagerly hunt for honor from their subjects instead, not ascribing honor to the Lord of all but diverting it to their own

[283]Here *oikonomia* could mean "the arrangement of his discourse" or "his plan of salvation." [284]Mt 15:9. [285]Jn 7:18.
[286]"Invention" is a rhetorical term referring to the process of discovering resources for arguments.

person. As a result, they now dare to transgress more easily.

So now, employing a different and more pointed approach, he gives them a bare and open rebuke. When charged with breaking the sabbath and enduring the most unjust accusation of transgression, he did not just convict them of offending against the law in individual points, but he convicted the whole people of the Jews of placing no value on the law of Moses. **[609]** Tell me, he says, you who condemn those who are eager to show mercy on the sabbath, you who render the most brutal decision against those who do well and pass sentence without restraint on the compassionate: Did not Moses, whom you always admire, give you the command that you must not murder? Did you not hear him saying, "You shall not kill the innocent and righteous"?[287] Why then do you grieve your own Moses by so readily transgressing the law decreed through him? The clear evidence and proof of this is the fact that you persecute me, even though I have done nothing wrong, and you are unjustly eager to kill one who can be accused of nothing that would warrant him suffering this.

The Savior's discourse, then, is quite emphatic, and he attacks the madness of the Jews most violently in this passage. He shows that they are sinking down, as if by unbridled impulses, to the point of condemning him for breaking the sabbath, while they themselves are transgressing and have decided to kill him. For this reason alone, they are falling into the worst sin of all. He all but cries out, On the sabbath day I healed the paralytic who had fallen into a bitter and incurable disease and was spent by an unbearable sickness. But for my good deed, I am condemned as though caught in the most shameful of all crimes. You even sentence me to death for it. What kind of punishment then, he says, will be devised for you, commensurate with such outrages? See, you too transgress the law. But your manner of transgressing is not like the charge against me since you are persuaded to act not for good, as I do, but with the intent to murder, the worst of all offenses. How then is Moses on your side in this matter, on account of whom I, though I heal, am judged? Did not he himself decree a law to you about this? Do you not then, after trampling on my **[610]** word, make light of transgression with your unjust thirst for blood? This is among the things Christ, then, might reasonably say to the unholy Pharisees.

He separates the law for now from his own person, even though he himself is the lawgiver, and ascribes it, as it were, to God the Father alone. Through him he brings maximum shame to the impudent Jews since they supposed that the Father was greater than he. Indeed, as we have often said, they did not yet acknowledge that he was God by nature, nor did they yet know the deep mystery of his *oikonomia* with the flesh. They marveled, rather, at the glory of Moses.

7:20-21 The crowd answered, "You have a demon. Who is trying to kill you?" Jesus answered them,

They perceive the accusations and, struck by the harsh words now coming from him, proceed to deny them. They do not renounce their murderous intent, but they are eager only to avoid the appearance of breaking the law, a boast that is rooted in mere conceit on the part of the Pharisees. Indeed, that is why Christ used to call them "whitewashed tombs," outwardly clothed in the beauty of artistic ingenuity but inwardly filled with the uncleanness of the dead.[288]

Now I think they say these things to take away the fear arising from his expectation to suffer something. They do this not to give him

[287]Ex 23:7. [288]Mt 23:27.

true assurance that he will not suffer but to draw him into a dangerous confidence, thinking to persuade him not to be intent on hiding from them. For then it would not be difficult to plot against him, or so they thought. They ignorantly supposed, since they did not know the one whom they were persecuting, that he would be subject to their evil plans and that even though he did not wish to suffer, he would be caught **[611]** like one of those who does not know the thoughts hidden in their minds. Their denial, then, is the fruit of their perversity and another form of blasphemy against Christ. By the very words with which they try to fend off what he said as untrue, they condemn him as a liar, adding "iniquity to their iniquity," as it is written.[289]

"I performed one work, and you are all amazed?"

We will read this passage as a question with a full stop. But we will not be ignorant of the skill in the words, which are pregnant with the wisest arrangement. Notice how, when he relates to the Jews the compassion he showed to the paralytic, he does not say incautiously, "I have healed the man on the sabbath, and you are amazed at this?" Instead, he says in a subdued manner and with a great deal of restraint, "I performed one work," thus soothing the unseasonable wrath of the multitude. It was not unlikely, after all, that they, cut by his breaking of the sabbath, would try to stone Jesus even now. For the crowd is without judgment, according to the Greek poets, and always prone to anger, both indulging in the gentlest agreement with whatever it wants and prone to unchecked rashness like a bull. It succumbs more swiftly than it should to reckless deeds with terrible results. Accordingly, he puts away any boasting about the deed (because that is the beneficial thing to do), and he uses the gentlest words. Applying great moderation he says, "I performed one work, and you are all amazed?" For this one deed, he says, even though it was performed for the healing and life of the man lying outstretched, you condemn the miracle worker as though he exhibited truly extraordinary **[612]** recklessness. And caring only for the honor of the sabbath, you do not grant the miracle any wonder. This, after all, would really have been more fitting. But because a precept of the law has been broken in some way, according to the ignorant supposition in your minds—not for any reasons that are minor or insignificant but for the healing and life of a man—you became unreasonably angry, though you ought to ascribe praise to him who is clothed with such great and God-befitting power. Through this as well, then, the people of the Jews are convicted of being uneducated in that they expended undue astonishment on the man who was healed and did not rather offer it to Christ, who miraculously healed him.

So we must understand that when he speaks to those of Israel and says, "I performed one work, and you are all amazed," he is again indirectly accusing them and insinuating this sort of thing: For this one transgression (as you see it), you greatly marvel at my intentions, as though I dared to offend against the lawgiver. How then do you think God is disposed toward you, when you offend against the law not just once but think nothing of transgressing it in matters for which you judge others?

7:22 "Moses gave you circumcision (not that it is from Moses but from the fathers), and you circumcise a man on the sabbath."

This saying is deep and the meaning of the passage inaccessible, but it will be clear because of the grace of the enlightener.

[289]Ps 69:27 (Ps 68:28 LXX).

Through many words, then, he outwits the Jews' lack of instruction and teaches them in various ways that they should not go off into inappropriate anger over the breaking of the sabbath [**613**] since the Son of Man is Lord of the sabbath. When he finally makes no headway because of the bad attitude of his hearers, he moves on to another way of framing the issue, and he now tries to make clear to them that the teacher Moses himself, the minister of the law, broke the sabbath law on account of circumcision, which extended from the custom of the fathers down to his own time. Thus with good reason, he too is ultimately shown to be a preserver of the fathers' custom, as it were. And since God works on the sabbath, he shows that he himself also works and that this is in no way a transgression of the sabbath since he always agrees with the one who begat him. That is why he also said, "My Father is still working, and I also am working."[290]

So in order that, when you see me working on the sabbath day, he says, you may not be astonished at my work as something strange and unexpected, "Moses gave you circumcision" on the sabbath, and he anticipated me in breaking the sabbath law. And for what reason? He did not think it would be right to dishonor, for the sake of the sabbath, the law decreed to the fathers and the custom that came from them. That is why a man is circumcised even on the sabbath. But if Moses thought it was proper to honor the custom of the fathers, and if he ranked this higher than the honor due to the sabbath, why have you vainly been thrown into confusion over me, and why are you astonished at me as though I were one of those who are accustomed to transgress the law heedlessly and contemptuously? You do this, he says, even though I do the same things as my Father, and I always agree with everything he deems right. And since he works on the sabbath, I do well to refuse being idle on the sabbath.

Now he maintains that Moses gave circumcision, although strictly speaking it was not from him but from the fathers, because the command was given to the fathers [**614**] that they should be circumcised, but the specifics of it were decreed through Moses with more detail and precision. Our forefather Abraham was circumcised, after all, but not on the eighth day, nor was a pair of turtledoves or two pigeons offered as a sacrifice for him, according to Moses' instructions. [**615**]

Chapter Six

A discussion of rest on the sabbath, showing in various ways what it means.

7:23 "If a man receives circumcision on the sabbath lest the law of Moses be broken, are you angry with me because I healed the whole man on the sabbath?"

This passage is difficult for the many to construe, and its subparts are not very clear. Therefore, we will speak about that first. We will read it piece by piece, leaving aside the overall structure of the passage, since this is how you will understand precisely what it means. Thus, he is saying, "If a man receives circumcision on the sabbath, are you angry with me lest the law of Moses be broken because I healed the whole man on the sabbath?" For a man does not receive circumcision on the sabbath "lest the law of Moses be broken." Rather, it is broken when the sabbath rest is not observed because of circumcision. As we taught earlier in anticipation of this point—or rather as the Savior himself said—circumcision is not from Moses but from the fathers. So for the sake of circumcision, which comes from the fathers, the law of Moses—I

[290]Jn 5:17.

mean, the sabbath law—is broken. Therefore, the words "lest the law of Moses be broken" must be joined with the Savior's words: "Are you angry with me," he says, "lest the law of Moses be broken because I healed the whole man **[616]** on the sabbath?"

Now that the division of this passage has been defined, we must proceed to the explanation of the meaning, even though it is exceedingly difficult to understand. Circumcision is a way of caring for a man, he says, and it surpasses the very ordinance of the sabbath because it was necessary for the sufferer to be healed. What then is the problem? How could the sabbath decree reasonably prevent the whole body from being healed since it already allows a violation without blame by a partial and slight healing? A man is circumcised, after all, and the sufferer is healed without accusation *on the sabbath*. In vain then, he says, are you indignant at the one who does greater works, charging him with transgression of the law when the law is not grieved even at being set aside by Moses for mere circumcision. By these things an argument is woven, persuading them to agree that they should not be vainly upset, since Moses has already become a type of this deed. Foolishly thinking they ought to support Moses, they were dragged down to the point of having to commit murder, giving no regard to his law.

7:24 "Do not judge by appearances, but judge with right judgment."

The law, he says, which you are eager to uphold, for the sake of which you were so inflamed to the point of savage wrath, explicitly cries out, "You shall not show partiality in judgment, for judgment belongs to God."[291] You then who condemn me as a transgressor because of the sabbath and who judge that it is quite fitting to be angry at this—show some concern for the honor of the law! You should be ashamed **[617]** at the message, "Do not judge by appearances, but judge with right judgment." If you place Moses outside the bounds of transgression and (quite rightly) think that he has no share in condemnation for it—even though he violates the sabbath regulation for the sake of circumcision which is from the fathers—then you free the Son from accusation as well who always agrees with the mind of the Father, consents to his will and is accustomed to do whatever the Father does. But if you condemn only the Son and do not judge Moses, he says, even though he is guilty of the same things you think I am guilty of regarding the sabbath, how will you not be caught trampling the divine law? How will you not be understood to be insulting the commands from above when, out of respect for certain people, you corrupt the statement about judging rightly and transgress it by making the one whom you respect out of favoritism greater than the divine commands?

Let the wise hearer note once again the admirable skill of our Savior Christ. When he is accused of breaking one law, he convicts them with a great many arguments of being transgressors, all but making that statement in the Gospels, "Why do you see the speck in your brother's eye but do not notice the log in your own eye?"[292] Judging others is therefore evil. "For in judging another, one condemns oneself," as it is written.[293] That is why the Savior himself also said, "Do not judge, and you will not be judged; do not condemn, and you will not be condemned."[294] We too say this in the matter before us, for Christ will not transgress in any way when he changes his own laws into whatever he wants and overlays the shadows of the law with the vibrant color of the truth, so that **[618]** the commands decreed to the ancients in a coarser fashion may ultimately be transformed into spiritual insight.

[291]Deut 1:17. [292]Mt 7:3. [293]Rom 2:1. [294]Lk 6:37.

Now that our discourse has flowed into the mention of the sabbath and circumcision, I think that next it will bring no less than the necessary amount of profit—at least to the one who is devoted to learning—to examine carefully what the seventh-day sabbath observance means and what is indicated by circumcision on the eighth day, and in addition to learn why circumcision is received even on the sabbath itself, thus not permitting the rest prescribed by the law. I will examine each point as well as I can and try to make it clear. The first topic before us will be that of the seventh day, or the sabbath and its rest. That way, there will be a most appropriate order of investigation. Therefore, let us now inquire about the first command decreed on this subject: how and in what manner it arose.

When God brought Israel out of slavery in Egypt, he called them to their original ancient freedom through the supremely wise Moses. And when he had miraculously brought them through the middle of the sea with their feet somehow dry and not wet, he commanded them to hurry to the promised land. When he had finally accustomed them to the necessity of cleansing and purifying themselves ahead of time in some way, he summoned them to an assembly at Mount Sinai. He descended on it in the form of fire and decreed laws for salvation, saying, "I am the Lord your God, who led you out of the land of Egypt, out of the house of slavery. You shall have no other gods except me. You shall not make for yourself an idol or any likeness that is in heaven above or on the earth below or in the waters beneath the earth. You shall not bow before them or worship them. For I am the Lord your God, a jealous God."[295] It was fitting—**[619]** it was fitting to start at that time to decree beneficial laws and to preinitiate the people with teaching leading to the knowledge of God once they had devoted themselves to service and obedience to God. For the knowledge of God is the root of all virtue, and faith is the foundation of piety. So he revealed himself and made himself manifest, as it were, by saying, "I am the Lord your God," and through knowledge he cultivated faith in them.

After he forbids the construction of idols and the worship of so-called gods, he shows them that their transgression will not go unpunished, and he sets before their eyes the penalty for departing from this, crying out, "You shall not take the name of the Lord your God in vain," that is, You shall not bestow on a vain idol the divine and most dread name, "for the Lord will not," he says, "acquit the one who takes his name in vain."[296]

After he said, then, that whoever is pleased to worship another god (whichever one it may be) and that whoever is pleased to enroll themselves under such a so-called god will be guilty of no small sin; and, after he threatened them in a manner commensurate with the fact that they were newly brought to faith and had a feebler understanding—he added and prescribed a second command, as it were, in the sequence. "Remember," he says, "the sabbath day to keep it holy. Six days you shall labor and do all your work, but the seventh day is a sabbath to the Lord your God. You shall not do any work on it."[297] Then he profitably shows whom they will imitate when they do this. "For in six days," he says, "the Lord made heaven and earth and the sea and all that is in them, but he rested on the seventh day. Therefore, the Lord blessed the seventh day and sanctified it."[298]

What then, someone might say now, did the sabbath law impart? Why has a second command been included immediately after the threat concerning **[620]** transgression? To this we say that it was fitting not only to threaten that the transgressors would suffer terrible

[295]Ex 20:2-5. [296]Ex 20:7. [297]Ex 20:8-10. [298]Ex 20:11.

things, and not only to secure Israel in piety by fear (since worshiping God in fear is more fitting for a slave), but also to show what they will be partakers of and what end they will reach who are firmly attached in love to him. He defines, therefore, and gives to them in type the promise of future good things. "For the law contains a shadow of the good things to come," as it is written,[299] and its form is shown to be a preparatory exercise for the truth. It commands that they rest on the last day of the week, that is, the sabbath, and that they cease from all their work and that they relax and practice rest on it. By this it signifies the rest and enjoyment that the saints will have at the end of the ages when those in Christ will cease from their life in this world, wash away the sweat of their good works and live a life without toil or any labor, according to what was said of them through the voice of the prophet, "They will forget their former tribulation, and it will not enter their heart, but eternal joy will be on their head. For praise will be on their head, and joy will take hold of them, but sorrow and grief and sighing have fled away."[300] They too then, in imitation of the creator who rested and ceased from the labors (so to speak) of creation, will rest from the toils of this life, ascending to the enjoyment that will be given by Christ at the end of the ages. I think this is the point of the rest commanded on the sabbath. **[621]**

Observe how the lawgiver says negatively, "You shall not worship other gods," but when he adds the neighboring command concerning the sabbath, he says, "Remember." Why? Because the time for not worshiping other gods was already at hand. (That is why he immediately commanded them to be diligent about this.) But through memory it was possible to see the things to come and to contemplate ahead of time with the mind what was already sketched in types.

Next, we must examine the following as well. After he has arranged with great care for the condition of our faith, he immediately adds the reminder of the promise at the end of the ages. After that, he finally decrees the other commands, I mean, "Honor your father and your mother," "You shall not murder," and the rest,[301] so that we may not think that we are justified by works or expect that the ungrudging bounty of God is a fruit of our own labors, but rather that we will have it by faith. That is why before the commands concerning the reverent way of life, grace has entered by faith as the immediate neighbor of the good things for which we hope.

The sabbath rest, then, signifies the life of the saints in rest and holiness when they will put off all that grieves them, cease from all their labors and enjoy blessings from God. Indeed, when the blessed Paul lectured to us about this and endeavored to inquire into the manner of the people's sabbath (and he did this quite well), he said this: "To whom did he swear that they will not enter his rest except to the unbelievers? So we see that they were unable to enter due to their unbelief."[302] Since some people thought that the land they entered after they left Egypt was the land of rest—even though the land of rest was understood as a type of the land that Christ will give to the saints **[622]** and which David calls "the land of the living"[303]—the most wise Paul tries to show that what was given as an inheritance to the Israelites at that time by the command of Joshua was a type of what is to be looked for. He forcefully proves that that land is to be taken as a type of the truth by bringing in an argument to demonstrate his claim. He says, "Since it remains for some to enter it, and those who formerly heard the good news did not enter it because of unbelief, again he sets a certain day, 'Today,' saying through David so long afterward, in the words already quoted,

[299]Heb 10:1. [300]Is 35:10. [301]Ex 20:12-17. [302]Heb 3:18-19. [303]Ps 27:13 (Ps 26:13 LXX).

'Today if you hear his voice, do not harden your hearts as in the rebellion.' For if Joshua had given them rest, he would not have spoken of another day after this."[304] Do you see how forcefully he refutes the apparent objection?

Now someone might immediately respond to this, using Jewish arguments to support their contention, "What are you saying, sir? Did not Joshua bring the people into the promised land? Did they not rest and keep the sabbath in it?" "Yes," he says, "but in type and imitation of the truth." After all, if the grace of God and the magnitude of his promise is circumscribed by this alone, and the hopes of Israel have been fulfilled in it, and if the letter of the law indicates nothing else besides this, how can another time of rest be defined through the blessed David, as though Joshua had not given them rest, even though David lived so long afterwards? After, then, he has wisely and quite shrewdly demonstrated that the items in the narrative are a type and image of spiritual things, he brings to light the still hidden and concealed meaning of the sabbath, adding, "So then there remains a sabbath rest for the people of God; for those who enter into his **[623]** rest also cease from their labors as God did from his."[305]

On this basis, then, how could anyone now disagree that the mind of the saints knows that the rest from labors (of works, I mean) is the sabbath observance? That is when the bright band of saints will revel in the good works that they did before in this life, just like the creator of all, who rested and rejoiced on the seventh day, as Wisdom says in the book of Proverbs, "I was the one in whom he delighted. Every day I rejoiced in his presence at all times, when he was rejoicing on completing the world, and he was rejoicing in the children of men."[306]

Therefore (for I will return once again to the beginning and review the point of the whole discussion), the sabbath rest indicates the toilless life of the saints. Without toil, God will bestow all good things on the saints at that time, and we will no longer commit sin, which is the origin of evil, because it will perish from us by its roots along with the one who always sows it in us, according to the statement, "No lion will be there, and no wicked beasts will go up on it, but a pure road will be there, and it will be called a holy road."[307] The mind of the saints, however, will retain all good things with ease. That is why those who gather sticks on the sabbath die by stoning, because they have wronged the truth in type.[308] Once we have ceased and have reached that rest, we will never leave that admirable way of life, illustrious in virtue, like they left their tent, nor will we gather sin, the food and mother of fire, like they gathered sticks because of their utter senselessness, not understanding the types pointing to the truth. **[624]** Therefore, they were pelted by the punishers with senseless stones, seeing that they were caught in great senselessness; thus they had the quality of their behavior inscribed in their punishment. It is clear, then, that at that time we will commit no loathsome sin, nor will we attain what is profitable by sweat.

This too we will see indicated once again in an enigma in the books of Moses. God showered down manna like dew on the Israelites in the desert, and he gave them the bread of angels, as it is written.[309] Then he decreed a command concerning it through the supremely wise Moses. He addressed them as follows: "Eat today. For today is a sabbath to the Lord. You will not find it in the plain. Six days you shall gather, but the seventh day is a sabbath. There will be none on that day."[310] He hints that before the end of the ages, it is fitting for us to gather by our toil what is profitable and

[304]Heb 4:6-8. Since the name for Joshua in Greek is Jesus, the last sentence of this verse implies that Jesus is the one who spoke of another day. [305]Heb 4:9-10. [306]Prov 8:30-31. [307]Is 35:9, 8. [308]Num 15:36. [309]Ps 78:25 (Ps 77:25 LXX). [310]Ex 16:25-26.

what nourishes us to eternal life, just as they, when they were wandering around the vast desert, gathered from everywhere the manna for nourishment. But on the seventh day, that is, at the end, the time for gathering what is beneficial has passed, and we will delight in what has already been supplied, according to the psalmist's statement, "You will eat the fruits of your labors."[311]

God the lawgiver, therefore, was not delighting in the shadows but was already looking ahead to the very image of the realities when he proclaimed that one must not work on the sabbath. But some despised the law decreed to them about this and recklessly did not refrain from offending the Lord of all. They resolved that it was all right for them to go and gather **[625]** manna even on the sabbath. And their audacity was not in thought alone, but it then led to deeds which seemed good to them. That is why the lawgiver next denounces them and says, "How long will you refuse to listen to my commands and my law? See, the Lord gave you this day as a sabbath. That is the reason he has given you two days worth of bread on the sixth day. Each one of you shall sit in your own house. Let none of you leave his place on the seventh day."[312] Do you see how, in this typological rest, he is fashioning for us ahead of time a life free from all sweat and toil when he permits them to do nothing at all on the sabbath? After all, he does not permit them to collect anything, but he adds to this that they must not leave their house to go anywhere and must not leave their places.

Next, we will set forth what he wants us to learn from this by bringing up a related statement that is like it. The blessed prophet Jeremiah addresses the Jews as follows: "Thus says the Lord, Guard your souls, and do not take up burdens on the sabbath day. Do not go out of the gates of Jerusalem. Do not carry burdens out of your houses on the sabbath day. Do not do any work. Sanctify the sabbath day just as I commanded your fathers."[313] And what do we learn from this? Having urged us before to a watchful habit, he commands us to guard our soul because in this way the duty of entering into the hoped-for sabbath observance would be easily accomplished. How many good things will come into view for those who possess this, he makes quite clear through the addition of the other items. **[626]** He does not allow anyone to be weighed down by a burden because no one at that time will take up the heavy burden of sin. It is the time of holiness when our old sin goes into utter destruction and each person's soul is renewed to a habit unswervingly devoted to virtue. However, he also does not permit them to go outside the gates of Jerusalem. And indeed, according to a true and right understanding, the bright chorus of the saints will dwell securely in the heavenly Jerusalem and will not leave the holy city but will be in it forever, held by the divine power so that they will never be able to run away from what is good once it is given to them. "For the gifts and call of God are irrevocable," according to Saint Paul.[314] At least when he says, "Each of you shall not leave your place," he seems to suggest this quite clearly. God the Father has many mansions, according to the Savior's statement[315] (and the holy tabernacle gloriously supplied the type of this since it had ten courtyards).[316] And a mansion will be given to each one according to their worthiness and in proportion to their good works. But those who come to be fully in possession of the dwellings there will live there forever. They will never proceed to fall from the blessings assigned to them by God's free gift.

And we will call in a true witness of this.

[311]Ps 128:2 (Ps 127:2 LXX). [312]Ex 16:28-29. [313]Jer 17:21-22. [314]Rom 11:29. [315]Jn 14:2. [316]Ex 36:8 (Ex 37:1 LXX). The LXX says that the tabernacle has ten curtains (αὐλαίας), but Cyril takes it as ten courtyards (αὐλάς).

The prophet Isaiah has spoken plainly about these matters, and he says this: "Your eyes will behold Jerusalem, a rich city, tents which will not be shaken or moved forever."[317] When he says that the tents in the rich city will not be shaken, he indicates the unchangeable continuance of it and dwelling in it. Jeremiah also says, however, "Do not **[627]** do any work on it," and, "Sanctify the sabbath day." As we have already often said, both statements concern the time of rest and refreshment, and that time is completely holy when it is dedicated as a feast to Christ.

Next, we will learn from other sources as well that we should not work on the sabbath but should put to an end, as it were, and let go of everything that calls us to sweat and toil. In Exodus it says, "For six years you shall sow your land and gather its harvest, but on the seventh year, you shall let it rest and leave it."[318] And in Leviticus, "When you enter into the land that I give you, the land that I give you will rest as a sabbath to the Lord. For six years you shall sow your field, and for six years you shall prune your vine and gather its fruit, but in the seventh year, the land shall rest as a sabbath to the Lord."[319] It is not the senseless land, after all, that he releases from toil, nor is it the land, strictly speaking, that he graces with the law concerning these matters. But by releasing the land, he brought about the prohibition on toil for those who possessed the land. In many ways, then, he signified to us the feast to Christ by which those who have lived in the fear of God will race up to the perfect and complete freedom that is in sanctification and the richest grace of the Spirit.

Next we will learn this also from the very commands of Moses. He has this: "When your brother or your sister, a Hebrew man or woman, is sold to you, they will serve you for six years, but in the seventh year you will release them."[320] So we who became slaves long ago to sin and who by taking pleasure in evil sold ourselves in a way to the devil, and who were justified in Christ by faith—we will ascend to the true and holy observance of the sabbath, clothed with the freedom that comes by grace and made to shine by the good gifts from God. **[628]**

CHAPTER SEVEN

A discussion of circumcision on the eighth day, showing in various ways what it means.

Now that we have sufficiently (I think) laid out the discussion of the sabbath to the best of our understanding, we will transfer the labor of our investigation to circumcision, which is the next topic. We have resolved to hunt down from all sides what is profitable, since it is fitting to do so. Indeed, it would be bizarre and not undeserving of extreme ridicule if one did not gladly and confidently give his entire life's work in exchange for the knowledge of these matters. We will consider spiritually what it indicated to the ancients in type, and then we will set it forth according to the measure that God supplies, who reveals all dark things and opens up for us hidden and invisible treasures.[321] For those who have already arrived at a state that lacks nothing and who have a more perfect understanding, it will be possible both to understand and to give discourses far better than this one. We, however, will set before our hearers what comes into our mind, even if it seems to be less than fitting. We do not violate brotherly love by being ashamed to seem inferior to others, but we know what is written: "Give opportunity to the wise, and they will be wiser. Instruct the righteous, and they will receive even more."[322]

Now the first law concerning circumcision was decreed **[629]** when God said to Abraham,

[317]Is 33:20. [318]Ex 23:10-11. [319]Lev 25:2-4. [320]Deut 15:12. [321]See Is 45:3. [322]Prov 9:9.

"You shall keep my covenant, you and your seed after you throughout their generations. And this is the covenant I will make between you and me and your seed after you throughout their generations: Every male shall be circumcised. And you shall circumcise the flesh of your foreskin, and it shall be for the covenant between me and you. And every male child of yours who is eight days old shall be circumcised."[323] After he decreed the law about this and commanded that they must surely circumcise the flesh of their foreskin, he makes clear that the transgression of the law is not without penalty, showing that this act is a type of a most essential mystery. For he adds next, "And my covenant will be in your flesh as an everlasting covenant. And the uncircumcised male, who is not circumcised in the flesh of his foreskin on the eighth day, that soul will be exterminated from his seed because he has broken my covenant."[324]

Now the divine Paul maintained that circumcision was given to the patriarch as a kind of sign and seal of the faith he had when he was uncircumcised. It was Paul's goal and fervent endeavor, it seems, to show that the call and righteousness of faith surpasses and predates every command of the law. With this argument, he barely managed to shame those of Israel and to convince them not to consider the righteousness of faith to be a transgression of the law but rather a return to that which was from the beginning, before all law. Yet at the right time, he brings around the force of his argument to what is immediately profitable and what is beneficial right now, and he shows that he knows of another kind of circumcision. Counseling the Jews to unlearn their delight in glorying in the flesh, **[630]** he writes, "A man is not a Jew who is one outwardly, nor is circumcision outward and in the flesh. Rather, a man is a Jew who is one inwardly, and circumcision is a matter of the heart, in the spirit and not the letter. His praise is not from people but from God."[325] With these words does he not persuade them to change their thoughts about this matter, and does he not want them to conclude that circumcision was given to their forefather not just as a "seal of the faith he had while he was still uncircumcised"[326] but to understand that it is something even greater than this, something spiritual?

We must investigate, then, and examine with care what circumcision in the spirit is, what the fleshly act should be understood to symbolize and why man is circumcised not arbitrarily on whatever day it happens to be, but only on the eighth day. Now it is obvious to everyone that since our aim is intent on being united with God through Christ the mediator, it is therefore altogether fitting for those who are ascending by faith to communion with the all-holy Lord first to be cleansed and sanctified in every way. We will take what God said to the holy Moses as an excellent image of such a cleansing: "Go down and warn the people, and sanctify them today and tomorrow, and have them wash their clothes. Let them be ready on the third day, for on the third day the Lord will descend on Mount Sinai."[327] By having them sanctify themselves first, he wants them to behave appropriately in all their ways, and by having them wash their clothes, he is emphasizing the cleansing of the body itself, since the body is a kind of garment and robe of the soul. **[631]**

Let me go back to the first and most necessary beginning of the argument: Since then it was necessary for those who were hurrying to communion with the holy God first to be sanctified in every way, according to his statement, "You shall be holy, for I am holy,"[328] he ordained for the ancients a symbol of sanctification through circumcision in the flesh. And we will explain how.

If we examine the nature of our affairs, we

[323]Gen 17:9-12. [324]Gen 17:13-14. [325]Rom 2:28-29. [326]Rom 4:11. [327]Ex 19:10-11. [328]Lev 19:2.

will find that pleasure precedes all sin. Some burning lust will call us to sin, always preceding the act itself. It first seizes the mind's judgment and so persuades us to come by a smooth road to the attainment of what we have chosen. Christ's disciple shows that our statement about these matters is true when he cries out, "No one, when tempted, should say, 'I am being tempted by God,' for God cannot be tempted with evil, and he himself tempts no one. But each person is tempted when they are lured and enticed by their own desires. Then desire when it has conceived gives birth to sin, and sin when it is full-grown brings forth death."[329] Do you see then how the birth of evil is first shaped in desire for things and how the seed of sin is first conceived in foreign pleasures?

That is why God the lawgiver commands the circumcising blade to be applied especially to that part of the body in which and through which lusts are born, so that you may learn through an enigma that it is impossible for us ever to appear pure unless, by receiving the sharpest working of the divine word in our heart and by admitting the sword of the Spirit[330] into our mind, we drive away the desire for every shameful act, never following **[632]** our own wills, even if they pretend to hold the sweetest enjoyment, but being persuaded to love and do only the will of God.

Since the truer circumcision brings such power to us, one could for good reason say to those who are accustomed to glorying only in the flesh, "Circumcise yourselves to God, and circumcise the hardness of your heart, men of Judah and inhabitants of Jerusalem."[331] The one who is circumcised in the flesh has been circumcised to the flesh alone, but the one who has received circumcision in the spirit by faith in Christ is truly circumcised to God alone.

We receive circumcision in the spirit which raises us to fellowship with God on the eighth day, that is, the day of Christ's resurrection. We take this fact as a sign that the circumcision of the spirit bestows life, and we agree through the act itself, in a way, that we will live with Christ, according to Paul's statement, "You have died, and your life is hidden with Christ in God. When Christ your life appears, then you also will appear with him in glory."[332] Will not one truly say, after all, that someone who avoids worldly pleasure for the sake of God will be dead to the world? The divine Paul showed himself to us as such a person when he said, "May I never boast except in the cross of Christ, through which the world has been crucified to me, and I to the world."[333] When we have become participants in him through the Spirit, who circumcises without hands all the uncleanness in us, we have died to the world, and we live a most excellent life to God.

Therefore, circumcision was on the eighth day because of the resurrection of Christ, and not before the eighth day. The gift of the Spirit, after all, is not before the resurrection **[633]** but after it, or at the same time as the resurrection, when he breathed on his disciples and said, "Receive the Holy Spirit."[334] For the Jews, then, circumcision by an iron knife was more fitting, since they were still slaves and subject to the law, the punisher. Iron is a sign of punishment. For us, however, who are free and spiritual, the purification by the Spirit is more appropriate. It drives out all defilement from our souls and brings in perfection in the brightness of godliness through faith.

By examining once again what was written about the patriarch Abraham, we will see that through the truer and spiritual circumcision, the boast of perfection in godliness is fulfilled. It is written, then, concerning our forefather Abraham, that when he was ninety-nine years old, God profitably instituted circumcision for him making this, too, a clear sign that circumcision is a kind of vestibule and entrance to

[329]Jas 1:13-15. [330]Eph 6:17. [331]Jer 4:4. [332]Col 3:3-4. [333]Gal 6:14. [334]Jn 20:22.

perfection in virtue, or rather clearly implying that no one will ever arrive at this who does not have the purification sketched in shadows by circumcision. The number one hundred is a symbol of perfection. Circumcision, then, is before perfection. When it precedes, it easily raises us to that perfection.

However, the benefits to us of circumcision (I mean the circumcision of the spirit) do not stop there. No, we will now find that this circumcision belongs only to those who are free in Christ. Those who have shaken off slavery to the devil and the yoke of sin are indeed free in Christ. They have burst their bonds, as it is written,[335] and clothed themselves in the glorious and untyrannical boast of righteousness, I mean the righteousness that is in faith in Christ. **[634]**

When we inspect the holy and divine Scriptures, we will find without a doubt that circumcision on the eighth day is fitting for the free, not for the slaves. Ishmael, the son born to the patriarch by the handmaid Hagar, was circumcised not on the eighth day but in his thirteenth year. It is written that Abraham circumcised Ishmael his son at thirteen years old[336] in order that the divine word may show us that the son of the slave woman Jerusalem, that is, Israel,[337] has fallen both from the eighth day and from the twelfth. He falls from the eighth day in that he refused to accept the saving proclamation of the resurrection that occurred on the eighth day, that is, the gospel of Christ by which without a doubt we are assisted to faith and circumcised in the spirit. And he falls from the twelfth in that in an enigma he drives away by unbelief the holy choir of the apostles, living his life with no taste or experience at all of their doctrine.

Such, then, is the servant. But Isaac, the free son of the free woman, is circumcised on the eighth day. The free children of the free woman, I mean the Jerusalem above,[338] have been enriched by receiving the eighth day, that is, the resurrection of Christ and the circumcision in the spirit. This circumcision has freed them from all sin and releases them from death (since it also frees from sin, through which and because of which there is death), and it transports them to the life of Christ.

Next, by studying the book called Exodus, we will easily see, in addition to what we have already said, that the destruction of death and the overturning of decay occur through the circumcision in the spirit. The blessed Moses **[635]** by God's command was sent to Pharaoh, the tyrant of the Egyptians, to announce that he should release Israel from their long bondage. Indeed, he set out to do what we just said, but "it came to pass," it says, "that an angel met him on the road by the inn and tried to kill him. And Zipporah took a stone, cut off her son's foreskin, and said, 'Here is the blood of the circumcision of my child!' And he departed from her because she said, 'Here is the blood of the circumcision of my child!'"[339]

Now listen to me carefully. The so-called angel tries to lay hands on Moses and kill him, but he withdraws from him in the nick of time and departs, put to shame by the circumcision of the child, which Zipporah carries out with a stone and which she says fulfilled what was necessary. For she cries out, "Here is the blood of the circumcision of my child!" and scares away the destroyer of Moses. But if there were no mystical meaning hidden in this passage, what credible sense, tell me, would it make when it says that the teacher Moses is saved by the circumcision of his son and that the destroyer, who pounced on Moses like a wild beast, desisted from his attack at the sight of blood and was held in check, as it were, and drew back?

Therefore (since I will proceed to this point first), the benefit, or boast, of his own circum-

[335]Ps 2:3. [336]Gen 17:25. [337]See Gal 4:25. [338]See Gal 4:26. [339]Ex 4:24-26.

cision was not sufficient for the salvation of the blessed Moses. Or rather, I should put it this way. The power of circumcision according to the law will not overturn death, which comes to everyone, evil and good, without distinction. But circumcision in the spirit, accomplished most excellently by Zipporah (that is, the church) on the new people (that is, believers in Christ), frightens death even against its will and overturns it while it is raging. **[636]**

How then, someone might ask (and quite reasonably), is Israel saved by the circumcision of the new people in the spirit, when they have not experienced it? To this we say, as far as Israel's refusal to receive the resurrection of Christ our Savior is concerned, death would have reigned forever. But since the believers received it, on their account the grace of the resurrection passed to the entire nature, extended in some sense to the whole through the circumcision in the spirit, even though there is a great difference between the resurrection of the one and the other.

Those who reject faith in Christ and by their unbelief commit an outrage against the bestower of life will gain from the resurrection only the power to live again. (They will live again for condemnation since they do not love Christ, who justifies.) But those who marvel at the Savior's resurrection and genuinely keep his commands will come out of the ground they are in "to the resurrection of life," as it is written.[340] The people who are circumcised in spirit, then, will transmit their own good even to unbelievers. Strictly speaking, the grace of the resurrection rightly belongs to that people, but they will transmit it also to others since God wills to save the entire nature by this means. As Paul says, just as we at one time were disobedient in order that, by the mercy shown to Israel, we might gain the grace of Christ through their obedience,[341] "so also they have now been disobedient in order that, by the mercy shown to us, they too might be shown mercy in turn,"[342] since Christ our Savior transmits to them too the good of his resurrection through our faith. The things that are more properly due the believers are given to the entire nature.

That is why **[637]** when the divine apostle Paul reveals to us the mystery of the coming resurrection, he too says that Christ will be raised as the first fruits. Indeed, he was raised from the dead first, but "then," Paul says, "at his coming those who belong to Christ"[343] will be raised too. He says that those who are in communion with him through faith must be raised before all the others, showing that the resurrection, strictly and properly speaking, belongs to them, even though it reaches the entire nature because God, out of his goodness and love for humanity, willed to destroy death completely.

Notice how Zipporah did not circumcise her child with an iron knife (since iron is an implement of punishment and fitting for those who are under the law, the punisher) but with a stone knife, as it is written,[344] understood as a type of Christ. By this is signified the altogether hard and unbreakable quality of the nature of the Only Begotten. Accordingly, God the Father called Christ adamant in the holy prophets, saying, "Behold, I appoint an adamant in the midst of my people Israel."[345] Adamant signifies to us in a figure that the divine and ineffable nature of the Word can never yield to those who resist it. So also the divine Joshua, when he was called to command after the leadership and death of Moses, purified the Israelites with a divine stone. And since he had to withstand the hand of the enemies, he quite rightly ordered them to arm themselves ahead of time, in a way,

[340]Jn 5:29. [341]εὐπειθείας. This statement would track better with Paul's argument in Rom 11:30 if one were to read ἀπειθείας, "disobedience" or "unbelief." [342]Rom 11:31. [343]1 Cor 15:23. [344]Ex 4:25. [345]Amos 7:8 (LXX).

through circumcision, knowing that only in this way would those who were on the verge of fighting be above falling and superior to death.

Thus it is written concerning him, "And the Lord said to Joshua, 'Make for yourself stone knives of sharp stone, and sit down and circumcise the sons of Israel.' And **[638]** Joshua made stone knives, and he circumcised the sons of Israel."[346] The word *stone* in this passage indicates to us the fixed, as it were, and indestructible quality of the Word of God, while the word *sharp* indicates his power to reach down keenly into all things and his razor-sharp activity, since Paul too, who is nourished in the holy and divine Scriptures, calls the divine Word "living and active, sharper than any two-edged sword," and he says that he pierces "to the division of soul and spirit."[347] And the one who is so keen and sharp, who reaches down into our hearts by his own Spirit, frees us from all impurity, and he renders us holy and blameless by circumcising in an ineffable way whatever fills us with extremely brutish behavior.

Look at what is in my opinion a crystal-clear image of the truth in this passage. Joshua[348] is the one who circumcises, and those who undergo it at his hand are "every young child," as it is written, "who this day does not know good or evil."[349] Those who left Egypt had God's wrath as the wages of their unbelief, and many kinds of punishment overtook them in the desert when the all-holy God for good reason decreed that he would not lead them into the land which he swore to their fathers. But the others after them, who were free from the charge of unbelief, supplied the type of the new people so that they received the circumcision in the spirit through Christ, since the original people, that is, Israel, went down to destruction, as we just said.

Furthermore, the new and noble people are circumcised beyond the Jordan at the command of Joshua, as it is written. The insight that comes from the truth is as follows: **[639]** We will never receive the circumcision of the heart by the Spirit as long as we have not yet been carried over the mystical Jordan but are still on the other side of the holy waters. But when the whole people was circumcised by the command of Joshua, the lawgiver immediately reveals the benefit of this act and says to the holy Joshua, "On this day I have removed from you the insult of Egypt."[350] In what respect, then, shall we grant that Israel is helped by circumcision? Or what sort of insult do we say was removed? It was their servitude, their susceptibility to oppression due to weakness and their labor in clay and brick. Do you see from what great evils the power of circumcision, understood spiritually, frees? It snatches the human soul from the hand of the devil. It frees and releases us from sin, which tyrannizes within us. And it renders us superior to all oppression from evil demons. Yes, it also releases us from clay and brick since it no longer allows us to be stained with the pleasures of the flesh or mixed with the toils of the earth, but it frees us from both death and decay. And these are not the only benefits of circumcision; it also makes us partakers in the divine nature[351] through participation in Christ our Savior.

To what has been said, the author of the book adds, "And the Israelites kept the Passover on the fourteenth day of the month, and they ate unleavened fresh bread made from the land's grain."[352] It is impossible, after all, to participate in the true lamb who takes away the sin of the world or to find the fresh unleavened food of the gospel proclamation without first crossing the mystical Jordan,

[346]Josh 5:2-3. [347]Heb 4:12. [348]In Greek, Joshua and Jesus are the same name. [349]Deut 1:39. [350]Josh 5:9. [351]2 Pet 1:4. [352]Josh 5:10-11.

receiving circumcision from the living [640] Word and rubbing off, as it were, the insult of Egypt like a stain on the soul, as we just explained it.

God loathes the one who is not yet circumcised, as one who is full of insult and uncleanness. He does not loathe the flesh, which he did not disdain to create, but he loathes the one who is healthy and complete, so to speak, when it comes to evil pleasures, because that person rejects nothing. We will learn this when we find him saying to holy Moses and to Aaron, "This is the law of the Passover. No foreigner shall eat of it. But every slave bought with money, you shall circumcise him, and then he shall eat of it."[353] He excludes the foreigner, indicating by this the one who has not yet been united with Christ by faith. But the one who is a slave to sin and sold to the devil, in a sense, he quite appropriately commands first to be circumcised and purified and then to taste the most holy flesh. After all, the pure will participate in Christ purely, as is appropriately[354] called out in our churches, "Holy things for holy people." For it is truly right and fitting, since Christ our Savior died for us and purified us not with sprinkling prescribed by the law but with his own blood, that we too should offer to him our own life and pay him a just debt by no longer living to ourselves but compensating him, as it were, with the complete consecration of our souls to holiness.

In the next passage, we will see that the precious blood and death of Christ, who died for all, has both saved us from every evil and has become the supplier of circumcision in the spirit, through which we gain union with God, who is over all. Something of this sort is written concerning the one who became commander after Moses, [641] I mean Joshua the son of Nun: "And it came to pass after these things that Joshua the son of Nun, the servant of the Lord, died at the age of a hundred and ten years. And they buried him at the border of his inheritance. In the tomb in which they buried him, they placed with him the knives of stone with which he circumcised the sons of Israel."[355] So the blessed Joshua died and was buried, but the knives were also profitably bound up with him in the tomb, serving as a type of circumcision, so that we might understand by this that the grace of circumcision in the spirit, which is the matchmaker for us of all heavenly goods, is bound up with the death of Christ our Savior.

Therefore, we will conceive of circumcision on the eighth day not as the Jews understand it but as the purification by the Spirit in faith and in the resurrection of Christ, the rejection of all sin, the taking away of death and decay, the supplier of sanctification and fellowship with Christ, the image of freedom and the way and the door to fellowship with God.

We have now collected from everywhere enough spiritual insights concerning these matters, and we have expended an appropriate discussion on each of the two topics, which were divided as seemed right. There now remains the task of saying why the spiritual reality of circumcision trumps, so to speak, even the honor of the sabbath. After all, circumcision is acceptable even on the sabbath, without worrying about the command to rest on it.

Now since the sabbath observance on the seventh day signifies relief and rest from all wickedness and respite from sin, and circumcision in the spirit signifies the same thing in a different way (since [642] I think that being freed from excessive desire and too much pleasure clearly produces rest from wickedness), not only will we find that circumcision

[353]Ex 12:43-44. [354]This particular word for "appropriately" (εὐρύθμως) literally means "with good rhythm," which may be an allusion to the rhythmic cadence of the phrase "holy things for holy people" (τὰ ἅγια τοῖς ἁγίοις). [355]Josh 24:29-30 (Josh 24:30-31 LXX).

in no way relaxes the sabbath law, but it is even a comrade in arms and all but meets at one and the same point, openly proclaiming that one ought to rest and cease from wickedness. So they are both the same thing, I mean circumcision and rest on the sabbath (as one might rightly surmise), because they both coincide in one purpose.

After all, we will certainly not adhere to the coarse type of the narrative, but we will attend to the sayings of the Spirit in a spiritual way. Without blame, then, the benefit of circumcision will be brought in even on the sabbath since, as the Savior says, "the priests in the temple profane the sabbath" by carrying out their priestly duties on it and not ceasing from their ordinary tasks, "and yet they are guiltless,"[356] as the judge himself has testified about them, indeed quite well and reasonably. What time could there be, after all, when we should cease from holy works and from things in which the deity delights? At what time would it not be harmful to abandon our determination for godliness? The sabbath rest, therefore, only entails a most praiseworthy rest and cessation from wickedness and loathsome sin. In no way does it prohibit us from delighting in holy works. It rightly permits us[357] instead to work hard at accomplishing whatever we think would benefit our own soul without blame.

You may see this same benefit brought in also by the power of circumcision. In the cutting off of the pleasures of evil, one sees the origin of resting from sin and a beginning of worship in the spirit and of the holiest way of life. The difference between them is small **[643]** but critical all the same. He does not command both to be performed on the seventh day, or on the eighth for that matter, and the instructions for each one give us to understand that there is some distinction. And this too has a meaning, and not an inelegant one, it seems to me. For resting from wickedness is not yet entirely expelling wickedness. The passions are often at rest in us. They are not completely expelled from our mind, but by sober reasoning they are led forcefully, as by a bridle, to a peace that is alien to them. Yes, they yield against their will to the labors of asceticism. But to shake off passion, insofar as a human can do this, is certainly something else besides this and far greater than resting from passions.

Now that the argument in these matters has been laid out, we move on finally to consider that we will never reach the expulsion of passions or of the sins that come from pleasure, which is what circumcision signifies, unless we first put an end to sins of action and put to rest, as it were, the motions of the mind that run toward sin. By using a step like this, as it were, we will easily rise to something still greater and higher, I mean the total cutting off of passions. Resting from passions seems to lie somewhat within our powers (since we may cease from evil by inclining our will to the better), but being freed from passions is not at all in our powers; rather, that would be a work that is proper to Christ, who suffered for us in order to refashion everyone to newness of life. Therefore, **[644]** circumcision was appropriately assigned the eighth day, the renewer day, so to speak, because it ushers in the time of the resurrection, while rest received the seventh day, its neighbor that is a little behind. That is because rest, which is temporary and happens at will, falls a little short of the complete cutting off of passions. **[645]**

---

[356]Mt 12:5. [357]Cyril uses the third person plural, but I have rendered the sentence in the first person plural to fit with the rest of the paragraph.

Chapters in the Fifth Book

1. Our affairs are not, as the Greeks ignorantly suppose, subject to hours by necessity, but we proceed by our own choice both to the good and to the opposite, and we are directed by the will of God; on the words "They tried to arrest him, but no one laid hands on him, because his hour had not yet come."
2. After the Savior's cross and at his resurrection from the dead, the Holy Spirit made his abode in us permanently; on the words "For as yet there was no Spirit, because Jesus was not yet glorified."
3. The suffering on the cross was not the work of Jewish might, nor did Christ die because of anyone's mistreatment, but he himself endured this willingly for us, in order to save everyone; on the words "These words he spoke in the treasury, as he taught in the temple, but no one arrested him because his hour had not yet come." **[646]**
4. The Son is God by nature, completely removed from likeness with creation, as far as his substance is concerned; on the words "You are of this world; I am not of this world."
5. The Son is not inferior in power and wisdom to God the Father, but he is his very wisdom and power; on the words "I do nothing on my own, but I speak these things just as the Father taught me." **[647]**

OUR FATHER AMONG THE SAINTS CYRIL ARCHBISHOP OF ALEXANDRIA ON THE GOSPEL ACCORDING TO JOHN

BOOK FIVE

7:25 Now some of the people of Jerusalem were saying, "Is not this the man whom they are trying to kill?"

Since it was the feast known as the feast of tabernacles in the law, and the Jews had gathered from the entire (so to speak) region in Jerusalem, because that is what the lawgiver decreed, Christ presented his teaching to everyone. He did not, of course, address only the city dwellers. So anyone who is devoted to hearing and learning must investigate what prompted the divine Evangelist to present all the rest of the Jews saying nothing, but to attribute this statement only to the Jerusalemites. We must investigate what they are contemplating and what they are thinking among themselves when they say this, because deep thought has gone into this statement. **[648]**

What then shall we say to this? Since Christ, the Savior of us all, performed a great many signs in the city and spent a rather long time in Jerusalem, some of those in the city were secretly convinced, and they quietly advanced to the point of believing in him. But they did not dare to love him openly or freely because they were fixed on the rashness of their leaders, and they were forced, not by their own will, into a harmful fear. The blessed Evangelist showed this clearly when he said in the foregoing that no one spoke openly about him "for fear of the Jews."[1] In this passage, he calls the leaders "Jews," shrinking, it seems to me, from bestowing the name of leaders on

Book 5 [1]Jn 7:13.

such hopeless men. When, then, our Savior Jesus Christ spoke openly, when he vigorously attacked the senselessness of the leaders, when he quite clearly convicted them of having no regard for the lawgiver, they all inclined (with great ease) to what seemed right to them, and they fell heedlessly into the desire to kill him as though that were nothing wicked, even though at that time he was enduring nothing unpleasant from those whose terrible deeds he was likely going to submit to.

Indeed, the inhabitants of Jerusalem take this very fact as a demonstration and confirmation of the God-befitting authority that is in him. Receiving this as a miracle in addition to his previous ones and heaping it on the preceding ones, they are driven by fervent emotions to the necessity of believing in him. That is why they say, in order to gain knowledge by right reasoning, "Is not this the man they are trying to kill?" Think about it: the inhabitants of Jerusalem all but raise their right hand on high, **[649]** wave it back and forth and point out the one who convicts them, while they ridicule the untamed rage of those people when they see that rage lulled to sleep not by sober reasoning (how could it be?) but by God-befitting power and authority.

We must also note that only the inhabitants of Jerusalem speak contrary to all the rest of the Jewish multitudes, and I will explain how that is. When Christ our Savior was explaining his most beautiful teachings, the Pharisees had stood by, cut to the heart at this, because their savage audacity was now exposed, and they were rushing to commit murder. Indeed, on this point he convicted them of breaking the law because they thought it would be proper to kill when he said, "Has not Moses given you the law? Yet none of you keeps the law. Why are you trying to kill me?"[2] The whole purpose of this statement is to target the heart of the leaders.

The common multitude, however, is struck. They thought the words were unbearable, and they answered very rashly, "You have a demon. Who is trying to kill you?"[3] But I think it is clear to all that Christ says these things because he saw the Pharisees' already murderous intent. How is it, then, that some deny it here and cry out, "Who is trying to kill you?" while the inhabitants of Jerusalem alone go against everyone else and say, "Is not this the man whom they are trying to kill?" And they do well to say "they" are trying so that the audacious deeds may be ascribed to the leaders alone.

Now a plausible explanation leads us to think that the rest of the Jewish people were ignorant of the intention of the rulers, but the inhabitants of Jerusalem, because they were with them most of the time and **[650]** lived in the same city and constantly met them, knew the unholy intention against Christ the Savior that filled them. And it happened that the bloodstained band of the Jews was accused not only by the voice of our Savior but now also by the very flock that was under them, which perished by their senselessness and was led over the cliffs. In fact, from what has been said, one may see the flock thirsting and kindled, as it were, to faith in Christ, lacking only a little leading. If they had obtained it, they would easily have received him as one who came to us from heaven. Those who have leadership, then, are responsible for the destruction of the sheep. The prophet Jeremiah too testifies about this when he cries out, "The shepherds became foolish and did not seek the Lord. Therefore, the whole flock had no understanding, and they were scattered."[4]

7:26 "Here he is, speaking openly to them, and they say nothing to him!"

[2]Jn 7:19. [3]Jn 7:20. [4]Jer 10:21.

They multiply words of assurance among themselves, and they arrive at a clearer demonstration, as it were, when they see Christ speaking freely and without danger. They are astonished for very good reason when they see those who were unholy for a long time brought to an undesired and unaccustomed patience and when they behold those who were violent practicing a gentleness that is foreign to them.

From this fact they draw reasonable inferences. They marvel at the forbearance of the leaders in matters that should not have provoked anger in the first place. By this they are found to accuse the leaders for their habit of uncritically attacking those who expound the most excellent teachings and for proceeding in anger against absolutely anyone who says something that disagrees with them, even if he agrees with the divine law. The arrogance of the Pharisees, after all, is always terrible, **[651]** and the audacity of their senselessness knows no bounds. Who then, they say, is this one who tames the Pharisees into their present condition? Who is this one who imposes sober reasoning as a bridle on their old uncontrollable anger? Who is this one who has so charmed them and lulls into gentleness those who like snakes always rear themselves up? "Here he is, speaking openly, and they say nothing to him."

He does not simply speak, they say, but he speaks "openly." I do not suppose anyone could rightly criticize their wrath for being still if the one they were seeking spoke against them secretly. Because they might not have learned about it, their wrath would not have been stirred up. But although his speech took place "openly" and proceeded with stinging criticisms (since this is what the word *openly* means), they not only refuse to be angry, even though they are quite susceptible to this disease, but they shrink even from words. For "they say nothing to him."

"Can it be that the rulers really know that he is the Christ?"

See how by reasonable thought and probable arguments they all but learn for themselves that they should believe. And they are distressed that the rulers already know who he is but nevertheless bury the acknowledgment of him in envious silence in order to avoid openly fighting against God and to keep themselves from shamefully treating him who came from above. If they did not really know, they say, "that he is the Christ," what persuaded them to put up with him as he freely accuses them, as he changes even the decrees of old by healing on the sabbath and as he vexes them without measure by openly saying, "Did not Moses give **[652]** you the law, yet none of you keeps the law?"[5] They put up with these things, even though they are in quite an unbearable state because of them and they are accustomed to attack vehemently even those who do them no harm. By going through all these considerations, then, the people compile faith in Christ little by little. And yet they attribute true knowledge to the rulers inasmuch as the rulers were brought up in the holy writings more so than they, and the rulers are better able than they to understand the mysteries in the divine Scriptures.

Notice that through all these things the people of the Jews were ready to follow their rulers without hesitation, and they would surely have been saved if they had been led to what is right by their leaders. Therefore, the leaders will undergo bitter punishment, since the Savior himself accused them saying, "Woe to you lawyers! For you have taken away the key of knowledge; you yourselves did not enter, and you hindered those who were entering."[6] For the word of those who teach rightly is a door, as it were, and a gate to the knowledge of God and a way that leads easily to all virtue. And the skill of the shepherd knows how to

[5]Jn 7:19. [6]Lk 11:52.

save the flock of sheep, just as the opposite easily destroys them and will carry the flock over the cliffs, even against their will.

7:27 "But we know where this man is from. But when the Christ comes, we will not know where he is from."

Not from external considerations alone does the mind of the Jerusalemites admit faith, or because their leaders had deemed the pain of criticism to be tolerable. Their mind quite profitably produced probable arguments **[653]** and was brought to a true conception of Christ through the God-befitting authority that was in him, and it was led not inelegantly to a true understanding of godliness. But their mind then failed to perceive that it was slipping back into the ignorance that was the foster brother of the Jews. Those who had investigated these things so well seem to want to hunt down the truth from every side, and they advance to the necessity of faith not only by the silence of their leaders and their unaccustomed meekness, but they also search the Holy Scripture itself. They are summoned to this search by their correct knowledge, but they make their inquiry of the mystery with absolutely no instruction or understanding. Just because they know "where he is from" who speaks boldly, that is, what village he comes from and what parents he was born from, they say that he is not the one foretold by the law. Then they add, "When the Christ comes, no one will know where he is from."

It is surely clear to everyone that their error in this too came from their lack of learning. But I suppose that we must search out the starting point from which they reach this conclusion. What, then, was it that persuaded those who had done a good job in their investigation of him to think that he was not the Christ just because his place of origin was not unknown? And why do they add, "When the Christ comes, no one will know where he is from"? After all, because of this they ultimately lose their understanding of the truth.

Now there is a statement about Christ in Isaiah: "Who shall declare his generation? For his life is taken from the earth."[7] The blessed prophet, making a statement about the Word of God, says "generation" instead of "being." Who, after all, could ever tell the mode of being of the Only Begotten? What tongue will declare the ineffable birth of the Son from the Father? **[654]** What mind will not be exhausted by this? *That* he was begotten of God the Father, we know and believe. But *how*, we say is inaccessible to every mind, and the investigation of it is most dangerous. For we must not investigate things that are too deep or search out things that are too difficult, but we must reflect on what we have been commanded[8] and have the unshakeable belief about God "that he both truly exists and rewards those who seek him."[9] However, we must not, as it is written, look into things beyond the mind and understanding—not only our own understanding but also that of the whole creation or even of every rational creature. Who then "shall declare the generation" of the Only Begotten? "For his life is taken from the earth,"[10] that is, the discussion of his being is clearly higher than all things that exist on the earth. Here he calls being "life."

This is what led the unintelligent mind of the Jews astray and made them wander from the truth about Christ. They did not realize, it seems, that there are two kinds of statements about him in the holy prophets. When they indicate that he will be present in this life with his flesh, they make clear his birth in the flesh from the virgin. "Behold, a virgin shall conceive and bear a son."[11] Yes, and they clearly proclaim where he will be born: "And you,

[7]Is 53:8. [8]Sir 3:21-22. [9]Heb 11:6. [10]Is 53:8. [11]Is 7:14.

Bethlehem, the house of Ephratha, are few among the thousands of Judah. Out of you, one shall come forth for me to be ruler in Israel, and his goings forth are from the beginning, from [655] eternity."[12] But when they are explaining, as far as possible, the ineffable birth from God the Father, they say either what we just said, "Who shall declare his generation? For his life is taken from the earth,"[13] or the phrase joined to the previous quote, "His goings forth are from the beginning, from eternity." Here "goings forth" indicates the shining of the Only Begotten as from a light and the procession, as it were, from his Father's substance before every age, day and moment.

The Holy Scripture, then, presents both to us. The divine writings both say where Christ will come from according to the flesh and honor with silence his unsearchable being from the Father. Therefore, how could one not rightly find the Jews to be immeasurably unlearned and laugh out loud and say, "One must not make an investigation about him based solely on not knowing the generation of Christ, but one must also base it on knowing who he is and where he comes from according to the flesh"?

7:28 Then Jesus cried out as he was teaching in the temple and said, "You know me, and you know where I am from."

As the people of Jerusalem were quietly whispering these things to each other (since they did not dare to "speak openly for fear of the Jews," as it is written),[14] Christ, in a God-befitting way, obtains knowledge of what they said. And since he considered it fitting to help the men, he immediately manifests divine activity in himself, and he clearly reveals that he has knowledge of all things. He lifts up his voice, even though earlier he was not accustomed to doing this, and he convicts them of not having a firm grasp of the divinely inspired Scripture. He makes what is secret and barely uttered the basis of his statement. [656] Then, by the very facts which made them foolishly think they should not believe, he forcefully persuades them that they should believe. That is the intention of what he says.

You marveled, he says, and you were quite right to do so, that there is a truly God-befitting power in me that easily calms the intention of the Jews, murderous though it may be. For they seek to kill me, as you yourselves truthfully and accurately remarked, and they have exceedingly great zeal for this. But as for me, he says, although I should leave and get as far away as possible from those who think it right to kill me, I pay no attention at all to their madness. On the contrary, I speak openly and accuse them of violating the law because they choose not to judge rightly, and I suffer absolutely nothing. They who were fierce from long ago are patient—but not of their own will, and this fact is not a fruit of their choice but of the power of my authority. I do not permit them to attempt their murderous intent against me ahead of time, even though they are raging and stirred up into an inhuman anger. You are astonished at these things then, he says, and quite reasonably so, and you say that the leaders truly know that I am the Christ.

You then followed sound reasoning in this matter and turned to the sayings of the divine Scripture. But when you ought to have been helped, confirmed in your conception of me, you experienced the opposite and took offense. Just because you know "where I am from" and from whom I was born, you have concluded, he says, that I am not the [657] Christ. Know then that "you know me and you know where I am from," that is, the divine Scripture has allowed you to know both me and where I am from. So just because you know, let's say, that I

[12]Mic 5:2. [13]Is 53:8. [14]Jn 7:13.

am a Nazarene or a Bethlehemite and that I am born of a woman, you should certainly not for that reason admit the disease of unbelief. Instead, you must begin from what was said about me, also regarding my birth in the flesh, and from there you must proceed to the understanding of the mysteries concerning me. You must not turn aside merely to a single statement of the prophet, who is pointing out my ineffable birth from God the Father.

"I have not come on my own, but he who sent me is true."

Next, in the form of a defense he strikes a furtive blow at those who were behaving outrageously because of their long unbelief. He weaves together his discourse with immeasurable skill and arranges it in every way so as not to give occasion to incite his hearers to reasonable indignation. Instead, by putting his words under the shadow of a certain obscurity, he steals away the greater part of their anger and takes the edge off their emotions. Why then, he says, when I have often explained and cried out explicitly that I have been sent from God the Father, do they still disbelieve? And why, just because they know his family according to the flesh, do they deny that he is the one foretold by the law and proclaimed in advance by the holy prophets? Why do they all but greet him with the words, You lie, sir; you came to us of your own will; do you not blush to employ falsely the name of the Father?

As he fends off, then, their slander on this point, he mixes accusation with his defense, and he says most excellently, **[658]** "I have not come on my own, but he who sent me is true." It is your custom, he says, you who dare all things with ease and proceed heedlessly to any action—even the most terrible actions—sometimes to prophesy falsely and, even though God has not sent you, to say that you have been sent by God. But I am not like you, and I will not imitate your well-worn audacity. I do not come "on my own" or self-sent like you. I have come from heaven. "He who sent me is true," certainly not like your lie-loving sender, the devil, whose spirit you receive when you dare to prophesy falsehoods. He who sent me is true, then, but he who incites you to fabricate words from God is not true. For he is a liar and the father of liars.[15]

We shall have no trouble seeing from the words of the prophets that false prophecy is in fact the norm for the Jews. The Lord of all says most clearly somewhere about them, "I did not send the prophets, yet they ran; I did not speak to them, yet they prophesied."[16] And again in Jeremiah, "The prophets prophesy lies in my name; I did not send them, I did not speak to them, I did not command them. They prophesy to you visions and auguries and prophecies of their own heart."[17] The arrogant Jews, then, are being accused here for attributing to Christ himself their own audacity against God, that is, false prophecy. Even the slightest disbelief of the one who cries out that he has been sent from God, from the Father—what else could this be than to cry out openly, You prophesy falsely, acting toward us the same way we act? **[659]**

7:29 "You do not know him, but I know him, because I am from him, and he sent me."

You just said, he says, "When the Christ comes, no one will know where he is from." All right, since you insist that you are correct to hold this opinion, I will agree with your statement on this matter. The Father, from whom I am, is true, but he is not known to you. Since, he says, you examine the mystery concerning me without any consideration except what is pleasing to you, and since you excuse yourselves from having to believe because you know who I am and where I come

[15]Jn 8:44. [16]Jer 23:21. [17]Jer 14:14.

from according to the flesh, you should receive faith for this very same reason when you discover that you do not know where I am from. I am from the Father, whom "you do not know" since you do not know the one who is from him, in whom alone the Father is seen. Whoever has seen the Son has seen the Father,[18] and whoever knows the Son is not ignorant of the one who begat him. Therefore, all their sophistical ingenuity is taken away by this. They are caught in their malice, no longer finding any pretext for unbelief. Instead, they reject knowledge solely out of their own stubbornness so that what is written may be shown true: "You have often seen and have not taken heed; your ears have been opened, but you have not heard."[19]

Since he was dealing with the statement of the Jews that "no one" will know where he is from when the Christ comes, he necessarily removed himself, as God, from the multitude of originate beings and from everything else to which the phrase "no one" might reasonably be applied, showing himself to be different in nature since, unlike them, he was not ignorant of the one who begat him, he says. On the contrary, he insisted that he knew both himself and his Father with total accuracy. For he is God from God the Father, and he has a wondrous **[660]** knowledge of these matters that is alien to us and proper to himself alone. For the Son knows the Father not as we know him, I mean not in the same way. The nature of originate beings approaches the sight of God to the point of conception alone, not surpassing the boundaries that are fitting for this nature, but it concedes to the divine nature, even unwillingly, that that nature is hidden in ineffable speech. But the Only Begotten, who arose from God the Father, sees his begetter completely in himself. And since he portrays the substance of his parent in his own nature, he knows him in a way that is impossible to say. For the things of God are unutterable. **[661]**

Chapter One

Our affairs are not, as the Greeks ignorantly suppose, subject to hours by necessity, but we proceed by our own choice both to the good and to the opposite, and we are directed by the will of God.

7:30 Then the Jews tried to arrest him, but no one laid hands on him, because his hour had not yet come.

The Pharisees are cut by his reproaches, and when they see that their silence on the matter is not without harm to their own stubbornness but is helpful to the crowds (since they were being persuaded that they should confess him to be the Christ), they are carried away to their usual audacity, and they once again thirst for blood. They reject reverence toward the law as completely useless to them. They place no value on the teachings of the Holy Scriptures. They do not consider the command, "You shall not kill the innocent and just,"[20] to be worth remembering, and so they are sick with a most unjust fury against Christ. But by divine power, the outcome is turned to the complete opposite of what they tried to do. "For the deceitful will catch no prey," as it is written.[21] They try to arrest him, as the Evangelist says, as though they had kept a voluntary and self-imposed silence at his rebukes, counteracting by their later wrath the appearance that he had held them back. That is because some of the Jerusalemites took this as proof of Jesus being **[662]** God by nature, saying, "Here he is, speaking openly to them, and they say nothing to him! Can it be that the rulers really know that he is the Christ?"[22] But he who "catches the wise in their craftiness"[23] renders

[18]See Jn 14:9. [19]Is 42:20 (LXX). [20]Ex 23:7. [21]Prov 12:27. [22]Jn 7:26. [23]1 Cor 3:19.

this audacity utterly ineffectual for those who planned the arrest, and he confirms for the crowds what they were talking about quietly in speculation and conjecture. The rulers are constrained by divine activity that puts a bridle on their unholy deeds and allows their plans to advance only to the point of attempting them.

The supremely wise Evangelist profitably presents in this passage the reason why they cannot carry out their proposed intention. "His hour," he says, "had not yet come." "Hour" in this passage means the time, that is, the time of his suffering and of the precious cross. To whom would it not be obvious from this that Christ would not have suffered at all if he had refused to choose suffering? For he went up on the cross not by Jewish arrogance but by his own will, for us and on account of us. That is why he says, rejecting the accusation of apparent powerlessness, "No one takes my life from me, but I lay it down of my own accord. I have the power to lay it down, and I have the power to take it up again."[24] As we just said, he did not endure the cross for us against his will. He himself offered himself as a holy sacrifice to God the Father, purchasing the salvation of all by his own blood.

That is also why he said in the gospel proclamation, "For their sakes I sanctify myself."[25] He says "sanctify" in this passage instead of "offer" and "dedicate," since what is offered **[663]** as a sacrifice to God is holy. And we will understand that he accepted being the sacrifice for all without any violence from anyone when we hear him saying to God the Father in the Psalms, "Sacrifice and offering you did not desire, but a body you have prepared for me. You took no pleasure in whole burnt offerings for sin. Then I said, 'Behold, I have come to do your will, O God. It is written about me in the chapter of the book.' "[26] Do you see how of his own accord he comes to his suffering for all? Behold, I have come, he says. I am not pursued by necessity that comes from another. He escapes, then, the present violence of the leaders, reserving his suffering for a fitting time and practicing a most God-befitting boldness in all things.

This is sufficient, I think, for the clarification of the passage before us. However, it is likely that some of those being initiated into the mysteries, when they hear that "his hour had not yet come," may from excessive levity slip into the mad folly of the Greeks so that they unreasonably suppose that human affairs are subject to hours and days and seasons. Therefore, I think it necessary to say a few words about this, since our aim is to be zealous in providing profit to the reader with every thought.

Now for the children of the church, who have been raised on the Holy Scriptures, I imagine that what Paul said as an accusation or wise rebuke to some who were so minded will be sufficient to refute the trickery of the Greeks and to enable us to jettison their foolishness: "You are observing days, and months, and seasons and years. I am afraid that I have labored over you in vain."[27] And indeed, apart from all subtle arguments, the one who is involved in this sort of foolishness **[664]** will destroy their own soul and will be caught dishonoring the originator of us all, to whom alone wise and learned reasoning attributes the steering of our affairs. Those who are incorrectly minded to hold those observances will overturn the order of providence. They believe that the Lord of all is no longer the dispenser of our affairs; instead, they end up attributing power over all things to seasons and hours. In so doing, they end up placing the creature over the creator; they rob the one who deserves all honor and glory and worship of the fairest attributes; they give to the creature what is above the creature and attribute to created beings those honors with which they ought to crown the creator.

[24]Jn 10:18. [25]Jn 17:19. [26]Ps 40:6-8 (Ps 39:7-9 LXX). [27]Gal 4:10-11.

And the charges against them will not stop there but will go further to something even more serious than this. They end up openly railing against the benevolent God and saying that the enemy of all sin is himself the worker of evil. For if time has been created by him—the hour, the day and the year—and if these intervals sometimes lead some people by necessity and by force into unintended wickedness so that they fall into misfortune because of it, how will our statement about this not show itself to be true? And what then becomes of what was said by the supremely wise Moses? "And God saw," he says, "all things that he had made, and behold, all of it was very good."[28] Now time is one of the "all things." And within time is the hour, day and year. If we say that what the eye of the divine nature saw was good actually introduced evil, how will we not admit outright that the Lord of all is found to be the creator of the most disgraceful things?

Now I think that those who are guilty of the offenses we just mentioned will already be blushing. But since it is likely **[665]** that some have chosen not only not to resist the senseless ideas of the Greeks but even to support them, let us examine the absurdity inherent in their teaching in another light also, and let us bring out the truth, amassing from reasoning useful assistance against their repulsive ideas. If as you say, sirs, we are compelled to something good because the season summons us by force and the hour coerces us, let's say, or we are compelled to good's opposite, it seems that reason is superfluous—reason which steers us regarding each of the acts, counseling us to avoid evil and ordering us to pursue what is praiseworthy. What profit, tell me, does reason have in the end, and what useful benefit comes from it, if I will be completely passive and will go even against my will wherever the hour summons me and wherever the season wishes to force me? It is fitting, then, just as they say the pilots of ships do, who have declared that there is no hope for the ship to be saved when it is endangered by a storm, to let go of every rope and cut loose the rudders, no longer exercising any skill in the situation, and so to entrust the ship to the force of the waves to be tossed by the sea.

There is no profit—none—as we just said, for those who want virtue, nor will any harm come to those who do evil unless we are repaid by God for each of our actions and receive a recompense in accordance with the quality of our actions. Will the hour, tell me, often decree the finest fortunes, and will the season uncritically do what is profitable to me, even if I am caught in the most disgraceful deeds? However, the season will sometimes allot nothing good **[666]** to some people but will inflict the hardest situation of all, so to speak, even on those who hold the conviction that they should especially honor the performance of good deeds.

But none of this will be so, perhaps someone will say; the hour and the season give to each one the fortune that fits them.

Does the season now rule over us, then? Will we ascribe the honor of providence to the hours, no longer giving any thought to God? Will we ask nothing from him in prayer but rather ask from the hour and the season? And then what? We will worship the creature rather than the creator,[29] and we will blasphemously ascribe the glory of the creator to what was made by him.

We will have no trouble seeing that this is disgraceful and the magnitude of the blasphemy has a repugnance more open than the women who are prostitutes, yet we will say what comes into our mind for the sake of profit. Superfluously, it seems, do the divine and human laws decree fitting punishments for those who love evil and bestow honors on those who make a valiant attempt to choose to live

[28]Gen 1:31. [29]Rom 1:25.

rightly. After all, if nothing whatsoever lies in our wills but everything happens by the necessities of the hours, which lead us inescapably and unavoidably to both, how could we still rightly say that the good deserve praise, and dispense the opposite to those who are not good, as their penalty? Why, tell me, do the laws compel us to depart from evil and zealously pursue the better if others hold the reins of our intentions and easily lead us wherever they want? They both say and desire that human affairs must be subject to the authority of the hours **[667]** without considering at all the absurdity that results from this.

Will they not say, even against their will, that the one who has command over all things on earth will be more wretched than the irrational animals themselves and will live in a pitiable state, and the one who ought to have first place because of his nature will now be ranked in second, or even in last place? If the animals by their autonomous impulses turn toward whatever they wish with nothing hindering them, and they let near them what they know to be good for them and avoid what usually harms them, while we serve the harsh master time and have the authority of the hours as an inescapable tyranny suspended over us like a staff, how is our condition not far worse than theirs?

Now the one who wants to advocate this position, or rather to utter lies, will probably blush, since the hours and the times were not created for any such purpose. But to deflect the stupidity of their doctrines, they will come and say, We do not characterize, sir, the hour or the time or the season as ruling human affairs, but we say that there are evil hours, and seasons too, which sometimes leap on us like furious winds, making us miserable.

To this we will reply, Your minds are frenzied, drunk with undiluted foolishness. How did it escape you once again that you are arming your mind against that substance which is above all? Will it not be an evildoer if something it created is evil? But since we have already addressed this, we will pass over it and be eager for you to convince us how the hour or the season could **[668]** harm us or, on the contrary, bring us joy. Does not God who directs all things wherever he wishes will for each thing its due, bringing either suffering or, on the contrary, joy?

We just heard you say that none of our affairs is under the authority of the hours, but rather some hours are evil by nature and come down on us all at once like a wind. I think, however, that it will not be difficult to show that your reasoning is full of the ultimate foolishness. Who doesn't know that intervals of twelve hours are obviously distributed between day and night, and that night and day do not come to one person and not another but pervade all things? So the interval that is evil by nature and inescapable would not be evil toward one and not another, nor would it bring harm to one, perhaps, or two, but equally to all on whom the interval of night or day would come.

How then is it possible that in a day, let's say, or in a single hour, one may see someone prospering, reveling with lots of people who know how to have a good time so as to live the good life and gather together feasting companions with great gusto, while others are in exactly the opposite condition so that someone is perhaps carried off to die miserably? What is the explanation, tell me, and how could it be possible that in a single hour or a single season, one person may be found in the former state and the other person in the latter? What will you say about that hour? Is it evil, or the opposite? I do not know what to say as I look at both people, the one reveling and the other a breathless and miserable corpse. Will not this teaching about the hours, then, be exposed as an ignorant myth and an invention of demonic madness? I think that everyone **[669]** will agree to this without hesitation and will condemn those who think this way.

We might well, I think, be content with what we have said, but so that I do not entrust everything to possibility and conjecture and leave some people a pretext for quibbling, I will move on to the interpretation of events, and from what has happened I will indisputably confirm the argument we have just rehearsed. Now the Assyrians once surrounded the holy city, I mean holy Jerusalem, and planned to besiege it. Their general, Rabshakeh, at one time tried to unnerve the mind of the soldiers in the city with deceptive words; at another time he planned to do this by threats. But the blessed Hezekiah, who holds the honor of kingship at the time, does not trust in his own armies but attributes the achievement of victory to the God of all, and through the most fervent prayer he kept asking for the aid that comes only from him. And God immediately inclined his ear to the righteous man and granted him grace in answer to his prayers. "And the angel of the Lord went forth," as it is written, "and slew a hundred and eighty-five thousand from the camp of the foreigners."[30]

What then, fine sir, will you say to this? In one night and at the same hour and moment, the Assyrian fell, destroyed by the hand of the angel, but the multitude of the inhabitants of Jerusalem were saved. The one was in extreme suffering, the other in joy and delight. Where is the power of the hour? How was it apportioned unequally to both? Did it bring about rejoicing for some and an evil death for others? You would not dare to call it two-natured and multiformed, even if you do utter exceedingly foolish ideas.

The same argument would hold for Dathan **[670]** and Abiram, who opposed the leadership of Moses and did not fear to leap unbidden to the rank of the holy priesthood, and went down with their whole household into the depths of the earth.[31] They were in Hades, but the rest of the assembly was preserved. But it was surely necessary, if the punishment was not at all from divine wrath but from the hour, that it burst forth not just on one part of the assembly but took hold of the entire assembly equally.

Therefore, let us not take the hour or the day or the season as the bestower of either grief or joy as far as their own nature is concerned, or however one might rightly speak of it. But let us understand benefit or harm from the hour or the season to occur when we proceed either wisely or ignorantly and meet with results that are either pleasant or not. For example, "There is a season for every matter," as it is written,[32] and knowing the seasons is most beneficial, while not knowing them is very harmful. One must not sail in winter, but it is not ignorant to do this during the summer. If we think about these matters this way, we will commit the rudder of our affairs to God, the master of all. After all, if, as the Savior truly says, the small and inexpensive sparrow will never fall into the snare apart from the knowledge of God the Father,[33] how could one so honored, who has attained authority over all, suffer anything contrary to God's knowledge or will, without providence decreeing what we have discussed in proportion to each person's way of life?

I will add something else to this that has just been shaken out of my memory, even though it is quite similar to the present matter, or rather calls for the same investigation for itself. And the solution is not difficult but **[671]** very easy to grasp, at least for one who has any intelligence at all and has their "faculties trained by practice to distinguish good from evil."[34] What then is this that we are talking about?

The people of Cana, who inhabited the land bordering Judea (that is, Galilee), once celebrated a wedding. And they invited the Lord to a lavish banquet, along with his

[30]Is 37:36. [31]Num 16:32-33. [32]Eccles 3:1. [33]Mt 10:29. [34]Heb 5:14.

mother and the holy disciples, and the reason for their feast was the marriage bed. But when the Lord was there, eating with those gathered in order to bless marriage which he had commanded, the wine began to run out for the guests. Since the Savior's mother has authority over her son because of his exceedingly great submission, and since she already knows by much experience that he has God-befitting power, she says, "They have no wine."[35] For she knew that it would take no effort for him to do whatever the nature of the situation required. But the Lord says to her, "Woman, what concern is that to you and me? My hour has not yet come."[36]

Now the mind that loves God and is free from monstrous opinions runs as far away as possible from Greek superstition and receives this statement in a reverent way. The time of my manifestation, he says (that is, by signs), has not yet come. Since he was God by nature, he was not unaware of the proper time for each matter. How could he be? But those who run to and fro out of complete ignorance (since evil is an easy path for the many) and who think that Christ himself is subject to the activity of the hours, as some foolishly say, will be caught here in their senselessness right before our eyes. They will be condemned for the absurdity of their opinions by the very arguments they thought would strengthen their case. If we grant that the nature of our affairs is subject to the activity of the hours and that this is the reason Christ says to his **[672]** mother, "My hour has not yet come," how, tell me, according to your repugnant and most foolish reasoning, does he grant her request when he does not yet have the activity of the hours on the side of his will? He obviously changes water into wine immediately, after all. But if you think that affairs must be subject to the authority of the hours, then the Lord should have made no attempt at all which the concurrence of the hours did not grant, right? He obviously did not think this way, however, but gave them his grace ahead of time, as it were. The power of the hour, then, was no hindrance, but Christ says this because the time has not yet come for his proclamation by miracles.

So we have been freed from your conjecture about this passage. When the "hour" is mentioned, let it be understood as that time which is fitting for every matter. The fact that we ourselves are free from the necessity of the hours is a subject that I think needs no more words. We have already gone through it sufficiently.

We will, however, now endeavor to show that we will find "hour" in the divine Scriptures to mean the proper time for each matter. The admirable Paul cries out and, mentioning the "hour," indicates its meaning: "And you know what time it is, how it is the hour for you to awake from sleep. The night is far gone, the day is at hand."[37] Notice how he puts "time" first and then adds "hour," using it to refer to the same thing, and nothing else. It was time for those now sleeping in sin to wake up, open their eyes to what is beneficial and be raised to a God-loving sobriety. **[673]**

7:31 Now many in the crowd believed in him and said, "When the Christ comes, will he be able to do more signs than this man has done?"

It is worth seeing how carefully this statement is arranged and how appropriately it follows after what came before. He said before that the Jews were trying to arrest him[38] and in their madness trap him with their nets for a very cruel and unseasonably contrived peril. Now he portrays the crowds believing, so that the evil machinations of the leaders against him may finally be acknowledged. So far are the

[35]Jn 2:3. [36]Jn 2:4. [37]Rom 13:11-12. [38]Jn 7:30.

people from wanting to rage against him that they now piece together an understanding of him from his miracles and explicitly acknowledge that they should pay attention to his teachings.

There was a report, it seems, buzzing across the entire race of the Jews and spread over their whole land that Christ would come to do mighty deeds. He would perform wonders beyond thought, and he would introduce teaching far more remarkable and superior than the teaching of the law. The Samaritan woman, for example, when she came to Jacob's well to draw water and was conversing with the Savior, said, "We know that the Messiah is coming, who is called Christ. When he comes, he will proclaim all things to us."[39] It is surely reasonable for us to apply the "we know" in this statement not to that woman alone, and if we apply it to the entire race of the Samaritans and Jews, we will confirm the statement we just made.

Those currently under consideration, then, since they see that the glorious hopes that are buzzing around about him do not surpass what is now present, all but say to each **[674]** other, For what mission has the law indicated to us that Christ would be revealed? What kind of man has the word of the holy prophets foretold? Clearly, he is a miracle worker and a most excellent instructor. And yet, we see that he who is now present is utterly outstanding in both. What higher signs remain for those who imagine something still greater? What difficult things has he been too weak to do? What miraculous deeds beyond thought has he not performed? In whom shall we still seek something greater? Let us see whether he does not reach the limit of all wonder! What is expected in the Christ that does not appear in this man? The refusal to believe is now shameless; laziness is reckless, and the case for delay for the sake of having to choose the best is utterly unpersuasive. Let God be confessed. The very nature of the facts demands it, even of those who are unwilling.

It would not be unsuitable or unbecoming, then, to place such a statement in the mouth of the Jews. We must note, however, that their obedience perished because of the stubbornness of the leaders. The one group was good at guessing, led by the glory of what he accomplished to the necessity of believing in him, awaiting only the judgment of the rulers concerning Christ. The other group was so savage in cruelty that they tried to mistreat him who was foretold for great hopes and who was accredited by what he already accomplished.

7:32 The chief priests and Pharisees heard the crowd muttering these things about him.

The multitudes are upset with their leaders, and for very good **[675]** reason. The people made a great outcry concerning Christ our Savior, not because he was a marvelous wonder worker beyond expectation or because he came speaking of matters superior to the worship of the law but because he was not yet accepted by the chief priests and Pharisees. This despite the fact that he had glory equivalent to what was said about Christ and was in no way inferior to what the common reports announced about him, or even what the word of the holy prophets foretold. Therefore, they justly accuse their leaders of being overcome by envy rather than truly thinking of the salvation of the people. And since the discussion of blame in this matter is widespread, it does not escape the notice of the rulers. The multitude has given them offense, it seems, since that multitude is now understandably astonished at the Lord, thirsts intensely to believe in him and is already refusing to bear the yoke of the

[39]Jn 4:25.

leaders' violence. It is practicing, so to speak, to do what is said in the Psalms, "Let us burst their bonds and cast their yoke from us."[40] By not subjecting the mind of the people to the commands of the law but rather to their own inventions, and by "teaching human precepts as doctrines,"[41] they left the straight and well-beaten road and sent to the cliffs and pits those who were even now ready to be saved and who were being led on their own to right reasoning.

And the chief priests and Pharisees sent officers to arrest him.

Although the law declares, "You shall not kill the innocent and righteous,"[42] and it clearly shouts up and down, "You shall not follow the majority in wrongdoing,"[43] the guardians of the law want to kill. They are overbearing when it comes to regarding the law of Moses as holy, **[676]** and they are accustomed to reprimanding everyone else if they do not think the same way. But here they think nothing of the law, and spurning, as it were, what is most precious to them, they are eager to catch in their nets the one who has done no wrong at all but is rather accredited by his very deeds to be the Christ.

But surely, someone will reasonably say, if the unholy leaders of the Jews were learned in the divine oracles and knowledgeable in the divine law, they should have addressed the crowds to overturn their outcry on this subject with fitting arguments. They should have fended off all suspicions of envy and changed the crowds' thinking to what it should be, if the crowds seemed to have been at all subverted by the leaders when the crowds were full of good guesses about Christ. The leaders should have confirmed those guesses with the testimony of the prophets and, in short, going through all the divine Scriptures, they should have washed away the accusations of the crowds and taught the truth about Christ, since they knew more. But since they find no defense from that source, and since they are ashamed of the Holy Scripture in that they find it accusing them along with the crowds, they fall into a shameless rage and try to take Christ away, since they are not able to convict him of any offense.

And what is most intolerable of all, this intention belongs not just to anyone, but the audacity belongs to the chief priests, who go along with the opinion of the Pharisees, even though they ought to lead them because of the superiority they had in the priesthood. Since they rank first because of this, they ought to show themselves leaders in good intentions and start with counsel that is not opposed to God. But **[677]** since good intentions were foreign to them, and they threw the divine law behind their own imagination, they were carried only to that which pleased their uncritical impulses. "The head has become the tail," as it is written.[44] The leader follows, and agreeing with the unholiness of the Pharisees, he now makes an unbridled attack against Christ.

But the attack of the wicked against the virtuous is always found to be utterly baseless, and their method of attack is essentially crippled because it does not depend on plausible arguments based on fair questions, hindered as it is by the singular disease of envy. They cannot compete with the great deeds of the virtuous, nor can they attain equal glory through equal courage, nor can they be in any better condition at all through better deeds. Therefore, they fall into savage thoughts, and they foolishly arm themselves against the praises of those who surpass them, zealous for the destruction of what disgraces them. Evil is always accused by juxtaposition with the better. But instead, they should surely desire to match them with equal actions and rush to imitate the praiseworthy in thought and deed.

[40]Ps 2:3. [41]Mt 15:9. [42]Ex 23:7. [43]Ex 23:2. [44]Deut 28:44.

But the Pharisees were likely bitter. They learned that the crowds were muttering and murmuring among each other, "Is not this the man whom they are trying to kill? Here he is, speaking openly to them, and they say nothing to him! Can it be that the rulers know that he is the Christ?" When they learn this, they repel this suspicion with evil, their stepsister, by giving orders to bind him and by sending officers to carry it out. **[678]**

7:33 Jesus then said, "I am with you a little longer, and then I go to him who sent me."

Now he was not unaware, since the Lord is indeed God by nature, of the bloodthirsty audacity of the Pharisees and the unholy intention of the chief priests against him. With the eyes of his divinity, he sees the officers who were chosen by them to arrest him now present and mingled with the crowds. That is why he makes his statement general, as though addressed to all the people standing around, though in a way it is an answer to them in particular. Even so, he teaches much that is profitable in this statement. He threatens them cleverly, but he also convicts them of being mean-spirited about things that should please them. And he says that even if they succeed, their attempt will be frustrated in another way. How he does this, we will explain by going through the statement piece by piece.

When he says, "I am with you a little longer," he practically says outright: Tell me, why are you angry with me for spending a long time in the world? I am burdensome to you, I admit, and I am not at all agreeable to those who do not honor virtue. I dash to pieces whoever does not love God and smite the ungodly at times with rebukes. I am not unaware that I have cultivated hatred for myself, but do not lay out the net of death for me so early. I will be "with you a little longer." I will go up rejoicing when the time for suffering comes, and I will not allow myself to be with the evil because time spent with the bloodthirsty, he says, is not pleasant to me. I will depart from the ungodly, as God, but I will be with my own all the days of the world, even though I seem to be absent in the flesh.

When he says, "I go to **[679]** him who sent me," he indicates something like this: In vain, he says, did you sharpen the sword of your ungodliness against me. Why do you tear yourselves to pieces with useless counsel? Put away the arrow of envy; you shoot it for nothing. It will not subject life to death, nor will corruption be superior to incorruption. I will not be overcome by the gates of Hades.[45] I will not be with you as a corpse in a tomb. I will fly up to him from whom I come. I will ascend back to heaven and will be seen by both angels and humans as an accusation against your ungodliness. The one group will marvel at me ascending, while the other will greet me and say, "What are these wounds in your hands?" And I will say to them, "The wounds that I received in the house of my beloved."[46] The statement, then, has been made with great tact and outstanding gentleness as an example also for us.

For this reason Paul too says that the servant of God must not "be quarrelsome but kind to all, instructing his opponents with gentleness."[47] I think that the God-loving mind must be free from all tumult and from wild angry emotions and be committed to avoiding mean-spirited behavior like a fierce onslaught of waves. It must take pleasure in gentle thoughts as in tranquil weather, desire to live as much as possible in longsuffering, show itself patient to all, have an altogether good spirit and make no undignified statement against its enemies.

[45]See Mt 16:18. [46]Zech 13:6. [47]2 Tim 2:24-25.

7:34 "You will seek me, and you will not find me."

This too is said skillfully and with great tact. It indicates something that, taken at face value, is not difficult to **[680]** understand; still, it contains a keen mystery hidden in it. When he says that he will ascend to him who sent him, that is, to God the Father, he is saying that even if they still try to plot against him, even if they do not stop persecuting him, he will be completely beyond their reach since he is rushing into the very heavens.

But the truer meaning, hinted at enigmatically, is this: I, he says, was sent to bestow life on you, and I have come to remove death, which came by transgression, from human nature and patiently to bring back to God those who have fallen through sin. I have come to implant the divine and heavenly light in those in darkness and to "preach the gospel to the poor" and to give "recovery of sight to the blind, to proclaim liberty to the captives and to declare the acceptable year of the Lord."[48] But since it seems good to you in your senselessness to drive away the one who set before you such a rich enjoyment of heavenly blessings, after a little while I myself will return to him from whom I come, and you will have remorse and weep bitterly for yourselves, consumed by ineffectual regret. Even if you still desire to find the bestower of life, you will not be able to enjoy the one you long for then. Once I have departed and turned away from my love toward you, I will completely block from you the benefit of seeking.

We will find this sort of thing also in the preaching of the prophets about them. Someone says concerning those of Israel, "With sheep and calves they will go to seek the Lord, but they will not find him because he has withdrawn from them."[49] Those who refused to choose life when it was present and who by ignorant reasoning rejected the good that was in their hands—how **[681]** could they still be fit to receive it? And those who thought nothing of missing the moment—how could they be able to have the corresponding benefits out of season? After all, one must seek the benefits in and from the moment when it has arrived and is still present. But when the moment is already past and gone, the search for its benefits is then superfluous and vain. Indeed, the blessed Paul says, "Behold, now is the acceptable time; behold, now is the day of salvation,"[50] and, "While we have time, let us do good to all."[51] Now—now, I say! Those of a good disposition must not seek for the good of a moment when that moment is already past its prime but at the beginning, when it shows its presence in full bloom, as it were.

There is still much more to say about time from the Holy Scriptures, but I will leave that to those who are eager to work in searching it out. Now I will say a little something that is common and in use among us, yet has no small profit. They say that those who make pictures on tablets, when they represent a moment in human form, they depict the rest of the body however they want, but they draw the head only like this. They show it from behind as bald and very smooth, painting it with bright colors. But from the middle of the head, they hang long hair over the forehead, full and flowing in front. With this depiction they indicate that when a moment is present and greets us face to face, as it were, one may easily lay hold of it. But when it has already passed, how could it still be seized? It is bushy, as it were, and easy to grab while it is still present, but when it has gone, it no longer is that way. This is what the smoothness in the back indicates, all but mocking the hand of the one who wants to hold it. **[682]** Since, then, we no longer have the opportunity outside or after the moment, let us not fall asleep to good

[48]Is 61:1-2. [49]Hos 5:6. [50]2 Cor 6:2. [51]Gal 6:10.

opportunities when they are present, but rather let us awake, and let us not ignorantly rush to track down what is profitable once the search is profitless.

"And where I am, you cannot come." Next, he most cleverly excludes the race of the Jews from the kingdom of heaven, introducing words consistent with what he already said before, but at the same time burying a deep mystery within them. If we apply ourselves more simply to this statement and take a more superficial interpretation of it, we say that it indicates something like this: that they will in no way be able to apprehend him,[52] nor will he fall under their nets, because he has returned to the Father. Heaven is not accessible to them, after all, so how could the one who sits with God the Father himself be easy for those who seek him to capture? Now this particular interpretation is not deep; rather, it is more suitable for the levity of the Jews and better for their understanding, since they always think in a more earthly way.

However, the precise and hidden meaning of the words goes something like this: I, he says, when I have escaped the snare of your unholiness, will return to God the Father. I will surely precede my worshipers in my departure in order to make the way that leads upward accessible to them and to have them all with me. "But you cannot come where I am," that is, you will find yourselves without a share in the divine blessings, you will not participate in my glory, you will be alienated from ruling with the saints, [683] you will remain without a taste of the gift of hope, you will be excluded from the divine wedding feast, you will not see my festal assembly, you will not ascend to the mansions above, nor will you behold the beauty of the church of the firstborn. The city above will be unseen by you; you will not behold the riches of Jerusalem, for there my flock will glorify me, but "you cannot come." Heaven, after all, will not receive those who kill the Lord, nor will the cherubim open the gates of paradise to let in the people who are enemies of God, nor will a man guilty of irreverence toward God in any way win over the "flaming sword."[53] It recognizes only the reverent and honors the one who loves God, and it makes faith its covenant of peace.

We will bring this sort of insight to these words, tracking down from all sides the meaning that is true and fitting for the intelligent. But we will add a few things to this, showing for our profit that as many as ascend to a God-loving disposition will be with and feast with Christ, but those who concur with Jewish ignorance will not be in this situation—how could they be?—but will suffer bitter punishment for their unbelief. Therefore, let the divine Paul come in, crying out to those who have died to sin, "You have died, and your life is hidden with Christ in God. When Christ your life appears, then you also will appear with him in glory."[54] And again, laying out his discussion of the resurrection, he says, "And we who are alive, who are left, will be caught up together with them in the clouds to meet the Lord in the air; and so we will always be with the Lord."[55] We see the Savior himself saying similar things to his disciples. As he is feasting with them, he says, "I tell you I shall not drink again of this fruit of the vine, until [684] that day when I drink it anew with you in the kingdom of heaven."[56] And to the thief hanging with him, who at the very gates of death seizes the grace of the saints through faith in him, he says, "Truly, truly I say to you, today you will be with me in paradise."[57]

Those, then, who have honored him with faith will have no difficulty being with him. They will enjoy blessings beyond their imagi-

[52]Cyril's word choice in Greek here evokes Jn 1:5, "And the darkness did not overcome (apprehend) [the light]." [53]Gen 3:24. [54]Col 3:3-4. [55]1 Thess 4:17. [56]Mt 26:29. [57]Lk 23:43.

nation. But those who do not refrain from insulting him with their senselessness will go down in gloom to Hades, paying bitter penalties, even though they are wedding guests.[58] For "they will be cast out," as it is written, "into outer darkness."[59] Therefore, the Lord is speaking the truth in an enigma when he says to the Jews, "Where I am, you cannot come."

7:35 Then the Jews said to one another, "Where is this man going to go that we will not find him? Surely, he is not going to go to the Diaspora among the Greeks and teach the Greeks, is he?"

Do you see in these words the wretchedness of Jewish reasoning? Do you see the most pitiful guess of the earthbound mind? They do not say that he is going to ascend to heaven, even though they have explicitly heard, "I am with you a little longer, and then I go to him who sent me."[60] Instead, they imagine the land of the Greeks, as though the one who sent him was among those Greeks, to whom he promised to return.

With these words, the people of the Jews are prophesying, it seems, though they do not know what they are saying. Moved by some divine impulse, they bestow Christ on the land of the Gentiles, thinking as a suspicion what a little later will be true. After all, he really was about to go to the Greeks and teach them, spurning Jerusalem, the ungrateful **[685]** mother of the Jews.

Notice how they do not make a simple statement about this. They do not suspect only that he will go "to the Diaspora of the Greeks," but they maliciously add that he is going to "teach the Greeks" in order that their suspicion may beget for them a pretext for accusing him. For dealing with the Diaspora of the Greeks by going to their cities or lands was common and blameless in the eyes of the Jews. But to explain the law to aliens and to unveil the divine mysteries to the uninitiated was slanderous and not without blame in their eyes. Indeed, God found fault with some who were indifferent about this, saying through the prophet Jeremiah, "And they read the law to outsiders."[61] Pointedly, then, they say that "he is going to teach the Greeks," disparaging him on the grounds that he readily transgresses the law. And from what he had already done before on the sabbath day, they believe that it is his custom to do everything heedlessly, even if it violates the divine law, and he thinks nothing of it.

7:37 On the last day of the feast, the great day, Jesus stood up and cried out, "Let anyone who is thirsty come to me and drink!"

In this statement we must carefully investigate what the supremely wise Evangelist is hinting at with his exceedingly great attention to detail when he calls the last day of the feast "great," or what induced our Lord Jesus **[686]** Christ, as though by some necessary reason appropriate to that time, to say to the Jews especially on that day, "Let anyone who is thirsty come to me and drink." He might have used other words, such as "I am the light" or "I am the truth." But when he turned his explanation to the matter of faith, he introduced "drink" as a necessary, as it were, and fitting expression for a feast. So I will try to say a few things about the intention of the statement before us.

Now when God prescribed the regulations concerning the feast of tabernacles, he said to Moses, "On the fifteenth day of the seventh month, there shall be a feast of tabernacles to the Lord. And you shall offer whole burnt offerings and sacrifices for seven days, and the

[58]The manuscript has καίτοι τοῦ νυμφῶνος οὐκ ὄντες υἱοί. I follow Pusey's conjectural emendation by omitting the οὐκ.
[59]Mt 8:12. [60]Jn 7:33. [61]Amos 4:5 (LXX).

first day shall be a holy convocation for you."[62] Then, after prescribing for them the kinds of sacrifices, he added, "And on the fifteenth day of this seventh month, you shall offer whole burnt offerings to the Lord for seven days. The first day shall be a rest, and the seventh day shall be a rest. And on the first day you shall take palm branches and thick tree branches and the fruit of good trees and willows and the branches of the chaste-tree from the stream to rejoice."[63]

Although we have already in the second book gone through every part of the above cited passage and expended a long discussion on it, we will nevertheless recall it again briefly.[64] We said that the feast of the tabernacles indicates to us the thrice longed-for time of the resurrection. The taking of the branches and the fruit of the good tree and the rest indicate the recovery **[687]** of paradise about to be given us again through Christ. And since it is added at the end of the statement that everything should be taken from the stream and that we rejoice because of it, we said that our Lord Jesus Christ was compared with a stream in whom we will find all enjoyment and delight in hope, and in him we will rejoice in a divine and spiritual way. That he both is and is called spiritual "streams," the supremely wise psalmist testifies to us when he says to God the Father about us, "The children of men will hope in the shadow of your wings. They will be drunk on the fatness of your house, and you will give them drink from the stream of your delight."[65] And the Lord himself says somewhere in the prophets, "Behold, I turn to them as a river of peace, flooding them like streams."[66]

Now since the law called the first and the seventh day of the feast a "holy convocation," the divine Evangelist himself called it "great," not dishonoring, it seems, the common custom of the Jews. Since there is a mention of the stream in the instructions about the feast, the Savior shows that he himself is that stream foretold in the law and says, "Let anyone who is thirsty come to me and drink." See how he removes the mind of the Jews from the types in the letter and ingeniously transfers the figures to the truth, if they help with the truth in any way. I am, he says, the stream foretold by the lawgiver in the account of the feast. And since one must take branches of a willow and a chaste-tree and thick branches of a tree from the stream, **[688]** but Christ is not strictly the stream, nor is the figure of the feast truly in those things, then they would be symbols of spiritual realities that will be given to the pious by Christ.

But since we have dealt with these things more expansively in the second book, as we already said, we will not repeat ourselves but will move on to what comes next.

7:38 "Whoever believes in me, as the Scripture has said, out of their belly shall flow rivers of living water."

He shows that the reward of faith is vast and ageless, and he says that whoever does not disbelieve will revel in the richest graces from God. They will be so full of gifts from the Spirit that not only is their own mind made fat, but they can now overflow into the hearts of others, gushing forth God's good gifts like a flowing river to their neighbor too. He gave the same command to the holy apostles when he said, "Freely you have received, freely give."[67] The wise and holy Paul himself as well, desiring to be active in this, writes to us, "I long to see you that I may impart some spiritual gift."[68]

[62]Lev 23:34, 36, 35. [63]Lev 23:39-40. [64]Book 3, chapter 4, p. 178 above. On this passage the younger Pusey, Cyril's translator, has the following note: "S. Cyril does not appear to have more than touched very briefly on the subject in any part of this commentary that we have: it is treated at length, *de Adoratione* lib. xvii. pp. 619, 620." [65]Ps 36:7-8 (Ps 35:8-9 LXX). [66]Is 66:12. [67]Mt 10:8. [68]Rom 1:11.

You may see this extremely well in the holy Evangelists, but also in those who teach the gospel in the church, who pour out the ungrudging word of inspired teaching on those going to Christ through faith and so delight them spiritually. They no longer allow them to thirst after the knowledge of the truth, but with wise roaring, as it were, they all but shout it into the hearts of their students. That is why the psalmist, rejoicing over them in the Spirit, called out, "The rivers have lifted up, O Lord, the rivers have lifted up their voice!"[69] **[689]** The word of the saints has sounded forth something great and mighty, and "their voice has gone out to all the earth," as it is written, "and their words to the ends of the world."[70] God, the God and Lord of all, promised to supply such rivers to us, saying through the prophet Isaiah, "The beasts of the field will bless me, the owls and the daughters of ostriches, because I have given water in the desert and rivers in a waterless land to give drink to my chosen race, my people whom I preserved to declare my praises."[71] So it is clear that the Savior says that there will come forth from the belly of the believer rivers, that is, the special grace taught by the Spirit, which Paul mentions when he says, "To one is given through the Spirit the utterance of wisdom."[72]

In addition to this, it is also good to know that the Savior put this statement in his own words, not as it is presented in the Holy Scripture but rather interpreting the Scripture according to its meaning. We find somewhere, concerning all who honor and love God, that they will be like "a well-watered garden and a spring whose water does not fail."[73] What he says before to the woman of Samaria, he now states clearly. There he says, "Whoever drinks of this water will thirst again, but whoever drinks of the water that I will give them will never thirst. The water that I will give them will become a spring of water gushing up to eternal life."[74] But here he is aiming at the same meaning when he says, "Out of their belly shall flow rivers of living water." **[690]**

Chapter Two

After the Savior's cross and at his resurrection from the dead, the Holy Spirit made his abode in us permanently.

7:39 Now he said this about the Spirit, which those believing in him were to receive; for as yet there was no Spirit, because Jesus was not yet glorified.

The meaning of this passage demands sharp scrutiny, and to understand sufficiently the depth of the mystery would be an achievement of great acumen (and that just barely). Anyone who considers this and looks at each of the holy prophets would understandably have burning questions right away. How is it that "there was no Spirit" when there is clearly so great a chorus of prophets who are found to speak in the Spirit of the divine mysteries concerning Christ through long discourses? We do not, I assure you, stray so far outside appropriate thinking that we imagine that the mind of the saints was bereft of the Spirit. After all, both the fact of prophecy and the contents of the Holy Scriptures shame us and call us, almost by force, to believe that they were truly bearers of the Spirit.

Samuel, for example, says to Saul, "The Spirit of the Lord will come on you, and you will be turned into another man."[75] **[691]** And it is written of the blessed Elisha himself, "And it came to pass as the harpist played, that the hand of the Lord came on him."[76] And our Lord Jesus Christ himself testifies of the blessed David that he spoke mysteries in the

[69]Ps 93:3 (Ps 92:3 LXX). [70]Ps 19:4 (Ps 18:5 LXX). [71]Is 43:20-21. [72]1 Cor 12:8. [73]Is 58:11. [74]Jn 4:13-14. [75]1 Sam 10:6. [76]2 Kings 3:15.

Spirit.[77] One could easily pile up many similar statements by which one could quite readily see that the saints possess the Spirit. But in matters so clear, it seems superfluous or even burdensome to weary ourselves with long discourses. We must investigate carefully in what sense "there was no Spirit," since I think we must hold that the blessed Evangelist tells the truth.

Now what is really true, let God himself, the all-wise, know. We must not dare to meddle in things above us. But as far as one can see by pious reasoning, something of this sort comes to us. This rational earthly animal, I mean the human being, came into being in the beginning without corruption. The reason for his incorruption and the reason he remained in every virtue was clearly that the Spirit of God dwelt in him. "For he breathed into his face the breath of life," as it is written.[78] But by that ancient deception he turned to sin, and then little by little he subsequently increased it to the point where he endures the loss of the Spirit, along with the other blessings. And so he ultimately becomes not only subject to corruption but also prone to every sin.

Now when the framer of all resolved (quite beautifully) to "recapitulate all things in Christ"[79] and willed to return human nature once again to its original condition, he promised along with the other gifts also to give human nature the Holy Spirit. For there was no other way to get back to unshaken stability in **[692]** what is good. He defines, therefore, the time of the descent of the Spirit on us and promises, "In those days (namely, the days of our Savior), I will pour out (of my Spirit, that is) on all flesh."[80] And when the time of this lavish generosity brought the Only Begotten to the earth with the flesh in front of everyone, that is, when as a man he was born of a woman, as the Holy Scripture says,[81] God the Father gave the Spirit once again, and Christ was the first to receive the Spirit as first fruits of the renewed nature. "For John testified saying, 'I saw the Spirit descending from heaven, and it remained on him.'"[82]

But he received it in what sense? The statement demands investigation. Did he receive as one not having? We say no, by no means! The Spirit is the Son's own. He is not supplied from the outside, like the things of God that come to us from the outside; rather, the Spirit is naturally in the Son, just as he is in the Father, and he proceeds through the Son to the saints, apportioned by the Father to each one as is fitting. The Son is said to have received insofar as he has become human, and receiving is fitting for a human. In the same way the Son, being of God the Father and begotten of his substance even before the incarnation, or rather even before all ages, is not at all distressed that God the Father says to him when he has become human, "You are my Son; today have I begotten you."[83] The Father says that he who is God before time, begotten of him, has been begotten today so that in him the Father may receive us into adoption, since all of humanity is in Christ because he is human. Thus, he is said to give the Spirit to the Son, who has the Spirit as his own, **[693]** so that in him we may obtain the Spirit. For this reason "he takes on the seed of Abraham," as it is written, and is "made like his brothers in all things."[84] The Only Begotten, then, does not receive the Holy Spirit for himself, since the Spirit is of him and in him and through him, as we said before. But since he became human, he had the entire nature in himself so that he might transform it to its original condition and set it all right.

But this too must be investigated in addition to what we just said. We will see by going through sound reasoning and by confirming our conclusions from the words of the divine Scripture that Christ did not receive the Spirit

[77]Mk 12:36. [78]Gen 2:7. [79]Eph 1:10. [80]Joel 2:28. [81]Gal 4:4. [82]Jn 1:32. [83]Ps 2:7. [84]Heb 2:16-17.

for himself but rather for us in himself. For all good things come to us through him. Our forefather Adam did not preserve the grace of the Spirit, since he was turned by deception to disobedience and sin. And so in him our entire nature ultimately lost the God-given good. Therefore, God the Word, who knows no turning,[85] had to become human so that by receiving the Spirit as a human he might preserve the good permanently in our nature.

The divine psalmist himself will enter as an expositor of these mysteries to us. He says this to the Son: "You loved righteousness and hated unrighteousness. Therefore, God, your God, has anointed you with the oil of gladness above your companions."[86] Since, he says, you always loved righteousness (since you are righteous, O God, and can never be turned from this) and you always hated unrighteousness (since hating wickedness belongs to you by nature as you are the righteous-loving God), therefore God the Father has anointed you. You who have unchangeable righteousness as an excellence of your own nature could never be brought over to that which you don't know, **[694]** that is, sin. Since this is so, you have undoubtedly preserved in yourself for humanity (in that you have become human) the holy anointing from God the Father, that is, the Spirit.

The Only Begotten, then, became human for us so that in him, first of all, good gifts might return, and, second, so that the grace of the Spirit might be rooted and preserved firmly in our whole nature. It is as though the Only Begotten, being the Word of God the Father, lends us the immutability of his own nature, which we needed because human nature was condemned in Adam for not being able to remain unchanged. Indeed, it slipped quite easily into turning away. Just as in the turning of the first man, the loss of good gifts extends to the whole nature, in the same way, I think, in the one who knows no turning, the attainment of the lasting possession of the divine gifts will be preserved for the entire race.

But if we seem to any not to think and to say what is absolutely right, let them come forward and teach us why the Savior is called the second Adam in the divine Scriptures. In the first one, the human race proceeds from nonexistence into existence, but once it had come into existence, it ended up decaying because it broke the divine law. In the second one, that is, Christ, the human race returns to a second beginning, being refashioned into newness of life and returning to its original incorruption, since "if anyone is in Christ, they are a new creation," as Paul says.[87] Therefore, the renewing Spirit, that is, the Holy Spirit, has been given to us. He is the cause of eternal life after the glorification of Christ, that is, after the resurrection. That is when he burst the bonds of death, showed himself superior to all decay and returned to life, having our whole nature in himself in that he was a human being and one of us. **[695]**

And if you are curious about why the outpouring of the Spirit did not take place before the resurrection but after it, listen to this: Christ became the first fruits of the renewed nature at that time when, having no regard for the bonds of death, he returned to life, as we have just said. How then could those who come after the first fruits be brought to life before it? In the same way that a plant could not sprout from the earth if it did not come from its own root (since that is the source of the plant's growth), so also it would be impossible for us, who have our Lord Jesus Christ as the root of incorruption, to sprout before our root.

He showed that the time for the Spirit's descent to us is now here when, after his resurrection from the dead, he breathed on his disciples and said, "Receive the Holy Spirit."[88] Then the time of renewal was really at the

[85]See Jas 1:17. [86]Ps 45:7 (Ps 44:8 LXX). [87]2 Cor 5:17. [88]Jn 20:22.

doors, or rather inside the doors. Let the one who is devoted to learning now consider whether our statement about this matter too is true. In the beginning, as the Spirit bearer Moses said to us, the creator of all took dust from the ground, fashioned a man and "breathed into his face the breath of life."[89] And what is the breath of life but plainly the Spirit of Christ, who says, "I am the resurrection and the life"?[90] Since the Spirit, who can form and keep us in the divine imprint, flew away from humanity, the Savior graces us once again with this Spirit, bringing us back to that original dignity **[696]** and refashioning us into his image. That is why, you know, Paul too says to certain people, "My little children, for whom I am in the pain of childbirth until Christ is formed in you."[91]

Let us now consider (since I will take up the purpose of the statement) that in the holy prophets there was certainly an abundant and torchbearing Spirit, able to lead them to an understanding of the things to come and to a knowledge of things hidden. In those who believe in Christ, however, there is not simply a torch light from the Spirit, but we are confident that the Spirit himself dwells in us and takes up residence. Thus, there is good reason that we are called the temples of God, even though none of the holy prophets was ever called a divine temple.

How will we understand this, and what will we say when we hear our Savior Christ saying, "Truly, truly I say to you, among those born of women no one has arisen greater than John the Baptist, yet the least in the kingdom of heaven is greater than he"?[92] And what is the kingdom of heaven? Clearly, it is the giving of the Holy Spirit, according to the statement, "The kingdom of heaven is within you."[93] The Spirit, after all, makes his dwelling in us through faith. Do you see, then, how he ranks the one in the kingdom of heaven before everyone born of women, even if that one falls short of the perfect?

Let no one think that we make little of the glory of the virtue of those saints or say that the least are superior to them. We do not say that. The beauty of their behavior is incomparable. But for a clear understanding, let us briefly interpret our Savior's statement. The blessed Baptist was truly great, and he was outstanding in every virtue. He drove on to the very limits of the righteousness that is in us, **[697]** so that there is nothing further. But even in his condition, he needed Christ and said, "I need to be baptized by you, and do you come to me?"[94] Do you see how even though he was perfect, insofar as is possible for human beings and those born of women, he still asks to be re-created in a certain way and reborn by the Holy Spirit? Do you see how he yields the greater position to those reborn by saying that he himself needs this? After all, if he is in a superior position without being baptized, what persuaded him to ask for baptism? And if he knows that he will be in a better position when the baptism comes, how will he not attribute the greater position to those already baptized?

Therefore, Christ says that the one who is least in the kingdom of heaven, that is, the one who is already baptized, even though that person is not yet outstanding in works, is greater than John himself in this respect alone: while the blessed John was born of a woman, that person has been born of God, as it is written,[95] and has became a participant in the divine nature,[96] having the Holy Spirit dwelling in them and now being called a temple of God.

I will now return to the passage at hand. The Spirit was in the prophets because of the need for prophesying. But now through Christ he dwells in believers, beginning in him first when he became human. As God, there is no distance between him and the Spirit, who

[89]Gen 2:7. [90]Jn 11:25. [91]Gal 4:19. [92]Mt 11:11. [93]Lk 17:21. [94]Mt 3:14. [95]1 Jn 3:9; cf. 1 Jn 5:18. [96]2 Pet 1:4.

springs from him essentially and is his own. But he is anointed for us and is said to receive the Spirit as a human being, acquiring participation in the divine goods not for himself but for human nature, [698] just as we taught earlier. So when the divine Evangelist says to us, "For as yet there was no Spirit, because Jesus was not yet glorified," let us understand him to be indicating the full and complete dwelling of the Holy Spirit in human beings.

7:40-41 When they heard these words, some in the crowd said, "This is truly the prophet." Others said, "This is truly the Christ."

They are astonished at his God-befitting boldness, and when they see that his words no longer suit the measure of a human being, they run to their memory of the law, since it already foretold of Christ, saying that a prophet would be raised up like the supremely wise Moses who would bring the words of God to Israel. This is what God says concerning him to the holy Moses, "I will raise up for them a prophet like you from their brothers, and I will put my words in his mouth, and he will speak to them everything that I command him."[97] By the quality of his words, then, and the excellence of his speech, they say that he has now been revealed as the one foretold in the law. Who, after all, could appropriately say, "Let anyone who is thirsty come to me and drink,"[98] and, "Whoever believes in me, as the Scripture has said, out of their belly shall flow rivers of living water," except only the one who is God by nature? And this is the Christ.

But since the Jews think small thoughts about him, they simply call him "the prophet," not knowing the all-surpassing excellence of Emmanuel but measuring him as one of the others. [699] In this too they will be caught applying themselves without understanding to the interpretation of the law. They think that "the Christ" is different from "the prophet" in the law. It is not surprising that the people lack accuracy in this matter when the God-opposing multitude of the arrogant Pharisees is found to suffer from the same ignorance as the crowds. At one point they are amazed at the blessed Baptist and say, "Why then are you baptizing, if you are neither the Christ, nor Elijah nor the prophet?"[99] Although two are expected to come, I mean the prophet in the law (that is, Christ) and Elijah, they were looking for three because they thought the prophet was different from Jesus. Therefore, what was said through the prophet Ezekiel could fittingly be said of them, "Like mother, like daughter; you are the daughter of your mother."[100] For the people have the same sickness as their leaders.

However, it is good for us to notice that they were already prepared to believe, and they are persuaded by the Savior's words to marvel at him. But since they do not have leadership from their leaders, they are led down a path of thoughts that branches off. Some call him and already believe that he is "the Christ," others, "the prophet." For the word *truly*, which they add, gives the impression of a conclusion that is already settled and suggests a faith that has been received.

7:41-42 But some said, "Surely the Christ does not come from Galilee, does he? Has not the Scripture said that Christ comes from the seed of David and from Bethlehem, the village where David was?"

The Jews make no careless search concerning Christ. They go through every idea, and from [700] various ideas, they gather their understanding of the truth about him. They have already marveled at his words and taken the supreme confidence of his teaching as their

[97]Deut 18:18. [98]Jn 7:37. [99]Jn 1:25. [100]Ezek 16:44-45.

guide to think something great about him. Then they search the divine Scripture itself, thinking to find there the absolutely inerrant conception of him, for so is its nature. They believed, therefore, that he would be of the seed of the thrice-blessed David and that he would be revealed in Bethlehem of Judea, persuaded by the prophecies concerning this. "For the Lord swore a sure oath to David," the wise psalmist says somewhere, "and will not reject him: I will place the fruit of your loins on the throne."[101] And the prophet says, "And you, Bethlehem, the house of Ephratha, are few among the thousands of Judah. Out of you, one shall come forth for me to be ruler in Israel, and his goings forth are from the beginning, from eternity."[102]

The untutored knowledge of the Jews, however, went astray and was toppled concerning Christ merely because of Nazareth in Galilee, in which the Lord grew up according to common knowledge. One of the holy Evangelists, after all, says, "And he came to Nazareth, where he had been brought up."[103] But they did not know that he had been born in Bethlehem of Judea of the holy virgin, who was of the seed of David (since her family belonged to the tribe of Judah). Merely because the Lord grew up in Nazareth, they fall away from the truth and miss the saving reasoning.

7:43 So there was a division in the crowd because of him.

In vain they fight and are divided into different [701] opinions: some supposing that he is the prophet, others that he is the Christ. And the cause of their division is that they did not know the Christ, nor did they see the precision in the Holy Scriptures. Otherwise, they would have believed that Jesus is none other than the prophet in the law, and they would have given up their ill-timed dispute.

7:44 Some of them wanted to arrest him, but no one laid hands on him.

Those who had been sent by the chief priests and Pharisees to arrest the Lord made the dissension among the crowds with one another an opportune pretext for their daring deed. They supposed that the crowd would let them take him away without a fight, no longer caring what might happen to him since he had become an occasion for discord and fighting. They thought the crowd would surely be happy at his mistreatment. "But no one laid hands on him," not out of respect for him or because they restrained their anger with the bridle of reverence, but they are stopped only by his power, since he assigned his passion for us to its own time. Barely is the plan of the Jews conceived when it is restrained by hindrances from above. They could not attempt murder prematurely. They had to wait—even though they themselves were ungodly—for the time of ungodliness.

7:45 Then the officers went to the chief priests and Pharisees, who said to them, "Why did you not bring him?"

When those who had been sent to hunt down the Lord were unable to carry out any of their instructions, they returned to the leaders. [702] The leaders are very upset at the arrival of the officers when they see that they do not have the one they seek. Believing that what they suspected had already happened, they are struck with immeasurable fear. Since Christ occasioned amazement because of his extraordinary signs and his excellent oratory, they were consumed by envy, their foster sister. They had no small fear that the people of the Jews had decided that they should follow him, and so the people would escape from their hand. They thought this had already happened

[101]Ps 132:11 (Ps 131:11 LXX). [102]Mic 5:2. [103]Lk 4:16.

(since one is always ready to believe what one suspects), so they urgently ask, "Why did you not bring him?" What prevented you, they say, from bringing to completion what was pleasing to those in power? We are quite eager to learn everything. Sometimes we do not discern what grieves us, but in our eager desire we grasp for the perception even of things we abhor.

7:46 The officers answered, "No one has ever spoken like this."

It is truly fitting to say of Christ our Savior, "He catches the wise in their craftiness."[104] Behold, behold, as it is written, "He subverted their tangled plan,"[105] and he showed the whole nature of things to be turned upside down. From every side he unmasks the foul character of the leaders and exposes their unholy ways as weak and reckless, since they just won't stop fighting against God. Since both the chief priests and the Pharisees feared that the people of the Jews would be persuaded by the Savior's words, they send out officers to arrest him, thinking that getting Christ out of the way would alleviate their concern about him. [703] But their agents returned having experienced the very thing the rulers were afraid of. And the rulers learned unwillingly what probably made them shudder when they heard it, hearing unexpectedly from those speaking contrary to their opinion, "No one has ever spoken like this."

Since they say this as an excuse for not bringing the Lord, let us expand what they say into a discourse. Let us consider the clear meaning of their words from every angle. If we delight in the teaching of the Holy Scriptures, they say, if we boast that we have been taught the divine laws, if we admire wisdom as an other-worldly good, why do we irreverently drive away one so wise? And why do we inflict immeasurable harm on one whom we least ought to harm, even though we owe him a special love? Yes, and why do we subject our own heads to the threat of the law by thirsting for no reason to kill one who is innocent and righteous?[106] We think that the words of the officers probably produce this idea.

I, however, think that by examining "no one has ever spoken like this," one may say something still keener. What they are practically saying is this: It is not reasonable for you now to blame us for not being able to bring to you the one you seek. How could anyone compel a man against his will who, judging from his words, has divine nature? He was not speaking as a man, nor were the words that came from him fitting for a man, but they are suited without blame to one who is God by nature. Let anyone mention if they can remember, they say, whether any of the holy prophets was ever caught calling himself a stream. Who dared to say, "Let anyone who is thirsty come to me and drink"?[107] When did the great Moses say to us, "Whoever believes in me, out of their belly shall flow rivers [704] of the water of life"?[108] And yet we heard Jesus say these things. He who boasts in superhuman words without fear of danger, then, must be God by nature. Thus, how dangerous must it be for anyone to try and hunt down by force and violence the one who is above creation? How could he be captured by us against his will when he is as far above us as God is above humanity? The officers, then, put forward the words "no one has ever spoken like this" as a clear proof that the Lord is God by nature. And the enemy of God is struck from every side and is slain without realizing it by the very scheme which was supposed to achieve his desire.

7:47 The Pharisees answered them, "Surely you have not been deceived too, have you?"

[104]1 Cor 3:19. [105]Job 5:13. [106]See Ex 23:7. [107]Jn 7:37. [108]Jn 7:38.

It is quite likely that the officers intensely adhered to a Jewish mindset since they always learned from the Pharisees and shared their common opinion. They were constantly drenched with the words of their leaders and persuaded to think like them since they were always with them. When they arrived without bringing the Lord, however—stunned as they were beyond expectation, only now marveling at someone they should never have hated to begin with, believing that everyone else should be persuaded to their position—the anguished Pharisees say, "Surely you have not been deceived too, have you?" Understand that this statement is full of despair regarding the people. They are expressing their fear to the officers that the rest of the multitude who were not as steadfast as they were had already been deceived. The rest of the multitude of the flock, it says, who are not well-versed in the Holy Scriptures or fortified by adherence to us—we grant that they might be attached to him by unexamined **[705]** impulses and might be more easily carried away to listen to him because of what he has said and done. But how can it be that you have adopted this error as well? How is it that you yourselves have also been deceived? What drew you away from your love toward us, even though you have been hardened by the same unbelief as we have? The words of the Pharisees indicate something like this.

7:48-49 "None of the rulers or the Pharisees have believed in him, have they? But this crowd, which does not know the law—they are cursed."

They fall again into their usual arrogance, throwing the charge of ignorance at those who are amazed at Jesus as a wonder worker and an expositor of teachings worthy of God. They crown their own heads alone with erudition in the law and knowledge of the Holy Scriptures. Because they do not agree with those who rightly marvel at these things, they believe that they alone are full of virtue—as though the law commanded them to find fault with what is remarkable and to render a perverted judgment on matters that surpass wonder. They foolishly strut around and plunge themselves into total ignorance out of their excessive shallowness. By the very source from which they ought to recognize Jesus now present, they are caught harming themselves, and they "weigh down their collar," as it is written,[109] "for claiming to be wise, they became fools."[110]

It would have been far better to admit their ignorance of the law than believe and claim they had full knowledge of it—much better than the bitter punishment and inescapable misery that would be inflicted on them because they dishonored the one proclaimed by the very law itself. **[706]** For the one who knows their master's will, it says, and does not do it will be beaten with many blows, but the one who does not know it and does not do it will be beaten with few blows.[111] By claiming to know the law, then, they themselves pronounce the accusation against their unbelief, even as they ridicule the crowd as ignorant and claim that is why the crowd is caught by our Savior's miracles.

Then, when they are unable to persuade the crowd by their explanation of the law, they arrogantly insult them, calling those who are ready to understand uninstructed. This is always the custom of the more ignorant teachers who, having nothing to say about what they are asked, angrily rebuff the careful questioning of those who want to inquire. They say that the believers are "cursed," though this could have just as easily been said about themselves. Indeed, being cursed is more fitting for the unbeliever, since the lawgiver

[109]Hab 2:6 (LXX). [110]Rom 1:22. [111]Lk 12:47-48.

says clearly concerning the prophet, Christ our Savior, "And it shall be that whoever does not listen to whatever that prophet says in my name, that soul shall be utterly destroyed from its people."[112]

7:50-51 Nicodemus, who had gone to Jesus before and was one of them, said to them, "Does our law judge people without first giving them a hearing and learning what they do?"

Nicodemus is one of the leaders and is numbered among those who have authority. He is not wholly unbelieving, but neither does he completely oppose their senselessness. He has already been pricked, but his love for Christ is not yet free, though he feels some shame at the accusations of his conscience. I think that we have all learned that he came to Jesus by night and affirmed that he knew full well that the teacher had come from God and that no one could **[707]** perform such signs if he did not have God with him, since the blessed Evangelist expressly said this at the beginning.

Since, then, he marveled at Jesus along with the crowds, he is secretly stung by being called "cursed" along with them. Now conscience is a powerful persuader not to remain silent in matters that go against it. Upset by this, then, he returns the same insult to them, not yet openly, but having its force from the words of the law, so as not to answer them with a bare provocation. The law, he says, tells judges concerning each matter under investigation, "You shall inquire"[113] diligently and clearly whether the matter has occurred. But you have prematurely condemned those not yet called to trial, and before hearing from them at all you render such a hasty judgment. You then, he says, are more truly the cursed ones, since you despise the law. For it is written, "Cursed is everyone who does not abide by everything written in the book of this law and do them."[114]

Because he is angry at the Pharisees, who condemn the people merely for marveling at Jesus, he clearly agrees with the believers. He is still sick with a harmful shame and has not yet mixed boldness with his zeal, so he does not permit the faith within him to be seen openly. Instead, he puts on hypocrisy like a dark cloak and conceals the fact that he already supports Christ. And yet he is terribly sick.

We ought to believe fearlessly, glorying rather than being ashamed, practicing transparent openness **[708]** and avoiding servile hypocrisy. That is why, you know, the wise Paul decreed that one who rightly handles the word of truth must be an unashamed worker.[115] And he also says somewhere, revealing this virtue shining in himself, "I am not ashamed of the gospel, for it is the power of God for salvation to everyone who believes."[116]

Nicodemus's statement, then (for I will pick up where I left off), is precise. Why did he alone speak up and oppose the voices of the Pharisees, although their bloodthirsty group had many others in it? It is clear to all that since he was numbered among those who marveled at Christ, he is showing that those who wickedly lay a curse on those who least deserve it are cursed in return.

7:52 They replied to him, "You are not from Galilee too, are you? Look into it, and you will see that no prophet has arisen from Galilee."

Since you are a native Jew, it says, why do you pretend to have no knowledge of the Galileans, and why are you ignorant of our affairs just like those who do not know us at all? Since you have dealt intensively with the holiest Scriptures and you are well-versed in the decrees in the law, how did you not know, it

[112]Deut 18:19; Acts 3:23. [113]Deut 17:4. [114]Gal 3:10; Deut 27:26. [115]2 Tim 2:15. [116]Rom 1:16.

says, that one cannot look for a prophet from the Galileans? This, then, is the intention of the Pharisees' words.

But we must consider the following as well. Those who spit on the crowds for not knowing what they ought to know well and who reproach them for being exceedingly ignorant, loathing them and arrogantly calling them uninstructed—they are the ones who are afflicted with an even worse sickness, **[709]** differing in no way from their inexperience. When the crowds had received Christ's miracles and were piecing together faith in him little by little, they said at one point, "When the Christ comes, will he be able to do more signs than this man has done?"[117] But then they were drawn away from such a correct understanding and were tripped up merely by "Nazareth," which is located in the land of the Galileans, in which the divine Scripture declares that the Lord was brought up. That is why they said, "Surely the Christ does not come from Galilee, does he? Has not the Scripture said that Christ comes from the seed of David and from Bethlehem, the village where David was?"[118] But those who laughed out loud at the people's lack of instruction, and on that account called them cursed, were not superior to their ignorance. See, they themselves say, "Look into it, and you will see that no prophet has arisen from Galilee."

In response to these things, one may for good reason be moved against them and say, O you who yield victory in ignorance to no one, who lack knowledge and are hardened, where is the boast of your pride? Where is there a trace of wisdom in you? Where is the understanding that is fitting for those who are learned in the law? You should not have doubted concerning Christ our Savior; instead, you should have believed God the Father without any hesitation when he says to the holy Moses about Christ, "I will raise up for them a prophet like you from their brothers."[119]

Now the words "from their brothers"—does this not surely have to mean from the Jews and from Israel? You do not need accusers from the outside; you will convict yourselves of having no understanding. **[710]** When Christ our Savior was teaching and explicitly said, "I have come down from heaven not to do my own will but the will of him who sent me,"[120] you began to argue sharply, and, full of immense anger at this, you said, "Is this not Jesus, the son of Joseph, whose father and mother we know? How can he now say, 'I have come down from heaven'?"[121] Now since you have confessed plainly that you knew his father and mother well, you surely knew, I take it, that he is from the root of Israel. How, then, do you say that one who is from the Jews is a Galilean? How is one from Israel an alien? Growing up in the land of Galilee, after all, and having lived there for a time surely does not remove an Israelite from his race, since nothing prevents one who comes from the Galileans from being Jewish by race if he happens to go to the land of the Jews. In vain, then, do the conceited Pharisees say of Christ our Savior, "No prophet has arisen from Galilee." They should rather have investigated how one from the Jews could be a Galilean and so should have realized that he grew up in Nazareth, and not on that account depart from faith.

We must next observe that since they cannot criticize his miracles in any way, even though their hostility has been honed to the extreme, they oppose him only because of his country, since he was from Galilee, or so they suspected. Therefore, once their suspicion on this point has been allayed, their faith would be firm, if they were wise. **[711]**

8:12 Again, Jesus spoke to them, saying, "I am the light of the world."[122]

[117]Jn 7:31. [118]Jn 7:41-42. [119]Deut 18:18. [120]Jn 6:38. [121]Jn 6:42. [122]Cyril, along with most early manuscripts, does not have the pericope of the woman caught in adultery (Jn 7:53–8:11).

We said before that Jesus made a statement that was appropriate for what was written about the feast when, on the last day, he stood up and cried, "Let anyone who is thirsty come to me and drink,"[123] since he called to mind Moses' statement about the stream.[124] So also now he gives a most timely explanation that is called for by the nature of the situation. When he saw that the teachers shared in the crowds' foolishness and that those who ridiculed had the same sickness as the ones they ridiculed—that they were all baptized, so to speak, in the same night of ignorance, trying to get hold of his mystery but finding nothing at all—he brings the cause, as it were, of their ignorance into the open, crying out, "I am the light of the world." Although you go through all of Holy Scripture, he says, and think to test what is said about me by the prophets, you go far astray from the way of life. And no wonder. The one who reveals mysteries and enlightens the world and shines like the sun into the hearts of those who receive him is not in you. Whoever does not have the divine and spiritual light in them must surely walk in darkness and stumble on many absurdities because of it. We have already demonstrated that the Only Begotten is light by nature because he shone forth from God the Father, who is light by nature. That was in a long discussion in the first book, on the words "he was the true light."[125]

Now we must consider that he says he is the light not uniquely or solely of the Israelites but of the whole world. And with this he makes a point that is absolutely true. We say that he **[712]** is the one who inserts intellectual light into all of nature and who sows, like a deposit of seed, understanding appropriate for every human being who is called into existence, according to the statement about him, "He was the true light, which enlightens every person coming into the world."[126]

I think, however, that there is something subtle buried in his words. If his statement were not pregnant with something of this sort, he would only have needed to say, "I am the light." But since he has added "of the world," I think that he is hinting and now intends something like this: God was known only in Judea, and only in Israel was his name great.[127] Deep darkness, as it were, filled the rest of the whole earth, and no one in the world had the divine and heavenly light, except Israel alone.

But just as in ancient times, when all the nations in the world together were banished from the knowledge of God and lay, as it were, in a rank of their own, "the people of the Lord became his portion, Israel the line of his inheritance,"[128] so also later, when the intellectual sun was transferred to the whole world and the light was taken away from those of Israel and handed over to the Gentiles, Israel was found to be excluded from the whole. "For while they waited for light, darkness came on them," as it is written, "while they waited for brightness, they walked in gloom."[129] Not in vain, then, does the Savior say to the Pharisees, "I am the light of the world." He is cleverly threatening to depart from Israel and transfer his grace to the whole world and finally spread the ray of the knowledge of God on others.

Observe how, although before his hearers **[713]** he appeared as a human being and with flesh, he does not say, "In me is the light," but "I am the light." That is so no one divides Christ into a pair of sons[130] after the *oikonomia* of the incarnation. There is "one Lord, Jesus Christ," as Paul says,[131] both before the flesh and with the flesh. And the Word of God the Father is the one and only true Son, even when he became human, not counted apart from the temple that was taken from a woman. For the body is his own, and to divide

[123]Jn 7:37. [124]Lev 23:40. [125]See pp. 43-48 above. [126]Jn 1:9. [127]Ps 76:1 (Ps 75:2 LXX). [128]Deut 32:9. [129]Is 59:9. [130]This seems to be said in opposition to the interpretation regarding Christ prevalent at Antioch. [131]1 Cor 8:6.

him at all after the incarnation, at least when it comes to sonship, is not without a share of blasphemy. One must understand, however, that though we say that he was made flesh, we do not mean that the Word of God was clothed in flesh alone, but with the word *flesh* we indicate the whole human being.

"Whoever follows me will not walk in darkness but will have the light of life." Next, he persuades them to devote themselves to hunting down from all sides what is profitable and, even more, to be led by his ordinances rather than choosing to follow their own ignorance and bereave themselves of eternal life itself. He shows how great the profit will be for those who are obedient to him, since he is good by nature and "wants everyone to be saved and to come to the knowledge of the truth."[132]

But since as God he knew that they would speak against him, he fashions his statement in the image of ancient events, and from what happened to their ancestors he declares clearly that the desire to follow him will profit them greatly. It is written of the Israelites, "He led them with a cloud by day, and all night long with the illumination of fire."[133] When they were crossing the wide **[714]** desert hurrying to the promised land, a cloud was suspended over them by day like a roof driving off the sun's fire, by the divine will, that is; by night a pillar of fire led them, fighting off the darkness and marking out an unerring road for the travelers. Just as the people at that time avoided wandering and were brought right through straight and holy ground by following the fire as it set out and led them, giving no thought to night or darkness, so also "whoever follows me," that is, whoever walks in the steps of my teachings will in no way be in darkness but will attain "the light of life," that is, the revelation of the mysteries concerning me which is able to lead to eternal life.

Now since the Lord is a craftsman when it comes to words, he does not provoke the Pharisees by openly telling them that they will remain in darkness and die in their unbelief. They were already angry and not a little enraged. Instead, he says this in another way, turning the meaning of his words to the positive. He promises with these words that whoever has chosen to follow him "will have the light of life." With the very same words, he suggests in a concealed way that those who refuse to follow him will lose the light that is able to return them to life. Is it not clear to all and accepted without hesitation that those who flee from what brings joy must necessarily experience the opposite? The statement of our Savior, then, is true, and the words arranged by his skill are undoubted. **[715]**

8:13 Then the Pharisees said to him, "You are testifying about yourself; your testimony is not true."

The Pharisee is sluggish and dull, one of the most difficult people to lead into seeing the divinity of the Lord. He goes astray because of the flesh and thinks of nothing beyond what he sees. When he sees the Lord making statements that far surpass humanity and hears words that are most appropriate for God, he still thinks of a common man. He does not see the obvious indication of the divine nature; he does not open the eye of his mind to see Emmanuel. Who, after all, has the ability to say, "I am the light of the world," except the one and only one who is God by nature? Which of the holy prophets ever dared to make this statement? What angel ever let loose with such a claim? Let them inspect the entire divinely inspired Scripture, let them work over the holy and divine word, and let them show this to us.

[132] 1 Tim 2:4. [133] Ps 78:14 (Ps 77:14 LXX).

They give no thought, however, to what necessarily follows. They think they should contradict, and they proceed angrily to the only thing they know well: accusation out of a love of blame. They disparage him, claiming that he is not the light of the world, accusing what he says and asserting that his "testimony is not true." "For they are wise in doing evil, but they do not know how to do good."[134] They suppose they can deceitfully overturn his testimony, trying to invalidate it by mere custom instead of by the commands of the law.

Let them teach us where the law says that testimony about oneself is invalid? It is perhaps wearisome, and sometimes unbearable, for someone [716] to testify to their own outstanding qualities. Indeed, the wisest compiler of Proverbs says, "Let your neighbor praise you, and not your own mouth; a stranger, and not your own lips."[135] But what someone says about themselves is not at all shown to be false.

Let one of the Pharisees come forward and teach us what we should do with the blessed Samuel when he testifies about his own excellent qualities. Somewhere he defends himself to the Israelites, saying, "The Lord is witness among you and his anointed is witness this day that you have not found anything in my hands."[136] But if the law prevented one from testifying about oneself, how is it, tell me, that Samuel ignored it, even though the divine Scripture says of him, "Moses was holy, Aaron was among his priests, and Samuel was among those who call on him. They called on the Lord, and he heard them. He spoke to them in a pillar of cloud. They kept his testimonies and his commands which he gave them."[137] Do you see how he was joined to the blessed Moses because he had virtue commensurate with him, and how the Spirit testifies that he is a diligent keeper of the law? Could someone tell me, then, how he transgressed the law by testifying about himself? But he did not transgress. He is testified to as a keeper of the law, and he testified about himself. Therefore, the law does not forbid anyone to testify about themselves.

What else can we say when we see the blessed David saying, "O Lord my God, if I have done this, if I have repaid those who have repaid me evil"?[138] Yes, and what is more, the blessed Jeremiah says, "Lord Almighty, I did not sit in the company of mockers, but I acted prudently because of your hand."[139] And then the most wise Paul, even though he was "educated strictly in the law of the fathers," just as he himself somewhere [717] testified,[140] cries out explicitly, "I am not aware of anything against myself."[141]

Let the Pharisee, then, say regarding each of these, "You are testifying about yourself; your testimony is not true," since for those who do not refuse to rebuke the Lord of all himself, poor behavior toward the rest is a matter of course. But we say, taking up our topic again, that the Pharisees' opposition is not compelled by the commands of the law but is made only from prevailing custom and from behavior that does not seem to be appropriate for good people. Their opposition to the law, however, is abuse, stealing away those who already marvel at him and are persuaded that they should believe. They disparage him as a liar. They undermine the faith of those just mentioned by denying that he is the true light. In so doing, those wretches pour the destruction of blasphemy down on their own heads.

8:14 Jesus answered and said to them, "If I testify about myself, my testimony is true, because I know where I came from and where I am going."

When Christ said that what he is, he is by

[134]Jer 4:22. [135]Prov 27:2. [136]1 Sam 12:5. [137]Ps 99:5-7 (Ps 98:5-7 LXX). [138]Ps 7:3-4 (Ps 7:4-5 LXX). [139]Jer 15:16-17. [140]Acts 22:3. [141]1 Cor 4:4.

nature and truly (since he announced explicitly, "I am the light of the world"), the reckless multitude of the Pharisees thought he was lying. In their extraordinary ignorance, they did not know that when some explain their own nature and say what is in them essentially, we should not suppose, if we are thinking reasonably, that they do so out of boasting. Nor should we say that they are hunting for empty glory. They are simply indicating clearly what they truly are.

For example, **[718]** we say that when an angel, indicating their own nature, says, "I am an angel," and when a human, showing what they are, says, "I am a human," yes and even if one should clothe the sun with a voice and it should teach us what belongs to its own nature saying, "I run the circuit of the heavens, and I send shining light to those on earth," no one will reasonably suppose that they are testifying about what does not belong to them, but rather that they are testifying to what they really are by nature. In the same way, I think, in the case of Christ our Savior, even if he calls himself light, he is speaking the truth and will not be found to boast in something external to him any more than they were.

The many, then, who are yoked together to ignorance and who do not understand Emmanuel suppose that he is seeking glory. They attack him as though one of us and do not shudder to say, "Your testimony is not true," to the one who does not know how to lie. For "no deceit was found in his mouth," as it is written.[142] But he had to lead the erring who had gone far astray from the truth and were departing from sound reasoning. He had to tell them patiently that they had missed the mark of what is fitting when they impiously ascribed love of lying to the one who is from above and begotten of God the Father.

"My testimony is true," he says, "even if I testify about myself." Human beings are sometimes found to have a desire, from self-love, to testify about their own excellent qualities, even if they should happen not to have any, since that nature is prone to slip into evil. But I, he says, do not have the ability to suffer the same sicknesses as those from the earth. "I know where I am from," that is, light from light, true God from true God the Father, having the nature that is inaccessible to weakness. Even though I became human, he says, because of my love for **[719]** humanity, I will not on that account be found bereft of God-befitting honor. I remain what I am by nature, that is, God. Clear proof of this is the fact that I know "where I am going." I will ascend to the heavens, to the Father from whom I am. This, I think, anyone would say applies not to a person like one of us but to God by nature, even though he became human. The words "I know where I came from," then, hint that the Son is by nature from God the Father, while the words "where I am going" are a proof of his God-befitting authority. As God, he will ascend above the heavens, as Paul says.[143]

At the same time this statement has a threat that fits with the unholiness of the Jews, even if it is not crystal clear. With these words he is seen to say that very soon he will surely depart from their race. And when he has left them bereft of the divine light, he will prepare them for the ignorance and deep darkness to come. He says this more clearly to them in other words: "While you have the light," he says, "walk in the light, so that the darkness may not overtake you."[144]

8:15 "You judge according to the flesh; I judge no one."

Again we find the Lord of all using a gentleness that is most worthy of love. He does not repay with equal wrath those who blaspheme him, even though he knew that they deserved

[142]1 Pet 2:22. [143]Eph 4:10. [144]Jn 12:35.

to suffer bitter punishments. He imitates the gentlest of physicians, and in this too I think there is good reason to marvel at him. They often think nothing of the insults of the sick but endure them with utmost patience as they apply their skill to help them. They remove what causes the pain, and though sometimes railed at, they explain what contributes to health and persuade them to be diligent in doing what is good for them as they bring to light the cause of the illness. **[720]**

Our Lord Jesus Christ puts up with those who blaspheme him and, though railed at, he helps them and binds up the wounds of those who insult him. Yes, and he recounts most clearly why it is that they suffer the charge of unbelief in him. "You," he says, "judge according to the flesh," that is, you err (and quite understandably so) because you look only at this flesh, even though you ought to be paying attention to the magnificence of the deeds. Since you believe that I am one of you because I am clothed with your flesh, you are terribly deceived. And since you do not consider the deep mystery of the *oikonomia* with the flesh, you make a most ill-advised judgment about me, claiming that the truth is telling a lie. But I will put off judging you for another time. "For God did not send his Son into the world to judge the world, but that the world might be saved."[145]

Now I think the question before us has been given an elegant solution. But one may still go through other considerations and refine its meaning as far as possible. "You," he says, "judge according to the flesh; I judge no one." Since you have nothing at all to accuse, he says, and you could not very well denounce my miracles, you disparage them only because of the flesh. Since I am seen by you as a human being, you irreverently classified me as nothing. But I, he says, do not condemn you for this reason. I will not write you off just because you are humans by nature, and you will not pay a penalty to the judge for that reason. I will not rebuke the nature. I do not condemn my own creation. I say there is no transgression in humans from their being human. You, however, **[721]** because of the flesh consider me to be nothing, and that is why you condemned me. I, by contrast, have not thought of you in that way; instead, I understand that a human being is a great and honorable thing, even though it has been made of the earth. Although I am true God and in the form of the Father who begat me, I humbled myself, taking on the form of a slave, and became human.[146] And for that alone, I am now condemned by you, though I myself condemn no one for this. "Yet even if I do judge, my judgment is just and true, because it is not I alone who judge, but I and the Father who sent me."[147]

Well then, perhaps someone who thinks contrary to the church's teachings will say, is it for this reason alone that the Son knows how to judge rightly: that the Father is in him when he does it? If this is truly how it is, what finally prevents us from saying that the Son is directed toward uprightness in some way by the will of the Father, not having this perfectly or being able to act irreproachably on his own?

What then shall we say in response to their words? Your thought is irreverent, sirs, and is perfectly appropriate only for Jewish senselessness. The Son does not say this as one who does not have the ability to judge rightly of himself. The psalmist will testify to him, saying in the Spirit, "God is a righteous judge."[148] And to show that there is no other judge besides him, he himself will enter as a witness for us in the Gospels, when he says, "The Father judges no one, but he has given all judgment to the Son."[149] Has God the Father, then, given judgment to one who does not know how to judge rightly? But I suppose that anyone would grant that it would be the most

[145]Jn 3:17. [146]See Phil 2:6-8. [147]Jn 8:16. [148]Ps 7:11 (Ps 7:12 LXX). [149]Jn 5:22.

extreme folly of all to think this way [722] concerning the righteousness of the Father, that is, the Son.[150] The Father knows his own offspring. He has given him the judgment, and by giving it he clearly testifies to his ability to judge justly. It is therefore perfectly clear that he says that the Father will judge with him not as though he himself were too weak to judge justly; rather, this statement is pregnant with a meaning that is related to and follows from what was said above.

We will clearly say, then, what he wishes to indicate. You, he says, O leaders and teachers of the Jews, have made a wicked and most unjust judgment about me. Just because of "the flesh," you suppose that you should consider me nothing, even though I am God by nature. I, however, when I begin to judge you, will not issue such a decision against you. It is not because you are human by nature that I will decide that you should be punished. Rather, I condemn you justly, having the Father as a cojudge, in agreement with me in all things.

And why? Because you did not receive the one who comes from heaven. You have not stopped insulting the one who was sent from the Father, as though he were one of you. You disparaged me, who came for the salvation of all, merely because of the flesh, completely spurning the law that was always dear to you. Where, tell me, does Moses command that you should condemn someone because they are human by nature? Therefore, you both judge and think unjustly. You do not, after all, have the law in agreement with you in these matters, but you alone dare every terrible deed without the inspiration of the divine will. But not so with me. I have the Father in myself. He concurs and agrees with me about everything concerning you. So I judge most justly when I hand over your whole country to desolation [723] and bury it in the misfortunes of war—yes, and expel from the very kingdom of heaven those who have so raged against the one who wants to save them and for that reason has come in human form.

8:17-18 "In your law it is written that the testimony of two people is true. I testify about myself, and the Father who sent me testifies about me."

Having said that God the Father will judge with him and will agree in condemning those who blaspheme against him, he understands the pair of persons as something else that is profitable. I, he says, will not refuse to declare what I am by nature. I am the light of the world. And I should not seem to any to be boasting at all because I am not glorying in qualities that are foreign to me but in those that belong to me essentially. But if in saying this, I do not seem worthy to receive from you acknowledgment that I speak the truth, because I am alone and I have testified about myself, I will bring in God the Father, who works and witnesses with me about my qualities. He performs miracles with me (he says) as you see, and he works with me. As far as the human nature is concerned, I would not be able to do anything if I were not God by nature. But insofar as I am from the Father and have the Father in me, I confess that I can do all things, and I have the testimony of the nature of him who begat me. Since I have him in myself by identity of substance, I proceed to do all things without hindrance.

For our Lord Jesus Christ has from [724] the divine nature all-creative power as God, even though he appeared as a human being. And he is testified to by the Father since he has the Father as a coworker in all things, according to his statement, "I do nothing on my own,"[151] but the Father who remains in me "himself does the works."[152] And we hold that the Father works with the Son, but not in the sense that

[150]See 1 Cor 1:30. [151]Jn 8:28.

the Father imports some other power of his own to the Son, who is perhaps weak, for the accomplishment of the works. If we think that, we might as well concede that both the power of the Father and that of the Son are surely imperfect, at least if it took both of them to accomplish any of the miracles, as though one were not sufficient for the need. But if we consider and receive his statement more reverently, we will say that since in the Father and the Son there is one divine nature and the exact same authority and power of the same nature, the works of God the Father will surely be those of the Son, and the works of the Son, in turn, will be those of God the Father.

He says, "I do nothing on my own," not as a servant or underling or one who ranks as a disciple, waiting for a command or instruction from the Father to proceed to perform miracles. Rather, he is indicating with the greatest precision that he has sprung from the substance of God the Father; he has emerged like light ineffably and without beginning from his innermost bosom; he is eternally with him; he both is and is understood to be the image and imprint of his hypostasis. So he has the same mind, so to speak, and activity as him in all things. In order to teach clearly that he has the same will as his Father in all things, he says, "I do nothing on my own." It is as though he said, I do not go off to some will of my own that is not in God the **[725]** Father. Whatever the nature of the Father wills and thinks, these things are surely in me as well, since I shone forth from his bosom, and I am the true fruit of his substance.

Now these matters are difficult to explain. And that which is sometimes unattainable to the understanding itself cannot without effort be made clear by the tongue. Nevertheless, by bringing these matters to a reverent interpretation, as far as possible, we will gain for ourselves a heavenly reward and thus preserve our mind unwounded and unmoved by diversions to anything else.

We must note that the Savior, by adding in his statement to the Jews, "In your law it is written," persuades the Pharisees by force to accept the pair of persons. "I testify about myself," he says, and I will call in the Father as well. Will you therefore accept the pair of witnesses before you, as established by the letter of the law, or will you look only at your envy of me and fail to keep the law that you admire?

8:19 Then they said to him, "Where is your Father?"

Here too most especially may anyone, I think, with good reason cry out against the ignorance of the Jews, uttering that statement of the prophet, "Behold, a foolish and senseless people."[153] After lengthy and repeated discussion with them by Christ our Savior, who mentions again and again God the Father in heaven, the wretches fall into such senselessness that they dare to say, "Where is your Father?" They give absolutely no thought to God the Father who is in heaven, but they look around and seek Joseph, believing that he and no one else has to be Christ's father.

You see, then, **[726]** how this people has rightfully been called truly foolish and senseless. They cannot so much as raise the eye of their understanding above earthly matters, so they prove true that which is said of them, "Let their eyes be darkened that they may not see, and bend their back forever."[154] The backs of irrational animals are bent since they have this form from their nature, and there is nothing upright in them. But the mind of the Jews too became animal-like in a certain way. It always stoops down and sees nothing heavenly.

Do we not deduce and figure out the truth about them as we are perfectly guided by the

[152]Jn 14:10. [153]Jer 5:21. [154]Ps 69:23 (Ps 68:24 LXX).

very fact of their statement about this? After all, if they were in any way thinking of God the Father in heaven, how could they have looked for the incorporeal in a place? How, tell me, are they not fighting with all of divine Scripture when they say most unadvisedly of God who fills all things, "Where is he?" This, despite the fact that the divine psalmist—recounting his description of God to the best of his ability—attributes to him the power to fill all things. "Where shall I go," he says, "from your Spirit, and where shall I flee from your countenance? If I ascend to heaven, you are there. If I descend to Hades, you are there. If I take up my wings of the dawn and go to the farthest limits of the sea, even there your hand will guide me, and your right hand will hold me."[155] Yes, and the God of all himself shows us clearly that he does not have a nature circumscribed by place when he says this to the unholy Jews: "Do I not fill heaven and earth? says the Lord. What house will you build me? Or what is my resting place? Heaven is my throne, and earth is my footstool."[156] One may therefore see that the Jews are completely unlearned when they say to Christ the Savior, "Where is your Father?" Unless [727] they are making this statement about the one thought to be his father according to the flesh, they are talking nonsense here.

It is indeed likely, however, that the words of the Jews are hinting at some other deeper meaning. Since they thought that the holy virgin committed adultery before marriage, they rail in this way most bitterly against Christ, on the grounds that he does not even know who he comes from, saying "Where is your Father?" This is nonsense.

Jesus answered, "You know neither me nor my Father. If you knew me, you would know my Father."

The statement is true and can in no way be accused of being false. Those who suppose that the Christ is really from Joseph, or at any rate from fornication, and do not know that the Word has shone forth from God the Father—how will they not with good reason hear, "You know neither me nor my Father"? If they had known the Word who shone forth from God the Father and who came to be in the flesh for us, according to the divine Scripture, they would also have known his Father. The most accurate knowledge of the Father arises through the Son in those who want to learn, as he himself maintained somewhere, saying to God the Father, "I have made your name known to humanity."[157] And again, "Knowledge of you has been made wonderful by me."[158] Since we know the Son, from him we know the one who begat him. The reference to the other is included in both. When the Father is named, the recollection of his offspring surely comes along; and with a reference to the Son, mention of his begetter comes along as well. That is why, you know, the Son is like a door and a way leading to the knowledge [728] of the Father. Thus, he also says, "No one comes to the Father except through me."[159] We must first learn, as far as possible, what the Son is by nature. Then in this way, we will have a good understanding of the archetype from its image and exact imprint. That is because the Father is seen in the Son, and he appears in the nature of his own offspring as in a mirror.

Now if this is true (and it is), let the God-fighting Arian be ashamed. The imprint of his essence must be like him in every conceivable way lest one suppose that something other than what the Father is, is shining forth unaltered in the Son. And if he loves to be known in the Son and appears in him, then the Son is surely of the same substance and knows that he is in no way inferior to his own inherent glory. After all, he would not have

[155]Ps 139:7-10 (Ps 138:7-10 LXX). [156]Jer 23:24; Acts 7:49. [157]Jn 17:6. [158]Ps 139:6 (Ps 138:6 LXX). [159]Jn 14:6.

willed that we believe him to be less than that which he is by nature. But since he loves and wills this, how is it not necessary to confess that the Son is in every way like the Father in order that through him one may also know the begetter, as we already said, and by ascending rightly from the image to the archetype, be able to have an irreproachable conception of the holy Trinity? In this way, then, whoever knows the Son knows the Father as well.

Consider too how when the Lord speaks the truth to the Jews, he weaves another device into his statement. By saying clearly, "You know neither me nor my Father," he lures the mind of the Jews not to think only human thoughts about him or indeed to think that he is truly the son of Joseph who was associated with him according to the *oikonomia;* rather, he lures them into investigating and considering: Who is the Word in the flesh, and who is his natural Father? **[1]**

Chapter Three

The suffering on the cross was not the work of Jewish might, nor did Christ die because of anyone's mistreatment, but he himself endured this willingly for us, in order to save everyone.

8:20 These words he spoke in the treasury, as he taught in the temple, but no one arrested him, because his hour had not yet come.

The most wise Evangelist offers a defense concerning the saving passion for our benefit. He shows that the death on the cross came about not by human force—or at any rate that Jesus did not suffer death by the violence of another against his will—but by offering himself for us as a spotless sacrifice to God the Father because of the love he had for us. Since it was necessary for him to suffer (since this is how the imported decay and sin and death would be overturned), he gave himself as a ransom in place of the life of all. So which words in this passage deal with the saving passion? And what benefit does the meaning of the passage intend to produce? Listen.

Christ, he says, "was speaking these words" not outside Jerusalem, or in a neighboring city or in a fairly insignificant town or village of Judea, but he stood in the treasury itself, **[2]** that is, he was talking about these things right in the middle of the very temple, in the holy place itself. But although the Pharisees were cut to the heart and extraordinarily upset at his words, they did not "arrest him," even though they could have done so quite easily at the time since he was, as I said, in their nets.

What then persuaded those who were raging like wild beasts to be silent even against their will? What was it that stopped their anger? How was the bloodthirsty heart of the Pharisees enchanted? "His hour," it says, "had not yet come," that is, the time of his death was not yet at hand—not a time determined by someone else for Christ the Savior or (as the lying myths of the Greeks say) cast on him by fate (or rather by the "hour," to use their nonsensical term) but a time determined by him in agreement with God the Father. Since he is true God by nature and can't fall short of what is fitting for that, he knew very well how long he would live in the flesh with those on earth and when he would go to heaven, after destroying death by the death of his own flesh.

The fact that death has not been imposed by the violence of others on him who is life by nature is, I think, surely clear to the wise. After all, how could the bonds of death have prevailed over him who is life by nature? The Lord himself testifies somewhere, saying, "No one takes my life from me; I lay it down of my own accord. I have authority to lay it down, and I have authority to take it up again."[160] If the time that he must surely undergo death were determined by someone else by force, how would we find him in a position of authority **[3]** to lay down his life of his own accord? It would have been taken even against his will, if his passion were not in his own power. But if he lays it down of his own accord, then we shall see that his suffering was not in the power of someone else but in his will alone. And when he saw that the proper time for his death was at hand, then he yielded to the madness of the Jews to be carried off to their designs for him.

So let not the arrogant Pharisee boast of his own daring deeds or let him be puffed up and recklessly say, If Christ were God by nature, how is it that he did not escape my nets? How did he not elude my hands? Those who love him will answer, Your net was not so strong. It would not have been difficult for God, who rules all things, to crush your snare and to slip through the net of your impiety. But his suffering was the salvation of the world. His suffering was the undoing of death. The great cross contained the overthrow of sin and decay. Knowing these things as God, he submitted himself to your unholy audacity. What, tell me, prevented you from netting him then, when you were gnashing your teeth at him while he was teaching in the treasury? And if conquering Christ was an accomplishment of your power, why did you not take him prisoner then? But you stood there, unmasked with your pure anger thirsting for blood, but carrying out none of your plans. That's because the one who complied with your madness, which is like an unbreakable bridle, did not yet will to suffer. One may reasonably say this in response to the itching tongue of the Jews and will thus shame them—even against their will—into not boasting about what least deserves boasting.

One may also marvel at the holy Evangelist (and for good reason) when he notes at just the right time [4] and says clearly that the Savior "taught these things in the temple," by the treasury, "and no one arrested him." It is as though he is testifying to Jesus' words that he spoke to the Jews when they were there to arrest him, "Have you come out with swords and clubs to arrest me like a robber? Day after day I sat in the temple teaching, and you did not seize me."[161] Surely no reasonable person would suppose that he blamed the Jews because they did not bring his suffering on him prematurely or because they let the right time slip by and were slow to advance, as it were, to shed blood. Rather, he accuses them of foolishly thinking that they would prevail even against his will and be able to take by force the one who cannot suffer unless he should will it. "For I sat in the temple teaching, and you did not seize me." I did not will it then, but even now you would not have prevailed in this attempt if I had not submitted myself willingly to your hands.

Through all these things, then, it is possible to see that putting the Lord to death was not the work of Jewish might. One should attribute the attempt to their unholy audacity, but one should attribute to Christ the Savior the will to suffer for all in order that he may rescue all and, having purchased them with his own blood, present them to God the Father. "For God was," as Paul says, "in Christ reconciling the world to himself,"[162] and in forgiveness restoring that which has fallen from friendship with him to what it was in the beginning.

8:21 Again he said to them, "I am going away, and you will search for me, and you will die in your sin."

Christ declares quite aptly in these words that we must seize the present moment for whatever [5] profit we can get from it. It brings no profit to be late in what is good or to plan after the fact for what is beneficial; instead, it inflicts mourning that befits laziness. Since

[160]Jn 10:18. [161]Mt 26:55. [162]2 Cor 5:19.

our Lord is good and gentle, as it is written,[163] he bears with those who dishonor him, helps those who insult him and as God is found superior to all human pettiness. Yet, for their good he does threaten to depart from them. He says clearly, "I am going away," in order to implant in them a more spirited mind and to sharpen them to march on to faith, as they consider that they should not leave the redeemer without having the benefit of his work while he is present, and in order to make them now more ready for obedience.

After he cried out, "I am going away," and threatened to withdraw from the whole nation, he joined to this the loss they would accrue from it, according to the *oikonomia*. "You will die in your sins," he says. And we will see that the fact of the matter shows this statement to be true. After all, those who have not at all received him who came to us from heaven to justify everyone by faith—how will they not indisputably die in their sins? Those who have not received the one who can cleanse them—how will they not have eternal pollution from their impiety? To die without being redeemed but still weighed down by the weight of sin—who doubts where that will send the human soul? The depths of Hades, I am sure, will receive such a one, and they will continue on in great darkness. Yes, and they will inhabit fire and flames and for good reason be numbered among those spoken of somewhere by the voice of the prophet, "Their worm will not die, and their fire will not be extinguished, and they will be **[6]** a spectacle for all flesh."[164] In order that they might avoid the trial of these things, Christ kept calling them in multiple ways to turn swiftly from their accustomed unbelief, not simply saying that he would depart and go away but also setting before them, as the occasion demands, what a great misfortune they would endure from this. "You will die," he says, "in your sins."

Since he inserted in the middle of the statement the words "and you will seek me," but up to this time we do not find the Jews seeking him, we will reasonably arrive at some such meaning as the following, since he must be telling the truth. Even though, while they are still in the body and still having fun with the pleasures of the flesh, they do not seek redemption because of their very great senselessness, yet when the wretches fall into Hades and come into the places of punishment, when they are in the evils themselves, then—then they will seek him, even against their will. "For there is weeping there," he says, "and gnashing of teeth."[165] Each of those there, in all likelihood, bewails their laziness in doing good and practically utters the statement in the book of Proverbs, "I did not listen to the voice of my teacher and my instructor."[166] "Therefore," as Paul says, "while a promise of entering his rest remains, let us fear lest any of you seem to have fallen short of it."[167] We must run so that we may obtain it.[168] We must not insult with unbelief the one who rescued us from bitter slavery, but we must accept him and with open hands seize grace.

"And where I am going, you cannot come." Not only will they die in their sins, he says, but he clearly declares that they will remain outside the blessings of the kingdom and not ascend to the mansions above. After all, those **[7]** who did not receive him who came from above—how could they follow him as he goes above? Double, therefore, not singular, is the punishment of the unbelievers. Just as those who come down with bodily illness must undergo and endure the terrible pain of suffering and in addition must be deprived of the pleasures of health, in the same way and not otherwise, I think, those who have gone to Hades and are suffering there a punishment equal to their sins must both endure the tribulation of their

[163]Ps 86:5 (Ps 85:5 LXX). [164]Is 66:24. [165]Mt 8:12. [166]Prov 5:13. [167]Heb 4:1. [168]1 Cor 9:24.

punishment and lose the enjoyment of the hope of the saints. Most excellently, then, does our Lord Jesus Christ say not only that they will die in their sins but also that they will not ascend to the mansions above. He binds them as with a double cord and hurries to drag them away from their evil purpose.

On every side he saves the lost, binds up the broken and rights the fallen, since these acts are characteristic of the good shepherd, who readily gives his life for the salvation of the sheep. As he does these things, he announces to his disciples, "I will go and prepare a place for you, and I will come again and take you with me,"[169] showing that even heaven itself will be accessible to the saints and teaching that the mansions above have been prepared for those who love him. But to those who have chosen not to believe in him, he rightly and appropriately says, "Where I am going, you cannot come." Who, after all, could ever follow the all-holy Christ when they do not desire the purification that is by faith? Or how will one who is still defiled and who has not scrubbed off the filth of their own passions be with the Lord, who loves humanity? "What communion does light have with darkness?" as Paul says.[170] I think they ought to be holy **[8]** who want to say to the all-holy God, "My soul clings to you."[171]

I think this present meaning is suited, not inelegantly, to the passage before us. But if, when we look into the matter, we must view it differently and say something else in addition to this, we will not hesitate to do so. "Where I am going, you cannot come." Since I am true God, I am absent from no one, but I fill all things. And though I am with all things, I dwell especially in heaven, enjoying the company of the holy spirits. But since I am also the loving creator of all, I could not bear the loss of my creatures. I saw that humanity had gone to complete destruction. I perceived that it had fallen into death from sin. I had to stretch out a helping hand to the prostrate. I had to assist in every way the conquered and falling.

How, then, was it fitting to save the lost? It was fitting for the physician to be with those in danger. It was fitting for life to be with the dying. It was fitting for light to dwell with those in darkness. But it was not possible for you, who are human by nature, to fly up to heaven and dwell with the Savior. So I myself have come to you. I often heard the saints crying, "Bow your heavens, Lord, and come down."[172] So I bowed the heavens, he says, and have come down. In no other way was it possible for you to even hope to get there. I am still patiently spending time with you, so lay hold of life vigorously and be cleansed by faith, while the one who can authoritatively have mercy is present. For I will go, yes, and return where "you cannot come." And if you seek the bestower of salvation at the wrong time as an **[9]** afterthought, you will not find him. You may see what follows from this. You will surely die in your sins and, weighed down by your own transgressions, you will finally dwell in gloom in the prison of death, there to pay the penalty for your prolonged unbelief. The Savior, then, is good and has a great love for humanity. He drives the Jews by fear of future evils, even against their will, to be saved.

8:23 And he said to them, "You are from below; I am from above."

Now perhaps someone who has a more studious mind and is accustomed to praising quite subtle divine teachings will say, What induced our Lord Jesus Christ, who just addressed the Jews and said, "I am going away, and you will search for me,"[173] to add (as something called for by the situation), "You are from below; I am from above"? These words seem somehow

[169]Jn 14:2-3. [170]2 Cor 6:14. [171]Ps 63:8 (Ps 62:9 LXX). [172]Ps 144:5 (Ps 143:5 LXX). [173]Jn 8:21.

not to follow very well from those above, yet they are full of a hidden *oikonomia*.

He is God, and he has no need, as the divine Evangelist John himself says somewhere, "that one should testify about anyone; for he himself knew what was in everyone."[174] He pierces "to the division of soul and spirit, joints and marrow, and he judges the thoughts and intentions of the heart."[175] Therefore, he was not unaware of the unlearned conjectures of the Jews. Their mind is thick and sluggish, so when they heard the Savior's statement, "I am going away," they ignorantly thought either that he would leave Judea and flee somewhere or that he was saying something like, While I am alive and around you, believe, lest death should befall me. The words "I am going away," after all, are commonly **[10]** taken to suggest this too.

And it is no surprise that the Jews have fallen into such foolish counsel that they think this sort of thing about Christ. They did not acknowledge, after all, that he was God by nature; when they saw only his earthly body, they kept thinking that he was a human being, one of us. That is why the Savior rebuked them and said, "You judge according to the flesh."[176] He therefore takes them away from such puerile and earthbound notions and teaches them that they are entertaining these considerations not of one who comes into being and decays but of one who is from above and begotten of God the Father in truth. Therefore dying, he says, and fleeing will not apply to me, for I am from above, that is, God from God (since God is above all), but these will belong more fittingly to you. You are from below, that is, of a nature that is subject to death and that falls under the sway of decay and fear. Concerning me then, he says, leave your own weakness behind and do not think such thoughts. The slave does not have honor equal to the Lord, nor does that which is from below and of the earth have honor equal to the one who is from above and begotten of God the Father.

Wise reasoning will convince us that "from above" refers to the Son's begetting from God the Father. When understood of a place, "from above" indicates that which is from heaven. But if he comes only from heaven, there is nothing in the Son that surpasses the creation that is below and subject to God since most of the angels, you know, as they are sent to serve,[177] descend from heaven above and walk below as they manage some of the affairs on earth. And the Savior is a witness to us of this when he says, "Truly, truly, I say to you, **[11]** you will see heaven opened and the angels of God ascending and descending on the Son of Man."[178]

Since, therefore, the angels too come down from above from heaven, why does Christ add an empty boast as though that were something great, surpassing the whole creation (I mean that he came from above)? But one may see without the slightest sweat or toil who the Only Begotten is by nature and what the angels are who are with him. Therefore, "from above" has to signify to us not this coming down from heaven that is common to him and the angels but that the Son shone forth from the highest nature that surpasses all things. And so "from above," in the case of the Only Begotten alone, indicates nothing other than the fact that he is from God by nature. Though all things are said to be and exist from God, the Son has this special quality above all: that he is from the very substance of the Father by begetting, not by creation like the creatures. **[12]**

Chapter Four

The Son is God by nature, completely removed from likeness with creation, as far as his substance is concerned.

[174]Jn 2:25. [175]Heb 4:12. [176]Jn 8:15. [177]Heb 1:14. [178]Jn 1:51.

8:23 "You are of this world; I am not of this world."

With these words he has shown quite well and clearly how one should understand "above" and "below." Since it was likely that the Pharisees, who could understand nothing, would approach his words in too corporeal a manner and take "above" and "below" to refer to places, thereby straying into many different conceptions, our Lord Jesus Christ beneficially strips his statement of all obscurity, like a garment that seemed to be wrapped around it, by subsequently presenting to them more clearly what he had said enigmatically. "You," he says, "are from this world," that is, from below. "I am not of this world." This, then, is what "above" means. God surpasses everything that comes into being, not by spatial exaltation (since it is silly and utterly senseless to conceive of something incorporeal in a place); rather, he outstrips originate beings by the ineffable superiority of his nature. The Word says that he is not a work but a fruit and offspring of this nature. Notice how we do not catch him saying, "I have come into being and have been created from above," but "I am," so that he demonstrates both where he is from and that [13] he was always with his own Father. Since he is, just as the Father is, and he who is, is eternally with the one who is, let the foolishness of the heterodox tell us how he was not.

But perhaps the enemy of the truth will rise up against us and say, Christ did not say without qualification, "I am not of the world," but by adding "this," he has indicated precisely that there is another world, the spiritual world, from which he can be.

So the Son is among the creatures (since this is what your statement, sir, amounts to for us), and the creator will surely be classified among those things that have an originate nature. You think you have freed yourself from the charge of blasphemy by conferring on him an angelic, perhaps, and slave-befitting honor. Do you not know that even though you grant him the highest status and standing, beyond that which could be understood of the holy angels, and even though you confess him to be higher than every rule, authority and throne, yet because you believe he is originate, you will insult him no less? There is no account whatsoever of superiority over others that brings honor to the Only Begotten so long as he is at all conceived of as created. He has glory not because he ranks higher than others but because he is not originate but is rather God from God by nature. You, however, number him who beamed forth from God, and therefore is God, among originate creatures, and you consider him part of the world—if not this world, perhaps, then another. (Contrived distinctions between worlds will make no difference at all when it comes to being created.)

Do you not blush, then, to count the Word, who sits with the one who begat him, among the guards and those who stand before him? Do you not hear Gabriel saying to Zechariah, "I am Gabriel, who stands [14] in the presence of God, and I have been sent to speak to you,"[179] and Isaiah, "I saw the Lord of Sabaoth sitting on a high and exalted throne, and seraphim standing around him"?[180] What a marvel! The prophet gazed on the Son and called him the Lord of Sabaoth. He presents him in the rank of king, guarded by the highest powers. That Isaiah clearly beheld the glory of the Only Begotten, the wise John will testify, saying, "Isaiah said this because he saw his glory and spoke about him."[181] For this reason the divine Paul too arrives at a most precise understanding of the mystery both from the Son sitting with God the Father and his being called Son by nature. Gathering together knowledge from this insight about

[179]Lk 1:19. [180]Is 6:1-2. [181]Jn 12:41.

him, Paul says, "For to which of the angels has he (namely, God the Father) ever said, 'You are my Son; today I have begotten you'?"[182] With the words "I have begotten," he indicates that the Son is God from God by nature. And again, "To which of the angels has he ever said, 'Sit at my right hand'?"[183] By saying these things, he surely does not accuse God the Father either of being in the habit of doing anything unjust or of dishonoring the nature of the angels when he determined to honor that nature in second place after the Son.

But what prevents God the Father, perhaps someone will say, since he is righteous and good, from seating even the nature of the angels with himself? This would be the case if the Son is at all among originate beings and of the same kind as them, at least when it comes to being created, even though by some excellent qualities he surpasses the measure that belongs to them, just as they, let's say, surpass us. But God the Father is not unjust when he commands the angels to stand before him. He gives this dignity to their nature, while he has his own Son seated with him, since he knows himself to be by nature God, and he knows that his own offspring is not alien to his substance. **[15]** How then is he still originate? How is he from the originate world and not rather in the condition in which the true God would be, namely, beyond all things both conceived of and acknowledged to exist in every world?

But since you put forward, as something great and invincible, the fact that Christ makes a distinction when he says, "I am not of this world," and you maintain that by "this" he is indicating to us another world and saying he is from there, let us next see whether you are depending on unsound reasoning, persuaded to reason and think these things only by your flippancy. "This" (or "of this," as the case may be) and anything we use as a pronoun is demonstrative and is not necessarily indicative of another at all. For example, the blessed Baruch, indicating to us the one and only God, says, "This is our God; no other can be thought of in comparison with him."[184] But if "this" is at all indicative of another, how would no other have been thought of in comparison with him? And when the righteous Simeon prophesies the mystery of Christ, he says, "Behold, this one is set for the falling and rising of many dead[185] in Israel, and for a sign that is spoken against."[186] Yet to whom is it not utterly clear that the righteous one says "this" not to direct us away from other persons but to refer singularly, if I may put it this way, to the one now present and appointed for this? Therefore, when Christ says, "I am not of this world," he does not at all say this because he is from another world, but he is defining and establishing in a more corporeal way two places, as it were: I mean the place of originate nature and the place of the nature that is ineffable and above all human substance. And he decrees that the Jews remain in the place of originate things when he says, "You are from this world." But he separates himself completely from the things that come into being, and he attaches himself to the other place (I mean the place of the divine nature) **[16]** by saying, "I am not of this world." So in order to contrast, for our knowledge, the divine nature with the world, he assigns "this" to the latter and assigns himself to God, who has begotten him, and to the substance that utterly surpasses all things.

"But God the Father will do no wrong to the nature of the angels," says the heretic, "if he does not honor it to the same degree as he honors the Son. After all, variety in creation,

[182]Heb 1:5. [183]Heb 1:13. [184]Bar 3:35 (Bar 3:36 LXX). [185]The word *dead* is in Cyril's Greek here, but he does not include it later in the commentary when this same passage from Luke is quoted. Cyril may have been quoting from memory and been thinking of the "resurrection of the dead." [186]Lk 2:34.

or the assignment to each thing of its appropriate glory, in no way shows God to be unjust, since we ourselves were less than the angels in a certain way, and we still confess God to be just. The way, then, that we compare with the angels is the way the angels compare with the Son. They concede to him, as one who is better than they, greater honor than they themselves have."

But sir, we will then reply, shaming the unlearned heretic—even though we are removed from the glory of the angels, since we are inferior to their piety, and even though there is great variety and diversity in creation with one thing having more honor and another having less according to the will of the creator, yet the fact of being created is common to all, and in this respect nothing at all is greater or less than another. That an angel surpasses a human in honor and glory is nothing marvelous, or that an archangel surpasses an angel. We will find, however, that the power to ascend to the glory of the creator of all belongs to none of the creatures. No originate being will be God by nature, nor will the slave have equal honor with the Lord, sitting and ruling with him.

What measure of honor, then, will there be for the Son, who according to you is originate and from the spiritual world? God-befitting honor? How will that which is of the same kind as the creatures mount up to the same glory as the one who is by nature God, despite the fact that God **[17]** says, "My glory will I not give to another"?[187] What, tell me, drove the devil out of the heavenly courts? Was it his thirst for honor that belongs to originate nature, though better and greater than the measure that belonged to him, that was the basis of the accusation against him? Or was it rather that he dared to say, "I will be like the Most High"?[188] He imagined that what was made could ascend to the nature of its maker and that he would be enthroned with God, who has power over all things. Therefore, he has fallen like lightning, as it is written, from heaven.[189]

But when you spring on us with such ramshackle arguments, you give no thought to the fact that the Son, who according to you is from some world and therefore is part of creation, is called by God the Father to a level of honor to sit with him, though his substance in no way bestows this on him, nor does it call him to the dignity that is due and fitting for that position. For he receives by grace, if your babbling is correct, his position above creation.

Away with this blasphemy, man. We will not be so minded. May God prevent it! We believe that angels and archangels and those higher still are honored differently according to the authority and will of the supremely wise God, who assigns a just decree to each originate being. But we will not imagine that the Son by nature is among these. He does not have his glory by grace as an external addition, but he has it because he is from the substance of God the Father, true God from the one who is true God by nature. He both sits and rules with him, having all things under his feet as God. From the Father and with the Father, he is above all creation in a God-befitting way. That is why **[18]** he rightly heard, "All things are your servants."[190]

Since he is found on all sides to be true God, it is surely clear that he is not "from this world," that is, originate. The "world" in this passage signifies to us the entire nature of created beings, carrying the comparison from a part to the whole (the whole being understood as the property of being created), just as God of course excluded himself from all connaturality with creation when he said in the prophets, "For I am God and not a human being."[191] And just because he said that he is not a human like us, we will surely not for that

[187]Is 42:8. [188]Is 14:14. [189]Lk 10:18. [190]Ps 119:91 (Ps 118:91 LXX). [191]Hos 11:9.

reason classify him as an angel or some other originate being, but going from part to whole, we will confess that God is by nature something other than all originate beings. This is how I think we must reverently understand the difficult things that come our way. "For we see in a mirror through an enigma," as Paul says.[192]

8:24 "I told you that you would die in your sins."

After he overturned with a few words the most ill-advised conjecture of those who were thinking this way, and after he then refuted those who were speaking foolishness against him, he returns, as it were, to the original intention of his speech. And when he takes it up again, he shows them what evils they will be in and what they will fall into if they irrationally reject faith in him. This too is quite appropriate for a wise and capable teacher. I think that a teacher should not be contentious about the ignorance of his hearers or take his concern for them lightly, even if they should be completely unprepared, let's say, to receive the knowledge of his teaching. But he should circle around and say the same things again, or rather many times, and cycle through the same words. **[19]**

The persevering ploughman, when he has turned up the ground and expended no small amount of labor on it and poured seed into the furrows, sometimes sees that some seed is ruined, so he returns to the plough and does not shrink back from sowing over the seed that is now ruined. He missed his goal the first time, but the same would surely not happen the second time, at least. The divine Paul too engages in the same practice when he says somewhere, "To say the same things to you is not troublesome for me, and to you it is a safeguard."[193] Do you see how the teacher is found to be superior to sluggishness, and then the hearers often develop safe practices as a result? Beneficially, then, does our Lord Jesus Christ repeat his statement to the Jews and insist that the penalty for not believing in him will be no small thing. The unbelievers must surely "die in their sins," he says. And no one doubts that dying in one's sins is a heavy burden because it will deliver the human soul to the all-consuming fire.

"For unless you believe that I am, you will die in your sins."

He explains his beneficial statement more precisely. He makes the way of salvation crystal clear and shows them what road to travel to ascend to the life of the saints and to arrive at the city above, the heavenly Jerusalem. Not only must one believe, he says, but he insists that one will have to believe in him. For we are justified when we believe in him as God from God, as Savior and redeemer and king of all and truly Lord. **[20]**

You will die then, he says, if you do not "believe that I am." And the "I," he says, is he of whom it is written in the prophets, "Be enlightened, be enlightened, Jerusalem, for your light has come, and the glory of the Lord has risen on you."[194] "I am," he says, the one who long ago commanded people to depart from the diseases of the soul and promised the healing that comes from love in the statement, "Turn, you children given to turning, and I will heal your bruises."[195] "I am" the one who declared that you be graced with the ancient God-befitting kindness and incomparable forbearance, which is why I cried out, "I am, I am the one who blots out your sins, and I will remember them no more."[196] "I am," he says, the one who also says through the prophet Isaiah, "Wash yourselves, make yourselves clean. Remove your iniquities from your hearts before my eyes. Cease from your iniquities. Come, let us reason together, says the Lord.

[192] 1 Cor 13:12. [193] Phil 3:1. [194] Is 60:1 (LXX). [195] Jer 3:22. [196] Is 43:25.

Though your sins be as crimson, I will make them white as snow. Though they be like scarlet, I will make them white as wool."[197] "I am," he says, the very one of whom the prophet Isaiah says somewhere, "Go up to a high mountain, you who preach the gospel to Zion; lift your voice with strength, you who preach the gospel to Jerusalem. Lift it up, do not be afraid. Behold, your God. Behold, the Lord comes with strength, and his arm with authority. Behold, his reward is with him, and his work is before him. Like a shepherd he will shepherd his flock. He will gather the lambs with his arm and comfort those who are with child."[198] And again, "Then will the eyes of the blind be opened and the ears of the deaf will hear. Then will the lame leap like a deer and the tongue of the stammerers speak clearly."[199] "I am," he says, the one of whom it is written, "Suddenly [21] the Lord, whom you seek, will come into his temple, the angel of the covenant, whom you desire. Behold, he is coming, says the Lord, and who will bear the day of his arrival? Or who will stand at his appearing? He will come in like fire in a furnace and like the soap of the fullers."[200] "I am," he says, the one who through the voice of the psalmist promises to offer myself as a sacrifice to God the Father himself for the salvation of all, crying out, "Sacrifice and offering you did not desire, but a body you prepared for me. You were not pleased with whole burnt offerings and sin offerings. Then I said, 'I have come. It is written about me in the chapter of the book. I have come to do your will, O God.'"[201] "I am," he says, also the same one the law announced through Moses when he said, "The Lord your God will raise up for you a prophet like me from your brothers. Listen to him. This is in accordance with everything you asked of the Lord your God on Mount Horeb on the day of the assembly."[202]

Therefore, you will perish for good reason, he says, and you will pay a most just penalty to the judge, since due to the colossal unholiness of your ways, you had nothing to do with the one who was announced beforehand to you through many saints and testified to by the works that I do. Indeed and in truth, no argument will rescue those who do not believe in him from punishment, since the divinely inspired Scriptures are filled with testimonies and words about him, and he himself furnishes by his works a splendor that is in harmony with what was prophesied long ago.

8:25 They said to him, "You? Who are you?"

Their words, mixed with the fiercest anger, proceed from false pretenses. They are eager to ask not so they may learn and believe but so that they may practically leap on Christ with their great ignorance. [22] He just says "I am," without adding that he is God from God or anything else that indicates the glory that is within him. In a subdued way and without any boasting, he says only this: "I am," leaving it to the better instructed to add the rest.

But they go on to the wildest unbridled madness, and from limitless arrogance they practically cut off the Savior's statement before he is finished. They rebuke him, as it were, and interrupt him and say, "You? Who are you?"[203] This was obviously a way of saying, "You do not dare to think of yourself more highly than we know you are, do you? We know that you are the son of the carpenter, a worthless poverty-stricken man, insignificant to us and of no importance whatsoever." They condemn, then, the Lord for being nothing since they look only at his family according to the flesh.

But the greatness of his deeds and his begetting from above from God the Father do not so much as enter their minds. From this

[197]Is 1:16, 18. [198]Is 40:9-11. [199]Is 35:5-6. [200]Mal 3:1-2. [201]Ps 40:6-8 (Ps 39:7-9 LXX). [202]Deut 18:15-16. [203]I am punctuating this sentence the way Cyril says he wants it punctuated (see below) rather than the way Pusey's Greek text punctuates it. Perhaps Pusey is punctuating it to make it conform to his Greek New Testament.

they could have recognized that he is God by nature. After all, who could have performed deeds fitting for God alone? Is it not one who himself is also God by nature? Christ performed these deeds. Therefore, he was and is God, even when he has come to be in the flesh for the salvation and life of all. But since they are persuaded only by their own bad counsel and take no account of our divine and God-breathed Scriptures, they disparage him for the very qualities for which they should have given thanks, without knowing "what they are saying or the things about which they are making assertions."[204]

Placing a question mark for emphasis after the "you," and throwing back what is known as the acute accent,[205] we take the word as a question asked with astonishment. They say "You?" meaning, "You who are nothing at all and known by us to be so, **[23]** a poor man from poor parents—how do you have anything glorious to say about yourself? What is worthy of mention about you?" For nothing in such audacity is foreign to Jewish madness.

Jesus said to them, "It is because I spoke to you at the beginning."

I am dishonored, he says, even though I call you to eternal life, to the forgiveness of sins, to getting rid of death and decay, to sanctification, to righteousness, to glory, to boasting of adoption by God. Even though I want to crown you with all these things, I am classified as nothing, and so I am considered by you to be worthless. I suffer these insults justly, he says, because I said something to you "at the beginning," because I told you ahead of time something that could help you, and I wanted to save those who were about to descend into such wickedness that they delighted in rendering bitter repayment to the one who had elected to save them.

Christ seems to be hinting at something else for us as well by these words. It was right, he says, that I not speak to you at all "at the beginning" but that I bestow this on those who would most readily delight in my words and without delay submit their necks to the gospel teachings. And by this he is referring to the multitude of the Gentiles. When we imagine him saying this, however, we will also be on guard against the words of the adversaries. Perhaps one of those who habitually fight against Christ will say, "If he had to speak not to the Jews at the beginning, but rather to the Gentiles, then the Son missed what was appropriate, since he did the former rather than the latter." But then we will reply, The Son does not change his own will or that of the Father when he says this, **[24]** nor does he depart from action that is appropriate for the *oikonomia*, since God would not have willed anything that was not altogether appropriate to happen. By saying that it was not right to speak to you at the beginning, or to lay a foundation, as it were, for you of saving teaching, he is showing that both he and the Father are by nature true and devoted to humanity. See, he graced the unholy Jews with his saving word, even though they did not deserve it, and he put the multitude of the Gentiles in second place, even though they were quite ready to make it their aim both to believe him and obey him.

What then persuaded him to put the stiff-necked Jewish people ahead of the others in rank and honor? To them he promises his coming through the holy prophets; to them grace was due on account of their fathers. That is also why he said, "I was sent only to the lost sheep of the house of Israel,"[206] and to the Syrophoenician woman, "It is not right to take the children's bread and throw it to the dogs."[207] For this reason, therefore, Israel has

[204]1 Tim 1:7. [205]Both the question mark and the acute accent in Greek make the word *you* interrogative. [206]Mt 15:24. [207]Mt 15:26.

been honored and ranked ahead of the Gentiles, even though it has the more perverse disposition. However, when it failed to recognize the Lord of all and the fulfiller of the promised blessings, the grace of the teaching finally went over to the Gentiles. It was right for the Lord to have addressed them "at the beginning" and at first, not because there was a promise to their fathers but because of their obedience.

8:26 "I have much to say about you, and much to judge."

The Jews pounced on him and condemned him, even though they had nothing at all to accuse him with. They were haughty just because of the [25] poverty of his birth according to the flesh and for this reason said that he was nothing. Therefore, he mildly shamed them, having said above more openly, "You judge according to the flesh; I judge no one."[208] It is reasonable for "judging according to the flesh" to have this meaning. After all, those who marvel only at earthly matters do not perceive the blessings of heaven. They look only at the glory of this life and admire the wealthy or the one who boasts in other petty glories. But those who carefully distinguish the natures of things according to the law of God say that that person is truly worthy of love and admiration who has the will to live according to the counsel and will of the creator. Low position according to the flesh will do no harm to the soul of one who is accustomed to doing good, while glory in this life and the splendor of riches will be of no help to those who refuse to live rightly. They judge, therefore, according to the flesh, as we just said—they judge as those who do not look at holiness and are not accustomed to test their conduct or their manners but turn their mind aside only to earthly matters and count someone worthy of all admiration who is brought up in wealth and luxury. You then, O deranged leaders of the Jews, even though you are instructed by the law of Moses in careful judgment, denounce him for no reason and condemn the one who was shown to you by many miracles to be God, just because of the poverty of his flesh.

I, however, will not imitate your lack of instruction, nor will I pass such judgment against you. Human nature, after all, is nothing at all. What might this perishable earthly body be? Rottenness and the worm and nothing else. But I will not condemn you for this reason; nor because you are human by nature [26] will I decide that you should be rejected. "I have much to say about you, and much to judge," that is, the full charge against you is mounting. I will not accuse you for only one fault but for many, and in no case will I lie as you do. I have to judge you as unbelievers, as arrogant, as insulters, as enemies of God, as senseless, as thankless, as wicked, as loving pleasure rather than habitually loving God, as "receiving glory from one another but not seeking the glory that is from the one and only,"[209] as setting fire to the spiritual vineyard, as not correctly feeding the flock entrusted to you by God, as not leading people to the one proclaimed by the law and the prophets, that is, me. The Savior could utter such statements to the Jews, but by adding, I still "have much to say about you, and much to judge," he subtly threatens them that the one who seems to them to be nothing because of the flesh will one day appear as their judge.

"But the one who sent me is true, and what I heard from him I speak to the world."

After saying good-bye to the ignorance of the Jews, and having no regard for those who dared to rail against him without restraint, he returns to what he was saying at the beginning, reserv-

[208]Jn 8:15. [209]Jn 5:44.

ing the judgment against them and open discourse on this matter not for the present time but rather for the proper time, preserving the proper aim for the manner of his advent. For he "did not come to judge the world but to save the world," as he himself says somewhere.[210] That is why he carries on his exhortation, both holding fast to what is fitting for him and repeating the word that calls them to salvation.

In this point, **[27]** it is quite right for us to marvel at both the measure of his patience and the exceeding love for humanity that is in him. For this reason, Peter too writes concerning him, "When he was reviled, he did not revile in return; when he suffered, he did not threaten; but he entrusted himself to him who judges justly."[211] Therefore, I will now spend, he says, my discourse on you, not as you are accustomed to do (in love of blame and concern for nothing good), but I have reserved my judgment of you for the proper time, and I will keep to what is profitable for you and will not stop caring for you, even though you foolishly insult me because of your senselessness.

Now I just said to you, "I am the light of the world. Whoever follows me will not walk in darkness but will have the light of life."[212] At this you were unreasonably angered and sprang on me sharply, crying out intemperately, "You testify about yourself; your testimony is not true."[213] Then to this I said, "Even if I testify about myself, my testimony is true because I know where I came from and where I am going."[214] But if I seem hard to bear when I say these things to you, if you cannot receive my testimony concerning the dignities that accrue to me by nature, still "the one who sent me is true, and what I heard from him I speak to the world." I say the same things, he says, as the Father who sent me. I utter what is in harmony with his words when I say that I am light by nature. What, therefore, I heard God the Father saying about me "I speak to the world." So if I am lying, as you say, and my testimony is not true, you certainly must say that the Father lied first. But "he is true." Therefore, I have not lied.

And if you are not persuaded by my words about myself, then respect the words of him who sent me, he says. What did he say about me? "Behold a man, Dayspring is his name."[215] And again, to those **[28]** who worship him, "But the sun of righteousness will arise for you who fear my name, and healing will be in his wings."[216] Indeed, concerning me, whom you insult though you do not know me, he says, "Behold, I have given you as a covenant for the people, as a light to the Gentiles."[217] But that I am a light for you, he said with the words, "Be enlightened, be enlightened, O Jerusalem, for your light has come, and the glory of the Lord has risen on you."[218] I heard the Father who sent me making these statements about me, and for this reason I say that I am the light of the world. But you judged me incorrectly and disparaged me just because of my flesh, and for this reason you have the audacity to say repeatedly, "You testify about yourself; your testimony is not true."[219]

Therefore (since it is appropriate to summarize the entire meaning of the passage before us), he shows that the Jews are fighting directly against God. They are fighting not only against his words but also against the decree of the Father. That is because the Father knows that his own Son is light by nature and for that reason calls him "dayspring" and "sun of righteousness." But they reject the truth and by their unbelief call down destruction on their own heads. They "call good evil," and therefore "woe" will justly follow them.[220]

8:27 They did not understand that he was speaking to them about the Father!

[210]Jn 12:47. [211]1 Pet 2:23. [212]Jn 8:12. [213]Jn 8:13. [214]Jn 8:14. [215]Zech 6:12. [216]Mal 4:2 (Mal 3:20 LXX). [217]Is 49:6. [218]Is 60:1 (LXX). [219]Jn 8:13. [220]Is 5:20.

Next, the Spirit bearer is stunned by the Jews' lack of perception, and quite rightly so. What could be more senseless than those who, after a long and repeated discourse about God the Father, do not think of him at all when they hear our Savior saying, "But the one who sent me is true"?[221] So we must discuss what their excuse is [29] and why the blessed Evangelist says that the Jews did not understand that Christ was referring to God the Father in this statement.

Since the Savior had said to them, "If you knew me, you would know my Father as well,"[222] the Evangelist introduces those who are ignorant of the Son as ignorant of the Father as well in order that in this case too the Son may be found telling the truth, since the Son is a door, as it were, and a gate to the knowledge of the Father. That is why he also said, "No one comes to the Father except through me."[223] Since the mind ascends from the image to the archetype, it forms a conception of that archetype from what it encounters. It was necessary, then, to show that the Jews understood nothing about the Father because they were not willing to be led up from the knowledge of the Son to the understanding of his Father. This is why the Evangelist indicates, almost passionately, that when Christ says, "The one who sent me is true," "they did not understand that he was speaking to them about the Father!"

8:28 "When you have lifted up the Son of Man, then you will know that I am."

He imitates the finest physicians and lays bare the cause of the sickness that is in their soul, and he clearly reveals what prevents them from vigorously advancing to understanding and faith in him. Since they were looking only at the flesh and at his origin from there, they were misled into thinking little of him. And since they had this veil over the eyes of their mind, they would not have known that he was God even though he appeared as a human being. Therefore, he addressed them as the situation demanded, saying, "When you have lifted up the Son of Man, then you will know that I [30] am," that is, When you have ceased from your petty and earthly conception of me, when you have thought of me in an exalted and heavenly way and have believed that I am God from God, even though for your sakes I became a human being like you, then you will know clearly that I am the light of the world, for that is what I just said to you. After all, he says, what could prevent him who is fully admitted to being true God from also being the light of the world? Surely no one will descend to such a depth of madness and audacity that they then dare to say, "Your testimony is not true,"[224] because they will in no way accuse whatever he who is true God by nature says.

It is quite clear, then, also from the Savior's words, that if we have a low conception of him and consider him to be a mere human being, by nature bereft of divinity, we will surely and in all likelihood disbelieve him and not accept the Savior and redeemer. What then is the consequence of this? We have fallen away from hope. If salvation is by faith, but faith is gone, what will save us now? But if we believe and lift up the Only Begotten to a God-befitting height, even though he became human, we will journey with a fair wind, as it were, and speed across the rough sea of life, and we will sail to the city above, there to receive the rewards of believing.

Another view of the same passage.
"When you have lifted up the Son of Man, then you will know that I am."
Though he has drowned the anger of the Jews with many good words, he sees that it is no less

[221]Jn 8:26. [222]Jn 8:19. [223]Jn 14:6. [224]Jn 8:13.

violent. [31] They do not stop blaspheming heedlessly. Yes, at one point they consider his words invalid, and they irreverently call him a liar. After all, to say, "Your testimony is not true"[225]—what else could that be than this? Then at another time, they hotly opposed him when out of love for them he explained matters of salvation. This is why he said, "Unless you believe that I am, you will die in your sins."[226] They met those words, which came from love, with words coming from senselessness and said, "You? Who are you?"[227]

Those, then, who have wallowed in such sheer unreasoning anger needed a sobering word to persuade them to have more measured thoughts and to put a bridle on their tongue, even against its will. For this reason he threatened them, saying with utter clarity that they would not escape the punishment for their impiety. Even though for the time being they see him patient, yet when their impiety toward him reaches its terrible goal, that is, death and the cross, they will be subject to a most fearful penalty and receive in return an intolerable circumstance, namely, that of war with the Romans, which happened to them after the Savior's cross by God's wrath from above. The Savior indicated even more clearly to them that they were about to undergo the most terrible experiences somewhere when he said at one time to a weeping woman, "Daughters of Jerusalem, do not weep for me, but weep for yourselves and your children."[228] Again at another time, "When you see Jerusalem surrounded by armies, then you will say to the mountains, 'Cover us,' and to the hills, 'Fall on us.' "[229] The sufferings of war so overcome the Jews that every form of death becomes sweeter and more desirable than those trials. Their deportation from their country, [32] the enslavement of its inhabitants, the most savage slaughter, the famines in every city and the eating of children within them Josephus too relates in his writings.

Therefore, he says, after you have betrayed the Son of Man to the cross, when you endure the retributive punishment and pay the penalty corresponding to your audacity against me, "then," weeping, "you will know that I am" the one with all power, that is, God. If one sparrow will not enter the fowler's snare apart from the will of God, how will a whole country, he says, and a beloved nation go to such complete destruction unless almighty God has surely willed this to happen? Contempt for God is evil, therefore, and dreaded; it leads to an abominable end. Therefore, Paul too rebukes certain people, saying of God, "Or do you despise the riches of his kindness and forbearance and patience? Do you not realize that God's kindness leads you to repentance? But by your hard and impenitent heart, you are storing up wrath for yourself on the day of wrath."[230]

Another view of the same passage.
Christ spent a long time living with the Jews. He addressed them in practically every synagogue, discoursed with them on every sabbath, presented them often and ungrudgingly with profitable teaching, and in so doing he continually called them to illumination by the Spirit. In particular, since he is true God by nature, he said, "I am the light of the world."[231] But they most foolishly opposed him when he said these things. "You," it says, "testify about yourself; your testimony is not true."[232] And the rashness of the Jews does not stop at contradiction in words, [33] nor does their untamable audacity end merely with their love of railing at him, but recklessly going through all savagery, they finally handed him over to death and the cross. But since he was life by nature, he broke the bonds of death and rose from the dead. He then for good reason departs from the brutality of the Jews. His

[225]Jn 8:13. [226]Jn 8:24. [227]Jn 8:25. [228]Lk 23:28. [229]Lk 21:21; 23:30. [230]Rom 2:4-5. [231]Jn 8:12. [232]Jn 8:13.

departure from Israel was completely just and, transferring himself to the Gentiles, he called everyone to the light and gave new sight to the blind.[233]

Now it happened that after Christ our Savior's death on the cross, the understanding of the Jews was darkened, in that the light had departed from them, but the hearts of the Gentiles were enlightened, since the true light shone on them. "When," therefore, "you have lifted up the Son of Man," he says, "then you will know that I am," which means, I will wait for the consummation of your impiety. I will not bring wrath on you ahead of time. I will accept suffering and death. Even this I will endure in addition to the rest. But when you have handed over to the cross "the Son of Man," whom you considered to be a mere man, "then you will know," even against your will, he says, that I did not lie when I said "I am" the light of the world. When you see yourselves in darkness but the uncountable multitude of the Gentiles enlightened because of my coming to them, how will you not finally agree, even against your will, that I am truly the light of the world?

No one doubts that the Savior was going to depart from the synagogue of the Jews because it has been accomplished and done. Yet one may see it in some way, or rather in a clear way, from his words, "While you have the light, walk in the light, so that darkness may not overtake you."[234] **[34]** The waning and withdrawal of the light generates darkness, while the arrival of the light makes darkness disappear. Therefore, Christ is revealed to be the true light because he darkened the Jews by his withdrawal from them, and he enlightened the Gentiles by his arrival among them. And the dreadful trials were a bitter lesson for the Jews.

Another view of the same passage.
"When you have lifted up the Son of Man, then you will know that I am."

Since you look only at the flesh, he says, you believe that I am a mere man, and you think that I am one like you, but the honor and glory of the divinity do not even come into your mind. Therefore, you will have the clearest sign that I am truly God from God and light from light: your own dreaded and lawless audacity, the cross and the death of the flesh on it. For when you see the outcome of your foolishness frustrated and the snare of death crushed in pieces (since I will rise from the dead), then even against your will you will finally have to agree with the words I spoke to you and confess that I am God by nature. I will be superior to death and decay, and since I am life by nature, I will raise my temple. But if conquering death and overcoming the meshes of decay are characteristic of him who is God by nature and of no one else, how will I not thereby (with all contradiction and doubt removed) be shown to conquer all things **[35]** mightily and without effort? Therefore, the Savior said that his cross would be a sign to the Jews and the clearest proof that he is by nature God.

You may see him clearly saying this in other places as well. After he had performed many countless wonders, the Pharisees approached him to test him and said, "Teacher, we want to see a sign from you."[235] But he, since he saw the thoughts going on inside them and was not unaware of their bitter plans, says, "A wicked and adulterous generation seeks for a sign, and no sign will be given to it except the sign of the prophet Jonah. Just as Jonah was in the belly of the great fish for three days and three nights, so the Son of Man will be in the heart of the earth for three days and three nights."[236] Do you hear how to the Jews seeking a sign to prove that he is true God (even though they said this to test him), he says that no other sign will be shown to them except the sign of the prophet Jonah, that is, the three-day death

[233]Is 61:1 (LXX). [234]Jn 12:35. [235]Mt 12:38. [236]Mt 12:39-40.

and the resurrection from the dead? What sign of God-befitting authority could be so great and clear as conquering death and overturning decay, even though by divine sentence it had mastery over human nature? That nature heard in Adam, "Earth you are and to earth you will return."[237] But Christ the Savior had the authority both to put an end to his own wrath and by blessings to overturn death, which had conquered because of his curse.

The Jews' final act will teach clearly that they shuddered greatly at the sign of the resurrection as a powerful persuasion that Christ was true God. When they learned about the Savior's resurrection and that he was not found in the tomb, **[36]** they became exceedingly terrified and fearful and planned to buy false testimony from the soldiers with large sums of money. They gave them silver to say, "His disciples came and stole him while we were sleeping."[238] Great, then, is the sign of the resurrection, containing indubitable proof that Jesus is God. At this, the hard and unbending heart of the Jews was thrown into confusion. **[37]**

Chapter Five

The Son is not inferior in power and wisdom to God the Father, but he himself is his wisdom and power.

8:28 "I do nothing on my own, but I speak these things just as the Father taught me."

He speaks in a more human fashion since the Jews cannot understand any other way, nor can they bear to hear full-strength, God-befitting words from him. At such words, they are found to hurl stones at him, identifying his blasphemy to be the fact that, though he was a human being, he made himself God.[239] He takes away, therefore, the excess of God-befitting honor and removes much of the splendor from his words in this statement so as to adapt himself well to the weakness of his hearers. Since he searches their mind and finds that they do not know that he is God, he makes his statement appropriate for a human being so that their thoughts may not be ignited with anger against him again and they may not foolishly flee from learning even a little from him. You will know, then, he says, "when you have lifted up the Son of Man, that I am." Likewise, you will also know that "I do nothing on my own, but I speak just as the Father taught me."

What, tell me, is the use of these words, perhaps someone will say, and what does Christ teach us in them? **[38]** So we will answer, accurately and reverently drawing out the sense of each statement. You have not stopped denouncing my deeds, he says, as deeds performed in rashness and unholiness. You often condemned me on the grounds that I do not refrain from transgressing, that my practice is to act in a way that is out of harmony with the lawgiver. After all, I freed the paralytic from such a great infirmity. I had mercy on a man on the sabbath. But, he says, when I saw you who love to find fault with what you ought to admire and who go far astray from what befits me, even as I just explained to you what pertains to salvation, I tried to persuade you to advance to the desire of participating in the light. Then I showed you the true light. I explained my nature to you and said, "I am the light of the world,"[240] but you, acting and plotting most thoughtlessly, rose up against my words, lost all restraint and dared to say, "Your testimony is not true."[241] When, then, you have lifted up the Son of Man, that is, when you encompass him with death and see that he is greater than the bonds of death (for I will rise from the dead since I am by nature God), then you will know that "I do nothing on my own," he says,

[237]Gen 3:19. [238]Mt 28:13. [239]Jn 10:33. [240]Jn 8:12. [241]Jn 8:13.

"but I speak just as the Father taught me."

When you see that the Son too is God by nature, you will learn that I by no means hold my own opinion, but my will is always in accord with God the Father. Whatever he does, I myself do not shrink from doing, and I say whatever I know he says. That is because I am of the same substance as the one who begat me. I healed the paralytic on the sabbath, and you were bitter about this. But I also showed you the Father working on the sabbath. I said, "My Father **[39]** is still working, and I also am working."[242] Therefore, "I do nothing on my own." Again I said, "I am the light of the world,"[243] but you thought I was saying something out of harmony with the Father. In this too I put you to shame, showing that he says about me, "Behold, I have established you as a covenant of the people, as a light of the Gentiles."[244] In vain, therefore, do you accuse the one who always wills in agreement with the Father, who does nothing out of harmony with him and who indeed cannot bear to speak what does not come from him. This is the meaning I think we should attach to this passage.

But perhaps the bitter beast will pounce on us, that is, the enemy of Christ (I mean the Arian). He will likely cry out and come and say, When the discourse is proceeding on a fair course, sir, what makes you push it the other way to what seems right only to you? Do you not blush to steal away the force of the truth? Look, the Son clearly maintains that he does nothing on his own, but what he learns from the Father, this he also speaks. Thus, he recognizes that his Father is in a higher position than he is.

What then, most excellent sir (such a person will hear in return)—is the Son then supplied with might and understanding from the Father so that he can both act and speak without blame? How then is he any longer God by nature when he borrows his power and understanding from another, just as the nature of creatures does? In the case of those who have their origin from nothing, everything that comes to belong to them is completely a gift from God. But it is not so in the case of the Son. The divine Scripture both recognizes and proclaims him to be true God. I, at least, think that all good things must perfectly belong to the one who is God by nature. But something that does not perfectly possess **[40]** every single marvelous attribute—how could that be by nature God? Just as incorruptibility and immortality must surely belong to him by nature and not from the outside or as something imported, the same is true also for total perfection and lack of nothing in all good things.

But if, sir, according to your unholy and unlearned reasoning, the Son is imperfect in his ability both to perform God-befitting acts and to speak what is right, and yet he is the power and wisdom of the Father according to the divine Scripture, this accusation will apply to the Father rather than to him. If you understand matters this way, you will be saying that God the Father is no longer perfect in power, nor is he perfectly wise. You see, then, the depths to which the rashness of your ignorance sinks.

I marvel that this too escapes your reasoning: how, tell me, will God the Father supply power to his own power? Or how could he make his own wisdom wiser? Either one must say that he always ascends to the greater and progresses little by little to some power that is even greater than the strength that is within him (which is completely stupid and impossible), or one must impiously suppose that he is strengthened by someone else. How could the Son still be called the "Lord of powers," and how could he still be understood to be wisdom and power, if he is strengthened (as you claim) and made wise by someone else?

[242]Jn 5:17. [243]Jn 8:12. [244]Is 42:6.

Away with this blasphemy and absurd reasoning! Either grant outright that the Son is a creature so that you may have the entire divinely inspired Scripture crying out against you, or, if you believe that he is by nature God, then grant—grant, I say!—that he perfectly possesses the attributes of the divine nature. It belongs to the property of his nature that he is not weak in any respect, nor does he fall short of the highest wisdom, **[41]** but he is by nature wisdom itself and power itself. But in wisdom, nothing comes by teaching; nor in the first power, strictly understood, would we ever see power brought in from the outside.

In order that we may test Christ's statement with greater precision by examining the very nature of the facts, we will add the following to what has been said. What deed has the Only Begotten, who has been made human, done that is so great that it surpasses his own power? I suppose it is likely that some would say that he fittingly made the statement, as one who borrowed power from God the Father, "I do nothing on my own," because he drove out a demon, he released the paralytic from his disease, he freed the leper from his suffering, he gave sight to the blind, he satisfied an innumerable multitude with five loaves, he lulled the raging sea to sleep with a word, and he raised Lazarus from the dead. Shall we say, then, that what he demonstrates in these deeds is even greater than his own power?

How then, tell me, did he fix the sky, which is so great, and spread it out like a tent to dwell in?[245] How did he lay the foundation of the earth? How did he become the maker of the sun and moon and the objects in the firmament? How did he create the angels and archangels, thrones and dominions, and the seraphim as well? He who in such great and supernatural deeds needed neither power nor wisdom from another—how could he have been powerless in such small deeds? Or how could he who is praised as wisdom by the holy prophets have needed someone to teach him what he should say to the Jews?

I hear one of them saying, "It is the Lord who made the earth by his strength, who set up the world by his wisdom and by his understanding stretched out the sky."[246] In addition to **[42]** this, the divine Daniel also says, "May the name of the Lord be blessed forever because wisdom and understanding and strength are his."[247] But if strength and wisdom are his, as the prophet says, who will any longer endure the babbling of the heterodox, who say that the wisdom and power of the Father is supplied with both power and wisdom from another?

If we were saying, says the heterodox, that it is someone else who supplies the Son what is lacking in his power or who teaches him, you would have been right to denounce our words, with the recognition that you were defending him as one insulted. But since we say that God the Father has given him these things, what pretext for grievance do you still have from this?

Now if you think that no wrong will be done to the Son, regarding your claim that he is by nature unlike[248] the one who begat him, even though he is said to be supplied by him in some way, remember, man, your recent statement, and be persuaded by this not to take offense. Grant to him that he is in all things equal to the one who begat him and in no way or respect whatsoever inferior to him. But if this drags you away from right reasoning and persuades you to think what is not lawful concerning him, why do you try in vain to outwit us with such unsound words? It will make no difference at all whether God the Father himself, or someone else besides him, is

[245]Is 40:22. [246]Jer 10:12. [247]Dan 2:20. [248]Ἀνόμοιον. A feature of the Eunomian position that distinguished it from earlier Arians was the claim that the Son was unlike (ἀνόμοιος) the Father. That is why Eunomians are also called Anomoians. Earlier Arians had claimed that the Son was of a "similar substance" (ὁμοιούσιος) as the Father, but not the same substance (ὁμοούσιος).

said to give something to the Son. Once he is charged with receiving something, what good will it do him if the person of the giver should be exceedingly illustrious? What difference will it make, tell me, to one who seeks to avoid a blow, whether he happens to be beaten with a wooden rod [43] or a gilded one? After all, the good does not consist in a particular kind of suffering but in not suffering at all. Since the Son, then, is proven to lack both power and wisdom when he is shown to receive something from him and by this fact already accrues the entire accusation, how is it not utterly silly that we should distract our hearers with a din of stale words and by devices of deception smear over the accusation by reckoning that no one else, but only the Father, must be admitted to be his supplier?

Furthermore, I am astounded that, though you think you are wise and well practiced at making fine distinctions with words foreign to the subject, this still escaped you: that when you disparage the imprint of God the Father, that is, the Son, you have determined to accuse not so much the Son himself as much as the one whose imprint he is, who must of necessity be however he is seen to be in the Son.

But the voice of the Son will force you, says the heterodox, to agree even against your will to what he did not disdain to say. For he himself has confessed that he does nothing on his own, but whatever he may be taught by God the Father, this he speaks.

As for you, noble sir, let even what is spoken correctly be considered incorrect, since you have denied the light of the truth. We, however, will follow our own path and set a high value on the Only Begotten, as is our custom. We will attend to the passage before us with the reverence that is appropriate in our view. If the Only Begotten had said, "I do nothing on my own, but by receiving power from God the Father I both work wonders and amaze people," even this statement would be such that it shows he should by no means be accused on its account, yet our opponent would have seemed somehow more reasonable to oppose us with it. [44] But since he says simply and absolutely, without addition, "I do nothing on my own," we will surely not say that he is accusing his own nature of being in any way weak but that he is indicating something else that is true and free from accusation.

So that we may see precisely what he is saying, we will transfer the meaning of his statement to a human example: let there be two men (having the same nature, that is) of equal strength and like-minded with each other. Then let one of them say, "On my own I do nothing." Now would he say this because he is weak or unable to do anything at all on his own or because he and the other are like-minded and agree in all things and are yoked together? It seems to me that in the case of the Son too, you should think this way, or rather in a way that far exceeds this. After all, when the Jews irrationally pounced on him as he worked miracles and accused him up and down of breaking the sabbath and charged him with breaking the law, he showed that God the Father was like-minded with him and agreed with him in all things, skillfully putting to shame the unbridled rage of the unbelievers. For it was likely that some would now shrink from wanting to accuse him since he said that he does all things in accordance with the Father's will, and he pointed out his own will in that of the Father. And the fact that the Son does everything in accordance with the Father's will proves that he is not an inferior underling but that he is of him, in him and of the same substance.

Since he is the very wisdom and living counsel of the Father, he confesses that he does nothing other than whatever the Father may will, whose wisdom and counsel he is, since even the understanding in us does nothing on its own but carries out everything that we decide to do. The example is minor in comparison with [45] the reality, but it does have an image of the truth that is not obscure. Just as the understanding in us is not considered to be something other than us, in the same way I think the wisdom of God the Father, that is, the Son, is not something other than him (I mean as far as the identity of substance and exact likeness of nature are concerned; of course, the Father is still the Father, and the Son is the Son, subsisting on their own).

When he says further, "I speak these things just as the Father taught me," let no one think that the Son needs any instruction about anything, since the absurdity of the reasoning in that thought is enormous. Instead, the force of his statement means something like the following. The Jews, who were not able to understand anything good, were not only offended when he worked miracles, but one may see them in the same condition whenever anything God-befitting was uttered. Indeed, when he said truthfully, "I am the light of the world," they were cut to the heart and thought that they needed to do audacious and terrible deeds. But our Lord Jesus Christ, in order to convict them of raging at this in vain, says that his words are those of God the Father, only he uses a more human expression: "taught."

Without subtle insight, however, we will not find the meaning of his statement. Now if the enemies of the truth should perhaps not accept what is human, they do a great injustice to the *oikonomia* with the flesh. (For the Only Begotten humbled himself, becoming human, and for this reason often speaks as a human.) Let them recognize, however, that the statement, "I speak just as the Father taught me," will in no way injure the Son, as far as his God-befitting dignity is concerned. We will show from every angle that this statement of his is sound and well-spoken.

Let that accuser of pious teaching answer us [46] as we ask, Who, tell me, teaches a newborn baby to use the human voice? Why does a baby never roar like a lion or imitate some other irrational animal? But nature, the teacher, fashions the offspring after the property of the sower, and it must and surely will proceed to that common sound to which all are accustomed. It is therefore possible to learn from nature without being taught, since the entire (so to speak) property of the sower is loaded into the offspring.

That, therefore, is the sense in which the Only Begotten himself affirmed in this passage that he learned from the Father. What nature is for us, this God the Father surely and for good reason should be understood to be for him. And just as we, since we are human beings from human beings, speak in a human fashion as we learn from nature without being taught, so also he, since he is God from God by nature, learned (so to speak) from his own nature to speak as God and to say God-befitting things, which is what "I am the light of the world" is. What he knows himself to be because he is from the Father (since he is light from light), this he said that he learned from him, since he has a kind of untaught education in God-befitting words and deeds from the property and nature of the one who begat him, just as he ascends by necessary laws to willing and saying the same as the Father in all things. How, after all, could those who have one nature not indisputably have identity in will and equality and likeness in speech?

Now this statement is surely true in the case of God, but not in our case. Divergences of customs, differences in wills and the violence of passions all drag us away from the limits of what is fitting. But the divine and incomprehensible nature, since it is always the same and [47] is fixed immovably in its own good qualities—what turn toward something else could it make? How will it not surely run straight toward its goal and both say and do what is fitting for it? Since the Only Begotten, then, is of the same substance as his begetter and preeminent in the dignities of the one divine nature, he will, no doubt, surely and necessarily do whatever the Father himself may do. This is what "doing nothing on his own" means. He will surely speak the words of the one who begat him, not as an underling or one who takes orders or a disciple but as one who possesses as a fruit of his own nature the fact that he uses the words of God the Father. By this, the statement that he says nothing on his own is made clear and distanced from all invective.

8:29 "And the one who sent me is with me, and he has not left me alone."

With this he shows clearly that he expounds the will of God the Father, since he himself has no other will than the one that is in the Father. (How could he? He himself is the living and hypostatic counsel and will of the one who begat him, according to what was said in the book of Psalms by one of the saints, "You guided me with your counsel,"[249] and again, "Lord, with your will supply power to my beauty,"[250] for all good things in Christ belong to those who love him.) Instead, he brings what is in God the Father into our knowledge. Just as for us, the word that is spoken[251] and poured forth through the tongue makes clear what is in the depth of our mind (both receiving like a kind of lesson the will in our mind regarding any given subject and impelled by it [48] to speak accordingly), so also let us reverently assume that, although he surpasses the force of this example, the Son, since he himself is both the Word and wisdom of God the Father, speaks what is in the Father. And since he is not anhypostatic, like a human word, but he really exists and lives, having his own existence in the Father and with the Father, he says here that he is not "alone," but the one who sent him is "with him."

Now when he says "with me," he is indicating something that is both God-befitting and mystical. We will certainly not imagine that he says this because the one who begat him is with him just as God might be with a prophet, let's say, that is, guarding him by his power and helping him by his favor or through enlightenment by the Spirit stirring him up to prophecy. No, in this statement he uses the phrase "with him" in a different sense. "The one who sent me," he says (that is, God the Father), has the same nature as I do.

You should understand the passage in Isaiah about Christ along the same lines: "Know, you Gentiles, and be conquered; for God is with us."[252] Although this passage could also apply to those who place their hope of salvation in him, nevertheless it says "God with us" not as though one should perhaps suppose that God will be an underling or an assistant but because he will be "with us," that is, from us. For the Word of God has become human, and by this we have all been saved. We have shattered the bonds of death, and we have stripped off the decay that comes from sin, since God the Word, who was in the form of God, has come down to us and has come to be with us. So just as [49] in this passage we understand "God with us" to mean that the Word of God the Father has come to be in the same nature as we are, so also here when Christ says, "The one who sent me is with me, and he has not left me alone," we will preserve the same correlation in our interpretation, and we will clearly take him to be mystically signifying that (as we just said before) God the Father is of the same nature as I am, "and he

[249]Ps 73:24 (Ps 72:24 LXX). [250]Ps 30:7 (Ps 29:8 LXX). [251]προφορικός. Cyril is here employing the Stoic distinction between λόγος ἐνδιάθετος (a thought in the mind) and λόγος προφορικός (a thought expressed in words), though he does not use the term ἐνδιάθετος in this passage. Patristic authors commonly use this distinction to unpack the implications of the fact that the Son is the λόγος (Word) of the Father, as Cyril does here. In his comments on Jn 1:2, Cyril opposes the way that Eunomius employed this distinction (Book 1, chapter 4, p. 20-28 above). [252]Is 8:9-10 (LXX).

has not left me alone." Indeed, it would truly have been impossible for me not to have God the Father, from whom I have been begotten, wholly with me.

And perhaps someone will ask a question out of a desire to learn and say, Why does the Savior say such things, or, what induced him to come to this explanation?

To this we shall reply, showing that, as the situation demands, he profitably adds this statement to what he already said. Since he said, "I speak these things just as the Father taught me,"[253] he now needs to show that the Father is with him and of the same substance as he is, so that he may be believed to speak his words as God speaking the words of God, impelled by the natural property of his begetter to speak what is God-befitting, just as human children have from nature a kind of untaught education, as we have said above, and truly know what belongs to human nature. One must not be offended, then, when the Son says that he learned something from the Father. For he will not for this reason be less than him, nor will he be found to be alien to him, as they claim.

Let us consider the matter further with the following reasoning. The definition of an essence is not determined by knowing or not knowing but by what each item is by nature. Take, for example, Paul and Silvanus. Let Paul know and be instructed perfectly in the mystery of Christ, but let Silvanus be somewhat less so than **[50]** Paul. Are they dissimilar, then, in nature? Will Paul surpass Silvanus as far as the principle of their nature is concerned since he knew the depth of the mystery to a greater degree than Silvanus did? No, I do not think anyone would be so foolish that they would ever imagine their natures to be different because of greater or lesser knowledge. Since, therefore, matters of substance are carefully evaluated not on the basis of learning or teaching anything, as we have said, it will do no harm to the Son, regarding the fact that he is God by nature, when he says that he learned something from his Father. He will not on that account depart from consubstantiality with him, but he remains completely what he is, that is, God from God and light from light.

But perhaps you will say, How is that? The Father is greater in knowledge, since that is why he teaches the Son. We shall respond that we have already shown with many words that the wisdom of the Father has no need of learning or teaching, and by stringing together many arguments on this point, we have repeatedly proven that their position ends up in limitless blasphemy.

Next, we need to make the following point to you as well: the Son takes special pains always to diminish his own dignity and not to speak in a way that is too God-befitting, on account of the form of a slave and the humility he took on from it for us. After all, where has he come down to, where did he come from and where did he go, if he never speaks in a lowly fashion or in a way that is not completely commensurate with God-befitting glory? That is why, you know, he is often presented[254] not knowing as man what he knows as God. You will see this clearly in the story of Lazarus of Bethany, who was dead for four days and already stinking but whom he brought back to life with miraculous power and with a most God-befitting voice. **[51]** Note, however, the *oikonomia* fashioned in this act. He knows that Lazarus has died, and he says this ahead of time, as God, to his disciples. Yet in a human way he asked, "Where have you laid him?"[255] O wondrous deed! He who lived far from Bethany and was not ignorant as God that Lazarus

[253]Jn 8:28. [254]σχηματίζεται. This verb has resonances with the Christ hymn of Phil 2. Christ is "found in form (σχήματι) as a man" (Phil 2:7), and so, according to Cyril, he is "presented" (σχηματίζεται) by the Scriptures as not knowing some things. [255]Jn 11:34.

had died—how was he asking to learn where the tomb was? Now you will say (and you are quite right) that he was feigning the question, as it were, arranging something profitable according to the *oikonomia*. In this case too, then, understand that he is speaking according to the *oikonomia* when he says that what he knows as God, he learned from the Father. In order not to permit the madness of the Jews to be stirred up further, and in order to keep the wrath of the unlearned in check, he does not present them with a purely God-befitting statement, even though it would be more fitting for him to do so.

Since they still thought he was a mere human being, he mixes, as it were, the dignity of his divine nature with words that are appropriate for a human being, and he says according to the *oikonomia*, with more moderation than his station demands, "I always do what is pleasing to him."[256] In this case too, I ask you, understand that there is a solution to what seems difficult. Observe that he is clearly and correctly interpreting the words "I do nothing on my own."[257] The reason, he says, that I testified that I do nothing on my own (when I spoke to you just now) is that my custom and practice is to do nothing out of harmony with God the Father and to intend nothing except what is pleasing to my parent. It is clear, then, that we should understand the fact that the Son does nothing on his own only in this sense: that he always does what is pleasing to God the Father, so that if he happened to do anything contrary to the will of his Father, he would have done it on his own. Therefore, he insisted in this statement that he does nothing on his own, not because he is inferior to the Father's virtue or because he is unable to accomplish anything by his own strength, **[52]** but because he is always of the same mind and will as his Father in all things, and he takes care never to do anything alone and separately, as it were.

We will certainly not sink to bizarre thoughts and imagine that the Son is exhibiting some volitional or habitual virtue in these words. No, he is instead exhibiting the fruit of an unchanging nature that does not require divine help in counseling to do anything. In the case of creatures, since they can turn toward what is inferior and yield to changes from the better to the worse, the good would be a fruit of a God-worshiping and virtue-loving will. But in the case of the substance that is divine and over all, this is not so. Since all change and turning have been removed and have no place, the good will be the fruit of an unalterable substance, just as heat in fire or cold in snow. Fire, after all, obviously does not have its proper activity in the will, but its activity is natural and essential. Fire cannot be otherwise unless it is forced into action by the will of the creator.

The Only Begotten, then, says these things not as we would. We and all other rational creatures are ruled by a choice that we make to press on to do what is pleasing to God the Father, but the Only Begotten says these things as one who is following the laws of his own nature and who does not know how to think or do anything other than what is in the will of the one who begat him. How, after all, could the consubstantial and one divine nature ever at all disagree with itself? Or how could it do anything that displeases it, as though anything had the power to turn it aside to something else? Although God the Father subsists on his own of himself, **[53]** and so too the Son and the Spirit, the holy and consubstantial Trinity will not be torn apart into complete division, but the whole fullness thereof will ascend to one nature of divinity.

We must consider this as well, that no argument could reasonably pull the Son down from his natural identity with the Father just

[256]Jn 8:29. [257]Jn 8:28.

because he maintained that he "always does what is pleasing to him," but rather, since he is consubstantial with him, this is why he will be acknowledged as God from God by nature, as well as true God. Who, tell me, will think the things of God in a God-befitting and unchanging way, except he who is by nature God? Or who could always accomplish what is pleasing to him, unless he has a nature that is beyond the reach of the worse, and he has as his possession the exceptional dignity of the divine nature, I mean being unable to sin?

Concerning creatures it has been said, "Who will boast of having a pure heart, or who will be so bold as to say they are pure from sins?"[258] And elsewhere the Scripture extends the statement to the utmost extremity, saying, "Even the stars are not pure in his sight."[259] For the angels, even though they are far removed from our condition and have a more stable position with respect to virtue, have not kept "their own position."[260] Because some of them have been completely torn from there and have fallen into sin, the entire nature of rational creatures is convicted of being receptive to sin and of being powerless to avoid sharing in the turn toward the worse. Furthermore, the rational and god-like living creature on the earth fell not after a long time but in the first Adam. Therefore, freedom from change and turning has been completely denied to creation, as well as the power to be that way by nature. That is fitting only to the one who is truly God.

But this shines forth full well in the Son. "For he committed no sin," as Paul says, [54] "nor was any deceit found in his mouth."[261] Therefore, the Son is God and by nature from God, who cannot sin or be turned or ever overstep what is fitting to his own nature. So when he confesses that he "always does what is pleasing" to the Father, let no one take offense or think that the one from the Father is inferior to the Father, but let them rather think reverently that he who is God from God by nature ascends to the same will, so to speak, and the same action as his parent.

8:30 As he was saying these things, many believed in him.

Next, the wise Evangelist marvels that Christ often employs lowly speech due to the weakness of his hearers, and he usually accomplishes something great from it. Although as God he can say anything and fashion a discourse that has free and royal authority over all, he measures his words and catches many in his net, bringing them to faith, and persuades many others to learn from him more zealously. Therefore, the Savior's practice is not in vain, I mean, that he speaks to the crowds in a more human fashion. Some of the more unlearned showed no small audacity and were prone to desert him when they saw a man but heard God-befitting words.[262] But since he was God and man in one, having without blame the authority pertaining to both and able to speak without offense in whatever way he wished, he did quite well to adapt to the frivolity of his hearers. Often and in various ways, he made statements about himself that were fitting for a human being, such as "I do nothing on my own," and related statements. Since they understood nothing at all and [55] approached the words without investigation, they went to the common meaning that the many have ready at hand, and they thought he was saying, By receiving power from God I work miracles, and, He is with me because "I always do what is pleasing to him."[263]

The accursed enemies of the truth, then, have the same mind as the unholy Jews. Opposing the dogmas of piety and loving contention, they think little of the Lord. And seizing what was said beautifully and accord-

[258]Prov 20:9. [259]Job 25:5. [260]Jude 6. [261]1 Pet 2:22. [262]See Jn 6:67. [263]Jn 8:29.

ing to the *oikonomia*, in order to destroy the glory and authority in it, they steal away the beauty of the truth. It seems they do not remember Paul, who says that we must "destroy arguments and every proud obstacle raised up against the knowledge of God, and take every thought captive" to Christ and in obedience to him.[264] And they are unaware of the statement concerning the divine oracles made by one of the prophets somewhere, "Who is wise and will understand these things? Or who is intelligent and will discover these things?"[265] If there were not some exceedingly great obscurity over the surface of the words and some deep dark veil floating over them, what would be the need of searching for a wise and intelligent person who could find the meaning of them?

But that is enough on this for now. Instead, we will take something useful from the passage before us and discuss that. Not everyone, but "many," as the Evangelist says, believed Christ as he spoke these things. Even though he is true God, and there is nothing that is not completely laid bare before his eyes, and he knows with great accuracy that he will not capture everyone and bring them to faith, yet he keeps bearing with them and lavishing long discourses on those who come to him, giving us a most beautiful [56] example by this too, and offering himself as a pattern to the teachers of the church. Even if perhaps not everyone should benefit (because of their own depravity), we must not be sluggish in leading them to what is profitable, since it is likely that some will gain motivation from it.

If we bury the talent that has been given to us, that is, the grace of the Spirit, in unfruitful silence, as it were, we will be like the wicked steward who says carelessly to the master of the house, "I knew that you were a hard man, reaping where you did not sow and gathering where you did not scatter seed, so I was afraid and buried my talent. Here you have what is yours."[266] But to what end that wretched man came, and what penalty he exacted of him, the one who is devoted to learning surely knows, having encountered it more than once in the Gospel writings. We will take this to heart, then. Let us rightly consider that the one appointed for this work should get rid of all sloth (in the task of teaching, I mean) and not look down on it in any way, even if not everyone is persuaded by his words; instead, he should rejoice in whoever he may gain by his work.

It is fitting too to consider with all sobriety the statement of our Savior, "A student is not above the teacher or a slave above their master. It is enough for a student to be like their teacher and a slave like their master."[267] Now if the Lord does not persuade everyone because of the perversity and hard-heartedness of his hearers, who will blame our speech for being feeble when it demands assent that is by choice and not by necessity? [57]

8:31 Then Jesus said to the Jews who had believed in him, "If you remain in my word, you are truly my disciples."

He demands of those who believed in him a firm and fixed disposition and a readiness to remain in the good once they have chosen it. This is what faith in him is all about. Wavering displays utter senselessness and the inability to gain profit because "a double-minded person is unstable in all their ways," as it is written.[268] But being eager to hold on to what is profitable is truly wise and most beneficial. As far as the obvious meaning is concerned, then, he says this: If they desire to obey his words, then they will surely also be called his disciples.

As far as the hidden meaning is concerned, however, he indicates this: when he says, "If

[264]2 Cor 10:4-5. [265]Hos 14:9 (Hos 14:10 LXX). [266]Mt 25:24-25. [267]Mt 10:24-25. [268]Jas 1:8.

you remain in my word," he is clearly drawing them away from the teachings of Moses gently and in an appealing way and removing them from their adherence to the letter. He is commanding them to be devoted no longer to what was said and done in type but rather to his word, which is clearly the evangelical and divine proclamation. Of course, he was also speaking to us through the holy prophets, but they were mediators, that is, those through whom he was communicating his words to us. The gospel proclamation, however, should be understood to be his word, strictly speaking, since we find that it comes to us not through another but through him. That is why, you know, the incarnate one says, "I myself am the one who speaks; I am present."[269] Paul too will give further testimony when he says in the epistle to the Hebrews, "In many and various ways, God spoke long ago **[58]** to our ancestors by the prophets, but now in these last days, he has spoken to us by his Son."[270] Thus, the Son has become the one who himself brings teaching to us in the last times of the age. For this reason, I say, the gospel teaching should be called his word strictly speaking.

It would have been fitting for him to say more nakedly, as it were, and openly, You who have received faith in me—even though you received it only recently—have nevertheless acknowledged him who is proclaimed to you from the beginning through the law and the prophets. Attach yourselves no longer to the types of Moses, and stop being convinced that you should adhere to the shadows of the law. Abandon your resolve that the power of salvation is in any way in those shadows; rather, that power is in the spiritual teachings and gospel proclamation I provide.

However, it was not unlikely, no rather it was undoubtedly the case, that after receiving the faith only just now (and that just barely) and having their mind shaken up and ready for a change, they would not have put up with such words or endured them at all, since they were prone to anger—as though the supremely wise Moses were being insulted by these words and nullified because his ancient decrees were being despised. They would easily have turned to their characteristic audacity and, ever supporting Moses, would have placed no value on the desire to believe any longer in Christ.

According to the *oikonomia*, then—albeit still obscurely—he contrasts the teachings of Moses with his own words. In other words, he cites the proclamation of the gospel over against the law and places the new teachings on a far superior level than the old, saying, "If you remain in my word, you are truly my disciples." Those who shine with a full faith, who have received the gospel teaching into their mind without hesitation, **[59]** who do not think too highly of the shadow of the law—they are truly disciples of Christ. But those who do not come to him in this way mock themselves. They cannot truly be his disciples, and for this reason they have fallen away from salvation. And so the blessed Paul writes explicitly to those who foolishly want to be justified by the law after faith, "You have been cut off from Christ, you who want to be justified by the law; you have fallen away from grace."[271] Single-minded faith, then, is marvelous and precious, as is the desire to follow Christ closely. These things pull us from the shadows of the law into the knowledge of him and transform what was said enigmatically into spiritual instruction. That is because the mystery about him is proclaimed through the law and the prophets.

8:32 "And you will know the truth, and the truth will set you free."

This statement is still obscure and not very clear, but it labors to give birth to the same

[269]Is 52:6. [270]Heb 1:1. [271]Gal 5:4.

meaning as the previous one, and though it is put together in a different way, it will take us through the same considerations. It too persuades them, once they have believed, gladly to rise up and leave the worship of the law. And instructing them that the shadow leads to knowledge of him, it persuades them to leave types and enigmas behind and proceed resolutely to the truth itself, that is, Christ the redeemer and the giver of true freedom. "You will know the truth," he says, as you remain in my words, and from knowing the truth, you will find the benefit that comes from it.

Understand, then, I ask you, that our Lord is saying something like this to the Jews (since I think it is necessary to expand the meaning in the passage for the benefit of the readers): You endured bitter slavery in Egypt, he says, **[60]** and heavy labor consumed you when you had gone into bondage under Pharaoh. But you cried out at that time to God, and you moved him to have mercy on you. You lamented the misfortunes that were on you, and you sought a redeemer from heaven. Then I visited you right away, and I brought you out of an alien land. I rescued you from the most savage tyranny, and I called you to freedom. I portrayed for you my mystery in the slaughter of the sheep in order that you might learn of your helper and redeemer, and I commanded it at that time to prefigure the salvation through blood. For you were saved by anointing both yourselves and the lintels with the blood of the lamb.[272] Therefore, when you have advanced a little ways beyond the types, when you know the truth, you will surely and truly be free. And let no one doubt this, he says. If the ancient type bestowed such blessings on you, how will the truth not grant an even richer grace?

Nothing prevents us from supposing that Jesus is saying something like that to the Jews, with his statement broadening into a wider meaning. It is likely, however, that some other sense as well shines forth to us from this passage. The law of Moses prescribed baptisms and sprinklings, but to the one who happened to be captured and to fall into the pit of sin, it commanded the sacrifice of a young bull or a sheep to take away the blame for each one's sin.[273] But these are of no use for washing away sin. They could never free the condemned from blame or release those who have trampled the divine law from having to be punished. What good will the sacrifice of oxen do for a transgressor? What profit could one find in **[61]** the slaughter of sheep? Which of these will be pleasing to God when he is insulted, as far as the transgression of the law is concerned?

Hear him say, "Do I eat the flesh or bulls or drink the blood of goats?"[274] He also says clearly to the Jews, "Gather together your whole burnt offerings and your sacrifices and eat flesh, for I did not speak to your ancestors about whole burnt offerings and sacrifices, but I gave them this command: Judge with a just judgment."[275] It is completely useless, then, to approach through blood. That cannot wash away the stain ground into a person from sin. He will confirm this again when you see him saying to Jerusalem, the mother of the Jews, through the voice of Jeremiah, "Why did my beloved commit abominations in my house? Will prayers and holy flesh remove your evil from you? Will you escape through these?"[276] "For it is impossible for the blood of bulls and goats to take away sins," as Paul says.[277] But because they were concerned with vain worship and hurried to perform their profitless approaches [to the altar] through blood or their gifts, they were for good reason expelled from the divine court. He will teach us this clearly also through the voice of Isaiah: "You shall no longer trample my court. If you bring fine flour, it is vain. Incense is an abomination to me."[278]

[272]Ex 12:7. [273]Lev 4–5. [274]Ps 50:13 (Ps 49:13 LXX). [275]Jer 7:21-23. [276]Jer 11:15. [277]Heb 10:4. [278]Is 1:12-13.

True salvation, then, is not in them (in the ordinances of the law, I mean). Nor could one gain from there the thrice longed-for freedom (from sin, I mean). But when we leap just above the types and focus on the beauty of worship in the spirit and recognize "the truth," that is, Christ, we are justified through faith in him. [62] And when we are justified, we pass over to true freedom, no longer ranked as slaves, as we were before, but as children of God. John testifies to this when he says about Christ and those who believe in him, "As many as received him, to them he gave the power to become children of God."[279] Profitably, then, our Lord and Christ does not allow those who believe in him to continue marveling at the shadows in the law (since there is nothing in them that is helpful or that bestows true freedom); instead, he tells them to know "the truth." For through this, he says, they will be entirely freed, according to the meaning of his words.

8:33 "We are Abraham's seed, and we have never been slaves to anyone. How can you say, 'You will be made free'?"

Next they laugh at our Savior's promise, or rather, they are angry with him because they feel insulted. After all, how could we who have no share of slavery, they say, need someone to call us to freedom and to supplement us with what we already have? They are unaware, though they are accustomed to think they are wise, that their forefather Abraham did not come from a father who was notable in the eyes of the world, nor was he the most renowned among those who are admired in this life, but he was made illustrious only through faith in God. "Abraham believed God," it says, "and his faith was reckoned to him as righteousness, and he was called the friend of God."[280] You see then quite clearly the cause of the glory that is in him. Since he has been called the friend of the almighty God, he has for this reason become great [63] and famous. His faith was reckoned to him as righteousness, and the righteousness of faith has become his basis for freedom before God. Therefore, when he was justified by believing, that is, when he shook off the low birth that is from sin, then he shone forth illustrious, noble and free. Foolishly, then, the Jews reject the grace that frees the very founder of their race and advance only to the one who was freed by it. But considering neither where his glory comes from nor where it looks to, they dishonor the bestower of what is most excellent in him. Though they have forsaken the fount of all nobility, they think highly of the one who participates in this fount.

They will also be caught boasting in vain that they have never been slaves to anyone, and their statement about this will no less be proven false. After all, they were slaves to the Egyptians for 430 years, and by the grace from above they were just barely brought out from the house of bondage and from the iron furnace, as it is written,[281] that is, from the oppression of the Egyptians. They were also slaves to the Babylonians and the Assyrians when they picked up the whole country of the Jews and Jerusalem itself and transferred Israel completely to their own country. In no respect, then, is the statement of the Jews sound. In addition to being ignorant of their truer slavery, I mean sin, they completely deny the other lower slavery and have a mind that is accustomed to think highly of nothing.

8:34 The Savior answered them, "Truly, truly, I say to you, whoever commits sin is a slave to sin."

He lifts those who are carnal and looking only at [64] corporeal matters out of their ignorance and leads them to more spiritual matters. He

[279]Jn 1:12. [280]Jas 2:23. [281]Deut 4:20.

transports them to a completely fresh and unexpected teaching, as it were, pointing out the hidden slavery that they were unaware of for a long time. He wisely passes by the fact that they are lying when they say, "We have never been slaves to anyone,"[282] and he does not mention that they boast in vain about the nobility of their forefather, so that he does not seem to incite those who are already prone and much inclined to anger to do what is not right.

He proceeds, as it were, to what is necessary and what they really need to learn. He says that whoever commits sin is "a slave to sin." He is basically saying this: A human being, my friends, is a composite animal on the earth, composed, namely, of soul and body. Fleshly slavery pertains to the flesh, while that which is in the soul and is inflicted on the soul has sin as its barbarian mother. So the power of rulers will procure someone's release from fleshly slavery, but freeing from sin should fittingly be attributed to God alone; it attaches to no one else. Therefore, he persuades them to think reasonably and to desire real and true freedom, and thus to seek not for the glory of their ancestor, which profits nothing on this issue, but to seek God alone, who rules over his own law. The transgression of that law creates sin, which is the one who rears up slavery in the soul.

But our Lord Jesus Christ seems to be convicting them—still subtly and in a very veiled way—of thinking highly of a man and of supposing that the blessed Abraham was altogether free. By showing more generally that everyone who "commits **[65]** sin is a slave to sin," he puts Abraham himself in the snare as a slave to sin at one time. After all, he was justified not as one who was righteous but as one who was called to the freedom of being justified when he believed God. We say this not at all to be contentious about the glory of that righteous man but because there is no human being who has not experienced the dart of sin. Even the one reputed to be great surely bore the yoke of sin. As it is written, "There is no one righteous, for all have sinned and fall short of the glory of God."[283] But the glory of God, in addition to other things, is to be utterly unable to fall into sin, which of course is reserved for Christ alone. For he alone has become "free among the dead"[284] since he committed no sin, even though he came to be among the dead, that is, he was classified with human beings, over whom the death of sin once had mastery.

Therefore (since I will summarize the main point of the statement), the Lord was hinting that the blessed Abraham himself, who was once enslaved to sin and was set free through faith alone in Christ, was not sufficient to pass on this spiritual nobility to others, since he is not authorized with the power to free others when he did not on his own put off the slavery of sin. Nor did he bestow freedom on himself; he received it from another, namely, from Christ himself, who justifies. **[66]**

8:35 "The slave does not remain in the house forever. The son remains forever."

After showing that the one who is subject to sin is not free but under bitter slavery, he profitably adds what will happen to the one who has loved slavery, and conversely, what will come from God to the one who has chosen to live lawfully and for this reason has been ranked among the children of God. "The slave," he says, "does not remain in the house forever." In fact, the slave will rush off into outer darkness, there to pay the penalty for a life without freedom. "The son," by contrast, "remains forever." Once they have enjoyed the glory of adoption, they will remain in the presence of God. At no time will they be cast out of the court of those who are firstborn;

[282]Jn 8:33. [283]Rom 3:10, 23. [284]Ps 88:4 (Ps 87:5 LXX).

rather, they will live there for a long, unending time.

You will understand his statement accurately if you propose that the parable in the Gospels be read in which Christ, it says, will stand the goats on his left and the sheep on his right and will send the goats away, saying, "Depart, you cursed, into the eternal fire prepared for the devil and his angels."[285] But he will gather the sheep to himself and will gladly receive them, crying out, "Come, you who are blessed by my Father, inherit the kingdom prepared for you from the foundation of the world."[286] By goats, he means the fruitless multitude of those who love sin, while by sheep, he means the choir of the pious, laden with the fruit of righteousness as with wool. Thus, the one who bears the disgrace of slavery will be cast out of the kingdom of heaven like **[67]** a useless and utterly menial vessel,[287] while everyone who cherishes living rightly and thus has been ranked among the children of God will be received and remain in it.

It is likely that in saying these things, the Lord is also hinting to them that those who have no concern for the freedom that is by faith will undoubtedly leave the holy and divine court, that is, the church. As one of the prophets says, "I will throw them out of my house."[288] The very nature of events testifies that what was announced beforehand about them has reached its fulfillment. "For the daughter of Zion was left like a tent in the vineyard, like a storehouse in a cucumber field," as it is written.[289] The temple has fallen and has been completely pulled down, and those who did not "remain" in it "forever" have gone out. In its place the church of the Gentiles has gone up and been raised up, as it were, because of Christ. Those who have been called through faith to divine adoption remain forever in it. And the boast of the church will never end or cease because the souls of the righteous are leaving earthly matters behind and sailing to the city above, the heavenly Jerusalem, the church of the firstborn "who is our mother," as Paul says.[290]

When we examined the statement about slavery and were eager to track down the truth by every means, we said that Abraham himself was numbered among the slaves, excluding not even him from the limits of our contemplation because of Christ's general statement, "Everyone who commits sin is a slave to sin."[291] Come, then, and let us follow up on our own words and **[68]** explain the force of what has been said.

The Jews were being conceited and puffed up, putting forward Abraham as a kind of head and fount of their own nobility. But the idea that they ought to seek the freedom that comes by grace from above did not even enter their minds. They were "blind fools," as the Savior says.[292] Christ, then, wants to show them, as the occasion demands, that something that is a slave by nature is not adequate to free others or even itself. How will that which lacks freedom, as far as its nature is concerned, grant freedom to itself? And that which borrows grace for itself from another—how could it be sufficient to give grace to others? The power to set free will be appropriately ascribed and belong only to him who is God from God by nature. He gives clear proof, then, that everything that does not "remain forever," that is, everything that does not remain always the same, must be and be acknowledged to be a slave. Everything that comes into being will surely also be subject to decay. And whatever is this way will be a slave, namely, a slave of God who has called it into existence, since it was said to him concerning creatures, "All things are your slaves."[293] The statement about this is general, but the one part belongs to the whole, that is, the

[285]Mt 25:41. [286]Mt 25:34. [287]See Rom 9:21. [288]Hos 9:15. [289]Is 1:8. [290]Gal 4:26. [291]Jn 8:34. [292]Mt 23:17. [293]Ps 119:91 (Ps 118:91 LXX).

blessed Abraham and humanity in general. But the property of remaining forever gives a clear sign that the only begotten God who shines forth from God is king and Lord of all. After all, who else could remain always the same and establish himself in the constancy of eternal things, except the one who is God by nature?

In this way, the divine psalmist too showed us that creation is a slave, but God the Word, who shone forth from God the Father, is king and Lord. Extending his thought from a part to the whole of creation, he says of both **[69]** the heavens and the natural Son respectively, "They will perish, but you remain. They will all wear out like a garment; you will change them like a cloak, and they will be changed. But you are the same, and your years will have no end."[294] Do you see how it is true quite beautifully and harmoniously also in these passages that the slave "does not remain forever, but the Son remains," and that "not remaining" is a proof that whatever receives that attribute is a slave? Analogously the other part, that is, "remaining forever," would be a clear sign that whoever is truly and strictly speaking the subject of these words is Lord and God.

Now the psalmist was sufficient to testify on behalf of our words. But since, as it is written, "every matter shall be established by the mouth of two or three witnesses,"[295] let us show that, in addition, the blessed Jeremiah too thinks and speaks in harmony with these ideas. From the fact that every created thing decays, he shows that it is therefore a slave. And from the fact that he remains and is unchangeable, the Son shows himself to be God by nature, and it is clear that he is therefore also Lord. Jeremiah says somewhere to him, "You sit forever, and we perish forever."[296] That is because at every moment, that which comes into being will be perishable, at least by virtue of being made, even if by the power of God it should not perish; but God will sit forever. The sitting mentioned here suggests the stability and unchanging permanency of his substance together with its concentration, and his magnificence in royal form and reality. For the act of sitting depicts these things.

Therefore (since I will return to the beginning), from the fact that the blessed Abraham does "not remain forever" he shows that he is corruptible and originate. **[70]** He died, after all and in a way departed from his Lord's house, that is, this world. Correspondingly from this, he wants him to be understood to be a slave, not having sufficient power to grace others with freedom. From the fact that the Son "remains forever," however, he now says clearly that he is God from God by nature. And it would surely follow from this that he is king and Lord. What is planned in the *oikonomia* from the distinction we just mentioned will be shown clearly in the passage that follows.

8:36 "If the Son makes you free, you will be free indeed."

The power to make free belongs only, he says, to the Son by nature, the one who is truly free and removed from all slavery, and to no one else at all besides him. Since he is by nature wisdom and light and power, he makes wise what can receive wisdom, he enlightens what needs light, and he empowers what lacks power. In the same way, since he is God from God, the genuine and free fruit of the substance that rules over all, he supplies freedom to whomever he wishes. Now no one could become truly free from the one who does not have freedom by nature. But when the Son himself wills to "make them free" by implanting his own good quality,[297] they will be called "free indeed," since they received that dignity from the one who has the power to give it, and

[294]Ps 102:26-27 (Ps 101:27-28 LXX). [295]2 Cor 13:1. [296]Bar 3:3. [297]Namely, the quality of freedom.

not from one of those who borrow from another and are enlightened, so to speak, by foreign graces.

The preceding explanation is most necessary, then, and those who are eager to pay studious attention to this distinction will derive great profit from it. Such a distinction was necessary [71] for us to understand where we must seek divine nobility and to learn that the one who has the power to make us free is indeed the Son. Let those who rejoice in worldly honors take care not to be puffed up by arrogant thoughts, and let them not run down the glory and grace of the saints, even though some are insignificant and come from insignificant parents according to the flesh. Seeming to be illustrious in human eyes is not sufficient for nobility before God; rather, a well-adorned life and virtuous conduct render a person "free indeed" and noble. "Joseph was sold as a slave," as it is written,[298] but even so he was free, radiant with the nobility of his soul. Esau, by contrast, was born of a free father and was free, but by the shamefulness of his conduct he demonstrated a mind fit for a slave. Therefore, the ones who are noble before God, as we just said, are not those who have riches and are flooded with a superabundance of possessions and delight in the splendid honors of the world but those who are illustrious in holy life and lawful conduct.

8:37 "I know that you are Abraham's seed, but you are trying to kill me because my word finds no place in you."

After showing them in various ways that their boastful attitude based on their kinship to Abraham is utterly empty and useless, he says this so they may seek the true nobility that is dear to God. For God does not look at the flesh. As Christ our Savior himself says, "The flesh profits nothing."[299] Instead, he accepts the nobility of soul and counts it praiseworthy. And he recognizes that people have true kinship when the similarity of their deeds or the identity of their conduct gathers them together into one virtue, as it were, [72] and gives them an august reputation by the visible equality of their good deeds. Correspondingly, the opposite is true as well. After all, how else are we who are from the earth and "formed from clay," as it is written,[300] said to be from the Lord of all, as when Paul says, "We are God's offspring"?[301] Everyone agrees that we have become related to him due to the flesh in the mystery of Christ, but it is possible to see that this is true in another way as well. When we think his thoughts and resolve in no cursory manner to live piously, we will be called children of God, who is over all. And when we shape our mind to his will, as far as possible, this is how we are truly related to his likeness and most exact image.

We will clearly recognize that God takes the likeness and exact image of works and conduct to have the force of being related by family when we closely examine the holy words and inspect the Holy Scripture. In the time of Jeremiah the prophet, there arose a certain false prophet, by the name of Shemaiah of Nehelam,[302] who belched forth things from his own heart, as it is written, and not from the mouth of the Lord.[303] Since there was a great multitude of other false witnesses and false prophets wandering among the crowds and drawing them away to what is not right, God the Lord of all finally became angry, and rightfully so. So after expending many words on Shemaiah and declaring in more detail what penalty he would pay for this audacity, he finally adds, "I will punish Shemaiah and his family, those who do deeds similar to his."[304] Do you hear how [73] he

[298]Ps 105:17 (Ps 104:17 LXX). [299]Jn 6:63. [300]Job 33:6. [301]Acts 17:29. [302]Jer 29:24 (Jer 36:24 LXX). [303]Jer 23:16. [304]Jer 29:32 (Jer 36:32 LXX). It is not clear where Cyril gets the words "those who do deeds similar to his," but he later claims they are in the text.

sees the fact of being related in similar works? How could the just judge have punished Shemaiah's fleshly family along with him, even though they do not behave like him (at least as far as evil is concerned), despite the clear statement in the prophet Ezekiel, "The soul that sins will die"?[305] Therefore, in order that such a thing may not be understood of God, as soon as he mentioned "family" he immediately added, "those who do deeds similar to his," thus defining being related in terms of identity of actions.

In order to see that the statement is true also of the Jews themselves, we recall the words of John, I mean the holy Baptist. To show them that their boast of being related to Abraham is stale, he says, "Do not say among yourselves, 'We have Abraham as our father,' for God is able from these stones to raise up offspring for Abraham."[306] Since God said to him, "I will multiply your offspring as the stars of heaven,"[307] the people of the Jews, relying on the utter inability of the promiser to lie, grew arrogant and expected that they would never fall away at all from being related to their ancestor, in order that the divine promise might be kept, it says. But the blessed Baptist obliterates this hope of theirs when he states clearly that God is able "from these stones to raise up children for Abraham."[308] The blessed Paul agrees with this too when he says this: "For not all who are descended from Israel belong to Israel, and not all are the children of Abraham because they are his descendants."[309] Since, then, it is shown to be true on all sides that God recognizes kinship in terms of manner and behavior, it is clearly vain to boast in holy and good ancestors while falling short of and being far removed from their virtue.

That is why the Lord says to the Jews, with good reason, [74] "I know that you are Abraham's seed, but you are trying to kill me because my word finds no place in you." Yes, he says, when I look only at the flesh and I examine where the people of the Jews sprang from, then I too see that you have come from the seed of Abraham. But when I consider the beauty of his behavior and attitude, I see that you are foreigners and no longer related, he says. "You are trying to kill me," after all, even though your forefather, in whom you now boast, was no murderer. And what is worse and most lawless of all, I am persecuted by you for no good reason. Indeed, you are utterly unjust in your desire to kill me. For this reason alone you plotted to do away with me: "because my word finds no place in you," even though it was calling you to salvation and life. "It finds no place in you" because of the sin that has dwelt within you and has left no place, as it were, for being advised and exhorted to do good. The Jews, then, are all alike murderers and utterly unjust judges, since they decree that he is worthy of death who has done nothing wrong, or rather, who is determined to help and zealous to save them. How then are they still related to the righteous and good Abraham, when they are just as far from the good that is in him and when they have strayed just as far from imitating his conduct as vice is removed and separated from virtue, as anyone would grant?

8:38 "I speak what I have seen with my Father. As for you, do what you have heard from your Father."

He said that the word coming from him had no place among the Jews, and he explained that for this one reason they were incited against him, or rather, he convicted them of wanting to kill him. [75] He adds these thoughts as well out of necessity, and next I will explain why. He was not unaware, it seems, that some of the Jews would rise up and oppose his

[305]Ezek 18:4. [306]Mt 3:9. [307]Gen 22:17. [308]Mt 3:9. [309]Rom 9:6-7.

words, that they would belch forth the madness that is in them and say, Some people do want to kill you, but it is not in vain (as you claim). There are good reasons that they feel compelled to do this. Their motives are pious, and their zeal contains nothing that can be justly accused. Your word has no place in them because you made it dissonant with God. You teach us another error, he says, and you draw us away from the way of the law and lead us to what seems right to you alone.

As the Jews are surely whispering these ideas in secret or thinking them to themselves, the Lord replies to them because he knows the thought processes in their hearts. Therefore, he says, "I speak what I have seen with my Father." I have closely examined the nature of my Father. I have often seen of myself and in myself the one who begat me, and I have become a beholder of his will. I have seen (through innate knowledge, that is) what works he loves, and these are what I am speaking to you. I will be found to say nothing at all that is dissonant, nor have I commanded anything other than what is pleasing to him. I have been earnest in calling my hearers to those things. In so doing, I did not depart from what is mine (since what is his is in me; and what is mine is in him). But if I seem false to you and I am thought to lead you astray from the divine teachings—even though I am this way by nature and I agree with God the Father in all things—let the charge be dismissed and cast away your suspicion. "Do what you have heard from your Father." He has spoken to you through Moses. Fulfill his command. You heard him say, "You shall not slay the innocent and righteous."[310] How then [76] are you "trying to kill me," in violation of the Father's command?

But we can take "do what you have heard from your Father" in another way as well. He has spoken to you through the prophets,[311] he says. You heard him say, "Rejoice greatly, O daughter of Zion; proclaim it aloud, O daughter of Jerusalem. Behold, your king comes to you, righteous and having salvation, riding a colt the foal of a donkey,"[312] and again through the voice of Isaiah, "Get up to a high mountain, you who bring good news to Zion; lift up your voice with a shout, you who bring good news to Jerusalem. Lift it up, do not be afraid! Behold, your God. Behold, the Lord is coming with strength, and his arm with power. Behold, his reward is with him, and his work is before him. Like a shepherd he will feed his flock, and with his arm he will gather the lambs, and he will comfort those who are with child."[313] Obey, then, the Father's commands and receive the one who is announced beforehand. Honor by faith the one who has been proclaimed ahead of time. Let at least the Father's words have sway in you.

He says that one must realize that the law belongs to God the Father, even though it was spoken by him through messengers. With this statement, he does not exclude himself from the giving of the law, but he yields to the assumptions of the Jews, who believe that is how it is, and he does not fight against their assumption due to the *oikonomia*. He often shamed them, when they did not receive him, by bringing up the Father's name.

8:39 They answered and said to him, "Our father is Abraham."

How ignorant can they be—with minds withered into unbelief and looking only for a fight! Though Christ our Savior agrees [77] and clearly says, "I know that you are Abraham's seed,"[314] they still persist along this train of thought. As though someone were arguing and opposing them and saying that they are not from the seed of Abraham according to the flesh, they say again, "Our father is Abraham."

[310]Ex 23:7. [311]See Heb 1:1. [312]Zech 9:9. [313]Is 40:9-11. [314]Jn 8:37.

And they do not blush to repeat the same words over and over. Perhaps they think they ought not yield to Battus,[315] although they are outstanding emulators of that man's babble.

Maybe, however, they have a preposterous pretext for this, and next we will discuss what that is. When the Lord said, "I speak what I have seen with my Father,"[316] they did not understand that he was referring to God the Father. Instead, they thought he was talking about either the righteous Joseph or some other earthly man, since they were ridiculing him and holding him in very low esteem. The holy virgin conceived the divine infant not by marital intercourse but "by the Holy Spirit," as it is written.[317] And being ignorant at first of the way of the *oikonomia*, the blessed Joseph "planned to divorce her quietly," as Matthew says.[318] It was not completely unknown to the Jews, however, that the holy virgin conceived before marriage and intercourse; yet they certainly did not know that it was by the Holy Spirit. They thought that she was corrupted by one of the Gentiles. Thus, they had no right understanding of Christ. Some thought, in their senselessness, that he was begotten as the child of another father who had corrupted the holy virgin, while others chalked him up to being merely a bastard son to Joseph, not a true son. So when he says, "I speak what I have seen with my Father,"[319] they were not in any way thinking of God; instead, they took it that he was referring to some earthly father. [78]

They imagined that he was trying to move them away from honoring their ancestor, and they suspected that he was ascribing the honor due to another—even the most ancient honor of the patriarchate—to his own family. So they answer him in a contentious and vehement manner, saying, "Abraham is our father." It is as though they were saying, Even if you drench us with wise words, sir, even if you make our ears ring with your extraordinary miracles and hit us hard with mighty deeds beyond our understanding, you still will not displace us from our ancient boast. We will not register your father as the founder of our race. We will not ascribe that glory to another, nor will we take new founders of the race in exchange for the old ones.

It is no wonder, and it is no stretch to believe, that the Jews fell into such foolishness, since they supposed that he was a mere man, and they called him "the carpenter's son,"[320] disparaging him in many ways and ranking the king and Lord of all as a nobody. We will see quite clearly in what follows that they had no right conception of the holy virgin, thinking that she was defiled by someone.

8:39-40 Jesus says to them, "If you were the children of Abraham, you would do what Abraham did. But as it is, you are trying to kill me, a man who has spoken the truth to you which I heard from God. This Abraham did not do."

In order to soothe the rashness of the Jews by every way and word, so to speak, Christ addresses them in a veiled way, not offering an open reproach but one mixed with gentle words, in various and subdued ways charming their wrath. But when he sees that they are completely senseless and understand nothing of what he is saying, he then frees his words from the veil and strips off all covering. You must, he says—if [79] you believe that being classified as "children of Abraham" is the highest honor—you must be eager to imitate his ways. You must follow in the footsteps of your ancestor's admirable virtue. You must also love and emulate his obedience. He heard God saying, "Depart from your land and from

[315]Battus means "Stammerer." It was the name of a king of Cyrenê and forms the basis of the New Testament term βατταλογέω, which means "babble" (Mt 6:7). [316]Jn 8:38. [317]Mt 1:18. [318]Mt 1:19. [319]Jn 8:38. [320]Mt 13:55.

your kindred, and come into a land that I will show you."[321] Without any delay in carrying out what was decreed, he immediately left his country and arrived at a foreign land that he did not know, relying on the mercy of the one who ordered him to go. And when he had reached the finish line of life, so to speak, and had lived to his hundredth year, he heard, "You will have seed."[322] Without hesitation, he placed fervent faith in the one who was speaking, paying no attention to the weakness of the flesh but recognizing the power of the one who declared this. He heard that he was to offer his beloved son as a sacrifice to God, and he immediately prevailed over his natural desires and subordinated his love for the young man to the divine command. I find the complete opposite of this behavior in you. "For you are trying to kill me," he says, "because I have spoken to you things from God. This Abraham did not do." He did not insult the one speaking to him with unbelief. He did not try to do anything that would grieve him. How then are you still "children of Abraham," since you have departed as far from his love for God as the difference in your actions indicates?

Observe how he arranges his statement. He does not say here that he has heard the truth "from the Father" but "from God," since, as we just said, they were dragged down by their immeasurable foolishness to untrue conceptions about him. They thought that he was speaking of some earthly father. He also does exceedingly well to call himself "man" when he is talking about dying. **[80]** Thereby, he completely preserves his incorruptibility as God by nature, yet he does not separate his temple from himself but exists as one Son, even when he has become a man. And so he says that he has spoken "the truth," since the Savior's statement teaches us to practice piety no longer in types and figures; instead, it persuades us to love true and spiritual worship.

Now when he says "which I heard from the Father," we should by no means be offended. Since he says that he is a "man," he speaks in a way that is fitting for men. As he is said to die as man, so also let him be said to "hear" as man. It is likely, however, that by "hearing" he means his inherent knowledge of the will of his progenitor. After all, it is the custom of the divinely inspired Scriptures themselves often to speak this way about God. When it says "and the Lord heard,"[323] we will in no way ascribe to him a separate sense of hearing that belongs to him, as is the case among us. That is because the divine nature is simple and free from all composition. Rather, we will take hearing as knowledge and knowledge as hearing. There is nothing compound in what is simple, as we have said.

We will also offer a third explanation of these words, not departing from our fitting goal. God the Father said somewhere to the most holy Moses concerning Christ, "I will raise up for them," that is, for the Israelites, "a prophet like you from among their brothers, and I will put my words in his mouth, and he will speak to them everything that I command him."[324] For this reason, I think, our Lord Jesus Christ says that he heard the truth from the Father and spoke it to the Jews, at the same time convicting them of fighting against God the Father himself and **[81]** showing clearly that he is the one whom the lawgiver promised before to raise up for them.

8:41 "You do the deeds of your father."

After he has shown that the Jews are completely different in their behavior from the founder of their race, and far removed from his love for God, he rightly strips off their idle fleshly boast. After explicitly stating that they should not be classified as his children, he

[321]Gen 12:1. [322]Gen 15:4-5. [323]Mal 3:16, for example. [324]Deut 18:18.

assigns them to another father like them, and he defines the likeness of deeds as a kind of family bond, teaching that those of good disposition should be joined with the good and declaring that those who live wickedly ought to have as fathers those who have been condemned for the same things. Just as those who have chosen to live excellently (and for this reason are even now called saints) can call God their Father without danger since they are eager to imitate him—as far as this is possible for human beings—so also the evil one would rightly be registered as the father of evil people since they form the image of his wickedness and perversity in their way of life.

The one who begets from himself is not the only one considered a father by the divine Scriptures; the one who has anybody conformed to his own conduct is also considered a father. He is for that reason said to be their father. Thus the divine Paul too writes to certain people, "I have begotten you in Christ Jesus through the gospel."[325] Therefore, just as some are conformed both to God and to the holy fathers through the similarity and holiness of their conduct (as we said), so also some are rendered like-minded both with the devil and with those who live like him, suffering this because of their own depravity. **[82]** The saints are fathers to the saints, while the wicked go[326] with the wicked, as is most fitting. Those who in holiness receive the divine impression, so to speak, in their souls and who have the boldness that befits children will for good reason say, "Our Father, who art in heaven."[327] The wicked, however, will be placed with the father who is like them, begotten, as it were, through likeness to him into the same depravity. That is why Christ defines and names another father for the Jews besides the holy Abraham. Who this is, he does not yet explicitly say.

Then they said to him, "We are not born of fornication! We have one father, God."
I have already said that the audacious Jews were prone to succumbing to the disease of bitter and unholy conceptions about Christ the Savior.[328] They thought that the holy virgin, I mean the mother of the Lord, had been defiled and that she was found to be pregnant not by the Holy Spirit or by power from above but by someone earthly. They did not believe and had absolutely no understanding. They either had no regard for the prophetic writings (even though they heard explicitly, "Behold, the virgin will conceive and bear a son"),[329] or they looked only to the flesh and followed the order of events usually with us and did not think of the nature that works beyond reason, for which nothing is difficult and everything it decides is easy. And so they thought that there is no other way a woman can become pregnant than by coming together and having intercourse with a man. Sick with such a supposition, the wretches dared to slander the birth through the Spirit of the divine and **[83]** wondrous offspring. Since he excludes them from being related to Abraham and assigns them to another father, they are livid, and the anger in them foams up without restraint. They rail at him, saying, "We are not born of fornication! We have one father, God." In a veiled way, they are saying something like this: You have two fathers, and you were not born of an honorable marriage. We, however, have one father, God.

But one ought to look and examine carefully what foolishness they are suffering from in this statement as well. Because of their own wickedness and depravity, the just judge does not count them even among Abraham's children. Yet they advance to such a point of madness that they call God their father, perhaps because of the statement in the books of Moses, "Israel is my firstborn,"[330] but they

[325]1 Cor 4:15. [326]τρεπόμενοι. There is a lacuna in one manuscript, so the text is uncertain. [327]Mt 6:9. [328]See pp. 360-61 above. [329]Is 7:14. [330]Ex 4:22.

pay no attention to what was said through the voice of Isaiah, "Woe to apostate children, says the Lord."[331]

One may reasonably ask what it was that now induced the Jews to say no longer, "Our father is Abraham," or, "We have one father, Abraham," but to go straight up to "one God." It seems to me that they were thinking something like this. When they insinuated with their railing against the Lord that his mother had been defiled before her marriage, they ascribed to him two fathers, so they had to try to claim the title of one as a kind of accomplice to their malice toward him. With the same words by which they insist that they have "one father, God," they obliquely reproach the Lord for having two, placing the two over against the one, as it were. They were calculating that if they said they have one father, Abraham, they would be completely denying the others, I mean Isaac and Jacob and his twelve sons. If they did that, they would then seem to be **[84]** arming against themselves and fighting against their own boast and intentions by alienating Israel from the nobility of the fathers. Thus in the end, they would seem to be going along with the Lord's statement. Fleeing, then, the damage that appears to accrue to them from this, they no longer say, "We have one father, Abraham," but they ascribe to themselves "one father, God." They are so enchanted by the treacherous pleasures of their ranting that they stumble into even greater blame, as they who are artisans of impiety dare to claim as a father him who is the enemy of all impiety.

8:42 Jesus said to them, "If God were your father, you would love me, for I came from God and now I am here."

With these words, the Lord does not take away the power of any to be ranked as the children of God;[332] instead, he shows to whom that boast would properly belong, and he shows that it will be found especially to belong to the saints. He also convicts the insolent Jew of being especially senseless. I came forth, he says, as the one true natural Son (of God the Father, that is). All others are counted as children because they are conformed to me and ascend to my glory, for images are always patterned after their archetypes. How then, he says, can you be numbered among the children of God at all, since you do not believe in him who sprang from God and who molds people into his form? Not only do you not love him, but you even dishonor him, not in one way but in many. And those who have not received the imprint of God the Father—how could they at all be conformed to him? Above all, he says, not just anyone can without blame call God their father. That belongs only to those whose excellent piety toward him flashes like lightning, and to no one **[85]** else. I have come from heaven to counsel you in excellent matters, and my word calls you to be conformed to God. If you really had a serious desire to have God as your father, surely you would also have loved me, your guide and teacher on that path, the one who gives you the opportunity to be like the one true Son, the one who takes those who receive him and conforms them to himself through the Holy Spirit. In sum, he says, how could those who boast that they belong to God's household not love him who came from God? How, tell me, will they honor the tree who loathe the fruit that is begotten of it? "Either," he says, "make the tree good and its fruit good, or make the tree bad and its fruit bad."[333] If therefore the tree (that is, God the Father) is noble and you know how to siphon his splendor onto your own heads, why did you not love his fruit, believing it to be like him?

This passage, then, has a bitter reproof of the Jews (since it shows them to be liars, for when they try to call God their father, they are

[331] Is 30:1. [332] See Jn 1:12. [333] Mt 12:33.

very far removed from the virtue of those who are called to this because they do not love the one who is from God by nature). At the same time it profitably makes mention of the ineffable birth so that they may be caught in their impiety by this statement as well, when they call him a lowborn bastard. Now if the words "I came from God" indicate his ineffable and timeless birth from the Father, then by adding "now I am here," he is indicating his entrance into this world with the flesh. One would surely not say that God the Word first beamed forth from God the Father **[86]** when he became human (for this is what some of the unholy heretics thought). Instead, they will rather take the statement in a fitting way and understand it reverently. Just because he joined the phrases (I mean "I came" and "now I am here"), that certainly does not mean that the Word of the Father is contemporaneous with the birth of the flesh; rather, we will preserve what is appropriate to each referent. We believe that the first birth of the Word from God is understood to be timeless and beyond thought, and that is what is presented in the words "I came from God." But his second birth, that is, the one according to the flesh, is presented in the words "I have not come on my own, but he sent me." I became flesh like you, that is, I became a human being, and I arrived in this world by the good will of God the Father to talk with you about the things of God and to make known to you, who do not know, the things that are in accordance with his will. But, he says, you did not love him who was revealed to you from the divine counsel as Savior and guide. How then will you still be called children of God, or how will you obtain the grace of being in his household, since you do not honor the one who is from him?

It is indeed likely that the Lord is hinting at something through these words as well, and he is eager to silence the people of the Jews, who are barking at him in vain. We will explain briefly what, then, he is hinting at.

Many among the Jews placed no value on the fear of God but admired and accepted only human honors. Overcome by shameful lucre, they dared to prophesy "speaking from their own hearts, and not from the mouth of the Lord," as it is written.[334] And indeed the Lord of all himself accused them, saying, "I did not send the prophets, I did not speak to them, and yet they prophesied."[335] Yes, he threatened to do terrible things to them, **[87]** crying out, "Woe to those who prophesy from their own hearts and see nothing at all!"[336] Shemaiah was such a man, the one who opposed the words of Jeremiah with his own lie, who took a wooden yoke, shattered it and said, "Thus says the Lord, I will shatter the yoke of the king of Babylon."[337]

So when Christ our Savior says, "As it is, you are trying to kill me, a man who has spoken the truth to you which I heard from God,"[338] the Jews began to murmur. And not knowing who he really was, they thought he was a false prophet. This is why they were hardened so that they then dared to rail against him, and they so fiercely wanted to kill him that they even pressed on to do it. Therefore, he profitably frightens them, saying that he did not come on his own, as was the habit of false prophets, but that he was sent from God. He does this to cut short their audacity, as by one and the same statement he deflects the reputation of being a false prophet and teaches that they will sustain immeasurable punishment when they not only dishonor the one sent from God the Father but even dare to plot his murder.

This, then, is the explanation of the passage before us. But now it is quite likely that the heretics will turn this statement into a kind of food for their impiety. They will perhaps

[334]Jer 23:16. [335]Jer 23:21. [336]Ezek 13:3. [337]Jer 28:2 (Jer 35:2 LXX). Cyril has Shemaiah instead of Hananiah. Shemaiah is mentioned, however, in Jer 29:24 (Jer 36:24 LXX). [338]Jn 8:40.

accuse the substance of the Only Begotten and think that it is inferior to the Father because of the statement about being sent from him. Let such people call to mind, however, the manner of the *oikonomia* that we just mentioned, and let them remember Paul crying out concerning the Son, "Who being in the form of God did not consider equality with God something to be exploited, but emptied himself, taking on the form of a slave, being born in human likeness. And being found in human form, he humbled himself and became obedient unto death."[339] **[88]**

Now if he humbled himself willingly (with the Father's consent and agreement, as it were), what accusation will he incur as he brings the path of the *oikonomia* to its completion in the way that was necessary? But if, because of the mention of being sent, you think that the Son is inferior to the Father, how, tell me, does one who is inferior (in your ignorant view) invariably accomplish the things of God? Where does inferiority manifest itself in him, since he perfectly possesses all that belongs to his progenitor and has God-befitting power to the fullest extent?

Therefore, he will not be understood to be inferior because he was sent, but being God from God truly and by nature (since he is the wisdom and power of the Father), he is sent to us (just as the light of the sun that is dispersed from it) to make wise that which lacks wisdom, that thus at length what is weak may be raised up through him and receive power to know God the Father and be led upwards to all virtue. For all the most beautiful characteristics of the human nature have been brought to light through Christ alone. There is nothing at all servile, then, in Christ, save only his form according to the flesh—or better, his power and authority over all is God-befitting, even though the Word, beautifully conformed to the measure of humility, takes human form for us.

8:43 "Why do you not understand what I say? It is because you cannot bear to hear my word."

What we have often said, we will say again because it is profitable for the reader. After all, it does no harm when our discourse goes through what is beneficial, even if it does so quite often. **[89]** Now it is the custom of Christ the Savior not to accept completely the words that seethe from the tongue of those who do not believe in him but rather to look into their hearts and inner realms and to fashion answers to the thoughts still turning in the depths of their heart. Since human beings do not see the thoughts of another, they have to accept the spoken word. Not so with God. Since he knows all things, he takes the thought for the voice.

Now when the Lord said to the Jews that he has not come on his own (as is the custom of those who approach prophecy from their own thoughts and not from the divine Spirit) but that he has been sent from God, they then imagine or discuss among themselves or secretly whisper to each other, Many prophets have spoken the things of God and have brought the words of the Spirit to us, but we find nothing among them that is like what this man's words contain. He completely removes us from the worship of the law and transfers us to another practice and introduces to us a foreign way of life. Therefore, his word is clearly dissonant and irreconcilable with the ancients.

It is likely that because he saw them thinking these things, he, showing that he is by nature God and seeing the thoughts in their hearts, grasps their thoughts and says, "Why do you not understand what I say? It is because you cannot bear to hear my word." I am not unaware, he says, that you cannot comprehend my words or teaching, but I will

[339]Phil 2:6-8.

explain to you the cause of this fact and clearly set before you the hindrance. "You cannot bear to hear my word."

When he says "you cannot," he convicts them of being lax toward the perfect good because they were previously overcome by their passions. Love of pleasure causes the mind to lose its nerve, and the **[90]** unbridled tendency toward the base enfeebles the sinews of the heart and renders it powerless and completely dispirited—at least when it comes to the ability to accomplish virtue. So since they were already weakened by their tendency toward baseness and ruled by their passions, he says, "You cannot bear to hear my word." "For the ways of the Lord are straight," as it is written, "and the righteous will walk in them, but the godless will lose their strength in them."[340]

You will find that what was said elsewhere to the Pharisees is related, "How can you believe when you accept glory from one another and do not seek that glory that comes from the one who alone is God?"[341] In this passage too, their inability to believe indicates the voluntary weakness of their understanding or the fact that their mind has already been overcome by love of glory. We also find what Paul says to be true of the Jews, "Those who are unspiritual do not receive the things of the Spirit of God, for they are foolishness to them."[342] Therefore, since they were unspiritual, they considered him to be foolishness when he was calling them to be saved and teaching them an excellent way of life and guiding them beautifully to be able to please God, who loves virtue, to whom be all honor, glory and might, to ages of ages. Amen.

[340]Hos 14:9 (Hos 14:10 LXX). [341]Jn 5:44. [342]1 Cor 2:14.

Subject Index

Scripture Index